Reprints of Economic Classics

THE LITERATURE OF POLITICAL ECONOMY

The LITERATURE of POLITICAL ECONOMY

A CLASSIFIED CATALOGUE

Of

Select Publications in the Different Departments of That Science

with

Historical, Critical, and Biographical Notices

By JOHN R. McCULLOCH

AUGUSTUS M. KELLEY, PUBLISHERS

First edition 1845
(London: Longman, Brown, Green and Longmans, 1845)

Reprinted 1991 by
AUGUSTUS M. KELLEY, PUBLISHERS
Fairfield NJ 07704-0008

Library of Congress Cataloging-in-Publication Data

McCulloch, J. R. (John Ramsay), 1789-1864.
The literature of political economy.
p. cm. — (Reprints of economic classics)
Reprint. Originally published: London : Longman, Brown, Green and Longman, 1845.
Includes indexes.
ISBN 0-678-01457-4
1. Economics—Bibliography. I. Title. II. Series.
Z7164.E2M3 1991 [HB161]
016.33 86-7466

Manufactured in the United States of America

PREFACE.

THOSE who have got together a considerable number of works in any department of science or literature, or who have bestowed any pains in tracing its history, can hardly fail to be struck, on the one hand, with the indications and explanations of sound principles and doctrines to be found among its earlier cultivators, and on the other, with the continued revival of exploded errors and fallacies. But if this be true in general, it is most especially so in all that relates to politics and national economy. Writers on such subjects, like those who undertake to instruct or lead the public in other departments of human knowledge, are sometimes imperfectly informed, and sometimes prejudiced, and incapable of communicating any useful information. Exclusive, however, of the common sources of error, there is another which, if not peculiar to those who discuss political questions, is found in them more frequently than in most others, and is far more productive of deceptive and unprincipled works. We allude to the discrepancy which sometimes exists between the real or supposed interests of the writers, or of their employers, and those of the public. Those who cultivate mathematical and physical sciences, or who devote themselves to literature or metaphysics, have rarely any selfish motive to bias their judgment, and to tempt them to conceal or pervert the truth. But it is not so with those who engage in political and economical discussions.

Every abuse, and every inexpedient or unjust institution or regulation, operates as a bounty on the production of false theories and sophistical publications; for, though injurious to the public, abuses are almost always productive of advantage to a greater or smaller number of individuals, who, when they are attacked, undertake their defence; and having enlisted a portion of the press, and probably, also, a corps of itinerant orators, into their service, labour by means of fallacious representations to make it appear that the abuses are beneficial to and should be supported by the public. Party influence is another copious source of delusion and error: measures being approved or censured, not because of their being consistent with or adverse to the public interests, but because they happen to have been proposed or opposed by the leaders of the party to which the writer or speaker is attached. And though in the end truth is sure to prevail over error, the history of this and most other countries shows that these attempts to make the worse appear the better cause—to make what is injurious be regarded as beneficial—and what is beneficial be regarded as injurious—have not unfrequently been attended with long-continued success. Hence, while the knowledge of the books that may be advantageously consulted is of considerable use in most departments of study, it is of paramount importance in those having relation to the conduct of public affairs.

Besides contributing to hinder the public judgment from being misled in matters that may deeply affect the national interests, such knowledge may be of material service to those about to engage in this field of inquiry. Whether a writer or a speaker undertakes to unfold principles, to set them in a novel and more striking light, or to recommend their application, he should know what has been already undertaken, what has been accomplished, and what remains for discovery and elucidation. The following work gives sundry examples of the inconveniences resulting from the want of this information, by exhibiting able men engaged in the investigation of principles and the development of laws which had been previously established and traced, and putting forward speculations as original which had been long before the public.

No attempt, that we are aware of, has hitherto been made to supply English readers with this knowledge. So that in endeavouring to furnish the public with an index to the select and really useful Literature of Political Economy, we may not unreasonably, perhaps, expect to meet with some indulgence for the defects unavoidable in a first attempt in a matter so extensive and so difficult.

It will be seen from the preceding remarks that no one needs take up this book in the expectation of finding in it anything like a complete list or catalogue of the various publications in the different departments of this science. Such a work would be bulky in the extreme; and would also, we incline to think, be of little value. We have proceeded on a principle of selection; and neglecting the others, have, with few exceptions, noticed those works only which appear to have contributed to develope sound principles, or to facilitate their adoption. It would, however, be idle to suppose, considering the myriads that have been published on commerce, corn-laws, money, the poor, and other subjects, that we have specified all the English works (for we have been less particular about the others) which deserved notice, or which have promoted the improvement of the science. At the same time we can safely say that our deficiencies in this respect have not been the result of carelessness and inattention. For many years past we have taken every means in our power, by collecting books and otherwise, to become acquainted with the history of the science, and with the leading publications in its different departments. And we have not omitted any work, of the existence of which we were aware, or which was present to our recollection, that appeared to be of any material importance. Perhaps, indeed, it may be thought by some that we have noticed too many rather than too few publications.

In addition to those that have conduced to elicit true principles, or to facilitate their application, we have specified a few of the works in which erroneous theories and opinions have been most ingeniously and ably defended, or which have had considerable practical influence. But we have been sparing in our references to this class of publications, and have taken no notice of those recommending a reduction of the standard of money, the issue of inconvertible paper, the employment of a double standard of value, and similar crudities. Neither have we referred to any work merely because it happened to be scarce: it must have had something else than rarity to recommend it to a place in our pages.

The works are ranged in classes, or divisions, though, no doubt, it is difficult to say to which of these some books really belong. The latter mostly follow each other, in chronological order, according to the date of their publication, separating between the English, French, Italian, &c.

If we have succeeded in our object, this work will be in some measure a history of Political Economy, as well as a critical catalogue of the principal economical works. It contains short notices of the rise of some of the principal theories, and of the circumstances which appear at different periods to have strongly determined public opinion upon economical questions, and given birth to classes of books. Without such notices, indeed, no just estimate could be formed of the latter.

But apart from these considerations, the history of this science has peculiar claims to attention. It is for the most part conversant with matters that belong to the every-day occupations and business of mankind; and some of its more important conclusions appear to be opposed to the most obvious deductions. Under such circumstances it cannot be uninteresting to trace the rise of new opinions, to observe the strong prejudices with which they have to contend, the errors that are often engrafted upon them, the mode in which one idea leads to another, and the generally slow and difficult process by which true doctrines come to be finally established, and their justness universally admitted.

It has been said, "*Vous ne devez jamais lire un livre, que vous ne sachiez quel en a été l'auteur, le temps auquel il a écrit, sa vie, l'estime qu'on en fait, et quelle en est la bonne impression.*"* But the authors of many valuable treatises in this science are wholly unknown; and it is often all but impossible to learn anything respecting others, with whose names only we are acquainted. We have, however, endeavoured to supply the information on which so high a value has been set, whenever it could be had, or appeared to be of consequence.

The criticisms we have ventured to make are in most instances very brief, being intended to give merely a general idea of the works to which they refer, without entering into a minute or detailed examination of their merits or defects. We have endeavoured to characterise them fairly, according to the view we take of the principles of the science; and shall regret should it appear that we have misapprehended or underrated any work of merit.

* Lami, 'Entretien VI. sur les Sciences,' prefixed by Camus to his catalogue.

When the name of the author of a work is included between brackets, it shows that it was published anonymously. When the word volume is used in describing a work, it shows that it is what is called a book; and when it is omitted, it shows that it is a tract or pamphlet, that is, a work of not more than about 150 or 180 pages.

The whole, or some portion, of the titles of the principal works is printed thus, in **Egyptian characters.**

To facilitate the consultation of the work a very complete double index has been added to it; the first portion of which comprises the names of the authors and individuals referred to, and the second those of the books and tracts.

*** We propose publishing, in 3 or 4 vols. 8vo., a Collection of some of the most important and curious Tracts referred to in this work, including, also, a few not noticed.

CONTENTS.

CHAPTER I.

CHAPTER II.

Commerce and Commercial Policy.

CHAPTER III.

CHAPTER IV.

CHAPTER V.

CHAPTER XVII.

CHAPTER XVIII.

CHAPTER XIX.

CHAPTER XX.

INDEX.

CORRECTIONS, &c.

Page 21, the name of the author, J. B. Say, is omitted in the title of the 'Traité d'Economie Politique, &c.'

„ 32, *for* Don Sempere y Guarinas, *read* Don Sempere y Guarinos.

„ 32, *for* Don Alvaro Florez Estrado, *read* Don Alvaro Florez Estrada.

„ 46. The 'Essai sur l'Etat du Commerce d'Angleterre' was written by M. Butel-Dumont, author of the 'Théorie du Luxe' (see p. 34 and p. 62), &c. (Correspondance de Grimm, i. 320.)

„ 134. It should have been stated that Gibbon refers in terms of high commendation to the Discourse of Greaves on the Roman Foot and Denarius, and to Hooper's Inquiry into Ancient Measures. Miscellaneous Works, v. 67.)

„ 151. The name of the author, M. Ameilhon, is omitted in the title of the 'Histoire du Commerce et de la Navigation des Egyptiens, &c.'

„ 253. Mr. Chalmers has given in the 1st edition of his 'Comparative Estimate' (see p. 217), lengthened extracts from the work of Sir Matthew Hale on the 'Primitive Origination of Mankind.'

THE LITERATURE

OF

POLITICAL ECONOMY.

CHAPTER I.

TREATISES ON POLITICAL ECONOMY IN GENERAL, OR ON SOME OF ITS FUNDAMENTAL PRINCIPLES.

"Political Economy* may be defined to be the science of the laws which regulate the production, accumulation, distribution, and consumption of those articles or products that are necessary, useful, or agreeable to man, and which, at the same time, possess exchangeable value."—*Principles of Political Economy*, p. 1.

THOUGH various works of considerable merit had appeared on commerce, money, and other subjects comprised within the limits of this science, it was not treated as a whole or in a scientific manner till about the middle of last century. It was entirely neglected in antiquity; and after the revival of arts and industry in modern Europe, gold and silver were almost universally regarded as the only real wealth. Having been used for ages as money, or as the *marchandise bannale* for which commodities were usually exchanged, the attention came to be transferred from the money's worth to the money itself—from the objects in view in making exchanges to the means by which they were effected. This delusion was not general merely, but universal; so that legislators, and those who speculated on the increase of national riches, almost exclusively applied themselves to a consideration of the most likely means for increasing the supply of the precious metals; and these, in the vast majority of cases, resolved themselves, directly or indirectly, into the prevention of their exportation, and the encouragement of their importation. Owing, however, in part, to the natural progress of society, and in part to the operation of peculiar circumstances that will be noticed in the course of this work, it began to be discovered, towards the end of the sixteenth and in the course of the seventeenth century, that there were periods of frequent

* From οικος, a house or family, and νομος, a law. Hence Political Economy may be said to be to the state what domestic economy is to a single family.

occurrence when gold and silver might be advantageously sent abroad; that the laws by which it was sought to prevent this being done were no better than so many attempts to "hedge in the cuckoo;" and that wealth really consisted in the supply of all sorts of useful and desirable products, and not in that of bullion only. It is surprising, indeed, how a different opinion should ever have been entertained by intelligent persons, seeing that it is all but obvious that an individual or a state well supplied with food, and with other useful and desirable commodities, would be rich and prosperous, though entirely unprovided with gold and silver; whereas the largest supplies of the latter, without the means of exchanging them for the former, would be of little or no advantage, and would be wholly unable to provide for the subsistence even of a single individual.

After the deep-rooted and wide-spread fallacy with respect to the paramount importance of the precious metals had been detected and exposed, the ground was cleared for the investigation of the true principles of the science; but various circumstances conspired to mislead, for a lengthened period, the greater number of those who turned their attention to this subject. Too much influence continued to be ascribed to legislation and arrangement. The real sources of wealth and prosperity were in consequence overlooked; and governments and individuals persevered in seeking in foreign trade and commercial regulations for that opulence which wholly springs from the judicious application of labour, which is always most efficient when most free. Gradually, however, sounder views began to prevail, and the foundations of the science were at length firmly established.

Hobbes seems to have been one of the first who had anything like a distinct perception of the real source of wealth. At the commencement of the 24th chapter of the *Leviathan*, published in 1651, he says, "The *nutrition* of a commonwealth consisteth in the *plenty* and *distribution* of *materials* conducing to life.

"As for the plenty of matter, it is a thing limited by nature to those commodities which, from (the two breasts of our common mother) *land* and *sea*, God usually either freely giveth, or for labour selleth to mankind.

"For the matter of this nutriment consisteth in animals, vegetables, minerals, God hath freely laid them before us, in or near to the face of the earth, so as there needeth no more but the labour and industry of receiving them, insomuch that *plenty dependeth* (next to God's favour) *on the labour and industry of man.*"

Locke, however, had a much clearer apprehension of this doctrine. His *Essay on Civil Government*, published in 1689, is in fact the earliest work in which the true sources of wealth and value are distinctly pointed out. "Let any one consider," says he, "what the difference is between an acre of land planted with tobacco or sugar, sown with wheat or barley, and an acre of the same land lying in common, without any husbandry upon it, and he will find that the improvement of labour makes the far greater part of the value. I think it will be but a very modest computation to say, that of the products of the earth useful to the life of man, *nine-tenths* are the effects of labour; nay, if we will rightly consider things as they come to our use, and cast up the several expenses about them, what in them is purely owing to nature, and what to labour, we shall find, that in most of them, *ninety-nine hundredths* are wholly to be put on the account of labour.

"To make this a little clearer, let us but trace some of the ordinary provisions of life through their several progresses, before they come to our use, and see how much of their value they receive from human industry. Bread, wine, and cloth are things of daily use and great plenty; yet, notwithstanding, acorns, water, and leaves or skins, must be our bread, drink, and clothing, did not labour furnish us with these more useful commodities; for whatever bread is more worth than acorns, wine than water, and cloth or silk than leaves, skins, or moss, that is wholly owing to labour and industry; the one of these being the food and raiment which unassisted nature furnishes us with, the other, provisions which our industry and pains prepare for us; which how much they exceed the other in value, when any one hath computed, he will then see how much labour makes the far greatest part of the value of things we enjoy in this world: and the ground which produces the materials is scarce to be reckoned in, as any, or at most but a very small part of it; so little that even amongst us, land that is wholly left to nature, that hath no improvement of pasturage, tillage, or planting, is called, as indeed it is, *waste;* and we shall find the benefit of it amount to little more than nothing.

"An acre of land that bears here twenty bushels of wheat, and another in America which, with the same husbandry, would do the like, are, without doubt, of the same natural intrinsic value (utility); but yet the benefit mankind receives from the one in a year is worth 5*l.*, and from the other possibly not worth *one penny*, if all the profit an Indian received from it were to be valued and sold here; at least I may truly say not $\frac{1}{1000}$. 'Tis labour then which puts the greatest part of the value upon land, *without which it would scarcely be worth anything.* 'Tis to that we owe the greatest part of all its useful products; for all that the straw, bran, bread of that acre of wheat is more worth than the product of an acre of as good land which lies waste, is all the effect of labour. For 'tis not merely the ploughman's pains, the reaper's and thrasher's toil, and the baker's sweat, is to be counted into the bread we eat: the labour of those who broke the oxen, who digged and wrought the iron and stones, who felled and framed the timber employed about the plough, mill, oven, or any other utensils, which are a vast number, requisite to this corn, from its being seed to be sown to its being made bread, must all be charged on the account of *labour*, and received as an effect of that; nature and the earth furnished only the almost worthless materials as in themselves. 'Twould be a strange catalogue of things that industry provided, and made use of, about every loaf of bread before it came to our use, if we could trace them. Iron, wood, leather, bark, timber, stone, bricks, coals, lime, cloth, dyeing drugs, pitch, tar, masts, ropes, and all the materials made use of in the ship that brought away the commodities used by any of the workmen to any part of the work; all which 'twould be almost impossible, at least too long, to reckon up."

Locke has here all but completely established the fundamental principle which lies at the bottom of the science of wealth. Had he carried his analysis a little further, he could hardly have failed to perceive that, however useful, water, leaves, skins, and other spontaneous productions of nature have no *value** except what they owe to the labour required for their appropriation. The value of water to a man on the bank of a river depends on the labour necessary to raise it to his lips; and its value, when carried ten or twenty miles off, is equally dependent on the labour necessary to convey it there; and so in the case of gold and silver, and of everything else. The rarest and the commonest products in an unwrought state, and in their original locality, are equally the free gift of nature. Whatever value the finest gold vase may possess is wholly derived from the labour required to extract the metal from the bowels of the earth, and to smelt, refine, and work it up into the magnificent article into which it has been fashioned. It has been said that the value of the mainspring of a watch is a thousand,

* By value we always mean *value in exchange.* What has been called value in use is only another and awkward expression for *utility.*

or two thousand, times greater than that of the raw material of which it is made; but in truth it is infinitely greater, for the raw material, being the spontaneous gift of nature, has no value. The miner has only to dig his way to it; when he has done this he gets it for the lifting: so that the value of the material depends in this as in every other case, on the labour expended upon it, and on nothing else. Nature is not niggard or parsimonious. Her rude products, powers, and capacities are all offered gratuitously to man. She neither demands nor receives an equivalent for her favours. An object which may be appropriated or adapted to our use, without any voluntary labour on our part, may be of the very highest utility; but as it is the free gift of nature, it is impossible it can possess the smallest value.

But though Locke gave, in the passage referred to above, a far more distinct and comprehensive statement of the fundamental principle that labour is the grand source of value, and consequently of wealth, than is to be found even in the 'Wealth of Nations,' it was but little attended to either by his contemporaries or by subsequent inquirers. Locke was not himself aware of the vast importance of the principle he had developed; and three quarters of a century elapsed before it began to be generally perceived that an inquiry into the means by which labour might be rendered most efficient was the object of that portion of political economy which treats of the production of wealth.

It will be seen in the course of this work that the true principles and real influence of commerce, or of the exchange of products and services between individuals of the same and of different nations, and also of the division and combination of employments, had been fully ascertained and exhibited previously to the middle of last century. The theory of money and banks had also been successfully elucidated, and other subordinate departments of the science had been inquired into and illustrated with more or less success; but notwithstanding this progress, the opinions of the best informed writers, by whom the analysis of Locke was wholly overlooked, respecting the nature and sources of wealth, continued to be confused and contradictory; the science was not treated as a whole or in a systematic manner; and that great and most difficult branch which relates to the distribution of wealth, or to the laws which determine rent, profits, and wages, was all but entirely neglected.

The first attempt to produce a systematic treatise on political economy was made by M. Quesnay, a French philosopher, distinguished for the subtlety and originality of his understanding, and the integrity and simplicity of his character. At an early period of his life he was struck with the depressed state of agriculture in France, and set himself to discover the causes which had prevented its making that progress which the industry of the inhabitants, the fertility of the soil, and the excellence of the climate seemed to insure. In the course of this inquiry he speedily discovered that the prevention of the exportation of corn, and the preference given in the policy of Colbert to manufactures and commerce over agriculture, formed the most powerful obstacles to the progress and improvement of the latter. But Quesnay did not satisfy himself with exposing the injustice of this preference, and its pernicious consequences: his zeal for the interests of agriculture led him not merely to place it on the same level with manufactures and commerce, but to raise it above them by endeavouring to show that it is the only species of industry which contributes to the riches of a nation. Founding on the indisputable fact that everything which ministers to our wants or desires must be originally derived from the earth, Quesnay assumed, as a self-evident truth, and as the basis of his system, that the *earth is the only source of wealth;* and held that labour is altogether incapable of producing any new value, except when employed in agriculture, including under that term fisheries and mines. The changes produced by the powerful influence of the vegetative powers of nature, and his inability to explain the origin and causes of rent, confirmed him in this opinion. The circumstance that, of all who engage in industrious undertakings, none but the cultivators of the soil pay rent for the use of natural agents, appeared to him to prove that agriculture is the only species of industry which yields a nett surplus (*produit net*) over and above the expenses of production. Quesnay allowed that manufacturers and merchants are highly useful; but, as they realise no nett surplus in the shape of rent, he contended that the value which they add to the raw material of the commodities they manufacture, or carry from place to place, is barely equivalent to the value of the capital or stock consumed by them during the time they are necessarily engaged in these operations. These principles being established, Quesnay proceeded to divide society into three classes: the *first* or *productive* class, by whose agency all wealth is produced, consists of the farmers and labourers engaged in agriculture, who subsist on a portion of the produce of the land reserved to themselves as the wages of their labour, and as a reasonable profit on their capital; the *second* or *proprietary* class consists of those who live on the rent of the land, or on the *nett surplus produce* raised by the cultivators after their necessary expenses have been deducted; and the *third* or *unproductive* class consists of manufacturers, merchants, menial servants, &c., who subsist entirely on wages paid them by the other two classes, and whose labour, though exceedingly useful, adds nothing to the national wealth. It is obvious, supposing this classification made on just principles, that all taxes must fall on the landlords. The third or unproductive class have nothing but what they receive from the other two classes, who pay them only what is required to enable them to subsist, and continue their services; and if any deduction were made from the fair and reasonable profits and wages of the husbandmen, or *productive class*, it would paralyse their exertions, and spread poverty and misery throughout the land, by drying up the only source of wealth. Hence it necessarily follows, on this theory, that the entire expenses of government, and the various public burdens, must, however imposed, be in the end defrayed out of the *produit net*, or rent of the landlords; and consistently with this principle, Quesnay proposed that all existing taxes should be repealed, and that a single tax (*impôt unique*), laid directly on the nett produce, or rent of the land, should be imposed in their stead.

But, however much impressed with the importance of agriculture over every other species of industry, Quesnay did not solicit for it any exclusive favour or protection. He successfully contended that the interests of the agriculturists, and of all the other classes, would be best promoted by establishing a system of perfect freedom. "Qu'on maintienne," says he, in one of his general maxims, "l'entière liberté du commerce; car la police du commerce intérieur et extérieur la plus sure, la plus exacte, la plus profitable à la nation et à l'état, consiste dans LA PLEINE LIBERTÉ DE LA CONCURRENCE." Quesnay showed that it could never be for the interest of the proprietors and cultivators of the soil to fetter or discourage the industry of merchants, artificers, and manufacturers; for the greater their liberty the greater will be their competition, and their services will in consequence be rendered so much the cheaper. Neither, on the other hand, could it ever be for the interest of the unproductive classes to harass or oppress the agriculturists by preventing the free exportation of their products, or by any sort of restrictive regulations. When the cultivators enjoy the greatest degree of freedom, their industry, and consequently their nett surplus produce (the only fund whence any accession of national wealth could ever be derived), will be augmented to the greatest possible extent. According to this "liberal and generous system" (*Wealth of Nations*, p. 303), the establishment of perfect liberty, perfect security, and perfect justice is the only, as it is the infallible, means of securing the highest degree of prosperity to all classes.

"On a vu," says the ablest expositor of this system, M. Mercier de la Rivière, "qu'il est de l'essence de l'ordre que l'intérêt particulier d'un seul ne puisse jamais être séparé de l'intérêt commun de tous; nous en trouvons une preuve bien convaincante dans les effets que produit naturellement et nécessairement la plénitude de la liberté qui doit régner dans le commerce, pour ne point blesser la propriété. L'intérêt personnel, encouragé par cette grande liberté, presse vivement et perpétuellement chaque homme en particulier de perfectionner, de multiplier les choses dont il est vendeur; de grossir ainsi la masse des jouissances qu'il peut procurer aux autres hommes, afin de grossir, par ce moyen, la masse des jouissances que les autres hommes peuvent lui procurer en échange. *Le monde* alors *va de lui-même;* le désir de jouir, et la liberté de jouir, ne cessant de provoquer la multiplication des productions et l'accroissement de l'industrie, ils impriment à toute la société un mouvement qui devient une tendance perpétuelle vers son meilleur état possible."—(*L'Ordre Naturel, &c.*, ii. 444.)

It would be inconsistent alike with the limits and objects of this work to enter into any lengthened examination of this very ingenious theory. It is sufficient at present to remark, that, in assuming agriculture to be the only source of wealth, because the matter or substance of commodities must be derived from the earth, Quesnay and his followers mistook altogether the nature of production, and really supposed wealth to consist of matter; whereas, in its natural state, matter is rarely possessed of any immediate or direct utility, and is invariably destitute of value. The labour required to appropriate matter, and to fit and prepare it for our use, is the only means by which it acquires value, and becomes wealth. The latter is not produced by making any additions to the matter of our globe, that being a quantity susceptible neither of augmentation nor diminution. All the operations of industry are intended to create wealth by giving utility to matter already in existence; and it has been demonstrated over and over again, that the labour employed in manufactures and commerce is, in all respects, as creative of utility, and consequently of wealth, as the labour employed in agriculture. Neither is the cultivation of the soil, as M. Quesnay supposed, the only species of industry which yields a surplus produce after the expenses of production are deducted. So long as none but the best of the good soils are cultivated, no rent, or *produit net*, is obtained from the land; and it is only after recourse has been had to poorer soils, and when, consequently, the productive powers of the labour and capital employed in cultivation begin to diminish, that rent begins to appear; so that instead of being a consequence of the superior productiveness of agricultural industry, rent is in fact a consequence of one piece of land being more productive than others.

The 'Tableau Economique,' comprising a set of formulæ constructed by Quesnay, intended to exhibit the various phenomena accompanying the production of wealth, and its distribution among the productive, proprietary, and unproductive classes, was published at Versailles, with accompanying illustrations, in 1758; and the novelty and ingenuity of the theory which it expounded, its systematic shape, and the liberal system of commercial intercourse which it recommended, speedily obtained for it a very high degree of reputation. It is to be regretted that the friends and disciples of Quesnay, among whom we have to reckon the Marquis de Mirabeau, Mercier de la Rivière, Dupont de Nemours, Saint Peravy, Turgot, and other distinguished individuals in France, Italy, and Germany, should, in their zeal for his peculiar doctrines, which they enthusiastically exerted themselves to defend and propagate, have exhibited more of the character of partisans than of (what they really were) sincere and honest inquirers after truth. Hence they have always been regarded as a sect, known by the name of *Economists*, or *Physiocrats;* and hence, also, the unusual degree of sameness by which their works are characterised.

We subjoin a list of the principal works published by the French Economists:—

TABLEAU ECONOMIQUE, et MAXIMES GENERALES du GOUVERNEMENT ECONOMIQUE. Par FRANÇOIS QUESNAY. 4to. Versailles, 1758.

THEORIE de l'IMPOT. Par M. de MIRABEAU. 4to. and 12mo. Paris, 1760.

LA PHILOSOPHIE RURALE. Par M. de MIRABEAU. 4to., and 3 vols. 12mo., 1763.

L'ORDRE NATUREL et ESSENTIEL des SOCIETES POLITIQUES. Par MERCIER de la RIVIERE. 4to., and 2 tom. 12mo. Londres (Paris), 1767.

SUR l'ORIGINE et PROGRES d'une SCIENCE NOUVELLE. Par DUPONT de NEMOURS. 8vo. Londres. (Paris.) 1767. A concise, clear, and popular view of the economical theory.

LA PHYSIOCRATIE, ou Constitution Naturelle du Gouvernement le plus avantageux au Genre Humain: Recueil des Principaux Ouvrages Economiques de M. Quesnay. Rédigé et publié par DUPONT de NEMOURS. 2 parties. Paris, 1767.

LETTRES d'un CITOYEN à un MAGISTRAT, sur les Vingtièmes et les autres Impôts. Par M. l'ABBÉ BAUDEAU. 1 vol., 12mo. 1768.

MEMOIRE sur les EFFETS de l'IMPÔT INDIRECT; qui a remporté le Prix proposé par la Société Royale d'Agriculture de Limoges. (Par SAINT PERAVY.) 1 vol., 12mo. 1768.

REFLEXIONS sur la FORMATION et la DISTRIBUTION des RICHESSES. Par TURGOT. 8vo. 1771, and reprinted in his works. This is the best of all the works founded on the principles of the Economists; and is in some respects the best work on the science published previously to the 'Wealth of Nations.'

ABRÉGÉ des PRINCIPES de l'ECONOMIE POLITIQUE. Par Mgr. LE MARGRAVE de BADE. 8vo. Carlsruhe. (Paris.) 1772. This royal brochure, which consists of fifty-one pages, gives a pretty good tabular summary of the leading points in Quesnay's system.

DE l'ORDRE SOCIAL; Ouvrage suivi d'un Traité Elémentaire sur la Valeur, l'Argent, la Circulation, l'Industrie, et le Commerce intérieur et extérieur. Par M. le TROSNE. 1 vol. 8vo. Paris, 1777.

THE JOURNAL d'AGRICULTURE and the EPHEMERIDES du CITOYEN contain many valuable articles contributed by Quesnay and other leading Economists.

The 'Ephémérides,' begun in 1767 and discontinued in 1775, was first conducted by the Abbé Baudeau, and subsequently by Dupont. It was published monthly, and two numbers make a considerable duodecimo volume. The authors were all disciples of Quesnay, and zealous Economists. Their discussions embraced only the moral and political sciences; many branches of which they have treated with much ability and acuteness. There is a valuable *Eloge* of Quesnay in one of the numbers for 1775, written by the Conte d'Albon. The following extract from the approbation given by the *Censeur* to the third number for 1770 is curious: "J'exhorte," says he, "de nouveau les auteurs de ce Journal, à résister à la tentation de critiquer. Le bonheur du citoyen tient à sa confiance. On peut et l'on doit quelquefois avertir en secret ceux qui sont préposés à l'administration. *Mais on ne doit prêcher aux particuliers que leur propre réforme, et non celle de l'état.*"

Quesnay, whose early education had been all but entirely neglected, subsequently became an eminent physician, and published several works on various branches of medicine and surgery, some of which continue to be held in high estimation. He became, in 1744, through the influence of his all-powerful friend Madame de Pompadour, consulting physician to Louis XV., and had apartments assigned to him in the Tuileries, and the palace at Versailles. Having been born and brought up in the country, Quesnay entertained a marked affection for the cultivators of the soil; and this circumstance most probably gave a bias to his theoretical inquiries. The articles *Fermier* and *Grains*, which he contributed to the 'Encyclopédie' in 1756 and 1757, contain the earliest development of his peculiar views.

Quesnay enjoyed in a high degree the friendship and esteem of his contemporaries. "Il étoit," says Madame du Hausset, "un grand génie, suivant l'opinion de tous ceux qui l'avoit connu et de plus un homme fort gai. Il aimoit causer avec moi de la campagne; j'y avois été élevée, et il me faisoit parler des herbages de Normandie et du Poitou, de la richesse des fermiers, et de la manière de cultiver. C'étoit le meilleur homme du monde, et le plus éloigné de la plus petite intrigue. Il étoit bien plus occupé à la cour de la meilleure manière de cultiver la terre que de tout ce que s'y passoit." (*Melanges*, p. 343.)

"Tandis," says Marmontel, "que les orages se formoient et se dissipoient au-dessous de l'entresol de Quesnay, il griffonnoit ses axiomes et ses calculs d'économie rustique, aussi tranquille, aussi indifférent à ces mouvemens de la cour, que s'il en eût été à cent lieues de distance. Là bas, on décidoit de la paix, de la guerre, du choix des généraux, du renvoi des ministres; et nous, dans l'entresol, nous raisonnions d'agriculture; nous calculions le *produit net*, ou quelquefois nous dînions gaiement avec Diderot, d'Alembert, Duclos, Helvétius, Turgot, Buffon; et Madame de Pompadour, ne pouvant pas engager cette troupe de philosophes à descendre dans son salon, venoit elle-même les voir à table et causer avec eux."

Dr. Smith was well acquainted with Quesnay. He frequently met him during his residence at Paris in 1766; and while he bears testimony to the "modesty and simplicity" of his character, he has pronounced his system to be, "with all its imperfections, the nearest approximation to the truth that has yet been published upon the subject of Political Economy." (*Wealth of Nations*, p. 307.) So highly, indeed, was Smith impressed with a sense of his merits, as a man and a philosopher, that it was his intention, had he not been prevented by Quesnay's death, to have inscribed to him the *Wealth of Nations.* (Stewart's *Account of the Life and Writings of Smith.*)

Quesnay expired in his lodgings in the palace of Versailles in December, 1774, in the 80th year of his age.

Though it be impossible to question the originality of Quesnay, it is certain he had been anticipated in several of his peculiar doctrines by some

English writers of the previous century. The fundamental principles of the economical system are distinctly stated in a tract entitled 'Reasons for a limited Exportation of Wool,' published in 1677. "That it is of the greatest concern and interest of the nation," says the author of the tract, "to preserve the nobility, gentry, and those to whom the land of the country belongs—at least much greater than a few artificers employed in working the superfluity of our wool, or the merchants who gain by the exportation of our manufactures, is manifest. 1. Because they are the *masters and proprietaries of the foundation of all the wealth in this nation, all profit arising out of the ground, which is theirs.* 2. *Because they bear all taxes and public burdens*, which in truth are only borne by those who buy and sell not, all sellers raising the price of their commodities, or abating of goodness, according to their taxes." (p. 5.)

In 1696 Mr. Asgill published a treatise entitled 'Several Assertions proved, in order to create another Species of Money than Gold,' in support of Dr. Chamberlayne's proposition for a Land Bank. The following extract from this treatise breathes, as Stewart has justly observed in his 'Life of Smith,' the very spirit of Quesnay's philosophy:—

"What we call commodities is nothing but land severed from the soil—*man deals in nothing but earth.* The merchants are the factors of the world, to exchange one part of the earth for another. The king himself is fed by the labour of the ox; and the clothing of the army and victualling of the navy must all be paid for to the owner of the soil as the ultimate receiver. All things in the world are originally the produce of the ground, and there must all things be raised."

These passages are interesting, as exhibiting the first germs of the theory of the Economists. But there is no ground whatever for supposing that Quesnay was aware of the existence of either of the tracts referred to. The subjects treated of in them were of too local a description to excite the attention of foreigners; and Quesnay was too candid to conceal his obligations, had he really owed them any. It is probable he may have seen Locke's treatise on 'Raising the Value of Money,' where the idea is thrown out that all taxes fall ultimately on the land. But there is an immense difference between the suggestion of Locke and the well-digested system of Quesnay.

We subjoin from the work of Dupont, 'Sur l'Origine et Progrès d'une Science Nouvelle,' a short statement of the various institutions the Economists held to be necessary for the good government of a country.

"Voici le résumé de toutes les institutions sociales fondées sur l'ordre naturel, sur la constitution physique des hommes et des autres êtres dont ils sont environnés.

"*Propriété personnelle*, établie par la nature, par la nécessité physique dont il est à chaque individu de disposer de toutes les facultés de sa personne pour se procurer les choses propres à satisfaire ses besoins, sous peine de souffrance et de mort.

"*Liberté de travail*, inséparable de la propriété personnelle, dont elle forme une partie constitutive.

"*Propriété mobiliaire*, qui n'est que la propriété personnelle même, considérée dans son usage, dans son objet, dans son extension nécessaire sur les choses acquises par le travail de sa personne.

"*Liberté d'échange*, de commerce, d'emploi de ses richesses, inséparable de la propriété personnelle et de la propriété mobiliaire.

"*Culture*, qui est un usage de la propriété personnelle, de la propriété mobiliaire, et de la liberté qui en est inséparable: usage profitable, nécessaire, indispensable pour que la population puisse s'accroître, par une suite de la multiplication des productions nécessaires à la subsistance des hommes.

" *Propriété foncière*, suite nécessaire de la culture, et qui n'est que la conservation de la propriété personnelle et de la propriété mobiliaire, employées aux travaux et aux dépenses préparatoires indispensables pour mettre la terre en état d'être cultivée.

" *Liberté de l'emploi de sa terre*, de l'espèce de sa culture, de toutes les conventions relatives à l'exploitation, à la concession, à la rétrocession, à l'échange, à la vente de sa terre, inséparable de la propriété foncière.

" Partage naturel des récoltes, *en reprises des cultivateurs*, ou richesses dont l'emploi doit indispensablement être de perpétuer la culture, sous peine de diminution des récoltes et de la population ; et *produit net*, ou richesses disponibles dont la grandeur décide de la prospérité de la société, dont l'emploi est abandonné à la volonté et à l'intérêt des propriétaires fonciers, et qui constitue pour eux le prix naturel et légitime des dépenses qu'ils ont faits, et des travaux auxquels ils se sont livrés pour mettre la terre en état d'être cultivé.

" *Sûreté*, sans laquelle la propriété et la liberté ne seraient que de droit et non de fait, sans laquelle le *produit net* serait bientôt anéanti, sans laquelle la culture même ne pourrait subsister.

" *Autorité tutélaire et souveraine*, pour procurer la sûreté essentiellement nécessaire à la propriété et à la liberté ; et qui s'acquitte de cet important ministère, en promulguant et faisant exécuter les loix de l'ordre naturel, par lesquelles la propriété et la liberté sont établies.

"*Magistrats*, pour décider dans les cas particuliers quelle doit être l'application des loix de l'ordre naturel, réduites en loix positives par l'autorité souveraine ; et qui ont le devoir impérieux de comparer les ordonnances des souverains avec les loix de la justice par essence, avant de s'engager à prendre ces ordonnances positives pour régle de leurs jugemens.

" *Instruction publique et favorisée*, pour que les citoyens, l'autorité, et les magistrats ne puissent jamais perdre de vue les loix invariables de l'ordre naturel, et se laisser égarer par les prestiges de l'opinion, ou par l'attrait des intérêts particuliers exclusifs qui, dès qu'ils sont *exclusifs*, sont toujours malentendus.

" *Revenu public*, pour constituer la force et le pouvoir nécessaire à l'autorité souveraine ; pour faire les frais de son ministère protecteur, des fonctions importantes des magistrats, et de l'instruction indispensable des loix de l'ordre naturel.

" *Impôt direct*, ou partage du produit net du territoire entre les propriétaires fonciers et l'autorité souveraine ; pour former le revenu public d'une manière qui ne restraigne ni la propriété ni la liberté, et qui par conséquent ne soit pas destructive.

" *Proportion essentielle et nécessaire de l'impôt direct* avec le produit net, telle qu'elle donne à la société le plus grand revenu public qui soit possible, et par conséquent le plus grand degré possible de sûreté, sans que le sort des propriétaires fonciers cesse d'être le meilleur sort dont on puisse jouir dans la société.

" *Monarchie héréditaire*, pour que tous les intérêts présens et futurs du dépositaire de l'autorité souveraine, soient intimement liés avec ceux de la société par le partage proportionnel du *produit net*."

Despite the defects in this system, there can be no question that the labours of the Economists powerfully contributed to accelerate the progress of the science. It was now found to be necessary, in reasoning on subjects connected with national wealth, to subject its sources, and the laws which regulate its production and distribution, to a more accurate and searching analysis. In the course of this examination, it was speedily ascertained that both the mercantile and economical theories were erroneous and defective; and that, to establish the science on a firm foundation, it was necessary to take a much more extensive survey, and to seek for its principles, not in a few partial and distorted facts, or in metaphysical abstractions, but in the connexion and relation subsisting among the various phenomena manifested in the progress of civilisation.

It was not till 1767 that any English work appeared on political economy which had any pretensions to be considered as a systematic or complete view of the subject. This distinction is due to the following treatise:—

An Inquiry into the Principles of Political Œconomy; being an Essay on the Science of Domestic Policy in Free Nations. By Sir James Steuart, Bart. 2 vols., 4to. London, 1767.

Though intended to serve as an exposition, or systematic view, of the principles of the mercantile system, this work is by no means destitute of enlarged and ingenious views. The first book, which treats of the mutual action and reaction of population and agriculture, contains several passages in which the true theory of population is set in the most striking light. There are also many judicious observations interspersed throughout the rest of the work, more especially in those parts which treat of money and exchanges. It must however be acknowledged that, even when sound, the statements and reasonings are singularly tedious and perplexed. The author had no correct idea of the real sources of wealth, or of the means by which they may be rendered most productive; and even as an exposition of the mercantile system, his work is inferior to the *Lezioni* of Genovesi (see chapter on Commercial Works), published three years previously. Though well acquainted with Steuart, Smith has not once referred to his treatise: and if we except those parts of the first book which treat of population, he could have gleaned little from it which he might not have found in other works.

Sir James Steuart published in 1772, at the request of the East India Company, 'The Principles of Money as applied to the Coin of Bengal,' in 4to.; and this and some other treatises are included in an edition of his works, in 6 vols. 8vo., published in 1805. Sir James Steuart died in 1780.

But all previous works on political economy were now about to be thrown into the shade by the appearance of the 'Wealth of Nations,' a work which did for this science what the great work of Grotius did for public law.

An Inquiry into the Nature and Causes of the Wealth of Nations. By Adam Smith, LL.D. 1st ed., 2 vols., 4to. London, 1776. The last ed. revised by the Author, 3 vols., 8vo. London, 1788.

——— A New Edition, with Notes, and an Additional Volume, by David Buchanan. 4 vols., 8vo. Edinburgh, 1817.

——— A New Edition, with a Life of the Author, an Introductory Discourse, Notes, and Supplemental Dissertations, by J. R. M'Culloch, Esq. 4 vols., 8vo. Edinburgh, 1828.

This last edition was republished, with numerous corrections and additions, including several new Dissertations, in a handsome 8vo. volume, double columns. London, 1839.

The subjoined extract from the preface to this edition will give the reader some idea of the objects which the editor had in view in undertaking it:—

1. "The majority of those who refer to any work of authority or celebrity being anxious to learn something of the author, a sketch is given of the life of Dr. Smith. This is principally abridged from Dugald Stewart's valuable memoir, but a few remarks and some facts gleaned from other sources have been added.
2. "Following the life is an introductory discourse, in which an attempt is made to trace the rise and progress of the science of wealth down to the publication of the 'Wealth of Nations;' to estimate the principal merits and defects of that work; and to point out the distinguishing steps in the subsequent history of the science. This is the only sketch of its kind in the English language; and it seemed to be necessary to enable the reader fairly to estimate the services rendered by Dr. Smith in this department of human knowledge, and to do justice to those who, in less enlightened times, laid the foundations of that liberal system of commercial policy that has done so much to promote the well-being of mankind; and to those who, at a later period, have assisted in bringing the science to the advanced state in which we now find it.
3. "Numerous foot-notes are subjoined to the text. These are sometimes of a controversial character; but their principal purpose is to point out the more prominent changes that have occurred in the laws, customs, and institutions referred to by the author. The supplemental notes or dissertations are given together at the end of the volume. The latter have a twofold object in view, being partly intended to make the reader aware of the fallacy or insufficiency of the principles Dr. Smith has sometimes adopted, and partly to exhibit a view of the principal discoveries and improvements made in the science of wealth, and of the more important changes introduced into our economical legislation since the close of the American war. They also embrace several additional speculations on subjects of general interest and importance."

The 'Wealth of Nations' gives Adam Smith an undoubted claim to be regarded as the founder of the modern system of political economy, and to be classed amongst the most eminent benefactors of his species. The excellence of this great work is obvious from the fact of its having exercised a more powerful and beneficial influence over the public opinion and legislation of the civilized world, since its appearance, than has ever been exercised by any other publication. It owes this high distinction to a variety of causes, but principally perhaps to the general soundness and liberality of its leading doctrines; to their bearing upon the most important affairs and interests of nations and individuals; and to the admirable manner in which they are expounded. Nor is it the least of the author's merits that he has pointed out and smoothed the route, by following which subsequent philosophers have been able to perfect much that he left incomplete, to rectify the mistakes into which he sometimes fell, and to make many new and important discoveries.

The 'Wealth of Nations' was the first work in which the science was treated in its fullest extent, and in which the fundamental principles that determine the production of wealth were established beyond the reach of cavil and dispute. In opposition to the Economists, Dr. Smith has shown that labour is the only source of wealth; and that the wish by which all individuals are actuated, of augmenting their fortunes and rising in the world, is the cause of wealth being saved and accumulated; he has shown that labour is productive of wealth when employed in manufactures and commerce, as well as when it is employed in the cultivation of the land; he has traced the various means by which labour may be rendered most effective, and has given an admirable analysis and exposition of the prodigious additions made to its powers by its division among different individuals, and by the employment of capital and machinery in industrious undertakings. He has also shown, in opposition to the commonly received opinions of the merchants and statesmen of his time, that wealth does not consist in the abundance of gold and silver, but in that of the various necessaries, conveniences, and enjoyments of human life; that it is, in all cases, sound policy to leave individuals to pursue their own interest in their own way; and that in prosecuting branches of industry advantageous to themselves, they necessarily prosecute such as are at the same time advantageous to the public. He has shown, with a force of reasoning and an amplitude of illustration that leaves little to be desired, that the principles of the mercantile or exclusive system are at once inconsistent and absurd; and that every regulation intended to divert industry into particular channels, or to determine the species of intercourse to be carried on between different parts of the same country, or between distant and independent countries, is impolitic and pernicious, subversive of the rights of individuals, and adverse to the progress of real opulence and lasting prosperity. "The statesman," he observes, "who should attempt to direct private people in what manner they ought to employ their capitals, would not only load himself with a most unnecessary attention, but assume an authority which could safely be trusted not only to no single person, but to no senate or council whatever, and which would nowhere be so dangerous as in the hands of a man who had folly and presumption enough to fancy himself fit to exercise it."

But, however excellent, still it cannot be denied that there are errors, and those too of no slight importance, even in those parts of the 'Wealth of Nations' which treat of the production of wealth. So long as Dr. Smith confines himself to a statement of the advantages resulting from the freedom of industry, and of the mischiefs occasioned by the attempts that have so frequently been made to fetter its operations, and to force it into certain channels in preference to others, his principles and reasonings are equally sound and conclusive, but they are less so in other instances. He does not say that such branches of industry as are found to be most for the advantage of individuals are necessarily, at the same time, most for the advantage of the public. His leaning to the system of the Economists (a leaning perceptible throughout his work) made him so far swerve from his own principles as to admit that individual advantage is not always a true test of the public advantageousness of different employments. He considered that agriculture, though not the only productive employment, is the most productive of any; that the home trade is more productive than a direct foreign trade; and the latter than the carrying trade! It is clear, however, that these distinctions are fundamentally erroneous. A state being nothing but a collection of individuals, it follows that whatever is most advantageous to them individually must be so also to the collective body; and it is obvious that the interest of the parties will always prevent them from engaging in manufactures and commerce unless when they yield as large profits, and are consequently as publicly beneficial, as agriculture.

Dr. Smith made a very great improvement on the system of the Economists by showing that the labour of manufacturers and merchants is productive; but his theory on this important point is, notwithstanding, incomplete and defective. He limits his idea of productive labour to that which is "fixed and realised in some vendible commodity;" whereas all labour should plainly be deemed productive, if it yield a return to the labourer without lessening the wealth of the society. In fact it is only through the security and protection afforded by the exertions of some of those placed by Smith in the unproductive class, that the supply of those material products, on which he exclusively fixed his attention, can ever become considerable, or that society can emerge from barbarism, and attain to opulence.

But the principal defect in the 'Wealth of Nations,' and the source whence most of the errors which pervade portions of it have been derived, consists in the erroneous opinions of Smith with respect to value and rent. He appears to have supposed that the value of commodities depended indifferently either upon the quantity of labour required to produce them, and bring them to market, or upon the value of such labour, and that consequently a general rise of wages led to a general rise of prices. But there is an immeasurable difference between the expressions which Smith supposed were identical; and Mr. Ricardo changed the whole aspect of the science by pointing out this difference, and showing that the value of commodities does not depend, in any degree, on the value or price of labour, but solely on the *quantity thereof* by which they are produced. It is singular indeed that the previous theory should have imposed on Adam Smith, and maintained its ground, for so long a period. A little reflection will suffice to convince every one that variations in the rate of wages, or in the value of labour, occasion a different distribution of the produce of industry —increasing the share of the labourer, and diminishing that of his employer, or conversely; and that they can do nothing more than this. Could a hatter, for example, if wages rose 10 per cent., get 10 per cent. more shoes, corn, or anything else, in exchange for hats? Certainly not; for the same rise that affects the hatter equally affects the producers of other things. The rise would diminish profits, but it is evident it would have no influence over prices.

The arrangement of the 'Wealth of Nations' has been described as perplexed and illogical, and it must be confessed that this censure is in a considerable degree well founded. The thread of the investigation is often interrupted to make way for digressions upon some collateral topic; but though these have frequently only a very slight connexion with the main subject of investigation in the chapter in which they are placed, they uniformly turn upon some of the most important points in moral and political science. They are evidently the favourite topics of the author, who has displayed in their treatment all that comprehensive sagacity which formed the distinguishing feature of his mind. Although, therefore, it must be admitted that these digressions are not always introduced in the best and most natural manner, they notwithstanding add materially to the value of the work, and have greatly increased the number of its readers, by rendering it as interesting as it is instructive, and recommending it to those who might have felt indisposed to study a more scientific and logically arranged treatise, had it abounded less in discussion and illustration.

Sir James Mackintosh has made the following just and discriminating remarks on the great works of Grotius, Locke, Montesquieu, and Smith:—"'The Treatise on the Law of War and Peace,' 'The Essay on the Human Understanding,' 'The Spirit of Laws,' and 'The Inquiry into the Causes of the Wealth of Nations,' are the works which have most directly influenced the general opinion of Europe during the two last centuries. They are, also, the most conspicuous landmarks in the progress of the sciences to which they relate. It is remarkable that the defects of all these great works are very similar. The leading notions of none of them can, in the strictest sense, be said to be original, though Locke and Smith in that respect surpass their illustrious rivals. All of them employ great care in ascertaining those laws which are immediately deduced from experience, or directly applicable to practice; but apply metaphysical and abstract principles with considerable negligence. None pursues the order of science, beginning with first elements, and advancing to more and more complicated conclusions: though Locke is, perhaps, less defective in method than the rest. All admit digressions which, though often intrinsically excellent, distract attention, and break the chain of thought. None of them are happy in the choice, or constant in the use, of technical terms; and in none do we find much of that rigorous precision which is the first beauty of philosophical language.

"Grotius and Montesquieu were imitators of Tacitus—the first with more gravity—the second with more vivacity; but both were tempted to forsake the simple diction of science, in pursuit of the poignant brevity which that great historian has carried to a vicious excess. Locke and Smith chose an easy, clear, and free, but somewhat loose and verbose, style—more concise in Locke—more elegant in Smith—in both exempt from pedantry, but not void of ambiguity and repetition.

"Perhaps all these apparent defects contributed in some degree to the specific usefulness of these great works; and, by rendering their contents more accessible and acceptable to the majority of readers, have more completely blended their principles with the common opinions of mankind."*

Adam Smith was a native of Kirkcaldy, in the county of Fife, where he first saw the light on the 5th of June, 1723. He received his academical education partly at Glasgow and partly at Oxford. During the three seasons ending with 1750 he delivered courses of lectures at Edinburgh on Rhetoric and Belles-Lettres. In 1751 he was appointed professor in the University of Glasgow, where he continued to reside till 1763, when he was appointed tutor to the Duke of Buccleugh. He accompanied the latter to France; and acquired, during his stay at Paris, the friendship of Quesnay, Turgot, Helvetius, the Abbé Morellet, and other distinguished individuals. After his return to Scotland, in 1766, he remained for nearly ten years in the greatest seclusion at Kirkcaldy, engaged in the completion of his great work, of which, however, the foundations had been laid at Glasgow. Subsequently to the appearance of the 'Wealth of Nations,' in 1776, Smith resided for about two years in London; but having been appointed a Commissioner of Customs for Scotland, the latter years of his life were spent in Edinburgh, where he expired in July, 1790. Besides the 'Wealth of Nations,' Dr. Smith was the author of the 'Theory of Moral Sentiments,' one of the best and most eloquent works on moral science, and of some minor publications, the best known of which is his 'Letter to Mr. Strahan,' containing an account of the death and a character of his friend Mr. David Hume. The Life of Smith has been written, and some details given in illustration of his habits and the simplicity of his character, by the late Mr. Dugald Stewart.

An Inquiry into the Nature and Origin of Public Wealth, and into the Means and Causes of its Increase. By the Earl of Lauderdale. 1st ed., 1 vol. 8vo. Edinburgh, 1804. 2nd and improved ed., 1 vol. 8vo. Edinburgh, 1819.

The author of this Inquiry, James the eighth Earl of Lauderdale, celebrated in early life for his ultra-democratical opinions, died in 1839,

* Article on Stewart's View of the Progress of Metaphysical, Ethical, and Political Science, in the 71st No. of the Edinburgh Review.

in the eightieth year of his age. He was, also, the author of tracts on the Currency, the Sinking Fund, and other subjects. This work attracted when first published, most probably from the author's rank and reputation as a politician, a good deal of attention. It was ably reviewed, in an article ascribed to Mr. (now Lord) Brougham, in the 4th volume of the 'Edinburgh Review.' His Lordship was unwise enough to publish a reply to this article, in a pamphlet entitled 'Observations by the Earl of Lauderdale on the Review of his Inquiry into the Nature and Origin of Public Wealth in the eighth number of the "Edinburgh Review," 8vo., Edinburgh, 1804.' This produced a rejoinder from the reviewer, in which the noble author was treated with no little severity, in 'Thoughts suggested by Lord Lauderdale's Observations upon the "Edinburgh Review,"' 8vo., London, 1805.

The Principles of Political Economy and Taxation. By DAVID RICARDO, Esq. 1st ed., 1 vol., 8vo. London, 1817.—3rd ed., 1 vol., 8vo. London, 1821.

This is a most able, original, and profound work. Its appearance formed a new æra in the history of the science. Exclusive of many valuable correlative discussions, Mr. Ricardo has traced the source and limiting principle of exchangeable value, and has exhibited the laws which determine the distribution of the various products of art and industry among the various ranks and orders of society. The powers of mind displayed in these investigations, the dexterity with which the most abstruse and difficult questions are unravelled, the sagacity displayed in tracing the operation of general principles, in disentangling them from such as are of a secondary and accidental nature, and in perceiving and estimating their remotest consequences, have never been surpassed, and will for ever secure the name of Ricardo a conspicuous place amongst those who have done most to unfold the mechanism of society, and to perfect this science.

Mr. Ricardo was the first to perceive the error into which Smith had fallen, in supposing that the effects consequent upon an increase or diminution of the wages paid for the labour employed in the production of commodities were the same with those consequent upon an increase or diminution of the quantity of such labour. He showed that variations of profits or wages, by affecting all commodities to the same, or nearly the same extent, would either have no influence over their exchangeable value, or, if they had any, it would depend on the degree in which they occasionally affect some commodities more than others. And as it had been already shown that rent is not an element of cost or value, it follows that the cost or value of all freely produced commodities, the stock of which may be indefinitely increased, abstracting from temporary variations of supply and demand, depends wholly on the quantity of labour required to produce them and bring them to market, and not upon the rate at which that labour may be paid; so that, supposing the labour required to produce any number of commodities to remain constant, their cost and value will also remain constant, whether wages really fall from 3*s.* to 1*s.*, or really rise from 3*s.* to 5*s.* or 7*s.* a-day. This is the fundamental theorem of the science of value, and the clue which unravels the laws that regulate the distribution of wealth. Its discovery has shed a flood of light on what was previously shrouded in impenetrable mystery; and the apparently knotty and hitherto insoluble questions regarding the conflicting action and reaction of wages and profits on each other and on prices, have since ceased to present any insuperable difficulties. What the researches of Locke and Smith did for the production of wealth, those of Ricardo have done for its value and its distribution.

The establishment of general principles being Mr. Ricardo's great object, he has paid comparatively little attention to their practical application, and sometimes he has wholly, or in a great measure overlooked the circumstances by which they are occasionally countervailed. In illustration of this we may mention, that society being laid under the necessity of constantly resorting to inferior soils to obtain additional supplies of food, Mr. Ricardo lays it down that, in the progress of society, raw produce and wages have a constant tendency to rise and profits to fall. And this, no doubt, is abstractly true. But it must at the same time be observed, that while on the one hand society is obliged constantly to resort to inferior soils, agriculture is on the other hand susceptible of indefinite improvement; and this improvement necessarily in so far countervails the decreasing fertility of the soil; and may, and in fact very frequently does, more than countervail it. Mr. Ricardo has also very generally overlooked the influence of increased prices in diminishing consumption and stimulating industry, so that his conclusions, though true according to his assumptions, do not always harmonise with what really takes place. But Mr. Ricardo's is not a practical work, nor was it any part of his object to show on what these discrepancies depended. It is not even a systematic treatise, but is principally an inquiry into and elucidation of certain fundamental principles, most of which had previously been undiscovered. And though it be often exceedingly difficult, or, it may be, all but impossible, to estimate the extent to which these principles may in certain cases be modified by other principles and combinations of circumstances, it is obviously of the greatest importance to have ascertained their existence. They are so many land-marks to which to refer; and can never be lost sight of even in matters most essentially practical.

The brevity with which Mr. Ricardo has stated some of his most important principles, their intimate dependence on each other, the fewness of his illustrations, and the mathematical cast he has given to his reasonings, render it sometimes not a little difficult for readers unaccustomed to such investigations readily to follow him. But those who give to his works the attention of which they are so worthy, will find that he is remarkably consistent in the use of terms, and that he is as logical and conclusive as he is profound and original. It was the opinion of Quintilian, that the students of eloquence who were delighted with Cicero, had made no inconsiderable progress in their art, and the same may, without hesitation, be said of the students of political economy who find pleasure in the works of Ricardo: *Sciat se non parum profecisse cui RICARDO valde placebit.*

After acquiring a large fortune on the Stock exchange, with the universal esteem and respect of his competitors, Mr. Ricardo retired from business soon after the peace of 1815. In 1810 he published his earliest work: 'The High Price of Bullion a Proof of the Depreciation of Bank Notes' (see *post*); and, as stated above, his 'Principles' appeared in 1817. In 1819 he entered the House of Commons, where he speedily attained to high distinction. He died in September, 1823, when only 51 years of age—a life long enough for his own fame and fortune, but far too short for the interests of science and of sound legislation.

ELEMENTS of POLITICAL ECONOMY. By JAMES MILL, Esq. 2nd ed., 1 vol., 8vo. 1824.

This work, by the distinguished author of the 'History of British India,' is a *résume* of the doctrines of Smith and of Ricardo with respect to the production and distribution of wealth, and of those of Malthus with respect to population. But it is of too abstract a character to be either popular or of much utility. Those secondary principles and modifying circumstances, which exert so powerful an influence over general principles, are wholly, or almost wholly, overlooked by Mill. But though their consideration might be omitted in an original work like that of Ricardo, it is not so easily excused in an elementary treatise. The object of the latter is not to make discoveries, but to exhibit the connexion, dependence, and real influence of the principles, whether primary or secondary, that are known to be in operation; and this is not to be done by looking only at one set and neglecting the others. The science is very far from having arrived at the perfection Mr. Mill supposed. Any one, indeed, may state generally how certain principles operate; but in the vast majority of instances it is extremely difficult, and sometimes quite impossible, to foresee the mode or the degree in which they may be countervailed by others, or to conjecture what may be the remote results of their combined action.

THE PRINCIPLES of POLITICAL ECONOMY, considered with a View to their Practical Application. By the Rev. T. R. MALTHUS, A.M. 1st ed., 1 vol. 8vo. London, 1820. 2nd ed., with a Life of the Author, by Dr. OTTER, late Bishop of Chichester. 1 vol. 8vo. London, 1836.

Mr. Malthus's reputation rests wholly on his essay on Population (which see), and was not increased by this or any one of his other publications, excepting, perhaps, the Essay on Rent. The work now referred to consists of a series of disquisitions, generally of a controversial character, on subjects belonging to and connected with political economy. Certainly, however, it has no pretensions to be regarded as an exposition of its principles, either in a practical or scientific point of view. Though frequently learned and ingenious, the reasonings are, for the most part, perplexed and inconclusive. Mr. Ricardo left a manuscript volume of observations on this work, principally in reply to the interminable criticisms of Mr. Malthus on his peculiar doctrines. These, however, were speedily and easily disposed of by Mr. de Quincey and others. Malthus never, in fact, thoroughly understood the Ricardian theory of value, or had any clear perception of the doctrines he was so ready to assail; so that his attacks on them could not be otherwise than feeble and futile.

An Essay on the Production of Wealth. With an Appendix in which the Principles of Political Economy are applied to the Actual Circumstances of this Country. By ROBERT TORRENS (Colonel TORRENS), Esq., F.R.S. 1 vol. 8vo. London, 1821.

Well-written, ingenious, and generally sound; but this, like the greater number of the author's works, has rather too many illustrative examples, which are not always very happily chosen or easy to follow.

Conversations on Political Economy, in which the Elements of that Science are familiarly explained. By Mrs. MARCET. 1 vol. post 8vo. 1st ed., London, 1817, and frequently reprinted.

This is on the whole, perhaps, the best introduction to the science that has yet appeared.

A DISCOURSE on the RISE, PROGRESS, PECULIAR OBJECTS, and IMPORTANCE of POLITICAL ECONOMY. With an Outline of a Course of Lectures on the Principles and Doctrines of that Science. By J. R. M'CULLOCH, Esq. 8vo. Edinburgh, 1825.

DEFINITIONS in POLITICAL ECONOMY. By the Rev. T. R. MALTHUS, A.M., &c. 1 vol. post 8vo. London, 1827.

This work was reviewed in an Edinburgh Journal soon after it was published; and the estimate there given of its merits has since been abundantly confirmed by the judgment of the public.

LECTURES on the ELEMENTS of POLITICAL ECONOMY. By THOMAS COOPER, M.D. 2nd ed., 1 vol. 8vo. Columbia, S.C., 1829.

This work, though not written in a very philosophical spirit, is the best of the American works on political economy that we have met with.

LECTURES introductory to a COURSE on the SCIENCE of POLITICAL ECONOMY. By Dr. WHATELEY, Archbishop of Dublin. 1 vol. 8vo. London, 1831.

ON POLITICAL ECONOMY in connexion with the MORAL STATE and MORAL PROSPECTS of SOCIETY. By the Rev. THOMAS CHALMERS, D.D. 1 vol. 8vo. Glasgow, 1832.

This work displays in an eminent degree that tendency to rash generalization, and that striking declamatory style, which, however unsuitable to works of this description, has materially contributed to the popularity of the author's other writings. The principles which pervade the work are mostly borrowed from the Economists and Mr. Malthus; and are frequently either wholly unsound or carried to such an extreme as to become inapplicable and absurd. It however contains some ingenious disquisitions. It was reviewed in the 'Edinburgh Review' (vol. lvi. pp. 52–72). Dr. Chalmers replied to the reviewer in a pamphlet, in which he ineffectually endeavoured to vindicate his doctrines from the objections urged against them.

PRINCIPLES OF POLITICAL ECONOMY, deduced from the Natural Laws of Social Welfare, and applied to the Present State of Great Britain. By G. POULETT SCROPE, Esq., M.P. 1 vol. 12mo. London, 1833.

A work of considerable talent and acuteness; but its theories and reasonings are, in many instances, not a little questionable.

An Outline of the Science of Political Economy. By N. W. SENIOR, Esq., A.M. From the Encyclopædia Metropolitana. 4to. London, 1836.

An able, comprehensive, and admirably written essay. We incline, however, to think that the learned author has confined the objects of the science within too narrow limits, and that he has taken an incorrect view of the principles and of the nature of the evidence on which it is founded. We have shortly stated our reasons for being of this opinion in the preface to the 'Principles of Political Economy.'

PRINCIPLES OF POLITICAL ECONOMY. By H. C. CAREY, Esq. 4 Parts, in 3 vols. 8vo. Philadelphia, 1837–40.

Part I. Treats of the Laws of the Production and Distribution of Wealth.
II. ———— Causes which retard Increase in the Production of Wealth, and Improvement in the Physical and Moral Condition of Man.
III. ———— Causes which retard Increase in the Numbers of Mankind.
IV. ———— Causes which retard Improvement in the Political Condition of Mankind.

This work is written in a fair and candid spirit, and is the fruit of a good deal of reading and research. But it is crude and indigested, being deficient in criticism, and without any clear or well defined principles. For the most part, indeed, the conclusions are deduced from statistical and other statements of very questionable authority, and which admit of various interpretations. It is, consequently, of little value. Even the portion which treats of production is infected with sundry grave errors; and these become still more numerous and important in the other parts of the work.

The Principles of Political Economy. With some Inquiries respecting their Application, and a Sketch of the Rise and Progress of the Science. By J. R. M'Culloch, Esq. 1st ed., 1 vol. 8vo. Edinburgh, 1825. 3rd ed., greatly enlarged and improved, 1 vol. 8vo. Edinburgh, 1843.

The Logic of Political Economy. By Thomas de Quincey, Esq. 1 vol. 8vo. Edinburgh and London, 1844.

This very clever work is intended to unravel intricacies and to expose sundry errors in the application of the Ricardian theory of value. It would, however, have been more popular and successful had it been less scholastic. It is right to be logical, but not to be perpetually obtruding logical forms and technicalities on the reader's attention. This sort of affectation is little noticed in a brief essay, like the 'Templars' Dialogues' (see *post*); but in a goodly sized volume, like the present, it becomes tiresome and repulsive.

Essays on some Unsettled Questions of Political Economy. By John S. Mill, Esq. (Author of the System of Logic). 8vo. London, 1844.

Traité des Richesses, contenant l'Analyse de l'Usage des Richesses en général, et de leurs Valeurs; les Principes et les Loix naturelles de la Circulation des Richesses, de leur Distribution, du Commerce, de la Circulation des Monnoies et de l'Impôt; et des Recherches Historiques sur les Révolutions que les Droits de Propriété, publics et particuliers, ont éprouvées en France depuis l'Origine de la Monarchie. (Par M. Isnard.) 2 vol. 8vo. Londres (Lausanne), 1781.

Though (like its title) desultory and wanting in precision, this is a learned and valuable work. M. Isnard is one of the few continental authors of his time who dissented entirely from the system of the Economists; and who justly contends that manufactures and commerce are really productive; and that, even if it were possible, it would be most unjust and inexpedient to lay all taxes on the land. He has also examined, at considerable length and with considerable acuteness, the various apologies that have been made for imposing restrictions on the exportation of certain commodities, and on the importation of others, and has shown that they are in every case sophistical and unfounded. And farther, he has ably vindicated the employment of machinery from the objections that have sometimes been urged against it. The second volume of the work is principally occupied with inquiries respecting taxation; in reference to which there is an elaborate account of the mode in which property was acquired, and the conditions and burdens under which it was held in different periods of French history, and especially at the epoch when this work was published.

DICTIONNAIRE d'ECONOMIE POLITIQUE de l'ENCYCLOPEDIE METHODIQUE. 4 vol. 4to. Paris, 1784-1788.

This immense work includes political geography and diplomacy, as well as political economy. It was edited by M. Demeunier, but some of the principal articles were contributed by M. Grivel, a zealous Economist. It is not of much value.

Traite d'Economie Politique, ou Simple Exposition de la Manière dont se Forment, se Distribuent, et se Consomment les Richesses. 1re ed., 2 vol. 8vo. Paris, 1802. 5me ed., 3 vol. 8vo. Paris, 1826.

This work would deserve to be respectfully mentioned, were it only for the influence which it has had in diffusing a knowledge of the true principles with respect to the production of wealth and the freedom of industry throughout the Continent. It is well arranged, clearly written, and easily understood. But, except in so far as respects the inquiry relating to gluts, Say has left the science in precisely the same state in which he received it from Adam Smith. He appears, indeed, to have taken the limits of his own vision for those of the horizon, and to have supposed that the science had attained in his hands to its highest possible perfection! It is difficult otherwise to account for his obstinately refusing to profit by the important discoveries of Ricardo and others. The first edition of his work, published in 1802, is in fact nearly as good as the last edition, published in 1826; though all that great branch of the science which treats of the distribution of wealth and the principles of taxation had been completely changed in the interim. The distinguishing merit of Say is that of a skilful exponent of truths and principles already known and fully established. Whatever seemed to open new views, or to clash in any degree with doctrines to which he had already assented, was sure, how well soever it might be established, to encounter his hostility.

His principal merit in a scientific point of view consists in his showing, in a more satisfactory manner than it had been done previously, that effective demand depends upon production.* And it is easy to see that such must be the case. An excess of a particular commodity, or of a few commodities, may be occasionally produced; but it is quite impossible that there should be an excess of every commodity. Abstracting from the disturbing influence of changes in the quantity and value of money, and of political regulations, if the market be encumbered and a difficulty experienced in effecting the sale of commodities, we may be assured that the fault is not in producing too much, but in the production of commodities which either do not suit the tastes of the buyers, or which we cannot ourselves consume. If we attend to those

* This principle had been previously advanced by Tucker, in his 'Queries on the Naturalization Bill,' p. 10; by Mengotti, in his 'Dissertazione sul Colbertismo,' p. 31; and still more clearly by the author of the tract entitled 'Sketch of the Advance and Decline of Nations,' 8vo., London, 1795.

two grand requisites—if we produce such commodities only as may be taken off by those to whom they are offered, or such as are directly available to our own use, we may increase the power of production ten or twenty times, and be as free of all excess as if we diminished it in the same proportion. A glut never originates in an increase of production, but is, in every case, a consequence of the misapplication of that power, or of the producers not properly adapting their means to their ends. They wished, for example, to obtain silks, and offered cottons in exchange: the holders of silks were, however, already sufficiently supplied with cottons, but were in want of woollens. Hence the cause of the glut, which consists not in over-production, but in the production of cottons which were not wanted, instead of woollens which were. Let this error be rectified, and the glut will disappear. Even though the holders of silks were supplied with cottons, cloth, and every other commodity in the power of the demanders to offer, the principle for which we are contending would not be invalidated: for, if those who want silks cannot obtain them in exchange for woollens, or such other commodities as they either have or can produce, they will abandon the production of the commodities which they do not want, and apply themselves directly to the production of those which they do want, or of substitutes for them. In no case, therefore, can an increased facility of production be attended with inconvenience. We might with equal truth pretend that an increased fertility of the soil, and an increased salubrity of climate, are injurious. Such commodities as are carried to market are produced only that they may be exchanged for others; and, under the circumstances supposed, the fact of their being in excess affords a conclusive proof that there is a corresponding deficiency in the supply of those they were intended to buy or be exchanged for. A universal glut of all sorts of commodities is impossible; every excess in one class must be countervailed by an equal deficiency in some other class. "To suppose that there may be a production of commodities without a demand, provided these commodities be of the right species, is as absurd as to suppose that the revenues of the several individuals composing the society may be too great for their consumption." (Sketch of the Advance and Decline of Nations, p. 82.)

M. Say expired at Paris on the 16th November, 1832, in his 67th year. He was highly esteemed by his friends.

Traite d'Economie Politique. Par M. le Comte DESTUTT DE TRACY. 1 vol. 12mo. Paris, 1823.

This treatise appeared at first, in 1815, in 8vo., as the 4th volume of the author's 'Traité d'Idéologie,' but was separately published in 12mo. in 1823. With the exception, perhaps, of the 'Traité d'Economie Politique' of Say, this was at the date of its publication the best work on the science that had appeared in France; and it continues to be highly worthy of study and attention. The nature of production has never been so well explained as in the following paragraphs:—

"Toutes les opérations de la nature et de l'art se réduisent à des transmutations, à des changemens de *formes* et de *lieux*. Non-seulement nous ne créons jamais rien, mais il nous est même impossible de concevoir ce que c'est que *créer* ou *anéantir*, si nous entendons rigoureusement par ces mots, *faire quelque chose de rien*, ou *réduire quelque chose à rien;* car nous n'avons jamais vu un être quelconque sortir du néant ni y rentrer. De là cet axiome admis par toute l'antiquité: rien ne vient de *rien*, et ne peut redevenir rien. Que faisons-nous donc par notre travail, par notre action sur tous les êtres qui nous entourent? Jamais rien qu'opérer dans ces êtres des changemens de forme ou de lieu qui les approprient à notre usage, qui les rendent utiles à la satisfaction de nos besoins Voila ce que nous devons entendre par *produire;* c'est donner aux choses une utilité qu'elles n'avaient pas. Quel que soit notre travail, s'il n'en résulte point d'utilité, il est infructueux; s'il en résulte, il est *productif.*

"Il semble d'abord, et beaucoup de personnes le croient encore, qu'il y a une production plus réelle dans le travail qui a pour objet de se procurer les matières premières, que dans celui qui consiste à les façonner ou à les transporter; mais c'est une illusion. Lorsque je mets quelques graines en contact avec l'air, l'eau, la terre et différens engrais, de manière que du concours et des combinaisons de ces élémens il résulte du blé, du chanvre, du tabac, il n'y a pas plus de création opérée que quand je vais prendre le grain de ce blé pour le convertir en farine et en pain; les filamens de ce chanvre, pour en faire successivement du fil, de la toile et des vêtemens; et les feuilles de ce tabac, pour les préparer de façon à pouvoir les fumer, les mâcher ou les prendre par le nez. Dans l'un et l'autre cas il y a production d'utilité, car tous ces travaux sont également nécessaires pour remplir le but désiré, la satisfaction de quelques-uns de nos besoins."

M. de Tracy has also successfully shown the error of supposing that there is any real or substantial difference between agricultural, and manufacturing and commercial industry: "Le vrai est tout uniment que tous nos travaux utiles sont productifs, et que ceux relatifs à l'agriculture le sont comme les autres, de la même manière que les autres, par les mêmes raisons que les autres, et n'ont en cela rien de particulier. Une ferme est une véritable manufacture; tout s'y opère de même, par les mêmes principes et pour le même but. Un champ est un véritable outil, ou si l'on veut, un amas de matières premières, que l'on peut prendre s'il n'appartient à personne, et qu'il faut acheter, ou louer, ou emprunter, s'il a déjà un maître. Il ne change point de nature, soit que je l'emploie à faire fructifier des graines, ou à y étendre des toiles pour blanchir, ou à tout autre usage. Dans tous les cas, c'est un instrument nécessaire pour un effet qu'on veut produire, comme un fourneau, ou un marteau, ou un vaisseau. La seule différence de cet instrument à tout autre, c'est que, pour s'en servir, comme il ne peut pas se déplacer, il faut l'aller trouver, au lieu de le faire venir à soi."

M. Destutt Tracy's work was published before the true theory of rent and of profits had been explained; so that it is in some important respects incomplete and defective. But speaking generally, it is equally sound and liberal; it is concisely and forcibly written, without any sort of pretension, or any attempt at over-refinement.

Cours d'Economie Politique, ou Exposition des Principes qui déterminent la Prospérité des Nations. Par M. Henri Storch. 1re ed., 6 vol. 8vo. Pétersbourg, 1815. 2de ed., avec des Notes de M. Say. 4 vol. 8vo. Paris, 1823.

This work was written at the request of Alexander, late Emperor of Russia, for the instruction of his brothers, the Grand Dukes Nicholas (the present emperor) and Michael. It would, we believe, be no easy task to refer to another instance of a work, produced under anything like similar circumstances, and in all respects so unexceptionable. Besides an exposition, derived principally from Smith, Say, and other high authorities, of the circumstances most favourable to the production of wealth, and the advantages resulting from the freedom of commerce and industry, the work contains various disquisitions on important subjects, some of which have received but little attention from the English and French ecomomists. Among others, the accounts of slavery in Ancient Rome and in modern Europe, particularly Russia, and of the paper money of the different continental states, are extremely interesting and valuable. We said of this work about twenty years ago, that "without the remotest intention of depreciating the labours of others, we conceive we are fully warranted in placing it at the head of all the works on political economy ever imported from the Continent into England;"* and we do not know that we have any very good reason for being at present of a different opinion.

The notes added by Say to the edition published at Paris in 1823 are of very little value, and are written in a conceited manner, and with an air of superiority, which is alike misplaced and ludicrous. In 1824 Storch published, at Paris, a supplementary volume, entitled *Considérations sur la Nature du Revenu National*, 8vo., in the preface to which he refers to Say with considerable bitterness; though, as we have seen, not without provocation.

Exclusive of the above, Storch is the author of a valuable Statistical Account of Russia, and of a Picture of Petersburgh.

RECHERCHES sur la NATURE et les CAUSES de la RICHESSE des NATIONS. Traduit de l'Anglois d'ADAM SMITH, avec des Notes et Observations par M. le MARQUIS GARNIER. 2de ed., 6 vol. 8vo. Paris, 1822.

There were two previous translations of the 'Wealth of Nations' into French; but the present is universally allowed to be the only one worthy of the original. Garnier belonged to the economical school, and his notes are written with a corresponding bias. But they are, notwithstanding, learned and ingenious, and embody much curious information, especially of a historical kind. Their great defect consists in their being opposed to the new doctrines respecting rent and profit, and in their representing the 'Wealth of Nations' as perfect in the very parts in which it stands most in need of correction.

DICTIONNAIRE d'ECONOMIE POLITIQUE. Par M. GANILH. 1 vol. 8vo. Paris, 1826.

Ganilh published several works on subjects connected with Political Economy, of which Blanqui says the Dictionary is *le plus mauvais*. We doubt, however, whether it be really entitled to this distinction. In truth they are universally good for nothing.

Traite d'Economie Politique, Ouvrage traduit de l'Allemand de M. SCHMALZ, par M. JOUFFROY. 2 vol. 8vo. Paris, 1826.

This work is written on the principles of the Economists, the writer not appearing to have been at all aware of the important discoveries of Ricardo and others by whom he had been preceded. But though of little or no value as a scientific treatise, it is in other respects entitled to very high praise. M. Schmalz has not proposed to solve what Burke truly calls the finest problem in legislation, that is, to determine "what the State ought to take upon itself to direct by the public wisdom, and what it ought to leave, with as little interference as possible, to individual exertion." He has, however, made various observations on the principles by which the interference of government should be regulated; the subjects in regard to which it is most necessary; and the extent to which it should be carried. And we are not aware that these important matters have been anywhere more ably handled; and the proper objects, degree, and limits of interference more satisfactorily ascertained. In these respects the work is most valuable. It was reviewed, and considerable extracts made from it, in the 48th volume of the 'Edinburgh Review.'

NOUVEAUX PRINCIPES d'ECONOMIE POLITIQUE; ou, de la Richesse

* Discourse on Political Economy, second edition, Edinburgh, 1825, p. 93.

dans ses Rapports avec la Population. Par M. DE SISMONDI. 2de éd., 2 vol. 8vo. Paris, 1827.

The deserved reputation of M. Sismondi as an historian has procured for this work, and his *Etudes sur l'Economie Politique* (2 vol. 8vo., Paris, 1838), a degree of attention which would not otherwise have been awarded to them. We may concede to M. Sismondi that the state of the labouring classes, even in the richest and most advanced countries, is not by any means so prosperous as might be wished. Still, however, these classes have gained immensely by the progress that has been made in civilization and the arts, though, had it been otherwise, the principles M. Sismondi has laid down, were they acted upon, would increase their misery a hundredfold, at the same time that they would sink every other class to the same level of hopeless barbarism. He finds fault with the employment of machinery, with competition, and, in fact, with everything most conducive to the increase of national wealth! His crude and contradictory reasonings have, however, been refuted over and over again;* and were it not for his other works, those now referred to would be as completely forgotten as the anti-social paradoxes of Rousseau or the Political Justice of Godwin.

ECONOMIE POLITIQUE; ou, Principes de la Science des Richesses. Par M. DROZ. 1 vol. 8vo. Paris, 1829.

One of the best elementary works on the science in the French language.

COURS d'ECONOMIE POLITIQUE PRATIQUE, &c. Par M. J. B. SAY. 6 vol. 8vo. Paris, 1828-29.

The principles advanced in this work are substantially identical with those in the *Traité d'Economie Politique*, the only difference being in the different treatment of the subjects and the illustrations.

MELANGES et CORRESPONDANCE d'ECONOMIE POLITIQUE. Ouvrage posthume de M. J. B. SAY. 1 vol. 8vo. Paris, 1833.

This volume consists principally of letters, in which various points of political economy are discussed between M. Say on the one part, and Messrs. Dupont de Nemours, Ricardo, Malthus, Tooke, &c., on the other.

The *Traité d'Economie Politique* of M. Say, and his *Cours*, have been published (the former in 1 vol. and the latter in 2 vols. royal 8vo.) at Paris, in 1841, being vols. ix. x. and xi. of the *Collection des Principaux Economistes*, now in the course of publication in that city.

Histoire d'Economie Politique en Europe, depuis les Anciens jusqu'à nos Jours. Par M. ADOLPHE BLANQUI. 2de éd. 2 vol. 8vo. Paris, 1842.

The works of Boeckh and of Dureau de la Malle on the public economy of the Athenians and Romans (see chapter on Miscellaneous Works), and those of Heeren on the Commerce of Ancient Nations, comprise the best accounts of the political economy of antiquity. The sketch of it given by Blanqui in the present work is brief and superficial; but his accounts of the political economy of the middle ages and of modern times are more carefully elaborated, and are interesting and valuable.

TRAITÉ d'ECONOMIE NATIONALE (Théorie de l'Economie Poli-

* Edinburgh Review, vol. xxxv. pp. 102-123; Principles of Political Economy, third edition, pp. 190-219, &c.

tique). Traduit de l'Allemand de M. CH. H. RAU. 1 vol. grand in-8vo. Bruxelles, 1840.

This work has been very popular in Germany, but it is not of a kind that would succeed in this country, being frittered down into endless divisions and subdivisions. It discovers a wide range of indiscriminate reading, all sorts of books being referred to as if they were entitled to equal credit. The author appears to be, on the whole, attached to the principles of Smith. He rejects the theory of rent, as explained by Ricardo and others; and he also dissents from the doctrine which makes the cost or value of freely-produced commodities depend on the quantities of labour required to produce them and bring them to market. He has, in consequence, no clear or accurate ideas in regard to many of the most important departments of the science, so that his work, from the want of fixed and sound principles, and the number of references to facts and books of very questionable authority, is better fitted to confuse and puzzle than to instruct and enlighten.

COURS D'ECONOMIE POLITIQUE, fait au Collège de Nanci, par M. MICHEL CHEVALIER. 1 vol. 8vo. Paris, 1842.

Principally devoted to an illustration of the advantages resulting from the employment of machinery, and from the facility of communication by roads, canals, railways, &c. M. Chevalier is the author of one of the best works on the United States, entitled *Lettres sur l'Amérique du Nord*, 2 vol. 8vo., Paris, 1837.

Cours d'Economie Politique. Par M. ROSSI. 2de éd., 2 vol. 8vo. Paris, 1843.

An able and liberal, but not a complete or systematic work. M. Rossi has set the new theory of rent in a clear point of view. Like most French writers he approves of the law of equal succession, and of the subdivision of the land which has resulted from it; and he contends that, by associating together, the properties of small proprietors may be farmed according to the most approved systems of agriculture. We believe, however, that any such supposition is much more visionary than anything else; and though we do not deny that the law of equal succession, and the subdivision of a country into small properties, have some advantages, we are well convinced that the disadvantages very greatly preponderate. For proofs of this, see note on the disposal of property by will, in the edition of the 'Wealth of Nations' by the author of this work.

Recherches sur la Nature et les Causes de la Richesse des Nations. Par ADAM SMITH, traduction de Garnier. Avec une Notice biographique, et des Notes des principaux Commentateurs. Par M. BLANQUI. 2 vol. grand in-8vo. Paris, 1843.

This work makes vols. v. and vi. of the *Collection des Principaux Economistes.*

Meditazioni sulla Economia Politica, di CONTE PIETRO VERRI. 1ma ed., 1 vol. 8vo. Milano, 1771.

Verri, who is by far the most distinguished of the Italian economists, belonged to a noble family of Milan, where he was born in 1728, and where he died in 1797. The work now referred to had the most decided success, having gone through no fewer than six or seven editions within two years from its publication. It is written with great brevity and clearness. Verri demonstrated the fallacy of the opinions entertained by the Economists respecting the superiority of agricultural labour; and showed that all the operations of industry resolve themselves into modifications of matter already in existence. He also laid it down that the great practical problem of that part of political economy which treats of the production of wealth, "*si è accrescere al possibile l' annua riproduzione col minor possibile travaglio, ossia data la quantità di riproduzione ottenerla col minimo travaglio; data la quantità del travaglio ottenere la massima riproduzione; accrescere quanto più si può il travaglio e cavarne il massimo effetto di riproduzione.*" It is to be regretted that he did not trace the consequences of the principle here distinctly stated, by inquiring into the means by which labour may be rendered most efficient, and that he has omitted all notice of the division and combination of employments, and of the introduction and improvement of machinery. His object, however, was not so much to produce a systematic treatise, as to show the impolicy of restrictions, especially of those restraining the freedom of the corn-trade, and of those growing out of the privileges of corporations, internal custom-houses, &c.

Verri's other treatises are also most valuable. The *Riflessioni sulle Leggi vincolanti principalmente nel Commercio de' Grani* (see post) is one of the ablest essays in favour of the unlimited freedom of the corn-trade hitherto published.

The economical works of Verri are comprised in the 15th, 16th, and 17th vols. of the modern part of the *Economisti Italiani.*

ELEMENTI di ECONOMIA PUBBLICA, di Marchese CESARE BECCARIA. Vol. 2nda delle Opere di Beccaria. 2 vol. 8vo. Milano, 1821.

Beccaria's famous treatise on crimes and punishments (*Dei Delitti e delle Pene*) appeared in 1764, and perhaps no other work ever became so immediately popular, while few have had a more beneficial influence. The author was soon after invited by the Empress Catherine to enter the Russian service; but the Austrian Government prevented his emigration by creating in 1768, in Milan, a class of public economy under the title of *Scienze Camerale*, of which he was appointed professor, with a handsome salary. The introductory discourse delivered at the opening of this class, on the 9th of January, 1769, was published separately; and having been translated into English, appeared at London in the course of the same year.* Soon after this, Beccaria published the first part of his *Ricerche intorno alla Natura dello Stile.* In 1771 he was appointed to a situation in the Government, the duties of which appear to have subsequently occupied the greater portion of his attention. At all events his future labours as an author were confined to the publication of a tract on a uniform system of measures, and to the arrangement of the returns obtained under the census of the Milanese in 1786. He was carried off by an apoplexy in 1793.

The *Elementi di Economia Pubblica* were published, for the first time, in 1804, by Custodi, in the collection of the *Economisti Italiani*, and occupy the 11th and the greater part of the 12th vols. of the modern series. They consist of his lectures delivered at Milan. He states that he intended his course should embrace the philosophy of agriculture, manufactures, commerce, finance, and public policy. Owing,

* A Discourse on Public Œconomy and Commerce, by the Marquis Cæsar Beccaria, &c., 8vo., London, 1769. This Discourse is neither worthy of the author, the subject, nor the course to which it was an introduction. It is indeed a very poor performance.

however, to the limited space within which it had to be confined, or to his attention having been diverted from it to other matters, the first two subjects have only been treated of with any degree of fulness, while the last two are wholly omitted. But notwithstanding their incompleteness, and the defects of their plan, the *Elementi* are enriched with some valuable disquisitions, and would have done credit, at the epoch when they were written, to any one less liberal and enlightened than the author of the treatise on crimes and punishments, but are hardly what might have been expected from the latter. Beccaria adopts the theory of the Economists with respect to the unproductiveness of manufactures and commerce. (See the notice prefixed to his works in the *Economisti Italiani;* Pecchio, *Storia dell' Economia Pubblica,* p. 144, &c.)

The Italians have a great many economical works, especially with reference to money. The best of these works were published, in a chronological series, by the Baron Custodi, in the Collection entitled **Scrittori-Classici Italiani di Economia Politica,** 50 vol. 8vo., Milano, 1803-1816, a publication which does honour to Italy. Exclusive of the treatises of Verri and Beccaria noticed above, some of the other treatises comprised in this collection will be noticed in other parts of this work. In the meantime we subjoin a list of the works of which it consists:—

Parte Antica.

Vol. I. (1.) Breve Trattato delle Cause che possono far abbondare li Regni d' Oro e d' Argento dove non sono Miniere, di Antonio Serra.
(2.) Discorsi e Relazioni sulle Monete del Regno di Napoli, di Gian-Donato Turbolo.
II. (1.) Lezione delle Monete, di Bernardo Davanzati.
(2.) Discorso sopra le Monete e della vera Proporzione tra l' Oro e l' Argento, di Gasparo Scaruffi.
III. Della Moneta Trattato Mercantile, di Geminiano Montanari.
IV. (1.) Trattato de' Tributi, di Carlo Antonio Broggia.
(2.) Trattato delle Monete considerate ne' rapporti di legittima Riduzione di Circolazione e di Deposito, di Carlo Antonio Broggia.
V. (1.) Trattato delle Monete—continuazione.
(2.) Due Frammenti estratti dal Trattato Politico della Sanità.
VI. Osservazioni sopra il Prezzo legale delle Monete, di Pompeo Neri.
VII. Documenti annessi alle Osservazioni sopra il Prezzo legale delle Monete, di Pompeo Neri.

Parte Moderna.

Vol. I. (1.) Elogio di Salustio Antonio Bandini, scritto da Giuseppe Gorani.
(2.) Discorso Economico scritto dall' Arcidiacono Salustio Antonio Bandini.
(3.) Saggio sopra il Commercio, di Francesco Algarotti.
II. (I.) Dissertazione sopra il Commercio, di Girolamo Belloni.
(2.) Saggio sopra il Giusto Pregio delle Cose della Moneta e sopra il Commercio dei Romani, di Gio. Francesco Pagnini.
III. Della Moneta, di Ferdinando Galiani, libro I. e II.
IV. „ „ „ „ „ III. IV. e V.
V. Dialogues sur le Commerce de Blés, par l'Abbé Ferdinand Galiani.
VI. (1.) Continuation des Dialogues.
(2.) Estratto del Discorso sulla Perfetta Conservazione del Grano, scritto e pubblicato per ordine e sotto il nome di Bartolommeo Intieri, da Ferdinando Galiani.

Vol. VII. Lezioni di Economia Civile, di Antonio Genovesi.
VIII. Lezioni—continuazione.
IX. (1.) Lezioni—continuazione.
(2.) Opuscoli di Economia Politica, di Antonio Genovesi.
X. Continuazione degli Opuscoli Economici, di Antonio Genovesi.
XI. Elementi di Economia Pubblica, di Cesare Beccaria.
XII. (1.) Elementi—continuazione.
(2.) Della Riduzione delle Misure di Lunghezza all' Uniformita' per lo Stato di Milano, Relazione del Consigliere Cesare Beccaria presentata al Magistrato Camerale.
XIII. (1.) Dell' Origine e del Commercio della Moneta e dei Disordini che accadona nelle Alterazioni di essa, Dissertazione di Gian-Rinaldo Carli.
(2.) Digressione su la Proporzione Media fra i Metalli Monetati estratta dalla Dissertazione sulle Monete di Gian-Rinaldo Carli.
(3.) Del Valore e della Proporzione de' Metalli Monetati con i Generi en Italia Prima delle Scoperte dell' India col confronto del Valore e della Proporzione de' Tempi nostri, Dissertazione di Gian-Rinaldo Carli.
XIV. (1.) Osservazioni Preventive al Piano Intorno alle Monete di Milano, di Gian-Rinaldo Carli.
(2.) Nuove Osservazioni su la Riforma delle Monete, di Gian-Rinaldo Carli.
(3.) Relazione del Censimento dello Stato di Milano, di Gian-Rinaldo Carli.
(4.) Breve Ragionamento sopra i Bilanci Economici delle Nazioni, di Gian-Rinaldo Carli.
(5.) Del Libero Commercio de' Grani, Lettera di Gian-Rinaldo Carli al Presidente Pompeo Nero.
XV. Meditazioni sulla Economia Politica di Pietro Verri, con Annotazioni di Gian-Rinaldo Carli.
XVI. (1.) Sulle Leggi Vincolanti principalmente nel Commercio de' Grani Riflessioni di Pietro Verri.
(2.) Dialogo sul Disordine delle Monete nello Stato di Milano nel 1762, di Pietro Verri.
(3.) Estratto del Progetto di una Tariffa della Mercanzia per lo Stato di Milano presentato al Magistrato Camerale da Pietro Verri.
XVII. (1.) Memorie Storiche sulla Economia Pubblica dello Stato di Milano, di Pietro Verri.
(2.) Osservazioni sulla Tortura e singolarmente sugli effetti che produsse all' occasione delle Unzioni Malefiche, alle quali si attribui la Pestilenza che devastò Milano l' anno 1630, di Pietro Verri.
(3.) Varj Opuscoli di Economia Pubblica di Pietro Verri ed altri due di diversi Autori relativi alle di lui Opere.
XVIII. Lettre Scelte sull' Agricoltura, sul Commercio e sulle Arti, di Antonio Zanon.
XIX. (1.) Apologia della Mercatura, Lettere di Antonio Zanon.
(2.) Estratto del Trattato dell' Utilità Morale, Economica e Politica delle Accademie di Agricoltura, Arti, e Commercio, di Antonio Zanon.
XX. (1.) Estratto de' Pensieri sopra l' Agricoltura, di Ferdinando Paoletti.
(2.) I Veri Mezzi di render Felici le Società, di Fernando Paoletti.
XXI. Della Economia Nazionale, libri sei, di Giammaria Ortes.
XXII. Della Economia—continuazione.

Vol. XXIII. Lettere di Giammaria Ortes in proposito del suo libro della Economia Nazionale.
XXIV. (1.) Riflessioni sulla Popolazione delle Nazioni per rapporto all' Economia Nazionale, di Giammaria Ortes.
(2.) Delle Scienze Utili e delle Dilettevoli per rapporto alla Felicità Umana Ragionamento, di Giammaria Ortes.
(3.) Calcolo sopra il Valore delle Opinioni e sopra i Piaceri e i Dolori della Vita Umana, di Giammaria Ortes.
(4.) Lettere di Giammaria Ortes al Conte Francesco Algarotti e al Sig. Auditore Michele Ciani.
XXV. (1.) Errori Popolari intorno all' Economia Nazionale considerati sulle presenti Controversie tra i Laici e i Chierici in ordine al Possedimento, de' Beni, di Giammaria Ortes.
(2.) Lettere sulla Religione e il Governo de' Popoli, di Giammaria Ortes.
XXVI. Lettere sulla Religione—continuazione.
XXVII. Dei Fidecommessi a Famiglie e a Chiese e Luoghi Pii in proposito del Termine di Mani-morte introdotto a questi ultimi tempi nell' Economia Nazionale, libri due, di Giammaria Ortes.
XXVIII. Esame Economico del Sistema Civile, di Filippo Briganti.
XXIX. Esame Economico—continuazione.
XXX. (1.) Dell' Armonia Politico-Economica tra la Città e il suo Territorio, di Giambattista Gherardo d'Arco.
(2.) Dell' Annona, di Giambattista Gherardo d'Arco.
XXXI. (1.) Dell' Influenza del Commercio sopra i Talenti e i Costumi, di Giambattista Gherardo d'Arco.
(2.) Risposta al Quesito: Se in uno Stato di Terreno Fertile favorir debbasi maggiormente l' Estrazione delle Materie prime, ovvero quella delle Manifatture, di Giambattista Gherardo d'Arco.
(3.) Del Diritto ai Transiti, di Giambattista Gherardo d'Arco.
(4.) Dissertazione sopra il Quesito: Se in uno Stato di Terreno Fertile favorir debbasi maggiormente l' Estrazione delle Materie prime, ovvero quella delle Manifatture, del Dottor Giovanni Scottoni.
XXXII. Delle Leggi Politiche ed Economiche, di Gaetano Filangieri.
XXXIII. (1.) Della Moneta Saggio Politici di Giambattista Vasco.
(2.) Delle Università delle Arti e Mestieri Dissertazione, di Giambattista Vasco.
(3.) Mémoire sur les Causes de la Mendicité et sur les Moyens de la supprimer, par J. B. Vasco.
XXXIV. (1.) La Felicità Pubblica considerata nei Coltivatori di Terre Proprie di Giambattista Vasco.
(2.) L' Usura Libera, di Giambattista Vasco.
XXXV. (1.) Risposta al Quesito: Quali siano i Mezzi di provvedere al Sostentamento degli Operai soliti impiegarsi nel torcimento delle sete ne' filatoj, qualora questa Classe d' uomini cosi utile nel Piemonte viene ridotta agli estremi dell' indigenza per Mancanza di l' Avoro cagionata da Scarsezza di Seta, di Giambattista Vasco.
(2.) Annunzj ed Estratti sopra Diversi Oggetti di Economia Politica, di Giambattista Vasco.
XXXVI. (1.) Del Commercio de' Romani dalla Prima Guerra Punica a Costantino, Dissertazione, di Francesco Mengotti.
(2.) Il Colbertismo ossia della Liberta di Commercio de' Prodotti della Terra, Dissertazione, di Francesco Mengotti.
XXXVII. Riflessioni sulla Pubblicà Felicità relativamente al Regno di Napoli, di Giuseppe Palmieri.

Vol. XXXVIII. (1.) Osservazioni sulle Tariffe con Applicazione al Regno di Napoli, di Giuseppe Palmieri.
(2.) Della Ricchezza Nazionale, di Giuseppe Palmieri.
XXXIX. (1.) Memoria sulla Liberta' del Commercio diretta a risolvere il Problema proposto dall' Accademia di Padova sullo stesso Argomento, di Melchiorre Delfico.
(2.) Riflessioni sulle Monete, di Giambattista Corniani.
(3.) Della Legislazione relativamente all' Agricoltura discorsi due recitati nella Pubblica Accademia Agraria di Brescia li 1 Maggio e 11 Settembre, 1777, di Giambattista Corniani.
(4.) Essai sur les Valeurs, par Maurice Solera.
XL. (1.) Annona ossia piano Economico di Pubblica Sussistenza di Domenico, di Gennaro Cantalupo.
(2.) Riflessioni sull' Economia e l'Estrazione de' Frumenti della Sicilia fatte in occasione della Carestia dell' Indizione III. 1784 e 1785, dal Marchese Caraccioli.
(3.) Memoria sulla Libertà del Commercio del Grani della Sicilia, presentata A. S. M. il re di Napoli, da Saverio Scrofani.
(4.) Riflessioni sopra le Sussistenze desunte da' Fatti osservati in Toscana, di Saverio Scrofani.
XLI. Riforma degl' Istituti Pii della Città di Modena, di Lodovico Ricci.
XLII. (1.) Sopra la Materia Frumentaria Discorso, di Pompeo Neri.
(2.) Osservazioni sul Lusso del Marchese Giuseppe Palmieri.
(3.) Tre Nuove Lettere sulla Economia Nazionale, di Giammaria Ortes.
(4.) Continuazione delle Riflessioni sulla Popolazione, di Giammaria Ortes.
(5.) Capitoli Inediti del Ragionamento di Giammaria Ortes delle Scienze Utili e delle Dilettevoli.
XLIII. (1.) Elenco degli Autori e delle l'oro opere contenute in questa Raccolta degli Economisti Classici Italiani.
(2.) Indice Analitico Generale degli Economisti Italiani.

DELLE SCIENZE ECONOMICHE, Idee Teoriche e Pratiche, in ogni Ramo d' Amministrazione privata e pubblica, del Signor MELCHIORRE GIOJA. 4 vol. 4to. Milano, 1815-17.

Storia della Economia Pubblica in Italia, ossia Epilogo Critico degli Economisti Italiani, precedato da un' Introduzione, di CONTE PECCHIO. 1 vol. 8vo. Lugano, 1829.

This work may be regarded as supplementary to the *Economisti Italiani*, inasmuch as it contains biographical and critical notices of the authors and works comprised in that collection. Though written with a strong national bias, it may on the whole be reckoned a pretty fair, as well as a rapid and spirited, sketch of the works of the Italian economists.

This work was translated into French, and published at Paris in 1 vol. in 1830.

DISCURSO SOBRE ECONOMIA POLITICA. Por Don ANTONIO MUNOZ. 1 vol. 12mo. Madrid, 1769.

It is generally believed that Muñoz was not the name of the real author of this work, which contains some ingenious disquisitions. But, whatever might have been the ability and information of the writer, it would be little better than absurd to expect that anything approaching to a good treatise on Political Economy should have been published in

Spain previously to its invasion by the French under Napoleon. Such a treatise must have condemned half the institutions of the country; and have shown that they were the real causes of the decline of the monarchy, and of the poverty, idleness, and barbarism of the people. Assuredly, however, the dungeons of the State or of the Inquisition would have speedily closed on any individual who should have had the hardihood to compose such a work, while the censorship of the press would have hindered its publication. The high station and influence of Ustariz and Campomanes enabled them to write with a degree of freedom which would have been extremely dangerous to persons in an inferior position. But they were obliged to omit all notice even of some most crying and gigantic economical abuses—such, for example, as the vast possessions engrossed by the clergy and the monastic orders, and to touch very gently on others. A really good and useful work on Political Economy can only appear, and its principles can only be carried into effect, in an enlightened country.

PROYECTO ECONOMICO, en que se proponen varias Providencias dirigidas a promover los Intereses de España. Por Don BERNARDO WARD. 1 vol. 8vo. Madrid, 1789.

INVESTIGACION de la NATURALEZA y CAUSAS de la RIQUEZA de las NACIONES. Por ADAM SMITH. Traducido al Castellano, con varias Notas é Ilustraciones relativas á España, por Don JOSEF A. ORTIZ. 4 vol. 4to. Valladolid, 1794.

The notes contain a good deal of curious information in relation to various points in the economical history of Spain.

BIBLIOTECA ESPANOLA ECONOMICO-POLITICA. Por Don J. SEMPERE Y GUARINAS. 4 vol. post 8vo. Madrid, 1801-21.

CURSO di ECONOMIA POLITICA. Por Don ALVARO FLOREZ ESTRADO. 2da ed., 2 vol. 8vo. Paris, 1831.

A work wholly, or almost wholly, made up of extracts from Smith, Say, and other distinguished writers.

The following works, though embracing only limited portions of the science, treat of matters of such importance, as respects its principles, that they may perhaps be most properly noticed in this place.

Essays, Moral, Political, and Literary. Part II. (By DAVID HUME, Esq.) 1 vol. small 8vo. Edinburgh, 1752.

Among others in this volume are essays on Commerce, Interest, Balance of Trade, Money, Jealousy of Trade, and Public Credit. They display the same felicity of style and illustration that distinguish the other works of their celebrated author. His views of the commercial intercourse that should subsist among nations are alike enlightened and liberal; and he has admirably exposed the groundlessness of the prejudices then entertained against a free intercourse with France, and the fear of being deprived, were commercial restraints abolished, of a sufficient supply of bullion. The masterly essay of the 'Populousness of Ancient Nations' will be noticed in another part of this work.

AN INQUIRY into the NATURE and PROGRESS of RENT, and the Principles by which it is regulated. By the Rev. T. R. MALTHUS. 8vo. London, 1815.

AN ESSAY on the APPLICATION of CAPITAL to LAND. With Observations showing the Impolicy of any great Restriction of the Importation of Corn. By a FELLOW of UNIVERSITY COLLEGE, OXFORD (Sir EDWARD WEST, afterwards a Judge in the Supreme Court of Bombay). 8vo. London, 1815.

The true theory of rent was elucidated in these pamphlets, which, by a curious coincidence, were published nearly at the same period. There is probably no good ground for impeaching the originality of either writer; but, however this may be, it will be afterwards seen that the theory of rent developed in these tracts had been discovered and fully explained by Dr. James Anderson, in a tract on the 'Corn Laws,' published in 1777, and in other works of the same author. (See post, chapter on the Corn Trade.)

THE MEASURE of VALUE STATED AND ILLUSTRATED. With an Application of it to the Alterations in the Value of the English Currency since 1790. By the Rev. T. R. MALTHUS. 8vo. London, 1823.

Dialogues of Three Templars on Political Economy, chiefly in relation to the Principles (respecting Value) of Mr. RICARDO.

These dialogues, which have not been separately published, appeared in the 'London Magazine' for April and May, 1824. They were written by Mr. de Quincey, and are unequalled, perhaps, for brevity, pungency, and force. They not only bring the Ricardian theory of value into strong relief, but triumphantly repel, or rather annihilate, the objections urged against it by Malthus, in the pamphlet now referred to and his Political Economy, and by Say, and others. They may, indeed, be said to have exhausted the subject.

A CRITICAL DISSERTATION on the NATURE, MEASURE, and CAUSES of VALUE; chiefly in reference to the Writings of Mr. RICARDO and his Followers. By the Author of Essays on the Formation and Publication of Opinions (SAMUEL BAILEY, Esq. of Sheffield). 1 vol. crown 8vo. London, 1825.

The conditions essential to an invariable measure of exchangeable value were first clearly pointed out in this dissertation: but, however ingenious and acute, Mr. Bailey does not appear to have properly appreciated the Ricardian theory of value, or to have succeeded in any degree in shaking its foundations. The Dissertation was criticised with uncalled for asperity, in an article in the 'Westminster Review;' to which the author replied in a pamphlet entitled 'A Letter to a Political Economist, occasioned by an article in the Westminster Review, on the subject of Value,' by, &c., crown 8vo., London, 1826.

AN ESSAY on the DISTRIBUTION of WEALTH, and on the SOURCES of TAXATION. By the Rev. RICHARD JONES, A.M. 1 vol. 8vo. London, 1831.

Perhaps it was hardly necessary to notice this work, which consists principally of a series of irrelevant and inapplicable criticisms on the theory of rent, as explained by Mr. Ricardo. It was reviewed and fairly appreciated in an article in the 54th volume of the 'Edinburgh Review,' to which we beg to refer such of our readers as may wish for further information on the subject.

Theorie du Luxe, ou Traité dans lequel on entreprend d'établir que le Luxe est un Ressort non-seulement utile, mais même indispensablement nécessaire à la Prospérité des Etats. 2 parties, 1 vol. 8vo. (Paris) 1771.

This ingenious work, though published anonymously, was written by M. Butel Dumont (see 'Biographie Universelle'), author of a very learned and able treatise '*Sur l'Administration des Terres chez les Romains*,' 1 vol. 8vo., Paris, 1779, and of other publications. He endeavours to show, and, we think, successfully, that luxury, or a taste for all sorts of improved accommodations, is the grand source of industry and civilization; and that all attempts to restrain this taste, whether by sumptuary laws or otherwise, are necessarily pernicious.

CHAPTER II.

COMMERCE AND COMMERCIAL POLICY.

§ I. Works on Commerce in General.

"On peut dire, sans crainte d'être soupçonné d'exaggération, que le commerce est le plus solide fondement de la société civile, et le lien le plus nécessaire pour unir entr'eux tous les hommes de quelque pays et de quelque condition qu'ils soient. Par son moyen, le monde entier semble ne former qu'une seule ville et qu'une seule famille. Il y fait régner de toutes parts une abondance universelle. Les richesses d'une nation deviennent celles de tous les autres peuples. Nulle contrée n'est stérile, ou du moins ne se sent de sa stérilité. Tous ses besoins lui sont apportés à point nommé du bout de l'univers, et chaque région est étonnée de se trouver chargée des fruits étrangers que son propre fonds ne pouvoit lui fournir, et enrichie de mille commodités qui lui étoient inconnues, et qui cependant font toute la douceur de la vie."—*Rollin, Hist. Ancienne*, v. 509, ed. 1740.

Commerce (from *commutatio mercium*) is the exchange of one sort of produce or service for some other sort of produce or service.

Exchanges of this description have their rise in the nature of man, and the circumstances under which he is placed, and their origin is coeval with the formation of society. The varying powers and dispositions of different individuals dispose them to engage in preference in particular occupations; and in the end every one finds it for his advantage to confine himself wholly or principally to some one employment, and to barter or exchange such portions of his produce as exceed his own demand, for such portions of the peculiar produce of others as he is desirous to obtain, and they are disposed to part with. The division and combination of employments is carried to some extent in the rudest societies, and it is carried to a very great extent in those that are most improved; but to whatever extent it may be carried, commerce must be equally advanced. The division of employments could not exist without commerce, nor commerce without the division of employments: they mutually act and react upon each other. Every new subdivision of employments occasions a greater extension of commerce; and the latter cannot be extended without contributing to the better division and combination of the former.

But the external circumstances under which different individuals are placed, vary still more than their natural powers or tastes. One set inhabit a rich fertile plain suitable for the growth of corn, and other culmiferous crops; another set inhabit a mountainous district, the soil of which is comparatively sterile, but which is well fitted for rearing cattle; another set are planted upon the margin of a river, or arm of the sea, abounding in every facility for carrying on the business of fishing; and so on. Now it is obvious that though the individuals belonging to any particular district had not established a division of labour amongst themselves, it would be highly for their advantage to establish one with those occupying other districts, the productions of which are materially different from their own. When the inhabitants of Newcastle apply themselves principally to the coal trade, those of Essex to the raising of wheat, and those of Wales and the Highlands of Scotland to the raising of cattle and wool, each set avail themselves in carrying on their employments of the peculiar powers of production conferred by providence on the districts they occupy; and by exchanging such portions of their produce as exceed their own consumption, for the surplus articles raised by others, their wealth, and that of every one else, is immeasurably increased. It is in this *territorial division of labour*, as it has been happily designated by Colonel Torrens, that the main advantage of commerce consists. In commercial countries each individual may not only enter at pleasure on such pursuits as he deems most advantageous, but the entire population of districts and provinces are enabled to turn their energies into those channels in which they are sure to receive the greatest assistance from natural powers. Suppose England were divided into separate parishes, or even counties, surrounded respectively by Bishop Berkeley's wall of brass, and having no intercourse with each other, in what a miserable situation should we be! Instead of 2,000,000, London could not, under such circumstances, contain 20,000 inhabitants, and these would be exposed to numberless privations of which we have no idea. Unless the territorial division of labour were carried to some extent, the division of employments amongst individuals occupying the same district could be but imperfectly established, and would be of comparatively little use. It is only when individuals are able both to gratify their tastes, and to avail themselves of the varying capacities of production given to different districts, that the benefits of commerce can be fully appreciated, and that it becomes the most copious source of wealth as well as the most powerful engine of civilization.

The trade carried on between individuals of different countries is founded on precisely the same circumstances—the differences of soil, climate, and productions, on which is founded the trade between different districts of the same country. One country, like one district, is peculiarly fitted for the growth of corn; another for the cultivation of the grape; a third abounds in minerals; a fourth has inexhaustible forests; and so forth:—

> "Hic segetes, illic veniunt felicius uvæ;
> Arborei fetus alibi, atque injussa virescunt
> Gramina. Nonne vides, croceos ut Tmolus odores,
> India mittit ebur, molles sua thura Sabæi;
> At Chalybes nudi ferrum, virosaque Pontus
> Castorea, Eliadum palmas Epiros equarum?
> Continuo has leges æternaque fœdera certis
> Imposuit natura locis."—*Georg.* lib. i. line 54.

Providence, by thus distributing the various articles suitable for the accommodation and comfort of man in different countries, has evidently provided for their mutual intercourse. In this respect, indeed, foreign trade is of far more importance than the home trade. There is infinitely less difference between the products of the various districts of the most extensive country than there is between the products of different and distant countries; and the establishment of a territorial division of labour amongst the latter is, therefore, proportionally advantageous.

"As the same country is rendered richer by the trade of one province with another; as its labour becomes thus infinitely more divided, and more productive than it could otherwise have been; and as the mutual interchange of all those commodities which one province has and another wants multiplies the comforts and accommodation of the whole, and the country becomes thus in a wonderful degree more opulent and more happy; so the same beautiful train of consequences is observable in the world at large—that vast empire of which the different kingdoms may be regarded as the provinces. In this magnificent empire, one province is favourable to the production of one species of produce, and another province to another. By their mutual intercourse, mankind are enabled to distribute their labour as best fits the genius of each particular country and people. The industry of the whole is thus rendered incomparably more productive; and every species of necessary, useful, and agreeable accommodation is obtained in much greater abundance, and with infinitely less expense."—(Mills's Commerce Defended, p. 38.)

It would far exceed the limits, and be at variance with the objects of this work, to enter into any detailed examination of the reasonings by which it has been attempted to defend the restrictions so generally imposed on commerce. Happily their sophistry and fallacy have been repeatedly demonstrated. It might, indeed, be as well attempted to show the advantage of inferior means of transit, of bad roads, and of oppressive tolls! Unless it could be satisfactorily established that those by whom regulations are enacted have a better understanding of what has a tendency to promote the wealth and industry of their subjects than themselves, it is difficult to see on what ground (apart from considerations of national security) restrictions on the freedom of commerce are to be vindicated. The merchants who import French wine and Polish corn do so only in the laudable view of benefiting themselves, and the country to which they belong, by supplying it with desirable articles at a comparatively low price; and if they have miscalculated the loss they will have to sustain, will speedily put a stop to the trade without any interference on the part of government. It may be necessary for fiscal purposes, and in order fairly to equalise public burdens, that duties should be laid on the principal articles that enter into the commerce between nations; and there can be no doubt that certain articles may be and indeed should be more heavily taxed than others. But, how much soever they may be varied, it may be laid down as a general rule, to which there are very few exceptions, that duties on importation and exportation should never be imposed for the purpose of protection or preference. The principle of *laissez faire* is, in commercial matters, the only general rule by which to abide. It is the duty of government to preserve at all times the just rights and privileges of all classes of its subjects; but if it go one step farther it will certainly lay itself open to the charge of acting partially by some and unjustly by others, and will require very peculiar reasons to justify its conduct.

Hence, in all ordinary cases, it is alike the duty and the policy of government to abstain from all interference with the trade carried on by its subjects. To the clamourers for protection they may always answer, that they would be happy to meet their wishes, provided they could do so without injuring others, but that that being impossible, they feel themselves bound not to interfere, but to allow every one to reap the profit or abide by the loss of the speculations into which he may enter.

THE MERCHANTS MAPPE OF COMMERCE, wherein the universal manner and matter of Trade is compendiously handled, &c., by LEWIS ROBERTS, Merchant. 1 vol. folio. London, 1638.

THE TREASURE OF TRAFFICKE, or a DISCOURSE of FORRAIGNE TRADE, &c., by LEWIS ROBERTS, Merchant and Captaine of the City of London. 4to. London, 1641.

The first of these works is a sort of encyclopædia of the art or practice of commerce. It contains notices of the principal commercial towns, and of the commodities usually found in them; their coins and exchanges; the manner of keeping their accounts and transacting business; and a variety of other particulars, comprising a fuller and better account of the trade of the world than any that had then appeared. According to the custom of the time various sets of laudatory verses are prefixed to the work, among which is one by Izaak Walton. This work went through several editions, and must, when it appeared, have been a useful acquisition to the counting-house.

The other work is intended to show the nature and advantages of commerce, and the means by which it might be facilitated. It is creditable to the author that he should be found at this early period in favour of the free exportation of gold and silver. This tract is remarkable from its containing the first, or one of the first notices of the cotton manufacture. "The towne of Manchester in Lancashire must also be herein remembered, and worthily for their incouragement commended, who buy the yarne of the Irish in great quantity, and weaving it, returne the same againe in linnen into Ireland to sell: neither doth their industry rest here, for they buy cotton wool in London, that comes first from Cyprus and Smyrna, and at home worke the same and perfect it into fustians and vermilions, dimities, and other suche stuffes; and then returne it to London, where the same is vended and sold, and not seldom sent into forrain parts, who have means at far easier termes to provide themselves of the said first materials."—p. 33.

Englands Treasure by Forraign Trade, or the Balance of our Forraign Trade is the Rule of our Treasure. Written by THOMAS MUN of London, Merchant, and now published for the common good by his Son, JOHN MUN of Bearsted, in the county of Kent, Esq. 1st ed. 1 vol. 8vo. London, 1664, and frequently republished.

Having been referred to by Dr. Smith, this work has attracted, even in recent times, considerable attention. Though published in 1664, it had been written many years previously. Mr. Mun's son, in the dedication to Lord Southampton, prefixed by him to the work, says, that his father "was, *in his time*, famous among merchants," a mode of expression which he would hardly have used, had not a considerable period elapsed since his father's death: and Misselden, in his 'Circle of Commerce,' published in 1623 (p. 36), refers to Mun's Tract on the East India Trade, and speaks of its author as an accomplished and *experienced* merchant. Perhaps, therefore, we shall not be far wrong in assuming that this treatise was written so early as 1635 or 1640. At all events the doctrines which it contains do not differ materially from those which he had previously maintained in his pamphlet in defence of the East India Company, published in 1609; and some of the expressions are identical with those in the petition presented by that body to Parliament in 1628, which was written by Mun.

Mun may be considered as the earliest expositor of what has been called the MERCANTILE SYSTEM of commercial policy. It was found to be indispensable to the profitable carrying on of the trade to India, and the East generally, that the exportation of gold and silver, which had hitherto been prohibited, should be permitted. But though Mun, in accordance with the prejudices of his time, admitted that the precious metals were the only real wealth a country could possess, he contended that their exportation might be safely allowed, provided the *balance of payments* were in our favour; that is, provided the total value of the exports exceeded the total value of the imports; for in that case, said Mun, the balance must be paid in bullion, and our riches will annually increase by its amount! It would be useless to take up the reader's time by entering into any lengthened statements illustrative of the hollowness of this theory. Every body is now aware that the circumstances which determine the importation and exportation of bullion are the same with those which determine the importation and exportation of other things; and that though the balance of payments were 10 or 20 millions in our favour, or against us, not a single ounce of bullion would be imported or exported if there were any other article whatever that might be imported or exported with greater advantage. Everybody is also aware that but little bullion can be exported from one country and imported into another, without so raising its value in the exporting and lowering it in the importing country as to put an end to its transfer. And everybody further knows that in all ordinary cases the value of the imports *must* considerably exceed the value of the exports; and that the excess of the former (and not its defect) is the measure of the profit realised in the trade with the foreigner. But, such as it was, this theory kept its ground for a lengthened period, and was all but universally assented to by merchants and legislators. Hence the bounties and premiums so frequently given on the exportation of domestic produce, and the formidable difficulties thrown, by means of prohibitions and heavy duties, in the way of importing foreign produce; and hence, also, the fact that though its principles have been completely overthrown, it still continues to exercise a powerful practical influence.

ENGLAND'S INTEREST and IMPROVEMENT, consisting in the Increase of the Store and Trade of this Kingdom. By SAMUEL FORTREY, Esq. 8vo. 1st ed. 1663; 2nd do. 1673.

The author of this tract is stated by Roger Coke to have been a gentleman of the king's bed-chamber. It contains a good argument in favour of enclosures, and the author is favourable to the policy of allowing foreigners to settle in the kingdom, to hold lands, and to enjoy the other privileges of Englishmen, under such restrictions as Parliament may think fit to enact. But this tract is chiefly remarkable for its having powerfully assisted in raising and perpetuating that prejudice against the trade with France, which resulted not long after in its almost total prohibition. Fortrey gives the substance of a statement which he alleges (but without quoting any authority for the fact) had been presented to the King of France (Louis XIV.), in which the value of the commodities exported from France to England is estimated at above 2,600,000*l.*, and that of the commodities exported from England to France at about 1,000,000*l.*; showing, says he, that our trade with France occasions a "clear loss" of 1,600,000*l.* to this kingdom! (pp. 22, 25). And this vague and worthless statement, which perhaps originated in the imagination of the writer, appears to have been generally acquiesced in at the time; and Fortrey's authority was referred to over and over again, especially during the discussions on the commercial treaty agreed upon with France towards the conclusion of Queen Anne's reign, in vindication of that *felo de se* policy by which we laboured but too successfully to suppress what had previously been, and would, but for our interference, have continued to be, the most extensive and advantageous branch of our commerce.

Four Treatises by Roger Coke, viz.:—

1. A Treatise wherein is demonstrated that the Church and State of England are in equal danger with the Trade of it. 4to. London, 1671.

2. Reasons of the Increase of the Dutch Trade, wherein is demonstrated from what Causes the Dutch govern and manage Trade better than the English, &c. 4to. London, 1671.

3. England's Improvement, in *Two Parts* (the first part relates to the strength and wealth, and the latter to the navigation of the kingdom). 4to. London, 1675.

4. How the Navigation of England may be Encreased and the Soveraignty of the British Seas more secured to the Crown of England. 4to. London, 1675.

These treatises, written by a descendant of Lord Coke, the famous lawyer, proceed on the hypothesis that the population and industry of England were at the time (1671-75) in a declining condition, occasioned principally by the plague and the emigration of settlers to the colonies and to Ireland. The truth is, however, that there was no depopulation. and that the kingdom was then more wealthy and prosperous than at any former period. But though wrong in his suppositions respecting the state of the country, Mr. Coke recommended several measures fitted to promote its improvement, such as the naturalization of foreign Protestants, the repeal of the laws prohibiting the importation of cattle from Ireland,* the opening of corporations, &c. Coke contends that the Navigation Act had been injurious to trade; and that the Act of the 43rd of Elizabeth, providing for the employment of the poor, had also been in various respects productive of mischief. He appears, like most of his contemporaries, to have placed the fullest confidence in Fortrey's statements with regard to the trade with France.

Englands Great Happiness, or a Dialogue between Content and Complaint, wherein it is demonstrated that a great part of our Complaints are causeless, &c. By a real and hearty Lover of his King and Country. 4to. Lond. 1677.

This is a very remarkable tract; its author having been very far in advance of the prejudices of his time. Were it to be re-written at this moment, the only changes which it would be proper to make would be in the style, and even these would be inconsiderable. We subjoin a specimen:—

" *Compl.*—You speak plain; but what think you of the French trade, which draws away our money by wholesale? Mr. Fortrey, whom I have heard you speak well of, gives an account that they get 1,600,000*l.* a year from us.

" *Cont.*—'T is a great sum; but, perhaps, were it put to a vote in a wise Council, whether for that reason the trade should be left off, 't would go in the negative. For paper, wine, linen, Castile soap, brandy, olives, capers, prunes, kidskins, taffaties, and such like, we cannot be without; and for the rest, which you are pleased to style *Apes* and *Peacocks* (although wise Solomon rankt them with gold and ivory), they set us all agog, and have increased among us many considerable trades. * * I must confess, I had rather the French would use

* These statutes, 15 Charles II. c. 8 and 18 Charles II. c. 2, though most inimical to the interests of England as well as Ireland, kept their place on the statute-book till 32 Geo. II. c. 11.

our goods than money, but if not, I WOULD NOT LOSE THE GETTING OF TEN POUND BECAUSE I CAN'T GET AN HUNDRED; and I don't question but when the French get more foreign trade, they'll give more liberty to the bringing in foreign goods. I 'll suppose John-a-Nokes to be a butcher, Dick-a-Styles an Exchange man, yourself a lawyer; will you buy no meat or ribbands, or your wife a fine Indian gown or fan, because they will not truck with you for indentures which they have need of? I suppose no; but if you get money enough of others, you care not though you give it away *in specie* for these things: I think 't is the same case with the French trade."

The author is in fact a decided and intelligent opponent of all commercial restraints, and of all laws for restraining, or in anywise limiting private expenditure; and is favourable to the immigration of foreigners, and the practice of enclosing, &c. Perhaps, however, the spirit of this remarkable tract may be best inferred from the titles of some of the Dialogues. Among others, we have "To export money our great advantage;" "The French trade a profitable trade;" "Variety of wares for all markets a great advantage;" "High living a great improvement to arts;" "Invitation of foreign arts a great advantage;" "Multitudes of traders a great advantage;" "The word Impossible a great discourager of arts;" &c. But how conclusive soever, its influence was too feeble to arrest the current of popular prejudice. In the year after its publication (1678) the importation of French commodities was prohibited for three years. This prohibition was made perpetual in the reign of William III. when the French trade was declared to be a *nuisance!*—a principle, if we may so call it, which has been acted upon down to our own times.

BRITANNIA LANGUENS, or a Discourse of Trade: showing the Grounds and Reasons of the Increase and Decay of Land, Rents, National Wealth and Strength, &c. 1 vol. *post* 8vo. Lond. 1680.

This work bears in various respects a strong resemblance to that of Coke, but is shorter, and written in a less affected manner. The author labours to show that trade, manufactures, and agriculture were in a very depressed, or, as he calls it, "consumptive" condition, occasioned partly by the exportation of treasure, partly by the operation of the Navigation Laws, the monopolies of the East India Company and other trading associations, corporation privileges, &c., and partly by the excess of the importation of luxuries from France and other countries. But, like the depopulation of Coke, the depression which the author laments, and of which he endeavours to assign the causes, had no existence in fact; and how much soever their progress may have been retarded by the institutions and circumstances referred to, trade, industry of all sorts, and wealth had rapidly increased in the interval between the Restoration and 1680. In proof of this we may refer to the authentic statements in Sir Josiah Child's 'Treatise on Trade,' and Sir William Petty's 'Political Arithmetic,' respecting the increase in the rent and price of land; the facility with which London was rebuilt after the great fire; the increase of towns and buildings in other parts of the country; the improvement in the style of living: and the increase in the customs'-duties, the produce of which (at the *old* rates) had risen from 421,582*l.* in 1661, to 635,562*l.* in 1680 (Chalmers's Estimate, p. 49, ed. 1802). The reasonings and statements by which the author endeavours to show how the results, which he deplores, had been brought about, and how they might best be obviated, exhibit a curious mixture of truth and error, intelligence and prejudice.

A New Discourse of Trade, &c. By Sir JOSIAH CHILD, Bart. 5th ed. 1 vol. 12mo. Glasgow, 1751.

The first edition of this work was published in a small 4to. tract in 1668. The second edition, which was very much enlarged, appeared in 1690.

Sir Josiah Child was one of the most extensive, and (judging from his work) best informed merchants of his time. The argument in the 'New Discourse,' to show that colonies do not depopulate the mother country, is as conclusive as if it had proceeded from the pen of Mr. Malthus; and the reasoning in defence of the naturalization of the Jews discovers a mind greatly superior to existing prejudices. There are also some excellent observations on the laws against forestalling and regrating; on those limiting the number of apprentices and preventing the exportation of bullion; and on corporation privileges, &c.

Some of the principles advanced by Child are so sound and so forcibly and concisely expressed that they assume the shape of maxims. Thus, in reference to population, he pithily observes, "Such as our employment is for people, so many will our people be" (p. 174, ed. 1690). In remarking on the inefficacy of the laws to prevent the clandestine exportation (*running*) of wool, he says, "They that can give the best price for a commodity shall never fail to have it by one means or other, notwithstanding the opposition of any laws, or interposition of any power by sea or land, of such force, subtilty, and violence is the general course of trade" (p. 129). In another place he says, in illustration of the dependence of the different branches of industry, "Land and trade are twins, and have always, and ever will, wax and wane together: it cannot be ill with trade but land will fall, nor ill with land but trade will feel it" (Preface). And he truly states that "the folly of suffering idleness to suck the breasts of industry needs no demonstration."

The radical defect of Child's treatise consists in its having been written to exhibit the advantages which he supposed would result from lowering the legal rate of interest to 4 per cent. He was led into this error by his admiration of the policy of the "wise Dutch;" and by his mistaking the lowness of interest in Holland for the principal cause of her wealth, when, in truth, it was the effect of her comparatively heavy taxation.

Sir Josiah Child had great influence in the East India Company, and published several tracts in defence of that association, the principles advanced in which are similar to those in the 'Discourse.'

Discourses upon Trade, principally directed to the Cases of the Interest, Coynage, Clipping, and Increase of Money. (By Sir DUDLEY NORTH, brother to the Lord Keeper Guildford.) 4to. London, 1691.

This tract contains a more able and comprehensive statement of the true principles of commerce than any that had previously appeared, either in the English or any other language. North, who had been extensively engaged in the Turkey trade, is throughout the intelligent advocate of commercial freedom. He is not, like the more eminent of his predecessors, well informed on one subject, and erroneous on another. His system is consentaneous in its parts, and complete. He shows that, in commercial matters, nations have the same interests as individuals; and forcibly exposes the absurdity of supposing that any trade advantageous to the merchant can be injurious to the public. His opinions respecting a seignorage on the coinage of money, and the advantage of sumptuary laws, then very popular, are equally enlightened.

The principles advocated in this tract are announced in the preface, as follows:—

"That the whole world as to trade is but as one nation or people, and therein nations are as persons.

"That the loss of the trade with one nation is not that only separately considered, but so much of the trade of the world rescinded and lost; for all is combined together.

"That there can be no trade unprofitable to the public; for if any prove so, men leave it off; and wherever the traders thrive, the public, of which they are a part, thrives also.

"That to force men to deal in any prescribed manner may profit such as happen to serve them; but the public gains not, because it is taking from one subject to give to another.

"That no laws can set prices in trade, the rates of which must and will make themselves. But when such laws do happen to lay any hold, it is so much impediment to trade, and therefore prejudicial.

"That money is a merchandise, whereof there may be a glut as well as a scarcity, and that even to an inconvenience.

"That a people cannot want money to serve the ordinary dealing, and more than enough they will not have.

"That no man will be the richer for the making much money, nor have any part of it, but as he buys it for an equivalent price.

"That the free coynage is a perpetual motion found out, whereby to melt and coyn without ceasing, and so to feed goldsmiths and coyners at the public charge.

"That debasing the coyn is defrauding one another, and to the public there is no sort of advantage from it; for that admits no character, or value, but intrinsic.

"That the sinking by alloy or weight is all one.

"That exchange and ready money are the same, nothing but carriage and re-carriage being saved.

"That money exported in trade is an increase to the wealth of the nation; but spent in war, and payments abroad, is so much impoverishment.

"In short, that all favour to one trade, or interest, is an abuse, and cuts so much of profit from the public."

Unluckily this admirable tract did not obtain any considerable circulation. Indeed it would appear from the statements in the very interesting *Life* of the author, by his brother, the Hon. Roger North (p. 179), that it had been designedly suppressed; and it was for a lengthened period supposed to be entirely lost. Fortunately, however, this supposition has turned out to be incorrect. A copy of the tract, which had found its way into the library of the late Rev. Rogers Ruding, author of the 'Annals of the Coinage,' was purchased at the sale of his books by a gentleman of Edinburgh, who printed a few copies for distribution among his friends. We have since stumbled upon two copies of the original edition.

An Essay on the probable Methods of making the People Gainers in the Balance of Trade. By the Author of the Essay on Ways and Means (Dr. Davenant). 1 vol. 8vo. London, 1699.

For a notice of Davenant's works, see *post*, Art. Miscellaneous.

Spectator, No. 69, 19th May, 1711.

This number contains an essay by Addison, in which the advantages of commerce are beautifully illustrated. We are sure our readers will be gratified by the perusal of the following extract from this admirable paper.

"Nature seems to have taken a particular care to disseminate her blessings among the different regions of the world, with an eye to this mutual intercourse and traffic among mankind, that the natives of the several parts of the globe might have a kind of dependence upon one another, and be united together by their common interest. Almost every degree produces something peculiar to it. The food often grows in one country, and the sauce in another. The fruits of Portugal are corrected by the products of Barbadoes, and the infusion of a China plant is sweetened by the pith of an Indian cane. The Philippic Islands give a flavour to our European bowls. The single dress of a woman of quality is often the product of an hundred climates. The muff and the fan come together from the different ends of the earth. The scarf is sent from the torrid zone, and the tippet from beneath the Pole. The brocade petticoat rises out of the mines of Peru, and the diamond necklace out of the bowels of Indostan.

"If we consider our own country in its natural prospect, without any of the benefits and advantages of commerce, what an uncomfortable spot of earth falls to our share! Natural historians tell us that no fruit grows originally among us, besides hips and haws, acorns and pig-nuts, with other delicacies of the like nature; that our climate of itself, and without the assistances of art, can make no further advances towards a plum than to a sloe, and carries an apple to no greater a perfection than a crab: that our melons, our peaches, our figs, our apricots and cherries, are strangers among us, imported in different ages, and naturalized in our English gardens; and that they would all degenerate and fall away into the trash of our own country, if they were wholly neglected by the planter, and left to the mercy of our sun and soil. Nor has traffic more enriched our vegetable world than it has improved the whole face of nature among us. Our ships are laden with the harvest of every climate: our tables are stored with spices, and oils, and wines: our rooms are filled with pyramids of china, and adorned with the workmanship of Japan: our morning's draught comes to us from the remotest corners of the earth: we repair our bodies by the drugs of America, and repose ourselves under Indian canopies. My friend Sir Andrew calls the vineyards of France our gardens; the Spice Islands our hot-beds; the Persians our silk-weavers; and the Chinese our potters. Nature, indeed, furnishes us with the bare necessaries of life, but traffic gives us a great variety of what is useful, and at the same time supplies us with everything that is convenient and ornamental. Nor is it the least part of this our happiness, that whilst we enjoy the remotest products of the North and South, we are free from those extremities of weather which give them birth; that our eyes are refreshed with the green fields of Britain, at the same time that our palates are feasted with fruits that rise between the tropics.

"For these reasons, there are not more useful members in a commonwealth than merchants. They knit mankind together in a mutual intercourse of good offices, distribute the gifts of nature, find work for the poor add wealth to the rich, and magnificence to the great. Our English merchant converts the tin of his own country into gold, and exchanges his wool for rubies. The Mahometans are clothed in our British manufacture, and the inhabitants of the frozen zone warmed with the fleeces of our sheep.

"When I have been upon the 'Change I have often fancied one of our old kings standing in person where he is represented in effigy, and looking down upon the wealthy concourse of people with which that place is every day filled. In this case how would he be surprised to hear all the languages of Europe spoken in this little spot of his former dominions, and to see so many private men who, in his time, would have been the vassals of some powerful baron, negotiating like princes for greater sums of money than were formerly to be met with in the royal treasury! Trade, without enlarging the British territories, has given us a kind of additional empire: it has multiplied the number of the rich, made our landed estates infinitely more valuable than they were formerly, and added to them an accession of other estates as valuable as the lands themselves."

The BRITISH MERCHANT, or Commerce preserved. By Mr. CHARLES KING. 3 vols. 8vo. Lond. 1721.

For an account of this work see *post*, section on Commercial Treaties.

A SURVEY of TRADE, in four Parts; with Considerations on Money and Bullion. (By WILLIAM WOOD, Esq.) 1 vol. 8vo. Lond. 1718.

Mr. William Wood, celebrated from his connexion with the famous patent issued to him in 1722, for supplying Ireland with 100,000*l.* worth of copper coins, has been commonly taken for the author of this work, which has, in consequence, excited some attention. Such, however, was not the case, it having been written by the Mr. William Wood who afterwards became secretary to the Commissioners of Customs. (Chalmers' Estimate, p. 92, ed. 1802.)

In respect to the project for supplying Ireland with copper, we may mention that it was vehemently opposed by Swift in his 'Drapier's Letters;' and the hostility against it in Ireland, though not resting on any very good foundation, was so violent and so universal, that government was in the end obliged to cancel the patent; a compensation of 3000*l.* a year, for eight years, being allowed to Wood to indemnify him for his loss. Though said by Swift to be a "hardware man," and a "low mechanic," "Copper Wood" was really in opulent circumstances, being an extensive proprietor and leaseholder of mines and iron-works.—(See Anderson's History of Commerce, anno 1722; Coxe's Life of Sir Robert Walpole, 8vo. ed., i. 377; the Drapier's Letters in Swift's Works, &c.)

A PLAN of the ENGLISH COMMERCE, being a complete Prospect of the Trade of this Nation, as well the Home Trade as the Foreign. (By DANIEL DEFOE.) 1st ed. 1 vol. 8vo. Lond. 1728; 2nd ed. 1 vol. 8vo. Lond. 1730.

This work is full of information; and, though desultory, it is ably written, and contains sundry passages in which the influence of trade and industry in promoting the well-being of the labouring classes and the public wealth is set in the most striking point of view. In the work of Gee, referred to below, the commerce and manufactures of the country are erroneously represented as being in a declining and, in some respects, ruinous condition; but in the present work it is shown that they had continued progressively to increase, and were then, in fact, more flourishing than at any former period. It would seem, however, that, when conscious of the contrary, people are well pleased to be represented as being in an unprosperous condition. At all events, while the work of Gee enjoyed a large share of popularity, and has been often quoted as an authority, the incomparably superior work of Defoe was comparatively neglected. What is called the second edition is merely the first edition with a new title-page and a brief appendix.

The TRADE and NAVIGATION of GREAT BRITAIN considered; showing that the surest way for a Nation to increase in Riches is to prevent the Importation of such Foreign Commodities as may be raised at Home, &c. By JOSHUA GEE. 1st ed. 1 vol. 8vo. Lond. 1730; 6th ed. 1 vol. 12mo. Glasgow, 1735.

The title of this work sufficiently explains its principles and objects. As mentioned above, the account given in it of the state of our trade is, for the most part, as deceptive as the means suggested for its improvement are illiberal and inefficient. Its author, who was extensively engaged in trade, was a principal contributor to the 'British Merchant.'

A DISCOURSE on TRADE and other Matters relative to it. By JOHN CARY, Esq., Merchant of Bristol. 1 vol. 8vo. London, 1745.

Portions of this work had been previously published so early as 1696. The principles advanced in it do not differ materially from those of the 'British Merchant.' Among other matters, the author investigates "what foreign trades are profitable and what not!" However little it deserved such an honour, this work was made the foundation of a French publication entitled

ESSAI SUR L'ETAT DU COMMERCE D'ANGLETERRE. 2 vol. post 8vo. Paris, 1755.

The latter, however, contains much additional matter, and is in all respects a more valuable work than that of Cary.

AN ESSAY on the TRADE and IMPROVEMENT of IRELAND. By ARTHUR DOBBS, Esq. In 2 Parts. 8vo. Dublin, 1729–1731.

This essay contains some interesting statements respecting the trade and population of Ireland, and its state at the period to which it refers. The author, who represented Carrickfergus in the Irish parliament, having visited London in 1730, was introduced to Sir Robert Walpole, by Primate Boulter, as follows:—"The gentleman who waits upon you with this letter is Mr. Dobbs, one of the members of our House of Commons, where he, on all occasions, endeavours to promote his Majesty's service. He is a person of good sense, and has for some time applied his thoughts to the trade of Great Britain and Ireland, and to the making of our colonies in America of more advantage than they have hitherto been; and has written his thoughts on these subjects, which he is desirous to offer to your consideration."—(Boulter's Letters, ii. 17.)

Dobbs exerted himself and spent much money in promoting the discovery of a north-west passage. In 1753 he was appointed governor of North Carolina. His active life closed at Cape Clear on the 26th of March, 1765, in the 84th year of his age. (We have borrowed part of these details from a note by George Chalmers, Esq., in his copy of Dobbs's Essay.)

An Essay on the Causes of the Decline of the Foreign Trade, consequently of the VALUE of LANDS in BRITAIN, and on the Means to restore both. (By Sir MATTHEW DECKER.) 1 vol. 4to. London, 1744. Reprinted, 1 vol. 12mo. Edinburgh, 1756.

The author of this work was an extensive merchant; and like Sir Josiah Child in the previous age, and Mr. Tooke in our own, conferred lustre on the mercantile character by the ability and liberality displayed in his writings. He erred, indeed, in supposing that trade was declining. No doubt its increase for some years previously to the publication of this work was but slow, though there certainly was no retrogression. But despite this error, there are few if any of the older works on commerce that have so many well-founded claims to attention, or that embody so many enlightened, ingenious, and original views. Decker is an intelligent and uncompromising enemy of all sorts of restrictions, monopolies, and prohibitions. To give full freedom to industry, he proposed that the privileges of corporations should be abolished, and the existing taxes repealed, and replaced by licence duties, or duties for leave to use or consume certain articles. The following extracts will give an idea of the spirit which pervades the work, and of the ability with which it is written:—

"Trade cannot, will not be forced: let other nations prohibit by what severity they please, interest will prevail; they may embarrass their own trade, but cannot hurt a nation, whose trade is free, so much as themselves. Spain has prohibited our woollens; but, had a reduction of our taxes brought them to their natural value only, they would be the cheapest in Europe of their goodness, consequently must be more demanded by the Spaniards, be smuggled into their country in spite of their government, and sold at better prices; their people would be dearer clothed with duties and prohibitions than without, consequently must sell their oil, wine, and other commodities dearer; whereby other nations, raising the like growths, would gain ground upon them, and their balance of trade grow less and less. But should we, for that reason, prohibit their commodities? By no means; for the dearer they grow, no more than what are just necessary will be used; their prohibition does their own business; some may be necessary for us; what are so, we should not make dearer to our own people; some may be proper to assort cargoes for other countries, and why should we prohibit our people that advantage? *Why hurt ourselves to hurt the Spaniards?* If we would retaliate effectually upon them for their ill-intent, handsome premiums given to our plantations to raise the same growths as Spain might enable them to supply us cheaper than the Spaniards could do, and establish a trade they could never return. Premiums may gain trade, *but prohibitions will destroy it.*"—(p. 163, ed. 1756.)

Decker applies the same argument to expose the injurious influence of the restraints on the trade with France. "Would any wise dealer in London," he asks, "buy goods of a Dutch shopkeeper for 15*d.* or 18*d.* when he could have the same from a French shopkeeper for 1*s.*? Would he not consider that by so doing he would empty his own pockets the sooner, and that in the end he would greatly injure his own family by such whims? And shall this nation commit an absurdity that stares every private man in the face? . . . The certain way to be secure is to be more powerful, that is, to extend our trade as far as it is capable of; and, as restraints have proved its ruin, to reject them and depend on freedom for our security, bidding defiance to the French, or any nation in Europe that took umbrage at our exerting our natural advantages."—(p. 184.)

Proposals made by His late Highness the Prince of Orange, to their HIGH MIGHTINESSES the STATES GENERAL, and to the States of HOLLAND and WEST FRIEZELAND, for Redressing and Amending the Trade of the Republic. Translated from the Dutch. 8vo. London, 1751.

After the war terminated by the treaty of Aix-la-Chapelle, the attention of the government of Holland was forcibly attracted to the state of the shipping and foreign commerce of the republic. They had been gradually declining since the beginning of the century; and the discovery of means by which this decline might be arrested, and the trade of the republic, if possible, restored to its ancient flourishing condition, became a prominent object in the speculations of every one who felt interested in the public welfare. In order to procure the most correct information on the subject, the Stadtholder, William IV., addressed the following queries to the principal merchants, desiring them to favour him with their answers:—

"1. What is the actual state of trade? and if the same should be found to be diminished and fallen to decay, then, 2. To inquire by what methods the same may be supported and advanced, or, if possible, restored to its former lustre, repute, and dignity."

In discussing these questions, the merchants were obliged to enter into an examination, as well of the causes which had raised the commerce of Holland to the high pitch of prosperity to which it had once attained, as of those which had occasioned its subsequent decline. It is stated, that, though not of the same opinion upon all points, they, speaking generally, concurred as to those that were most important. When their answers had been obtained, and compared with each other, the Stadtholder had a dissertation prepared from them, and other authentic sources, on the commerce of the republic, to which proposals were subjoined for its amendment; and this dissertation and proposals (though the latter are alone referred to in its title), are given in the above pamphlet. Some of the statements advanced in it apply to Holland only; but most of them are of universal application, and are alike comprehensive and sound. The substantial benefits resulting from religious toleration, political liberty, and the freedom of industry, have seldom, indeed, been more clearly set forth than in this dissertation.

It begins by an enumeration of the causes which contributed to advance the commerce of the republic to its former unexampled prosperity; these the authors divide into three classes, the first embracing those that were natural and physical; the second, those they denominate moral; and the third, those which they considered adventitious and external, remarking on them in succession as follows:—

"I. The natural and physical causes are the advantages of the situation of the country, on the sea, and at the mouth of considerable rivers; its situation between the northern and southern parts, which, by being in a manner the centre of all Europe, made the republic become the general market, where the merchants on both sides used to bring their superfluous commodities, in order to barter and exchange the same for other goods they wanted.

"Nor have the barrenness of the country, and the necessities of the natives arising from that cause, less contributed to set them upon exerting all their application, industry, and utmost stretch of genius, to fetch from foreign countries what they stand in need of in their own, and to support themselves by trade.

"The abundance of fish in the neighbouring seas put them in a condition not only to supply their own occasions, but with the overplus to carry on a trade with foreigners, and out of the produce of the fishery to find an equivalent for what they wanted, through the sterility and narrow boundaries and extent of their own country.

"II. Among the moral and political causes are to be placed, The unalterable maxim and fundamental law relating to the free exercise of different religions; and always to consider this toleration and connivance as the most effectual means to draw foreigners from adjacent countries to settle and reside here, and so become instrumental to the peopling of these provinces.

"The constant policy of the republic to make this country a perpetual, safe, and secure asylum for all persecuted and oppressed strangers; no alliance, no treaty, no regard for, or solicitation of, any potentate whatever, has at any time been able to weaken or destroy this law, or make the state recede from protecting those who have fled to it for their own security and self-preservation.

"Throughout the whole course of all the persecutions and oppressions that have occurred in other countries, the steady adherence of the republic to this fundamental law, has been the cause that many people have not only fled hither for refuge, with their whole stock in ready cash, and their most valuable effects, but have also settled, and established many trades, fabrics, manufactories, arts, and sciences, in this country, notwithstanding the first materials for the said fabrics and manufactories were almost wholly wanting in it, and not to be procured but at a great expense from foreign parts.

"The constitution of our form of government, and the liberty thus accruing to the citizen, are further reasons to which the growth of trade, and its establishment in the republic, may fairly be ascribed; and all her policy and laws are put upon such an equitable footing, that neither life, estates, nor dignities depend on the caprice or arbitrary power of any single individual; nor is there any room for any person, who, by care, frugality, and diligence, has once acquired an affluent fortune or estate, to fear a deprivation of them by any act of violence, oppression, or injustice.

"The administration of justice in the country has, in like manner, always been clear and impartial, and without distinction of superior or inferior rank—whether the parties have been rich or poor, or were this a foreigner and that a native; and it were greatly to be wished we could at this day boast of such impartial quickness and despatch in all our legal processes, considering how great an influence it has on trade.

"To sum up all, amongst the moral and political causes of the former flourishing state of trade, may be likewise placed the wisdom and prudence of the administration; the intrepid firmness of the councils; the faithfulness with which treaties and engagements were wont to be fulfilled and ratified; and particularly the care and caution practised to preserve tranquillity and peace, and to decline, instead of entering on a scene of war, merely to gratify the ambitious views of gaining fruitless or imaginary conquests.

"By these moral and political maxims was the glory and reputation of the republic so far spread, and foreigners animated to place so great a confidence in the steady determinations of a state so wisely and prudently conducted, that a concourse of them stocked this country with an augmentation of inhabitants and useful hands, whereby its trade and opulence were from time to time increased.

III. "Amongst the adventitious and external causes of the rise and flourishing state of our trade may be reckoned—

"That at the time when the best and wisest maxims were adopted in the republic as the means of making trade flourish, they were neglected in almost all other countries; and any one reading the history of those times may easily discover, that the persecutions on account of religion throughout Spain, Brabant, Flanders, and many other states and kingdoms, have powerfully promoted the establishment of commerce in the republic.

"To this happy result, and the settling of manufacturers in our country, the long continuance of the civil wars in France, which were afterwards carried on in Germany, England, and divers other parts, have also very much contributed.

"It must be added, in the last place, that during our most burdensome and heavy wars with Spain and Portugal (however ruinous that period was for commerce otherwise), these powers had both neglected their navy; whilst the navy of the republic, by a conduct directly the reverse, was at the same time formidable, and in a capacity not only to protect the trade of its own subjects, but to annoy and crush that of their enemies in all quarters."

We believe the reader will agree with us in thinking, that these statements reflect the greatest credit on the merchants and government of Holland; and that nothing can be more correct and judicious than the account they give of the causes which contributed to render their country a great commercial commonwealth.

Many dissertations, or rather volumes, have been written to account for the decline of the commerce of Holland. But, if we mistake not, it may be principally ascribed to the gradual growth of commerce and navigation in other countries, and the oppressiveness of taxation at home. It is plain, that the operation of the former cause could not have been obviated by any policy the Dutch might have adopted; and, perhaps, we may say the same of the latter, inasmuch as the taxes were imposed to defray the interest of the loans contracted during the revolutionary struggle of the republic with Spain, and in her subsequent contests with France and England. But, how indispensable soever, the pernicious influence of this heavy taxation became obvious after the treaty of Utrecht, and is very forcibly pointed out in this dissertation. "Oppressive taxes," say its authors, "must be placed at the head of all the causes that have co-operated to the prejudice and discouragement of trade; and it may be justly said, that it can only be attributed to them that the trade of this country has been diverted out of its channel, and transferred to our neighbours, and must daily be still more and more alienated and shut out from us, unless the progress thereof be stopt by some quick and effectual remedy: Nor is it difficult to see from these contemplations on the state of our trade, that the same will be effected by no other means than *a diminution of all duties*.

"In former times this was reckoned the only trading state in Europe; and foreigners were content to pay the taxes, as well on the goods they brought hither, as on those they came here to buy; without examining whether they could evade or save them, by fetching the goods from the places where they were produced, and carrying others to the places where they were consumed: In short, they paid us our taxes with pleasure, without any farther inquiry.

"But since the last century, the system of trade is altered all over Europe: Foreign nations seeing the wonderful effect of our trade, and to what an eminence we had risen only by means thereof, they did likewise apply themselves to it; and to save our duties, sent their superfluous products beside our country, to the places where they are most consumed; and in return for the same, furnished themselves from the first hands with what they wanted."

But notwithstanding this authoritative exposition of the mischievous effects resulting from the excess of taxation, the necessary expenses of the state were so great as to render it impossible to make any sufficient reductions. And, with the exception of the transit trade carried on through the Rhine and the Meuse, which is in a great measure independent of foreign competition, and the trade with Java, most branches of the foreign trade of Holland, though still very considerable, continue in a comparatively depressed state.

A good, or even a respectable history of the commercial, colonial, and financial policy of Holland is a desideratum. It is a noble subject, and if well executed would be a work of the highest interest and value. It would, however, require a great deal of labour and research, and consequently of time. We gave a slight sketch of the progress of Dutch commerce, in the 51st volume of the 'Edinburgh Review.'

A Brief Essay on the Advantages and Disadvantages which respectively attend FRANCE and GREAT BRITAIN with regard to TRADE, &c. By JOSIAH TUCKER, M.A. 8vo. 3rd ed. London, 1753.

The 1st and 2nd editions, London, 1750 and 1751, were anonymous.

The author of this tract, who was rector of St. Stephens, Bristol, and dean of Gloucester, died in 1799, at the advanced age of 88. Besides that now referred to, Dr. Tucker was the author of various pamphlets on questions connected with the trade and domestic policy of the empire, most of which display great sagacity and vigour of mind. This essay, and the essays in defence of the naturalization of foreigners (see *post*), are, perhaps, the best of his publications. The injustice and impolicy of the restraints on the trade of Ireland, and the advantages of a union with that country, are, in the present tract, set in a clear point of view. The author is also strongly opposed to all sorts of monopolies, whether of trading companies or corporations; and he has strikingly illustrated the many advantages that might be expected to result (and which have in fact resulted) from the establishment of the warehousing system, the improvement of the high roads, the opening of canals, &c. It is singular, however, notwithstanding his general good sense, that Tucker should be found proposing the institution of "guardians of public morals," and "inspectors of manufactures;" the increase of population by the "taxing of batchelors," and such like expedients; the taxing of articles of "luxury and extravagance;" the granting of bounties on the export of manufactured goods; and avowing that "the whole science of gainful commerce consists in procuring a balance of gold or silver to ourselves from other nations!" He approved highly of Decker's proposal for commuting the subsisting taxes for licence duties. It is greatly to the credit of Tucker that he was amongst the earliest of our writers who entertained a just sense of the value of colonial possessions; and who clearly foresaw that we should lose nothing by the emancipation of the American colonies. His style is clear, forcible, and free from all pretensions. There is a good, though rather flattering notice of Tucker in the 'Penny Cyclopædia.'

THE ELEMENTS of COMMERCE, and THEORY of TAXES. (By JOSIAH TUCKER, M.A.: issued from Bristol, 10 July, 1755.) 1 vol. thin 4to.

This work, though printed, was not published, a few copies only having been circulated among the author's friends for their opinion and revision. It comprises 174 pages, and is but a small fragment of what it would have been had it been completed. The theory of taxation is not touched upon. The principles laid down in this fragment are identical with those in the author's other works. The copy in our possession has some notes by the Earl of Shelburne (afterwards first Marquis of Lawnsdowne); but they are not of much consequence.

REFLECTIONS on the EXPEDIENCY of OPENING the TRADE to TURKEY, &c. (By JOSIAH TUCKER, M.A.) 2nd ed. 8vo. London, 1755.

A VIEW of the MANNER in which TRADE and CIVIL LIBERTY affect each other. 4to. London, 1756.

A Vindication of Commerce and the Arts; proving that they are the Source of the Greatness, Power, Riches, and Populousness of a State, &c. By J— B—, M.D. 8vo. London, 1758.

This very able tract was written in answer to a 'Dissertation on the following subject: What Causes principally contribute to render a Nation Populous? And what Effect has the Populousness of a Nation on its Trade? being one of those to which were adjudged the prizes given by Lord Viscount Townsend to the University of Cambridge in 1756. By William Bell, M.A. 4to. Cambridge, 1756.' Mr. Bell contends that population will be greatest in those countries in which artificial wants are fewest and property most equally distributed, and in which the principal attention of the people is directed to the necessary arts, or to those connected with the supply of food and other indispensable accommodations; and he further endeavours to show that luxury and refinement, with the culture of the arts subservient thereto, and an extensive commerce, produce vice and debauchery, a disinclination to marriage, a general corruption of manners, and a decrease in the numbers of the people. But the learned author of the 'Vindication' has successfully defended commerce and the arts from these charges; and has conclusively shown that without their cultivation and the stimulus afforded by artificial wants, countries would be incomparably less populous, and mankind sunk in sloth and barbarism. Statements and reasonings similar to those of Bell have since been frequently reproduced; but we do not know that their shallow sophistry has ever been more completely disposed of than in this tract.

The Universal Dictionary of Trade and Commerce. By Malachy Postlethwayt, Esq. 2 large vols., fol., 1st ed., London, 1751; 4th ed., London, 1774.

Postlethwayt, who was a laborious and indefatigable writer, died in 1767, and the 4th edition of his book appears to be little else than a reprint of the 3rd edition, which appeared in 1766, a little before his death. The work is chargeable with the same defects as that of Savary (see below), of which, indeed, it is in great part a translation. The author has made no effort to condense or give consistency to the statements under different articles, which being mostly copied from other publications (generally without acknowledgment), are often not a little contradictory. The work is swelled out to a most inconvenient magnitude, by being filled with articles and statements that either have no connexion with commerce, or one that is so very slight as hardly to be appreciable.

Great Britain's Commercial Interest explained and improved. By Malachy Postlethwayt, Esq. 2nd ed., 2 vols., 8vo. London, 1759.

The Analysis of Trade, Commerce, Coin, Bullion, &c. By Philip Cantillon, late of the City of London, Merchant. 1 vol., 8vo. London, 1759.

The author adopts several of the views of Hume, whose Political Essays were published in 1752. His principles are for the most part liberal, and some of his speculations display considerable ingenuity. He is one of the few writers to whom Smith has referred.

A New Dictionary of Trade and Commerce. By Mr. Rolt (Richard Rolt), with the assistance of several eminent Merchants. 1 vol., fol. London, 1761.

A wretched compilation, without learning or talent of any kind. The only good thing in it is its preface, which was written by Dr. Johnson. The latter, however, never saw the work which he undertook to usher into the world. "I knew very well," said he, "what such a dictionary should be, and I wrote a preface accordingly."—(Boswell's Life of Johnson, i. 280, Pickering's ed.) But Rolt and his coadjutors (if he had any) had no such knowledge, and therefore the preface is quite misplaced.

A New and Complete Dictionary of Trade and Commerce, &c. By Thomas Mortimer, Esq., Vice-Consul for the Netherlands. 2 vols., fol. London, 1766.

This is perhaps a better book than that of Rolt, though inferior to that of Postlethwayt. It is crammed with articles on all manner of subjects, such as architecture, the natural history of the ocean, the land-tax, the qualifications of surgeons, &c., the relation of which to commerce is rather difficult to discover. Had these articles been of any value they might have been tolerated; but for the most part they are as worthless as they are out of place.

The success of Postlethwayt's dictionary no doubt led to the publication of the dictionaries of Rolt and Mortimer, which, most probably, were suggested by the booksellers.

AN ESSAY on TRADE and COMMERCE, containing Observations on Taxes, &c. 1 vol., 8vo. London, 1770.

This work is by the author of the tract entitled 'Considerations on Taxes as they are supposed to affect the Price of Labour,' &c., which see *post*.

THE ELEMENTS of COMMERCE, POLITICS, and FINANCE. By THOMAS MORTIMER, Esq. 1 vol., 4to. London, 1774.

Of little or no value.

FOUR TRACTS on POLITICAL and COMMERCIAL SUBJECTS. By JOSIAH TUCKER, D.D. 1 vol., 8vo. 3rd ed. London, 1776.

In the first of these very clever tracts, Tucker endeavours to show, and we think successfully, that a poor country, provided it have no considerable natural advantages on its side, has very little chance of being able to come into competition with a rich country in manufacturing industry. Capital, skill, and industry are the essentials of superiority. "A war," says Tucker, "whether crowned with victory or branded with defeats, can never prevent another nation from being more industrious than you are; and if they are more industrious they will sell cheaper, and consequently your former customers will forsake your shop and go to theirs, though you covered the ocean with fleets and the land with armies. In short, the soldier may lay waste, the privateer, whether successful or unsuccessful, will make poor; but it is the eternal law of Providence that the *hand of the diligent alone can make rich*.

"The greater industry of different nations enables them to be so much the better customers, to improve in a friendly intercourse, and to be a mutual benefit to each other. A private shopkeeper would certainly wish that his customers did improve in their circumstances rather than go behind-hand, because every such improvement would probably redound to his advantage. Where then can be the wisdom in the public shopkeeper, or trading people, to endeavour to make the neighbouring states and nations, that are his customers, so very poor as not to be able to trade with him?"—pp. 42, 43.

But that complete overthrow of the principles of the mercantile system, which the desultory attacks of previous writers had merely shaken, was now (1776) effected by the publication of the 'Wealth of Nations.' Every one capable of appreciating the justice of its reasonings, and who had no selfish motives to lead him to a different conclusion, felt satisfied that the protective or monopoly system was opposed to the progress of real opulence and lasting improvement; and that every deviation from the freedom of commerce, not required for the purpose of national security and defence, was an evil. But a lengthened period elapsed before this conviction became general. The interest which many had in the support of measures and institutions bottomed on the principles that had been attacked, and the apathy and ignorance of many more, prevented the publication of the

'Wealth of Nations' from having so immediate an effect as some perhaps might have anticipated. The demolition of the theory of the prohibitive system was sure, however, to lead, in the end, to very great practical changes. Happily Mr. Pitt became a convert to the new doctrines, and from this date the character of our commercial legislation began to alter; a new spirit was infused into the discussions on commercial and financial subjects that took place in Parliament; and the writers on such topics no longer talked of the balance of trade and the dicta of Mun, as if they were the only principles to which an appeal could be made.

New and Old Principles of Trade Compared; or, a Treatise on the Principles of Commerce between Nations. 8vo. London, 1784.

In this tract the author contrasts the principles and practical results of the old or monopoly system with the principles and results of the new or free commercial system, as expounded by Smith, Quesnay, Decker, and others; and shows the superiority of the latter in promoting the increase of wealth, and of friendly relations among nations.

Observations on the Commerce of the American States. By John, Lord Sheffield. 1 vol., 8vo. 2nd. ed. London, 1784.

The attention of the legislature of this country and of that of Ireland was occupied during a considerable portion of the session of 1785 in discussing a project of Mr. Pitt, for liberalising the intercourse between the two great divisions of the empire. Our readers are aware that for a lengthened period Ireland was debarred from all communication with the English colonies, and that her intercourse with this island was subjected to many vexatious restraints. The former prohibition was suppressed in 1782, when Ireland was rendered politically independent of Great Britain. Little, however, was then done for promoting the intercourse between Great Britain and Ireland, which continued to be subject to the most objectionable restrictions. Mr. Pitt was anxious for the abolition of the latter, and for facilitating, in as far as possible, the trade between both countries; and, in pursuance of this policy, government introduced a series of resolutions into the Irish parliament embodying and declaring the principles on which the proposed commercial arrangements between them should be made; and these, after a good deal of debate, were agreed to.

The resolutions being thus assented to in Ireland, Mr. Pitt introduced them to the British House of Commons on the 22nd February, 1785, and moved in an able speech that they should be adopted. But, however unexceptionable, the project excited the greatest jealousy among the manufacturing and commercial classes in England, whose real or pretended fears were warmly seconded by the opposition in parliament, who made no better an appearance in these debates than in those that took place in the following year on the commercial treaty with France. And so powerful was the hostility to the resolutions as originally introduced, that Mr. Pitt was obliged to consent to their being materially modified. But this having displeased the Irish parliament, the bill to carry the amended resolutions into a law was dropped, so that the trade between the two countries continued on its old footing down to the Union.

Those who may be inclined to place implicit confidence in the statements of manufacturers and practical men in regard to the injury they are likely to sustain by the opening of new markets and new sources of competition, will do well to look a little into the evidence given on this occasion. Owing to the want of coal, and the peculiar habits and condition of the population,

Ireland has few or no facilities for the prosecution of manufacturing industry. And yet one would be tempted to suppose, on reading the evidence referred to, that nothing but the prohibitory regulations, which it was then proposed to modify, prevented our manufacturers from leaving Lancashire and the West Riding of Yorkshire to establish themselves in Down and Dublin! So extraordinary, indeed, was the delusion, even among the most intelligent persons, that the late Sir Robert Peel, father to the present Sir Robert, stated that he had serious thoughts, if the ministerial project were carried, of removing a part at least of his works and establishments to Ireland!

Among the publications that originated in this controversy the following may be specified:—

OBSERVATIONS on the MANUFACTURES, TRADE, and PRESENT STATE of IRELAND. By JOHN, LORD SHEFFIELD. 1 vol., 8vo. London, 1785.

REPORT of the LORDS of the COMMITTEE of COUNCIL upon the Propriety of Reducing the Duties payable in Great Britain on the Importation of Goods of the growth and manufacture of Ireland, &c. 8vo. London, 1785.

THE PROPOSED SYSTEM of TRADE with IRELAND EXPLAINED. 8vo. London, 1785.

This pamphlet, which is understood to have been written by Mr. George Rose, contains an outline of the proposed system, and a reply to the principal objections that had been urged against it.

A REPLY to the TREASURY PAMPHLET entitled 'The proposed System of Trade with Ireland explained.' 8vo. London, 1785.

Ascribed to Mr. Eden (afterwards Lord Auckland), paymaster-general under the coalition administration.

AN ANSWER to the REPLY to the supposed TREASURY PAMPHLET. 8vo. London, 1785.

REFLECTIONS on the PRESENT MATTERS in DISPUTE BETWEEN GREAT BRITAIN and IRELAND, and on the Means of converting these Articles into Mutual Benefits to both Kingdoms. By JOSIAH TUCKER, D.D. 8vo. London, 1785.

In this tract Tucker expresses his belief that the rejection of Mr. Pitt's project might be made of advantage to both Great Britain and Ireland; that Ireland being an independent kingdom, and not subject to our navigation or colonial laws, might carry on a free trade with all the world; and that English merchants might, by using her ports and flag for carrying on their operations, trade to the East Indies and China, notwithstanding the monopoly of the East India Company; and might also import sugar and all sorts of colonial and other products from wherever they could be had cheapest. But plausible as this view of the matter may appear, it does not seem to have been in any degree realized. English ships might, no doubt, have been fitted out from Irish ports, as Tucker suggested, but he either did not know, or forgot to state, that the cargoes which such ships might bring home would be excluded from the markets of Great Britain; and this exclusion far more than countervailed any advantages to be derived from sailing under the Irish flag.

EUROPEAN COMMERCE, showing New and Secure Channels of Trade with the Continent of Europe, detailing the Produce,

Manufactures, and Commerce of Russia, Prussia, Sweden, &c. By J. JEPHSON ODDY. 1 vol., 4to. London, 1805.

A work deficient in philosophy, but which contains much practical information. The great changes that have taken place in the trade of the countries described in it since its publication, have, however, gone far to deprive it of its original value. It was reviewed in an article in the 8th vol. of the 'Edinburgh Review.'

The Milan and Berlin decrees, promulgated by Napoleon in 1806, followed up as they were by the orders in council of the British government of the 7th of January, and 11th and 25th of November, 1807, placed the intercourse with the Continent and the neutral trade under the greatest difficulties. At this period an ingenious gentleman, Mr. William Spence, undertook to allay the public anxiety by endeavouring to show that though Napoleon were to succeed in totally shutting us out of the Continent, it would be of no moment, inasmuch as our wealth and power were wholly independent of foreign trade! In this view he published the following pamphlet:—

BRITAIN INDEPENDENT of COMMERCE; or Proofs deduced from an Investigation into the true Causes of the Wealth of Nations, that our Riches, Prosperity, and Power are derived from sources inherent in ourselves, and would not be affected even though our commerce were annihilated. By WILLIAM SPENCE, Esq. 8vo. London, 1807.

Owing to the peculiar juncture of circumstances at the time, the nature of the statements put forth by Mr. Spence, and the little attention paid by the bulk of the people to such subjects, which disposed them to lend a willing ear to the wildest paradoxes, this pamphlet met with a ready sale, and went through several editions. To make any remark upon it would be paying rather an equivocal compliment to the discernment of the reader. It is enough to say that it is a mere *rifacciamento*, and even exaggeration, of the exploded errors of the Economists, consisting of a series of shallow sophisms which had been refuted over and over again, and which, in fact, contradict and refute themselves. It, however, elicited several answers, of which the following are the best:—

COMMERCE DEFENDED: an Answer to the Arguments by which Mr. Spence, Mr. Cobbett, and others have attempted to prove that Commerce is not a source of National Wealth. By JAMES MILL, Esq., (Author of the 'History of British India.') 8vo. London, 1808.

THE ECONOMISTS REFUTED; being a Reply to Mr. Spence's 'Britain Independent of Commerce.' By COLONEL TORRENS. 8vo. London, 1808.

This is among the earliest contributions to political economy of the gallant and learned author, who has since continued to be one of its most assiduous cultivators.

The most striking proof of the progress of liberal opinions, and of the overthrow of the old protective and prohibitive system of commercial policy, was given in 1820 by the presentation of several petitions to Parliament from the principal trading towns in the United Kingdom, praying for the establishment of a free commercial system. The best of these petitions, and that which preceded the others, was from the city of London. It was written by Thomas Tooke, Esq., author of the excellent work on 'Prices,' and was subscribed by most of the leading merchants of the day. This petition was laid before the House of Commons on the 8th of May, 1820—an epoch in the history of commerce which deserves to be commemorated. We believe we shall gratify our readers by laying the petition before them.

"To the Honourable the Commons, &c., the Petition of the Merchants of the City of London.

"Showeth,

"That foreign commerce is eminently conducive to the wealth and prosperity of a country, by enabling it to import the commodities for the production of which the soil, climate, capital, and industry of other countries are best calculated, and to export in payment those articles for which its own situation is better adapted.

"That freedom from restraint is calculated to give the utmost extension to foreign trade, and the best direction to the capital and industry of the country.

"That the maxim of buying in the cheapest market, and selling in the dearest, which regulates every merchant in his individual dealings, is strictly applicable, as the best rule for the trade of the whole nation.

"That a policy founded on these principles would render the commerce of the world an interchange of mutual advantages, and diffuse an increase of wealth and enjoyments among the inhabitants of each state.

"That unfortunately a policy the very reverse of this has been and is more or less adopted and acted upon by the government of this and every other country, each trying to exclude the production of other countries, with the specious and well-meant design of encouraging its own productions, thus inflicting on the bulk of its subjects, who are consumers, the necessity of submitting to privations in the quantity or quality of commodities, and thus rendering what ought to be the source of mutual benefit and of harmony among states a constantly recurring occasion of jealousy and hostility.

"That the prevailing prejudices in favour of the protective or restrictive system may be traced to the erroneous supposition that every importation of foreign commodities occasions a diminution or discouragement of our own productions to the same extent; whereas it may be clearly shown that the particular description of produce which could not stand against unrestrained foreign competition would be discouraged, yet as no importation could be continued for any length of time without a corresponding exportation, direct or indirect, there would be an encouragement, for the purpose of that exportation, of some other production to which our situation might be better suited; thus affording at least an equal, and probably a greater, and certainly a more beneficial, employment to our own capital and labour.

"That of the numerous protective and prohibitory duties of our commercial code, it may be proved that while all operate as a very heavy tax on the community at large, very few are of any ultimate benefit to the classes for whose benefit they were originally instituted, and none to the extent of the loss occasioned by them to other classes.

"That among the other evils of the restrictive or protective system, not the least is that the artificial protection of one branch of industry, or source of production, against foreign competition, is set up as a ground of claim by other branches for similar protection; so that if the reasoning upon which these restrictive or prohibitory regulations are founded were followed out consistently, it would not stop short of excluding us from all foreign commerce whatsoever. And the same train of argument which, with corresponding prohibitions and protective duties, should exclude us from foreign trade, might be brought forward to justify the re-enactment of restrictions upon the interchange of productions (unconnected with public revenue) among the kingdoms composing the union, or among the counties of the same kingdom.

"That an investigation of the effects of the restrictive system at this time is peculiarly called for, as it may, in the opinion of your petitioners, lead to a strong presumption that the distress which now so generally prevails is considerably aggravated by that system; and that some relief may be obtained by the earliest practicable removal of such of the restraints as may be shown to be most injurious to the capital and industry of the community, and to be attended with no compensating benefit to the public revenue.

"That a declaration against the anti-commercial principles of our restrictive system is of the more importance at the present juncture, inasmuch as in several instances of recent occurrence the merchants and manufacturers in foreign states have assailed their respective governments with applications for further protective or prohibitory duties and regulations, urging the example and authority of this country, against which they are almost exclusively directed, as a sanction for the policy of such measures. And certainly if the reasoning upon which our restrictions have been defended is worth anything, it will apply in behalf of the regulations of foreign states against us. They insist upon our superiority in capital and machinery, as we do upon their comparative exemption from taxation, and with equal foundation.

"That nothing would more tend to counteract the commercial hostility of foreign states than the adoption of a more enlightened and more conciliatory policy on the part of this country.

"That although, as a matter of mere diplomacy, it may sometimes answer to hold out the removal of particular prohibitions, or high duties, as depending upon corresponding concessions by other states in our favour, it does not follow that we should maintain our restrictions, in cases where the desired concessions on their part cannot be obtained. Our restrictions would not be the less prejudicial to our own capital and industry because other governments persisted in preserving impolitic regulations.

"That, upon the whole, the most liberal would prove to be the most politic course on such occasions.

"That, independent of the direct benefit to be derived by this country on every occasion of such concession or relaxation, a great incidental object would be gained, by the recognition of a sound principle or standard to which all subsequent arrangements might be referred; and by the salutary influence which a promulgation of such just views, by the legislature and by the nation at large, could not fail to have on the policy of other states.

"That in thus declaring, as your petitioners do, their conviction of the impolicy and injustice of the restrictive system, and in desiring every practicable relaxation of it, they have in view only such parts of it as are not connected, or are only subordinately so, with the public revenue. As long as the necessity for the present amount of revenue subsists, your petitioners cannot expect so important a branch of it as the customs to be given up, nor to be materially diminished, unless some substitute less objectionable be suggested. But it is against every restrictive regulation of trade not essential to the revenue; against all duties merely protective from foreign competition, and against the excess of such duties as are partly for the purpose of revenue, and partly for that of protection, that the prayer of the present petition is respectfully submitted to the wisdom of parliament.

"May it therefore," &c.

An EXAMINATION of the NEW TARIFF proposed by the Hon.

Henry Baldwin, by one of the People. (— CAMBRELENG, Esq.) 8vo. New York, 1821.

A well reasoned, conclusive tract.

TWELVE REPORTS from, with MINUTES of EVIDENCE taken before the Committees of the Houses of Lords and Commons in 1821, 1822, 1823, and 1824, on the Foreign Trade of the Country.

SUBSTANCE of two SPEECHES delivered in the House of Commons on the 21st and 25th of March, 1825, respecting the Colonial Policy and Foreign Commerce of the Country. By the Right Hon. WILLIAM HUSKISSON. 8vo. London, 1825.

Three Lectures on the Transmission of the Precious Metals from Country to Country, and on the Mercantile Theory of Wealth. By N. W. Senior, Esq. 8vo. London, 1828.

REPORT of a COMMITTEE of the CITIZENS of BOSTON and its Vicinity on DUTIES on IMPORTATIONS. 8vo. Boston, 1827.

PAPERS relative to AMERICAN TARIFFS; printed by order of the House of Commons. Folio. 1828.

REPORT of the COMMITTEE of the HOUSE of REPRESENTATIVES of the 8th of February, 1830, on COMMERCE and NAVIGATION. (Drawn up by Mr. CAMBRELENG.) 8vo. New York, 1830.

A forcible exposition of the mischievous influence of the restrictive system.

MEMORIAL of the COMMITTEE appointed by "The Free Trade Convention," held at Philadelphia in September and October, 1831. 8vo. New York, 1832.

The State of the Commerce of Great Britain, with reference to COLONIAL and other PRODUCE, for the year 1830. 8vo. London, 1831

For 1831 ,, ,, 1832

For 1832 ,, ,, 1833.

These states comprise, within a brief space, much valuable information set in the clearest point of view. They were compiled by Mr. Cook, of the firm of Trueman and Cook, brokers, for the use of their numerous friends and connexions; but having exceeded the limits within which mercantile circulars are usually confined, a few copies were printed for the use of the public. They are incomparably the best publications of their class that we have ever seen, and their discontinuance is much to be regretted.

A DIGEST of the EXISTING COMMERCIAL REGULATIONS of FOREIGN COUNTRIES with which the United States have intercourse, as far as they can be ascertained. Prepared in compliance with a Resolution of the House of Representatives of the 3rd of March, 1831. 3 vols. 8vo. Washington. 1833–36.

This, though less copious and complete, is a work of the same description as that of Mr. Macgregor mentioned below. It consists principally of translations of tariffs and other official documents, and of reports from the American consuls in foreign countries. We have not examined it with sufficient attention to give any opinion of its accuracy.

ON COMMERCE, ITS PRINCIPLES AND HISTORY. By J. R. M'CULLOCH, Esq. 8vo. London, 1833.

Published by the Society for the Diffusion of Useful Knowledge.

A STATISTICAL VIEW of the COMMERCE of the UNITED STATES of AMERICA, including an Account of Banks, Manufactures, Internal Trade, &c. By TIMOTHY PITKIN, Esq. 1 vol., 8vo. New-Haven, 1835.

REPORT on the COMMERCE of the PORTS of NEW RUSSIA, MOLDAVIA, and WALLACHIA, made to the Russian Government in 1835. By M. de HAGEMEISTER. Translated from the original. 1 vol., post 8vo. London, 1836.

A Dictionary, Practical, Theoretical, and Historical, of Commerce and Commercial Navigation. By J. R. M'CULLOCH, Esq. A new and much improved edition, 1 thick vol., 8vo. London, 1844.

Commercial Statistics: a DIGEST of the Productive Resources; Commercial Legislation; Customs Tariffs; Navigation, Port and Quarantine Laws and Charges; Shipping; Imports and Exports; Moneys, Weights, Measures, &c. of all Nations. By JOHN MACGREGOR, Esq., one of the Secretaries to the Board of Trade. 3 vols., folio. London, 1844.

THE YEARLY JOURNAL OF TRADE for 1844 and several previous Years. By CHARLES POPE, Comptroller of Accounts in the Port of Bristol. 1 vol. 8vo. London, 1844, &c.

This useful work gives the tariff, and the customs' regulations respecting the importation and exportation of different articles, port charges, &c., at the commencement of each year. It also specifies the principal changes that have taken place in commercial laws and regulations in the course of the previous year. It might, however, be advantageously shortened by the omission of irrelevant and useless matter.

LE NEGOCE D'AMSTERDAM. Par J. P. RICARD (a son of Samuel Ricard. See below). 1 vol., 4to. Amsterdam, 1722.

ESSAI POLITIQUE sur le COMMERCE. Par M. MELON. 1re éd. 1 vol. 12mo. Paris, 1734. A second and greatly improved edition was published at Paris in 1736.

The author, a native of Tulle, after being employed in various departments of the government, died at Paris in 1738. Voltaire has said of this work: "*C'est l'ouvrage d'un homme d'esprit, d'un citoyen, d'un philosophe; et je ne crois pas que du tems même de M. Colbert, il y eut en France deux hommes capables de composer un tel livre. Cependant il y a bien des erreurs dans ce bon ouvrage; tant le chemin vers la vérité est difficile.*"

This statement appears to be as true as it is well expressed. The opinions of Melon respecting the intercourse that should subsist among nations are, speaking generally, liberal, and in advance of those entertained by his countrymen at the time. But a large proportion of his book is occupied with discussions respecting money, and changes in the value of the coin; and he is uniformly almost the apologist of those reductions of the standard, so disgraceful to the governments by which they are practised, and so ruinous to their subjects. Indeed he lays it down as a maxim of law and of public policy, that government should always favour the debtors. *C'est une maxime de droit, qui est encore bien plus maxime d'état,* QU'IL FAUT TOUJOURS FAVORISER LE DEBITEUR (p. 221, ed. 1736). It is not easy to imagine anything more reprehensible than this. The only maxim for a state to act upon is to do *justice* to all parties; to preserve, in as far as possible, the purity and integrity of its coins; and to leave the creditors and the debtors to take care of themselves.

Melon's work was translated into English, and published with some useful notes under the following title:—

A POLITICAL ESSAY upon COMMERCE. Written in French by M. M****. Translated, with Remarks and Annotations, by DAVID BINDON, ESQ. 1 vol., 8vo. Dublin, 1739.

DICTIONNAIRE UNIVERSEL du COMMERCE, &c. Par Messrs. SAVARY. 3 vol., folio. Paris, 1748.

This work originally appeared at Paris in 1723, in 2 vols. folio, a 3rd vol. being added to it by way of supplement in 1730, which was incorporated with the former in the edition of 1748. An edition in 6 vols. folio was published at Geneva in 1750, which includes the '*Parfait Négociant*' of Jacques Savary, father of the authors of the Dictionary, and some additional articles, partly on commercial subjects, but principally on subjects connected with natural history. The last and best edition is that of Copenhagen, in 5 vols. folio, the first of which appeared in 1759, and the last in 1765. The additions to this edition consist for the most part of articles taken from the first 7 vols. of the *Encyclopédie.*

This was the first work of the kind that appeared in modern Europe; and has furnished the principal part of the materials for most of those by which it has been followed. The undertaking was liberally patronised by the French government, who justly considered that a Commercial Dictionary, if well executed, would be of national importance. Hence a considerable, and indeed the most valuable portion of the work is compiled from memoirs sent the authors, by order of government, by the inspectors of manufactures in France and by the French consuls in foreign countries.

More than half this work consists of articles altogether foreign to its proper object. It is in fact quite as much a dictionary of manufactures as of commerce, descriptions being given which are necessarily in most instances exceedingly incomplete, and which the want of plates often renders unintelligible, of the methods followed in the manufacture of the articles described. It is also filled with lengthened articles on natural history, the by-laws and privileges of different corporations, and a variety of subjects nowise connected with commercial pursuits. No one, however, need look into it for any development of sound principles, or for enlarged views. It is valuable as a repertory of facts relating to commerce and manufactures at the commencement of last century, collected with laudable care and industry; but its commercial geography and statistics are, even for the time, miserably defective; and it is pervaded by the spirit of a customs officer, without any philosophy and but little learning. "*Les principes généraux manquent à l'ouvrage de Savary, et souvent dans ses réflexions, il tend plutôt à égarer ses lecteurs qu'à les conduire, et des maximes nuisibles au progrès du commerce et de l'industrie obtiennent presque toujours ses éloges et son approbation.*"—(Morellet, Prospectus, p. 19.)

The work was commenced and principally compiled by M. Savary, inspector of customs at Paris, and, after his death in 1716, was completed by his brother the Abbé Savary, canon of St. Maur.

REMARQUES sur les AVANTAGES et les DESAVANTAGES de la FRANCE et de la GRANDE BRETAGNE, par Rapport au Commerce. Traduit de l'Anglois du Chevalier JOHN NICKOLLS. 3me. éd. 1 vol. 12mo. Paris, 1754.

This work is pseudonymous, having been originally written in French by M. Dangeul, on whom, though he has followed Tucker rather too closely, it reflects considerable credit.

RETABLISSEMENT des MANUFACTURES et du COMMERCE d'ESPAGNE. Traduit de l'Espagnol de Don Bernardo de Ulloa. Par FORBONNAIS (?). 1 vol., 12mo. Amsterdam (Paris), 1753.

ELEMENS du COMMERCE. Par FORBONNAIS. 2de. éd. 2 vol., 12mo. A Leyde (Paris), 1754.

A new and considerably improved edition appeared at Paris in 1796.

The author of this work was a laborious, conscientious, and useful writer. Unfortunately, however, he was a zealous adherent of the mercantile system; and consequently had no proper conception of the mode in which commerce contributes to increase national wealth.

ESSAI sur l'ETAT du COMMERCE d'ANGLETERRE. 2 vol., 12mo. Paris, 1755.

(See ante, p. 46.)

CONSIDERATIONS sur le COMMERCE, et en particulier sur les COMPAGNIES, SOCIÉTÉS, et MAITRISES. 1 vol. 12mo. Amsterdam, 1758.

An excellent little work, in which the impolicy of corporations with peculiar privileges, and of regulations for the prevention of fraud in manufactures, is conclusively shown.

MEMOIRES et CONSIDERATIONS sur le COMMERCE et les FINANCES d'ESPAGNE. 2 vol., 12mo. Amsterdam (Paris), 1761.

That portion of this work which relates to finance was written by Forbonnais. The other portion is said to be the work of a Spaniard.

PROSPECTUS d'un NOUVEAU DICTIONNAIRE du COMMERCE. Par M. l'ABBE MORELLET. 1 vol., 8vo. Paris, 1769.

This prospectus, which is undoubtedly one of the very best specimens of that class of works, was intended to exhibit the principles and plan of a Commercial Dictionary, in the compilation of which Morellet was then actively engaged, which was to extend to five, or perhaps six, volumes folio. And from his acknowledged learning and talent, the liberality of his views, and his capacity for laborious exertion, there can be no doubt, had the projected Dictionary made its appearance, that it would have been infinitely superior to that of Savary, or any other that had then been published. Morellet continued to occupy himself with this gigantic enterprise down to the Revolution, when he was compelled finally to abandon it. The work was begun under the auspices of M. Trudaine, intendant of finance, and was patronised by Messrs. Laverdy and Bertin, comptrollers-general. Morellet survived the massacres of the Revolution, and died at Paris in 1819, at the great age of 92. His large and valuable collection of commercial works was sold soon after his death; but we have not learned the fate of his manuscripts.

LE COMMERCE de la HOLLANDE, ou Tableau du Commerce des Hollandais dans les Quatre Parties du Monde. 3 vol., 12mo. Amsterdam, 1768.

LES INTERETS des NATIONS de l'EUROPE dévelopés relativement au COMMERCE. 2 vol., 4to. A Leide, 1766.

La Richesse de la Hollande. 2 vol., 4to. Amsterdam, 1778.

This and the two preceding works are by Acarias de Serionne, a French littérateur, who died at Vienna in 1792, at a very advanced age. Though diffuse in the extreme, and in some respects contradictory, they contain a great variety of curious and instructive details, especially the last, which is by far the most valuable. It is said, in the 'Biographie Universelle,' that M. Elie Luzac, a Dutch jurist, to whom we are indebted for the '*Remarques d'un Anonyme sur l'Esprit des Loix*,' and other works, was the author of the 'Richesse de la Hollande.' We have, however, been assured by an eminent Dutch economist, that this is an error, which most probably originated in the circumstance of Luzac having translated the work, to which he made considerable additions, into Dutch, and published it under the title of '*Hollands Rykdom*,' 4 vols. 8vo., at Leyden, in 1780.

Exclusive of the above, Serionne was the author of sundry other works, among which the 'Biographie Universelle' includes

LA RICHESSE de l'ANGLETERRE. 1 vol., 4to. Vienne, 1771.

But this we have not seen.

LE COMMERCE et le GOUVERNEMENT, considérés relativement l'un à l'autre. Par M. l'ABBÉ DE CONDILLAC. 1 vol., 12mo. Amsterdam (Paris), 1776.

This treatise is also included in the collective editions of the works of Condillac.

"Condillac," to borrow the expressions of Say, "a cherché à se faire un systême particulier sur une matière qu'il n'entendait pas; mais il y a quelques bonnes idées à recueillir parmi le babil ingénieux de son livre."—(Discours Prélim. Traité d'Economie Politique.)

TRAITÉ GENERAL du COMMERCE. &c. Par SAMUEL RICARD. 2 vol., 4to. Amsterdam, 1781.

This treatise, by a well-informed merchant of Amsterdam, was first published early in the century; but it was so much changed in subsequent editions that at length little remained of the original work, except the title. The edition now referred to is the most valuable; and when published was decidedly the best counting-house guide that had appeared, being, in this respect, infinitely superior to the dictionaries of Savary and Postlethwayt.

DE la BALANCE du COMMERCE. Par M. ARNOULD. 2 vol., 8vo. Paris, 1791.

TRAITÉ de la RICHESSE COMMERCIAL. Par M. SISMONDI. 2 vol., 8vo. Genève, 1803.

When this work appeared, Sismondi was a follower of Adam Smith, from whom he afterwards seceded.

DE l'INFLUENCE d'un GRANDE REVOLUTION sur le COMMERCE. Par M. LABOULINIERE. 1 vol., 8vo. Paris, 1808.

Dictionnaire du Commerce et de Marchandises, &c. Par Messrs. BLANQUI, A. CHEVALIER, PARISOT, &c. 2 vol., grand in-8vo. Paris, 1842.

LEZIONI di COMMERCIO, o sia di ECONOMIA CIVILE. Dell' ABATE ANTONIO GENOVESI. 2 vol., 8vo. Napoli, 1764.

These Lectures have been often reprinted, and are included in the *Economisti Italiani*.

This work is one of the best that has been written on the narrow and hollow principles of the mercantile system, and without the author having any clear idea of the real sources of wealth. It contains many interesting statements and ingenious discussions. There is, however, a great want of method in its plan; and the reader will have little difficulty in discovering that Genovesi was a theologian and a metaphysician, as well as a publicist.

The history of this work is rather curious. Genovesi was the intimate friend of the Abbaté Intieri, a Florentine, who is believed to have contributed to the treatise on money by Galiani (see *post*), and who was celebrated for the variety of his attainments, and his benevolence. Having resided long in Naples, as manager of the estates of the Corsini and Medici families in that kingdom, Intieri became familiar with many of the abuses with which every part of the administration was infected; and being strongly impressed with a conviction that the easiest, safest, and most effectual reform of these abuses would be brought about by rendering the public acquainted with the sources of national wealth and happiness, and of poverty and misery, he determined to show his gratitude to the Neapolitans for the kindness he had experienced during his residence amongst them, by instituting a course of lectures on public economy. In this view Intieri applied to the Neapolitan government for leave to found a professorship of public economy in the University of Naples, to which a salary of 300 scudi a-year should be attached, stipulating that the lectures should be delivered in the Italian language; that his friend Genovesi should be the first professor; and that after his death no individual in holy orders should be appointed to the chair. Government having assented to these conditions, Genovesi opened his class, the first, we believe, of the kind ever established, on the 5th of November, 1754. The lectures, which were very successful, were published, as already stated, ten years after, or in 1764. Genovesi died in 1769, at the age of 57. (See 'Biographie Universelle,' art. Genovesi; and the notice of his life prefixed to his works in the 14th vol. of the *Economisti Italiani*.)

DEL COMMERCIO de' ROMANI, dalla Prima Guerra Punica a Costantino, Dissertazione, di FRANCESCO MENGOTTI, coronata dall' Accademia delle Iscrizione e Belle Lettere di Parigi nel 1787.

IL COLBERTISMO, ossia della Liberta di Commercio de' Prodotti della Terra, Dissertazione di FRANCESCO MENGOTTI, coronata dall' Accademia di Georgofili di Firenze nel 1791.

These dissertations were printed in 2 vols. 12mo., at Milan, in 1802, and they are comprised in the 36th volume of the modern part of the 'Economisti Italiani.' By Colbertism Mengotti means the mercantile system of policy of which he is a strenuous opponent. Both Dissertations are respectable performances, but neither does justice to the subject of which it treats.

TÉORICA y PRACTICA del COMERCIO y MARINA. Por DON GERONYMO USTARIZ. 1st ed., 1 vol. 4to. Madrid, 1724; 3rd ed., 1 vol. folio, 1753.

A translation of this work into English, by John Kippax, B.D., in 2 vols. 8vo., was published in London in 1751; and a translation into French, by Forbonnais, in 1 vol. 4to., was published at Paris in 1753.

Though imbued with the prejudices of the mercantile system, the work of Ustariz is valuable for the information it affords respecting the internal policy, trade, and state of Spain from the reign of Charles V. downwards.

---

§ II. TRADE IN CORN, CORN LAWS, &c.

FOR a lengthened period the regulations with respect to the corn trade were framed in the view of directly promoting abundance and low prices. But, though the purpose was laudable, the means adopted for accomplishing it had, for the most part, an opposite effect. When a country exports corn, it seems, at first sight, as if nothing would increase her supplies so much as the prevention of exportation: and even in countries that do not export, its prohibition seems to be a prudent measure, and calculated to prevent the supply being diminished, upon any emergency, below its natural level. These are the conclusions that immediately suggest themselves upon this subject; and it requires a pretty extensive experience, an attention to facts, and a habit of reasoning upon such topics, to perceive their fallacy. These, however, were altogether wanting when the regulations affecting the corn trade began to be introduced into Great Britain and other countries. They were framed in accordance with what were supposed to be the dictates of common sense; and their object being to procure as large a supply of the prime necessary of life as possible, its exportation was either totally forbidden, or forbidden when the home price was above certain limits.

The principle of absolute prohibition seems to have been steadily acted upon, as far as the turbulence of the period would admit, from the Conquest to the year 1436, in the reign of Henry VI. But at the last-mentioned period an act was passed, authorising the exportation of wheat whenever the home price did not exceed 6*s*. 8*d*. (equal in amount of pure silver to 12*s*. 10¾*d*. present money) per quarter, and barley when the home price did not exceed 3*s*. 4*d*. In 1463, an additional benefit was intended to be conferred on agriculture by prohibiting importation until the home price exceeded that at which exportation ceased. But the fluctuating policy of the times prevented these regulations from being carried into full effect; and, indeed, rendered them in a great measure inoperative.

In addition to the restraints laid on exportation, it has been common in some countries to attempt to increase the supply of corn, not only by admitting its unrestrained importation from abroad, but by holding out extraordinary encouragement to the importers. This policy has not, however, been much followed in England. During the 500 years immediately posterior to the Conquest, importation was substantially free; but it was seldom or never promoted by artificial means: and during the last century and a half it has, for the most part, been subjected to severe restrictions.

Besides attempting to lower prices by prohibiting exportation, our ancestors attempted to lower them by proscribing the trade carried on by corn dealers. This most useful class of persons were looked upon with suspicion by every one. The agriculturists concluded that they would be able to sell their produce at higher prices to the consumers, were the corn dealers out of the way: while the consumers concluded that the profits of the dealers were made at their expense; and ascribed the dearths that were then very prevalent entirely to the practices of the dealers, or to their buying up corn and withholding it from market. These notions, which have still a considerable degree of influence, led to various enactments, particularly in the reign of Edward VI., by which the freedom of the internal corn trade was entirely suppressed. The *engrossing* of corn, or the buying of it in one market with intent to sell it again in another, was made an offence punishable by imprisonment and the pillory; and no one was allowed to carry corn from one part of the country to another without a licence, the privilege of granting which was confided by a statute of Elizabeth to the quarter sessions. But as the principles of commerce came to be better understood, the impolicy of these restraints grew more and more obvious. They were considerably modified in 1624; and, in 1663, the engrossing of corn was declared to be legal so long as the price did not exceed 48*s.* a quarter—(15 Chas. II. c. 7); an act which, according to Dr. Smith, has, with all its imperfections, done more to promote plenty than any other law in the statute book. In 1773, the last remnant of the *legislative* enactments restraining the freedom of the internal corn trade, was repealed.

The acts of 1436 and 1463, regulating the prices when exportation was allowed and when importation was to cease, continued, nominally at least, in force till 1562, when the prices at which exportation might take place were extended to 10*s.* for wheat and 6*s.* 8*d.* for barley. But a new principle—that of imposing duties on exportation—was soon after introduced; and, in 1571, it was enacted that wheat might be exported, paying a duty of 2*s.* a quarter, and barley and other grain a duty of 1*s.* 4*d.*, whenever the home price of wheat did not exceed 20*s.* a quarter, and barley and malt 12*s.* At the Restoration, the limit at which exportation might take place was very much extended; but as the duty on exportation was, at the same time, so very high as to be almost prohibitory, the extension was of little or no service to the agriculturists. This view of the matter seems to have been speedily taken by the legislature; for, in 1663, the high duties on exportation were taken off, and an *ad valorem* duty imposed in their stead, at the same time that the limit of exportation was extended. In 1670, a still more decided step was taken in favour of agriculture; an act being then passed which extended the exportation price to 53*s.* 4*d.* a quarter for wheat, and other grain in proportion, imposing, at the same time, prohibitory duties on the importation of wheat till the price rose to 53*s.* 4*d.*, and a duty of 8*s.* between that price and 80*s.* But the real effects of this act were not so great as might have been anticipated. The extension of the limit of exportation was rendered comparatively nugatory, in consequence of the continuance of the duties on exportation caused by the necessities of the Crown; while the want of any proper method for the determination of prices went far to nullify the prohibition of importation.

At the accession of William III. a new system was adopted. The interests of agriculture were then looked upon as of paramount importance: and to promote them, not only were the duties on exportation abolished, but it was encouraged by the grant of a *bounty* of 5*s.* on every quarter of wheat exported while the price continued at or below 48*s.*; of 2*s.* 6*d.* on every quarter of barley or malt, while their respective prices did not exceed 24*s.*; and of 3*s.* 6*d.* on every quarter of rye, when its price did not exceed 32*s.* (1 Will. and Mary, c. 12.) A bounty of 2*s.* 6*d.* a quarter was subsequently given upon the exportation of oats and oatmeal, when the price of the former did not exceed 15*s.* a quarter. Importation continued to be regulated by the act of 1670.

Much diversity of opinion has been entertained with respect to the policy of the bounty. That it was intended to raise the price of corn is clear, from the words of the statute, which states, "that the exportation of corn and grain into foreign parts, *when the price thereof is at a low rate in this kingdom*, hath been a great advantage not only to the owners of land, but to the trade of the kingdom in general; therefore,"-&c. Admitting, however, this to have been its object, it has been contended that the low prices which prevailed during the first half of last century show that its real effect had been precisely the reverse; and that it had, by extending tillage, contributed to reduce prices. But this could not really have been the case; for the extension of tillage must, by bringing inferior lands into cultivation, have in so far operated to raise the cost and price of corn. The fall in its price, that took place during the first half of last century, may, however, be sufficiently accounted for by the improvements in agriculture, the gradual consolidation of farms, the diminution of sheep husbandry, &c., combined with the slow increase of population. In point of fact, too, prices had begun to give way thirty years before the bounty was granted; and the fall was equally great in France, where, instead of exportation being encouraged by a bounty, it was almost entirely prohibited; and in most other Continental states. At the same time, however, we are by no means clear that a bounty on the exportation of corn is, in all cases, so injurious as has been represented. That it extends tillage, and somewhat increases the average price of corn, is true; but, on the other hand, it affords a certain degree of security against scarcity and injurious fluctuations of price. If there be no bounty on exportation, prices, in a country which grows in ordinary years nearly its own supply of corn, must sink to a comparatively low level in luxuriant years, for the excess of produce cannot be taken out of the market till the price fall so far below the level of other countries as to admit of exportation to them; and if two or three such seasons should follow in succession, as is commonly the case, the agriculturists would be involved in distress, a check would be given to improvements, and the extent of land under corn would, perhaps, be diminished. But with a bounty the fall is proportionally less; and the farmer being in so far protected against the injurious influence of a ruinously low price, prosecutes his business with greater zeal and vigour; and improvements being carried on, and a greater supply of corn raised, the chances of scarcity and high prices are proportionally diminished, and when they do occur their severity is abated.

A bounty in a country that generally exports, as was the case in England from 1690 down to 1750, does little more than impose a tax on the public merely to increase exportation, while in a generally importing country a bounty on exportation would be inoperative. But whenever the supply of corn in ordinary years nearly balances the demand, we incline to think that a reasonable bounty on exportation is advisable; and that by giving additional security and confidence to the corn-growers, it increases the home supply of corn and materially diminishes the chances and evils of scarcity.

If we be right in these remarks, it will be seen that the virtual abandonment of the bounty, in 1773, was inexpedient. It had then really begun to be useful, for the demand and supply of corn had then begun to be well nigh balanced, and scarcities were, therefore, to be apprehended, and should, in as far as practicable, have been provided against.

It may not be uninteresting to observe that this view of the bounty was taken by Dr. Johnson, in an essay on the "Corn Laws," supposed to have been written in 1766, but not published till 1808 (Works, x., 402, ed. 1823). It contains almost every thing that can be urged in favour of the bounty.

Three Tracts on the Corn Trade and Corn Laws. (By CHARLES SMITH, Esq.) 1 vol. 8vo. 2nd ed. London, 1766.

These tracts are by far the best of the earlier works on the corn trade. They embody much valuable information respecting the corn laws of England, and other countries, especially France; the prices, imports, and exports of corn; the sums paid in bounties on exportation; the numbers of the people using different sorts of corn, and the quantity used by each, &c. The first tract was published in 1758, and the second in 1759.

"The ingenious and well-informed author" of these tracts (Wealth of Nations, p. 224) was practically versed in the corn trade, having inherited extensive corn-mills at Barking, in Essex. He was killed by a fall from his horse in 1777. The tracts were republished, with a notice of the author, and some additional matter, by George Chalmers, Esq. 1 vol. 8vo. London, 1804.

THE EXPEDIENCY of a FREE EXPORTATION of CORN, with some OBSERVATIONS on the BOUNTY. (By ARTHUR YOUNG, Esq.) 8vo. London, 1772.

An Enquiry into the Nature of the Corn Laws, with a view to the new Corn Bill proposed for Scotland. (By JAMES ANDERSON, LL.D.) 8vo. Edinburgh, 1777.

The publication of this tract marks an important æra in the history of economical science, from its containing the earliest explanation that is anywhere to be met with of the real nature and origin of rent. And it is to be observed that the author did not stumble upon this great discovery as it were by chance, and without being aware of its value. On the contrary, nothing can be more complete and satisfactory than his analysis of the circumstances in which rent originates, and which occasion its increase and diminution; and he did not fail to recur again and again to the subject in subsequent publications. But despite their paramount importance to a right understanding of the principles of political economy, and of the constitution of society, Anderson's profound and original speculations do not appear to have attracted any attention from his contemporaries. Though published nearly at the same time as the 'Wealth of Nations,' Dr. Smith, to whom they might have been of essential service, did not profit by them in revising any subsequent edition of his great work; and so completely were they forgotten, that when, in 1815, Mr. Malthus and Sir Edward West published their tracts exhibiting the nature and progress of rent, they were universally believed to have, for the first time, discovered the laws by which it is governed; and perhaps their originality cannot be justly impeached, but whether this be so or not, it is at all events certain that the true theory of rent had been quite as well and as satisfactorily explained by Dr. Anderson in 1777 as it was by them in 1815. In proof of this we beg to subjoin the following extracts from this tract:—

"I foresee here a popular objection. It will be said that the price to the farmer is so high only on account of the high rents and avaricious extortions of the proprietors. 'Lower,' say they, 'your rents, and the farmer will be able to afford his grain cheaper to the consumer.' But if the avarice alone of the proprietors was the cause of the dearth of corn, whence comes it, I may ask, that the price of grain is always higher on the west than on the east coast of Scotland? Are the proprietors in the Lothians more tender-hearted and less avaricious than those of Clydesdale? The truth is, nothing can be more groundless than these clamours against men of landed property. There is no doubt that they, as well as every other class of men, will be willing to augment their revenue as much as they can, and therefore will always accept of as high a rent for their land as is offered to them. Would merchants or manufacturers do otherwise? Would either the one or the other of these refuse, for the goods he offers to sale in a fair open way, as high a price as the purchaser is inclined to give? If they would not, it is surely with a bad grace that they blame gentlemen for accepting such a rent for their land as farmers, who are supposed always to understand the value of it, shall choose to offer them.

"It is not, however, the rent of the land that determines the price of its produce, but it is the price of that produee which determines the rent of the land, although the price of that produce is often highest in those countries where the rent of land is lowest. This seems to be a paradox that deserves to be explained.

"In every country there is a variety of soils, differing considerably from one another in point of fertility. These we shall at present suppose arranged into different classes, which we shall denote by the letters A, B, C, D, E, F, &c., the class A comprehending the soils of the greatest fertility, and the other letters expressing different classes of soils, gradually decreasing in fertility as you recede from the first. Now, as the expense of cultivating the least fertile soil is as great or greater than that of the most fertile field, it necessarily follows, that if an equal quantity of corn, the produce of each field, can be sold at the same price, the profit on cultivating the most fertile soil must be much greater than that of cultivating the others; and as this continues to decrease as the sterility increases, it must at length happen that the expense of cultivating some of the inferior classes will equal the value of the whole produce.

"This being premised, let us suppose that the class F includes all those fields whose produce in oatmeal, if sold at 14*s.* per boll, would be just sufficient to pay the expense of cultivating them, without affording any rent at all; that the class E comprehended those fields whose produce, if sold at 13*s.* per boll, would free the charges without affording any rent; and that in like manner the classes D, C, B, and A, consisted of fields whose produce, if sold respectively at 12*s.*, 11*s.*, 10*s.*, and 9*s.* per boll, would exactly pay the charge of culture without any rent.

"Let us now suppose that all the inhabitants of the country where such fields are placed could be sustained by the produce of the first four classes, viz. A, B, C, and D. It is plain that if the average selling price of oatmeal in that country was 12*s.* per boll, those who possessed the fields D could just afford to cultivate them without paying any rent at all; so that if there were no other produce of the fields that could be reared at a smaller expense than corn, the farmer could afford no rent whatever to the proprietor for them; and if so, no rents could be afforded for the fields E and F, nor could the utmost avarice of the proprietor in this case extort a rent for them. In these circumstances, however, it is obvious that the farmer who possessed the fields in the class C could pay the expense of cultivating them, and also afford to the proprietor a rent equal to 1*s.* for every boll of their produce; and, in like manner, the possessors of the fields B and A could afford a rent equal to 2*s.* or 3*s.* per boll of their produce respectively. Nor would the proprietors of these fields find any difficulty in obtaining these rents; because farmers, finding they could live equally well upon such soils, though paying these rents, as they could do upon the fields D without any rent at all, would be equally willing to take the one as the other.

"But let us again suppose that the whole produce of the fields A, B, C, and D was *not* sufficient to maintain the whole of the inhabitants. If the average selling price should continue at 12*s.* per boll, as none of the fields E or F could admit of being cultivated, the inhabitants would be under the necessity of bringing grain from some other country to supply their wants; but if it should be found that grain could not be brought from that other country, at an average, under 13*s.* per boll, the price in the home market would rise to that rate, so that the fields E could then be brought into culture, and those of the class D could afford a rent to the proprietor equal to what was formerly yielded by C, and so on of others—the rents of every class rising in the same proportion. If these fields were sufficient to maintain the whole of the inhabitants, the price would remain permanently at 13*s.*; but if there was still a deficiency, and if that could not be made up for less than 14*s.* per boll, the price would rise in the market to that rate, in which case the field F might also be brought into culture, and the rents of all the others would rise in proportion.

"To apply this reasoning to the present case, it appears that the people in the Lothians can be maintained by the produce of the fields A, B, C, D, and E, but the inhabitants of Clydesdale require also the produce of the fields F: so that the one is under the necessity of giving, at an average, 1*s.* per boll more for meal than the other.

"Let us now suppose that the gentlemen of Clydesdale, from an extraordinary exertion of patriotism, and an inordinate desire to encourage manufactures, should resolve to lower their rents so as to demand nothing from those who possessed the fields E, as well as those of the class F, and should allow the rents of all the others to sink in proportion: would the prices of grain fall in consequence of this? By no means. The inhabitants are still in need of the whole produce of the fields F as before, and are under the necessity of paying the farmer of these fields such a price as to enable him to cultivate them. He must therefore still receive 14*s.* per boll as formerly; and as the grain from the fields E, D, C, B, and A, is at least equally good, the occupiers of each of these fields would receive the same price for their produce. The only consequence then that would result from this Quixotic scheme would be the enriching one class of farmers at the expense of their proprietors, without producing the smallest benefit to the consumers of grain—perhaps the reverse, as the industry of these farmers might be slackened by this measure."—pp. 45-48.

Dr. Anderson, the author of this profound and original pamphlet, was born at Hermandston, in Mid-Lothian, in 1740. He was long engaged in the business of farming in the neighbourhood of Aberdeen, the University of which conferred on him, in 1780, the honorary degree of LL.D. Having left Aberdeenshire in 1783, Anderson resided for some time in the vicinity of Edinburgh, where he projected and edited the 'Bee,' a respectable weekly publication. In 1797 he removed to London, where he edited 'Recreations in Agriculture, Natural History, Arts,' &c. In this work (vol. v. pp. 401-405) he gave a new and lucid exposition of the origin and causes of rent. Exclusive of this and another pamphlet, published during the scarcity in 1800 (see *post*), and of the periodical publications referred to above, Anderson was the author of various works, which, though now of little value, had, when they made their appearance, a powerful influence in forwarding improvement in Scotland. He died in 1808.

REPRESENTATION of the LORDS of the COMMITTEE of COUNCIL appointed for the Consideration of all Matters relating to Trade and Foreign Plantations, upon the present State of the Laws for regulating the Importation and Exportation of Corn. 4to. London, 1790.

In consequence of the statements and suggestions made in this Representation, a change, though of no great moment, was effected in the corn laws in the course of the ensuing year.

AN INQUIRY into the CORN TRADE and CORN LAWS of GREAT BRITAIN, and their INFLUENCE on the PROSPERITY of the KINGDOM. By ALEXANDER DIROM, Esq. 1 vol. 4to. London, 1796.

Thoughts and Details on Scarcity, originally presented to the Right Hon. William Pitt, in November, 1795. By the Right Hon. EDMUND BURKE. 8vo. London, 1800.

Mr. Burke protests, in the most energetic manner, in this celebrated tract, against all attempts to interfere, in seasons of scarcity, with the prices of corn or the wages of labour; and he shows that, though the pressure of scarcities may be alleviated, it is not possible by any scheme of charity to exempt the labouring classes from the privations and sufferings incident to such calamitous periods. Mr. Burke considered the shutting up of the distilleries as an ill-advised measure, "too precious a sacrifice to prejudice." His observations on this point, and on the consumption of ardent spirits, are highly interesting. We subjoin the following conclusive argument against a project, which has been repeatedly brought forward, for establishing warehouses in which supplies of corn should be stored up, at the public expense, in years of abundance, as a resource in years of scarcity.

"The construction of such granaries throughout the kingdom would be at an expense beyond all calculation. The keeping them up would be at a great charge. The management and attendance would require an army of agents, storekeepers, clerks, and servants. The capital to be employed in the purchase of grain would be enormous. The waste, decay, and corruption would be a dreadful drawback on the whole dealing; and the dissatisfaction of the people, at having decayed, tainted, or corrupted corn sold to them, as must be the case, would be serious.

"The climate (whatever others may be) is not favourable to granaries, where wheat is to be kept for any time. The best, and indeed the only good granary, is the rick-yard of the farmer, where the corn is preserved in its own straw—sweet, clean, wholesome, free from vermin and from insects—and comparatively at a trifle of expense. This, with the barn, enjoying many of the same advantages, have been the sole granaries of England from the foundation of its agriculture to this day. All this is done at the expense of the undertaker, and at his sole risk. He contributes to Government; he receives nothing from it but protection; and to this he has a *claim*.

"The moment that Government appears at market, all the principles of market will be subverted. I don't know whether the farmer will suffer by it, as long as there is a tolerable market of competition; but I am sure that, in the first place, the trading government will speedily become a bankrupt, and the consumer in the end will suffer. If Government makes all its purchases at once, it will instantly raise the market upon itself. If it makes them by degrees, it must follow the course of the market. If it follows the course of the market, it will produce no effect, and the consumer may as well buy as he wants: therefore all the expense is incurred gratis.

"But if the object of this scheme should be, what I suspect it is, to destroy the dealer, commonly called the middle-man, and by incurring a voluntary loss to carry the baker to deal with Government, I am to tell them that they must set up another trade, that of a miller or a mealman, attended with a new train of expenses and risks. If in both these trades they should succeed, so as to exclude those who trade on natural and private capitals, then they will have a monopoly in their hands, which, under the appearance of a monopoly of capital, will, in reality, be a monopoly of authority, and will ruin whatever it touches. The agriculture of the kingdom cannot stand before it.

"A little place like Geneva, of not more than from twenty-five to thirty thousand inhabitants, which has no territory, or next to none; which depends for its existence on the good-will of three neighbouring powers, and is of course continually in the state of something like a *siege*, or in the speculation of it, might find some resource in state granaries, and some revenue from the monopoly of what was sold to the keepers of public houses. This is a policy for a state too small for agriculture. It is not (for instance) fit for so great a country as the Pope possesses, where, however, it is adopted and pursued in a greater extent and with more strictness. Certain of the Pope's territories, from whence the city of Rome is supplied, being obliged to furnish Rome and the granaries of His Holiness with corn at a certain price, that part of the papal territories is utterly ruined. That ruin may be traced with certainty to this sole cause, and it appears indubitably by a comparison of their state and condition with that of the other part of the ecclesiastical dominions not subjected to the same regulations, which are in circumstances highly flourishing.

"The reformation of this evil system is in a manner impracticable; for, first, it does keep bread and all other provisions equally subject to the chamber of supply, at a pretty reasonable and regular price in the city of Rome. This preserves quiet among the numerous poor, idle, and naturally mutinous people of every great capital. But the quiet of the town is purchased by the ruin of the country, and the ultimate wretchedness of both. The next cause which renders this evil incurable, is the jobs which have grown out of it, and which, in spite of all precautions, would grow out of such things, even under governments far more potent than the feeble authority of the Pope.

"This example of Rome, which has been derived from the most ancient times, and the most flourishing period of the Roman Empire (but not of the Roman agriculture), may serve as a great caution to all governments, not to attempt to feed the people out of the hands of the magistrates. If once they are habituated to it, though but for one half-year, they will never be satisfied to have it otherwise. And having looked to government for bread, on the very first scarcity they will turn and bite the hand that fed them. To avoid that *evil*, government will redouble the causes of it, and then it will become inveterate and incurable." (pp. 28-31.)

Dispersion of Gloomy Apprehensions with respect to the Decline of the Corn Trade. By the Rev. John Howlett (vicar of Great Dunmow, in Essex). 8vo. London, 1797.

Besides that now referred to, Mr. Howlett published tracts on population, the poor, and other economical subjects, all of which are distinguished by ability, correct information, and good sense. We shall have occasion to notice most of them in other parts of this work.

The scarcity and high price of corn in 1800 and 1801, led to a revival of the old clamour against corn-dealers, forestallers, and regraters; and produced myriads of pamphlets, of which, however, very few deserve notice. Among these may be specified:—

An Investigation of the Cause of the present High Price of Provisions. By the Author of the 'Essay on the Principle of Population.' (Mr. Malthus.) 8vo. London, 1800.

In this tract Mr. Malthus, having endeavoured to show, or rather having taken for granted, that the deficiency in the harvest of 1799 would not account for the height to which the prices of corn had attained, proceeded to contend that "The attempt, made in most parts of the country, to increase the parish allowances in proportion to the price of corn, combined with the riches of the country, which have enabled it to proceed so far as it has done in this attempt, is, comparatively speaking, the sole cause which has occasioned the price of provisions in this country to rise so much higher than the degree of scarcity would seem to warrant, and so much higher than it would do in any other country where this cause did not operate." But, though the practice referred to in this paragraph must, no doubt, have had some influence, it is almost needless to add, that the deficiency of the crop neither was, nor could be, ascertained with anything approaching to precision; and, though it had, it would have been impossible to specify the influence of such deficiency on prices, as that must have depended on a host of all but inappreciable circumstances, exclusive of the one referred to by Malthus.

INQUIRY into the CAUSES and REMEDIES of the LATE and PRESENT SCARCITY and HIGH PRICE of PROVISIONS, in a LETTER to EARL SPENCER, K.G. 8vo. London, 1800.

A SHORT INQUIRY into the NATURE of MONOPOLY and FORESTALLING. By EDWARD MORRIS, Esq. 3rd ed., with additions. 8vo. London, 1800.

An Address to the Good Sense and Candour of the People in behalf of the Dealers in Corn, with Observations on a late Trial for Regrating. By Sir THOMAS TURTON, Bart. 8vo. London, 1800.

The preceding three, especially the last, are valuable pamphlets. The trial alluded to by Sir Thomas Turton was that of Rusby, a corn merchant, indicted for regrating, that is, for selling a quantity of corn on the same day, and in the same market, in which he bought it, at an advance of 2s. a-quarter. The statutes against forestalling, regrating, &c., having been (as already stated) repealed in 1772, Rusby was proceeded against at common law. The speech of the Chief Justice, Lord Kenyon, who presided at the trial, shows how little he had profited by the conclusive reasoning of Smith on this subject. Rusby was convicted; but, as some of the judges doubted whether regrating were really punishable at common law, he was not brought up for judgment. This is the last instance in which the judicial tribunals have debased themselves by pandering to the popular prejudices against one of the most useful classes of men in the community. No such action would now be entertained.

A Calm Investigation of the Circumstances that have led to the Present Scarcity of Grain in Britain, suggesting the Means of alleviating that Evil, and of preventing the Recurrence of such a Calamity in future. By JAMES ANDERSON, LL.D., &c. 8vo. London, 1801.

This pamphlet derives its principal claim to attention from its being written by the discoverer of the true theory of rent. Anderson was a decided friend to the protective system, and ascribed the increased importations of previous years, and the scarcity with which the country was then afflicted, principally to the virtual repeal of the bounty system in 1773. There can, however, be no manner of doubt that the importations in question were mainly occasioned by the extraordinary increase of the population after the peace of Paris in 1763, and that the scarcity of 1800 and 1801 was wholly a consequence of bad seasons. But though wrong in these respects, Anderson's statements with respect to the bounty are well worth attention.

REVIEW of the STATUTES and ORDINANCES of ASSIZE, which have been established in ENGLAND from the fourth year of KING JOHN, 1202, to the thirty-seventh of his present MAJESTY

(George III.). By G. Attwood, Esq., F.R.S. 4to. London, 1801.

From the year 1202, in the reign of King John, down to our own days, it was customary to regulate the price at which bread should be sold according to the price of wheat or flour at the time. An interference of this sort was supposed to be necessary, to prevent that monopoly on the part of the bakers which it was feared might otherwise take place. But it is needless, perhaps, to say that this apprehension was of the most futile description. The trade of a baker is one which may be easily learned, and which requires no considerable capital to carry on; so that, were those engaged in the business in any particular town to attempt to force up prices to an artificial elevation, the combination would be immediately defeated by the competition of others; and, even though this were not the case, the facility with which bread may be baked by private parties would of itself serve to nullify the efforts of any combination. But the assize regulations were not merely useless; they were in many respects exceedingly injurious: they rendered the price of flour a matter of comparative indifference to the baker; and they obliged the baker who used the finest flour, and made the best bread, to sell at the same rate as those who used inferior flour, and whose bread was decidedly of a lower quality. But these considerations, how obvious soever they may now appear, were for a long time entirely overlooked. According, however, as the use of wheaten bread was extended, it was found to be impracticable to set assizes in small towns and villages; and, notwithstanding the fewness of the bakers in such places gave them greater facilities for combining together, the price of bread was almost uniformly lower in them than in places where assizes were set. In consequence, partly of this circumstance, but still more of the increase of intelligence respecting such matters, the practice of setting an assize was gradually relinquished in most places; and in 1815 it was expressly abolished in London and its environs, in pursuance of the recommendation of a select committee of the House of Commons to that effect (see *post*), by an act of the legislature (55 Geo. III. c. 99). In other places, though the power to set an assize still subsists, it is seldom acted upon, and has fallen into disuse.

The average price of corn in 1800 and 1801 rose to the unprecedented height of 116*s.* 8*d.* the imperial quarter. And the extraordinary stimulus this rise gave to agriculture was evinced by the number of Enclosure Acts passed in these years and in 1802, by the conversion of grass lands into tillage, and so forth. In 1802, however, the price of corn sunk to 69*s.* 10*d.*, and in 1803 to 58*s.* 10*d.*; and the check that was in consequence given to improvements, and the distress in which many occupiers were involved, led to a demand on the part of the agriculturists for a new corn-law, which was accordingly enacted in 1804. This law imposed a prohibitory duty of 24*s.* 3*d.* per quarter on all wheat imported when the home price was at or below 63*s.*; between 63*s.* and 66*s.* a middle duty of 2*s.* 6*d.* was paid, and above 66*s.* a nominal duty of 6*d.* The price at which the bounty was allowed on exportation was extended to 50*s.*, and exportation without bounty to 54*s.* By the Act of 1791, the maritime counties of England were divided into twelve districts, importation and exportation being regulated by the particular prices of each; but by the Act of 1804 they were regulated, in England, by the *aggregate average* of the maritime districts; and in Scotland by the aggregate average of the four maritime districts into which it was divided. The averages were taken four times a year, so that the ports could not be open or shut for less than three months. This manner of ascertaining prices was, however, modified in the following session; it being then fixed that importation, both in England and Scotland, should be regulated by the average price of the twelve maritime districts of England.

AN ESSAY on the IMPOLICY of a BOUNTY on the EXPORTATION of GRAIN, and on the PRINCIPLES which ought to regulate the COMMERCE of GRAIN. (By JAMES MILL, Esq., Author of the 'History of British India.') 8vo. London, 1804.

Several impolitic restraints had been for a lengthened period imposed on the importation and exportation of corn between Great Britain and Ireland, but they were wholly abolished in 1806; and the Act of that year, the 46 Geo. III. c. 97, establishing a free trade in corn between the two great divisions of the empire, was not only a wise and proper measure in itself, but has powerfully contributed to promote the general advantage. The importations of corn from Ireland into Great Britain, which did not, previously to 1806, exceed from 300,000 to 350,000 quarters a-year, amount at present (1844) to about three millions of quarters!

An Inquiry into the Policy and Justice of the Prohibition of the Use of Grain in the Distilleries. By ARCHIBALD BELL, Esq. 8vo. Edinburgh, 1808.

An able pamphlet, strongly opposed to the prohibition.

AN INQUIRY into the STATE of NATIONAL SUBSISTENCE, as connected with the PROGRESS of WEALTH and POPULATION; to which is subjoined a DIGEST of the CORN LAWS. By W. T. COMBER. 1 vol. 8vo. London, 1808.

During the five years ending with 1813, the average price of wheat in England and Wales was as high as 5*l*. 7*s*. a quarter. This extraordinary high price was occasioned partly by the depreciation of the currency at the time, but principally by the circumstance of some of the crops in the period referred to having been deficient, and by the difficulties which the war threw in the way of importing corn. The latter were such as to increase the cost of freight and insurance to from *five* to *six* times their customary amount; and went far to secure an absolute monopoly of the British markets to the home grower. But the failure of the invasion of Russia by Napoleon, and the subsequent emancipation of the North of Europe, having again admitted of a free importation from the great corn-growing countries, large quantities of grain were brought into our ports; and prices fell rapidly in the latter part of 1813 and in 1814. Under these circumstances it became obvious that the prices realised during the latter years of the war could no longer be maintained; and that such rents as had been raised proportionally to the rise of prices would have to be reduced. The agriculturists, however, were very averse from an adjustment of this sort, and endeavoured to obviate the necessary consequences of the new state of things by imposing additional restrictions on importation. In this view committees of the Houses of Lords and Commons were appointed in 1814 to inquire into the depressed state of agriculture; and these recommended that the limit at which foreign wheat might be entered for consumption under a nominal duty should be raised to 80*s*. a quarter, and other grain in proportion. And a bill founded on these reports having been introduced into parliament was, after a great deal of opposition, passed into a law, the 55 Geo. III. c. 26.

An immense number of tracts and other publications appeared during the excitement occasioned by these proceedings. But the principal arguments on the one side and the other are embodied in the subjoined works:—

REPORTS and EVIDENCE from the COMMITTEES of the HOUSES of LORDS and COMMONS on the CORN LAWS. Folio. London, 1814–15

CONSIDERATIONS on the PROTECTION required by BRITISH AGRICULTURE, and on the INFLUENCE of the PRICE of CORN on EXPORTABLE PRODUCTIONS. By WILLIAM JACOB, Esq. 8vo. London, 1814.

OBSERVATIONS on the EFFECTS of the CORN LAWS. By the Rev. T. R. MALTHUS. 8vo. London, 1814.

THE GROUNDS of an OPINION on the POLICY of RESTRICTING the IMPORTATION of FOREIGN CORN. By the Rev. T. R. MALTHUS. 8vo. London, 1815.

In the first of these tracts Mr. Malthus compared the advantages and disadvantages that might be expected to result from continuing the corn laws on the footing on which they then stood, and from laying still greater restrictions on importation. His leanings were, however, obviously in favour of higher duties; and in his second tract he strongly recommends the latter. One of his principal arguments is the increase which he alleges a fall in the value of corn would occasion in the value of money, and, consequently, in the pressure of taxation. On this occasion Mr. Horner addressed a letter to Mr. Malthus, controverting his conclusions, which is given in the Memoirs of his Life (ii. 228); and he was publicly replied to by Mr. Ricardo in the following tract:—

AN ESSAY on the INFLUENCE of a LOW PRICE of CORN on the PROFITS of STOCK, with Remarks on MR. MALTHUS's last Two Publications. By DAVID RICARDO, Esq. 8vo. London, 1815.

The corn law of 1815 was warmly supported by the great majority of landholders in and out of parliament, and was, in fact, carried by their exertions. But it would, notwithstanding, be unjust not to mention that a large and respectable body amongst the landlords have always been opposed to restrictions on the trade in corn, and have uniformly thought that their interests were identified with those of the public, and would be best promoted by the abolition of restrictions on importation. A protest expressive of this opinion, subscribed by 10 peers, was entered on the Journals of the House of Lords, against the law of 1815. It is said to have been written by the late Lord Grenville, a distinguished and enlightened advocate of sound commercial principles; and having been frequently referred to, we take leave to lay it before the reader:—

" *Dissentient.*—I. Because we are adverse in principle to all new restraints on commerce. We think it certain that public prosperity is best promoted by leaving uncontrolled the free current of national industry; and we wish rather, by well considered steps, to bring back our commercial legislation to the straight and simple line of wisdom, than to increase the deviation by subjecting additional and extensive branches of the public interest to fresh systems of artificial and injurious restrictions.

" II. Because we think that the great practical rule, of leaving all commerce unfettered, applies more peculiarly, and on still stronger grounds of justice as well as policy, to the corn trade than to any other. Irresistible, indeed, must be that necessity which could, in our judgment, authorise the legislature to tamper with the sustenance of the people, and to impede the free purchase of that article on which depends the existence of so large a portion of the community.

"III. Because we think that the expectations of ultimate benefit from this measure are founded on a delusive theory. We cannot persuade ourselves that this law will ever contribute to produce plenty, cheapness, or steadiness of price. So long as it operates at all, its effects must be the opposite of these. Monopoly is the parent of scarcity, of dearness, and of uncertainty. To cut off any of the sources of supply, can only tend to lessen its abundance; to close against ourselves the cheapest market for any commodity must enhance the price at which we purchase it; and to confine the consumer of corn to the produce of his own country, is to refuse to ourselves the benefit of that provision which Providence itself has made for equalizing to man the variations of climate and of seasons.

"IV. But whatever may be the future consequences of this law at some distant and uncertain period, we see with pain that these hopes must be purchased at the expense of a great and present evil. To compel the consumer to purchase corn dearer at home than it might be imported from abroad, is the immediate practical effect of this law. In this way alone can it operate. Its present protection, its promised extension of agriculture, must result (if at all) from the profits which it creates by keeping up the price of corn to an artificial level. These future benefits are the consequences expected, but, as we confidently believe, erroneously expected, from giving a bounty to the grower of corn, by a tax levied on its consumer.

"V. Because we think the adoption of any permanent law for such a purpose required the fullest and most laborious investigation. Nor would it have been sufficient for our satisfaction, could we have been convinced of the general policy of a hazardous experiment. A still further inquiry would have been necessary to persuade us that the present moment is fit for its adoption. In such an inquiry, we must have had the means of satisfying ourselves what its immediate operation will be, as connected with the various and pressing circumstances of public difficulty and distress with which the country is surrounded; with the state of our circulation and currency, of our agriculture and manufactures, of our internal and external commerce, and, above all, with the condition and reward of the industrious and labouring classes of our community.

"On all these particulars, as they respect this question, we think that parliament is almost wholly uninformed; on all, we see reason for the utmost anxiety and alarm from the operation of this law.

"Lastly. Because, if we could approve of the principle and purpose of this law, we think that no sufficient foundation has been laid for its details. The evidence before us, unsatisfactory and imperfect as it is, seems to us rather to disprove than to support the propriety of the high price adopted as the standard of importation, and the fallacious mode by which that price is to be ascertained. And, on all these grounds, we are anxious to record our dissent from a measure so precipitate in its course, and, as we fear, so injurious in its consequences."

But though the limit at which foreign corn might be entered for consumption duty free was raised by the act of 1815 to 80*s*., the effect was not such as had been anticipated. The truth is that production had been so much increased previously to 1815 that we grew in average seasons, notwithstanding the increase of population, an adequate supply of corn for our consumption. Under these circumstances it is plain that though the restriction on importation raised prices in unfavourable seasons, it could not prevent them from falling to a ruinously low level in abundant years; so that, in fact, it increased those fluctuations that are as destructive of the interests of the agriculturists as of the other classes. In 1821 the price of corn sunk from the cause now stated to 56*s.* 1*d.*, and in 1822 to 44*s.* 7*d.*; and the distress of the agriculturists thence resulting led to a modification of the law of 1815.

REPORT and EVIDENCE from the SELECT COMMITTEE of the HOUSE of COMMONS on the LAWS relating to the MANUFACTURE, SALE, and ASSIZE of BREAD. Folio. London, 1815.

Report from and Minutes of Evidence taken before the Select Committee of the House of Commons on the Depressed State of Agriculture. Folio. London, 1821.

This Report, which was drawn up by Mr. Huskisson, contains a forcible exposition of the mischievous influence of the law of 1815; but it also contains some doubtful, or rather, we should say, erroneous, positions. Mr. Ricardo was a member of this committee, and not choosing to have his opinions identified with those of the Report, he published the following tract:

On Protection to Agriculture. By DAVID RICARDO, Esq., M.P. 8vo. London, 1822.

This is the best of Mr. Ricardo's tracts, and is, indeed, a *chef-d'œuvre.* The important questions respecting remunerating price, the influence of a low and of a high value of corn on wages and profits, the effect of taxation on agriculture and manufactures, the grounds on which restrictions on importation may be justified, with others of equal interest and difficulty, are all discussed in the short compass of 87 pages with a depth, precision, and clearness that have never been surpassed. Had Mr. Ricardo never written anything else, this pamphlet would have placed him in the very first rank of political economists.

A LETTER to the AGRICULTURISTS of the COUNTY of SALOP on the Present State and Future Prospects of Agriculture. By W. W. WHITMORE, Esq., M.P. 8vo. London, 1822.

An ESSAY on the DEPRESSED STATE of AGRICULTURE. By JAMES CLEGHORN (Editor of the 'Edinburgh Farmer's Magazine'). Published by order of the Highland Society. 8vo. Edinburgh, 1822.

OBSERVATIONS on the PRESENT STATE of LANDED PROPERTY, and on the Prospects of the Landlords and Farmers. By DAVID LOW, Esq. 8vo. Edinburgh, 1823.

PRICES of CORN and WAGES of LABOUR, with Observations, &c. By Sir EDWARD WEST (author of the Tract on Rent). 8vo. London, 1826.

A COMPENDIUM of the LAWS passed from time to time for REGULATING and RESTRICTING the IMPORTATION, EXPORTATION, and CONSUMPTION of CORN from the Year 1660, with Tables of Prices, &c. 8vo. London, 1826.

Cheap Corn best for Farmers, proved in a Letter to G. H. SUMNER, Esq., M.P. for Surrey. By ONE OF HIS CONSTITUENTS. 8vo. London, 1826.

This tract was written by Henry Drummond, Esq., the munificent founder of the chair of Political Economy in the University of Oxford.

An Essay on the External Corn Trade. By COLONEL TORRENS. 1 vol. 8vo., 4th ed. London, 1827.

"Among the most able of the publications on the impolicy of restricting the importation of corn, may be classed Major (now Colonel) Torrens's 'Essay on the External Corn Trade.' His arguments appear to me to be unanswered and to be unanswerable." (Ricardo, Political Economy, 3rd ed. p. 318.)

A Catechism of the Corn Laws, with a List of Fallacies and the Answers. (By COLONEL PERRONET THOMSON.) 8vo. London, 1827.

TWO REPORTS on the TRADE in CORN and the AGRICULTURE of the NORTH of EUROPE. By WILLIAM JACOB, Esq. Printed by order of the House of Commons in folio in 1826 and 1827.

These Reports contain a great deal of valuable information respecting the agriculture and statistics of the North of Europe.

Corn and Currency. An Address to the Landowners. By Sir JAMES GRAHAM, Bart., M.P. 8vo. London, 1827.

An exceedingly well-written, able pamphlet. Though for the most part unexceptionable, it contains some principles and suggestions of a doubtful description, which have been much, and sometimes not very fairly, animadverted upon. The suggestions in question do not, indeed, differ materially from those previously advanced by Lord Lauderdale (Further Considerations on the State of the Currency. 8vo. Edinburgh, 1813), and Mr. Malthus (see p. 76); and are in unison with the views which were at the time entertained by many well-informed persons. Happily, however, the estimates, which the distinguished author of this tract and the other parties referred to formed of the probable influence of the rise in the value of money subsequently to the late war, and of the fall in the prices of corn and most other articles, on the condition of the agriculturists and of the industrious classes generally, have proved to be in a great degree erroneous. But no one acquainted with the circumstances can wonder that such estimates should have been formed; or that it should have been *bonâ fide* proposed to mitigate what was believed to be the disastrous operation of the changes in question by imposing some portion of the sacrifice on the holders of funded property.

The system still acted upon of making the duties on corn vary inversely as the price, was introduced, in 1828, by the Act 9 Geo. IV. c. 60.

REPORT from and EVIDENCE taken before the SELECT COMMITTEE of the HOUSE of LORDS on the PRICE of Shipping FOREIGN GRAIN from FOREIGN PORTS. Folio. 1827.

FREE TRADE in CORN the REAL INTEREST of the LANDLORD and the TRUE POLICY of the STATE. By A CUMBERLAND LANDOWNER. 8vo. London, 1828.

AN INQUIRY into the EXPEDIENCY of the EXISTING RESTRICTIONS on the IMPORTATION of FOREIGN CORN; with Observations on the present Social and Political Prospects of Great Britain. By JOHN BARTON. 8vo. London, 1833.

LETTERS on the CORN LAWS and on the RIGHTS of the WORKING CLASSES, originally inserted in the Morning Chronicle, showing the Injustice and also the Impolicy, &c. (of the Corn Laws). By H. B. T. 8vo. London, 1834.

The late Mr. Deacon Hume, one of the Secretaries to the Board of Trade, who had the principal share in the consolidation of the Customs and Navigation Laws effected in 1825, is understood to have been the author of these letters. They are more liberal than philosophical; and involve some very questionable and, as we think, wholly untenable positions. Considering the manner in which the Corn Laws are dealt with in them, the conclusion seems rather impotent; for, instead of insisting upon the unconditional repeal of statutes which he tells us are subversive of the law of God, the rights of industry, and so forth, Mr. Hume proposes to compromise the question by imposing a duty of 10*s.* a quarter on *all* sorts of grain, to be annually reduced by 1*s.* a quarter till it is brought to 5*s.*, at which rate it is to remain stationary.

Influence of the Corn Laws as affecting all Classes of the Community, and particularly the Landed Interests. By James Wilson, Esq. 8vo. London, 1839.

One of the best and most reasonable of the late tracts in favour of the unconditional repeal of the corn laws.

The Effect of Restrictions on the Importation of Corn considered with Reference to the Landowners, Farmers, and Labourers. By G. R. Porter, Esq. (of the Board of Trade). 8vo. London, 1839.

Corn Laws: An Authentic Report of the late Important Discussions in the Manchester Chamber of Commerce on the Destructive Effects of the Corn Laws upon the Trade and Manufactures of the Country. 8vo. London, 1839.

A Letter to Kirkman Finlay, Esq., on the Importation of Foreign Corn, and the Value of the Precious Metals in Different Countries. By James Pennington, Esq. 8vo. London, 1840.

In 1841 Lord John Russell brought forward his unsuccessful proposal for amending the Corn Laws, by repealing the graduated scale of duties, and admitting foreign corn for consumption at all times, without regard to price, on paying a fixed duty of 8s. a-quarter on wheat, and other grain in proportion. On this occasion we published the following tract:—

Statements Illustrative of the Policy and Probable Consequences of the Proposed Repeal of the existing Corn Laws, and the Imposition in their Stead of a Moderate Fixed Duty on Foreign Corn, when entered for Consumption. By J. R. M'Culloch, Esq. 8vo. London, 1841.

This pamphlet, having had a very extensive sale, was honoured with answers by Sir J. C. Dalbiac, Mr. Taylor, and others.

A Few Words on the Corn Laws, wherein are brought under Consideration certain of the Statements which are to be found in the Third Edition of Mr. M'Culloch's Pamphlet on the Same Subject. By General Sir James Charles Dalbiac, K.C.H. 8vo. London, 1841.

AN ENQUIRY into the PRINCIPLES which ought to REGULATE the IMPOSITION of DUTIES on FOREIGN CORN, in answer, &c. By GEORGE TAYLOR, Esq., W.S. 8vo. Edinburgh, 1842.

We endeavoured to show in the above tract that in consequence of the agriculturists being more heavily burdened than the other classes of the community, they are entitled to insist, in the event of the ports being opened to importation, that a duty sufficient to countervail the peculiar burdens by which they are affected should be laid on all foreign corn when entered for consumption; and that this duty might be estimated at about 5*s.* per quarter on wheat, and other grain in proportion. It has, however, been contended by some of those who admit the justice of this view of the matter, that a fixed duty could not be levied in periods when prices are high; and that a duty varying inversely as the price of corn, and either ceasing or becoming nominal merely when the price is high, is the only one that can be safely adopted. But though it may seem paradoxical, it is, we believe, true (as we have elsewhere endeavoured to show) that prices in years of scarcity would not be perceptibly influenced by the payment of a moderate duty on importation; and that they would be quite as high were it repealed or suspended as they would be were it allowed to exert its full influence. It is easy to see that such would be the case. At present, if there were no duty, and no restrictions of any kind on importation, foreign corn of about the same quality as British corn might, in ordinary years, be imported from Dantzic and other corn-shipping ports, and sold to the miller for about 48*s.* or 50*s.* a quarter.* If, then, a fixed duty of 5*s.* were laid on imported corn, the price would have to rise to 53*s.* or 55*s.* a quarter before it would answer the foreigner to send corn to this country. But he would begin to export as soon as it attained this level; and if the price rose to 54*s.* or 56*s.*, its exportation would be peculiarly advantageous. The moment, however, that it is ascertained that any serious deficiency has taken place in our harvest, the price of corn, as everybody knows, rises far above this limit, most probably ranging, according to the presumed deficiency, from 65*s.* to 85*s.* or 90*s.* a quarter; but when such is the case, the duty ceases to have any influence over price, which is then wholly determined by the proportion between the supply and demand, without reference to the cost of the corn. Under such circumstances, the duty becomes, in fact, a deduction from the profits of the foreigner, so that its suspension would only add to the latter, without depressing prices.

An objection has, however, been made to this reasoning, founded on the different distances from which corn has to be brought in dear years. It is admitted that the duty would have no direct influence in such seasons over the prices or supplies of corn brought from the contiguous markets; but it is contended that, by obstructing importation from great distances, it would tend by lessening the supply to raise prices generally. But this statement is more ingenious than correct. The truth is, that the practical influence of a duty of 5*s.* a quarter, in the way now stated, would be quite inappreciable. Every person engaged in the corn trade knows, that when prices are 65*s.*, 75*s.*, or 85*s.* a quarter, the fact of there being or not being a duty of 5*s.* on importation would have no influence whatever over the quantities imported. The circle whence corn is brought in years of scarcity is too vast, and its margin too ill-defined, to be either sensibly expanded or circumscribed by adding 5*s.* to, or deducting the same sum from, our prices.

---

* For proofs of this, see Art. Corn Laws and Corn Trade in 'Commercial Dictionary.'

It appears, therefore, however much the conclusion may be at variance with popular prejudices, that a fixed duty on corn would be most onerous when prices are about the level at which importation can take place, or but a little higher. It would then, like the generality of customs duties, fall wholly on the importers, or on the consumers here; but when prices rise considerably above the level of profitable importation, the duty has no sensible influence over them, and falls wholly on the foreigner. Hence the repeal or suspension of the duty, when prices are high, would be most impolitic: it would be sacrificing revenue, not for the benefit of our own people, but for that of the growers and dealers in Poland, Russia, and other exporting countries.

Whatever amount of duty may be laid on foreign corn, for the equitable purpose of countervailing peculiar burdens laid on the corn raised at home, an *equivalent drawback* should be allowed on exportation. "In allowing," says Mr. Ricardo, "this drawback, we are merely returning to the farmer a tax which he has already paid, and which he must have to place him in a fair state of competition in the foreign market, not only with the foreign producer, but with his own countrymen who are producing other commodities. It is essentially different from a bounty on exportation, in the sense in which the word bounty is usually understood; for by a bounty is generally meant a tax levied on the people for the purpose of rendering corn unnaturally cheap to the foreign consumer: whereas what I propose is, to sell our corn at the price at which we can really afford to produce it; and not to add to its price a tax which shall induce the foreigner rather to purchase it from some other country, and deprive us of a trade which, under a system of free competition, we might have selected." *

Besides being, in our view of the matter, indispensable to meet the justice of the case, we are firmly persuaded that nothing would do so much to promote and secure the interests of agriculture as the opening of the ports, under such a duty as has been suggested, accompanied by an equal drawback. The granting of the latter is of more importance than is commonly supposed. Thanks to the spread of agricultural improvement, we now grow, in moderately favourable years, nearly as much corn as is sufficient for our supply; and in unusually productive years, such as 1822 and 1833, the home supply is so very abundant that the market is overloaded. This abundance is, however, under the peculiar circumstances of the case, a serious loss to the farmer; for, owing to our ordinary or average prices being above those of the Continent, the market cannot be relieved by exportation till they have fallen to a ruinously low level. Nine-tenths of the agricultural distress, of which we have heard so much at different periods since the peace of 1815, originated in the way now mentioned. Such revulsions would, however, be to a considerable extent obviated by granting a drawback of 5*s.* a quarter, inasmuch as it would, by facilitating exportation in unusually plentiful years, hinder prices from then falling to the extent they now necessarily do. Such a plan would, by checking all tendency to extremes, render agriculture and commerce comparatively secure; and would, in this way, promote the continued prosperity of both. (See *ante*, p. 67.)

But, however advantageous, the system of imposing fixed duties on importation was, as already stated, abandoned in 1828, when the plan of imposing duties varying indirectly as the price was introduced by the 9 Geo. IV. c. 60. But the scale of duties established by this Act was materially modified, and a corresponding approach made to a better system, in 1842, by the 5 Vict. 2 Sess. c. 14, by which the corn trade is at present regulated.

* Protection to Agriculture, p. 53.

INFORMATION CONCERNING the COST and SUPPLY of VARIOUS ARTICLES of AGRICULTURAL PRODUCE, &c., in VARIOUS PARTS of NORTHERN EUROPE. Obtained by JAMES MEEK, Esq., under instructions from Government. Printed by order of the House of Commons. Folio, 1842.

A carefully compiled paper, comprising much useful information.

VINDICATION of a FIXED DUTY on CORN, &c. By J. G. HUBBARD, Esq. 8vo. London, 1842.

HOW will FREE TRADE in CORN affect the FARMER? Being an EXAMINATION of the EFFECTS of CORN LAWS upon BRITISH AGRICULTURE. By C. G. WELFORD, Esq. 8vo. London, 1843.

CORN LAWS: THE CONSEQUENCES of the SLIDING SCALE EXAMINED and EXPOSED. Being the SUBSTANCE of a SPEECH delivered in the HOUSE of LORDS on the 14th of March, 1843. By LORD MONTEAGLE. 8vo. London, 1843.

FREE TRADE and PROTECTION. Being a TRACT on the "NECESSITY of AGRICULTURAL PROTECTION." By ARCHIBALD ALISON, Esq., F.R.S. (Author of the 'History of Europe during the French Revolution.') 8vo. Edinburgh and London, 1844.

The distinguished author of this tract ascribes the decay of agriculture in ancient Italy under the emperors, principally to the importation of corn from Egypt, Mauritania, &c. But, admitting such to be the fact, the inference drawn from it is wholly inapplicable to this country, inasmuch as the corn referred to was not imported to be sold at its fair price in an open market, but principally as tribute, to be *gratuitously distributed* among the population. It was this donation of corn, combined with the substitution of cultivation by slaves for cultivation by freemen,* the oppressiveness of taxation, and the licentiousness of the soldiery, that occasioned the decay of agriculture. Importation, in the modern sense of the word, had nothing whatever to do with it.

Mr. Alison has also very greatly exaggerated the advantages conferred on agriculture by the Corn Laws. Indeed it is very questionable whether it would be sensibly injured by their repeal. That such could not be the case is certain, unless the repeal of the Corn Laws were to be followed by a very heavy fall of prices. But no evidence has been, or can be, produced to show that their repeal would have any such effect. We have shown, in the 'Commercial Dictionary,' and in the tract referred to above, that, with a duty on importation of only 5*s*. or 6*s*. a quarter on wheat, and other grain in proportion, the opening of the ports would have little or no influence over our average prices. The truth is, that both their supporters and their opponents ascribe infinitely more influence to the Corn Laws than what really belongs to them. No doubt they tend, by restricting importation, to raise prices in bad years, at the same time that they increase the chances of those revulsions which are as injurious to the agriculturists

* Quænam ergo tantæ ubertatis causa erat? Ipsorum tunc manibus colebantur agri: at nunc eadem illa vincti pedes, damnatæ manus, inscripti vultus exercent.—(Plin. Hist. Nat. lib. xviii. c. 3.)

as to the other classes. But, thanks to the spread of agricultural improvement, their influence, in ordinary years, is now very inconsiderable.

Conformably to the policy of Colbert, which, in that respect, was most unfortunate for his country, the exportation of grain from France, except by special licence, was forbidden from the æra of his administration; and its circulation in the interior of the kingdom, or from province to province, was also subjected to many vexatious restraints. The powerful influence of these restrictions in depressing agriculture, and in occasioning the very scarcities they were supposed to obviate, forced itself, at length, on the public attention, and was set in the clearest point of view in several works, of which the best was the

Essai sur la Police Generale des Grains. (Par M. C. J. HERBERT.) 1 vol. 12mo. Berlin (Paris), 1755.

This is, in all respects, an excellent treatise; and may, indeed, be safely placed at the head of the works on commerce that had appeared in France, or any where else on the Continent, previously to the æra of Quesnay and the Economists. It is clearly and ably written; and contains every argument that could be advanced to show the pernicious consequences of restrictions on the corn trade, and the advantages of freedom, with the exception of those that may be deduced from the new doctrines as to rent and profits.

The influence of the above and other works on public opinion, and the approval of similar doctrines by the parliaments of several provinces, led, in 1763, to an edict being issued abolishing the restraints on the internal corn trade; and this was followed, in 1764, by another edict, authorising the exportation of corn whenever the home price was under certain limits. But, how singular soever it may now appear, these edicts were strongly objected to by a great and powerful party; and a rise of price which occurred soon after they were issued, in consequence of a succession of bad harvests, was ascribed to the licence given to exportation. And such was the influence of popular prejudice, on the one hand, coupled with the weakness and timidity of government, on the other, that the edict of 1764 was revoked in 1770, and a stop put to exportation except under peculiar circumstances.

The policy of these measures was discussed with great keenness; and an unusual number of works appeared on the subject of the corn-trade between 1760 and 1780. Of these the following are, perhaps, the most remarkable:—

DE L'EXPORTATION et de L'IMPORTATION des GRAINS. Par M. DUPONT. 1 vol. 8vo. Soissons et Paris, 1764.

LA LIBERTÉ du COMMERCE des GRAINS toujours Utile et jamais Nuisible. Par M. LE TROSNE. 1 vol. 12mo. Paris, 1765.

LETTRES à un AMI sur les AVANTAGES de la LIBERTÉ du COMMERCE des GRAINS, &c. 1 vol. 12mo. Amsterdam (Paris), 1768.

PRINCIPES sur la LIBERTE du COMMERCE des GRAINS. 8vo. Amsterdam (Paris), 1768.

OBSERVATIONS sur les EFFETS de la LIBERTÉ du COMMERCE des GRAINS, et sur ceux des Prohibitions. Par M. DUPONT. 1 vol. 8vo. Paris, 1770.

The above are all strongly in favour of the unlimited freedom of exportation.

Dialogues sur le Commerce des Bleds. 1 vol. 8vo. Londres (Paris), 1770.

These Dialogues were written by Galiani, Secretary to the Neapolitan Embassy at Paris. They are opposed to the system of the Economists, and to the unlimited freedom of the corn trade, though without approving of absolute prohibition. They are not, however, indebted for their celebrity to their philosophy, but to their vivacity, wit, and the brilliancy of their style. Perhaps no foreigner ever obtained so perfect a mastery over the delicacies of the French language as Galiani has displayed in these Dialogues. Voltaire said of them—*Il semble que Platon et Molière se soient réunis pour composer cet ouvrage.* And even Turgot, though hostile to the principles advanced by Galiani, said of the work in a letter to the Abbé Morellet:—"On ne peut soutenir une bien mauvaise cause avec plus d'esprit, plus de grâces, plus d'adresse, de bonne plaisanterie, de finesse même, et de discussion dans les détails. Un tel livre, écrit avec cette élégance, cette légèreté de ton, cette propriété, et cette originalité d'expression, et par un étranger, est un phénomène peut-être unique. L'ouvrage est très-amusant; et malheureusement il sera très-difficile d'y repondre de façon à dissiper la séduction de ce qu'il y a de spécieux dans les raisonnemens et de piquant dans la forme. Je voudrais avoir du temps, mais je n'en ai point; vous n'en avez pas non plus. Dupont est absorbé dans son journal; l'Abbé Baudeau repondra trop en économiste." (Mémoires de Morellet, i. 193.)

This was a pretty distinct intimation that in Turgot's opinion Morellet had better decline the task of confuting Galiani. But Morellet thought otherwise, and produced his

RÉFUTATION des DIALOGUES sur le COMMERCE des BLEDS. 1 vol. 8vo. Paris, 1770.

This, however, though a very respectable work, in which the heresies, contradictions, and misstatements of Galiani are detected and exposed, was little read, and had little effect. Voltaire might have successfully replied to Galiani. But the matter-of-fact statements and systematic reasonings of Morellet were not the sort of weapons with which to contend against the raillery and badinage of the Dialogues. To answer them was besides wholly useless. Their influence did not extend beyond the salons of Paris, where they were prized not for their substance but their form, their style and not their philosophy.

Turgot endeavoured to dissuade M. Teray, the minister by whom the edict of 1764 was revoked, from that step; and in this view addressed to him a series of letters illustrative of the advantages of a free trade in corn. Of these four have been happily preserved, and are printed in the 6th volume of the *Œuvres de M. Turgot*. The excellence of those that remain makes the loss of the others (three in number) be the more regretted.

DE la LÉGISLATION et le COMMERCE des GRAINS. 1 vol. 8vo. Paris, 1776.

This work, written by Necker, made when published some sensation. It adopts the *mezzo termine* policy of Galiani, but wants his brilliancy and pungency:—" Une doctrine populaire contre les monopoleurs et les riches et les propriétaires, une opinion en apparence mitoyenne et modérée, des déclamations contre l'esprit de systême, c'était-là tout l'ouvrage." Such is the character of this work given by Morellet (Mémoires, i. 236), who published a reply to it under the title of

ANALYSE de l'OUVRAGE de la LÉGISLATION et le COMMERCE des GRAINS. 1 vol. 8vo. Paris, 1776.

De la DISETTE et de la SURABONDANCE en FRANCE, des Moyens de prévenir l'Une en mettant l'Autre à Profit, et d'empêcher la trop grande Variation dans le Prix des Grains. Par M. LABOULINIÈRE. 2 vol. 8vo. Paris, 1821.

Travail consciencieux d'un magistrat éclairé.—(Blanqui.)

RAPPORT fait au NOM de la COMMISSION Chargée par la CHAMBRE des DÉPUTÉS d'examiner le PROJET de LOI sur les CÉREALES. Par le Baron DUPIN. 4to. Paris, 1831.

An able paper, favourable to the modified protective system established in France in regard to the corn trade.

RIFLESSIONI sulle LEGGI VINCOLANTI, principalmente nel COMMERCIO de' GRANI. Di Conte PIETRO VERRI. 1 vol. 8vo. Milano, 1796.

Though not published till 1796, this work was written in 1769. It has been several times reprinted, and is comprised in the 16th volume of the modern part of the *Economisti Italiani*.

This is a very learned, able, and conclusive treatise. The arguments of the writer are principally directed against restrictions on the exportation of corn, which were then enforced in the Milanese and most other parts of Italy. But they are equally applicable to restrictions on importation. The following paragraph leaves nothing to be desired:—

" La terra che abitiamo riproduce ogni anno una quantità corrispondente alla universale consumazione; il commercio supplisce col superfluo di una terra al bisogno dell' altra, e colla legge de continuità si equilibrano, dopo alcune oscillazioni, periodicamente bisogno ed abbondanza. Quei che suggeriscono i vincoli risguardano gli uomini sulla terra come ridotti a gettar il dado a chi debba morir di fame; risguardiamoli con occhio tranquillo e riceveremo idee più consolanti o vere, conoscendoci fratelli di una vasta famiglia sparsa sul globe, spinti a darci vicendevolmente soccorso, e provveduti largamente dal gran Motore della vegetazione a quanta fa d'uopo per sostenere i bisogni della vita. I soli vincoli artificiali, immaginata dalla timida ignoranza o dall' astuta ambizione, hanno ridotti gli stati ai timori della fame ed a soffrirla. L'uomo che ha meditato sulla società, vede che nella politica più giova il lasciar fare che il fare; che la libertà è l'anima dell' industria, la produttrice della concorrenza, la livellatrice de' prezzi, la conservatrice dell' abbondanza, la divinità preide, in somma, alla vita e alla prosperità delle nazioni."

The Italians have a great many other treatises on the corn trade, some of which are given in the *Economisti Italiani;* but such of them as we have seen are very inferior to that of Verri.

CONTARENI, de RE FRUMENTARIA, DISSERTATIO. 1 vol. 12mo. Vesaliæ, 1669.

This treatise is also printed in the 8th volume of the *Thesaurus Antiquitatum Romanorum* of Grævius.

---

§ III. COLONY TRADE, COLONIZATION, &c.

"Nec omnibus eadem causa relinquendi quærendique patriam fuit. Alios excidia urbium suarum, hostilibus armis elapsos, in aliena, spoliatos suis, expulerunt: Alios domestica seditio submovit: Alios nimia superfluentis populi frequentia, ad exonerandas vires, emisit: Alios pestilentia, aut frequens terrarum hiatus, aut aliqua intoleranda infelicis soli ejecerunt: Quosdam fertilis oræ, et in majus laudatæ, fama corrupit: Alios alia causa excivit domibus suis." (*Seneca, Consol. ad Helviam*, c. 6.)

IN Bacon's Essays, first published in 1597, is a short and admirable essay, entitled 'Of Plantations,' marked by his usual deep thought and nobleness of expression.

GROANS of the PLANTATIONS; or a True Account of their Grievous and extreme Sufferings by the many Impositions on Sugar. 4to. London, 1689.

The project for founding a Scotch colony on the west side of the isthmus of Darien or Panama produced a great many tracts. But as the interest attached to them was principally local, and has long ceased, it appears to be unnecessary to specify their titles; and we shall content ourselves with stating that this colony, which was attempted to be established in 1698, was projected by the same intelligent Scotch gentleman, Mr. William Paterson, who founded the Bank of England (see *post*), and was zealously patronised by all classes of his countrymen, who formed a joint-stock company, and subscribed large sums to carry the scheme into effect. The site of the proposed colony was, however, extremely ill-chosen; and even had it been otherwise, the project was most unsuitable for a country in the situation of Scotland at the time. It provoked the well-founded hostility of the Spaniards, and the bitter though unreasonable and unfounded jealousy of the English West India merchants and ship-owners, who either were or pretended to be seriously alarmed lest this new settlement, in an unoccupied and unhealthy country, should seriously injure their commerce and navigation. The selfish opposition of those interested parties to the project having been abetted by the English government, the king (William III.) disavowed the Darien Company, and orders were sent to the governors of the West Indian and American colonies, charging them not to permit any intercourse with the Scotch at Darien! In consequence of these vindictive measures, of the threatened attacks of the French and Spaniards, and of sickness, the settlement was abandoned. This event was most acutely felt by the Scotch, whose pride was mortified by the failure of a scheme, of the success of which they had formed the most exaggerated expectations; and many of whom were ruined by the loss of the sums they had embarked in it. (Laing's Hist. of Scotland, iv. 261-277; Burnet's Hist. of his Own Times, iii. 299, &c., ed. 1753.)

Proposals offered for the Sugar Planters' Redress, and for Reviving the British Sugar Commerce, in a Letter from a Gentleman of Barbadoes to his Friend in London. 4to. London, 1733.

The State of the Sugar Trade, showing the Dangerous Consequences that must attend any Additional Duty on Sugar. 4to. London, 1747.

An Account of the European Settlements in America. 2 vols. 8vo. London, 1757.

This work has been usually ascribed to the Right Hon. Edmund Burke; but it has been affirmed, apparently on good grounds, that it was partly written by his brother Richard and partly by their namesake, William Burke. Though a sketch merely, it is very comprehensive, embracing an account of the discovery of America, of the manners and customs of the Indians, and of the settlements of the different European powers both on the islands and on the continent. The author states in the preface, that his "principal view, in treating of the several settlements, was to draw everything towards their trade, which is the point that concerns us the most materially."

The following notice of Columbus's famous voyage is worthy of Edmund Burke, by whom, no doubt, it was written:—

"I do not propose to relate all the particulars of Columbus's voyage in a track now so well known, and so much frequented: but then there was no chart to direct, no lights from former navigators, no experience of the winds and currents particular to those seas. He had no guide but his own genius, nor anything to comfort and appease his companions, discouraged and mutinous with the length and hopelessness of the voyage, but some indications which he drew from the casual appearance of land-birds and floating sea-weeds, most of them little to be depended upon, but which this wise commander, well acquainted with the human heart, always knew how to turn to the best advantage. It was in this expedition that the variation of the compass was first observed; an appearance which has ever since puzzled all philosophers, and which at this time made a great impression upon Columbus's pilots; when in an unknown and boundless ocean, far from the road of former navigation, nature itself seemed altered, and the only guide they had left appeared to be on the point of forsaking them. But Columbus, with a wonderful quickness and sagacity, pretended to discover a physical cause for this appearance, which, though it did not satisfy himself, was plausible enough to remove something of the terrors of his mariners. Expedients of this kind were daily wanting, and the fertile genius of this discoverer invented them daily. However, by frequent use they began to lose their effect; the crew insisted on his returning, and grew loud and insolent in their demand. Some even talked of throwing the admiral overboard. His invention and almost his hopes were near exhausted, when the only thing that could appease them happened, the clear discovery of land, after a voyage of thirty-three days, the longest any man was known to be from sight of shore before that time."

A Summary, Historical and Political, of the first Planting, Progressive Improvements, and Present State of the British Settlements in North America. By William Douglass, M.D. 2 vols. 8vo. Originally published in Boston, New England, and reprinted in London in 1755.

"The honest and downright Dr. Douglass."—Adam Smith.

The Administration of the Colonies. By Thomas Pownall, Esq. 1 vol. 8vo. 2nd ed. London, 1765.

Candid and Impartial Considerations on the Nature of the Sugar Trade. By Dr. Campbell. 8vo. London, 1764.

The attempts to tax the colonies, which eventually terminated in the war of independence, led to the publication of myriads of tracts. By one party the right of the mother country to tax the colonies, and to regulate and coerce their trade, was stoutly asserted, while by others it was as stoutly denied. We shall only notice a few of these publications, most of which are now deservedly forgotten.

Considerations on the Trade and Finances of this Kingdom, &c. 4to. London, 1766.

This tract, ascribed to Mr. George Grenville, the author of the Stamp Act, contains a statement of the arguments for and against taxing the colonies, in which the author endeavours to show the futility of the latter.

Examination of Dr. Franklin at the Bar of the House of Commons. 8vo. London, 1766.

And in his works.

The Constitutional Right of the Legislature of Great Britain to Tax the British Colonies in America impartially stated. 8vo. London, 1768.

Letters from a Farmer in Pennsylvania to the Inhabitants of the British Colonies. 8vo. London, 1768.

Considerations on the Expediency of admitting Representatives from the American Colonies into the British House of Commons. 8vo. London, 1770.

Taxation no Tyranny, an Answer to the Resolutions and Address of the American Congress. (By Dr. Johnson.) 8vo. London, 1775.

And reprinted in all the editions of Johnson's works.

In this tract, which displays alike the strong sense and dogmatism of the author, the Americans and their pretensions are treated with very little respect.

Dr. Price's tracts on Civil Liberty and the War with America were published in 1776 and 1777. They are among the best, and were by far the most popular of the tracts on the side of the Americans. Price's reasonings are bottomed on the principle, that in free states there can be no legal taxation without representation. They also contain several interesting financial statements.

These tracts were published together, with a preface and additions, under the following title:—

Two Tracts on Civil Liberty, the War with America, and the Debts and Finances of the Kingdom, with a General Introduction and Supplement. By RICHARD PRICE, D.D., F.R.S. 1 vol. 8vo. London, 1778.

History of the Colonization of the Free States of Antiquity, applied to the Present Contest between Great Britain and her American Colonies. 4to. London, 1777.

This treatise was written by Mr. Barron, professor in the University of St. Andrew's, whose lectures on Belles Lettres and Logic were published (in 2 vols. 8vo.) in 1806, two years after his death. In the work referred to above the learned author endeavours to show that the ancients exercised the same sort of control over the trade of their colonies that has been exercised by modern states; and that "whenever they had power," they invariably imposed taxes or contributions on them. His object in these researches being, as he states it, to reconcile the American colonists to the exercise of this authority by the mother country, by showing that it was consistent with "the purest and most satisfactory precedents," and with the policy of those states which "enjoyed the most perfect civil liberty." But no one doubts that one country will, if it can, impose taxes on another, whether that other be a colony or not. Mr. Barron's "pure precedents" might have been of some use had he shown that it had been the practice in antiquity for colonies, powerful enough to resist the demands of the mother countries, voluntarily to submit themselves to taxation for the benefit of the latter! But, how inapplicable soever to the great controversy that was then about being settled by an appeal to arms, Mr. Barron's work is valuable for the light it throws on the colonial policy of the ancients, and for the attention which it drew to the subject. It elicited various answers, among which the next two tracts may be specified.

REMARKS on the ESSAY entitled the 'History of the Colonization of the Free States of Antiquity.' By JOHN SYMONDS, LL.D. 4to. London, 1778.

HISTORICAL REMARKS on the TAXATION of FREE STATES, in a Series of Letters to a Friend. (By Sir WILLIAM MEREDITH, M.P.) 4to. London, 1781.

Previously to its commencement, and during the course of the war, Dr. Tucker, Dean of Gloucester, published the following, among other tracts:—

1. THE RESPECTIVE PLEAS and ARGUMENTS of the MOTHER COUNTRY and of the COLONIES distinctly set forth, &c. 8vo. London, 1775.

2. A LETTER to EDMUND BURKE, Esq., M.P. for Bristol, Agent for the Colony of New York, &c. 8vo. London, 1775.

3. An Humble Address and Earnest Appeal to the Landed Interest, whether a Connection with or Separation from the American Colonies would be most for the Benefit of these Kingdoms. 8vo. Gloucester, 1775.

4. A Series of Answers to certain Popular Objections against separating from the Rebellious Colonies, and discarding them entirely. Being the Concluding Tract of the Dean of Gloucester on the subject of American affairs. 8vo. Gloucester, 1776.

5. Cui Bono? or an Inquiry what Benefits can arise to the English or Americans, the French, Spaniards, or Dutch, from the greatest Victories or Successes in the present War, in Letters addressed to M. Necker. 8vo. Gloucester, 1782.

In these and other tracts on the American contest, Tucker endeavoured to show that the differences between the mother country and the colonies were not of a kind that could be adjusted otherwise than by a complete separation, and that we should consult our interest by acknowledging their independence. But this judicious and sound advice was rejected with disdain even by those who were most opposed to the contest. The truth is that no nation ever voluntarily gives up any dominion, how worthless or costly soever. The god Terminus is immoveable except by force—

"Jovi ipsi regi noluit concedere."

He is never willingly brought nearer home. All concessions of independence to colonies must be compulsory, and are invariably obtained from the weakness or inability, not from the good sense, justice, or generosity of the mother country.

Political Annals of the Present United Colonies, from their Settlement to the Peace of 1763. By George Chalmers, Esq. 1 vol. 4to. (all that was published). London, 1780.

Lord Sheffield's Observations on the Commerce of the American States were published in 1784: see *ante*, p. 54.

A Descriptive Account of the Island of Jamaica, with Remarks on Slavery. By William Beckford, Esq. 2 vols. 8vo. London, 1790.

A Treatise concerning the Properties and Effects of Coffee. By Benjamin Moseley, M.D. Fifth Edition, with considerable additions. 8vo. London, 1792.

A Treatise on Sugar, with Miscellaneous Observations. By Benjamin Moseley, M.D. Second edition, with considerable additions. 1 vol. 8vo. London, 1800.

These are two very learned and able tracts. The merchants and others interested in the West Indian colonies are said to have rewarded the labours of the author by the present of a considerable sum of money; and he certainly had established a claim to some substantial mark of their gratitude.

An Inquiry into the Colonial Policy of the European Powers. By HENRY BROUGHAM, Esq. (now Lord BROUGHAM). 2 vols. 8vo. Edinburgh, 1803.

This, which was the earliest, is, perhaps, also the best of the many publications put forth by its prolific and versatile author. It has comparatively little of the exaggeration which characterizes his later writings. It evinces, also, considerable research. But as a scientific treatise it is extremely defective. We incline to think that the learned gentleman overrates the importance of colonies; at all events, he defends or extenuates the oppressive restrictions so frequently imposed on their trade, and which have uniformly been as injurious to the mother countries as to the colonies; and he contends, in vindication of these restrictions, that "the interests of traders in the employment of their capitals are by no means the same, in all cases, with the interests of the community to which they belong."—(I. 254.) No one need be surprised or need regret that, despite the celebrity of its author, such a work, if not actually dead-born, speedily sunk into oblivion.

THE WEST INDIA COMMONPLACE BOOK, compiled from Parliamentary and Official Documents; showing the Interest of Great Britain in the Sugar Colonies, &c. By Sir WILLIAM YOUNG, Bart., M.P. 1 vol. 4to. London, 1807.

AN INQUIRY into the STATE of the BRITISH WEST INDIES. By JOSEPH LOWE, Esq. 8vo. London, 1807.

The last and preceding work were reviewed in the eleventh volume of the 'Edinburgh Review.'

THE RADICAL CAUSE of the PRESENT DISTRESSES of the WEST INDIA PLANTERS Pointed out, &c. By WILLIAM SPENCE, Esq., F.L.S. 8vo. London, 1807.

A well-reasoned, and, indeed, unanswerable pamphlet. It was written by the author of 'Britain Independent of Commerce,' (see p. 56,) but in this case his principles are sound, and he is not led astray by a love of paradox.

AN ESSAY on the Nature of COLONIES and the CONDUCT of the MOTHER COUNTRY towards them. 8vo. London, 1811.

The History, Civil and Commercial, of the British West Indies. By BRYAN EDWARDS, Esq. The fifth edition, with a continuation. 5 vols. 8vo. London, 1819.

Edwards died in 1806, at the age of 57. He resided for a lengthened period in the West Indies, and after his return to England became a member of the House of Commons. The 'History of the West Indies' is well entitled to the popularity it has long enjoyed. The subject is varied and interesting; and though written in rather an ambitious style, with a strong bias in favour of the old colonial system, and a disposition to extenuate the cruelties that were too often inflicted on the slaves, it is a most valuable addition to our historical library. But the continuation, we are sorry to say, is quite unworthy of the original work and of the subject; and we do not know that any better service could be done to colonial and commercial literature than to publish an edition of Edwards's work that should complete the history and continue it to the present time. The establishment of the Black Republic of Hayti, the abolition of the slave-trade, the emancipation of the slaves in the

British colonies, with the present and probable future influence of that measure, and the wonderful progress made by Cuba and Porto Rico since the repeal of the restrictions on their trade, are all topics of great interest; and would supply materials for a work which, if executed in a philosophical spirit, with the requisite knowledge and ability, would be most important.

In 1822 and 1825 measures were brought forward by Mr. Robinson (now Lord Ripon) and Mr. Huskisson for the modification of the old colonial system, and for the repeal or diminution of the restraints and duties on the intercourse between the colonies in America and the West Indies and foreign countries. These measures were carried, though not without considerable opposition.

ON COLONIAL INTERCOURSE; with an Appendix, containing a Memorial to the Right Honourable the Board of Trade against opening the West Indies to Ships of the United States, with Tables of Comparative Prices, Tonnage, &c. By HENRY BLISS, Esq. 8vo. London, 1826.

Down to 1835 sugar from our possessions in India was charged, on being admitted to consumption in England, with a decidedly higher rate of duty than was imposed on sugar from the West Indies. This unfair preference was long and justly objected to; and in 1823 a vigorous effort was made by the parties interested in the India trade to have the duties equalised. On this occasion an animated controversy arose, and several pamphlets were published, of which the following embody the reasonings on the one side and the other:—

EAST and WEST INDIA SUGAR; or, a Refutation of the Claims of the West India Colonists to a Protecting Duty on East India Sugar. (By ZACHARY MACAULEY, Esq.) 8vo. London, 1823.

A STATEMENT of the CLAIMS of the WEST INDIA COLONIES to a PROTECTING DUTY against EAST INDIA SUGAR. 8vo. London, 1823.

A REPLY to the ARGUMENTS contained in VARIOUS PUBLICATIONS recommending an EQUALISATION of the DUTIES on EAST and WEST INDIA SUGAR. By JOSEPH MARRYAT, Esq., M.P. 8vo. London, 1823.

ON PROTECTION to WEST INDIA SUGAR. (By Sir GEORGE LARPENT, Bart) The 2nd edition contains a Reply to Mr. Marryat's Tract. 8vo. London, 1823.

SUBSTANCE of a DEBATE in the HOUSE of COMMONS on the 22nd of May, 1823, on the Motion of Mr. Whitmore, "That a Select Committee be appointed to Inquire into the Duties payable on East and West India Sugar." 8vo. London, 1823.

Among other speakers Mr. Ricardo supported the motion. It was, however, rejected by a large majority, and the distinction was continued, as already stated, till 1835, when the equalisation was effected.

In 1831 Lord [illegible] (now Earl Spencer) proposed, but without success, in the House of Commons, to reduce the discriminating duty in favour of colonial timber. This proposal elicited several pamphlets, among which were—

CONSIDERATIONS on the VALUE and IMPORTANCE of the BRITISH NORTH AMERICAN PROVINCES. By Sir HOWARD DOUGLASS, Bart. 8vo. London, 1831.

OBSERVATIONS on the PROPOSED ALTERATION of the TIMBER DUTIES, with Remarks on the Pamphlet of Sir HOWARD DOUGLASS. By JOHN REVANS. 8vo. London, 1831.

ON the TIMBER TRADE. By HENRY BLISS, Esq. 8vo. London, 1831.

One of the best tracts in opposition to an alteration of the duties.

England and America. A Comparison of the Social and Political State of Both Nations. (By E. G. WAKEFIELD, Esq.) 2 vols. 8vo. London, 1833.

The author of this work is understood to be the founder of what has been called the "New Colonization System," which is described at large in the 2nd volume. Many inconveniences had resulted from the inconsiderate manner in which large tracts of land had been granted in the colonies, sometimes to settlers and sometimes to persons of influence at home. These, however, might have been obviated in various ways, by limiting the extent of the grants to be made to settlers and others, by proportioning them to the capital of the settlers, by forfeiting the grants at the end of certain periods unless certain improvements were effected upon them, and so forth. But such expedients appear to have been too simple and obvious to be approved by Mr. Wakefield and his school. Almost all the hardships incident to colonization, and whatever is backward in our colonies, have, according to them, originated in the too great dispersion of the colonists; and hence, say they, the true remedy for these evils is to make the colonies as like old countries as possible; and to do this you have merely to cease making grants, and to exact a high price for the land! But this is not all; for while land in the colonies is thus to be rendered artificially dear, labour is to be rendered artificially cheap, by expending the price of the land in conveying pauper emigrants from this country to the colonies. In other words, take as much as you can, by exacting a high price for land, from the means of the settlers to employ labour, and then supply them with quantities of labour! Such being the nature of this project, we leave it to others to say whether anything can be imagined more contradictory of sound principle and common sense. But such as it is, it has been adopted in our legislation; and under its influence we have proceeded to exact a price of 20*s.* an acre for the downs of New South Wales, of which from 2 to 3 acres are required to feed a single sheep! Those who bought land on such terms have, of course, been ruined: and so far as we know, the only thing likely to be effected by keeping up this system either in Australia or our other colonies, is to divert emigrants possessed of capital from them to the United States.

A variety of other works have been published in illustration of the principles and supposed advantages of this system; but they do little else than repeat the arguments and reasonings in the present publication.

A SUMMARY of COLONIAL LAW, with the Practice of the COURT of APPEALS from the Plantations, Charters of Justice, Orders in Council, &c. By CHARLES CLARK, Esq., Bar. at Law. 1 vol. 8vo. London, 1834.

A compendious and useful work, which, however, would require to be occasionally republished.

STATISTICS of the COLONIES of the BRITISH EMPIRE in the West Indies, North and South America, Asia, Australia, Africa, and Europe. By MONTGOMERY MARTIN, Esq. 1 large vol. royal 8vo. London, 1839.

This work contains the substance of a previous work on the same subject, by the same author, in 5 vols. 8vo.

Lectures on Colonization and Colonies, delivered before the University of Oxford in 1839, 1840, and 1841. By HERMAN MERIVALE, A.M. 2 vols. 8vo. London, 1841.

Though not all that might be desired, this is certainly the most complete and best work on the subject in the English language.

On the Government of Dependencies. By G. C. LEWIS, Esq. 1 vol. 8vo. London, 1841.

A learned and valuable work on a subject which, though of the greatest interest, has been strangely neglected in this country.

DISSERTATION sur les DROITS des MÉTROPOLES GRECQUES sur les COLONIES, couronnée par l'Académie des Inscriptions et Belles Lettres. Par M. de BOUGAINVILLE. 1 vol. 12mo. Paris, 1745.

ESSAI sur les COLONIES FRANÇOISES. 1 vol. 12mo. Paris, 1754.

DE l'ETAT et du SORT des ANCIENNES COLONIES. (Par M. de STE. CROIX.) 1 vol. 8vo. Philadelphie (Paris), 1779.

One of the best works on the subject.

Histoire Philosophique et Politique des Etablissements et du Commerce des Européens dans les deux Indes. Par M. l'Abbé RAYNAL. Avec des planches. 4 vol. 4to., et 10 vol. 8vo. Genève, 1780.

Turgot has characterized this work as follows, in a letter addressed to the Abbé Morellet, then in England:—" Je suis curieux de savoir ce que les Anglois auront pensé de l'Histoire des deux Indes. J'avoue qu'en admirant le talent de l'auteur et son ouvrage, j'ai été un peu choqué de l'incohérence de ses idées, et de voir tous les paradoxes les plus opposés mis en avant et défendus avec la même chaleur, la même éloquence, le même fanatisme. Il est tantôt rigoriste comme Richardson, tantôt immoral comme Helvétius, tantôt enthusiaste des vertus douces et tendres, tantôt de la débauche, tantôt du courage féroce; traitant l'esclavage d'abominable, et voulant des esclaves; déraisonnant en physique, déraisonnant en métaphysique, et souvent en politique; il ne résulte rien de son livre sinon que l'auteur est un homme de beaucoup d'esprit, très-instruit, mais qui n'a aucune idée arrêtée, et qui se laisse emporter par l'enthousiasme d'un jeune rhéteur. Il semble avoir pris à tâche de soutenir successivement tous les paradoxes qui se sont présentées à lui dans ses lectures et dans ses rêves. Il est plus instruit, plus sensible, et a une éloquence plus naturelle qu'Helvétius; mais il est en vérité, aussi incohérent dans ses idées, et aussi étranger au vrai systême de l'homme." (Mémoires de l'Abbé Morellet, i. 222.)

But despite the sophistry, declamation, and paradoxes by which this work is disfigured, it contains much valuable matter respecting the colonial establishments o' the different European powers. Inasmuch, however, as the author rarely refers to authorities, his statements, even when well founded, cannot be safely depended upon by those who are ignorant of the sources whence they have been derived; so that the historical and statistical parts of the work have fallen, though undeservedly, into nearly the same discredit as the others.

Notwithstanding Raynal had the courage to address, in 1791, a letter to the National Assembly, in which he strongly censured the excesses by which the revolution had even then been disgraced, he was fortunate enough to escape falling a sacrifice to the vindictive jealousy of the Jacobin tribunals; and died in 1796.

COLLECTION de MÉMOIRES et CORRESPONDANCES OFFICIELLES sur l'ADMINISTRATION des COLONIES. Par M. MALOUET. 5 vol. 8vo. Paris, 1802.

An unequal but valuable publication.

Essai sur les Avantages a retirer des Colonies Nouvelles dans les Circonstances présentes. Par le Cit. TALLEYRAND.

Memoire sur les Relations Commerciales des Etats-Unis avec l'Angleterre. Par le Même.

These Memoirs were originally published in the *Mémoires de la Classe des Sciences Morales et Politiques de l'Institut National.*

M. de Talleyrand emigrated at an early stage of the Revolution to the United States, and the Memoirs now referred to, which he printed soon after his return to France, appear to have been suggested by his observations while in the New World. They are not unworthy of his high reputation. In the first Memoir he endeavours to point out the advantages France might derive by founding colonies on a proper footing, both as a means of extending her industry and trade, and of providing an outlet for her poor and discontented population. In the second Memoir, which may be regarded as a practical illustration of the doctrines laid down in the first, he shows the many advantages England continued to derive from her old colonies, notwithstanding their independence; and explains the circumstances which (in his opinion) occasioned the preference given, then as formerly, by the Americans to English products and English connexions.

A translation of the second Memoir into English was published under the title of 'Memoirs concerning the Commercial Relations of the United States with England. 8vo. London, 1806.' And both Memoirs were reviewed in an article in the sixth volume of the Edinburgh Review.

HISTOIRE CRITIQUE de l'ETABLISSEMENT des COLONIES GRECQUES. Par M. RAOUL ROCHETTE. 4 vol. 8vo. Paris, 1815.

ETAT des COLONIES et du COMMERCE des EUROPÉENS dans les DEUX INDES depuis 1783 jusqu'en 1821. Par M. PEUCHET. 2 vol. 8vo. Paris, 1821.

Notices Statistiques sur les Colonies Francaises. Imprimées par Ordre du Ministre Secrétaire d'Etat de la Marine et des Colonies. 2 vol. 8vo. Paris, 1837.

This work contains full and authentic details respecting the population, industry, trade, government, &c. of the French colonies, at the epoch of its publication.

ANNALES MARITIMES et COLONIALES; ou Recueil de Lois, Ordonnances, Règlemens, &c., et généralement de tout ce qui peut intéresser la Marine et les Colonies. 82 vol. 8vo. Paris, 1819-1843.

MONARQUIA INDIANA. Por Don JUAN DE TORQUEMADA. 3 vol. folio. Madrid, 1723.

RECOPILACION de las LEYES de los REYNOS de las INDIAS. 4 vol. folio. Madrid, 1756.

DICCIONARIO GEOGRAPHICO-HISTORICO de las INDIAS OCCIDENTALES O AMERICA: es a saber de los Reynos del Peru, Nueva España, Tierra Firme, Chile, y Nueva Reyna de Granada. Por Don ANTONIO DE ALCEDO. 5 vol. small 4to. Madrid, 1786-89.

This work was translated into English, with additions from more recent authors, by Mr. G. A. Thomson, and published at London in 1812-15, in 5 vols. 4to. The author was a native of Spanish America, and a captain in the Spanish guards. It must have been, when published, a useful and instructive work; but the changes in the countries and places described have been so numerous and extensive during the last thirty or forty years, and the additional information obtained respecting them so great, that the translation as well as the original work is now nearly obselete.

MEMORIAS HISTORICAS sobre la LEGISLACION y GOBIERNO del COMERCIO de los ESPANOLES con sus COLONIAS en las INDIAS OCCIDENTALES. Recopiladas por el Sr. Don ANTUNEZ y ACEVEDO, del Supremo Consejo de Indias. 1 vol. 4to. Madrid, 1797.

This work contains a good deal of valuable information. It is divided into five parts: whereof the first treats of the ports authorized to trade with the colonies; the second, of the ships engaged in the trade; the third, of the cargoes; the fourth, of the duties on exports and imports; and the fifth, of the parties permitted to engage in the trade. The Appendix includes several interesting documents.

Notwithstanding the vast numbers of emigrants that annually leave the United Kingdom for the colonies, there are but few works that treat expressly of emigration, it being generally treated as a branch of colonisation. In 1840 a Board of "Colonial Land and Emigration" Commissioners was appointed for the sale of lands in the colonies, and the superintendence of emigration; and their Reports, which are annually published, comprise the most authentic information with respect to the numbers and destination of emigrants, the cost of emigration, and the encouragement afforded to the different classes of emigrants in the different colonies. There is also a very extensive emigration to the United States; and there is every probability, unless the regulations with respect to the sale of lands in our colonies be materially modified, that the United States will continue gradually to absorb a larger proportion of the emigrants possessed of capital.

Observations on the Present State of the Highlands of Scotland, with a View of the Causes and Probable Consequences of Emigration. By the EARL of SELKIRK. 2nd ed. 1 vol. 8vo. Edinburgh, 1806.

This is a very able work; but it is more valuable for the information it gives with respect to the state of the Highlands in past times, and at the period when it was written, than for anything it contains peculiar to emigration. His Lordship has shown the groundlessness of the complaints made against those Highland gentlemen who encouraged emigration; and has shown that their conduct was not only highly advantageous to their estates, but also to the country and to the emigrants themselves.

THREE REPORTS from the SELECT COMMITTEE on EMIGRATION from the UNITED KINGDOM. Folio. 1826–27.

These Reports, with the evidence annexed thereto, contain much information in regard to emigration.

PAPERS respecting EMIGRATION to the different COLONIES. Printed by order of the House of Commons. Folio. 1842.

See also the Annual Reports of the Land and Emigration Commissioners.

---

§ IV. TRADE, HISTORY, AND CONDITION OF INDIA, CHINA, THE EASTERN ARCHIPELAGO, &c.

A DISCOURSE of TRADE from ENGLAND unto the EAST INDIES; answering to diverse Objections which are usually made against the same. By T. M. (THOMAS MUN.) 2nd impression, 4to. London, 1621.

We have not met with the 1st ed. of this tract; but we have seen it stated, though we cannot vouch for the fact, that it was published in 1609.

In this very ingenious tract Mun lays down those principles respecting the balance of trade which he afterwards expounded more at length in his 'England's Treasure by Forraign Trade,' previously referred to (p. 38). And founding on them, while he admits, in accordance with the prejudices of the time, the paramount importance of the precious metals, and that the increase of riches is to be measured by their increased importation, he makes out a good case in favour of permitting the exportation of gold and silver to the East.

In illustration of the advantages which the discovery of the passage to India by the Cape of Good Hope had conferred on the people of Europe, Mun gives (p. 10) accounts of the quantities and prices of the different Eastern articles brought to Europe as they were formerly bought at Aleppo, and as they were in his time put free on board the ships in Indian ports; and by these it appears that in all a saving of 953,543*l.* a-year had been effected by the change in the channels of the trade, of which a considerable share accrued to England.

Nearly at the same time that Mun's tract was published, another tract on the same subject made its appearance, entitled

THE DEFENCE of TRADE: in a LETTER to Sir THOMAS SMITH, Knight, Governour of the East India Companie, &c. From one of that Societie. 4to. London, 1615.

This tract, which was written by Sir Dudley Digges, contains some curious particulars. But it wants the ingenuity and originality which distinguish Mun's tract.

A TREATISE wherein it is DEMONSTRATED that the EAST INDIA TRADE is the MOST NATIONAL of all FOREIGN TRADES, &c. By Φιλοπάτρις. 4to. London, 1681.

The 'British Merchant' (i. 182) says that this tract was either written by Sir Josiah Child, or by his direction; and whoever compares it with his 'Discourse of Trade' (p. 41), will be satisfied that Sir Josiah was its author.

A keen controversy was carried on for some years previously to 1700 respecting the importation of East Indian silks and cotton stuffs. Those who wished to prevent their importation, resorted to the arguments uniformly made use of on such occasions; affirming that the substitution of Indian goods for those of England occasioned the ruin of our manufacturers, the exportation of the coin, and the general impoverishment of the kingdom! The merchants and others interested in the trade to India could not, as had previously happened to them in the controversy respecting the exportation of bullion, meet these arguments without attacking the principles on which they rested, and maintaining, in opposition to them, that it was for the public advantage to buy whatever might be wanted in the cheapest market. This sound principle was, in consequence, embodied in several petitions laid before parliament by the importers of Indian goods; and it was also enforced in several publications.

The principal tracts in this controversy were

AN ESSAY on the EAST INDIA TRADE in a LETTER to the MARQUIS OF NORMANBY. (By Dr. DAVENANT.) 8vo. London, 1696-97.

See notice of Davenant's works under the chapter *Miscellaneous Works.*

ENGLAND and INDIA INCONSISTENT in their MANUFACTURES; being an Answer to a Treatise entitled 'An Essay on the East India Trade.' (By JOHN POLLEXFEN, Esq.). 1 vol. 12mo. London, 1697.

Considerations upon the East India Trade. 8vo. London, 1701.

Republished with a new title-page, but without any other alteration, and entitled

THE ADVANTAGES of the EAST INDIA TRADE to ENGLAND CONSIDERED, wherein all the Objections, &c. to that Trade are fully Answered. 8vo. London, 1720.

Though rather tautological, this is a profound, able, and most ingenious tract. The author is probably the first who has conclusively shown the advantage of employing machinery, and cheaper methods of production, in the manufacture of commodities; and who has shown that such employment is not injurious, but advantageous to the labourers as well as to the other classes of the community. He has, also, set the powerful influence of the division of labour in the most striking point of view, and has illustrated it with a skill and felicity which even Smith has not surpassed, but by which he most probably profited. We subjoin a few extracts from this very remarkable work:—

"The *East India* trade destroys no profitable *English* manufacture; it deprives the people of no employment which we should wish to be preserved. The foundation of this complaint is, that manufactures are procured from the East Indies by the labour of fewer people than are necessary to make the like in England; and this shall be admitted. Hence it follows that, to reject the Indian manufactures that like may be made by the labour of more hands in England, is to employ many to do the work that may be done as well by few; is to employ all, more than necessary to procure such things from the East Indies, to do the work that may be done as well without 'em.

"A saw-mill, with a pair or two of hands, will split as many boards as thirty men without this mill; if the use of this mill shall be rejected, that thirty may be employed to do the work, eight-and-twenty are employed more than are necessary, so many are employed to do the work that may be done as well without 'em. Five men in a barge upon a navigable river, will carry as much as an hundred times so many horses upon the land, and twenty times as many men; if the navigation of this river shall be neglected, that the same carriage may be performed by land, nineteen in twenty of these men, and all these horses, are more than are necessary to do the work, so many are employed to do the work that may be done as well without them. So, if by any art, or trade, or engine, the labour of one can produce as much for our consumption, or other use, as can otherwise be procured by the labour of three; if this art, or trade, or engine shall be rejected, if three shall rather be employed to do the work, two of these are more than are necessary. Wherefore the people employed to make manufactures here, more than are necessary to procure the like from India, are people employed to do the work that may be done as well without 'em,—so many are employed to no profit of the kingdom.

"For, if the providence of God would provide corn for England, as manna heretofore for Israel, the people would not be well employed to plough, and sow, and reap for no more corn than might be had without this labour. If the same providence would provide us cloaths without our labour, our folly would be the same, to be carding, spinning, weaving, fulling, and dressing to have neither better nor more cloaths than might be had without this labour. Again, if Dantzick would send us corn for nothing, we should not refuse the gift, only that we might produce the same quantity of corn by the sweat of our brows. In like manner, if the East Indies would send us cloaths for nothing, as good or equivalent of those which are made in England by prodigious labour of the people, we should be very ill employed to refuse the gift, only that we might labour for the same value of cloaths which might be as well obtained by sitting still. A people would be thought extravagant, and only fit for Bedlam, which, with great stir and bustle, should employ itself to remove stones from place to place, at last to throw 'em down where at first they took 'em up. I think the wisdom of a people would be little greater which, having cloaths and victuals, and other necessaries of life, already provided sufficient for their use, should, nevertheless, abstain from the use of these things till after the penance of having carryd them seven miles upon their shoulders; so in no case are any number of people well employed, or to any profit of the kingdom, who only do the work which might be done as well without 'em, who, with great pains and labour, provide for their own, or for the use of other people, the same, or no better things than might be had without this pains and labour. Wherefore, to employ to make manufactures here in England more people than are necessary to procure the like from India, to employ so many to do the work which might be done as well without them, is to employ so many to no profit of the kingdom.

"We are very fond of being restrained to the consumption of English manufactures, and therefore contrive laws either directly, or by high customs, to prohibit all that come from India. By this time, 't is easie to see some of the natural consequences of this prohibition.

"It is to oblige the thing to be provided by the labour of many, which might as well be done by few; 't is to oblige many to labour to no purpose, to no profit of the kingdom, nay, to throw away their labour, which otherwise might be profitable. 'T is to oblige us provide things for our own consumption by the labour of many, when that of few would be sufficient. To provide the conveniences of life at the dearest and most expensive rates, to labour for things that might be had without. 'T is all one as to bid us refuse bread or cloaths, tho' the providence of God, or bounty of our neighbours, would bestow them on us; 't is all one as to destroy an engine, or a navigable river, that the work which is done by few, may rather be done by many. Or all these things may be comprehended in this, to prohibit the consumption of Indian manufactures, is by law to establish vain and unprofitable labour.

"As often as I consider these things, I am ready to say with myself, that God has bestowed his blessings upon men that have neither hearts nor skill to use them. For, why are we surrounded with the sea? Surely, that our wants at home might be supply'd by our navigation into other countries, the least and easiest labour. By this we taste the spices of Arabia, yet never feel the scorching sun which brings them forth; we shine in silks which our hands have never wrought; we drink of vineyards which we never planted; the treasures of those mines are ours in which we have never digged; we only plough the deep, and reap the harvest of every country in the world. * * *

"Arts, and mills, and engines, which save the labour of hands, are ways of doing things with less labour, and consequently with labour of less price, tho' the wages of men imploy'd to do them shou'd not be abated. The East India trade procures things with less and cheaper labour than wou'd be necessary to make the like in England; it is therefore very likely to be the cause of the invention of arts, and mills, and engines to save the labour of hands in other manufactures. Such things are successively invented to do a great deal of work with little labour of hands; they are the effects of necessity and emulation; every man must be still inventing himself, or be still advancing to farther perfection upon the invention of other men; if my neighbour, by doing much with little labour, can sell cheap, I must contrive to sell as cheap as he. So that every art, trade, or engine doing work with labour of fewer hands, and consequently cheaper, begets in others a kind of necessity and emulation, either of using the same art, trade, or engine, or of inventing something like it, that every man may be upon the square, that no man may be able to undersel his neighbour. And thus the East India trade, by procuring things with less, and consequently cheaper labour, is a very likely way of forcing men upon the invention of arts and engines, by which other things may be also done with less and cheaper labour, and therefore may abate the price of manufactures, tho' the wages of men shou'd not be abated.

"Again, the East India trade is no unlikely way to introduce more artists, more order and regularity, into our English manufactures; it must put an end to such of them as are most useless and unprofitable; the people imploy'd in these will betake themselves to others, to others the most plain and easie, or to the single parts of other manufactures of most variety; for plain and easie work is soonest learned, and men are more perfect and expeditious in it: And thus the East India trade may be the cause of applying proper parts of works of great variety to single and proper artists, of not leaving too much to be perform'd by the skill of single persons; and this is what is meant by introducing greater order and regularity into our English manufactures.

"The more variety of artists to every manufacture, the less is left to the skill of single persons; the greater the order and regularity of every work, the same must needs be done in less time, the labour must be less, and, consequently, the price of labour less, tho' wages shou'd not be abated. Thus, a piece of cloth is made by many artists; one cards and spins, another makes the loom, another weaves, another dyes, another dresses the cloth; and thus to proper artists proper parts of the work are still assign'd; the weaver must needs be more skilful and expeditious at weaving, if that shall be his constant and whole imployment, than if the same weaver is also to card and spin, and make the loom, and weave, and dress, and dye the cloth. So the spinner, the fuller, the dyer, or clothworker, must needs be more skilful and expeditious at his proper business, which shall be his whole and constant imployment, than any man can be at the same work, whose skill shall be pusled and confounded with variety of other business.

"A watch is a work of great variety, and 'tis possible for one artist to make all the several parts, and at last to join them all together; but if the demand of watches shou'd become so very great as to find constant imployment for as many persons as there are parts in a watch, if to every one shall be assign'd his proper and constant work, if one shall have nothing else to make but cases, another weels, another pins, another screws, and several others their proper parts; and, lastly, if it shall be the constant and only imployment of one to join these several parts together, this man must needs be more skilful and expeditious in the composition of these several parts, than the same man cou'd be if he were also to be imploy'd in the manufacture of all these parts. And so the maker of the pins, or wheels, or screws, or other parts, must needs be more perfect and expeditious at his proper work, if he shall have nothing else to pusle and confound his skill, than if he is also to be imploy'd in all the variety of a watch."

In No. 232 of the 'Spectator,' published the 26th of November, 1711, the construction of a watch is referred to in illustration of the saving of labour and expense that may be effected by employing different persons to execute different parts of a complex work. The writer in the 'Spectator' (supposed to be Mr. Henry Martyn) says the example was borrowed from "the admirable Sir William Petty." We have not, however, found any such example in such of Petty's works as we have met with; and it may, perhaps, have been taken from the pamphlet now referred to, though certainly not his.

But despite this able pamphlet it was enacted, in the course of the same year, that it appeared, by the Act 11th and 12th William III. c. 10, that the wear of wrought silks, and of printed or dyed calicoes, from India, Persia, and China should be prohibited, and a penalty of 200*l.* imposed on all persons having or selling the same! But notwithstanding this penalty the wear of printed calicoes gradually increased; and to avert this evil, as it was called, the 7th George I. c. 7 was passed, which absolutely prohibited the wear of printed calicoes, whether manufactured at home or abroad, under a penalty of 5*l.* on the wearer, and of 20*l.* on the seller. This extraordinary statute was so far modified about fifteen years after, that calicoes manufactured in Britain were allowed to be worn, "provided the warp thereof was entirely of linen yarn." We may add that this continued to be the law with respect to calicoes till after the introduction of Sir Richard Arkwright's inventions, when its impolicy became obvious to every one. And even when printed goods wholly made of cotton in Great Britain were permitted to be used, in 1774, they were loaded with a duty of *3d.* per square yard, an impost which ceased only in 1831! Certainly no great manufacture ever met with such step-dame-like treatment.

A NEW ACCOUNT of the EAST INDIES. By Captain ALEXANDER HAMILTON. 2 vols. 8vo. Edinburgh, 1727.

One of the best of the earlier accounts of India.

A COLLECTION of PAPERS RELATING to the EAST INDIA TRADE: wherein are shown the Disadvantages to a NATION by confining any TRADE to a CORPORATION with a Joint Stock. 8vo. London, 1730.

ANCIENT ACCOUNTS of INDIA and CHINA. By two MOHAMMEDAN TRAVELLERS of the Ninth Century. Translated from the Arabic, with Notes, Illustrations, and Inquiries, by RENAUDOT (in English). 1 vol. 8vo. London, 1733.

These 'Accounts,' which refer to the ninth century, are now ascertained to be portions only of a greater work. They are extremely curious, though not, perhaps, to be altogether depended upon. The notes and dissertations of Renaudot are very learned and interesting. The work appeared at Paris in 1718. (Biographie Universelle, art. Renaudot.)

A COLLECTION of LETTERS relating to the EAST INDIA COMPANY and to FREE TRADE. 1 vol. 8vo. London, 1754.

The history of the commerce with India previously to the discovery of the Cape of Good Hope, and of the discoveries, trade, and establishments of the Portuguese, Spaniards, English, Dutch, and other European nations in the East subsequently to that great event and down to about the middle of last century, occupies the whole of the 10th and the larger portion of the 9th and 11th vols. (8vo. ed.) of the 'Modern Universal History.' It was written by Dr. Campbell, who has in all cases resorted to and carefully compared the original authorities; and forms one of the most valuable portions of the great work to which it belongs.

REFLECTIONS on the GOVERNMENT of INDOSTAN, with a short SKETCH of the HISTORY of BENGAL, from 1738 to 1756. By LUKE SCRAFTON, Esq. 8vo. London, 1763; reprinted in 1770.

An interesting tract, particularly that portion of it in which the author gives a brief but striking account of the religion, customs, government, &c., of the native Indians, and of the Mohammedans.

CONSIDERATIONS on INDIAN AFFAIRS. By WILLIAM BOLTS, Esq. 4to. London, 1772.

A VIEW of the RISE, PROGRESS, and PRESENT STATE of the ENGLISH GOVERNMENT in BENGAL. By HENRY VERELST, Esq. 4to. London, 1772.

Mr. Verelst was Governor of Bengal from 1766 to 1769. To "undoubted integrity amid universal corruption," he added the distinction of entertaining the soundest views with respect to most branches of the Company's affairs. Besides much valuable information and remarks of a general character, Mr. Verelst has in this work successfully repelled the calumnious imputations of Mr. Bolts.

An Historical Disquisition concerning the Knowledge which the Ancients had of India, and the Progress of Trade with that Country prior to the Discovery of the Passage to it by the Cape of Good Hope. By WILLIAM ROBERTSON, D.D. 1 vol. 4to. London, 1791.

And since frequently reprinted in 8vo. in the different editions of Robertson's works.

This work, begun in the 68th year of Dr. Robertson's age, was brought to a conclusion within twelve months. But it "exhibits nevertheless, in every part, a diligence in research, a soundness of judgment, and a perspicuity of method not inferior to those which distinguish his other performances." (Dugald Stewart, 'Life of Robertson.')

The sovereigns of India, as of most other Eastern states, may be regarded as the real proprietors of the soil; the cultivators (in India called *ryots*) having, however, a perpetual and transferable right of occupancy so long as they pay the land-tax or rent demanded by the sovereign or head-landlord. But when the English took possession of Bengal there were, besides the ryots or occupiers of the soil, a superior class called *zemindars*, who seemed to occupy nearly the same place in India that the great landlords occupy in England; inasmuch as they collected the rents of the ryots, and paid out of them the tax due by the latter to government, reserving the surplus to themselves. Great doubts were, however, entertained respecting the real position and rights of the zemindars. One party contended that originally they were merely officers employed by government to collect the revenue; that their office had, in course of time, become hereditary; and that whatever powers they now exercised as landlords were so many usurpations of the rights either of the sovereign or of the ryots who held immediately of the sovereign. On the other hand it was contended that the zemindars were, subject to the crown, the real proprietors of the soil, the ryots or occupiers having no rights but such as had been derived from them. The principal reasonings on the one side and other of this curious and interesting controversy are embodied in the following works, viz.:—

AN INQUIRY into the NATURE of ZEMINDARY TENURES, in the LANDED PROPERTY of BENGAL. By JAMES GRANT, Esq. 4to. 2nd ed. London, 1791.

Against the proprietary rights of the zemindars.

DISSERTATION concerning the LANDED PROPERTY of BENGAL. By C. BOUGHTON ROUSE, Esq. 1 vol. 8vo. London, 1791.

In favour of the proprietary rights of the zemindars.

Practically, and in so far as respects the provinces of Bengal, Orissa, Bahar, and Benares (for in every other part of British India the matter is still *sub judice*), this question was settled in 1793 by Lord Cornwallis, who framed the *perpetual settlement* on the hypothesis that the zemindars were, under government, the real proprietors of the land. This, however, it is now generally admitted, was an erroneous assumption; and it may be regarded as sufficiently established that the zemindars were, previously to the perpetual settlement, merely hereditary revenue officers employed to collect the land-tax, and entitled to retain one-tenth thereof as compensation for their trouble and responsibility.

The grand defect of this settlement, which in other respects has been most advantageous to Bengal, consisted in no provision being made to secure the rights of the ryots, who were left to be dealt with by the zemindars as the latter pleased.

A right of private property in the soil, vested in one class or other of the cultivators, may be traced without difficulty in most parts of India. It is clearest and most considerable in the rudest parts of the country, and least distinct and least considerable in those that are most populous and most improved. Thus, it is tolerably perfect in Malabar, and nearly obliterated in Bengal, where the controversy respecting proprietary rights was first agitated.

It may, perhaps, be worth observing that the words *Ryot* and *Zemindar* are not native, but foreign: the first being the Arabic term for subject, the correlative of sovereign; and the second a Persian term, meaning literally a holder of land, but without implying in any degree the European acceptation of the word "landholder," that is, proprietor.

VOYAGES to the EAST INDIES by JOHN S. STAVORINUS, Esq., comprising a Full and Accurate Account of all the present and late Possessions of the Dutch in India. Translated from the Original Dutch by S. H. WILCOCKE. 3 vols. 8vo. London, 1798.

The author was a distinguished officer in the Dutch naval service. The work is valuable for the authentic information it affords respecting the state of the Dutch East India Company, and of the Dutch possessions in the East previously to the late war, which annihilated the former, and effected the most important changes in the condition of the latter.

THE PRINCIPLES of ASIATIC MONARCHIES. By ROBERT PATTON, Esq. 1 vol. 8vo. London, 1801.

AN ACCOUNT of the ISLAND of CEYLON; containing its History, Geography, Natural History, with the Manners and Customs of its various Inhabitants. By ROBERT PERCIVAL, Esq. 1 vol. 4to. London, 1803.

Travels in China, containing Descriptions, Observations, &c. made in a Journey through the Country from Pekin to Canton. By JOHN BARROW, Esq., F.R.S. (now Sir JOHN BARROW, Bart., Secretary to the Admiralty.) 1 vol. 4to., 2nd ed. London, 1806.

An able, instructive, and judicious work. We incline, however, to think that the author takes too unfavourable a view of the Chinese, and we are surprised that a person of his sagacity should place such implicit confidence in the accounts of the excessive population of the empire.

Remarks on the Husbandry and Internal Commerce of Bengal. (By H. T. COLEBROOKE, Esq.) 1 vol. 8vo. London, 1806.

The original work, of which this is in part a republication, issued from the press of Calcutta, in 1794, in 4to. It was the joint production of H.

T. Colebrooke, Esq., the most accomplished of all our orientalists, and of Mr. Lambert, an intelligent merchant of Calcutta. In its present form, the work contains only the portion contributed by Mr. Colebrooke, revised in 1803. Mr. Lambert's portion of the original work, which related to the manufactures and external commerce of Bengal, was not revised by its author, and has not been republished. Notwithstanding the lapse of nearly half a century since its publication, Mr. Colebrooke's account of the husbandry and internal commerce of Bengal continues to be by far the best and most trustworthy work on the subject.

Asiatic Researches. A work containing a great variety of Papers on the History, Antiquities, Language, Religion, Politics, Commerce, &c., of Hindostan. 12 vols. 8vo. London, 1801–18.

A Journey from Madras, through the Countries of Mysore, Canara, and Malabar. By FRANCIS BUCHANAN, B.D., F.R.S. 3 vols. 4to. London, 1807.

The best and most complete statistical account ever published of any part of India. It is especially full and particular on agriculture, arts, commerce, and natural history.

A DEMONSTRATION of the NECESSITY and ADVANTAGES of a FREE TRADE to the EAST INDIES, &c. By ROBERT RENNY, Esq. 2nd ed. 8vo. London, 1807.

ANNALS of the HON. EAST INDIA COMPANY, from the Establishment of the CHARTER in 1600 to 1707-8. By JOHN BRUCE, Esq., M.P. and F.R.S. 3 vols. 4to. London, 1810.

FIVE REPORTS of the COMMITTEE of the HOUSE of COMMONS appointed, in 1808, to Inquire into INDIAN AFFAIRS. Folio. London, 1810–13.

The **fifth** of these Reports, on the general management, history, and government of India, is, perhaps, the most valuable of all the parliamentary documents on our eastern empire. A glossary of names is added to it compiled by Sir Charles Wilkins.

The portion of the Fifth Report which relates to Bengal is understood to have been written by Mr. Davies, a Director of the East India Company, and previously a distinguished civil officer in the Company's service in Bengal. But the most elaborate portion of the work, being that relating to Madras, was drawn up by Mr. Cumming, one of the chief clerks in the Board of Control, remarkable for his minute and extensive knowledge of Indian affairs. Mr. Cumming's portion of the Report, including the Appendixes, contains a complete exposition of the principles and details of the ryotwar system of land-revenue; of which Sir Thomas Monro was the ablest advocate in India, and Mr. Cumming the most zealous in England.

The History of Sumatra: containing an Account of the Government, Laws, Customs, and Manners of the Native Inhabitants; with a Description of the Natural Productions, and a Relation of the Ancient Political State of the Island. By WILLIAM MARSDEN, F.R.S. 3rd ed. 4to. London, 1811.

This excellent work gives the best and most authentic account of the great island of Sumatra, and of the manners and usages of the several nations by which it is inhabited; more especially of the greatest and most wide-spread of these—the Malay.

The History of the European Commerce with India. By DAVID MACPHERSON, Esq. (Author of the 'Annals of Commerce.') 1 vol. 4to. London, 1812.

A valuable work, but inferior to the account of the European commerce with India in the 'Universal History.'

A SKETCH of the HISTORY of the EAST INDIA COMPANY, from its first formation till 1773, &c. By ROBERT GRANT, Esq. 1 vol. royal 8vo. London, 1813.

PAPERS respecting the NEGOCIATION with GOVERNMENT for a RENEWAL of the COMPANY'S CHARTER, from the 1st of March, 1814. Printed by order of the Court of Directors. 1 vol. 4to. London, 1813.

ORIENTAL COMMERCE: Containing a GEOGRAPHICAL DESCRIPTION of the PRINCIPAL PLACES in the EAST INDIES, CHINA, and JAPAN, with their Produce, Manufactures, Trade, &c. By WILLIAM MILBURN, Esq. 2 vols. 4to. London, 1813.

This work contains a great mass of useful information, especially with respect to the products and trade of the East. But the author rarely quotes his authorities, so that his statements have not the weight they would have had had they been properly authenticated.

CONSIDERATIONS on the PRESENT POLITICAL STATE of INDIA. By A. F. TYTLER, Esq. 2nd ed. 2 vols. 8vo. London, 1816.

DESCRIPTION of the CHARACTER, MANNERS, and CUSTOMS of the PEOPLE of INDIA. By the Abbé DUBOIS. 1 vol. 4to. London, 1817.

The History of Java. By THOMAS STAMFORD RAFFLES, Esq., late Lieut.-Governor of the Island and its Dependencies. 2 vols. 4to. London, 1817; and 2 vols. 8vo. London, 1830.

An important work, being, on the whole, the best account of this fine island that has yet appeared. It was principally compiled from materials supplied by the officers subordinate to the author, during the five years of his intelligent and successful government of the island. These materials do not, however, appear to have been sufficiently digested; and hence the discrepancy observable in some parts of the work, its diffuseness and prolixity.

The Travels of Marco Polo, a Venetian of the Thirteenth Century. Translated from the Italian, with Notes, by WILLIAM MARSDEN, F.R.S. 1 vol. 4to. London, 1818.

This is incomparably the best translation of the celebrated travels of Marco Polo, the precursor in discovery of Columbus and Vasco de Gama; and is, in all respects, one of the best edited books that has ever been published. It is enriched with an introduction and elaborate notes, in which the editor's varied learning and habitual fidelity are conspicuous.

History of British India. By JAMES MILL, Esq. 3 vols. 4to. London, 1817-18; and 6 vols. 8vo. London, 1820.

Mr. Mill's work has been very fairly characterised in the 31st volume of the 'Edinburgh Review:'—"Mr. Mill appears to possess, in perfection, the patient industry and habits of research which the work demanded; an acute and logical mind, with very little imagination or passion, and well stored with that sort of information which such a mind, combined with such powers of application, is apt to acquire. He seems perfectly familiar with the modern and ancient historians and orators, and to have studied diligently the progress of all the sciences connected with government and legislation, from the earliest speculations to their most recent advances. It is not difficult, after this character, to imagine how he has performed his task. Those parts in which picturesque description, and the power of warm and interesting narrative might have been displayed, are not made the most of by him. But in the careful investigation of facts, and of the inferences to be drawn from them, in illustrating his subject by help of the widest range of historical knowledge, in discriminating between the real and apparent causes of events, in the examination of policy, in the exposition of the motives of the actors and the consequences of their acts, in unfolding "the drift of hollow states hard to be spelled," he leaves little to be desired. Of partiality in bending facts or opinions in favour of any individual or any party, we have not discovered the least symptom; and though it may be invidious to pry into the causes of so good a quality, we are apt to attribute his merit, on this score, to his habits of thought as much as to his love of justice. He has evidently formed to himself a very high standard of attainable perfection in matters of government, and seems to entertain no little contempt for all practical statesmen. He is, therefore, nowise disposed to exaggerate the merits of persons with whom he feels so little in common. He is sparing of his censure and his praise; and the influence of no name or party can procure an exemption from his scrutiny for a fallacy or an error."

Soon after the publication of this great work, which had engrossed his principal attention for many years, Mr. Mill was appointed, much to the credit of the Directors, to an important situation in the India House, which he held till his death in 1836. Besides the 'History of India,' Mill was the author of various works, some of which are noticed in other parts of this treatise. He belonged to and was one of the ablest and most zealous adherents of the utilitarian school.

THE POLITICAL HISTORY of INDIA from 1784 to 1823. By Sir JOHN MALCOLM, G.C.B. &c. 2 vols. 8vo. London, 1826.

History of the Indian Archipelago, containing an Account of the Manners, Arts, Languages, Religions, Institutions, and Commerce of its Inhabitants. By JOHN CRAWFURD, Esq., F.R.S., late British Resident at the Court of the Sultan of Java. 3 vols. 8vo. Edinburgh, 1820.

The best work hitherto published on the Eastern Archipelago. His lengthened residence in Java gave Mr. Crawfurd the best opportunities for acquiring information, and his extensive learning, application, and ability enabled him to turn these opportunities to the best account.

A MEMOIR of CENTRAL INDIA; including Malwa and the adjoining Provinces. By Major-General Sir JOHN MALCOLM, G.C.B., K.L.S. 2 vols. 8vo. London, 1825.

This is, perhaps, the best of the various publications of its author. Sir John Malcolm's name will always maintain a respectable place in the annals of Indian diplomacy; but his published works are prolix and deficient in the vigour and reach of mind required in a philosophical historian.

AN INQUIRY into the EXPEDIENCY of applying the PRINCIPLES of COLONIAL POLICY to the GOVERNMENT of INDIA, &c. 1 vol. 8vo. London, 1822.

A FARTHER INQUIRY into the EXPEDIENCY of applying the PRINCIPLES of COLONIAL POLICY to the GOVERNMENT of INDIA, &c. 1 vol. 8vo. London, 1827.

These works were written by Major Gavin Young, a gentleman of talent and varied attainments.

No objection can be fairly made to the principle advanced in them, which, in fact, was adopted in the Act 3 and 4 Will. IV. c. 85 for renewing the charter. But the author has much overrated the practical importance of allowing Englishmen to settle in India. If, indeed, we reflect for a moment on the nature of the climate, the density of population, and the low rate of wages, it will appear to be little better than visionary to imagine that voluntary emigration to India should ever be carried on to any considerable extent. And despite the abolition of the former restrictions it has continued to be quite inconsiderable.

A Geographical, Statistical, and Historical Description of Hindostan and the Adjacent Countries. By WALTER HAMILTON, Esq. 2 vols. 4to. London, 1820.

The East India Gazetteer, containing Descriptions of the Empires, Kingdoms, Principalities, Cities, Towns, &c. of Hindostan and the Adjacent Countries. By WALTER HAMILTON, Esq. 2nd ed. 2 vols. 8vo. London, 1828.

Mr. Hamilton's works, especially the last, are compiled with great care and judgment, and are, indeed, of the highest authority.

An ANALYSIS of the LAWS and CONSTITUTION of the EAST INDIA COMPANY. By PETER AUBER, Esq. (Secretary to the Company). 1 vol. royal 8vo. London, 1827.

A Review of the Financial Situation of the East India Company in 1824. By H. ST. GEORGE TUCKER, Esq. (now a Director of the Company). 1 vol. 8vo. London, 1825.

A work evincing considerable ability and an intimate acquaintance with the subject. The author is strongly and, as we think, justly attached to the principles of the *perpetual settlement*; and he is decidedly opposed, and, as it appears to us, on equally good grounds, to the opposite or, as it is termed, *ryotwar* system, acted upon in the government of Madras. In this system the agents of government transact directly with the ryots or occupiers, without the intervention of zemindars, or other head landlords. But the former have no perpetual title to the soil; and their rents being subject to constant variations, their industry is paralyzed, the country makes no progress, and the revenue is stationary or declining.

Journeys through the Upper Provinces of India, and to Madras and the Southern Provinces, with Letters written in India By Bishop HEBER. 2nd ed. 2 vol. 8vo. London, 1828.

"Independently of its moral attraction, we are inclined to think it, on the whole, the most instructive and important publication that has ever been given to the world, on the actual state and condition of our Indian empire. Not only exhibiting a more clear, graphic, and intelligible account of the country, and the various races by which it is peopled, but presenting us with more candid, judicious, and reasonable views of all the great questions relating to its destiny, and our interests and duties with regard to it, than are anywhere else to be met with." (Edinburgh Review, xlviii. 314.)

REMARKS on the PHILIPPINE ISLANDS, and on their Capital, Manilla. By an ENGLISHMAN. 8vo. Calcutta, 1828.

This is a respectable publication; but there is no really good work on the Philippines in the English language. There can, however, be no question that they are naturally one of the finest and best situated groups of islands in the world. Their soil is in most parts of exuberant fertility; the climate is various, and they are, in great part, beyond the range of the typhoons; their products are varied and important, including sugar of the best quality, coffee, rice, indigo, tobacco, hemp, cotton, sago, &c.; they are mostly well-watered and readily accessible; the Malay portion of the inhabitants are distinguished by their vigour, activity, and industry; their situation is extremely favourable for carrying on an extensive commerce with China and the Eastern Archipelago; nor can there be a doubt, had these islands been occupied by the British instead of the Spaniards, they would have been a most important and valuable settlement. But notwithstanding the many gross and glaring defects in the government of the latter, the islands have recently been materially improved: that this must be the case is obvious from the fact of their population, trade, and commercial importance having rapidly increased.

A VIEW of the PRESENT STATE and FUTURE PROSPECTS of the FREE TRADE and COLONIZATION of INDIA. (By JOHN CRAWFURD, Esq.) 8vo. London, 1829.

SIX REPORTS from, with MINUTES of EVIDENCE taken before the SELECT COMMITTEE of the HOUSE of COMMONS on the Renewal of the Company's Charter, in 1831–32; being, 1st, Public; 2nd, Finance and Trade; 3rd, Revenue; 4th, Judicial; 5th, Military; and, 6th, Political and Foreign.

A GEOGRAPHICAL, HISTORICAL, and TOPOGRAPHICAL DESCRIPTION of INDIA. (By JOSIAH CONDER.) 4 vols. 12mo. London, 1830.

This work makes the 7th, 8th, 9th, and 10th vols. of the 'Modern Traveller;' and is, like the other parts of that excellent publication, ably executed.

Journal of an Embassy from the GOVERNOR-GENERAL of INDIA to the COURTS of SIAM and COCHIN-CHINA, exhibiting a View of the actual State of those Kingdoms. By JOHN CRAWFURD, Esq. F.R.S. &c., the Envoy. 2nd ed. 2 vols. 8vo. London, 1830.

Journal of an Embassy from the GOVERNOR-GENERAL of INDIA to the COURT of AVA (that is, the Burmese Court). By

JOHN CRAWFURD, Esq., F.R.S., &c., the Envoy. 2nd ed. 2 vols. 8vo. London, 1834.

This and the preceding work give not only the latest, but the best and most authentic accounts of the countries referred to; and have added most materially to our knowledge of a very large portion of Eastern Asia.

An Inquiry into some of the Principal Monopolies (especially those of Salt and Opium) of the East India Company. (By JOHN CRAWFURD, Esq.) 8vo. London, 1830.

Chinese Monopoly Examined. (By JOHN CRAWFURD, Esq.) 8vo. London, 1830.

OBSERVATIONS on the INFLUENCE of the EAST INDIA COMPANY'S MONOPOLY on the Price and Supply of TEA, and on the Commerce with India, China, &c. (By J. R. M'CULLOCH, Esq.) 8vo. London, 1831.

SKETCH of the RYOTWAR SYSTEM of REVENUE ADMINISTRATION. 8vo. London, 1831.

This is an explanation and defence of the ryotwar plan of assessing the land-tax. But despite the statements of the present and other apologists of the system, it appears to us to have almost every quality that an assessment should not have, and hardly one that it should have. We have stated our reasons for holding this opinion in the article INDIA (BRITISH) in the 'Geographical Dictionary;' and we beg to refer such of our readers as may wish for further information with respect to the ryotwar and other revenue systems of India to that article, and to the work of Mr. Tucker on the Finances of India, and the authorities there referred to.

INDIA; or, FACTS submitted to Illustrate the CHARACTER and CONDITION of the NATIVE INHABITANTS. By ROBERT RICKARDS, Esq. 2 vols. 8vo. London, 1832.

The Act of the 3 & 4 Will. IV. c. 85, for continuing the charter till 1854, terminated the Company's commercial character, by enacting that the Company's trade to China should cease on the 22nd of April, 1834, and that the Company should, as soon as possible after that date, dispose of their stocks on hand, and close their commercial business. The Company has, therefore, ceased to be in any degree a mercantile, and is now wholly a political body.

A Report on the Inland Customs and Town Duties of the Bengal Presidency. By C. E. TREVELYAN, Esq., of the Bengal Civil Service (now Assistant-Secretary to the Treasury). 1 vol. 8vo. Calcutta, 1835.

The publication of this elaborate and valuable report was, we believe, productive of the greatest advantage by contributing to the abolition of the oppressive duties that were previously imposed on the transit of goods from one part of India to another. These duties had existed from a very remote period, and, by obstructing the intercourse between its different districts, have been singularly pernicious. After the East India Company began to acquire a footing in India, they availed themselves of a favourable opportunity to procure an exemption from the transit-duties in favour of their own trade; "the goods which they imported being allowed to pass into the interior, and those which they purchased for exportation in the interior being allowed to pass to the sea, without either stoppage or duties." (Mill's 'India,' 8vo. ed., vol. iii. p. 289.)—They were not, however, long permitted to monopolise this privilege. Immediately after the victories of Clive had raised the Company to the situation of a great territorial power, their servants engaged largely in the inland trade, and endeavoured, partly by fraud and partly by force, to extend to their own goods the exemption from transit duties established in favour of those belonging to the Company. Every reader of Indian history is aware of the multiplied abuses and disturbances that grew out of this attempt of the Company's servants to release themselves from duties and charges that pressed with grinding severity on the natives, and, by consequence, to engross (for such was their object) the whole internal trade of the country. The company endeavoured to obviate the evil by strictly forbidding its servants from engaging in internal traffic. But its orders to this effect were long either totally disregarded, or but very imperfectly obeyed. At length, in 1788, Lord Cornwallis adopted the decisive and judicious measure of abolishing the duties. They were, however, again renewed in 1801. The exclusion of Englishmen from all participation in the interior traffic of the country having been gradually carried into complete effect for a lengthened period, they were less alive than they would otherwise have been to the injurious influence of the duties, so that their re-establishment met with comparatively little opposition. In 1810 a new tariff was introduced, by which the duties "were frightfully augmented;" and they continued from that epoch down to their recent abolition seriously to obstruct all sorts of internal traffic, and to oppose the most formidable obstacle to the improvement of the country.

Had the inland transit duties been productive of a large amount of revenue, that would have been some set-off against the enormous evils of which they were productive. But such was not the case. The expenses of collection, and the interruption of communication, were so very great, that the nett produce of the inland transit duties has been quite insignificant; so much so that, according to Mr. Trevelyan, it did not exceed, in the extensive province of Bengal, the miserable pittance of 27,500*l.* a year. (Report, p. 143.) We see no reason to doubt the accuracy of this statement; and, assuming it to be correct, we are warranted in affirming that there is not another instance to be found, in the history of taxation, of a tax so fruitful of mischievous results, and so barren of revenue. Happily, however, these are now matters of history, the duties having been again abolished, and, it is to be hoped, for ever.

The Town Duties were charged on the principal articles of consumption in twenty-three of the chief towns of Bengal. They were in many respects similar to the *octrois* in France; and, though not nearly so injurious as the internal transit duties, were productive of much inconvenience. We are glad, however, to have to state that they, as well as the transit duties, have recently been abolished; and that the internal trade of Bengal is now as free, in so far, at least, as statutory regulations can make it, as the internal trade of England—an emancipation which will, undoubtedly, be productive of the most beneficial results.

Notes on Indian Affairs. By the Hon. F. J. Shore. 2 vols. 8vo. London, 1837.

Exhibits some striking abuses connected with the revenue systems of India.

Political and Statistical Account of the British Settlements in the Straits of Malacca, Pinang, Malacca, and Singapore;

with a History of the Malay States on the Peninsula of Malacca. By T. J. NEWBOLD, Esq. 2 vols. 8vo. London, 1839.

The author resided three years in the countries described, and appears to have made diligent use of his opportunities for acquiring information.

The Chinese Repository (of Facts and Statements respecting the History, Statistics, Trade, &c., of China and the adjacent Countries). 4 vols. 8vo. Canton, 1834, &c.

This work, edited by the late Dr. Morrison, contains a great variety of valuable and curious papers.

CHINA OPENED; or, a Display of the Topography, History, Customs, Manners, Arts, Manufactures, Commerce, Literature, Religion, Jurisprudence, &c., of the Chinese Empire. By the Rev. CHARLES GUTZLAFF. 2 vols. 8vo. London, 1838.

A superficial, yet, on the whole, pretty good sketch of China and its inhabitants. But the author being a missionary, his views could hardly fail, though unconsciously, perhaps, to be unfavourably biassed in regard to some important particulars in the Chinese character and institutions.

ACCOUNT of the INTERIOR of CEYLON, and of its Inhabitants, &c. By JOHN DAVY, M.D. 1 vol. 4to. London, 1821.

REPORTS and DOCUMENTS connected with the Proceedings of the East India Company in regard to the Culture and Management of Cotton-wool, Raw-silk, and Indigo. Printed by order of the East India Company. 1 vol. 8vo. London, 1836.

AN HISTORICAL and DESCRIPTIVE Account of CHINA. By HUGH MURRAY, Esq., and other writers (in the 'Edinburgh Cabinet Library'). 3 vols. post 8vo. Edinburgh, 1836.

A useful compendium of information with respect to China and the Chinese.

The Chinese: a General Description of China and its Inhabitants. By J. F. DAVIS, Esq., F.R.S., &c., late His Majesty's Chief Commissioner in China. 1 vol. square 8vo. London, 1840.

Notwithstanding its brevity, this is undoubtedly the best work on China in the English language. Mr. Davis is now (1844) governor of Hong Kong, and chief superintendent of the British trade in China.

The Bengal and Agra Guide and Gazetteer, for 1841 and 1842. 4 vols. 8vo. Calcutta, 1841–42.

This work embodies a great deal of information respecting the statistics, government, finances, and condition of India.

History of the British Empire in India. By EDWARD THORNTON, Esq. 5 vols. 8vo. London, 1843–44.

A Gazetteer of the Countries adjacent to India on the North-west, including Scinde, Afghanistan, Beloochistan, the Punjab, &c. By EDWARD THORNTON, Esq. 2 vols. 8vo. London, 1844.

Voyage de Francois Bernier, Docteur en Médecine, contenant la Description des Etats du Grand Mogol; où il est traité de la Force, de la Justice, et des Causes Principales de la Décadence des Etats de l'Asie, et de plusieurs événemens considérables; et où l'on voit comment l'Or et l'Argent, après avoir circulé dans le monde, passent dans l'Indostan, d'où ils ne reviennent plus. 2 vol. 12mo. Amsterdam, 1679; *ibid.*, 1723; *ibid.*, 1725.

Notwithstanding the remoteness of its date, this work contains the most graphic and best account of the manners, customs, and institutions of the people of India hitherto published. Bernier was a pupil of Gassendi, a schoolfellow of Molière, and a collaborateur of Boileau. He was twelve years in India, during eight of which he acted as physician to the emperor Aurungzebe. Gibbon and Robertson quote him with the highest approbation; and Major Rennel calls him "the most instructive of all Indian travellers." He died at Paris in 1688.

Description du Royaume de Siam. Par M. de la LOUBERE, Envoyé Extraordinaire du Roy auprès du Roy de Siam en 1687 et 1688. 2 vol. 12mo. Paris, 1691.

This account of Siam continues to be held in the highest estimation, and is one of the best and fullest which early European voyagers have left us of any part of Asia.

Description Geographique, Historique, Chronologique, Politique, et Physique de l'Empire de la Chine et de la Tartarie Chinoise, avec Figures et un Atlas. Par le Père DUHALDE. 2 vol. folio. Paris, 1735.

An edition in 4 vols. 4to, comprising some additional matter, was published at the Hague in 1736. A translation into English appeared at London in 1742 in 2 vols. folio, but in this some retrenchments are made from the original work.

This work, in which the Chinese empire was for the first time exhibited in detail, was principally compiled from the printed and manuscript works of the Jesuits, and from reports made to Duhalde, who himself never visited China, by the members of the Society then in that country. Its principal defect is a want of critical sagacity, the biases and prejudices of the missionaries being treated with too much respect. But it is notwithstanding an elaborate, valuable, and, in most respects, accurate work. The author discovered the greatest diligence and perseverance in collecting what he believed to be the best materials, and in digesting them after they had been collected.

MEMOIRE sur la SITUATION ACTUELLE de la COMPAGNIE des INDES. Par M. l'Abbé MORELLET. 4to. Paris, 1769.

REPONSE au MEMOIRE de M. l'Abbé MORELLET sur la COMPAGNIE des INDES. (Par M. NECKER.) 4to. Paris, 1769.

EXAMEN de la REPONSE au MEMOIRE de M. l'Abbé MORELLET. Par le Même. 4to. Paris, 1769.

This controversy took place when the affairs of the French East India Company were in the most disordered state possible. Morellet, who contended for the abolition of the Company and the opening of the trade, had a decided advantage over his opponent, who appeared as the defender of the Company. The controversy was terminated by government adopting the suggestions of Morellet. The latter, indeed, had been invited to write his first Mémoire by M. d'Invaux, then Comptroller-general; and on the accession of Turgot to the ministry, he received a pension of 2000 livres a year for his services on this occasion. (Mémoires de Morellet, i. 178, &c.)

DU COMMERCE et de la COMPAGNIE des INDES. Par M. DUPONT. 2de éd. augmentée de l'Histoire du Système de Law. 1 vol. 8vo. Paris, 1769.

This is, perhaps, the ablest of the works to which this controversy gave rise. The account of the *systême*, though short, is remarkably clear and distinct; and, till M. Storch published his article on the same subject in his *Cours d'Economie Politique*, was the best of the shorter sketches of this curious chapter in the history of national folly and quackery.

VOYAGES d'un PHILOSOPHE. Par M. PIERRE POIVRE. 1 vol. 12mo. 3me éd. Paris, 1797.

These voyages consist of extracts from the papers of the author, published without his consent. Poivre followed the famous M. de la Bourdonnais in the government of the Isle de France (Mauritius) and the Isle de Bourbon. He is celebrated alike for the extent and solidity of his attainments, his benevolence and disinterestedness, the zeal and ability with which he laboured to promote the interests of those committed to his charge, and for the efforts he made to introduce new articles of culture into the islands, and to extend and facilitate their commercial transactions. He returned to France in 1773, and lived in dignified retirement till his death in 1786. The extracts in this work chiefly refer to the agriculture of the East. The edition referred to above is by far the best, having prefixed to it a valuable life of M. Poivre by Dupont de Nemours.

Voyages a Peking, Manille, et l'Isle de France, faits dans l'intervalle des Années 1784 et 1801. Par M. de GUIGNES, &c. 3 vol. 8vo. Paris, 1808.

This work is almost wholly occupied with an account of China. Its author was the son of M. de Guignes, who was deeply versed in Chinese literature, and to whom the learned world is indebted for the 'Histoire des Huns,' 5 vols. 4to., and other valuable works. Having resided for a lengthened period in China, and acquired a competent knowledge of the language, the young De Guignes accompanied the Dutch envoy, M. Titzing, in 1794, in the capacity of interpreter, from Canton to Pekin, and thence by a different road back to Canton. He had, therefore, peculiarly favourable opportunities for correctly appreciating the state of the country, and the history, condition, and attainments of the people; and his work appears to be eminently characterized by intelligence, moderation, and good sense. It is probable, indeed, that he may have carried his scepticism with respect to the high antiquity claimed by the Chinese, and their extraordinary population, to an unreasonable extent. His conclusions with respect to these points have, at all events, been fiercely assailed by the Abbé Grosier, in the Introduction to the following work:—

DE LA CHINE, ou DESCRIPTION GENERALE de cet EMPIRE, Rédigée d'après les Mémoires de la Mission de Pekin. La 3me éd., revue et considérablement augmentée. Par M. l'Abbé GROSIER. 7 vol., 8vo. Paris, 1818.

This work, which originally appeared in 1 vol. 4to., in 1786, was intended to serve as a Supplement to the translation, executed in Pekin, of the Chinese History, by the Jesuit Mailla, in 12 vols, 4to, published by Grosier. It met with considerable success, and a translation into English, in 2 vols. 8vo., appeared in 1788. The present edition is, however, so much improved and enlarged as to be almost a new work. The additions made to it were principally derived, as the author tells us, from the labours of the last Jesuit missionaries. It may, indeed, be regarded as a sort of new and modernized Duhalde; being, like the latter, deficient in criticism, and inclined to overrate the Chinese; but, taken as a whole, it is the most complete modern work on China.

Coup d'Œil sur l'Isle de Java et les autres Possessions Néerlandaises dans l'Archipel des Indes. Par M. le Comte HOGENDORP. 1 vol. 8vo. Bruxelles, 1830.

This is an excellent work. The author has united to the most extensive knowledge and enlightened views of commercial and colonial policy an intimate acquaintance with the capabilities and peculiarities of Java and the contiguous Dutch possessions, so that his work, at once philosophical and practical, liberal and judicious, is entitled to stand in the very first rank of such publications, along with those of Hamilton, Raffles, and Crawfurd. A new edition that should describe the extraordinary progress made by Java during the last dozen years would be most acceptable. But as it is, we know of no work relating to any Eastern country that is more instructive and deserving of attention.

Estado de las Islas Filipinas en 1810, brevemente descrito. Por TOMAS DE COMYN. 1 vol. 4to. Madrid, 1820.

This is a valuable work. The author, who resided eight years in the islands, has embodied a good deal of official information in tabular statements.

Estado de la Poblacion, &c., de las ISLAS FILIPINAS correspondente a el Año de 1818. Manila, 1820.

This is the fullest account we have seen of the Philippines. It is, in fact, an official publication of returns of the population, revenue, and commerce of the Spanish portion of the group.

---

§ V. NAVIGATION IN PEACE AND WAR, SHIPPING, CONSULS, &c.

THE MARITIME DICÆOLOGY; or Sea Jurisdiction of England. By JOHN EXON. 1 vol. folio, London, 1664.

THE LAWS, ORDINANCES, and INSTITUTIONS of the ADMIRALTY of GREAT BRITAIN, Civil and Military, comprehending, &c. 2 vols. 8vo. London, 1746.

Republished in 1767 with new title-pages.

During the war terminated by the treaty of Aix-la-Chapelle in 1748, British cruisers stopped and carried into English ports several Prussian merchant ships, on the alleged ground of their having enemies' property on board, or contraband articles. These cases having been inquired into, and adjudged in our courts of Admiralty according to the received principles of public law, the ships and goods were partly restored to the owners, and partly declared to be good prize. But the King of Prussia (Frederick the Great) being dissatisfied with these proceedings, resorted to the extraordinary step of appointing a Commission to inquire into the sentences pronounced against his subjects in the British courts; and this Commission having decided them to be erroneous, the King of Prussia proceeded to make reprisals for the alleged injustice done his subjects by retaining the interest due to certain British subjects for a loan made by them and secured upon the revenues of Silesia. The grounds on which his Prussian Majesty relied for his vindication in this affair were stated in an *Exposition des Motifs fondés sur le Droit des Gens*, &c., transmitted to the British Government.* The latter referred the *Exposition* and the dispatch of the Prussian minister by which it was accompanied, to the Judge of the Prerogative Court (Sir George Lee), his Majesty's Advocate General (Dr. Paul), and the Attorney and Solicitor Generals (Messrs. Ryder and Murray†), for their consideration and report. And these gentlemen having carefully considered the matter, agreed to a Report, dated the 18th of January, 1753, which is universally allowed to be one of the ablest, clearest, and most conclusive state papers that has ever been published. It was characterised by Montesquieu as a *réponse sans réplique;* ‡ and it is not going too far to say that it completely annihilates every statement and pretence by which the Prussian Government attempted to justify their proceedings. In regard to the extraordinary claim put forward by Prussia of rejudging cases that had been decided in our courts, the law officers observe :—

"Such a thing never was attempted in any country of the world before. *Prize, or not prize, must be determined by Courts of Admiralty belonging to the power whose subjects made the capture:* every foreign prince in amity has a right to demand that justice shall be done his subjects in these courts, according to the law of nations, or particular treaties, where any are subsisting. If, *in re minime dubia*, these courts proceed upon foundations directly opposite to the law of nations or subsisting treaties, the neutral state has a right to complain of such determination. But there never was, nor ever can be, any other equitable method of trial. All the maritime nations of Europe have, when at war, from the earliest times, uniformly proceeded in this way, with the approbation of all the powers at peace."

This Report having been inclosed in a letter of the Duke of Newcastle, dated the 8th of February, 1753, addressed to the Prussian minister, it is usually referred to as **'The Duke of Newcastle's Letter.'** It has been more than once reprinted; but it is incomplete and not easily understood unless it be accompanied with the *Exposition des Motifs*.

It is due to the King of Prussia to state that, on receiving this letter, he

---

* This paper was published with an English translation on the opposite page. in 8vo., London, 1752.

† Afterwards Lord Mansfield.

‡ Mr. Phillimore in his Letter to Lord Ashburton (p. 18) quotes this statement. referring the reader to the *Lettres Persannes*, let. 45. But there is not a word in these letters in relation to this subject, nor could there be, as they were published several years before this question occurred. The passage is contained in a letter to the Abbé de Guasco, dated 5th March, 1753. See 'Œuvres de Montesquieu,' vii. 400, ed. Paris, 1819.

abandoned his pretensions, and ordered the arrrears of interest due on the Silesian loan to be paid.

General Treatise of Naval Trade and Commerce founded on the Laws and Statutes of the Realm. 2 vols. 8vo. London, 1753.

A Discourse on the Conduct of the Government of Great Britain in respect to Neutral Nations. By Charles Jenkinson, Esq. (afterwards first Earl of Liverpool, and Author of the work on the Coinage). 8vo. London, 1758, and 1794.

In the war of 1756 the rule was enforced by Great Britain, that neutrals are not to be allowed to carry on a trade during war, from which they had been excluded during peace; and in conformity with this rule British ships of war made prize of the Dutch vessels which then conveyed the produce of the French West India islands to France, because they had been previously excluded from such trade. This rule has been much objected to, but the principle on which it is founded appears, notwithstanding, to be wholly unassailable. The reasonable claims of neutrals cannot surely be carried further than that they should be allowed to carry on their trade, during war, as they had been accustomed to carry it on during peace, except with places under blockade. But to concede to them the right to engage during war, in a trade in which they had not previously any right to engage, would not be preserving to them their former rights, but conceding them *new ones* which may be fairly withheld, and which, if conceded, would in effect enable them, by becoming the carriers and navigators of the belligerent who was weakest at sea, to defeat and nullify the efforts of the fleets and forces of the other, however superior. Lord Liverpool does not, however, argue the point on this special ground, but on the broad principle that enemies' goods, though on board neutral ships, are good prize. The tract is learned, moderate, and able.

De Jure Maritimo et Navali; or a Treatise of Affairs Maritime and of Commerce. By Charles Molloy, Esq. 1st ed London, 1682; 9th ed. 2 vols. 8vo. London, 1769.

This treatise continued to be the best English work on maritime law down to the publication of the work of Lord Tenterden.

In 1780, during the American war, Russia, Denmark, Sweden, Holland, and afterwards Prussia, conceived it would be a favourable opportunity, by taking advantage of the difficulties in which Great Britain was then involved, to effect a change in the law which had hitherto been acted upon by this country, France, and most maritime nations, with respect to the trade of neutrals during war. In this view they agreed to a treaty, in which, among other stipulations, they covenanted as follows:—

"1st. That it shall be lawful for any ship whatever to sail freely from one port to another, or along the coast of the powers now at war. 2nd. That all merchandise and effects belonging to the subjects of the said belligerent powers, and shipped on neutral bottoms, shall be entirely free, except contraband goods. 3rd. In order to ascertain what constitutes the blockade of any place or port, it is to be understood to be in such predicament when the assailing power has taken such a station as to expose to imminent danger any ship or ships that should attempt to sail out or in of the said ports. And 4th. No neutral ships shall be stopped without a material and well-grounded cause; and in such cases justice shall be done to them without loss of time; and besides indemnifying each and every time the party aggrieved, and thus stopped without sufficient cause, full satisfaction shall be given to the high contracting powers, for the insult offered to their flag."

It is obvious that such principles are wholly inadmissible; and that if they were conceded the commerce of any belligerent power might, though she were wholly destitute of ships of war, be carried on with nearly as little interruption during hostilities as during peace! and that, consequently, the superior fleets of another belligerent would be rendered of no value! The armed neutrality formed to carry these pretensions into effect was entirely directed against this country; but the war having terminated soon after, the project fell to the ground, and no notice was taken of it in the treaties of peace.

The project was again revived in 1800, by a new confederacy of the northern powers; but this also was soon after dissolved by the victory of Lord Nelson over the Danes on the 2nd of April, 1801.

In order to prevent enemies' ships saving themselves from attack by hoisting neutral flags, and in order to prevent neutral ships conveying articles contraband of war, the cruisers of belligerents have an undoubted right to visit and search all neutral ships; and all authorities, including even Hubner (De la Saisie des Bâtimens Neutres, i. 228), lay it down that neutral vessels refusing to submit to such visitation and search, may be lawfully captured and condemned. But the question becomes more difficult when neutral vessels sail under convoy; for in such cases it is contended that the assurance of the commander of the convoy that the merchant ships under his orders are really what they pretend to be, and that they have no contraband goods on board, should be deemed sufficient. This, however, is obviously a matter that must wholly depend on negotiation and arrangement; and is not a principle or rule that can be enforced by a neutral on a belligerent. A case of this sort occurred in 1798, when some Swedish ships, sailing under convoy and refusing to be searched, were taken possession of and carried into English ports. On the 11th of June, 1799, Sir William Scott (afterwards Lord Stowell) pronounced his famous judgment in this case, by deciding that the "Maria," one of the vessels in question, was good prize; his decision proceeding principally on the ground that, having made no compact with Sweden agreeing to take the assurance of the officers commanding Swedish ships of war that the merchant ships under their convoy had nothing contraband on board, the rights of Great Britain, as a belligerent, to visit and search Swedish merchantmen, remained entire. This occurrence helped to forward the armed neutrality; and besides the appeal to arms in which it terminated, each party endeavoured to support their pretensions by an appeal to the principles of public law, which led to the publication, among others, of the following works:—

LETTERS of SULPICIUS on the NORTHERN CONFEDERACY; with an Appendix of Documents, &c. 8vo. London, January, 1801.

These letters are popularly and ably written.

A Collection of Public Acts and Papers relative to the Principles of Armed Neutrality brought forward in 1780 and 1781. 1 vol. 8vo. London, 1801.

Among other papers contained in this very valuable volume are the Duke of Newcastle's Letter with the accompanying Report of the Law Officers of the Crown, and the judgment pronounced by Sir William Scott in the case of the Maria, referred to above. The latter produced the following tract:—

A Memoir on the Visitation of Neutral Vessels under Convoy; or, an Impartial Examination of a Judgment pronounced by the English Court of Admiralty, June, 1799, in the Case of the Swedish Convoy. 8vo. London, 1801.

This memoir is translated from the tract *Sur la Visite des Vaisseaux Neutres sous Convoi*, of J. F. W. Schlegel. Copenhagen, 1800.

Schlegel's tract was answered and refuted in the following tracts by Ward and Croke:—

A Treatise of the relative Rights and Duties of Belligerent and Neutral Powers in Maritime Affairs, in which the Principles of Armed Neutralities, and the Opinions of Hubner and Schlegel are fully discussed. By Robert Ward, Esq. 8vo. London, 1801.

A Treatise on Contraband, being a continuation of the preceding work. 8vo. London, 1801.

An Answer to Schlegel on the Visitation of Neutrals. By Alexander Croke, LL.D. 8vo. London, 1801.

Collectanea Maritima, being a collection of Public Instruments tending to illustrate the History and Practice of Prize Law. By Sir Christopher Robinson, D.C.L. 2 parts in 1 vol. royal 8vo. London, 1801.

Law of Shipping and Navigation, &c. By John Reeves, Esq. 1 vol. 8vo. London, 1792; 2nd ed., 1807.

Strictures on the Necessity of inviolably Maintaining the Navigation and Colonial System of Great Britain. By John, Lord Sheffield. 2nd ed., greatly enlarged, 1 vol. 8vo. London, 1806.

A Collection of Interesting and Important Reports and Papers on the Navigation and Trade of Great Britain, &c. Printed by order of the Society of Shipowners. 1 vol. 8vo. London, 1807.

War in Disguise, or the Frauds of Neutral Flags. (By James Stephen, Esq.) 8vo. London, 1806.

"This is a pamphlet of great merit, upon a subject of very general importance. It is written with uncommon talent and considerable eloquence; and is distinguished by that full and systematic argument, and also, perhaps, by that tone of confidence, anxiety, and exaggeration, which we expect to meet in the pleadings of a professional advocate."—(Edinburgh Review, viii. 1.)

The main object of the pamphlet is to recommend the enforcement of the rule of 1756, by excluding neutrals from all intercourse with the colonies that then belonged to France.

AN ANSWER to 'WAR IN DISGUISE;' or Remarks on the New Doctrine of England concerning Neutral Trade. 8vo. New York, 1806; reprinted in London in the course of the same year.

An Examination of the British Doctrine which Subjects to Capture (vessels engaged in) a Neutral Trade not open in time of Peace. Originally published in America, but reprinted in 8vo. London, 1806.

This is one of the best and ablest expositions of the arguments on the neutral side of this question. But to contend that war should put neutrals into a better position than they occupied during peace; and that after all the ships of war belonging to one of the belligerents have been swept from the sea by the superior forces of the other, the supply and trade of his colonies should, notwithstanding, be as regularly carried on by the novel intervention of neutrals, as they had been, previously to the war, by his own ships, are propositions, the unreasonableness of which must strike every impartial judge, and which are wholly subversive of the acknowledged rights of nations engaged in war. It is idle, indeed, to suppose that such pretensions should ever be admitted by any power able to protect and carry on her own commerce, or by any power which entertains any real respect for the best established principles of international law. And this is now in effect admitted by the ablest American jurists. "It is very possible," says Mr. Chancellor Kent, "that if the United States should hereafter attain that elevation of maritime power and influence which their rapid growth and great resources seem to indicate, and which shall prove sufficient to render it expedient for her maritime enemy (if any such enemy should ever exist) to open all his domestic trade to enterprising neutrals, we might be induced to feel more sensibly than we have hitherto done the weight of the arguments of the foreign jurists in favour of the policy and equity of the rule of 1756."—(Commentaries on American Law, i. 94.)

This is a pretty distinct intimation that in Mr. Kent's opinion justice is on the side of those who contend, that neutrals should not be allowed to carry on any trade during war, from which they were excluded during peace; and no one ever doubted, that when the Americans think it for their advantage to admit the reasonableness of this rule, they will be ready to do so, and probably even to deny that they ever were of a different opinion!

BELLIGERENT RIGHTS ASSERTED and VINDICATED against NEUTRAL ENCROACHMENTS; being an Answer to 'An Examination of the British Doctrine, &c.' 8vo. London, 1806.

ORDERS in COUNCIL; or an Examination of the Justice, Legality, and Policy of the new System of Commercial Regulations, with an Appendix of State Papers, Statutes, and Authorities. 8vo. London, 1808.

An Inquiry into the Causes and Consequences of the Orders in Council, and an Examination of the Conduct of Great Britain towards the Neutral Commerce of America. By ALEXANDER BARING, Esq., M.P. (now Lord Ashburton). 8vo. London, 1808.

A very able tract; rather too favourable to the pretensions of neutrals; but the best by far, in a commercial point of view, of those published on the interesting subject of which it treats.

A Treatise of the Law relative to Merchant Ships and Seamen. By CHARLES ABBOTT, Esq. (afterwards Lord TENTERDEN). 1st ed. 1 vol. 8vo. London, 1802.

An edition of this work was published with notes, and an appendix containing the recent statutes relative to shipping and navigation, by Mr. Sergeant Shee. 1 vol. royal 8vo. London, 1844.

This work is creditable alike to the talents, erudition, and liberality of its noble and learned author. It gives, within a brief compass, a clear and admirable view of the more important branches of our maritime law; and may be consulted with equal facility and advantage by the merchant, the general scholar, and the lawyer.

Reports of Cases in the High Court of Admiralty, commencing with the Judgments of the Right Hon. Sir WILLIAM SCOTT (Lord Stowell), from 1798 to 1808. By Sir CHRISTOPHER ROBINSON, D.C.L. 6 vols. royal 8vo. London, 1798-1808.

It has sometimes been alleged, though we believe with little foundation, that Sir William Scott conceded too much to the claims of belligerents. But, admitting him to have been in some degree insensibly biassed in favour of the latter, it detracts but little from the merit of his judgments, which are among the noblest monuments of judicial wisdom of which any country has to boast. "They will be contemplated," says Mr. Serjeant Marshall, "with applause and veneration as long as depth of learning, soundness of argument, enlightened wisdom, and the chaste beauties of eloquence hold any place in the estimation of mankind." (On Insurance, Prelim. Disc.)

The Law of Nations relative to the Legal Effect of War on the Commerce of Belligerents and Neutrals. By JOSEPH CHITTY. 1 vol. 8vo. London, 1812.

OPINIONS of Eminent LAWYERS on various POINTS of ENGLISH JURISPRUDENCE, chiefly concerning the Colonies, Fisheries, and Commerce of Great Britain, collected and digested from the Originals in the Board of Trade, and other depositories. By GEORGE CHALMERS, Esq. 2 vols. 8vo. London, 1814.

A SYSTEM of the SHIPPING and NAVIGATION LAWS of GREAT BRITAIN; and of the Laws relative to Merchant Ships and Seamen, and Maritime Contracts. By F. L. HOLT, Esq., Barrister at Law. 2nd ed. 1 vol. 8vo. London, 1824.

N.B.—Works on commercial law in general, such as those of Beawes, Chitty, Woolrych, &c., mostly include the subject of maritime law.

NAVIGATION LAWS: Speech of the Right. Hon. WILLIAM HUSKISSON in the House of Commons, on the 12th of May, 1825, on the State of the Shipping Interest. 8vo. London, 1825.

SHIPPING INTEREST: Speech of the Right Hon. WILLIAM HUSKISSON in the House of Commons on the 7th of May, 1827, on General Gascoyne's Motion on the Depressed State of the Shipping Interest. 8vo. London, 1827.

Though the general principles on which they are established vary but little, many of the regulations in the customs and navigation laws of this and other countries are perpetually changing, so that it is always necessary, in practical operations, to refer to the latest statute or enactment respecting them.

The right of visitation and search being hitherto regarded as a war right enjoyed exclusively by belligerents, questions with respect to its exercise formerly occurred only during periods when some of the great maritime powers were engaged in war; latterly, however, they have begun to be agitated during peace. This has principally arisen out of the efforts made by this country to suppress the slave trade, and from our having in this view endeavoured to persuade other nations to agree to a mutual right of visitation. It is clear, indeed, that though a nation should impose severe penalties on its subjects in the event of their engaging in the slave trade, still if it refuse to recognise the right of visitation they may probably so engage without its authorities knowing anything of the matter; and it is also evident that other parties might, by disguising their ships, and hoisting the flag of such nation, screen themselves from the consequence of their illegal conduct. A right of visitation in time of peace appears, indeed, to be indispensable for the prevention of piracy and the general security of navigation; for, if the mere showing of the colours of a state that refuses to acknowledge the right of visitation is to protect the vessel showing them from farther molestation, an impunity will be given to sea-robbers, and the security of navigation will be at an end.

It may perhaps be said that the presence of the cruisers of the state which refuses to acknowledge a right of mutual visitation will suffice to preserve the honour and purity of her flag! But this is plainly no security at all. Do the Americans, for example, keep cruisers in all the channels or passages of the Chinese and other Eastern seas? And is a Borneo pirate to escape from our cruisers, or those of any other nation, because she hoists American colours? Such a pretension would obviously be absurd: and yet it must be carried to this extent or abandoned, it being impossible to define the degree of suspicion that would warrant the stopping of ships under the flag of a country that had refused to recognise this right. It may be advisable, perhaps, to restrict the mutual right of visitation to suspected localities, or to make it applicable only to the ships navigating between certain latitudes and longitudes. But it is plainly for the common interest of all maritime and commercial countries that, under such limitations, this right should be recognised and made a part of the law of nations.

The instructions to the officers of British ships employed in the suppression of the slave trade are contained in a bulky folio volume, presented to both Houses of Parliament by Her Majesty's command in 1844.

Researches Historical and Critical in Maritime International Law. By JAMES REDDIE, Esq., Advocate. 1 vol. 8vo. Edinburgh, 1844.

Mr. Reddie has long been advantageously known by his attention to the civil law and the law of nations. In this work he traces the rise and progress of international maritime law from the earliest periods down to 1800. Another volume will include its history from the peace of Amiens down to the present time.

A Treatise on the Maritime Laws of Rhodes. By ALEXANDER C. SCHOMBERG, M.A. (an eminent Civilian). 8vo. Oxford, 1786.

The earliest system of maritime law of which we have any traces was compiled by the Rhodians, several centuries before the Christian æra. The most celebrated authors of antiquity have spoken in high terms of the wisdom of the Rhodian laws: luckily, however, we are not wholly left, in forming our opinion upon them, to the vague though commendatory statements of Cicero and Strabo.—(Cicero pro Lege Manilia; Strab. lib. xiv.) The laws of Rhodes were adopted by Augustus into the legislation of Rome; and such was the estimation in which they were held, that the Emperor Antoninus, being solicited to decide a contested point with respect to shipping, is reported to have answered, that it ought to be decided by the Rhodian laws, which were of paramount authority in such cases, unless they happened to be at variance with some regulation of the Roman law.—"*Ego quidem mundi dominus, lex autem maris legis id Rhodia, qua de rebus nauticis præscripta est, judicetur, quatenus nulla nostrarum legum adversatur. Hoc idem Divus quoque Augustus judicavit.*" The rule of the Rhodian law with respect to average contributions in the event of a sacrifice being made at sea for the safety of the ship and cargo, is expressly laid down in the Digest (lib. xiv. tit. 2); and the most probable conclusion seems to be, that most of the regulations respecting maritime affairs embodied in the compilations of Justinian have been derived from the same source. The regulations as to average adopted by all modern nations, are borrowed, with hardly any alteration, from the Roman, or rather, as we have seen, from the Rhodian law!—a conclusive proof of the sagacity of those by whom they had been originally framed. The only authentic fragments of the Rhodian laws are those in the Digest. The 'Jus Navale Rhodiorum,' published at Bâle in 1561, is admitted by all critics to be spurious.

Us et Coutumes de la Mer, contenant les Jugemens d'Oleron, les Ordonnances de Wisbuy, de la Hanse Teutonique, &c. Par ETIENNE CLEIRAC. 1 vol. 4to. Bordeaux, 1647; and with some additional Pieces, Rouen, 1671.

This collection was formerly highly esteemed, but it has now given way to that of Pardessus.

TRAITE GENERAL du DOMAINE de la MER, et Corps Complet des Loix Maritimes; comprenant ce qu'il y a de plus intéressant dans les écrits des Anciens et des Modernes. Par LECLERE. 1 vol. 12mo. Amsterdam, 1757.

De la Saisie des Batimens Neutres: ou, du Droit qu'ont les Nations Belligérantes d'Arrêter les Navires des Peuples Amis. Par M. HUBNER. 2 vol. 12mo. La Haye, 1759.

This is an acute and very clever work. Being a professor in a university (Copenhagen) in a country which would derive the greatest advantage from the recognition of the claims of neutrals, it was natural that Hubner should support their pretensions; and he is by far the ablest and most distinguished of those who have taken this side of the question. But no ability or ingenuity can ever reconcile the principle contended for by Hubner in this work, that the flag covers the cargo (*que le pavillon couvre la marchandise*) with the undoubted rights of belligerents.

Hubner was also the author of an *Essai sur l'Histoire du Droit Naturel*, 2 vol. 8vo., Londres, 1759. He died at Copenhagen in 1795.

Nouveau Commentaire sur l'Ordonnance de la Marine du Mois d'Août, 1681. Par M. René Josué Valin. 2 vol. 4to. La Rochelle, 1760, and again in 1766.

The *Ordonnance de la Marine* of 1681 comprises the most complete and well digested system of maritime jurisprudence that has ever appeared. It was compiled under the direction of Colbert, by individuals of great talent and learning, after a careful revision of all the ancient sea laws of France and other countries, and upon consultation with the different parliaments, the courts of admiralty, and the chambers of commerce of the different towns, so that it combines whatever experience and the wisdom of ages had shown to be best in the Roman laws, and in the institutions of the maritime states of modern Europe. The first Earl of Liverpool characterised it as "the wisest and best digested system of naval laws which the spirit of legislation hath ever yet produced."—(Discourse on Neutrals, p. 32.) And a still higher authority, the late Lord Tenterden, says, in the preface to his treatise on the *Law of Shipping*, "If the reader should be offended at the frequent references to this ordinance, I must request him to recollect that those references are made to the maritime code of a great commercial nation, which has attributed much of its national prosperity to that code—a code composed in the reign of a politic prince (Louis XIV.), under the auspices of a wise and enlightened minister, by laborious and learned persons, who selected the most valuable principles of all the maritime laws then existing, and which, in matter, method, and style, is one of the most finished acts of legislation that ever was promulgated."

Valin, the commentator of this celebrated Ordinance, was procurator for the king in the Court of Admiralty in La Rochelle, where he died in 1765; and besides being a profound lawyer, was distinguished by his taste in literature. The commentary is detailed and elaborate; and it is not easy to say which is most worthy of admiration—the learning or the sagacity and good sense of the writer. Lord Mansfield was indebted for no inconsiderable portion of his superior knowledge of the principles of maritime jurisprudence to a careful study of Valin's work.

That part of the *Code de Commerce* which treats of maritime affairs is copied, with very little alteration, from the Ordinance of 1681. Valin is also the author of a valuable work on prize law, entitled—

Principes de la Jurisprudence Francaise, concernant les Prises qui se font sur Mer. 2 vol. 8vo. La Rochelle, 1763.

Considerations sur l'Admission des Navires Neutres aux Colonies Françaises de l'Amerique en Tems de Guerre. 8vo. Paris, 1779.

This tract has been repeatedly referred to by the learned author of 'War in Disguise.'

Essai sur un Code Maritime Général pour la Conservation de la Liberté de la Navigation, et du Commerce des Nations Neutres en Tems de Guerre. 1 vol. 8vo. Leipsic, 1782.

Mr. Reddie has given a much fuller account of this work than it appears to be entitled to, in his 'Maritime International Law,' pp. 328-342.

Dissertation sur l'Influence des Loix Maritimes des Rhodiens. Par M. Pastoret. 8vo. Paris, 1784.

Essai concernant les Armateurs, les Prises, et les Reprises. Par MARTENS. 1 vol. 8vo. Gottingen, 1795.

This work was translated into English by Mr. T. H. Horne, and published in 8vo. London, 1801.

Droit Maritime de l'Europe. Par M. Dom. Alb. AZUNI. 2 vol. 8vo. Paris, 1805.

Azuni was a native of Sardinia, of which he has published a very good account. He was afterwards a judge of the tribunal of commerce at Nice, a deputy of the department of Genoa to the legislative body, and one of the presidents of the imperial court. He is the author of several other works, some of which we shall elsewhere notice. His treatises on maritime law, though of considerable value, evince the spirit of the time, and the prejudices under which they were written, by their strong bias against England.

Considerations sur les Droits Reciproques des Nations Belligerantes, et des Puissances Neutres sur Mer. Par M. JEAN N. TETENS. 1 vol. 8vo. Copenhague, 1805.

M. Tetens has emancipated himself from the prejudices in favour of the imaginary rights of neutrals by which the Northern jurists have been generally influenced, and has taken a comprehensive and very able view of the subject.

ORIGINE et PROGRES du DROIT et de la LEGISLATION MARITIME, &c. Par M. D. A. AZUNI. 1 vol. 8vo. Paris, 1810.

ESSAI sur les CONSULS. Par STECK. 1 vol. 8vo. Berlin, 1790.

DE L'ORIGINE et des FONCTIONS des CONSULS. Par BOREL. 2 vol. 8vo. St. Pétersbourg, 1807.

Pardessus says that the work of Steck is merely an extract from the 'Commentaire' of Valin; and that Borel has done little more than copy Steck!

CONSULAT de la MER, ou Pandectes du Droit Commercial. Par BOUCHER. 2 vol. 8vo. Paris, 1808.

This work, which never enjoyed any reputation, has been entirely set aside by that of Pardessus.

SYSTEME UNIVERSEL des ARMEMENS en COURSE et des CORSAIRES en tems de GUERRE. Par M. D. A. AZUNI. 1 vol. 8vo. Gênes, 1817.

Collection de Lois Maritimes Anterieures au XVIIIme Siecle. Par M. PARDESSUS. 5 vol. 4to. Paris, 1828-1839.

The extensive learning, industry, and good sense of M. Pardessus are conspicuous in every part of this publication. It has thrown into the shade and completely superseded every other collection of maritime laws. It contains the original text, with a French translation, of the spurious compilation entitled *Jus Navale Rhodiorum*, and of the *Consolato del Mare*, the *Rooles* of Oleron, the laws of Wisbuy, of the Hanse-Towns, and in fact of all the laws and fragments of laws relating to navigation from the earliest times: and these are accompanied with critical dissertations and notes, in which their authenticity and history are elaborately discussed; and their obscurities and apparent contradictions pointed out and explained. It is impossible, indeed, to speak in too high terms of this truly excellent work.

Manuel des Consuls. Par M. Miltitz. 5 parties 8vo. Londres et Berlin, 1837–42.

A work evincing extraordinary learning and the most extensive research; but crude, indigested, and overlaid with citations from all sorts of books and documents in reference to all sorts of subjects.

De' Doveri de' Principi Neutrali, verso i Principi Guerreggianti, e di questi verso i Principi Neutrali. Di Galiani. 1 vol. 4to. Napoli, 1782.

In this work, which was written by order of his government, Galiani supports the pretensions of neutrals in their fullest extent, with considerable talent, but with little knowledge of the rules and practices observed by maritime nations. It is therefore of no great authority, and has been fully answered by Lampredi.

Del Commercio dei Popoli Neutrali in tempo di Guerra. Di Lampredi. 2 Parte. Firenze, 1788.

Lampredi was professor of public law in the university of Pisa. This work, which is well reasoned, and of considerable authority, was translated into French by Peuchet, and published at Paris in 1802.

Biblioteca di Gius Nautico, contenente le Legge delle piu culte Nazioni, ed i Migliori Trattati Moderni sopra le Materie Maritime. 2 vol. 4to. Firenze, 1785.

Della Giurisprudenza Maritima Commerciale, Antica e Moderna. Di Piantanida. 4 vol. 4to. Milano, 1806.

Tratado Juridico-Politico sobre Pressas de Mar, y Calidades que deben Concurrir para hacerse legitimamente el Corso. Por Don Felix Joseph de Abreu y Bertonada. 1 vol. small 4to. Cadiz, 1746.

This valuable work, which is much less known in this country than it deserves to be,* was translated into French, and published in 2 vols. 12mo. Paris, 1758. It may, perhaps, be worth mentioning that the reports and approvals of the various censors and licensers by whom the original work was examined before its publication occupy no fewer than thirty-four pages! Some of them are choice specimens of pedantry. Abreu was for a while ambassador from Spain to this country; and he was also the compiler of the collection of the various treaties between the sovereigns of Spain and other powers, in 12 vols. folio, reckoned one of the best works of its class. He died in 1775.

Codigo de las Costumbres Maritimas de Barcelona, hasta aqui vulgarmente llamado Libro del Consolato, nuevamente traducido al Castellano, &c. Por Don Antonio de

---

* Mr. Reddie says he had never been able to procure a copy of the original work of Abreu. There is, indeed, a lamentable deficiency of such works in our public libraries.

CAPMANY. Con un Appendice qui contiene una Colleccion de Leyes y Estatutos de España, relativos a Ordenanzas de Comercio Naval, de Seguros Maritimos, &c. 2 vol. 4to. Madrid, 1791.

This work is worthy of the high reputation of its author. The first volume contains the original text of the *Consolato del Mare*, with a translation on the opposite page into modern Castilian; and, excepting that given in the more recent work of Pardessus, this is incomparably the best translation of the *Consolato* hitherto published. It is introduced by a Discourse in which Capmany discusses the origin and antiquity of the 'Consolato,' and in which he endeavours to show that it was compiled at Barcelona, between the years 1258 and 1266; and that it is founded upon and embodies the principal rules, regulations, and customs which the Barcelonese, Pisans, Venetians, and other commercial nations of the Mediterranean had adopted for their guidance in maritime affairs. (Discurso Preliminar, pp. xii.-xxv.)

Azuni (Droit Maritime de l'Europe, i. pp. 414-439) has endeavoured to show, in opposition to Capmany, that Pisa is entitled to the glory of having compiled the Consolato. But notwithstanding his ability and ingenuity, Pardessus and other able critics concur in thinking that he has not been able to shake the conclusions of Capmany. The Spanish origin of the Consolato is further corroborated in a very striking manner by the fact that the Consolato was first published in Catalan at Barcelona in 1502, and that the earliest Italian and French editions are, without any exception, translations from this.

Of the Consolato itself we may shortly observe that, notwithstanding its prolixity, and its frequent want of precision and clearness, the correspondence of the greater number of its rules with the ascertained principles of justice and public utility, gradually led, without the intervention of any agreement to that effect, to its being adopted as their code of maritime jurisprudence by all, or almost all, the nations surrounding the Mediterranean; and it still continues to be everywhere of high authority. Casaregis has said of it, though, perhaps, too strongly, "*Consulatus maris, in materiis maritimis, tanquam universalis consuetudo habuit vim legis inviolabiliter attenda est apud omnes provincias et nationes.*" (Disc. 213, n 12.)

Commentarii Peckii in tit. Digestorum et Codicis ad Rem Nauticam pertinentes, cum Notis Vinnii. 1 vol. 8vo. Amstelodami, 1668.

Prefixed to this edition is a copy of the pretended Rhodian laws (*Jus Navale Rhodiorum*), first published by Schard at Bâle in 1591.

Grotii, Mare Liberum. 1 vol. 18mo. Lugd. Batavorum, 1633.

In the same volume are the dissertations of Merula *De Maribus*, and of Boxhornius *Pro Navigationibus Hollandorum*. There are two editions of this date; one of 267 and the other of 308 pages; but the contents are the same in both, the types only being different. (Dupin.)

Seldeni, Mare Clausum, seu de Dominio Maris, libri duo. 1 vol. folio. Londini, 1635.

This work was translated into English, and published by order in folio. London, 1652 and 1668.

Loccenii, Libri Tres de Jure Maritimo et Navali. Ed. 2da. 12mo. Holmiæ, 1652.

Loccenius, a native of Holstein, was invited to Sweden by Gustavus Adolphus, by whom he was made Professor of History and Politics at Upsal. He published several works relating to the history and antiquities of his adopted country. The work now quoted comprises a well-digested summary of maritime law; and continues to be frequently referred to. Loccenius died in 1677.

STYPMANNI (J. F.), JUS MARITIMUM. 4to. Stralsundi, 1661.

KURICKE (REIN.), JUS MARITIMUM HANSEATICUM. 4to. Gotting., 1667.

Kuricke was also the author of a valuable treatise (see *post*), *De Assecurationibus*.

The works of Loccenius, Stypman, and Kuricke having become, especially the first, of rare occurrence, were published, with a preface, by Heineccius, in 1 vol. 4to., entitled *Scriptorum de Jure Nautico et Maritimo Fasciculus*. Hallæ-Magd. 1740. While, however, the works of Stypman and Kuricke were reprinted without alteration, sundry changes, as well of retrenchment as of addition, were made in that of Loccenius, so that the Stockholm edition of 1652 is the only one of authority.*—See Valin, Preface, p. xvi.

Wedderkopii, Introductio in Jus Nauticum. 1 vol. 4to. Flensburgi, 1757.

Pardessus calls this work *le plus parfait abrégé qui existe des principes du droit maritime.*

Heineccii, de Navibus ob Vecturam Vetitarum Mercium commissis, Dissertatio, in Collect. ejus Operum vol. ii. p. 310.

" Heineccius," says Mr. Manning,† " was equally remarkable for his great learning, and for the powerful understanding which he employed in deducing conclusions from his materials; and he brought the spirit of a philosopher to the consideration of law. He was a writer on morality as well as on jurisprudence, and he was above the suspicion of any influences which might bias the correctness of judgment which his education so qualified him to attain. If weight is due to any authority it is to that of Heineccius: and it is thus that he expresses himself, in his excellent treatise on maritime captures. Stating that the goods of a friend found on board the ship of an enemy should be released, he adds—" *Idem statuendum arbitramur, si res hostiles in navibus amicorum reperiantur. Illas posse capi, nemo dubitat, quia hosti in res hostis omnia licent, eatenus, ut eas ubicunque repertas sibi possit vindicare*" (C. ii. § 9.). It is impossible for any statement to be more distinct and decisive.

---

§ VI. COMMERCIAL LAW, PARTNERSHIP, &c.

CONSUETUDO vel LEX MERCATORIA; or the Ancient Law Merchant, &c. By GERARD MALYNES. 1st ed. 1 vol. folio. London, 1622.

---

* We are fortunate enough to have a copy of this edition.

† See his valuable work on the Law of Nations, p. 221.

This work was republished in 1686 with the following Treatises, viz.:—'Collection of Sea Laws;' 'Advice concerning Bills, by J. Marius;' 'Merchant's Mirrour, by R. Dafforne;' 'Introduction to Merchant's Accounts, by J. Collins, F.R.S.;' 'Accountant's Closet, by A. Lisset;' 'The Jurisdiction of the Admiralty of England, by P. Zouch;' 'Ancient Sea Laws of Oleron, Wisby, and the Hanse Towns, translated by G. Miege;' and the 'Sovereignty of the British Seas, by Sir John Burroughs.'

Malynes appears to have been either a Dutchman or descended of Dutch parents. The last-mentioned edition of his work, with the treatises appended to it, comprises a pretty complete body of the old law of commerce and commercial navigation. Malynes had a controversy respecting some points in the theory of exchange with Misselden (a merchant), which is now curious only as a specimen of the pedantry of both parties, and the extreme acrimony with which such matters were then discussed.

LEX MERCATORIA; or the Merchant's Companion. By G. JACOBS. 1 vol. 8vo. London, 1718.

LEX MERCATORIA REDIVIVA; or a Complete Code of Commercial Law. By WINDHAM BEAWES. 1st ed. 1 vol. folio. London, 1751.

The *Parfait Négociant* of Savary, originally published in 1675, formed the groundwork of this publication. It was, however, materially changed in subsequent editions. The 6th was by Chitty (but executed in a careless, slovenly manner), 2 vols. 4to., London, 1813.

A Practical Treatise on the Laws of Foreign and Inland Commerce, Manufactures, and Contracts, with an Appendix of Treaties, Statutes, and Precedents relating thereto. By JOSEPH CHITTY, Esq. 4 vols. royal 8vo. London, 1820-24.

A PRACTICAL TREATISE on the COMMERCIAL and MERCANTILE LAW of ENGLAND. By H. W. WOOLRYCH, Esq. 1 vol. 8vo. London, 1829.

COMMENTARIES on the LAWS of SCOTLAND, and on the PRINCIPLES of MERCANTILE JURISPRUDENCE, considered in relation to Bankruptcy, Competition of Creditors, and Imprisonment for Debt. By G. J. BELL, Esq., Professor of Law in the University of Edinburgh. 5th ed., 2 vols. 4to. Edinburgh, 1826.

REPORT on the LAW of PARTNERSHIP. By H. BELLENDEN KER, Esq. Printed by order of the House of Commons. Folio. 1837.

This Report and the evidence annexed to it embody much valuable information with respect to the law and constitution of partnerships. One of the principal objects of the reporter was to inquire into the expediency of authorising the formation of partnerships with limited responsibility, as in France and some other countries. Mr. Poulett Thomson (afterwards Lord Sydenham), then President of the Board of Trade, by whom Mr. Ker was employed to investigate this subject, was rather favourable to the principle of limited responsibility. But fortunately, as we think, it has been but little approved in this country; and the evidence of the principal bankers and merchants annexed to the Report is conclusive against it. We beg particularly to recommend Mr. Loyd's paper to those who take any interest in this question. It appears to us to exhaust and settle it; and we regret that our limits prevent our giving it a place in this work.

PRACTICAL TREATISE on the LAW of PARTNERSHIP, with an Appendix of Forms. By F. COLLYER, Esq. 2nd ed., royal 8vo. London, 1840.

PRACTICAL TREATISE on the LAW of PARTNERSHIP. By N. GOW, Esq. 3rd ed., 1 vol. royal 8vo. London, 1841.

THE LAW of JOINT STOCK COMPANIES; containing Chapters on Banking, Railway, Canal, Mining, Insurance, and other Companies, &c. By C. F. F. WORDSWORTH, Esq. 1 vol. 8vo. 3rd ed. London, 1842.

REPORT from and MINUTES of EVIDENCE taken before the SELECT COMMITTEE of the HOUSE of COMMONS appointed to Inquire into the state of the Laws respecting Joint Stock Companies (except those for Banking). Printed by order of the House of Commons. Folio. 1844.

This Report, including the evidence, throws a good deal of light on the practices followed by the getters up of bubble companies. This method of swindling has latterly been carried to a very great extent; and the ruin it has entailed on many persons, who have been prevailed upon or seduced, by their apparent respectability and reasonableness, to buy shares in the most worthless schemes, shows the expediency of some efficient measures being taken for preventing this sort of deception. This may be done by making the public aware who the parties engaged in joint stock schemes really are; and by facilitating the means by which they may be made responsible for fraud, concealment, or misrepresentation.

Mr. Bellenden Ker's Report is printed in the appendix to that now referred to.

The policy of imprisoning for the non-payment of debts fairly contracted has been much discussed in this and other countries; and the imprisonment of parties for debts of small amount has been very generally disapproved.* It has, no doubt, been alleged that the fear of imprisonment prevents people from contracting debts, and that without it, or some equivalent punishment, every sort of fraud would be practised. But we take leave to dissent entirely from these views. The fear of imprisonment is proved, by the number of persons who have been thrown into jails for the smallest sums, to have had no perceptible influence in the way now mentioned; while, on the other hand, it leads retail dealers and others to place an ill-founded confidence in its efficacy, and tends to hinder them from exercising a proper discretion in the granting of credits. This, in truth, is a case in which the principle of *caveat vendor* is the only one on which any reliance can safely be placed. Indeed, we should be disposed to go much further than the mere prevention of imprisonment; and believe it would contribute

* To prevent misapprehension it may be as well, perhaps, to state that the remarks in the text do not apply to cases of fraudulent bankruptcy, that is, to cases in which credit has been obtained by false representations, or in which the property of the bankrupt has been secreted, &c. Such frauds should be adequately and promptly punished, either by imprisonment or otherwise, as may be thought fit.

in no ordinary degree to the public advantage, were most descriptions of debts for sums less than 50*l.* placed beyond the pale of the law. We have elsewhere (Commercial Dictionary, article Credit) stated our reasons for being of this opinion, and we have seen nothing that should incline us to modify or alter it.

In the meantime, however, we are glad to have to state, that an Act of Parliament has been passed (7 & 8 Vict. c. 96) in the course of the present year (1844), which has taken from creditors the power to incarcerate debtors for debts under 20*l.* We have no doubt that this measure will be productive of many advantages; and it may probably pave the way for the introduction of still more extensive changes.

We do not know that the hardship and inexpediency of imprisonment for non-payment of debts fairly contracted have ever been set in a clearer light than by Dr. Johnson, in the 22nd and 38th Nos. of the 'Idler,' published in 1758. We subjoin a short extract from the former:—

"Those who made the laws have apparently supposed that every deficiency of payment is the crime of the debtor. But the truth is, that the creditor always shares the act, and often more than shares the guilt, of impolitic trust. It seldom happens that any man imprisons another but for debts which he suffered to be contracted in hope of advantage to himself, and for bargains in which he proportioned his profit to his own opinion of the hazard; and there is no reason why one should punish the other for a contract in which both concurred.

"Many of the inhabitants of prisons may justly complain of harder treatment. He that once owes more than he can pay is often obliged to bribe his creditor to patience, by increasing his debt. Worse and worse commodities, at a higher and higher price, are forced upon him; he is impoverished by compulsive traffic, and at last overwhelmed in the common receptacles of misery by debts which, without his own consent, were accumulated on his head. To the relief of this distress no other objection can be made, but that by an easy dissolution of debts fraud will be left without punishment and imprudence without awe, and that when insolvency should be no longer punishable credit will cease.

"The motive to credit is the hope of advantage. Commerce can never be at a stop while one man wants what another can supply, and credit will never be denied while it is likely to be repaid with profit. He that trusts one whom he designs to sue is criminal by the act of trust; the cessation of such insidious traffic is to be desired, and no reason can be given why a change of the law should impair any other.

"We see nation trade with nation, where no payment can be compelled. Mutual convenience produces mutual confidence; and the merchants continue to satisfy the demands of each other, though they have nothing to dread but the loss of trade."

Numerous works have been written on this subject, and it has been ably discussed in the following, among other, tracts:—

A Treatise on Civil Imprisonment in England, with the History of its Progress, and Objections to its Policy, &c. By Thomas Macdonald, Esq., Barrister-at-Law. 8vo. London, 1791.

Credit Pernicious. (By Archibald Rosser.) 8vo. London, 1823.

The Abolition of Arrest and Imprisonment for Debt Considered, in Six Letters addressed to a Constituent. By Benjamin Hawes, jun., Esq., M.P., 8vo. London, 1836.

The changes in the law respecting bankrupts have recently been so very numerous as to have rendered the greater number of the older works on the subject comparatively useless. The following is at present one of the best:—

THE LAW and PRACTICE of BANKRUPTCY, as altered by the New Statutes, Orders, and Decisions. By BASIL MONTAGU and SCROPE AYRTON, Esquires. A new Edition by HERBERT KOE and SAMUEL MILLER, Esquires. 2 vols. royal 8vo. London, 1844.

COMMENTARIES on the LAW of BAILMENTS, with Illustrations from the Civil and the Foreign Law. By JOSEPH STORY, LL.D. 1 vol. 8vo. London, 1839.

It is, we believe, generally admitted that the Americans have attained to higher distinction by their legal writings than by their efforts in any other liberal pursuit; and of those who have so distinguished themselves a very high place is occupied by the author of the present work. It is not certainly so classical or finished a performance as the essay of Sir William Jones on the same subject; but it takes in a wider field, and brings to the discussion of some of the more important points in commercial law a wide range of legal learning and a sagacity and sobriety of judgment not often met with. The following is also a very valuable work:—

COMMENTARIES on the LAW of PARTNERSHIP, as a Branch of Commercial and Maritime Jurisprudence; with occasional Illustrations from the Civil and Foreign Law. By JOSEPH STORY, LL.D. Royal 8vo. London, 1842.

CODE de COMMERCE, précédé des Discours de Messieurs les Orateurs du Conseil, &c. 1 vol. 8vo. Paris, 1807.

INSTITUTES du DROIT COMMERCIAL. Par M. DELVINCOURT. 2de éd., 2 vol. 8vo. Paris, 1823.

COURS de DROIT COMMERCIAL. Par M. PARDESSUS. 4me éd., 5 vol. 8vo. Paris, 1831.

Prefixed to the 1st vol. of the 2nd and 3rd editions of this excellent work is a very extensive catalogue of books on commercial law.

DE l'EMPRISONNEMENT pour DETTES, Considérations sur ses Rapports avec la Morale Publique, &c. Par M. BAYLE-MOUILLARD. (Ouvrage couronné par l'Institut). 1 vol. 8vo. Paris, 1836.

DIZZIONARIO UNIVERSALE ragionata della GIURISPRUDENZA MERCANTILE. Di Dom. Alb. AZUNI. 4 vol. 4to. Livorno, 1822.

DELLA SOCIETA CHIAMATA ACCOMANDITA, &c. Del Signor FIERLI. 2 vol. 8vo. Firenze, 1803.

"L'ouvrage que nous indiquons contient, en ce qui concerne les faillites des sociétés, des principes de droit commun fort importans."—Pardessus.

CASAREGIS, DISCURSUS LEGALES de COMMERCIO. 3 vol. folio. Florentiæ, 1719-29. 4 vol. folio. Venetiis, 1740.

This is a work of the highest authority. Pardessus calls Casaregis *le plus distingué de ceux qui ont traité les matières commerciales.*

---

§ VII. WEIGHTS AND MEASURES.

"Nolite facere iniquum aliquid in judicio, in regulâ, in pondere, in mensurâ. Statera justa et æqua sint pondera, justus modius æquusque sextarius."—*Levit.* xix. 35-36.

A DISCOURSE on the ROMAN FOOT and DENARIUS, from whence, as from two Principles, the Measures and Weights used by the Ancients may be deduced. By JOHN GREAVES, Professor of Astronomy in the University of Oxford. 1 vol. 8vo. Oxford, 1647. Reprinted in the 1st vol. of the Collection of Greaves' Miscellaneous Works. 2 vols. 8vo. London, 1737.

AN ESSAY towards the RECOVERY of the JEWISH MEASURES and WEIGHTS, comprehending their Moneys, by help of Ancient Standards, compared with ours of England. By RICHARD CUMBERLAND, D.D. (afterwards Bishop of Peterborough). 1 vol. 8vo. London, 1686.

Both the above works evince great learning, research, and ingenuity.

AN INQUIRY into the STATE of the ANCIENT MEASURES, the Attick, the Roman, and especially the Jewish, with an Appendix concerning our old English Money and Measures of Content. (By Dr. HOOPER, Bishop of Bath and Wells.) 1 vol. 8vo. Lond. 1721.

A STATE of the ENGLISH WEIGHTS and MEASURES of CAPACITY, as well Ancient as Modern; with some Considerations thereon: Being an Attempt to prove that the present Avoirdupois Weight is the Legal and Ancient Standard for the Weights and Measures of this Kingdom. By SAMUEL REYNARDSON, Esq., F.R.S. 4to. London, 1750.

Tables of ancient Coins, Weights, and Measures. By JOHN ARBUTHNOT, M.D. 2nd edit. with Observations on Dr. Arbuthnot's work, by BENJAMIN LANGWITH, D.D. 1 vol. 4to. London, 1754.

This work, though deficient in accuracy, is replete with curious information, and has been very generally referred to by later English writers who have had occasion to notice such subjects.

TWO REPORTS from the SELECT COMMITTEE of the HOUSE of COMMONS appointed to Inquire into the ORIGINAL STANDARDS of WEIGHTS and MEASURES, and the LAWS relating thereto. Folio. 1758 and 1759.

In 1742 the Royal Society had a yard made from a careful comparison of the standard ells or yards of the reigns of Henry VII. and Elizabeth, kept in the Exchequer. In 1758 an exact copy was made of the Royal Society's yard; which having been examined by the committee of the House of Commons now referred to, was reported by them to be equal to the standard yard, and marked as such: and this identical yard was made the standard of lineal measure in Great Britain by the Act 5 Geo. IV. c. 74; which also declared it to be in the proportion of 36 inches to 39·1393 inches of a pendulum vibrating seconds of mean time in the latitude of London at the level of the sea.

A PROPOSAL for UNIFORMITY of WEIGHTS and MEASURES in SCOTLAND, by the Execution of the Laws now in force, with Tables of the English and Scotch Standards, and of the customary Weights and Measures of the several Counties and Boroughs of Scotland, &c. 1 vol. 8vo. Edinburgh, 1779.

It was agreed upon by the 17th Article of the Union between the two kingdoms that the weights and measures of England should be used in Scotland. Very little attention was, however, paid to this stipulation. The greatest diversity continued to prevail among the weights and measures used in different parts of that kingdom, and the many inconveniences thence arising became more apparent as the country became more commercial. In consequence, various ineffectual efforts were made to introduce something like a uniform system. The present work (by a judge of the Court of Session, Lord Swinton) was intended to forward this desirable object. It gives a short statement of the law of Scotland on the subject of weights and measures, with tables and rules for the conversion of those used customarily in different parts of the country into the standard weights and measures of Scotland and England. But it appears to have had little or no influence.

In England, though the discrepancies were not so great, the same inconveniences had long been felt, from the diversity of weights and measures, as in Scotland, and efforts had early been made to obviate them. A law of King Edgar ordered that the same weights and measures should be used throughout the realm. There is a clause to the same effect in *Magna Charta;* and various Acts of Parliament were subsequently passed, enjoining the use of the same weights and measures, under severe penalties. But owing to the inveteracy of ancient customs, and the difficulty of enforcing new regulations, these statutes had a very limited influence, and the greatest variety continued to prevail, except in lineal measures. But the statute 5 Geo. IV. c. 74, seems to have effected what former statutes failed of accomplishing. It is partly, perhaps, indebted, in some measure, for its success to the more general conviction of the advantages that would result from the measure; but it owes it in a far greater degree to the moderate nature of the changes which it introduced. It made no alteration in the lineal measures previously in use. Neither did it affect the previously existing system of weights; both the Troy and the Avoirdupois weights having been preserved. The only changes were in the measures of capacity; and these, except in the case of the wine gallon, were not very considerable. Thus, the old ale gallon contains 282, the old wine gallon 231, and the Winchester bushel 2150·42 cubic inches, whereas the imperial gallon contains 277·274, and the imperial bushel 2218·192 ditto.

The Act 5 Geo. IV. c. 74 (17 June, 1824) was preceded by, and founded upon, 'Three Reports of Commissions appointed to consider the subject of Weights and Measures,' folio, 1819, 1820, and 1821; and upon the 'Reports of Select Committees of the House of Commons' (Sessions 1813-14, and 1821) on weights and measures.

The principal blemish in the statute 5 Geo. IV. c. 74, was the continuance and legitimation of the practice of selling by heaped measure. But this has since been abolished by the 5 and 6 Will. IV. c. 63, which also abolished the use of all local and customary measures.

Tables for converting the Weights and Measures hitherto in Use in Great Britain into those of the Imperial Standards, &c. By GEORGE BUCHANAN, Civil Engineer. 1 vol. 12mo. Edinburgh, 1829.

A carefully compiled and extremely useful publication. The local measures formerly used in the different Scotch counties are given, with the equivalents in Imperial measure.

The works of Kelly and Tate (see Works on Money, &c.) contain the most ample details with respect to the moneys, weights, and measures of foreign countries, and their equivalents in the moneys, weights, and measures of England. Unluckily, however, the work of Kelly, which is the most elaborate of its kind in our language, being published before the change effected in the measures of capacity in 1824, the foreign measures of capacity are converted into old ale and wine gallons, and Winchester bushels. Considerable changes have also taken place in the interval in the measures and coins of different foreign states, so that a new and thoroughly revised edition of Kelly's 'Cambist,' or a new work of the same kind, is a desideratum.

OBSERVATIONS on the EXPEDIENCY and PRACTICABILITY of Simplifying and Improving the MEASURES, WEIGHTS, and MONEY used in this Country, without materially altering the Present Standards. By C. W. PASLEY, C.B., Colonel of Engineers, &c. 1 vol. 8vo. London, 1834.

In consequence of the destruction of the standard yard by the fire at the House of Commons, a new Commission of scientific men was appointed, in 1838, to report on the steps to be taken for the restoration of standards of weight and measure, &c. This Commission made a Report in 1841. Among other matters the Commissioners strongly recommend the introduction of the decimal system of coinage, as well on its own account as a means of introducing a decimal scale of weights and measures. It may, however, be doubted whether any ultimate advantage would follow from the introduction of such a system, and it would, most certainly, occasion great immediate and, we believe, long continued inconvenience.

REPORT upon WEIGHTS and MEASURES. By JOHN QUINCY ADAMS, Secretary of State to the UNITED STATES (afterwards

President). Prepared in obedience to a Resolution of the Senate of the 3rd of March, 1817. 1 vol. 8vo. Philadelphia, 1821.

Colonel Pasley has spoken in very high terms of this work. "Mr. Adams," says he, "has thrown more light on the history of our old English weights and measures than all former writers on the same subject; and his views of historical facts, even when occasionally in opposition to the Reports of our own Parliamentary Committees, appear to me to be the most correct. For my own part, I confess that I do not think I could have seen my way into the history of English weights and measures in the feudal ages without his guidance."—(Preface, p. x.)

ESSAI sur le RAPPORT des POIDS ETRANGERS avec le Marc de FRANCE. Par M. TILLET. 1 vol. 4to. Paris, 1766.

TRAITÉ des MESURES ITINERAIRES ANCIENNES et MODERNES. Par M. D'ANVILLE. 1 vol. 8vo. Paris, 1769.

Metrologie, ou Traité des Mesures, Poids, et Monnoies des Anciens Peuples et des Modernes. Par M. PAUCTON. 1 vol. 4to. Paris, 1780.

At the æra of its publication this very learned work was universally admitted to be the most complete and important that had appeared on the subjects of which it treats; and though materially affected by the changes which have taken place in the interval, especially the introduction of the metrical system into France, it continues to be held in high estimation. Exclusive of the subjects which properly belong to a treatise on Metrology, it embraces a great variety of curious and profound discussions upon collateral topics, which, though they have added considerably to its bulk, have greatly increased its interest and value.

METROLOGIE, ou TABLES pour servir à l'intelligence des Poids et Mesures des Anciens, et principalement à Déterminer la Valeur des Monnoies Grecques et Romaines, d'après leur rapport avec les Poids, les Mesures, et le Numéraire actuel de la France. Par M. DE ROMÉ de L'ISLE. 1 vol. 4to. Paris, 1789.

The new or metrical system established in France subsequently to the Revolution, is founded on the measurement of the quadrant of the meridian, or of the distance from the pole to the equator. This distance having been determined with the greatest care, the ten-millionth part of it was assumed as the *mètre*, or unit of length, all the other lineal measures being multiples or submultiples of it, in decimal proportion. The mètre corresponds pretty nearly to the ancient French *aune*, or yard, being equal to 3·07844 French feet (*Pieds du Roi*), or 3·2808991 English feet, or 39·37079 English inches.

The unit of weight or *gramme*, is a cubic centimètre, or the 100th part of a mètre of distilled water of the temperature of melting ice: it weighs 15·434 English Troy grains. The kilogramme is very nearly equal to 2·2 lbs. avoirdupois; and to 2·68 lbs. Troy.

In order to express the decimal proportion, the following prefixes have been adopted: those for multiplying being Greek, and those for dividing Latin.

For multipliers,

The prefix *Deca* indicates	. . . . .	10 times.
—— *Hecto*	. . . . .	100 „
—— *Kilo*	. . . . .	1,000 „
—— *Myria*	. . . . .	10,000 „

On the contrary, for divisors,

The prefix *Deci* indicates the	. .	10th part.
—— *Centi*	. . . . .	100th „
—— *Milli*	. . . . .	1000th „

Thus, a *Décamètre* is	. . . .	10 mètres.
—— *Décimètre*	. . . .	the 10th part of a mètre.
—— *Kilogramme*	. . . .	1000 grammes, &c.

The *are*, or element of square measure, is a square décamètre, equal to 3·955 English perches. The *hectare*, or 100 ares, is equal to 2 acres 1 rod and 35 perches English.

The *stère*, or element of solid measure, contains 35·31658 cubic feet English.

The *litre*, or element of liquid measure, is a cubic décimètre, being equivalent to 1·76077 English Imperial pints. The hectolitre, or 100 litres, equals 22·009667 English Imperial gallons, or 26·481637 wine gallons.

MANUEL PRATIQUE et ELEMENTAIRE des POIDS et MESURES, des MONNAIES, et du CALCUL DECIMAL. Par M. TARBÉ. 1re éd. 1 vol. 8vo. Paris, 1799.

This work, which is entirely of a practical character, has been repeatedly reprinted. The last edition we have seen was in 1839.

TRAITÉ des MONNAIES, POIDS, MESURES, &c. Par ALTES. 1 vol. 8vo. Marseille, 1832.

Dictionnaire Universel des Poids et Mesures Anciens et Modernes, Contenant des Tables des Monnaies de Tous les Pays. Par HORACE DOURSTHER. 1 vol. grand in-8vo. Bruxelles, 1840.

For practical purposes this is the most extensive, complete, and best arranged work on weights, measures, and moneys that we have seen. Its value, however, must almost wholly depend on the care and accuracy with which it has been compiled, and we have not examined it with sufficient minuteness to give any opinion on this point; but we have had every reason to be satisfied with the accuracy of such parts of it as we have had occasion to look into.

DELLE MISURE d'ogni Genere, Antiche e Moderne. Di GIROLAMO CHRISTIANI. 1 vol. 4to. Brescia, 1760.

EDWARDUS BERNARD, D.D., DE MENSURIS et PONDERIBUS ANTIQUORUM. 1 vol. 8vo. Oxonii, 1683.

J. C. EISENSCHMIDII, de PONDERIBUS et MENSURIS VETERUM ROMANORUM, GRÆCORUM, HEBRÆORUM, &c. 1 vol. 12mo. Argentorati, 1737.

§ VIII. Book-keeping and Mercantile Accounts.

"The counting-house of an accomplished merchant is a school of method, where the great science may be learned of ranging particulars under generals, of bringing the different parts of a transaction together, and of showing at one view a long series of dealing and exchange. Let no man venture into large business while he is ignorant of the method of regulating books; never let him imagine that any degree of natural abilities will enable him to supply this deficiency, or preserve multiplicity of affairs from inextricable confusion."—*Johnson, Preface to Rolt's Dictionary.*

The Universal Accountant and Complete Merchant. By William Gordon. 3rd ed., 2 vols. 8vo. Edinburgh, 1774.

A work of this kind adapted to the present state of science and commerce is a desideratum.

Introduction to Merchandise, containing a complete System of Arithmetic, with an Account of the Trade of Great Britain. By Robert Hamilton, LL.D. (author of the work on the National Debt, see *post*). 1st ed. Edinburgh, 1777; but since frequently reprinted.

A work of the same description as the last, and of very considerable merit. Owing, however, to the want of any recent edition, it is now little in use.

A Complete System of Book-Keeping. By Benjamin Booth. 1 vol. thin 4to. London, 1799.

The Science of Book-Keeping Exemplified. By Mr. Jones. 1 vol. 4to. London, 1831.

A Practical Treatise on Accounts Mercantile and Official. By J. P. Cory, Esq. 1 vol. 8vo. London, 1840.

La Tenue des Livres rendue Facile. Par Degrange. 1 vol. 8vo. Paris, 1840.

Introduzione alla Pratica del Commercio. Folio. Livorno, 1759.

---

§ IX. Commercial Treaties.

Commercial treaties have been negotiated from a very remote æra, and a good deal more stress has been laid upon them than they would seem to deserve. During the middle ages, indeed, while aliens or foreigners were exposed to the most inhospitable treatment, being frequently even made liable for the debts and crimes of others, commercial treaties were of considerable advantage, inasmuch as they stipulated for the suspension of those barbarous customs, and procured for foreigners that protection and security so essential to the prosecution of commercial undertakings. After the establishment of good order, and the growing intercourse among nations had abated the prejudices against strangers, it might have been supposed that commercial treaties would have gradually fallen into disuse, or been restricted to a few simple regulations for facilitating mercantile transactions. But at the same time that the real importance of commercial treaties declined, they acquired an adventitious value in the estimation of politicians and merchants, and began to be employed as one of the most efficacious instruments of the mercantile system. They have not consequently, with a few exceptions, been entered into for the purpose of mutually modifying restrictions, and giving greater facilities to commerce, but because each party imagined they were gaining some peculiar advantage at the expense of the other! And hence almost all the commercial treaties negotiated during the last 200 years are full of stipulations respecting duties, the privileges to be enjoyed by the ships of either party in the ports of the other, &c. It is almost superfluous to add that these imaginary advantages have commonly proved either useless or positively pernicious. It cannot be for the public advantage to show any favour to one set of foreigners more than to another. Common sense suggests the propriety of dealing in preference with those who supply us best and cheapest with the articles we want. Now these, it is obvious, require no privileges. All that is necessary to the successful prosecution of the most extensive intercourse with them is to *let it alone*. We deal with them because we find it most for our advantage; and it is evident that, if we put an end to this intercourse, by giving artificial privileges to others, we injure ourselves, and force our people to forsake the cheap shop and to go to the dear! Such is the preposterous principle on which nine out of ten commercial treaties have been negotiated. They have not been employed to remove the obstacles that oppose commerce, but to give it an artificial direction, to force it into channels in which it would not naturally flow, and in which it is sure to be least beneficial.

But it may be said, perhaps, that though a commercial treaty stipulating for some peculiar privilege, be disadvantageous to the country making the concession, it is proportionally advantageous to the one in whose favour it is made. In point of fact, however, such is not the case. Reciprocity is the beginning, the middle, and the end of all commercial transactions. It is quite visionary to imagine that any nation will continue *bonâ fide* to grant to another an exclusive advantage, unless she obtain what she reckons a countervailing benefit; and if a commercial treaty stipulating for an exclusive privilege be really observed on the part of the country by which it is conceded, we may be assured that the concessions made by the country in whose favour the privilege is granted are sufficient fully to balance it.

The famous commercial treaty negotiated by Mr. Methuen with Portugal, in 1703, was long regarded as a master-piece of its kind. Such, indeed, was the estimation in which it was held in the reign of George I., that it is stated in the 'British Merchant,' a work of great authority at the time, that a statue ought to be erected to Mr. Methuen in every considerable town in the empire! So far, however, from these encomiums being deserved, it would be difficult to point out any transaction in the commercial history of the country that has been more injurious than this very treaty. Previously to 1700 British woollens had been admitted at a reasonable duty into Portugal, but at the epoch of the negotiation of this treaty they were excluded. The main object of Great Britain in entering into the treaty was to procure the repeal of this prohibition, which it effected, but at an enormous cost. The treaty being short and often referred to, we subjoin it:—

"I. His sacred royal Majesty of Portugal promises, both in his own name and that of his successors, to admit, for ever hereafter, into Portugal, the woollen cloths and the rest of the woollen manufactures of the British, as was accustomed till they were prohibited by law, nevertheless upon this condition:

"II. That is to say, that her sacred royal Majesty of Great Britain shall, in her own name and that of her successors, be obliged, for ever hereafter, to admit the wines of the growth of Portugal into Britain; so that at no time, whether there be peace or war between the kingdoms of Britain and France, anything more shall be demanded for these wines by the name of custom or duty, or by whatsoever other title, directly or indirectly, or whether they shall be imported into Great Britain in pipes or hogsheads, or other casks, than what shall be demanded for the like quantity or measure of French wines, deducting or abating a third part of the custom or duty. But if at any time this deduction or abatement of customs, which is to be made as aforesaid, shall in any manner be attempted or prejudiced, it shall be just and lawful for his sacred royal Majesty of Portugal again to prohibit the woollen cloths, and the rest of the British woollen manufactures."

A more improvident bargain on our part could not have been entered into. The repeal of the prohibition of woollens was of infinitely more importance to the Portuguese than to the English. It should also be observed that in its repeal Portugal made no peculiar concessions to us; for though she bound herself to admit our woollens on the same terms as before the prohibition, she did not bind herself to admit them on lower terms than those of France, Saxony, or any other country. And in return for this pitiful boon we bound ourselves "for ever hereafter" to drink inferior wine bought at a comparatively high price! But the influence of this treaty in increasing the cost and deteriorating the quality of wine, was perhaps the least of its mischievous consequences. By excluding one of the principal equivalents the French had to exchange for our commodities, it lessened their ability to become the purchasers of our goods, at the same time that it tempted them to adopt retaliatory measures against our trade, by either excluding our commodities altogether, or burdening them with prohibitory duties. It is owing more to the Methuen treaty than to anything else that the trade between Great Britain and France—a trade that ought to be the most extensive of any in the world—has been confined, down almost to yesterday, within such narrow limits as to be of very inferior importance.

Hume and Smith saw and pointed out the injurious operation of the Methuen treaty, and exposed the absurdity of our sacrificing the trade with France to that with so beggarly a country as Portugal. "Our jealousy and hatred of France," said Hume, "are without bounds. These passions have occasioned innumerable barriers and obstructions on commerce, where we are commonly accused of being the aggressors. But what have we gained by the bargain? We lost the French market for our woollen manufactures, and transferred the commerce of wine to Spain and Portugal, where we buy much worse liquor at a much higher price. There are few Englishmen who would not think their country absolutely ruined were French wines sold in England so cheap and in such abundance as to supplant ale and other home-brewed liquors. But, could we lay aside prejudice, it would not be difficult to prove that nothing could be more innocent, perhaps more advantageous. Each new acre of vineyard planted in France, in order to supply England with wine, would make it necessary for the French to take an equivalent in English goods, by the sale of which we should be equally benefited."—*(Essay on the Balance of Trade.)* Such, however, is the force of prejudice, that it was not till 1832 that the Methuen treaty was finally abolished and an end put to the discriminating duty on French wines.

In 1713 the Tory ministry, which negotiated and concluded the Treaty of Utrecht, concluded, also, a treaty of commerce and navigation with France: and whatever may be said of the other treaty, the latter appears to have been founded on just and fair principles; and there can be no doubt, had its provisions been carried into effect, that it would have been of singular advantage to both countries. It was stipulated in the treaty (Art. viii.) that the ships and goods of both parties should be placed in each other's ports and markets on the same footing as the ships and goods of the most favoured nations; and it was farther stipulated that (with one or two exceptions) the prohibitions enacted in both countries since 1664 should be repealed, and the tariffs of that epoch revived. Nothing could be more liberal and judicious than these regulations, under which an extensive and most beneficial commerce would certainly have grown up. But liberality, at least in commercial matters, was not then the order of the day. The leading merchants and manufacturers, who almost all belonged to the school of Mun and Fortrey, alleged that the treaty would be ruinous to our interests; that, as it set aside the Methuen Treaty, the Portuguese would exclude our woollens from their markets; that we should be deluged with French commodities; that our coin would be carried off by the unfavourable balance we should have to pay to France; and that our workmen would be thrown out of employment by the greater cheapness of French products. These false and contradictory allegations were all but universally believed, and were eagerly taken up by the Opposition in Parliament, and used as convenient weapons by which to assail the ministry. In consequence of the ferment and jealousy thus excited, and the unpopularity of the government, the bill to give effect to the treaty was rejected in the House of Commons by a majority of 194 to 185.

Owing to the odium attaching to the treaty, by far the greater number of the publications to which it gave rise are hostile to its provisions. It was however defended, though with little talent and in a subdued tone, by the celebrated Daniel Defoe, in a tract entitled

An Essay on the Treaty of Commerce with France, with necessary Expositions. 8vo. London, 1713.

And in the 'Mercator,' a paper published three times a week. The principal publication on the other side is entitled

The British Merchant, or Commerce Preserved. By Mr. Charles King. 3 vols. 8vo. London, 1721.

This work, which appeared in weekly numbers at the time when the treaty was under discussion, was written by some of the leading merchants of the day; but the papers being subsequently collected and published by Mr. Charles King, his name appears singly on the title-page. It enjoyed at the time a large share of popularity, and was for a while referred to as a work of authority. And it continues to deserve attention from the full exposition which it gives of the opinions and reasonings then current on commercial affairs, and which led the parliament and people to reject a measure which would have been productive of great immediate and of still greater permanent advantage. At present one has difficulty in believing that such shallow sophisms and contradictory misstatements should have been capable of influencing well-informed persons, and of obstructing a great public good.

The trade between England and France continued with but little variation on the footing on which it had been placed by the rejection of the treaty of 1713 down to 1786, when a change was effected under the auspices of Mr. Pitt, who was one of the first British statesmen who clearly perceived the vast advantage that would redound to both countries from their being permitted freely to avail themselves of their capacities for a commercial intercourse. The Count de Vergennes, French minister, participated in Mr. Pitt's sentiments, and negotiators being appointed by both parties, a commercial treaty was agreed upon in the above-mentioned year. It introduced a more liberal system into the trade between France and England, by moderating the severity of the duties and restrictions with which it was burdened; and its object being, by familiarising both parties with the many advantages derivable from a more extensive intercourse, to teach them to forget their animosities, and to feel an interest in each other's welfare.

The speech made by Mr. Pitt in vindication of this treaty is highly deserving of attention; and whether we refer to the soundness of its principles, or the ability with which they are enforced, is deserving of every commendation.

"France," said he, "was, by the peculiar dispensation of Providence, gifted, perhaps more than any other country upon earth, with what made life desirable, in point of soil, climate, and natural productions. It had the most fertile vineyards and the richest harvests. The greatest luxuries of life were produced in it with little cost, and with moderate labour. Britain was not thus blessed by nature; but, on the other hand, it possessed, through the happy medium of its constitution, and the equal security of its laws, an energy in its enterprise, and a stability in its exertions, which has gradually raised it to a high state of commercial grandeur; and not being so bountifully gifted by Heaven, it had recourse to labour and art, by which it had acquired the ability of supplying its neighbours with all the artificial embellishments of life, in exchange for their natural luxuries. Thus standing with regard to each other, a friendly connexion seemed to be pointed out between them, instead of that state of unalterable enmity which was falsely said to be their true political feeling towards one another."

Having refuted the commercial arguments against the treaty, Mr. Pitt inquired, in answer to an argument inculcating constant jealousy of France, "Whether, in using the word jealousy, it was meant to recommend to this country such a species of jealousy as should induce her either madly to throw away what was to make her happy, or blindly grasp at what must end in her ruin. Was the necessity of a perpetual animosity with France so evident and pressing, that for it we were to sacrifice every commercial advantage we might expect from a friendly intercourse with that country?—or was a pacific connexion between the two kingdoms so highly offensive that even an extension of commerce could not counterpoise it? The quarrels between France and Britain had too long continued to harass not only these two great nations themselves, but had frequently embroiled the peace of Europe; nay, they had disturbed the tranquillity of the most remote parts of the world: they had, by their past conduct, acted as if they were intended for the destruction of each other; but he hoped the time was now come when they would justify the order of the universe, and show that they were better calculated for the more amiable purposes of friendly intercourse and mutual benevolence." "Considering the treaty," he continued, "in a political point of view, he should not hesitate to contend against the too-frequently advanced doctrine, that France was, and must be, the unalterable enemy of Britain. To suppose that any nation was unalterably the enemy of another, was weak and childish. It had neither its foundation in the experience of nations nor in the history of man. It was a libel on the constitution of political societies, and supposed diabolical malice in the original frame of man."

The Opposition in parliament were decidedly hostile to the treaty. Mr. Fox, indeed, knew little or nothing of such subjects; but though he had understood them better, the result would probably have been the same; the presumption being that the chance of damaging the ministry by exciting a popular prejudice against them, would have been preferred to the greatest national advantage. It would, however, be unjust not to mention that the Marquis of Lansdowne (previously Earl of Shelburne), though generally opposed to the government, gave the most zealous and efficient support to the treaty, and successfully repelled the objections made against it.

At the same time, however, we are far from thinking that the treaty of 1786 should be taken for a model. The negotiators were too much influenced by old notions, and the treaty is encumbered with too many conditions. When a few stipulations are agreed upon for giving facility and security to the transactions of merchants, in the buying and selling of such commodities as are not prohibited, for securing their persons and properties in the event of hostilities breaking out, for the regulation of port-charges, &c., the most seems to be done that should be attempted in a commercial treaty. Such a compact may, indeed, bear that the goods and ships of the one party shall be admitted to the markets and ports of the other, on the footing of the most favoured nations—that is, that they shall not be loaded with discriminating duties; but here stipulations should stop. All commercial treaties, fixing the duties to be paid in either country, are radically objectionable. Every people should always be able to regulate its tariff as may seem best fitted to promote its own views, without being fettered by engagements with others. It may sometimes, indeed, be expedient to transact with a foreign country for the mutual abolition of duties or prohibitions; but this should be done by a convention for the particular object, the duration of which should be limited to a few years, so that at its termination each party may be free either to abide by it or to enact other regulations. It is absurd to attempt to bind an independent nation to a policy which it considers injurious, by a condition in a commercial treaty which is sure to be either openly or covertly defeated. The promotion of its own interest should be the object of every nation; and this will always be best done by dealing fairly and liberally with others, not by grasping at oppressive privileges.

The treaty of 1786, though highly advantageous to both parties, was very unpopular both in this country and in France. Among the tracts to which it gave rise on this side the Channel were—

Historical and Political Remarks upon the Tariff of the Commercial Treaty (with France), with Preliminary Observations. 8vo. London, 1787.

An able, though not a very conclusive tract, attributed to Mr. Eden, who negotiated the treaty.

A Complete Investigation of Mr. Eden's Treaty, as it may affect the Commerce, the Revenue, or the General Policy of Great Britain. 8vo. London, 1787.

A VIEW of the TREATY of COMMERCE with FRANCE, signed at Versailles 20th September, 1786. 8vo., 2nd ed. London, 1787.

The last two pamphlets are opposed to the treaty.

In France the treaty was attacked by the Chamber of Commerce of Normandy, and other bodies, and was ably defended by Dupont de Nemours and other writers; but it is enough to refer to the following works:—

OBSERVATIONS de la CHAMBRE du COMMERCE de NORMANDIE sur le Traité de Commerce entre la France et l'Angleterre. 8vo. Rouen, 1787.

LETTRE à la CHAMBRE du COMMERCE de NORMANDIE sur le MEMOIRE qu'elle a publié relativement au TRAITÉ de COMMERCE avec l'ANGLETERRE. (Par M. DUPONT.) 8vo. Rouen (Paris), 1781.

REFUTATION des PRINCIPES et ASSERTIONS contenus dans la LETTRE à la CHAMBRE du COMMERCE de NORMANDIE. Par M. D. P. Par la dite Chambre. 8vo. Rouen, 1788.

A good work on the principles, style, and history of commercial treaties is a desideratum. The best we have seen are Mascovius *De Fœderibus Commerciorum*, 4to., Leipsic, 1735; and Bouchaud, *Théorie des Traités de Commerce*, 12mo., Paris, 1777. But these are principally works of erudition, and were written before the sound principles of commercial policy had been unfolded. There is no good collection of commercial treaties in the English language; but the following work is valuable, from its containing the recent treaties in an accessible form.

A Complete Collection of the Treaties and Conventions and Reciprocal Regulations at present subsisting between Great Britain and Foreign Powers, and of the Laws, Decrees, and Orders in Council concerning the same, so far as they relate to Commerce and Navigation; to the Repression and Abolition of the Slave Trade; and to the Privileges and Interests of the Subjects of the High Contracting Parties. Compiled from Authentic Documents. By LEWIS HERTSLET, Esq. 5 vols. 8vo. London, 1820-1840.

There appears, however, to be no very good reason for mixing up the treaties relating to the slave trade with those relating to commerce in general; and we incline to think that it would be an improvement to divide the work into two separate works, one of which should contain the treaties, orders in council, &c., relating to commerce, and the other those relating to the slave trade.

We have inserted copies of the greater number of the existing commercial treaties between this country and foreign powers, in the Commercial Dictionary.

Recueil des Traités de Commerce et de Navigation de la France avec les Puissances Etrangères depuis la Paix de Westphalie en 1648, suivi du Recueil des Principaux Traités de même Nature conclus par les Puissances Etrangères entre elles. Par M. le Comte d'HAUTERIVE et le Chev. de CUSSY. 10 vol. 8vo. Paris, 1834-42.

An important and valuable publication.

---

§ X. HISTORY OF COMMERCE AND NAVIGATION.

NAVIGATION and COMMERCE, their ORIGINAL and PROGRESS. By J. EVELYN, Esq., F.R.S. 1 vol. small 8vo. London, 1674.

A brief and necessarily very imperfect sketch. It is introduced by some observations on the advantages of commerce and navigation, as exemplified in the instances of Holland, Venice, &c.

The Introductory Discourse to Churchill's Collection of Voyages, published in 1704, containing the history of navigation from the earliest periods down to that time, with a catalogue and account of the principal books of travels, has been usually ascribed to Locke, and is included in the later editions of his works. As Locke died in the same year in which this Discourse was published, it may be regarded as his last contribution to literature; and though it would be too much to say that it adds anything considerable to his fame, it certainly detracts nothing from it, but is worthy of the author of the 'Essay on the Human Understanding.' We subjoin the concluding paragraph of this interesting work. It shows that this great philosopher had nothing in common with those who affect to doubt whether the progress of navigation and discovery has been advantageous. That such notions should ever have been entertained is, indeed, singular. It is certain that but for this progress half the civilised world would at this moment have been occupied with the scanty population of a few half-starved savage hordes.

"After so long a discourse of voyages and discoveries, it may seem superfluous to treat of the advantages the public receives by navigation, and the faithful journals and accounts of travellers. The matter is natural, and no man can read the one without being sensible of the other; and therefore a few words may suffice on this subject, to avoid cloying the judicious reader with what is so visible and plain, and to save running out this introduction to an unreasonable length. What was cosmography before these discoveries but an imperfect fragment of science, scarce deserving so good a name? when all the known world was only Europe, a small part of Afric, and the lesser portion of Asia; so that of this terraqueous globe not one-sixth part had ever been seen or heard of. Nay, so great was the ignorance of man in this particular, that learned persons made a doubt of its being round; others no less knowing imagined all they were not acquainted with desert and uninhabitable. But now geography and hydrography have received some perfection by the pains of so many mariners and travellers, who, to evince the rotundity of the earth and water, have sailed and travelled round it, as has been here made appear, to show there is no part uninhabitable, unless the frozen Polar regions, have visited all other countries, though never so remote, which they have found well peopled, and most of them rich and delightful; and to demonstrate the *antipodes* have pointed them out to us. Astronomy has received the addition of many constellations never seen before. Natural and moral history is embellished with the most beneficial increase of so many thousands of plants it had never before received; so many drugs and spices; such variety of beasts, birds, and fishes; such varieties in minerals, mountains, and waters; such unaccountable diversity of climates and men, and in them of complexions, tempers, habits, manners, politics, and religions. Trade is raised to the highest pitch, each part of the world supplying the other with what it wants, and bringing home what is accounted most precious and valuable; and this not in a niggard and scanty manner, as when the Venetians served all Europe with spice and drugs from India, by the way of Turkey and the Red Sea; or as when gold and silver were only drawn from some poor European and African mines; but with plenty and affluence, as we now see most nations resorting freely to the East Indies, and the West yearly sending forth prodigious quantities of the most esteemed and valuable metals. To conclude, the empire of Europe is now extended to the utmost bounds of the earth, where several of its nations have conquests and colonies. These and many more are the advantages drawn from the labours of those who expose themselves to the dangers of the vast ocean, and of unknown nations, which those who sit still at home abundantly reap in every kind: and the relation of one traveller is an incentive to stir up another to imitate him, whilst the rest of mankind, in their accounts, without stirring a foot, compass the earth and seas, visit all countries, and converse with all nations."

An Historical and Chronological Deduction of the Origin (and Progress) **of Commerce,** from the Earliest Accounts to the Present Time. By ADAM ANDERSON, Esq. 2nd ed. 2 vols. folio. London, 1764.

This work is hardly, perhaps, worthy of the estimation in which it has been held. In his accounts of the commerce of the earlier ages, Anderson appears to have trusted too much to imperfect translations and modern compilations, and to have paid too little attention to original sources. He has consequently, to use the words of Macpherson, been betrayed in this part of his work "into innumerable errors and omissions."—(Preface.) But in his more modern portion these defects are much less obvious; and though his views of commercial subjects be not unfrequently narrow and illiberal, his statements of facts are carefully drawn up, and may in general be depended upon. The following work of Macpherson is wholly founded on that of Anderson, of which it may be considered as a new and revised edition. Macpherson has re-written the portion of Anderson antecedent to 1492; and besides abbreviating the succeeding portion, which is frequently not a little tedious, and improving the style, he has continued it from 1760 to 1801. Anderson was a native of Scotland, where he was born in 1692. Having come to London, he became a clerk in the South Sea House, in which establishment he continued for about forty years. He died in 1765.

Annals of Commerce, Manufactures, Fisheries, and Navigation. By DAVID MACPHERSON. 4 vols. 4to. London, 1805.

The author of this work, who during the latter part of his life was one of the deputy-keepers of the public records, died in 1816, in his 69th year. He was also author of the 'History of European Commerce with India' (p. 107), and of some other works.

The Commerce and Navigation of the Ancients in the Indian Ocean. By WILLIAM VINCENT, D.D., Dean of Westminster. 2 vols. 4to. London, 1807.

The first volume of this valuable work, originally published in 1797, contains an account of the voyage of Nearchus, the admiral of Alexander the Great, from the Indus to the Euphrates. This account, though not translated from, is principally founded on, the journal of the voyage given by Arrian (of Nicomedia), the historian of Alexander, in his book on India, the statements in the latter being compared with and illustrated by other ancient and a host of modern authorities.

The second volume principally consists of what is called the 'Periplus of the Erythræan Sea,' from an ancient work of that name, giving an account not merely of the coasts of the Red Sea, but also of those of Southern Arabia, Persia, and Western India. Neither the author nor the epoch of this work is ascertained. It has, indeed, been commonly ascribed to Arrian, the historian of Alexander, to whom, as stated above, we are indebted for the account of the voyage of Nearchus. But it is now generally admitted that there is no good ground for supposing Arrian to be its author. Dr. Vincent says it "certainly was not his;" and supposes it to have been the work of a Greek, a native of Egypt, and a merchant of Alexandria, prior to Arrian by about a century. But, whoever may have been the author of this Periplus, it is an extremely curious and interesting relict. Dr. Vincent makes it, as in the case of the voyage of Nearchus, the foundation of a lengthened work, embracing a detailed account of the navigation and trade of the ancients in the Red Sea and the Indian Ocean. Elaborate dissertations are annexed to this volume on the country of the Seres; the places and articles referred to in the magnificent account of the commerce of Tyre in the 27th chapter of the prophet Ezekiel; the compass of the Chinese, &c. (See also St. Croix, 'Examen Critique des Historiens d'Alexandre,' pp. 88—102, éd. 2de.; 'Penny Cyclopædia,' art. Arrian, &c.)

This work evinces throughout great industry, research, and good sense, and is a most valuable contribution to the geography of antiquity and the history of commerce. Its principal fault is its prolixity: it might certainly have been compressed, without injury to its merits, within smaller limits.

Dr. Vincent died in 1815, in his 77th year. The Deanery of Westminster was conferred upon him as a mark of the approval by the government of a tract of his entitled a 'Defence of Public Education,' 8vo. 1802.

HISTORICAL SKETCH of the PROGRESS of DISCOVERY, NAVIGATION, and COMMERCE, from the Earliest Periods to the beginning of the Nineteenth Century. By WILLIAM STEVENSON, Esq. 1 vol. 8vo. Edinburgh, 1824.

This work was originally intended to serve as a supplement to Kerr's Collection of Voyages and Travels, but it has no necessary connexion with the latter, and is, in all respects, an independent publication. The author, who filled the place of librarian to the Treasury, contributed some valuable statistical articles to the 'Edinburgh Encyclopædia,' and was possessed of much general information. This sketch appears, however, to have been hastily written, and wants the elaboration and research necessary to give real and permanent value to such works. Annexed to it is a valuable catalogue of voyages and travels.

ACCOUNT of the LEVANT COMPANY; with some Notices of the Benefits conferred upon Society by its Officers, &c. 8vo. London, 1825.

This tract, which contains some interesting details, was published on the dissolution of the Levant Company in 1825. But it derives its principal value from its containing a report of the speech made by Lord Grenville, Governor of the Company, on the occasion referred to. As this tract is not of common occurrence, we believe we shall gratify the reader by making the following extracts from Lord Grenville's speech :—

"The surrender of your charters is the second part of the proposal made to you by government. On this it is for you to determine. My own impressions, if you will permit me to state them to you, are strongly in its favour. The essential objects of those grants have either been provided for in the lapse of time by the full establishment of your commerce, or will be sufficiently answered by the arrangement of which I have already spoken. Little more would then remain to you, except the monopoly which excludes from the British commerce with the Levant all persons not admitted to the freedom of this Company. No useful purpose, either to yourselves or to the public, could, I think, be answered by the continuance of this invidious restraint. In your former position it was both necessary and just; those who bore the burthen of protecting this commerce could alone claim to share its benefits. But it will become wholly useless when you shall be relieved from the duties and expenses in contemplation of which it was originally created.

"And if the removal of such a restraint on any branch of trade is a measure, on general grounds of policy, not only unobjectionable but desirable, there are, in the circumstances of the present moment, two considerations which appear to me peculiarly and forcibly to recommend it to your adoption.

"The first of these arises from the rapidly increased, and I trust still more rapidly increasing, commercial prosperity of our country; an augmentation in which your own trade has already participated largely, and in the farther progress of which we have every reason to hope it will bear its full proportion. From this auspicious circumstance the whole fabric of the British empire, and every one of the numerous and extensive interests which it includes, are daily acquiring new strength and stability. To all the members, therefore, of such a community, and most especially to those who are by their own exertions so greatly instrumental in its advance, it peculiarly belongs to concur with zeal in whatever can conduce to objects of such inestimable value: it will be no less your pride than your interest to take your full share in the removal of every obstacle which in the slightest degree embarrasses or impedes the working of this great engine of national prosperity.

"The other consideration to which I adverted is of yet wider scope, and still more extensive importance. States and empires partake of the instability of all human affairs. We know not what revolutions our own free and happy country may in the lapse of ages be destined to experience. But whatever be her future fortunes, one boast she still may make, one wreath she has for ever secured to herself of imperishable glory. In the history of the human mind, and through every successive advance which man has yet to make in valuable and useful knowledge, never will it be forgotten that here the first seeds were sown of that experimental and practical philosophy, to which all subsequent improvements in science must trace back their origin. Neve will it cease to be recorded that here also the first lessons were given, the first great example manifested to the world, of social institutions founded on their true basis of religious and civil liberty.

"Nor is it a small addition to these benefits thus conferred upon mankind, nor will it lightly enhance the gratitude and admiration of posterity, that here also—in this favoured nursery of science, and of liberty, and as the natural consequence, of the joint cultivation and influence of both these inestimable blessings—here were first developed to statesmen and legislators the rights and the advantages of unrestricted trade. Whatever portion of human happiness shall hereafter result, and large, I trust, will that portion be, from the fixed establishment and universal diffusion of these great principles, from the undisturbed freedom of peaceful occupation, from the uncontrolled discretion in the application of each man's industry and capital, and from the open and unfettered intercourse of all the tribes and families of mankind, to Great Britain must all such blessings be referred: here first was it demonstrated that these are fundamental maxims of policy and justice; alike conducive to private happiness, productive of national prosperity, and consonant to all rightful exercise of public legislation.

"Nor is this all. To the glory of the discovery, to the merit of its first promulgation and establishment, we have now added the still higher praise of its general reception, its just and enlightened application. During a long and laborious public service, it has been my happiness repeatedly to concur both in the preparation and in the adoption of detached but considerable experiments, in which these principles were practically and successfully exemplified. But I esteem myself fortunate indeed to have lived to see the time when our sovereign and his parliament have now, first among all the legislatures of the world, sanctioned them by a definitive and solemn recognition. They are no longer unprofitable and barren speculations—the visions of theorists dreaming in their closets of public happiness and public justice never to be realised; they are the rules by which the British legislature has pledged itself from this time forth to administer all the unmeasurable interests committed to its charge; they are the foundations on which is henceforward to be rested the whole commercial prosperity of the greatest commercial empire which the sun has ever yet enlightened.

"I need not recapitulate to those who now hear me what has recently been accomplished in this course, by measures well considered and therefore gradual, but the pledges, I trust, of a systematic and undeviating perseverance in the same wise and benevolent design. When compared with so much more which still remains to be performed, these indeed are but of small extent and limited operation. To judge rightly of their value we must estimate them by the prejudices which were to be surmounted, and by the advantages of which they have already been productive. In those advantages you have yourselves partaken largely, and they have extended themselves to almost every other class of British merchants. And if in the long and honourable career which is still open to the adversaries of commercial restriction, monopoly, and preference, the same spirit shall animate, the same resolution uphold the legislature, if full and uncompromising effect be finally given to a system thus confirmed by experience, thus sanctioned by public applause, not this age, nor this country alone, will have reason to bless our exertions. There is no period so remote, there is no nation so barbarous, in which we may not confidently anticipate that these successful researches of British philosophy, this auspicious example of British policy, will become, under the favour of Providence, a pure and ample source of continually increasing human happiness.

"The deep interest with which I view this prospect, and the glowing hopes which it excites, have led me much farther than I had intended. I will not detain you longer, by explaining what you all feel, the close connexion of these topics with the questions now before you. In such an assembly of British merchants as I now address, deliberating in the centre of this great metropolis of the commerce of the world, can I be deceived in the belief, that an eager and earnest desire will be expressed in your language, and manifested by your conduct, to follow up to the utmost this beneficial and happy system of public policy; carrying into full execution, in so far at least as depends on you, the gracious recommendation from the throne, the wise determination of parliament, for the removal of every restraint by which the native freedom of trade is still unnecessarily, and therefore unjustly, fettered!"

THE HISTORY of MARITIME and INLAND DISCOVERY. (By — COOLEY, Esq.) 3 vols. foolscap 8vo. London, 1830.

A comprehensive and well written sketch of the progress of discovery by sea and land from the earliest ages.

Historical Researches into the Politics, Intercourse, and Trade of the Carthaginians, Ethiopians, and Egyptians. From the German of A. H. L. HEEREN, Professor of History in the University of Gottingen. 2 vols. 8vo. Oxford, 1832.

Historical Researches into the Politics, Intercourse, and Trade of the Principal Nations of Antiquity. From the German of A. H. L. HEEREN, &c. 3 vols. 8vo. Oxford, 1833.

Vol. I. of this work comprises Asiatic Nations, Persians.
II.—Babylonians, Phœnicians, Scythians.
III.—Indians.

Though involving a great variety of elaborate researches respecting the language, religion, policy, and other particulars of the nations referred to in these works, the elucidation of their commerce, and of the modes in which it was carried on, are the objects to which the author appears to have given the greater part of his attention, and in the prosecution of which he is generally allowed to have been most successful. The commerce of the ancient world, especially that carried on previously to the occupation of Egypt by the Greeks and the ascendancy of the Romans, was principally carried on by land: and Heeren has displayed equal sagacity and learning in tracing the circumstances on which this early commerce depended, and which also determined the formation and the routes of the caravans. These are of a more permanent character than might at first, perhaps, be supposed. The greater part of the commerce of Africa continues to be carried on at this day for much the same objects and by nearly the same routes by which it was carried on 3000 years ago; and this also is the case, though in a less degree, with a considerable portion of the internal trade of Asia. The discovery of the route by the Cape of Good Hope and the improvement of navigation have, however, effected the most extraordinary changes in the channels of the commerce carried on between India and Europe, and the ruins of Palmyra, and other ancient emporiums, show at once the powerful influence of the flow and of the ebb of the commercial tide.

HISTOIRE du COMMERCE et de la NAVIGATION des ANCIENS. Par M. HUET, Evêque d'Avranches. 1re éd. 1 vol. 12mo. Paris, 1716; 2de éd. 1 vol. 8vo. Lyon, 1763.

Huet is said to have written this work at the solicitation of Colbert; but, though a useful sketch, it is neither worthy of the subject nor of the learning and celebrity of the author.

ESSAI de l'HISTOIRE du COMMERCE de VENISE. 1 vol. 12mo. Paris, 1729.

Histoire du Commerce et de la Navigation des Egyptiens, sous le Regne des Ptolemees, Ouvrage qui a remporté le prix de l'Académie des Inscriptions et Belles Lettres. 1 vol. 12mo. Paris, 1766.

A valuable dissertation upon one of the most interesting portions of the commercial history of antiquity.

ESSAI sur la MARINE des ANCIENS, et particulièrement sur leurs Vaisseaux de Guerre. Par M. DESLANDES. 1 vol. 12mo. Paris, 1768.

RECHERCHES sur le COMMERCE; ou Idées relatives aux Intérêts des différens Peuples de l'Europe. 2 vol. en 4 part., 8vo. Amsterdam, 1778.

This work is principally occupied with very learned and curious researches respecting the prices of commodities, labour, &c., previously to and after the discovery of America; the variations in the coins of different countries, and such like topics.

HISTOIRE RAISONNÉE du COMMERCE de la RUSSIE. Par M. SCHERER. 2 vol. 8vo. Paris, 1788.

DE la LIGUE HANSEATIQUE, de son Origine, ses Progrès, &c. Par MALLET. 1 vol. 8vo. Genève, 1805.

A rapid and superficial, but useful work. A good account of the constitution and history of the Hanseatic League is given in the third part of the *Art de Vérifier les Dates*, 8vo. ed. vol. viii. pp. 202-312.

TABLEAU CHRONOLOGIQUE et MORAL de l'HISTOIRE UNIVERSELLE du COMMERCE des ANCIENS, &c. Par JULLIEN du RUET. 2 vol. 4to. Paris, 1809.

RECHERCHES sur l'ORIGINE de la BOUSSOLE. Par M. DOM. A. AZUNI. 2de éd. 1 vol. 8vo. Paris, 1809.

The common opinion is that the compass was invented by Flavio Gioia, a citizen of the once famous republic of Amalphi, near the beginning of the fourteenth century. Robertson has adopted this opinion, and regrets that contemporary historians furnish no details of the life of a man to whose genius society is so deeply indebted.—(Hist. of America, vol. i. p. 47, 8vo. ed.) But though Gioia may have made improvements on the compass, he has no claim to be considered as its discoverer. Passages have been produced from writers who flourished more than a century before Gioia, in which the polarity of the needle, when touched by the magnet, is distinctly pointed out. Not only, however, had this singular property been discovered, but also its application to the purposes of navigation, long previously to the fourteenth century. Old French writers have been quoted ('Fabliaux par Legrand,' ii. 26; Macpherson's 'Annals of Commerce,' anno 1200; and the present work of Azuni, p. 135) that seem fully to establish this fact. But whatever doubts may exist with respect to them, cannot affect the passages which Capmany (Questiones Criticas, pp. 73-132) has given from a work of the famous Raymond Lully (De Contemplatione), published in 1272. In one place Lully says, "as the needle, when touched by the magnet, naturally turns to the north" ("sicut acus per naturam vertitur ad septentrionem dum sit tacta a magnete"). This is conclusive as to the author's acquaintance with the polarity of the needle; and the following passage from the same work—"as the nautical needle directs mariners in their navigation" ("sicut acus nautica dirigit marinarios in sua navigatione," &c.)—is no less conclusive as to its being used by sailors in regulating their course. There are no means of ascertaining the mode in which the needle Lully had in view was made use of. It has been sufficiently established (see the authorities already referred to) that it was usual to float the needle, by means of a straw, on the surface of a basin of water; and Azuni supposes, and Capmany contends, that we are indebted to Gioia for the card, and the method now followed of suspending the needle; improvements which have given to the compass all its convenience, and a very large portion of its utility. But this part of Capmany's Dissertation, though equally learned and ingenious, is by no means so satisfactory as the other. It is difficult to conceive how mariners at sea could have availed themselves of a floating needle; but, however this may be, it seems most probable that Gioia improved the construction of the compass; and that, the Amalphitans having been the first to introduce it to general use, he was, with excusable partiality, represented by them, and subsequently regarded by others, as its inventor.

Azuni has conclusively shown, in the work now referred to, that there is no good foundation for the opinions of those learned persons who ascribe the invention of the compass, some to the Chinese, and others to the Arabians.

MEMOIRES pour Servir à l'HISTOIRE de la PIRATERIE. Par M. AZUNI. 1 vol. 8vo. Gènes, 1816.

HISTOIRE du COMMERCE entre le LEVANT et l'EUROPE depuis les CROISADES jusqu'à la Fondation des Colonies d'AMERIQUE. Par M. DEPPING. 2 vol. 8vo. Paris, 1830.

A learned work, honoured with the approbation of the Academy *des Inscriptions et Belles Lettres.*

DELLA DECIMA e delle altre GRAVEZZE, della MONETA, e della MERCATURA de' FLORENTINI sino al Secolo XVI. 4 vol. 4to. Lisbonna e Lucca, 1765–66.

Depping says of this work—"Non seulement on y a inséré beaucoup de renseignemens et de chartes, mais on y a publié les traités précieux de deux marchands Florentins du 14me et du 15me siècles, sur les usages du commerce de leurs temps. Le moyen âge n'a rien fourni d'aussi instructif sur la même matière que ces deux traités, qui exposent le mouvement commercial de toutes les contrées."—Préface à l'Histoire du Commerce du Levant, &c.

STORIA FILOSOFICA e POLITICA delle NAVIGAZIONE, del COMMERCIO, e delle COLONIE degli ANTICHI, nel MAR NEGRO. Di FORMALEONI. 2 vol. 8vo. Venezia, 1788.

This work was translated into French, and published at Venice in 2 vols. 12mo. in the course of the subsequent year.

STORIA del COMMERCIO e della NAVIGAZIONE, dal PRINCIPIO del MUNDO. Da MICHELE di JORIO. 4 vol. 4to. Napoli, 1778.

This work only reaches to the æra of Augustus.

STORIA del COMMERCIO e NAVIGAZIONE dei PISANI. Di Signor LOR. CANTINI. 2 vol. 8vo. Firenze, 1797.

STORIA CIVILE e POLITICA del COMMERCIO de' VENEZIANI. Di Signor C. A. MARIN. 8 vol. 8vo. Venezia, 1798–1800.

This work is unworthy of its title. It contains, indeed, a great many valuable statements; but it is exceedingly prolix; and while unimportant and trivial subjects are frequently discussed at extreme length, many of great interest are either entirely omitted, or are treated in a very brief and unsatisfactory manner. The commercial history of Venice remains to be written; and were it properly executed it would be an invaluable acquisition.

Memorias Historicas sobre la Marina, Comercio, y Artes de la antigua ciudad de Barcelona. Por Don ANTONIO de CAPMANY. 4 vol. 4to. Madrid, 1779–91.

This work, which is a model of its kind, comprises a larger body of important and well-digested information respecting the early commerce and commercial institutions of Barcelona, and the Mediterranean ports generally, than is elsewhere to be found. The first two volumes contain the history of commerce, arts, &c.; the last two being a collection of documents relative thereto.

Exclusive of the above and of the *Costumbres Maritimas* (see p. 127), Capmany is the author of the work entitled *Questiones Criticas sobre varios Puntos de Historia Economica, Politica, y Militar*, 1 vol. 4to. Madrid, 1807.

In this work Capmany has conclusively shown the total fallacy of the still repeated statements respecting the flourishing state of agriculture, manufactures, and commerce in Spain, in the reigns of Ferdinand and Isabella, Charles V., and Philip II. He has also successfully investigated several interesting points in the history of science and civilization, such as the invention of the compass (see p. 152), the introduction of gunpowder and artillery, the ships of the middle ages, &c. We made considerable use of this work in compiling the article Spain, in the 'Geographical Dictionary.'

Antiguedad Maritima de la Republica de Cartago, con el Periplo de su General Hannon. Traducido del Griego è illustrado por Don P. R. CAMPOMANES. 1 vol. small 4to. Madrid, 1756.

One of the best works on the history and trade of Carthage. Dr. Falconer says in the preface to his translation of the voyage of Hanno (8vo. London, 1797), that none of the libraries, to which he had access, including the Bodleian, contained either this work of Campomanes, or its translation into French.

WERDENHAGEN, de REBUS PUBLICIS HANSEATICIS Earumque CONFŒDERATIONE. 1 vol. folio. Francofurti, 1641.

CHAPTER III.

MONEY, BANKS, EXCHANGES, &c.

"Origo emendi vendendique à permutationibus cœpit. Olim enim non ità erat nummus; neque aliud merx, aliud pretium vocabatur; sed unusquisque, secundùm necessitatem temporum ac rerum, utilibus inutilia permutabat, quando plerumque evenit ut quod alteri superest alteri desit. Sed quia non semper, nec facile concurrebat, ut cum tu haberes quod ego desiderarem, invicem haberem quod tu accipere velles, electa materia est, cujus publica et perpetua æstimatio difficultatibus permutationi æqualitate quantitatis subveniret; eaque materia formâ publicâ percussa, usum dominiumque non tam ex substantiâ præbet quàm ex quantitate; nec ultra merx utrumque, sed alterum pretium vocatur."—*Digest.* lib. xiii. tit. I., *de Contr. Empt.* leg. 1.

A Speech made by Sir Robert Cotton before the Lords of His Majesties most Honourable Privy Council touching the Alteration of Coyn. (From *Cottoni Posthuma.*) 8vo. London, 1679.

This speech was originally printed in 1641 (4to.) as the speech of Sir Thomas Rowe at the Council-table, in July 1640, with respect to brass money; but there is not a sentence in the speech that has any reference to any such subject, the whole relating to a project for enfeebling the standard of the coin. It was again printed in 1651, with some additions, as the speech of Sir Robert Cotton at the Council-table, the 2nd of September, 1626: and as it is known that a project for reducing the standard was then entertained, it seems most probable that Sir Robert Cotton was its real author. But, to whichever of these learned persons the honour may belong of making this speech, it is not too much to say that the injustice and impolicy of debasing the standard have never been more successfully demonstrated.

A Discourse of Coin and Coinage, &c. By Rice Vaughan, late of Grayes-Inn, Esq. 1 vol. 12mo. London, 1675.

Republished with a new title-page, as a 2nd ed. in 1696.

It appears from the dedication (to Henry Earl of Clarendon) that this was a posthumous publication, and it is probable it had been written several years before it was printed. It is a valuable treatise, superior to any other that had then been published on the same subject.

Quantulumcunque; or a Tract concerning Money, addressed to the Marquis of Halifax, by Sir William Petty. 4to. (London), 1682. It was republished in 1695, but has been most improperly omitted in the collection of Petty's tracts published at Dublin in 1769.

In this short but interesting tract Petty shows the folly of expecting that any real advantage should result in our trade with foreigners from lowering the value of the coin, and of supposing that a country can be drained of its cash by an unfavourable balance. He also strongly condemns the laws limiting the rate of interest, justly observing that there might as well be laws to limit the rate of exchange or of insurance.

During the greater part of the seventeenth century the silver coins were in a very bad condition, the new and heavy coins issued from the mint having, for the most part, been soon after either exported or melted down, while those which remained in circulation were much degraded and defaced by wear, clipping, rubbing, &c. This arose principally from gold being overvalued as compared with silver, which, by making it for the interest of people to pay their debts in gold, occasioned the melting down and exportation of the silver coins of full weight; and partly from the vitiated state of the great bulk of the silver coins with which the people were acquainted, hindering the few new and standard coins that were met with from exchanging in the market for a greater quantity of goods than the others. But, however occasioned, the degradation of the silver coins attained to a maximum in the early part of the reign of William III.; and very great public inconvenience having been occasioned by the debased state of the coin, its reformation became indispensable.

On this occasion Mr. Lowndes, Secretary to the Treasury, recommended that in order to prevent the future melting and exportation of the coins the mint price of silver should be raised from 5*s*. 2*d*. to 6*s*. 5*d*. an ounce, or that instead of 62*s*. no fewer than 77*s*. should be coined out of the pound troy of silver bullion, being a degradation of the standard to the extent of 24.2 per cent. Happily, however, this project was powerfully opposed by Locke; and the views of the latter being espoused by government, or rather by Mr. Montague (afterwards Lord Halifax), then Chancellor of the Exchequer, the degradation of the standard was averted.

It is true that in no very long time most part of the coins that were issued during the great recoinage in 1696, 1697, and 1698 were either exported or melted down. But that was not a consequence of the standard being adhered to, but of the continued overvaluation of gold as compared with silver, and of the circumstance of no seignorage being charged upon the coin. In consequence of this exemption, coin, though really worth more (from the coinage) than bullion, only passed at the same value as the latter; and was consequently exported the moment the exchange became unfavourable. And it is not a little singular that notwithstanding its obvious defects, this practice should have been persevered in down to 1816. The following are the titles of the principal publications having reference to this recoinage:—

Some Considerations of the Consequences of the Lowering of Interest and Raising the Value of Money, in a Letter to a Member of Parliament. (By John Locke, Esq.) 1 vol. 12mo. London, 1691.

Short Observations on a Printed Paper entitled 'For encouraging the Coining Silver Money in England, and after for Keeping it here.' (By John Locke, Esq.) 12mo. London.

A Report (to the Lords of the Treasury), containing an Essay for the Amendment of the Silver Coins. (By William Lowndes, Esq., Secretary to the Treasury.) 8vo. London, 1695.

Further Considerations concerning Raising the Value of Money, wherein Mr. Lowndes' Arguments for it in his late Report are particularly examined. (By JOHN LOCKE, Esq.) 1 vol. 12mo. London, 1698.

A DISCOURSE concerning COINING the NEW MONEY LIGHTER, in Answer to Mr. LOCKE's 'Considerations about Raising the Value of Money.' By NICHOLAS BARBON, Esq. 12mo. London, 1696.

In this tract Barbon has pointed out sundry errors into which Locke had fallen, and he has the further merit of having demonstrated the fallacy of the then prevalent opinions with respect to the balance of trade, and of having shown that bullion is never sent abroad in payment of an unfavourable balance unless it be at the time the cheapest and most profitable article of export. But although Barbon showed that the circumstances which determine the value of bullion, and which regulate its importation and exportation, differ in no respect from those applicable to other commodities, he contended that the value of coins (or of bullion in the shape of coin), depended on the stamp affixed to them by government; and consequently, that "money will be of as good value to all intents and purposes when it is coined lighter." This gross and unaccountable error destroyed the influence of Barbon's tract; and was most probably the cause of the oblivion into which it very soon fell, and of its never having attracted that attention to which, on other accounts, it was entitled.

DECUS et TUTAMEN; or our New Money as now coined in full Weight and Fineness proved to be for the Honour, Safety, and Advantage of England. 12mo. London, 1696.

This is a valuable and an extremely rare tract. The copy in our possession belonged to the Rev. Rogers Ruding, author of the work on the Coinage.

Previously to 1640 it had been customary for the principal merchants of London, when they happened to have on hand any considerable quantity of cash or bullion, to send it to the mint for safe custody. But in that year the king having seized upon the cash in the mint (about 200,000*l.*), it ceased, of course, to be a place of deposit; and the merchants began soon after to place their money with the goldsmiths, who were generally people of capital, and whose premises were secure and well watched. This led by easy steps to the introduction of the trade of private banking; the merchants soon beginning to send orders to the goldsmiths with whom their money was deposited, to pay their bills when due, and also sending them bills of which they were to receive payment, and to place the produce to their account. For a while the businesses of goldsmiths and bankers continued to be combined; but they were gradually more and more separated, till at length some opulent houses confined themselves entirely to the business of banking, that is, to keeping the money of individuals and paying and receiving their bills; discounting the bills of merchants and others; giving interest on the money deposited in their hands provided it were allowed to lie for a certain period, &c. The goldsmiths and bankers began, also, after the Restoration, to make advances to government in anticipation of the different branches of the revenue and on the security of Treasury Bills, &c. (Anderson and Macpherson, *Annis* 1645, 1664, 1672, &c.)

It may be worth mentioning that the first run upon the bankers took place in 1667; being a consequence of the panic caused by the Dutch fleet entering the Thames, and destroying the ships at Sheerness and Chatham.

This, however, was but a trifling inconvenience compared with what the bankers had soon after to sustain. They had advanced to government in loans, mostly at short dates, on various descriptions of securities, the sum of 1,328,526*l.* at 8 per cent. It could hardly, however, be supposed that a profligate prince like Charles II., destitute alike of honesty and honour, should make any great efforts to provide for the liquidation of the claims of the bankers. But his contempt for his engagements went further than could have been anticipated; and in January, 1672, he took the extreme step of shutting up the exchequer, putting a stop of course to all further payments to the bankers, but declaring, at the same time, that the stoppage should only be for a year, and that the interest on the debt would be punctually paid! It is almost needless to add that no attention was paid to this declaration, and that the debt continued unpaid till, in the reign of William III., the arrears of interest were provided for, and the debt itself funded and made redeemable on paying a moiety of the original sum, or 664,263*l.*! It was long before the bankers recovered from this blow.

Between the Restoration and the establishment of the Bank of England, in 1694, various projects were brought forward for establishing a bank on a large scale. Of these the most patronized was that of Dr. Chamberlen, a celebrated accoucheur, foı the institution of a land bank, but the projects of Mr. John Briscoe and Mr. Robert Murray were not materially different. These persons appear to have entertained the notion, which was also entertained by the famous John Law, that it was enough for the establishment of paper money that it should be issued on adequate security, such as land and other fixed property. But every body is now aware that security is not, by itself, sufficient to maintain the value of notes; that, however secured, they can only be issued in certain quantities; and that to prevent their being issued in excess, it is necessary to make them convertible into gold at the pleasure of the holders. It was fortunate, therefore, that Chamberlen's scheme, though strongly supported, came to nothing.

The BANK OF ENGLAND, which has long been the principal bank of deposit and circulation, not in this country only, but in Europe, was, as stated above, founded in 1694. Its principal projector was Mr. William Paterson, an enterprising Scotch gentleman. Government being at the time much distressed for want of money, partly from the defects and abuses in the system of taxation, and partly from the difficulty of borrowing, because of the supposed instability of the revolutionary establishment, the Bank grew out of a loan of 1,200,000*l.* for the public service. The subscribers, besides receiving *eight* per cent. on the sum advanced as interest, and 4000*l.* a year for the expense of management, in all 100,000*l.* a year, were incorporated into a society denominated the *Governor and Company of the Bank of England;* the charter is dated the 27th of July. And it was enacted in the same year in which the Bank was established, by statute 6 William and Mary, c. 20, that the Bank "shall not deal in any goods, wares, or merchandise (except bullion), or purchase any lands or revenues belonging to the crown, or advance or lend to their Majesties, their heirs or successors, any sum or sums of money by way of loan or anticipation, or any part or parts, branch or branches, fund or funds of the revenue, now granted or belonging, or hereafter to be granted to their Majesties, their heirs and successors, other than such fund or funds, part or parts, branch or branches of the said revenue only, on which a credit of loan is or shall be granted by parliament."

Among the works introductory to and having reference to this subject were:—

THE TRADESMAN'S JEWEL; or, a Safe, Easie, Speedy, and Effectual Means for the Incredible Advancement of Trade, and Multiplication of Riches, &c., by making Bills become current instead of Money. (By W. POTTER.) 4to. London, 1659.

AN EXPEDIENT for TAKING AWAY all IMPOSITIONS, and for RAISING a REVENUE without TAXES, by creating BANKS for the ENCOURAGEMENT of TRADE. By FRANCIS CRADOCKE, Merchant. 4to. London, 1660.

PROPOSALS to the KING and PARLIAMENT; or a Large Model of a Bank, showing how the fund of a Bank may be made without much Charge or any Hazard, that may give out Bills of Credit to a vast Extent, &c. By MATTHEW LEWIS, D.D. 4to. London, 1678.

A SHORT ACCOUNT of the intended BANK of ENGLAND. 4to. London, 1694.

This tract was written by Michael Godfrey, Esq., first Deputy-Governor of the Bank, and one of the most active coadjutors of Paterson in its formation.

A PROPOSAL for a NATIONAL BANK, consisting of Land, or any other valuable Securites or Depositums, &c. By ROBERT MURRAY, *Gent.* 4to. London, 1695.

SEVERAL ASSERTIONS proved in order to create Another Species of Money than Gold. 8vo. London, 1696.

For a remarkable passage in this tract (which was written by John Asgill, Esq., M.P.), having reference to the theory of the Economists, see p. 9.

ANGLIÆ TUTAMEN, or the Safety of England; being an Account of the Banks, Lotteries, Mines, Diving, Draining, Metallic, Salt, Linen, Lifting, and sundry other Engines, and many Pernicious Projects now on foot, tending to the Destruction of Trade and Commerce, and the Impoverishing of this Realm. By a PERSON OF HONOUR. 4to. London, 1695.

This is a curious tract. It shows that the public were then infected with the same mania for all sorts of quackish schemes that attained to such a height in 1722, and, a century later, in 1825.

CONFERENCES on the PUBLIC DEBTS by the WEDNESDAYS CLUB in FRIDAY STREET. (By Mr. WILLIAM PATERSON.) 4to. London, 1695.

This tract gives an account of the proceedings connected with the establishment of the Bank of England.

The accounts of Paterson are obscure and contradictory. He was a native of the parish of Tinwald, in Dumfriesshire, where he first saw the light in 1660; but of his early life and adventures little appears to be known.

Burnet says he was "a man of no education" (Hist. of His Own Times, iii. 217, ed. 1753); but other accounts say he was bred for the church, and he must have been a person of some consideration, having more than once represented Dumfries in the Scotch parliament. He visited, though the reason for his doing so is not clear, the West Indies in the earlier part of his career; and he has been represented as having associated with the buccaneers, and learned from them his habits of daring enterprise (Burnet, *ubi supra*). Of his talents no doubt can be entertained; and not long after founding the Bank of England, he projected the ill-fated colony at Darien (see p. 87). The failure of this project involved Paterson in very heavy losses; but such, according to Anderson, was the opinion of his merits and services entertained by the House of Commons, that they voted him, in 1713, 18,241*l*. 10*s*. 10¾*d*., as a compensation for his losses (Anderson, *anno* 1695). This account corresponds ill with the statements of those who represent Paterson as surviving the Darien scheme for many years, pitied and respected, but totally neglected, by his countrymen.

THE CONSTITUTION of the OFFICE of LAND CREDIT declared in a DEED. By HUGH CHAMBERLEN, M.D., and others. Enrolled in Chancery, A.D. 1696. 12mo. London, 1698.

In 1696, during the great recoinage, the Bank was involved in considerable difficulties, and was even compelled to suspend payment of her notes, which were at a heavy discount. Owing, however, to the judicious conduct of the directors, and the assistance of government, the Bank got over the crisis. But it was at the same time judged expedient, in order to place her in a situation the better to withstand any adverse circumstances that might afterwards occur, to increase her capital from 1,200,000*l*. to 2,201,171*l*. In 1708, the directors undertook to pay off and cancel one million and a half of Exchequer bills they had circulated two years before at 4½ per cent., with the interest on them, amounting in all to 1,775,028*l*.; which increased the permanent debt due by the public to the Bank, including 400,000*l*. then advanced in consideration of the renewal of the charter, to 3,375,028*l*., for which they were allowed 6 per cent. The Bank capital was then also doubled or increased to 4,402,343*l*. But the year 1708 is chiefly memorable, in the history of the Bank, for the act that was then passed, which declared, that during the continuance of the corporation of the Bank of England, "it should not be lawful for any body politic, erected or to be erected, other than the said Governor and Company of the Bank of England, or for any other persons whatsoever, united or to be united in covenants or partnership, exceeding the number of six persons, in that part of Great Britain called England, to borrow, owe, or take up any sum or sums of money on their bills or notes payable on demand, or in any less time than six months from the borrowing thereof."—This proviso, which had a powerful operation on banking in England, is said to have been elicited by the Mine-adventure Company having commenced banking business, and begun to issue notes.

It has been pretty generally imagined, from the private banking companies in the metropolis not issuing notes, that they were legally incapacitated from doing so. But the clause in the act of 1708, which has been the only restriction on the issue of notes, applied generally to all England, and had no peculiar reference to London. The fact that banks with six or fewer partners have not issued notes in the metropolis, as well as in the provinces, is, therefore, ascribable either to their being aware that their notes would obtain no considerable circulation concurrently with those of a great association like the Bank of England, or from their believing that their issue would not be profitable.

Money and Trade Considered, with a Proposal for Supplying the Nation with Money. 8vo. Edinburgh, 1705.

This tract was written by John Law, of Lauriston, the founder of the Mississippi scheme, of which, indeed, it contains the germ. It was reprinted at Glasgow in 1760, in 12mo.

Report by Sir Isaac Newton on the State of the Coinage. 4to. London, 1717.

In pursuance of the recommendation in this Report the value of the guinea was reduced from 21*s*. 6*d*. to 21*s*.; but being still overvalued, as compared with silver, about $1\frac{19}{31}$ per cent., gold continued to be the principal currency of the country, and silver coins of standard weight and purity were either melted down or exported (Liverpool on Coin, p. 85).

An Historical Account of the Establishment, Progress, and State of the Bank of Scotland; and of the Several Attempts that have been made against it, and the Several Interruptions and Inconveniences which the Company has encountered. 4to. Edinburgh, 1728.

This tract was published the year subsequent to the incorporation of the Royal Bank of Scotland; and is chiefly, in fact, occupied with a prejudiced one-sided account of the circumstances that led to the foundation of the latter. Inasmuch, however, as the Bank of Scotland has been of essential service to the part of the empire in which it is established, and has served as a model for the numerous banks since established in Scotland, we may, perhaps, be excused for taking advantage of this opportunity to lay before the reader the following brief notice of its history.

The Bank of England having been projected by a Scotchman (Mr. Paterson), it was but fair that the Bank of Scotland should be projected by an Englishman, and such was the fact, Mr. John Holland,* merchant of London, being its founder. It was established by Act of the Scotch Parliament (Will. III., Parl. 1, § 5) in 1695, by the name of the Governor and Company of the Bank of Scotland. Its original capital was 1,200,000*l*. Scotch, or 100,000*l*. sterling; distributed in shares of 1000*l*. Scotch, or 83*l*. 6*s*. 8*d*. sterling, each. The Act exempted the capital of the bank from all public burdens, and gave it the exclusive privilege of banking in Scotland for twenty-one years. The objects for which the bank was instituted, and its mode of management, were intended to be, and have been, in most respects similar to those of the Bank of England. The responsibility of the shareholders was and is limited to the amount of their shares.

The capital of the bank was increased to 200,000*l*. in 1744; and was enlarged by subsequent Acts of Parliament, the last of which (44 Geo. III., c. 23) was passed in 1804, to 1,500,000*l*., its present amount. Of this sum, 1,000,000*l*. has been paid up. The last mentioned Act directed that all sums relating to the affairs of the bank should henceforth be rated in sterling money, that the former mode of dividing bank-stock by shares should

* It has been repeatedly stated that Paterson, the founder of the Bank of England, was also the founder of the Bank of Scotland. But there is no foundation for any such statement. The fact of the bank being established by Holland is mentioned expressly in the above, and in other contemporary publications, and in the records of the bank.

be discontinued, and that, for the future, it should be transferred in any sums or parcels. On the union of the two kingdoms in 1707, the Bank of Scotland undertook the recoinage, and effected the exchange of the currency in Scotland: it was also the organ of government in the issue of the new silver coinage in 1817.

The Bank of Scotland is the only Scotch bank constituted by Act of Parliament. It began to establish branches in 1696, and issued notes for 1*l.* so early as 1704. The bank also began at a very early period to receive deposits on interest, and to grant credit on cash accounts; a minute of the directors, with respect to the mode of keeping the latter, being dated so far back as 1729. It is, therefore, entitled to the credit of having introduced and established the distinctive principles of the Scotch banking system, which, whatever may be its defects, is probably superior to any other hitherto established. Generally speaking, the Bank of Scotland has always been conducted on sound and liberal principles, and has been productive, both directly and as an example to other banking establishments, of much public advantage.

It may be worth mentioning, that the Act of Will. III., establishing the Bank of Scotland, declared that all foreigners who became partners in the bank, should, by doing so, become, to all intents and purposes, naturalised Scotchmen. After being for a long time forgotten, this clause was taken advantage of in 1818, when several aliens acquired property in the bank in order to secure the benefit of naturalisation. But, after being suspended, the privilege was finally cancelled in 1822.

MONEY ANSWERS ALL THINGS: or an Essay to Make Money sufficiently Plentiful amongst all Ranks of People, and Increase our Foreign and Domestic Trade, &c. By JACOB VANDERLINT. 8vo. London, 1734.

Dugald Stewart has referred to this tract in the appendix to his Life of Adam Smith, and has quoted from it some passages illustrative of the advantages of commercial freedom, which he says "will bear a comparison both, in point of good sense and of liberality, with what was so ably urged by Hume twenty years afterwards in his Essay on the Jealousy of Trade." Vanderlint closes his tract with an argument in favour of the repeal of the existing taxes, and the substitution in their stead of a territorial tax, an idea borrowed from Locke, and subsequently adopted by the Economists.

TABLES of ENGLISH GOLD and SILVER COINS, with their Weights, Intrinsic Values, &c. By MARTIN FOLKES, Esq. 1 vol. 4to. London, 1745.

Mr. Folkes having died in 1754, a new and much improved edition of these valuable Tables, illustrated with numerous plates of coins, edited by Dr. Andrew Gifford, was published in 1 vol. 4to. London, 1763.

AN HISTORICAL ACCOUNT of ENGLISH MONEY, from the Conquest to the Present Time. By S. M. LEAKE, Esq., Clarenceux King at Arms. Second Edition, with great Additions and Improvements. 1 vol. 8vo. London, 1745.

A third edition of this valuable treatise, with some supplementary matter, was published in 8vo. London, 1793.

A Discourse concerning the Currency of the British Plantations in America, especially with regard to their Paper Money. 8vo. Boston, 1740; reprinted at London in 1751.

This essay is especially valuable for the ample information which it gives respecting the paper currency of the American colonies, and also for the soundness of its principles. The causes of the depreciation of paper, and the mischiefs of which it is productive, are set in a very striking light.

An Essay towards an Historical Account of Irish Coins, and of the Currency of Foreign Monies in Ireland; with an Appendix. By James Simon, of Dublin, Merchant, F.R.S. 1 vol. 4to. Dublin, 1749.

Snelling published a short Supplement to this standard work, which is sometimes bound up with it, and is embodied in the edition published at Dublin in 1810. The latter, however, is less valuable than the original edition. A very excellent judge, the Rev. Rogers Ruding, has said that Simon's work is "the most valuable of all the publications on the coinage of any part of the United Empire." (Annals, i. 11. Orig. 4to. ed.)

A Treatise upon Money, Coins, and Exchanges, in regard both to Theory and Practice (principally the latter). By John Hewitt. 1 vol. 8vo. London, 1755.

An Essay on Money and Coins. (By Joseph Harris, Esq., Assay Master of the Mint.) Two Parts. 1 vol. 8vo. London, 1757-58.

This is one of the very best treatises on money and coins that has ever been published. It is clearly and ably written; and, in addition to an exposition of the principles that determine the value of coins and the course of exchange, it contains some good illustrations of the influence of commerce, and of the division of labour in furthering the increase of wealth. Part II. is principally occupied with an examination and refutation of the various statements that have been, from time to time, put forward in vindication of a degradation of the standard. Harris died in 1764.

Reflections on Coin in General, on the Coins of Gold and Silver in Great Britain in particular, on those Metals as Merchandise; and also on Paper passing as money. 4to. London, 1762.

This tract contains, within a brief space, a singularly clear and neat summary of the principles that should be kept in view in the issue of coins. It also shows the cause, arising from the over-valuation of gold as compared with silver, why silver coins of full weight were melted down and exported; and it further shows the advantage of using only one metal, and that the most precious, for the standard of the currency, and of employing paper as a substitute for gold.

Snelling's Works, viz.—

1. A View of the Silver Coin and Coinage of England from the Norman Conquest to the Present Time, with Plates. Folio. London, 1762.

2. A View of the Gold Coin and Coinage of England from Henry III. to the Present Time, with Plates. Folio. London, 1763.

3. A View of the Copper Coin and Coinage of England, with Plates. Folio. London, 1766.

4. The DOCTRINE of GOLD and SILVER COMPUTATIONS, in which is included that of the Price of Money, the Proportion in Value between Gold and Silver, &c. 8vo. London, 1766.

5. A VIEW of the COINS at this Time CURRENT throughout EUROPE, exhibiting the Figures of more than 300 on 25 Copperplates, &c. 8vo. London, 1766.

6. MISCELLANEOUS VIEWS of the COINS Struck by ENGLISH PRINCES in FRANCE, Counterfeit Sterlings, &c., with Plates. Folio. London, 1769.

7. A VIEW of the ORIGIN, NATURE, and USE of JETTONS or COUNTERS, &c., with Plates. Folio. London, 1769.

8. A SUPPLEMENT to Mr. SIMON'S ESSAY on IRISH COINS. (2 plates and 8 pages letterpress.) 4to. London, 1770.

9. A VIEW of the SILVER COIN and COINAGE of SCOTLAND from Alexander I. to the Union of the Two Kingdoms, with Plates. Folio. London, 1774.

This work was published after Snelling's death.

Snelling is one of the most esteemed numismatical writers that this country has produced. His works are all valuable, and indeed indispensable to every good collection. Original copies of some of them have become rather rare, but reprints of these may, for the most part, be easily had. Snelling had a shop in Fleet Street, where he carried on business as a dealer in coins and medals. He died on the 2nd May, 1773.

The CONNEXION of the ROMAN, SAXON, and ENGLISH COINS, deduced from Observations on Saxon Weights and Money. By WILLIAM CLARKE, M.A. 1 vol, 4to. London, 1767.

There is in this work (pp. 54-65) a very good account of the ancient trade of the Black Sea. Mr. Clarke was father to the celebrated traveller, Dr. Clarke.

CONSIDERATIONS on MONEY, BULLION, and FOREIGN EXCHANGE; being an Inquiry into the Present State of the British Coinage. 8vo. London, 1772.

OBSERVATIONS on the Present State (1730) of our GOLD and SILVER COINS. By the late JOHN CONDUIT, Esq., M.P., Master of the Mint; from an Original Manuscript formerly in the possession of the late Dr. Swift. 8vo. London, 1774.

A CRITICAL INQUIRY into the LEGALITY of the Proceedings consequent to the late GOLD ACT. 8vo. London, 1774.

PRECIPITATION and FALL of Messrs. DOUGLAS, HERON, and Co., late Bankers, Ayr. 1 vol. 4to. Edinburgh, 1778.

The bank of Messrs. Douglas, Heron, and Co. commenced business at Ayr in November, 1769, and had branches in Edinburgh and Dumfries. Dr. Smith has shortly but satisfactorily explained the circumstances which occasioned its ruin (Wealth of Nations, p. 137). It suspended payments on the 25th of June, 1772, when, though it had not been three years in operation, and though its paid-up capital amounted to only 128,000*l.* (80 per cent. of 160,000*l.*), it had incurred obligations for no less than 800,000*l.*, viz., 600,000*l.* of debt accumulated in London, and 200,000*l.* of outstanding notes.

The large private fortunes of the partners enabled them, in the end, to discharge all claims upon the bank. The whole loss incurred before its affairs were finally wound up is said to have amounted to about 400,000*l.*

An Essay on Medals; or an Introduction to the Knowledge of Ancient and Modern Coins and Medals, especially those of Greece, Rome, and Britain. By John Pinkerton. 1st ed. 2 vols. 8vo. London, 1784; 3rd and best ed. 2 vols. 8vo. London, 1808.

This work, though deformed by the dogmatism and self-conceit of the author, is one of the most useful publications on the subject of which it treats. Pinkerton is said to have been under considerable obligations in getting up this book to his learned friends Mr. Douce, and Mr. Southgate of the British Museum.

Numismata Scotiae, or a Series of the Scottish Coinage from the Reign of William the Lion to the Union. By Adam de Cardonnel, F.A.S. 1 vol. 4to. Edinburgh, 1786.

Remarks on the Coinage of England from the Earliest to the Present Times, with a View to point out the Causes of the present Scarcity of Silver Coin, &c. By Walter Merrey. 8vo. Nottingham, 1789.

The first great destruction of bank paper occasioned by a contraction of the currency consequent to its previous over-issue, took place in 1792-3. Previously to 1759, the Bank of England did not issue any notes for less than 20*l.*: but having then commenced the issue of 10*l.* notes, her paper was gradually introduced into a wider circle, and the public became more habituated to its employment as money in ordinary transactions. The distress and embarrassment that grew out of the American war proved exceedingly unfavourable to the formation of country banks, or of any establishments requiring unusual credit and confidence. No sooner, however, had peace been concluded than everything assumed a new face. Agriculture, commerce, and especially manufactures, into which Watt and Arkwright's inventions had been lately introduced, immediately began to advance with a rapidity unknown at any former period; so that the public confidence, which had been very much weakened by the disastrous events of the war, was soon fully re-established. The extended transactions of the country required fresh facilities for carrying them on; and in consequence a bank was erected in every market-town, and in almost every village. The prudence, capital, and connexions of the individuals who set up these establishments were but little attended to. The great object of a large class of traders was to obtain discounts; and the bankers of an inferior description were equally anxious to accommodate them. All sorts of paper were thus forced into circulation, and enjoyed nearly the same degree of esteem. The bankers, and those with whom they dealt, had the fullest reliance on each other. None seemed to suspect that there was anything hollow or unsound in the system. Credit of every kind was strained to the utmost; and the available funds at the disposal of the bankers were reduced far below the level which the magnitude of their transactions required to render them secure.

The catastrophe which followed might easily have been foreseen. The currency having become redundant, the exchanges took an unfavourable turn in the early part of 1792; and the Bank of England having been, in consequence, obliged to narrow her issues, a violent revulsion took place in the latter part of 1792 and the beginning of 1793. The failure of one or two great houses excited a panic which proved fatal to myriads more. When this revulsion began, there were about 350 country banks in England and Wales, of which about 100 were compelled to stop payment, and upwards of 50 were totally destroyed, producing by their fall an extent of misery and bankruptcy that had until then been unknown in England.

"In the general distress and dismay," says Macpherson, "every one looked upon his neighbour with caution, if not with suspicion. It was impossible to raise money upon the security of machinery, or shares of canals; for the value of such property seemed to be annihilated in the gloomy apprehension of the sinking state of the country, its commerce, and manufactures: and those who had any money, not knowing where they could place it with safety, kept it unemployed and locked up in their coffers. Amidst the general calamity, the country banks, which multiplied greatly beyond the demand of the country for circulating paper currency, and whose eagerness to push their notes into circulation had laid the foundation of their own misfortunes, were among the greatest sufferers, and, consequently, among the greatest spreaders of distress and ruin among those connected with them; and they were also the chief cause of the drain of cash from the Bank of England, exceeding any demand of the kind for about ten years back. Of these banks above one hundred failed, whereof there were twelve in Yorkshire, seven in Northumberland, seven in Lincolnshire, six in Sussex, five in Lancashire, four in Northamptonshire, four in Somersetshire," &c.*

Attempts have sometimes been made to show that this crisis was not really occasioned by an excess of paper having been forced into circulation, but by the agitation caused by the war then on the eve of breaking out. But there do not seem to be any good grounds for this opinion. The unerring symptoms of an overflow of paper—a fall of the exchange, and an efflux of bullion—exhibited themselves early in 1792, or about twelve months before the breaking out of hostilities. Mr. Chalmers states that none of the great houses that failed during this crisis had sustained any damage from the war.† The efforts of the country bankers to force their paper into circulation occasioned the redundancy of the currency; and it was on them, and the country traders and dealers dependent on them, that the violence of the storm chiefly fell. "And this circumstance is alone sufficient to show, that the cause of our commercial maladies arose at home, without infection from abroad; that it arose from the fulness of peace, without the misfortunes of war."‡

It is of importance to remark, inasmuch as it illustrates some of the principles that have been already, and some that will hereafter be noticed, that antecedently to this crisis the Bank of England had no notes for less than 10*l*., nor the country banks for less than 5*l*. in circulation. The issue of low notes had indeed been expressly forbidden by repeated acts of Parliament; and it was perhaps supposed that this limitation of their value would prevent them from being issued in excess, and driving gold coin from

---

* Annals of Commerce, vol. iv. pp. 266-7.

† Comparative Estimate, &c. p. 226, ed. 1812.

‡ Ibid. p. 228.

circulation. But if such notions were really entertained, the result showed their fallacy. The ease with which supplies of paper were procured from the country bankers, occasioned its employment in an immense number of transactions previously carried on by means of specie; and ultimately occasioned that overflow of the currency and fall of the exchange which led to the crisis.

ADDRESS to the PROPRIETORS of the BANK of ENGLAND. By ALEXANDER ALLARDYCE, Esq., M.P. 4to. London, 1798.

THOUGHTS upon a NEW COINAGE of SILVER, more especially as it relates to the Alteration in the Division of the Pound Troy. By a BANKER. 8vo. London, 1798.

A PROPOSAL for RESTORING the ANCIENT CONSTITUTION of the MINT, so far as relates to the Expense of Coinage, &c. By the Rev. ROGERS RUDING, B.D. (Author of the 'Annals of the Coinage.') 8vo. London, 1799.

Written to recommend the imposition of a seignorage on the coin. But the circumstance of the expense of the coinage being defrayed by the public, though an improvident arrangement, was not, as Mr. Ruding appears to suppose, the principal cause of the scarcity and degraded state of the silver coin: that, as we have already shown, was mainly occasioned by the overvaluation of gold.

We have anticipated, in the view of bringing together the principal works on the coinage, one of the most important epochs in the history of the currency of this country—the suspension of cash payments at the Bank of England in 1797. Owing partly to events connected with the war in which we were then engaged—to loans to the Emperor of Germany—to bills drawn on the Treasury at home by the British agents abroad—and partly, and chiefly, perhaps, to the advances unwillingly made by the Bank to Government, which prevented the directors from having a sufficient control over their issues,—the exchanges became unfavourable in 1795, and in that and the following year large sums in specie were drawn from the Bank. In the latter end of 1796, and beginning of 1797, considerable apprehensions were entertained of invasion, and rumours were propagated of descents having been made on the coast. In consequence of the fears that were thus excited, runs were made on the provincial banks in different parts of the country; and some of them having failed, the panic became general, and extended itself to London. Demands for cash poured in upon the Bank from all quarters; and on Saturday, the 25th of February, 1797, she had only 1,272,000*l*. of cash and bullion in her coffers, with every prospect of a violent run taking place on the following Monday. In this emergency an order in council was issued on Sunday, the 26th, prohibiting the directors from paying their notes in cash until the sense of parliament had been taken on the subject. And after parliament met, and the measure had been much discussed, it was agreed to continue the restriction till six months after the signature of a definitive treaty of peace.

As soon as the order in council prohibiting payments in cash appeared, a meeting of the principal bankers, merchants, traders, &c. of the metropolis, was held at the Mansion House, when a resolution was agreed to, and very numerously signed, pledging, as had been done in 1745, those present to accept, and to use every means in their power to make bank-notes be accepted, as cash in all transactions. This resolution tended to allay the apprehensions that the restriction had excited.

Parliament being sitting at the time, a committee was immediately appointed to examine into the affairs of the Bank; and their report put to rest whatever doubts might have been entertained with respect to the solvency of the establishment, by showing that at the moment when the order in council appeared the Bank was possessed of property to the amount of 15,513,690*l.* after all claims upon her had been deducted.

Much difference of opinion has existed with respect to the policy of the restriction in 1797; but, considering the peculiar circumstances under which it took place, its expediency seems abundantly obvious. The run did not originate in any over-issue of bank-paper, but grew entirely out of political causes. So long as the alarms of invasion continued, it was clear that no bank-paper immediately convertible into gold would remain in circulation. And as the Bank, though possessed of ample funds, was without the means of instantly retiring her notes, she might, but for the interference of Government, have been obliged to stop payment; an event which, had it occurred, must have produced consequences in the last degree fatal to the public interests.

It had been generally supposed, previously to the passing of the Restriction Act, that bank-notes would not circulate unless they were immediately convertible into cash; but the event showed, conformably to principles that have since been fully explained, that this was not really the case. Though the notes of the Bank of England were not, at the passing of the Restriction Act, publicly declared to be legal tender, they were rendered so in practice, by being received as cash in all transactions on account of Government, and of the vast majority of individuals. For the first three years of the restriction their issues were so moderate, that they not only kept on a par with gold, but actually bore a small premium. In the latter part of 1800, however, their quantity was so much increased that they fell to a discount of about 8 per cent. as compared with gold, but they soon after rose nearly to par; and it was not until 1808 that the decline of their value excited any considerable attention.

Few, if any, measures ever occasioned so much discussion in parliament and out of doors as the Restriction Act. We shall enumerate a few of the tracts to which it gave rise.

OBSERVATIONS on the ESTABLISHMENT of the BANK of ENGLAND, and on the PAPER CIRCULATION of the COUNTRY. By Sir FRANCIS BARING, Bart. 8vo. London, 1797.

An able tract in favour of the policy of the restriction. The author, however, clearly perceived that the value of bank-notes could not be maintained, now that the obligation to pay them on demand was done away, unless they were issued in moderate quantities; and he even goes so far as to recommend, in the view of guarding against abuse, and their depreciation from excess, that the *maximum* amount of notes which the Bank should be allowed to issue should be fixed by law at a sum not materially greater than the amount then in circulation. (p. 73.)

A LETTER to the Right Hon. WILLIAM PITT on the INFLUENCE of the STOPPAGE of ISSUES in SPECIE at the BANK of ENGLAND on the Prices of Provisions and other Commodities. By WALTER BOYD, Esq., M.P. 2nd ed. with Notes and a Preface. 8vo. London, 1801.

Mr. Boyd contends in this letter, "that a great increase of bank-notes has taken place since February, 1797; that such an increase could not have happened in the same period, if the Bank had been bound to observe the fundamental principles of its institution, namely, to pay its notes in specie on demand; and that there is the highest probability that the increase of bank-notes is the principal cause of the great rise in the price of commodities and every species of exchangeable value" (p. 7). Sundry answers were made to Mr. Boyd's tract, but of these it is needless to do more than refer to

Observations on the Publication of Walter Boyd, Esq., M.P. By Sir Francis Baring, Bart. 8vo. London, 1801.

Sir Francis Baring contends in this tract that the additions made by the Bank to her issues in the period since the restriction, had not been greater than were required by circumstances; and that it was quite impossible they could have the effects ascribed to them by Mr. Boyd.

An Enquiry into the Nature and Effects of the Paper Credit of Great Britain. By Henry Thornton, Esq., M.P. 1 vol. 8vo. London, 1802.

This work contains a greater amount of practical and useful information with respect to the pecuniary transactions carried on in the country than had ever previously been communicated to the public. Its author having been long a director and also governor of the Bank of England, was placed in the most favourable position for acquiring accurate information respecting the various subjects of which he treats. His position appears, however, to have biassed, though perhaps unconsciously, his judgment; his statements and reasonings having an evident leaning in favour of the Bank, and being intended to vindicate the policy of the restriction on cash payments from the objections of Mr. Boyd and others. But though we agree with Mr. Thornton in thinking that that measure was indispensable at the time when it was passed, he has produced no arguments sufficient to show that it should have been continued after the alarms of invasion (in which the drain on the Bank for gold originated) had subsided; and it is needless to add that he has wholly failed in showing that there is or can be any real security other than their conversion into coin at the pleasure of the holders, for that limitation of the amount of bank-notes which he admits is necessary to sustain their value. Mr. Thornton ascribes the fall of the exchange in 1800 and 1801 to payments abroad on account of the war, and the heavy importations of corn. These circumstances will not, however, account for the rise in the mint price of bullion in these years—a rise which showed conclusively that the currency was depreciated. Mr. Horner wrote an elaborate article upon this book in the first number of the Edinburgh Review. Mr. Thornton was a member of the Bullion Committee in 1810, and contributed a portion of the Report.

The Utility of Country Banks Considered. 8vo. London, 1802.

Thoughts on the Effects of the Bank Restrictions. By Lord King. 1st ed. 8vo. London, 1803. The 2nd edition enlarged, with some Remarks on the Coinage. 8vo. London, 1804.

At the time when this tract was published, the circumstances which determine the value of paper money, though they had been well explained by Adam Smith and others, were not generally understood. The Restriction Act was comparatively recent; and the fall of the exchange and the rise in the mint price of bullion from 1799 downwards had been ascribed by Mr. Thornton and various practical authorities to the influence of deficient harvests, war expenditure, and other circumstances unconnected with the issue of paper. It was, therefore, of great importance with a view to the information of the public and the proper conduct of the Bank of England, that the principles which really determine the value of paper money, and the tests by which its depreciation may be satisfactorily ascertained, should be clearly stated; and this Lord King did in the tract now referred to. He showed by a reference to the exchange with Ireland, where notes had been issued to a much greater excess than in England, that its currency was certainly depreciated as compared with the currency of this country; and he further showed by similar reasoning that the currency of Great Britain was itself depreciated as compared with the precious metals; and that this depreciation was occasioned by its being issued in too great quantities. The tract is written in a temperate, philosophical spirit, without any of that acerbity which marks some of the other performances of its author; and though the doctrines which it expounds have been since frequently stated with greater precision, brevity, and force, and corroborated by a far wider and more conclusive experience, Lord King deserves to be remembered as being one of the ablest as well as earliest of those writers who led the way in the bullion controversy, and the soundness of whose principles was at length fully recognised by the legislature. This tract was reviewed by Mr. Horner in the 2nd volume of the Edinburgh Review, and has been reprinted in the 'Selections' from Lord King's Speeches and Writings published in 8vo. in 1844. His lordship expired on the 4th of June, 1833, in the 58th year of his age.

For several years previously to the restriction on cash payments the exchange between Dublin and London had varied very little from par. But subsequently to that event it became gradually very unfavourable to Dublin, and in January, 1804, it was no less than 10 per cent. against the latter. Under these circumstances a Committee of the House of Commons was appointed to inquire into "the state of Ireland, as to its circulating paper, its specie, and current coin, and the exchange between that part of the United Kingdom and Great Britain." And this Committee having taken evidence agreed to a Report, dated June, 1804, which deserves especial attention, from the striking nature of the facts which it lays before the public, and the able manner in which they are explained and commented upon. The Committee show, by a careful inquiry into the circumstances, that there was nothing in the trade of Ireland to render the exchange unfavourable to her; and they then proceed to trace its fall to its true source, the depreciation of Irish bank paper, occasioned by the excess of its issue by the Bank of Ireland and other banks. In corroboration of this view of the matter, they state that the notes of the Bank of Ireland had increased from between 600,000*l.* and 700,000*l.*, in March, 1797, to the unprecedented amount of 2,986,999*l.* on the 1st of January, 1804! And they go on to show, that by limiting the issue of bank paper in Ireland, or by making it convertible, at the pleasure of the holder, into Bank of England paper, the exchange would be forthwith restored to par. The evidence of Messrs. Colville and Marshall attached to this report is peculiarly valuable.

About the same time that the Report appeared Messrs. Parnell and Foster published the following tracts, in which they take the same view of the matter.

Observations upon the State of Currency in Ireland, and upon the Course of Exchange between Dublin and London. By Henry Parnell, Esq. (afterwards Sir Henry Parnell, Bart.) 8vo. Dublin, 1804.

In this tract Mr. Parnell directs the reader's attention to a fact, established in the clearest manner by the returns laid before the Committee, which is equally striking and conclusive. It appears that while the exchange between London and Dublin, where bank paper only was in circulation, was 10 per cent. against Ireland, the exchange between London and Belfast, which had a metallic currency, was about 3 per cent. in favour of Ireland! And there was, at the same time, an internal exchange between Dublin and Belfast equally in favour of the latter and against the former! Is it possible to imagine anything more decisive of the question?

An Essay on the Principle of Commercial Exchanges, and more particularly of the Exchange between Great Britain and Ireland; with an Inquiry into the Practical Effects of the Bank Restrictions. By JOHN LESLIE FOSTER, Esq. 8vo. London, 1804.

In this very able treatise Mr. Foster gives the earliest explanation of the real nature and influence of absentee expenditure that we have met with.

"Let us suppose the case of a single absentee proprietor, who has an estate in Ireland of the value of 20,000*l.* per annum; his rents must be remitted to him either in gold or in bills of exchange; if they are remitted in gold, an increase of Irish produce must be sent out to recover specie to an equal amount, as indispensable to the circulation of Ireland; and, therefore, may be considered as having been sent out, in the first instance, in discharge of that remittance. The reason that such should be the inevitable consequence of a balance of debt has been already so fully stated that it is unnecessary to repeat it; but the fact is that the remittances to absentees seldom or never are made in specie. This was fully admitted in the evidence taken by the Select Committee. Even in the north of Ireland, where the rents are paid in gold, the gold does not leave the country. The remittances, for a reason which shall be stated hereafter, are made in bills at a course of exchange not sufficiently high to tempt the gold out of the country; but when the remittances are made in bills of exchange, it is so obvious that they are ultimately paid for in Irish produce that it is scarcely necessary to illustrate it; for if the bill of exchange be drawn in Ireland upon London, and bought by the agent in Ireland to be remitted to the proprietor, it has necessarily been drawn in consequence of a demand which the Irish exporting merchant has upon England. If, on the other hand, the bill be drawn by the absentee in London, on his agent or banker in Dublin, it cannot be sold on the Exchange in London unless to some merchant who has imported, or is going to import, commodities from Ireland; or if we suppose, that, for want of a purchaser in London, the bill is remitted to Ireland in the first instance for payment, and that specie is in consequence exported, still that must occasion an exportation of produce to recover specie to an equal amount.

"Perhaps the most correct mode of considering the effect of the absentees in the abstract would be, that, had they continued in Ireland, they would have given birth to a quantity of produce equal in value to their rents, and consumed it in Ireland; but that living in England, they still give birth to an equal amount of Irish produce, but consume it in England. The productions of Irish industry, and the consumption of it, are equal in both cases; but in the latter the produce passes through the Customhouse in its way to the consumer, and therefore falls under observation; but though the quantities produced and consumed in both cases appear to be the same in value, they are certainly different in the nature of the items of which they are composed.

"The Irish produce which would have been consumed in Ireland, had the proprietor remained at home, would have been such as his taste and pleasure should have dictated; but on his emigration they become such as the foreign market shall demand. The consumers also are different; for it is not to be supposed that the absentee spends his income in the purchase of Irish commodities: on the contrary, he spends his Irish rents in the encouragement of English industry; but then he is the cause that others become the consumers of Irish produce of another description, and to an equal amount. The Irish producers are also different. Had the proprietor remained at home, he would have called forth industry probably on his own estate, and in its immediate neighbourhood; but when settled in England, the proprietor of an estate in Munster may perhaps, to a much greater degree, encourage the industry of Ulster. It is he indeed that gives birth to the quantity of produce, but the quality must be decided by the demand of the foreign market. It is this circumstance, perhaps more than any other, which has made the absentee the object of jealousy in Ireland. The traveller who sees the neglected fields and miserable habitations of his tenants, often can trace out, by ditches and hedges, the line of demarcation between the estates of the absentee and the resident; but as he cannot see, so he omits to recollect the circumstance, that the prosperity of the tenants of the resident may possibly be in consequence of the demand for their produce occasioned by the absentee."—pp. 23-26.*

A Treatise on the Coins of the Realm, in a Letter to the King (George III.), by CHARLES EARL of LIVERPOOL. 1 vol. 4to. Oxford, 1805.

In 1798, in consequence of an address of the House of Commons, recommending a new copper coinage, a committee of the Privy Council was appointed to inquire generally into the state of the coins, the constitution of the mint, &c. The first Earl of Liverpool was a member of this committee, and prepared the draft of a report to be laid by them before his Majesty; but though printed, for some reason or other, the report does not appear to have been made, and the draft was subsequently thrown by his lordship into its present form. It is a work of great and deserved authority; and comprises in a reasonable compass a greater amount of information respecting the coins of the kingdom, and a more comprehensive and elaborate exposition of the principles on which the coinage should be conducted, than is perhaps to be met with in any other publication. The present mint regulations, which work extremely well, were adopted in exact conformity with the suggestions offered by Lord Liverpool in this treatise.

The depreciation of bank-notes in England, as indicated by the excess in the market price of gold above its mint price, had been but inconsiderable from 1803 down to 1808, not exceeding from 2½ to 4 per cent. But, in the latter part of 1808 this depreciation began to increase; and the market price of bullion continued to rise, and the exchange to fall throughout 1809 and 1810. Among those whose attention was directed by these circumstances to the state of the currency, the most able and conspicuous was Mr. Ricardo, who then made his *début* as an author, by publishing a series of letters on the subject in the Morning Chronicle, the first of which appeared on the 6th of September, 1809. Having subsequently collected the Letters, and given them a more systematic form, Mr. Ricardo published them in a pamphlet, which appeared early next year, entitled

* We had not seen this work, and consequently were not aware of the existence of this striking passage, when we had the honour to be examined, in 1825, before a Committee of the House of Commons on absentee expenditure.

The High Price of Bullion a Proof of the Depreciation of Bank-Notes. By DAVID RICARDO, Esq. 8vo. London, 1810.

The 4th and best edition of this tract, published in 1811, has an appendix in which Mr. Ricardo has succesfully vindicated some of his statements from objections that had been made to them in the 'Edinburgh Review.'

In this tract Mr. Ricardo showed that redundancy and deficiency of currency are only relative terms; and that so long as the currency of a particular country consists exclusively of gold and silver coins, or of paper immediately convertible into such coins, its value can neither rise above nor fall below the value of the currencies of other countries, by a greater sum than will suffice to defray the expense of importing foreign coin or bullion, if the currency be deficient; or of exporting a portion of the existing supply, if it be redundant. But when a country issues inconvertible paper notes (as was then the case with England) they cannot be exported to other countries in the event of their becoming redundant; and whenever, under such circumstances, the exchange with foreign states is depressed below, or the price of bullion rises above its mint price, more than the cost of sending coin or bullion abroad, it shows conclusively that too much paper has been issued, and that its value is *depreciated from excess.*

An ENQUIRY into the EFFECTS produced on the NATIONAL CURRENCY and RATES of EXCHANGE by the BANK RESTRICTION BILL, explaining the Cause of the High Price of Bullion, &c. By ROBERT MUSHET, of His Majesty's Mint. 8vo. London, 1810.

Though posterior to Mr. Ricardo's Letters, this tract preceded the publication of the Bullion Report. It is sound and able; showing that the currency was depreciated from excess, and that that depreciation was the cause of the high market-price of bullion, and of the fall of the exchange.

The public attention being now fully awake to the subject, and the exchange continuing to fall, Mr. Horner moved in the House of Commons, on the 19th of February, 1810, that a Select Committee be appointed to "Inquire into the Cause of the High Price of Gold Bullion, and to take into Consideration the State of the Circulating Medium and of the Exchanges between Great Britain and Foreign Parts." The motion was agreed to; and the committee, which comprised some of the ablest men in the House, having examined a great number of witnesses, agreed to a report, which being presented to the House on the 8th of June, was soon after published in various forms.

Though not wholly exempt from error, without any pretensions to originality, and not very skilfully put together, the **'Bullion Report'** is nevertheless one of the most valuable papers that has ever proceeded from a committee of the legislature. It was principally written by Mr. Horner, but partly also by Messrs. Huskisson and Thornton, and embodies a comprehensive view of the principles which determine the value of paper money. The committee expressed their conviction, founded on elaborate statements and reasonings, that the paper currency was depreciated from excess; and recommended as the only means by which the evil could be checked, and the value of paper maintained on a par with gold, that cash payments should be resumed within the space of two years. Such being the character and recommendation of the Report, we need not wonder that its publication should have been the signal for a violent and long-continued controversy. The principles laid down in it were said to be contradicted by the evidence; and besides being strenuously opposed by the government, and the greater number of bankers, merchants, and practical men, were assailed by a host of writers. All the great authorities were, however, on the other side; and among these Mr. Ricardo, Mr. Blake, and Mr. Huskisson ably and successfully defended the Report. At length, in 1819, the triumph of the Bullionists, and of sound principles, was completed by the legislature reverting to cash payments at the old standard. We proceed to specify a few of the all but innumerable tracts that followed the publication of the 'Bullion Report.'

Observations on the Principles which regulate the Course of Exchange, and on the Present Depreciated State of the Currency. By WILLIAM BLAKE, Esq., F.R.S. 8vo. London, 1810.

This is one of the very best pamphlets to which the Bullion controversy gave birth. It contains a masterly exposition of a most important but at the same time complex and difficult subject. Mr. Blake has enumerated the various circumstances, whether arising out of the state of trade or of the currency, that determine the "course of exchange;" and has traced with equal skill and sagacity the mode in which they operate, and set their respective and combined influence in the clearest light.

The Question respecting the Depreciation of the Currency Stated and Examined. By WILLIAM HUSKISSON, Esq., M.P. 8vo. London, 1810.

There is nothing new in this tract, the doctrines in it being identical with those of Mr. Ricardo, Mr. Mushet, Mr. Blake, and the Bullion Report. But these have nowhere been stated with greater or perhaps equal clearness, and in a way so likely to recommend them to the public attention.

PRACTICAL OBSERVATIONS on the REPORT of the BULLION COMMITTEE. By CHARLES BOSANQUET, Esq. 8vo. London, 1810.

Many of the facts and conclusions in this pamphlet appear to be completely at variance with those in the Bullion Report; and as Mr. Bosanquet, who was an eminent merchant, represented them as having been deduced from a careful examination of the theoretical notions of the Committee by the test of experiment and observation, they were well fitted to make, and did make, a considerable impression, which however was not destined to be of long duration.

Reply to Mr. Bosanquet's 'Practical Observations on the Report of the Bullion Committee.' By DAVID RICARDO, Esq. 8vo. London, 1811.

This is perhaps the best controversial essay that has ever appeared on any disputed question of Political Economy. In it Mr. Ricardo met Mr. Bosanquet on his own ground, and overthrew him with his own weapons. He examined the proofs which Mr. Bosanquet had brought forward of the pretended discordance between the facts stated in his own pamphlet, which he said were consistent with experience, and the theory laid down in the Bullion Report; and showed that Mr. Bosanquet had either mistaken the cases by which he proposed to try the theory, or that the discrepancy was only apparent, and was entirely a consequence of his inability to apply the theory, and not of anything erroneous or deficient in it. The victory of Mr. Ricardo was perfect and complete; and the elaborate errors and misstatements of Mr. Bosanquet served only, to use the words of Dr. Coppleston, "to illustrate the abilities of the writer who stepped forward to vindicate the truth." (First Letter to the Right Hon. Robert Peel by one of his Constituents, p. 61.)

This tract affords a striking example of the ascendancy which those who possess a knowledge both of principle and practice have over those who are familiar only with the latter; and though the interest of the question which gave rise to it has now subsided, it will always be read with delight by those who are not insensible of the high gratification which all ingenuous minds must feel in observing the ease with which a superior intellect clears away the irrelevant matter with which a question has been designedly embarrassed, reduces false facts to their just value, and traces and exhibits the constant and active operation of the same general principle through all the mazy intricacies of practical detail.

Owing partly to the luxuriant crop of 1813, and partly and chiefly, perhaps, to the opening of the Dutch ports, and the renewed intercourse with the continent, the prices of corn sustained a very heavy fall in the latter part of that year and the beginning of 1814. And the want of confidence and alarm amongst the country bankers and their customers, produced by this fall, occasioned such a destruction of country paper as has seldom been paralleled. In 1814, 1815, and 1816, no fewer than 240 country banks stopped payments, and *eighty-nine* commissions of bankruptcy were issued against these establishments, being at the rate of *one* commission against every *ten and a half* of the total number of country banks in 1813! The failures that then occurred were the more distressing, as they chiefly affected the industrious classes, frequently swallowing up in an instant the fruits of a long life of laborious exertion. Thousands upon thousands, who had, in 1812, considered themselves affluent, found they were destitute of all real property, and sunk, as if by enchantment, and without any fault of their own, into the abyss of poverty! Mr. Horner, the accuracy of whose information will not be disputed, stated, in his place in the House of Commons, that the destruction of country bank paper in 1815 and 1816 had given rise to a universality of wretchedness and misery, which had never been equalled, except perhaps by the breaking up of the Mississippi scheme in France.

Had the country banks been established on solid foundations, or had they possessed capital equal to the extent of their business, the fall of prices which took place in 1813 and 1814 would have done comparatively little injury. Had such been the case, the bankers would have been able to withdraw a portion of their notes from circulation, and to bear any losses that might have been entailed on them by the difficulties in which the agriculturists were so suddenly involved. Unluckily, however, many country bankers had, in their eagerness to get their notes into circulation, left themselves without the means of meeting any emergency. And their fall, by generating suspicions as to the stability of others, had exactly the same effects as were produced by the early failures in 1793. It occasioned a want of confidence and a run upon most of the other banks; so that what would otherwise have been a mere decline in the price of agricultural produce, affecting only the agriculturists and their dependents, was, in consequence of the insecurity of provincial banks, changed into a revulsion that spread bankruptcy over the whole kingdom.

The destruction of country bank paper in 1814, 1815, and 1816, by greatly reducing the total amount of the currency, raised its value, in 1816, almost to a par with gold. And this rise having materially facilitated a return to cash payments, and ample experience having been had of the injurious consequences of fluctuations in the value of money, a conviction began to be very generally entertained of the expediency of terminating the restriction on cash payments at the Bank of England. This was happily effected in 1819, by the act 59 George III. cap. 78, commonly called Peel's Bill, from its having been introduced and carried through the House of Commons by Mr. (now Sir Robert) Peel.

The policy of this act, or rather of that part of it which enacted that cash payments should be resumed at the old standard, has been much questioned. But we are satisfied that it was a wise and politic measure; and that it has not had the injurious consequences attributed to it. The destruction of country bank paper had, as already seen, raised the value of the currency to within about 3 per cent. of the standard; so that the act of 1819 did little more than maintain the currency at the elevation to which it had been raised by accidental circumstances. It had, moreover, been declared by the legislature, that cash payments were to be resumed at the end of the war; and none but the strongest possible reasons would have justified a departure from this pledge, and from the ancient standard of the country. The objectors to the measure contend, indeed, that it has been most injurious: they allege that instead of 3 or 4 per cent., the difference between gold and paper at the time, the measure really added from 25 to 30 per cent. or more to the value of the currency; and they appeal in proof of this extraordinary assertion to the fall that has taken place in the price cf corn, colonial produce, and most other articles since 1819. But it has been shown over and over again, that this statement is wholly fallacious: corn and other articles have fallen in price, not because money rose in value, but because the cost of their production has been diminished by the introduction of improved processes into their manufacture, the abolition of monopolies, and the opening of new and cheaper markets. It is, in fact, impossible to point out a single article that has sunk in price since 1819, the fall of which may not be completely accounted for by circumstances connected with its production or supply, and having no reference whatever to the value of money. If we suppose that the act of 1819 added 5 per cent. to the value of the currency, we shall not be within but beyond the mark.

But admitting that the act of 1819 had some of the mischievous consequences ascribed to it by its opponents, that would add nothing to the plea of those who are now urging its repeal. The restored standard has (1844) been maintained for twenty-five years; and ninety-nine out of every hundred existing contracts have been entered into with reference to it. To set it aside would not be to repair former injustice, if such were committed, but to commit it afresh—to perpetrate an abuse in 1845 for no better reason than the allegation that a similar abuse had been perpetrated in 1819! So long as there is either common sense or common honesty in parliament, we are pretty secure against an attempt of this sort succeeding. Latterly, indeed, the clamours for a reduction of the standard have in a great measure died away.

Proposals for an Economical and Secure Currency, with Observations on the Profits of the Bank of England. By David Ricardo, Esq. 8vo. London, 1816.

In this tract Mr. Ricardo brought forward his ingenious proposal for superseding the use of gold coin by making bank-notes exchangeable for gold bars of the standard purity at the mint price of gold. The object of this proposal was to save the heavy expense of a gold currency, while, by making it immediately convertible into bullion, a security was provided that the value of the paper currency should correspond with that of gold. This plan was acted upon for a short period; and was abandoned principally, we believe, from the facility with which forged or spurious notes for 1*l.* and 2*l.* got into circulation.

Annals of the Coinage of Britain and its Dependencies, from the Earliest Period of Authentic History to the End of the Fiftieth Year of His Majesty King George III. By the Rev. ROGERS RUDING, B.D. 4 vols. 4to. London, 1817.

A 2nd ed. of this elaborate work in 6 vols. 8vo. with a 4to. vol. of plates, bringing down the history to 1818, was published in 1819. Mr. Ruding died in 1820, in his 69th year; and since his death a new edition of the 'Annals' has been published in 3 vols. 4to., with additional notes, tables, and plates, under the superintendence of J. Y. Akerman, Esq.

"This important work, on the compilation of which Mr. Ruding bestowed no ordinary amount of laborious research, contains a chronological history of the monetary affairs of this country, the constitution of the mint, the process of coinage, and the numerous and often ineffectual measures adopted to prevent the deterioration and counterfeiting of money. It also embraces an account, geographically arranged, of all the mints and exchanges formerly existing in various parts of the kingdom; and a description of the coins illustrated by a series of more than 100 plates, including those previously published in the tables of English gold and silver coins, by Martin Folkes, Esq., which were lent by the Society of Antiquaries for the purpose." (Penny Cyclopædia, Art. Ruding, Rogers.)

We have previously seen that Ruding published a tract in 1798, containing a proposal for reverting to the ancient constitution of the mint by charging a seignorage on the coins. He appears, however, both in that pamphlet and in the present work, to have all but wholly overlooked the principal cause of the debased state of the silver coins from the reign of Charles II. down to 1816, which consisted in the employment of a double standard, and in gold being overvalued by our mint regulations as compared with silver. So long as this was the case, it is plain that no silver coins of the standard purity and weight would remain in circulation (see p. 156). But, under the existing mint regulations, adopted in 1816, conformably to the recommendation of Lord Liverpool (see p. 172), this conflicting action has been completely obviated. Silver was then made a merely subsidiary currency, being legal tender to the extent only of 40*s.*, so that it cannot displace or come into competition with gold, which, since that period, has been the only standard in law as it was previously in fact: and silver being also charged, since 1816, with a seignorage of $6\frac{14}{31}$ per cent., nothing is to be gained by melting it down or by its exportation. There has been, contrary to Ruding's anticipations, very little forgery of the coins in circulation since 1816.

REPORTS from and EVIDENCE taken before the COMMITTEES of the HOUSES of LORDS and COMMONS on the Expediency of the BANK of ENGLAND resuming CASH PAYMENTS. Folio, 1819.

ELEMENTARY THOUGHTS on the BULLION QUESTION, the NATIONAL DEBT, the RESOURCES of GREAT BRITAIN, &c. 8vo. Barnstaple, 1820.

"The correct views on the Bullion question, and some other points of the science of Political Economy, are neatly explained in a small work which the author has sent me in print, but which he says he does not mean to publish. I have, however, advised him to publish it in the usual way, and I think he will do so." (Private Letter of Mr. Ricardo.)

A SERIES of TABLES exhibiting the GAIN and LOSS to the FUNDHOLDER arising from the FLUCTUATIONS in the VALUE of the CURRENCY from 1800 to 1821. By ROBERT MUSHET, Esq. 8vo. London, 1826.

The price of corn, which had been very much depressed in 1821 and 1822, rallied in 1823; and this circumstance contributed, along with others peculiar to that period, to promote an extraordinary rage for speculation. The issues of the country banks being in consequence too much extended, the currency became redundant in the autumn of 1824; and the exchanges having been depressed, a drain for gold began to operate upon the Bank of England.* But the directors of the Bank having entered, in the early part of that year, into an engagement with government to pay off such holders of 4 per cent. stock as might dissent from its conversion into a 3½ per cent. stock, they were obliged to advance a considerable sum on this account after the depression of the exchange. This tended to counteract the effect of the drain on the Bank for gold; and, in consequence, the London currency was not very materially diminished till September, 1825. When, however, the continued demand of the public on the Bank for gold had rendered money scarce in the metropolis, the pressure speedily extended to the country. Such of the provincial banks—and they were a numerous class—as had been originally established without sufficient capital, or had conducted their business upon erroneous principles, began to give way the moment they experienced an increased difficulty of obtaining pecuniary accommodations in London. The alarm, once excited, soon became general; confidence and credit were, for a while, almost wholly suspended; and *sauve qui peut* was the universal cry. In the short space of six weeks above seventy banking establishments were destroyed, notwithstanding the very large advances made to them by the Bank of England; and the run upon the Bank, for cash to supply the exigencies of the country banks, was so heavy, that she was well nigh drained of all the coin in her coffers, and was obliged to issue about a million of 1*l.* and 2*l.* notes she happened to have on hand.

In order to guard against a recurrence of the wide-spread mischief and ruin produced by this and the previous bankruptcies of the country banks, it was resolved, in 1826, with consent of the Bank of England, to make a change in the law of 1708 limiting the number of partners in banking establishments to six only. And it was accordingly enacted, that thenceforth any number of partners might form themselves into associations for carrying on the business of banking; but such associations were not to be allowed to issue notes anywhere within sixty-five miles of London. The Bank of England had withdrawn her 1*l.* and 2*l.* notes from circulation soon after 1821; and it was now enacted that the circulation of all local notes for less than 5*l.* should cease, in England and Wales, from 1829. The directors of the Bank of England came, at the same time, to the resolution of establishing branches in some of the principal towns.

These measures were accompanied by the publication of

REPORTS from and EVIDENCE taken before SELECT COMMITTEES

* We endeavoured to show, in an article in the Scotsman newspaper, what would be the probable consequences of this drain; and our anticipations were more than realised.

of the HOUSES of LORDS and COMMONS on PROMISSORY NOTES in SCOTLAND and IRELAND.

CONSIDERATIONS on the STATE of the CURRENCY. By THOMAS TOOKE, Esq., F.R.S. 2nd ed. 8vo. London, 1826.

ELEMENTARY PROPOSITIONS on the CURRENCY. By HENRY DRUMMOND, Esq. 3rd ed. with Additions. 8vo. London, 1826.

An ATTEMPT to EXPLAIN from FACTS the EFFECT of the ISSUES of the BANK of ENGLAND upon its own Interests, Public Credit, and Country Banks. By ROBERT MUSHET, Esq. 8vo. London, 1826.

OBSERVATIONS on PAPER MONEY, BANKING, OVERTRADING, &c. By Sir HENRY PARNELL, Bart., M.P. 8vo. London, 1827.

A PRACTICAL TREATISE on BANKING, containing an Account of the London and Country Banks, the Joint Stock Banks, &c. By JAMES WILLIAM GILBART. 8vo. London, 1827.

An ADDRESS to the PROPRIETORS of BANK STOCK, the London and Country Bankers, and the Public in general, on the AFFAIRS of the BANK of ENGLAND. 8vo. London, 1828.

A Letter to Lord Grenville on the Effect ascribed to the Resumption of Cash Payments on the Value of the Currency. By THOMAS TOOKE, Esq., F.R.S. 8vo. London, 1829.

On the Currency in Connexion with the Corn Trade, and on the Corn Laws, in a Second Letter to LORD GRENVILLE. By THOMAS TOOKE, Esq., F.R.S. 8vo. London, 1829.

Three Lectures on the Cost of Obtaining Money, and on some Effects of Private and Government Paper Money. By N. W. SENIOR, Esq., A.M. 8vo. London, 1830.

The Universal Cambist and Commercial Instructor, being a full and accurate Treatise on the Exchanges, Coins, Weights and Measures of all Trading Nations and their Colonies; with an Account of their Banks, Paper Currencies, &c. By PATRICK KELLY, LL.D. 2nd and best ed., 2 vols. 4to. London, 1831.

The most complete work of its class in the English language. It should, now, however, be thoroughly revised.

Historical Sketch of the Bank of England, with an Examination of the Question as to the Prolongation of the Exclusive Privileges of that Establishment. (By J. R. M'CULLOCH, Esq.) 8vo. London, 1831.

A Plain Statement of the Power of the Bank of England, and of the Use it has made of it; with a Refutation of the Objections made to the Scotch System of Banking, and a Reply to the 'Historical Sketch of the Bank of England.' (By Sir H. PARNELL, Bart., M.P.) 8vo. London, 1832.

LECTURES on the COINAGE of the GREEKS and ROMANS, delivered in the University of Oxford. By EDWARD CARDWELL, D.D. 1 vol. 8vo. Oxford, 1832.

REPORT from the COMMITTEE of SECRECY appointed by the House of Commons to INQUIRE into the EXPEDIENCY of RENEWING the CHARTER of the BANK of ENGLAND, and into the System on which the Banks of Issue in England and Wales are conducted. Folio, 1832.

In pursuance of the recommendation of this committee, the Act 3 and 4 William IV. c. 98, was passed, by which the charter of the Bank of England was prolonged, under certain conditions, till 1855, with a proviso that it might be dissolved on twelve months' notice after the 1st of August, 1845.

The overtrading that took place in 1835 and 1836, and the adverse exchange and heavy drain for bullion on the Bank of England in these years and in the early part of 1837, coupled with the bankruptcy of some of the great joint-stock banks, continued to attract an unusual degree of attention to the currency. And this attention was further kept alive by the renewed drain for bullion in 1839, and by the mercantile distress of 1841 and 1842. It now became obvious to all reflecting persons that the mere convertibility of bank-notes into coin at the pleasure of the holder was no effectual security against overissue; for, though immediately convertible paper cannot be depreciated as compared with gold at home, its overissue depreciates the whole currency gold as well as paper, and occasions a fall of the exchange and a demand upon the Bank for bullion for exportation. It was then also fully established that few or none of the country or joint-stock banks paid any attention to the exchanges in the regulation of their issues, and that the latter were frequently increased when they should have been diminished, and when, in fact, the Bank of England was diminishing her issues. And it was further seen that we had not really gained any security, by the measures adopted in 1826, against a recurrence of the events of 1793 and 1815; that the stipulation that bank-notes should be paid on presentation in gold, was frequently disregarded; and that the establishment of joint-stock banks was wholly ineffectual to protect the public against loss by the fraud or bankruptcy of the issuers of notes.

The HISTORY and PRINCIPLES of BANKING. By J. W. GILBART, Manager of the London and Westminster Bank. 1 vol. 8vo. 1st ed. London, 1834; 2nd and improved ed. London, 1835.

Though partial to joint-stock banks, and not always to be relied on in matters of principle, this and the other publications of Mr. Gilbart noticed below, contain much useful information, presented in a clear, compendious form.

The HISTORY of BANKING in IRELAND. By J. W. GILBART. 1 vol. 8vo. London, 1836.

In the course of this year (1836) we contributed to the 'Edinburgh Review' (vol. lxiii.) an article on 'Joint-Stock Banks and Companies.' Our object in this article was threefold, viz. to trace and exhibit the circumstances in which the spirit of speculation and the multiplication of joint-stock companies by which the period was characterised, had originated; to show the mischievous consequences that would result from adopting a proposal brought forward and strongly recommended by Mr. Clay (now Sir William Clay, Bart.) for limiting the responsibility of partners in banks; and to exhibit the sort of agency by which joint-stock banks were sometimes organised, and the serious public injury that could not fail to arise from the abuse or mismanagement of such associations.

REPORT from the SECRET COMMITTEE of the HOUSE of COMMONS on JOINT-STOCK BANKS, with Minutes of Evidence, Appendix, &c. Folio, 1837.

The Causes and Consequences of the Pressure upon the Money Market, with a Statement of the Action of the Bank of England from the 1st of October, 1833, to the 27th of December, 1836. By J. HORSLEY PALMER, Esq. 8vo. London, 1837.

A very important pamphlet, written by one of the most intelligent and most experienced gentlemen in the direction of the Bank of England. Mr. Palmer had explained in his evidence before the Commons' Committee on the renewal of the Bank charter in 1832, the line of conduct which the Bank pursued in conducting her business as an issuer of money. And this, shortly stated, may be said to have been to endeavour to keep in the Bank's coffers a supply of bullion equal to a third part of her total liabilities, including securities as well as notes; to retain about an equal amount of securities; and to allow the contraction and expansion of the currency to be effected by the public demanding bullion from or carrying it to the Bank. Mr. Palmer's object in the present tract was to show that the Bank had, during the period referred to, adhered to this line of conduct; and that the continued drain upon the Bank for bullion had originated partly in the negotiation of foreign loans, partly in the change then effected in the mint regulations of the United States, and partly and principally in the multiplication of joint-stock banks, and in the increased issues of those establishments, which nullified the contraction of the circulation that would otherwise have been effected by the Bank of England.

Mr. Palmer's pamphlet elicited various replies, of which the ablest and by far the best was that of Mr. Loyd, *argentariorum sui sæculi facile princeps*, who made his first appearance as a writer on currency on this occasion.

Reflections suggested by a Perusal of Mr. J. Horsley Palmer's Pamphlet on the 'Causes and Consequences of the Pressure on the Money Market.' By SAMUEL JONES LOYD, Esq. 8vo. London, 1837.

Mr. Loyd concludes this pamphlet by directing the attention of the public to the following points:—

1. "The propriety of securing, strengthening, and, if possible, extending the monopoly, as regards currency, of the central issuer, with the view of rendering the indirect control which she can exercise over subordinate issuers more powerful and effectual.
2. "The propriety of making some gradual approach towards the separa-

tion of banking functions from the management of currency, with the view of rendering the body which undertakes the latter duty free from all conflicting interests and motives, and at the same time making her responsibility distinct and complete, and the nature of her proceedings simple and easily understood.

3. "The propriety, in the meantime, of a distinct separation in the accounts of the Bank of the management of currency from every other branch of her business, of subjecting the superintendence of this department to a separate Committee of Currency, and of associating with this Committee a representative of the Government, whose presence should always be requisite to constitute this Committee efficient for business.

"The effect of such a regulation would be to check that tendency, which will inevitably exist in every body which combines the functions of banking with the issue of paper-money, to consider the amount of her issues as liable to vary in accordance with her own wants, and to be rendered subservient to her own convenience; thus neglecting, or at least partially suspending, that one great principle, by an exclusive reference to which all paper issues ought to be regulated. The presence of a member of the Government in all the deliberations of this Committee would prevent the Bank in any tendency to abuse her power over the currency for the promotion of her banking purposes, and the Bank would exercise a similar restraint over the Government. Add to this a full and intelligible publication of the proceedings of this Committee, and the public will thus be enabled to exercise a sufficient control over this body, in any case in which it may be conceived that the two parties united can have a common interest in neglecting their duty to the public."

Reply to the Reflections, &c., of Mr. S. Jones Loyd, on the Pamphlet entitled 'Causes and Consequences of the Pressure upon the Money Market.' By J. Horsley Palmer, Esq. 8vo. London, 1837.

A Letter to the Right Hon. Lord Viscount Melbourne, on the Causes of the Recent Derangement in the Money Market and on Bank Reform. By R. Torrens, Esq., F.R.S. (Colonel Torrens.) 8vo. London, 1837.

Further Reflections on the State of the Currency, and the Action of the Bank of England. By S. Jones Loyd, Esq. 8vo. London, 1837.

Thoughts upon the Principles of Banks, and the Wisdom of Legislative Interference. 8vo. London, 1837.

One of the best tracts in opposition to interference with banking.

The History of Banking in America; with an Inquiry how far the Banking Institutions of America are adapted to this Country; and a Review of the Causes of the Recent Pressure on the Money Market. By J. W. Gilbart. 1 vol. 8vo. London, 1837.

The reader will lose little by overlooking the last two heads of this publication.

Remarks on Some Prevalent Errors with respect to Currency and Banking. By G. Warde Norman, Esq. 8vo. London, 1838.

A sound and able tract by a most intelligent director of the Bank of England.

MONEY and its VICISSITUDES in VALUE, as they affect NATIONAL INDUSTRY and PECUNIARY CONTRACTS. By the Author of 'The Rationale of Political Representation,' &c. (SAMUEL BAILEY, Esq., of Sheffield). 1 vol. 8vo. London, 1837.

A DEFENCE of JOINT STOCK BANKS and COUNTRY ISSUES. By the Author of 'Money and its Vicissitudes in Value.' 8vo. London, 1840.

The subject discussed in the first of these works is one of much interest and importance, but we doubt whether Mr. Bailey has thrown much new light upon it. The reasonings in defence of the unrestricted issue of notes by country banks are not distinguished by any peculiar novelty or vigour, and have been refuted over and over again.

Remarks on the Management of the Circulation, and on the Condition and Conduct of the Bank of England, and of the Country Issuers during the year 1839. By SAMUEL JONES LOYD, Esq. 8vo. London, 1840.

The best, perhaps, of Mr. Loyd's tracts.

A Letter to J. B. Smith, Esq., President of the Manchester Chamber of Commerce. By S. J. LOYD, Esq. 8vo. London, 1840.

Effects of the Administration of the Bank of England. A Second Letter to J. B. SMITH, Esq., President of the Manchester Chamber of Commerce. By S. J. LOYD, Esq. 8vo. London, 1840.

Mr. Loyd has done in these tracts for Mr. Smith and the Manchester Chamber of Commerce what Mr. Ricardo did for Mr. Bosanquet.

In consequence of the general attention that had been drawn to the subject, and the differences of opinion that prevailed on some subordinate points, a Select Committee of the House of Commons was appointed in March 1840 to inquire into "The Effects produced on the Circulation of the Country by the various Banking Establishments issuing Notes payable on Demand."

This Committee made two Reports of Evidence, portions of which are very valuable. In his examination Mr. Loyd set the characteristic differences between bank-notes and bills and checks in so clear a point of view that there is but little chance of their being again confounded, even by those least conversant with such subjects.

A Letter to Charles Wood, Esq., M.P., on Money and the Means of Economising the Use of it. By G. W. NORMAN. Esq. 8vo. London, 1840.

The Silver Coins of England Arranged and Described, with Remarks on BRITISH MONEY previous to the Saxon Dynasties (Illustrated with numerous Plates). By EDWARD HAWKINS, F.R.S., &c. 1 vol. 8vo. London, 1841.

The Modern Cambist, forming a Manual of Foreign Exchanges, &c. By WILLIAM TATE. 4th ed. 1 vol. 8vo. London, 1842.

An accurate and very useful work.

LETTERS on CURRENCY. Addressed to the Right Hon. F. T. Baring, by J. W. COWELL, Esq., B.A. 8vo. London, 1843.

The Currency and the Country. By J. G. HUBBARD, Esq. (a Director of the Bank of England). 8vo. London, 1843.

A valuable tract in favour of a single bank of issue.

An Inquiry into the Currency Principle, the Connexion of the Currency with Prices, and the Expediency of a Separation of Issue from Banking. By THOMAS TOOKE, Esq., F.R.S. 8vo. London, 1844.

Decidedly the ablest tract in opposition to the recent measures.

We have now arrived at an important epoch in the history of the currency. On the 6th of May, 1844, Sir Robert Peel brought forward, in the House of Commons, his project for a renewal of the Bank charter, and for effecting some material reforms in the state of the currency and the banking system. An outline of the measures he then proposed is given in the speeches referred to below. They are most important; and though it be impossible to foresee their exact working, yet, in as far as a conjecture may be formed beforehand, it may be pretty confidently presumed that it will be a great improvement on the late system. Sir Robert Peel has adopted the suggestion of Mr. Loyd, for making a complete and entire separation between the banking and issuing departments of the Bank of England. The Bank is to be allowed to issue 14,000,000*l.* of paper upon securities; and whatever additions she may make to this amount can only be made upon the deposit of an equivalent amount of bullion. More frequent and complete returns are also to be published of the amount of bullion in the coffers of the Bank, and of other particulars of her condition. The maximum future circulation of the existing joint-stock and other banks is to be limited to the average amount of their circulation during the twelve weeks preceding the 27th of April, 1844; and such joint-stock banks as may be organised in future are to be subject to the provisions in the late act, the 7th and 8th Victoria, c. 113, for regulating such associations. The names of the partners in joint-stock and other bank associations are to be periodically published.

These regulations will certainly be a powerful check on over-issue and over-trading; and will go far to enforce an immediate and systematic contraction of paper whenever the exchange becomes unfavourable. No doubt, however, they leave some things to be amended. We confess our inability to discover why some restriction should not have been laid on the issue of bank post-bills by the Bank of England as well as on the issue of bank-notes, inasmuch as the former may be, and perhaps will be, substituted for the latter. The new regulations prevent an increase in the amount of the provincial currency, and are, in so far, highly advantageous; but they do not in any degree improve its quality, the public continuing exposed, as formerly, to losses against which they have no means of providing through the bad faith or mismanagement of its issuers. But, considering the circumstances, the wonder is that so much has been accomplished. It may, indeed, be safely affirmed that no measure deeply affecting so many and such powerful interests, and introducing such extensive changes, was ever brought into parliament and carried through it with so little difficulty. This is to be ascribed to the skill with which the measure was prepared, and which reflects the highest credit on the administrative ability of Sir Robert Peel. Had he attempted more, had he suppressed all local issues, or required security for their payment, he would probably have lost or endangered the great advantages he has secured, and which have paved the way for a single bank of issue.

It would be unjust to dismiss this subject without observing how deeply the public is indebted to Sir Robert Peel for his whole conduct with respect to the currency. It may be truly said of him, *monetam in justum valorem restituit.* It was mainly owing to his exertions and his influence that the act of 1819, which restored our old standard, and saved the country from the indelible disgrace of a fraudulent bankruptcy, was carried. He has also steadily opposed the schemes and projects of those who have been clamouring for a change in the mint regulations, and for the contradictory absurdity of a double standard. And he has now gone far to complete the great work he so auspiciously began in 1819, by improving the system of the currency; and providing, in as far as circumstances would admit, against those mutations in the quantity and value of money that have been, and always will be, so extremely injurious.

Speeches of the Right Hon. Sir Robert Peel, Bart., in the House of Commons, May 6th and 20th, 1844, on the Renewal of the Bank Charter, and the State of the Law respecting Currency and Banking. 8vo. London, 1844.

An Inquiry into the Practical Working of the proposed Arrangements for the Renewal of the Charter of the Bank of England, and the Regulation of the Currency, &c. By ROBERT TORRENS, Esq. (Colonel TORRENS), F.R.S. 8vo. London, 1844.

Thoughts on the Separation of the Departments of the Bank of England. By S. J. LOYD, Esq. 8vo. London, 1844.

Mr. Loyd's tracts are all excellent, being admirable alike for the uniform soundness of their doctrines, the perfect acquaintance of the author with the details of the subject, their skilful arrangement, and the graces of their style. Since Ricardo no writer on currency has combined the same wide range of theoretical and of practical information as Mr. Loyd, or has been so able to detect plausible fallacies, and to elicit and illustrate true principles, however obscured by sophistry, prejudice, or interest.

ON the REGULATION of CURRENCIES, and the WORKING of the NEW BANK CHARTER ACT, &c. By JOHN FULLARTON, Esq. 1 vol. 8vo. London, 1844.

The following are amongst the best legal works relating to notes, bills of exchange, &c.

SUMMARY of the LAW of BILLS of EXCHANGE, CASH BILLS, and PROMISSORY NOTES. By Sir JOHN BAYLEY. 5th ed., with considerable additions, by F. BAYLEY, Esq. 1 vol. 8vo. London, 1830.

PRACTICAL TREATISE on BILLS of EXCHANGE, CHECKS on BANKERS, PROMISSORY NOTES, CASH NOTES, &c. By JOSEPH CHITTY, Esq. 9th and best ed. 1 vol. royal 8vo. London, 1840.

TRAITÉ du CONTRAT et des LETTRES de CHANGE. Par M. PARDESSUS. 2 vol. 8vo. Paris, 1809.

FRANCKII (J. C.), INSTITUTIONES JURIS CAMBIALIS. Ed. optima. 1 vol. 8vo. Jenæ, 1751.

HEINECCII (F. G.) ELEMENTA JURIS CAMBIALIS. Ed. optima. 1 vol. 8vo. Nuremberg, 1787.

CONSIDERATIONS on the CURRENCY and BANKING SYSTEM of the UNITED STATES. By ALBERT GALLATIN. 8vo. Philadelphia, 1831.

This is a valuable pamphlet; but a great deal of light has since been thrown on the defects and vices of the American banking system.

A SHORT HISTORY of PAPER-MONEY and BANKING in the UNITED STATES, &c. By WILLIAM M. GOUGE. 1 vol. 8vo. Philadelphia, 1833.

A work which gives a variety of striking and curious details, illustrative of the frauds committed in the getting up and managing of the American banks.

ON CREDIT, CURRENCY, and BANKING. By ELEAZAR LORD. 8vo. New York, 1834.

In so far as respects general principles, the positions in this tract are mostly unexceptionable; but the practical measures suggested are of a very different description.

THE CREDIT SYSTEM of FRANCE, GREAT BRITAIN, and the UNITED STATES. By H. C. CAREY, (author of the work on Political Economy, see p. 19). 8vo. London and Philadelphia, 1838.

ANSWERS to the QUESTIONS, What constitutes Currency? What are the Causes of Unsteadiness of the Currency? and What is the Remedy? By H. C. CAREY. 8vo. Philadelphia and London, 1840.

It is needless to say more of Mr. Carey's lucubrations than that his panacea for the fraud, bankruptcy, and other evils, of which the American system of banking is the prolific source, is neither more nor less than the repeal of all restrictions, of whatever kind, on the formation and management of banks! After this it is not, perhaps, too much to expect that Mr. Carey may favour us with an essay, showing that all restrictions on the issue of coins, weights, and measures should also be repealed. In the mean time, however, we may state that it is completely in the power of the Americans, if they be so disposed, to adopt measures effectual to insure the payment of notes by the issuers, and the equality of their value. And it is some consolation to know that till they do this their banking system will be ten times more injurious to themselves than to those who may deal with them.

BANKS, BANKING, and PAPER CURRENCIES. By R. HILDRETH. 1 vol. 8vo. Boston, 1840.

A feeble apology for the worst parts of the American banking system.

The THEORY of MONEY and BANKS investigated. By GEORGE TUCKER, Professor of Moral Philosophy in the University of Virginia. 1 vol. 8vo. Boston, 1839.

A respectable work; but the proposals of the author, even if they were adopted, would do little, if anything, to obviate the scandalous abuses in the banking system of the United States. He does not propose taking security from the issuers of notes, though it has been shown over and over again that, where private parties and associations are permitted to issue notes, nothing short of this can be of any material service. The various regulations that have been enacted in the United States, ordering banks to have a certain portion of their capital paid up before they commence business, to publish returns of their assets and obligations, to submit their books to the examination of public inspectors, and so forth, have all been found to be in fact worse than worthless. Such regulations cannot be enforced; so that their real effect is, by giving an appearance of credit and respectability to the worst description of banks, to lull suspicion, and facilitate fraud.

But the state-legislatures may compel all banks that issue notes to give full security for their payment. A regulation of this sort may be easily made effectual. And if the Americans have any wish to put down swindling, and to give that solidity and respectability to their banks of which they are at present so entirely destitute, they will make haste to adopt and enforce it.

Traité Historique des Monnoyes de France, avec leurs Figures, depuis le Commencement de la Monarchie jusqu'à Présent. Par M. Le Blanc. 1 vol. 4to. Paris, 1690.

Reprinted at Amsterdam in the same form in 1692, with the addition of a *Dissertation sur quelques Monnoies de Charlemagne, Louis le Débonnaire, Lothaire et ses Successeurs, frappées dans Rome.*

A learned, well-arranged, and valuable work. It refers only to the coins of the kings of France; that portion which related to the coins of the great feudal lords and nobility not having been printed. Le Blanc condemns in no measured terms, and sets in the most striking light, the evils France has suffered from the constant changes in the value of the coin.

"Ces changemens, je l'avoue, sont surprenans, car s'il y a quelque chose dans le monde qui doive être immuable, c'est la monnoye, puisqu'elle est la mesure de tout ce qui entre en commerce parmi les hommes. Quelle confusion n'y aurait-il pas dans un état où l'on changerait fréquemment les poids et les mesures? Sur quel pied et avec quelle assurance pourrait-on traiter les uns avec les autres, et quels peuples voudraient négocier avec des gens qui vivraient dans ce désordre? Cependant cela n'a pas empêché que la monnoye, qui est la plus précieuse et la plus importante des mesures, n'ait changé en France presque aussi souvent de valeur que nos habits sont accoutumés de changer de mode." (p. xvii., ed. Amsterdam.)

Essai sur les Monnoies, ou Réflexions sur le Rapport entre l'Argent et les Denrées. (Par M. DUPRÉ de ST. MAUR.) 1 vol. 4to. Paris, 1746.

This work would, perhaps, have been more properly placed along with works on Prices. It is full of elaborate researches with respect to the value of money at different periods; and contains tables exhibiting the successive variations in the quantity of silver in the coins, and the prices of a great variety of commodities from the early part of the 13th down to near the middle of the 18th century. Dr. Smith has borne testimony to "the diligence and fidelity" with which M. de St. Maur has formed his table of prices. (Wealth of Nations, p. 85.)

RECHERCHES sur la VALEUR des MONNOIES, et sur le PRIX des GRAINS, avant et après le Concile de Francfort (1409). (Par M. DUPRÉ DE ST. MAUR.) 1 vol. 12mo. Paris, 1762.

May be regarded as supplementary to the preceding work.

TRAITÉ des MONNOIES, et de la JURISDICTION de la COUR des MONNOIES, en Forme de Dictionnaire. Par M. ABOT DE BAZINGHEN. 2 vol. 4to. Paris, 1764.

TRAITÉ de la CIRCULATION et du CRÉDIT. (Par M. PINTO.) 1 vol. 8vo. Amsterdam, 1771.

See the Chapter on Revenue and Finance.

De la CAISSE d'ESCOMPTE. Par le Comte de MIRABEAU. Avec le Postscriptum, &c. 1 vol., 8vo. (Paris), 1785.

For an account of the Caisse d'Escompte, see Storch, iv. 151.

De la BANQUE d'ESPAGNE, dite de ST. CHARLES. Par le COMTE de MIRABEAU. 1 vol. 8vo. Paris, 1785.

An energetic remonstrance against the establishment of the bank in question, which had the consequences foretold by Mirabeau.

De la CONSTITUTION MONÉTAIRE, précédé d'OBSERVATIONS sur le RAPPORT du COMITÉ des MONNAIES, et suivi des LOIS MONÉTAIRES, présentée à l'Assemblée Nationale. Par M. MIRABEAU l'Aîné. 8vo. Paris, 1790.

M. Storch has given in the fourth volume of his *Cours d'Economie Politique*, Paris, 1823 (see *ante*, p. 23), an extremely good account of the paper money and of the principal banks of the different continental states. It were much to be wished that some competent hand would continue this account down to the present time.

CONSIDÉRATIONS GÉNÉRALES sur l'EVALUATION des MONNAIES GRECQUES et ROMAINES, et sur la VALEUR de l'OR et de l'ARGENT avant la Découverte de l'AMÉRIQUE. Par M. LETRONNE. 4to. Paris, 1817.

A very learned treatise, in which Letronne examines and endeavours to refute some of the positions laid down by Garnier in his Memoirs on the Value of the Ancient Moneys of Account, afterwards embodied in his *Histoire de la Monnaie*.

HISTOIRE de la MONNAIE depuis les Temps de la plus haute Antiquité jusqu'au Règne de Charlemagne. Par M. le MARQUIS GARNIER. 2 vol. 8vo. Paris, 1819.

M. Garnier has also subjoined some valuable notes in regard to the value of money in antiquity and in the middle ages to his excellent translation of the 'Wealth of Nations.'

MANUEL UNIVERSEL, à l'Usage des NÉGOCIANS; ou, Traité des Monnaies, Poids, et Mesures. Par M. NELKENBRECHER. Traduit de l'Allemand. 1 vol. 8vo. Bruxelles, 1830.

BREVE TRATTATO delle CAUSE che possono far abbondare li REGNE d' ORO e d' ARGENTO dove non sono miniere; coll' Applicazione al REGNO di NAPOLI: diviso in Tre Parti. Di ANTONIO SERRA. 1 vol. 8vo. Napoli, 1613.

This treatise, which had become extremely rare, has been reprinted in the 1st vol. of the *Economisti Italiani.*

This work has been extravagantly eulogised by Galiani in his treatise *Della Moneta* (2da ed. p. 410), and by Pecchio in his *Storia dell' Economia Pubblica* (p. 63). These writers affect to consider Serra as the earliest modern author who entertained sound views of political economy; and Galiani prefers him not merely to Melon but even to Locke! Nothing, however, as it appears to us, can be more entirely unfounded than the claims of Serra to these distinctions. The truth is that there is an incomparably clearer appreciation and analysis of the grand source of wealth in the statement made by Locke, in the Essay on Civil Government, in illustration of the influence of labour in establishing a right of property (see p. 2), than is to be found in all the writings of all the Italian economists from Serra down to those of the present day. Serra, indeed, hardly had a notion of the means by which public wealth is really augmented; and in proof of this it is enough to state that he prefers manufacturing industry to agriculture, because, according to him, a manufacturing nation is more likely to have large quantities of produce to export, and with which to buy and bring home gold and silver! Galiani was a zealous adherent of the mercantile system; and but for this he certainly was (how much soever he might be biassed in favour of his countryman) too clearsighted to have so much as dreamed of putting such a man on a level with Locke. It would not be more absurd to put Mun and Gee on a level with Smith.

Little is known of Serra except that he was a native of Cosenza in Calabria, and that his book was written in prison; but we are ignorant of the reasons for his imprisonment, and of his subsequent history.

DISCORSI e RELAZIONE sulle MONETE del REGNO di NAPOLI. Di GIAN DONATO TURBULO. Napoli, 1616, 1618, &c.

These discourses are partly reprinted in the 1st vol. of the *Economisti Italiani.*

Galiani has formed a much more impartial estimate of Turbolo than of his contemporary Serra: "Fu il Turbolo oscurissimo nel suo stile, e tratto la materia più di maestro di zecca, che da filosofo legislatore; ma non lascio d' inculcare molte verità che o non si vollero intendere, o furono disadattamente, e quasi a rovescio messe in pratica" (Della Moneta, ediz. 2da, p. 409). The Italian writers, and Turbolo among the rest, deserve credit for having opposed all tampering with the currency. The arguments they employ to show the injustice and impolicy of a reduction of the standard, are similar to those made use of by Sir Robert Cotton in his speech before the Privy Council in 1626 (see p. 155). The latter, however, states them with incomparably greater brevity and force.

Della Moneta, Libri Cinque. Di FERDINANDO GALIANI. 1 vol. 4to. 1ma ed. Napoli, 1750; 2da ed. 1780.

This is the best of the many treatises published in Italy on Money. The first edition, which was anonymous, appeared when the reputed author was only about twenty-one years of age, and is certainly a very remarkable performance for so young a person. It has, however, been suspected that Galiani was very largely indebted in the publication of this work to the assistance of his well-informed friends the Abbaté Intieri (see p. 64) and the Marquis Rinuccini; and this suspicion derives strength from the elaborate character of the work, and from its being written in a grave, philosophical style, without any of the vivacity and wit which distinguish the *Dialogues sur le Commerce de Bleds*, and other works of Galiani. But, by whomsoever written, the work is learned and able. Say (Disc. Prélim. Economie Politique) ascribes to Galiani the doctrine afterwards adopted as the groundwork of the 'Wealth of Nations,' that labour is the grand source of wealth. But we have already seen (p. 2) that this doctrine had been most admirably developed by Locke more than half a century previously to the æra of Galiani; and as the latter was well acquainted with Locke's writings, the fair presumption is that he was indebted to him for his knowledge of this fundamental principle, of which, however, he failed to perceive the important consequences. It is singular that so intelligent a writer should have been deeply imbued with some of the worst prejudices of the mercantile system. Indeed he does not hesitate to affirm *che oggi, che il mondo e pieno d' abitatori, uno non può arrichire senza che altri impoverisca* (ed. 1780, p. 291). The economical writings of Galiani occupy 4 vols. of the *Economisti Italiani*.

Galiani was a native of Chieti, in Abruzzo citra, where he was born in 1728. He died at Naples in 1787.

LEGGI e COSTUMI del CAMBIO. Di POMPEO BALDASSERONI. 3 part. 4to. Modena, 1805.

ECKHEL (J. H.), **Doctrina Numorum Veterum.** 8 vol. 4to. Vindobonæ, 1792–98.

A supplement to this work, in 1 vol., was published at Vienna in 1826.

"Ce bel ouvrage, dans lequel l'auteur a embrassé la numismatique toute entière, en a disposé les différentes parties dans le meilleur ordre, les a soumises à la critique la plus savante et la plus ingénieuse, et a dissipé les ténèbres dont plusieurs étaient encore couvertes, a mis le comble à sa gloire littéraire; mais il n'a pas eu le temps d'en jouir: il mourut le 16 mai, 1798, peu de jours après la publication de son dernier volume, et avant que l'opinion des savans, toujours un peu lente à manifester lorsqu'il s'agit de juger des ouvrages aussi solides et aussi profonds que celui d'Eckhel, eût pu justifier dans son esprit cette satisfaction intime qui est le prix, si non le plus brillant, du moins le plus sûr et le plus flatteur des grands travaux littéraires. Tant que les bonnes études et le goût de l'antiquité, de ses écrivains et de ses monumens, seront en honneur, l'ouvrage de la science des médailles sera le flambeau qui éclairera cette vaste région des connaissances. Des découvertes nouvelles pourront compléter et enrichir l'ouvrage d'Eckhel; on pourra remarquer et corriger quelques fautes qui lui sont échappées dans les détails; mais la perfection du plan général, l'étendue des recherches, la justesse de la critique, le choix et la sobriété dans les citations, rendront à jamais ce livre précieux pour ceux qui aiment à s'instruire profondément dans un genre de connaissances si intimement lié à l'histoire, et si propre à exciter une docte curiosité. On ne cessera d'admirer la sage distribution que l'auteur a faite des matières—distribution par laquelle, pour éviter les redites et donner des aperçus plus généraux, il a placé, dans des prolégomènes et dans des traités joints à chaque partie de l'ouvrage, l'examen des questions difficiles et les recherches qui forment l'ensemble de la théorie numismatique. Cette lecture, attachante par l'intérêt du fond, l'est encore par la clarté et les graces du style qui est si coulant et si naturel, que l'ouvrage, pour tout lecteur qui entend le latin, lui semble écrit dans sa langue maternelle." (Biographie Universelle, article de M. Visconti.)

RASCHE (J. C.) **Lexicon Universæ Rei Numariæ Veterum,** præcipue GRÆCORUM ac ROMANORUM, cum OBSERVATIONIBUS ANTIQUARIIS, GEOGRAPHICIS, CHRONOLOGICIS, &c. 12 vol. 8vo. Leipzic, 1785–94.

A supplement to this work, but comprising only the first 9 letters of the alphabet, was published at Leipzic, in 2 vols. 8vo., in 1802 and 1805.

Besides this very elaborate work Rasche published several other works on the coins of the ancients. He officiated for more than forty years as a clergyman in Saxony, and died in 1805, in the 72nd year of his age.

CHAPTER IV.

PRICES.—INFLUENCE OF ENCLOSURES ON PRICES.

Chronicon Preciosum, or an Account of English Gold and Silver Money; the Price of Corn and other Commodities; and of Stipends, Salaries, Wages, Jointures, Portions, Day-Labour, &c., in England, for Six Hundred Years last past. By Bishop FLEETWOOD. 1st ed. 1 vol. 8vo. London, 1707. 2nd and best ed. 1 vol. 8vo. London, 1745.

This work contains the best account of prices published in England previously to that given by Sir F. M. Eden. (See below.)

It appears from the returns obtained under the Population Acts, that the population of England and Wales declined during the first ten years of last century; and that it increased very slowly from 1720 down to 1760. About the latter period, however, the great extension of our trade and industry gave a powerful stimulus to population, which was still further increased after the peace of Paris in 1763. So much was this the case, that nearly 800,000 individuals were added to the population between 1760 and 1770! But agriculture having made no corresponding progress prices began to rise; and the prices of wheat at Eton, which amounted, at an average, to 37*s*. 2¼*d*. per Windsor quarter during the five years ending with 1763, rose, at an average of the next five years, to 54*s*. 10*d*. per ditto, and did not again fall back to their former level. Owing to the want of any authentic information respecting the progress of the population, which, indeed, was then generally supposed to be falling off, it was not a little difficult to give any plausible explanation of the rise of prices. That, however, did not prevent the subject from being elaborately discussed; and a great many tracts were published, the authors of which endeavoured, some with more and some with less success, to explain the circumstances that had occasioned the rise, and how it might best be obviated.

THE CAUSES of the DEARNESS of PROVISIONS Assigned; with effectual Methods of Reducing the Prices of them. Humbly submitted to the Consideration of Parliament. 8vo. Gloucester, 1766.

This tract is usually ascribed to Dr. Tucker, and we are afraid truly. It is imbued with the grossest prejudices, being full of complaints of the "engrossing of farms," "selling by sample," the "iniquities of millers," "forestalling," and such like grievances. One could hardly suppose it possible that such trash should have been indited by the author of the tracts on Naturalization.

REFLECTIONS on the PRESENT HIGH PRICE of PROVISIONS; and the Complaints and Disturbances arising therefrom. 8vo. London, 1766.

The author of this tract says little of the causes of the rise of prices; but contends warmly against all interference with the free competition of the buyers and sellers in the market, and finds great fault with the countenance given by persons in superior stations to the clamour and outrages of the mob.

THOUGHTS on the CAUSES and CONSEQUENCES of the PRESENT HIGH PRICE of PROVISIONS. (By SOAME JENYNS, Esq.) 8vo. London, 1767.

In this very flimsy publication Jenyns contends that the cause of the increased price of corn was to be found in the increased abundance of money; that the former had not become dear, but that the latter had become cheap. Owing most probably to Jenyns having a seat at the Board of Trade his tract had a considerable sale, and excited some attention.

AN ANSWER to the Pamphlet entitled 'Thoughts on the Causes, &c.' 8vo. London, 1768.

An Enquiry into the Causes of the Present High Price of Provisions, in Two Parts. 1 vol. 8vo. London, 1767.

This is, perhaps, the ablest of the many treatises published about this period on the rise of prices. It contains, indeed, not a few principles and conclusions that are quite untenable. But the comprehensiveness of the author's views, and the liberal and philosophical spirit by which the work is pervaded, make it both valuable and interesting. It was written by the Rev. Nathaniel Forster, D.D., rector of All Saints, Colchester, and affords ample evidence of his talent and zeal for the public good.

AN ENQUIRY into the PRICES of WHEAT, MALT, and occasionally of other Provisions; of Land and Cattle, &c., as sold in England from the year 1000 to the year 1765. (By MICHAEL COMBRUNE, Esq., Brewer.) 1 vol. thin folio. London, 1768.

SERIOUS REFLECTIONS on the HIGH PRICE of PROVISIONS, in which is contained a candid Inquiry into the True Causes of the Present Scarcity, &c. 8vo. London, 1768.

AN ESSAY on the CAUSES of the PRESENT HIGH PRICE of PROVISIONS, as connected with Luxury, Currency, Taxes, and the National Debt. 8vo. London, 1773.

This tract was written by the Rev. Mr. Dickson, of Whittingham, author of the work on the Husbandry of the Ancients, see *post*.

An Inquiry into the Connection between the Present Price of Provisions and the Size of Farms; with Remarks on Population, as affected thereby. To which are added, Proposals for preventing future Scarcity. By A FARMER. 8vo. London, 1773.

This is a very remarkable tract. The author shows that the high prices of corn and other articles of provision were not occasioned by the engrossing of farms, the arts of jobbers and regraters, and such like causes, to which they were commonly ascribed; but that they were occasioned by the increased demand arising out of the improved mode of living, the increased number of horses, and (he might have added, as having more influence than all the others) the rapid increase of population. In the view of increasing the supply of corn and other farm produce, he recommends the enclosure, subdivision, and culture of wastes and commons; and he farther recommends that the royal forests should be parcelled out, and partly granted to cottagers, and partly sold to the public. And these things being done, he next proposes, as the most indispensable measure of all, that the perfect freedom of the corn trade should be established by repealing all duties and restrictions whatever, either on exportation or importation. He shows, by comparing prices at home and abroad, that this freedom would be in no degree injurious to the British farmers; that they prefer "a regular certain profit to chance speculative gains;" and that the freedom of the corn trade, by contributing to steady and equalize prices, would give them increased security. The tract is written in a moderate philosophical spirit, without any of the dogmatism and abuse of others, which so frequently disfigure the lucubrations of those who entertain similar views. The concluding chapter gives an account of the corn trade of Amsterdam.

CONSIDERATIONS on the PRESENT EXORBITANT PRICE of PROVISIONS, &c. By FRANCIS MOORE. 8vo. London, 1773.

The great increase in the number of horses was, according to Mr. Moore, the principal cause of the rise of prices; which consequently were to be reduced by imposing such a tax on horses as would discourage their use, and make oxen be employed in their stead in field labour.

The copy of this tract in our possession was once the property of Mr. Isaac Reed, who has inserted in it the following notice:—

"The author is a linendraper in Cheapside. It was he who took it into his foolish head that coaches and waggons might be constructed so as to go without horses as well and as fast as with. After spending great sums of money in experiments, and subjecting himself to much ridicule, he showed a degree of prudence nobody expected from him by abandoning all his ridiculous schemes, and returning to his business."

This was written in 1776; and in little more than half a century thereafter the object which Moore had in vain essayed to effect was satisfactorily accomplished; coaches and waggons being made to travel without horses not only as well as with, but incomparably better!

To whatever other causes the increase of prices might have been ascribed, one could hardly have imagined that the extension of enclosures would have been of the number. Indeed, if there be one thing that has contributed more than another to the vast increase that has taken place in the produce of England since the middle of last century, it has been the enclosure of wastes and the division and enclosure of commons. The reasons why such should be the case are too obvious to require being pointed out. And yet, how unaccountable soever it may now appear, the practice of enclosing is denounced in a great number of the tracts published between 1760 and 1790, as a prominent cause of the rise of prices. It is put forward with much confidence in the next two tracts:—

A POLITICAL ENQUIRY into the CONSEQUENCES of ENCLOSING WASTE LANDS, and the CAUSES of the PRESENT HIGH PRICE of BUTCHERS' MEAT; being the Sentiments of a Society of Farmers in ——shire. 8vo. London, 1785.

CURSORY REMARKS upon ENCLOSURES. By a Country Gentleman. 8vo. London, 1786.

But the unfounded allegations and fallacious reasonings in these pamphlets were completely disposed of by Mr. Howlett in the following conclusive and indeed unanswerable tract:—

Enclosures a Cause of Improved Agriculture, of Plenty and Cheapness of Provisions, of Population, and of both Private and National Wealth; being an Examination of two Pamphlets, &c. By the Rev. JOHN HOWLETT, Vicar of Great Dunmow, Essex. 8vo. London, 1787.

Sir F. M. Eden's 'State of the Poor' was published in 1797. The Appendix to the third volume of this standard work contains by far the most complete and authentic table of prices in the English language. The source whence every fact is taken is distinctly specified, so that it is of the highest authority. There is also an extensive table of prices in the Appendix to Macpherson's 'Annals of Commerce.'

A DETERMINATION of the AVERAGE DEPRESSION of the PRICE of WHEAT in WAR, below that of the preceding PEACE; and of its Readvance in the following, &c. By J. BRAND, C.L., M.A., &c. 8vo. London, 1800.

Written to show that the war was not the cause of the high price of corn in 1800; and that the influence of war is rather to reduce than to raise its price. But this, it is plain, is a matter with respect to which no uniform rule can be laid down, inasmuch as the influence of war over prices wholly depends on the degree in which it may affect the supply of corn and the demand for it; and this can never be appreciated beforehand, and may vary in every possible way.

THE QUESTION of SCARCITY plainly STATED, and REMEDIES CONSIDERED; with Observations on Permanent Measures to keep Wheat at a more regular Price. By ARTHUR YOUNG, Esq., F.R.S. 8vo. London, 1800.

This tract contains various statements respecting the supply and consumption of corn, the deficiency occasioned by the failure in the crop, &c. Little stress can, however, be laid on such statements. It is the besetting sin of statistical inquirers to affect precision and accuracy where there can be neither; and to deceive the public, by giving to their loose and often worthless guesses an arithmetical form.

AN INQUIRY into the RISE of PRICES in EUROPE, during the last Twenty-five Years, compared with that which has taken place in ENGLAND; with Observations on the Effects of High and Low Prices. By ARTHUR YOUNG, Esq., F.R.S. 8vo. London, 1815.

In this tract, which was written in his old age, Young endeavours to show that the rise of prices from 1790 down to 1815 had been about as great in most parts of the Continent as in this country; and that, therefore, it had not been occasioned by anything peculiar to ourselves, such as restrictions on importation and the depreciation of the currency. But the facts before Young were far too few in number, and of too questionable a description, to warrant his drawing any such sweeping conclusions. The price of every article bought and sold in England was in so far raised by the depreciation of the currency; but there were, at the same time, an infinity of other circumstances by which the prices of all commodities were some more and some less affected, and which in certain cases more than countervailed by their depressing influence the depreciation, while in others they added to its effect.

REMARKS on FIAR PRICES and PRODUCE-RENTS. By J. H. MACLEAN, Esq., Advocate. 8vo. Edinburgh, 1825.

We may avail ourselves of this opportunity to state, that by "fiar prices" is meant the prices of the various kinds of grain in the different counties of Scotland, as determined by juries summoned by the sheriffs for the purpose. The juries, which consist of persons experienced in such matters, usually meet in February or March; and having examined witnesses and returns of sales, and taken such other means of informing themselves as they may think necessary, specify in their verdict the average prices of the various descriptions of grain in the county during the previous year: and the sums stipulated to be paid to the proprietors of estates in lieu of produce-rents, and to the clergy in lieu of grain, &c., are determined by the results of these verdicts. They are consequently of very great importance in Scotland; and we incline to think that the introduction of some such method of ascertaining local prices into England would be productive of many advantages. No doubt also the prices of butchers' meat, wool, and such like articles, and of ordinary farm labour, of which there is no authentic record, might be ascertained at the same time and by the same means as the prices of corn, with but little additional trouble. The origin of the "fiars" is not very satisfactorily ascertained; but they appear to have been "struck" so early as the end of the sixteenth or the beginning of the seventeenth century, and have been since regularly continued.

THOUGHTS and DETAILS of the HIGH and LOW PRICES of the Thirty Years from 1793 to 1822. By THOMAS TOOKE, F.R.S. 2nd ed. 1 vol. 8vo. London, 1824.

The History of Prices, and of the State of the Paper Circulation from 1798 to 1837, &c. By THOMAS TOOKE, Esq., F.R.S. 2 vols. 8vo. London, 1838.

A History of Prices, and of the State of the Circulation in 1838 and 1839, &c.; being a Sequel to the foregoing work. By THOMAS TOOKE, Esq., F.R.S. 1 vol. 8vo. London, 1840.

These works (or rather the last two, which include the first) embody a great mass of information with respect to the prices of most articles, and the commercial and pecuniary history of the empire during the lengthened and eventful period of forty-six years, ending with 1839. Mr. Tooke's great experience as a merchant, and his intimate acquaintance with the principles of economical science, have enabled him to disentangle and clear up some very complicated phenomena, and to throw a great deal of light on most of the subjects within the range of his inquiries. We cannot, however, help thinking that he has laid too much stress, in accounting for fluctuations of price, on variations in the supply and in the cost of corn and other articles referred to, and too little on variations in the quantity and value of money, and on the different degrees of facility with which discounts and loans have been obtained at different periods. The influence of the latter has, no doubt, been sometimes very greatly exaggerated; but it is not, therefore, to be neglected or undervalued. But, supposing this criticism to be well founded, the defect detracts only in a very slight degree from the great and substantial merits of the 'History of Prices.' It is a standard work; and is valuable alike to practical and speculative inquirers.

The 'Traité de Métrologie' of Paucton (p. 137), and the 'Essai sur les Monnoies' of Dupré de St. Maur (p. 188), contain, especially the first, very elaborate tables of prices.

CHAPTER V.

ROADS, CANALS, RAILWAYS, &c.

NEXT to the introduction of money, and of weights and measures, the formation of roads and canals, especially the first, gives the greatest facility to commerce, and contributes more powerfully, perhaps, than anything else to the progress of improvement. They have been denominated national veins and arteries; and the latter are not more indispensable to the existence of individuals than improved communications are to a healthy state of the public economy. It were vain to attempt to point out in detail the various advantages derived from the easy means of communication that exist in Great Britain. There is not a single district that is not indebted to others for a large part of its supplies, even of some of the bulkiest commodities. Besides the coal, metals, minerals, timber, corn, &c., conveyed from one part of the empire to another by sea, immense quantities are conveyed from place to place in the interior by roads and canals; and every improvement effected in the means of conveyance has obviously the same effect upon the cost of commodities that have to be conveyed as an improvement in the methods by which they are raised or manufactured. Without our improved roads and canals the great inland manufacturing towns with which England is studded, such as Manchester, Leeds, Birmingham, Sheffield, Bolton, Preston, &c., could not exist. But by their intervention the inhabitants are able to obtain the rude products of the soil and of the mines almost as cheap as if they lived in country villages. There is thus nothing, or next to nothing, to detract from the advantages which the inventive and enterprising artisan may expect to realise from resorting to these great hives of industry; and, owing to the gigantic scale on which all sorts of industry are conducted in them, the scope afforded for the employment of the most powerful machines, and the appropriation of particular sets of workmen to every separate process, however minute, manufacturing industry is carried to a degree of perfection that almost exceeds belief.

The system of making and repairing roads by contributions of forced labour appears to have formerly extended itself all over Europe. In England it was made the subject of legislative enactment in the reign of Philip and Mary; and from that epoch down to the latter part of the seventeenth century, highways of all kinds were constructed and kept in repair by annual assessments of six days' compulsory labour of the inhabitants. It is needless to dwell on the obvious inexpediency of such a system. But the practice of constructing tolls on the great roads, the produce of which was to be expended on their repair, did not commence till the reign of Charles II., and was not carried to any very considerable extent till so late as 1767. It was then applied to the great roads to all parts of the country, the contributions of compulsory labour being thenceforth appropriated to the cross or country roads; and it is a curious fact that these contributions continued to be rendered in England down to 1835, when they were commuted for an equivalent county-rate, whereas in Scotland they were commuted early in the reign of George III.

It may be worth mentioning that when the plan for extending turnpike roads from the metropolis to distant parts of the country was in agitation, the counties in the neighbourhood of London petitioned Parliament against it, alleging that the remoter counties would be able, from the comparative cheapness of labour in them, to sell their produce in London at a lower rate than they could do; and that their rents would be reduced, and cultivation ruined, by the measure! Luckily this selfish and short-sighted opposition proved ineffectual; and instead of being injurious to the counties adjoining the metropolis, the improvement of the roads has been quite as beneficial to them as to those at a distance, inasmuch as, by providing for the indefinite extension of the city, it has rendered it a far better market for their peculiar productions than it would have been had its growth been checked, which must have been the case long ago had the improvements in question not been made.

CONSIDERATIONS on ROADS. 8vo. London, 1734.

DISSERTATION concerning the HIGH ROADS. By — PHILIPS. 8vo. London, 1737.

OBSERVATIONS on the STATE of the HIGHWAYS, and on the Laws for Amending and keeping them in Repair. By JOHN HAWKINS. 8vo. London, 1763.

CONSIDERATIONS on the ACTS of PARLIAMENT relative to HIGHWAYS in SCOTLAND, and on the New Scheme of a Tax in lieu of Statute Labour. 8vo. Edinburgh, 1764.

An ESSAY on the NATURE and METHOD of ascertaining the SPECIFIC SHARES of PROPRIETORS upon the INCLOSURE of COMMON FIELDS, with an INQUIRY into the means of PRESERVING and IMPROVING the PUBLIC ROADS of this KINGDOM. (By the Rev. HENRY HOMER.) 8vo. London, 1767.

REPORT from the SELECT COMMITTEE of the HOUSE of COMMONS appointed to Inquire into the Acts now in force regarding the Highways in England and Wales, &c. Folio, 1810-11.

An Essay on the Construction of Roads and Carriages. By R. L. EDGWORTH, Esq. 1 vol., 8vo. London, 1812.

Observations on Roads. By J. L. M'ADAM, Esq. 8vo. London, 1822.

The publication of this work, though it be in various respects erroneous, effected a salutary revolution in the system of road-making, by establishing the superior advantages, in respect of durability, smoothness, and consequent lightness of draught, of roads covered with a layer of stones broken into small pieces, without any admixture of sand, clay, gravel, or other material. This practice had been followed for a lengthened period in the construction of roads in Switzerland, Sweden, and some other countries, but M'Adam was the first by whom it was introduced into England. Roads covered in this way are said to be *macadamized*. But to have a really good and lasting road it is not only necessary that the surface should be formed in the way recommended by M'Adam, but it is farther necessary that a dry and sound foundation should be provided for the upper stratum, and that the surface of the road should be regularly convex. By undervaluing the importance of these indispensable conditions, M'Adam showed he had no very intimate knowledge of the principles of the art of which he so greatly improved the practice.

REPORTS of the SELECT COMMITTEES of the HOUSE of COMMONS of 1819 and 1823, on the Highways of the Kingdom.

A Treatise on Roads, wherein the Principles on which they should be made are explained and illustrated. By the Right Hon. Sir HENRY PARNELL, Bart. 2nd ed., 1 vol., 8vo. London, 1838.

This is the best and most complete treatise on the subject. Sir Henry Parnell was the intimate friend of Telford, the celebrated engineer; and the principles and recommendations embodied in this work were those acted upon by Telford in the construction of the great road from London to Holyhead, generally allowed to be one of the most perfect works of its kind.

Owing partly to the late rise of extensive manufactures and commerce in Great Britain, but more perhaps to the insular situation of the country, no part of which is very distant from the sea, or from a navigable river, no attempt was made in England to construct canals till a comparatively recent period. The efforts of those who first began to improve the means of internal navigation were limited to attempts to deepen the beds of rivers, and to render them better fitted for the conveyance of vessels. So early as 1635 a Mr. Sandys of Flatbury, Worcestershire, formed a project for rendering the Avon navigable from the Severn, near Tewkesbury, through the counties of Warwick, Worcester, and Gloucester, "that the towns and country might be better supplied with wood, iron, pit-coal, and other commodities." This scheme was approved by the principal nobility and landowners in the counties referred to; but the civil war having broken out soon after, the project was abandoned, and does not seem to have been revived. After the Restoration, and during the earlier part of last century, various acts were at different times obtained for cheapening and improving river navigation. For the most part, however, these attempts were not very successful. The current of the rivers gradually changed the form of their channels; the dykes and other artificial constructions were apt to be destroyed by inundations; alluvial sand-banks were formed below the weirs; in summer, the channels were frequently too dry to admit of being navigated, while at other periods the current was so strong as to render it quite impossible to ascend the river, which at all times indeed was a laborious and expensive undertaking. These difficulties in the way of river navigation seem to have suggested the expediency of abandoning the channels of most rivers, and of digging parallel to them artificial channels, in which the water might be kept at the proper level by means of locks. The Act passed by the legislature in 1755, for improving the navigation of Sankey Brook on the Mersey, gave rise to a lateral canal of this description, about 11¼ miles in length, which deserves to be mentioned as the earliest effort of the sort in England.

But before this canal had been completed, the celebrated Duke of Bridgewater,* and his equally celebrated engineer, the self-instructed James

* This truly noble person expended a princely fortune in the prosecution of his great designs; and, to increase his resources, is said to have restricted his

Brindley, had conceived a plan for the formation of canals independent altogether of natural channels, and intended to afford the greatest facilities to commerce, by carrying them across rivers and through mountains, wherever their construction was practicable.*

The Duke was proprietor of a large estate at Worsley, 7 miles from Manchester, in which were some very rich coal-mines, that had hitherto been in a great measure useless, owing to the cost of carrying coal to market. Being desirous of turning his mines to some account, it occurred to his Grace that his purpose would be best accomplished by cutting a canal from Worsley to Manchester. Mr. Brindley, having been consulted, declared that the scheme was practicable; and an Act having been obtained, the work was immediately commenced. "The principle," says Mr. Phillips, "laid down at the commencement of this business reflects as much honour on the noble undertaker as it does upon his engineer. It was resolved that the canal should be perfect in its kind; and that, in order to preserve the level of the water, it should be free from the usual construction of locks. But in accomplishing this end many difficulties were deemed insurmountable. It was necessary that the canal should be carried over rivers, and many large and deep valleys, where it was evident that such stupendous mounds of earth must be raised as would scarcely, it was thought by numbers, be completed by the labour of ages; and, above all, it was not known from what source so large a supply of water could be drawn, even on this improved plan, as would supply the navigation. But Mr. Brindley, with a strength of mind peculiar to himself, and being possessed of the confidence of his great patron, contrived such admirable machines, and took such methods to facilitate the progress of the work, that the world soon began to wonder how it could be thought so difficult."

Before the canal from Worsley to Manchester had been completed, it occurred to the Duke and his engineer that it might be practicable to extend it by a branch, which, running through Chester parallel to the Mersey, should at length terminate in that river, below the limits of its artificial navigation; and thus afford a new, safer, and cheaper means of communication between Manchester and its vicinity and Liverpool. The execution of this plan was authorised by an Act passed in 1761. This canal, which is above 29 miles in length, was finished in about five years. It was constructed in the best manner, and has proved equally advantageous to its noble proprietor and the public.

"When the Duke of Bridgewater," says Dr. Aikin, "undertook this great design, the price of carriage on the river navigation was 12*s.* the ton from Manchester to Liverpool, while that of land-carriage was 40*s.* the ton. The Duke's charge on his canal was limited, by statute, to *six* shillings; and together with this vast superiority in cheapness, it had all the speed and regularity of land-carriage. The articles conveyed by it were likewise much more numerous than those by the river navigation. Besides manufactured goods and their raw materials, coals from the Duke's own pits were deposited in yards at various parts of the canal for the supply of Cheshire; lime,

---

own personal expenses to 400*l.* a year! But his projects were productive of great wealth to himself and his successors; and have promoted, in no ordinary degree, the wealth and prosperity of his country. He died in 1823. There is a very able and interesting notice of the Duke of Bridgewater in the Number of the 'Quarterly Review' for March, 1844.

* There is a good account of Brindley in Aikin's 'Biographical Dictionary.' His intense application, and the anxiety of mind inseparable from the great enterprises in which he was engaged, terminated his valuable life at the early age of 56.

manure, and building materials, were carried from place to place; and the markets of Manchester obtained a supply of provisions from districts too remote for the ordinary land conveyances. A branch of useful and profitable carriage, hitherto scarcely known in England, was also undertaken, which was that of passengers. Boats, on the model of the Dutch treckschuyts, but more agreeable and capacious, were set up, which, at very reasonable rates, and with great convenience, carried numbers of persons daily to and from Manchester along the line of the canal."—(Aikin's 'Description of the Country round Manchester,' p. 116.)

The success that attended the Duke of Bridgewater's canals stimulated public-spirited individuals in other districts to undertake similar works. Mr. Brindley had early formed the magnificent scheme of joining the great ports of London, Liverpool, Bristol, and Hull, by a system of internal navigation: and, though he died in 1772, at the early age of fifty-six, he had the satisfaction to see his grand project in a fair way of being realised, and it was not long after fully completed. Indeed, with the exception of Holland, England has long had a more extensive command of artificial navigation than any other country; and no small portion of the wonderful progress she has made since 1770 in manufacturing industry may be ascribed to this circumstance. Scotland and Ireland have also been intersected by canals; and it may be doubted whether any great example has ever been more vigorously and successfully followed up than that of the Duke of Bridgewater.

The History of Inland Navigations, particularly those of the Duke of Bridgewater, showing their Utility and Importance. 8vo. London, 1766.

An interesting tract written during the progress of the Duke's works.

A General History of Inland Navigation, Foreign and Domestic. By John Phillips. 1 vol., 4to. London, 1792.

The fourth edition of a useful and well-executed abridgment of this work, bringing down the information to the date of its publication, was published in 1 vol. 8vo. London, 1804.

The Political Economy of Inland Navigation, Irrigation, and Drainage. By William Tatham. 1 vol., 4to. London, 1799.

Historical Account of the Navigable Rivers, Canals, and Railways throughout Great Britain. By Joseph Priestley, Esq. 1 vol., 4to. London, 1831.

This valuable work is accompanied by a large, well engraved, and accurate map of the canals, railways, &c., of Great Britain.

But vast as have been the advantages derived from the formation of improved roads and canals, they are now in some measure thrown into the shade, and appear to be inferior to those that have been and, most likely, will be derived from the construction of railways traversed by locomotive engines. The effect of railroads in diminishing friction is familiar to every one; and they have long been used in various parts of this and other countries, particularly in the vicinity of mines, for facilitating the transport of heavy loads. But it is only since the application of locomotive engines as a moving power, that they began powerfully to attract the public attention, and that their value has been fully appreciated. These engines were first brought into use on the Darlington and Stockton railway, opened on the 27th of December, 1825; but it was not till the opening of the railway between Manchester and Liverpool that the vast importance of this novel means of intercourse was fully perceived. This splendid work, though now far surpassed in magnitude by other railroads, cost nearly a million sterling. It has the advantage of being nearly level; for, with the exception of a short distance at Rainhill, where it is inclined at the rate of 1 foot in 96, there is no greater inclination than in the ratio of 1 foot in 880. The length of the railway is about 31 miles; and it was usual from its opening to perform this journey in handsome carriages attached to the locomotive engines in one hour and a half, or less! So far, indeed, as respects the facility of passing from the one to the other, this railway has brought Manchester and Liverpool as near to each other as the western part of London is to the eastern part!

The opening of this railway having more than verified the most sanguine anticipations as to the success of such undertakings, and gone far, in fact, to strike time and space out of the calculations of the traveller, gave an extraordinary stimulus to similar undertakings in all parts of the country; and there are now hardly any two considerable places in Great Britain, how distant soever, which have not already been connected, or which it is proposed to connect by railways. An immense number of companies have been formed, and a very large amount of capital subscribed, for carrying on these undertakings; and though, as was to be anticipated, some of them appear to have been commenced or projected without due consideration, and hold out very indifferent prospects to the subscribers, there can be no doubt that the country will profit very largely by the railway system, the facility of intercourse having been prodigiously extended, at the same time that the greater number of the principal lines of road have proved, in a pecuniary point of view, exceedingly beneficial to the parties engaged in them.

A Statement of the Claim of the Subscribers to the Birmingham and Liverpool Railroad to an Act of Parliament. By Joseph Parkes (Parliamentary Solicitor). 8vo. London, 1825.

A very interesting tract, containing various details illustrative of the rapid growth of manufactures and of the internal trade of the country.

Among the greater lines of railway now (1844) existing, may be specified that from London to Manchester and Liverpool, which has been already extended to Lancaster, and will certainly, at no distant period, be farther prolonged to Carlisle and Glasgow; but, taking it as it now stands, it is one of the greatest public works ever executed in any country, and is a striking result of the wealth, science, and civilisation of modern times. The railway from London to Bath, Bristol, and the south-western counties is also a magnificent work, and is, in some respects, superior to any other in the kingdom. Among the other leading railways may be specified those from London to Southampton, Brighton, and Dover; the Eastern Counties, Midland, North Midland, and North of England railways; and those from Carlisle to Newcastle, from Edinburgh to Glasgow and Ayr, with a host of others.

But, notwithstanding the vast advantages which the opening of so many new and improved lines of communication by canals and railways has conferred on the country, we cannot help thinking that these advantages might have been greater, and that in the instance of railway legislation, the public interests have been overlooked to a degree that is not very excusable. It is, we admit, no easy matter to decide how far the interference of government should be carried in matters of this sort. But, at all events, this much is obvious, that when parliament is called upon to pass an act authorising private parties to execute a railway or other public work, it is bound to provide, in as far as practicable, that the public interests shall not be prejudiced by such act, and that it should be framed so that it should not, either when passed, or at any future period, stand in the way of the public advantage. We believe, however, that a little consideration will serve to satisfy most persons that this important principle has, in the case of railways, and indeed of most descriptions of public works, been, in this country, until very recently, all but wholly neglected. We have remarked upon this subject in the 'Commercial Dictionary' as follows:—

"The practice is for a railway act to authorise the company in whose favour it is granted, to appropriate a certain line of road, and to charge certain specified rates of toll on the passengers and goods to be conveyed by such road, not for fifteen, twenty, or even fifty years, but *in all time to come!* Now, as it appears to us, this is a singularly injudicious arrangement on the part of the public. There is, between any two or more places that may be named, a certain railway line that is preferable to any other that can be pointed out. The probability is that this line will in all cases be the first to be selected; and the act that gives it up to a company confers on the latter a virtual and substantial monopoly. The rates of charge imposed by the act are calculated to remunerate the projectors, supposing every thing to remain on its present footing. But the probability is that manufactures and population, in the places communicating by most lines of railway, will continue to increase in time to come, as they have done in time past; and it is all but certain that great improvements will be effected in the construction of roads and engines. Whatever, therefore, may be the chances of success at the outset, the fair presumption is, that most great lines of road will in the end be exceedingly productive. But if we continue to abide by the present system, the public will be effectually excluded from all participation in these prospective advantages; and a few private associations will be able to make enormous profits, by monopolising improvements, and keeping up the expense of transit at an exorbitantly high level. It is idle to trust to competition to remedy a grievance of this sort. There may only be one practicable line of railway between two places; and if so, no other can, of course, come into competition with it. But though this were not the case, a company in possession of the best line might, if an opposition were threatened, reduce its rates till the opposition was defeated, and then raise them to the old level. Supposing, however, that a second road is made, its managers would most likely come to an understanding with the first, so that the tolls, instead of being reduced by the instrumentality of the new road, may be raised; and were it otherwise, the question is, was the second road really necessary? Could not the first road have sufficed for the whole traffic to be carried on by both lines? If this be the case, it is clear the second road has been merely resorted to as a device for reducing the tolls charged on the first; as a means, in fact, for doing that, by an outlay of some hundreds of thousands, or, it may be, millions of pounds, which might have been quite as effectually done by limiting the duration of the act authorising the first road, or by inserting a clause in it providing for the periodical revision of the tolls.

"We are clear, indeed, that no act, authorising a private association to construct a railway or canal, to lay down gas-pipes, to convey water into a town, or for any such purpose, should ever be passed without reserving to parliament power periodically to revise the tolls granted under it. Such revision would secure to the public a participation in future improvements, not in the contemplation of the parties when the project was entered upon; and it would do this without in any degree clogging the spirit of enterprise. Undertakings of this sort are not engaged in because there is a vague expectation, or even a considerable probability, of their yielding 20 or 30 per cent. profit some thirty or forty years hence; but because it is believed that they will immediately, or in the course of a few years, yield a reasonable profit—that is, a return of 8, 10, or 12 per cent. The chances of realising more than this at the distance of twenty or twenty-five years are rarely taken into account, and are worth very little indeed. This, however, is *all* that would be taken away by the revision in question; and, while a reservation of this sort would not stand in the way of any legitimate enterprise, the history of several of our existing companies shows that it may come to be of essential service to the public. Had this principle been formerly acted upon in the formation of companies for the execution of public works, the charges on some of the principal lines of canal might, long since, have been reduced to less than half their present amount; and the water brought into the city of London by the New River Company might have been sold for less than one fourth part of what it now costs; and so in a vast number of cases.

"It has been objected to the proposal now made, that the reserving to the public of power to revise the charges on railways, and other public works, would be of no use, inasmuch as the parties would contrive so to swell their charges as to make their revenue appear not more than a fair return on their outlay. And such, most probably, would be the case, were the statements of the parties to be taken without examination. But who ever proposed that this should be done? If charges are to be revised, government must be authorised to appoint parties to inquire carefully into the management of all concerns with which it is proposed to interfere: and it would be the duty of such parties to proscribe every useless expense, and to ascertain how the railway could be carried on, supposing it were wrought under a system of open competition, and at the least expense, and to frame their report accordingly.

"We do not even know that it is now too late to interfere with existing railways, in some such way as has been here suggested. Suppose it were enacted that it should be lawful for government to revise the rates of charge, and to lay down new regulations for the government of all railways at twenty-five or thirty years hence, very little injury would be done to the existing interests of individuals, at the same time that provision would be made for securing those of the public. The fact that the rates of charge on the Birmingham and Great Western Railways were to be revised, and most probably reduced, in 1870 or 1875, would have little or no influence over the present value of shares in these concerns; and such being the case, the proposed reduction could entail no real injury on the railway proprietors, inasmuch as those who may not choose to be subject to future revision may withdraw at present from the concerns with little or no loss."

It is the more singular that nothing should have been done to protect the public interests in this matter, seeing that the subject was brought under the consideration of Parliament in 1836, by Mr. Morrison, who gave a remarkably clear and able statement of the principles on which acts for railways, and such like public works, should be framed, and who also showed the loss and inconveniences that would, most probably, result from their not being enforced.

Railroads; Speech of James Morrison, Esq., in the House of Commons, 17th May, 1836, on moving a Resolution relative to the Periodical Revision of Tolls and other Charges on Railroads and other Public Works. 8vo. London, 1836.

But though Mr. Morrison's speech was very favourably received, nothing was done in the matter. The public attention was again called to the subject by the author of a tract entitled

RAILWAY REFORM, its Expediency and Practicability considered, &c. 8vo. London, 1843.

The author of this elaborate pamphlet proposes that government should buy up all the railways at the prices of the day, take them into its own charge, and subject them to an economical and uniform system of administration! But it is needless to discuss such a project. Even if it were desirable, which it certainly is not, it is almost superfluous to add, that there is not so much as the vestige of a chance of its ever being carried into effect.

The necessity of providing for the conveyance of the mail, and the expediency of endeavouring to provide against accidents, drew at length the attention of government to the subject. In the course of last session an act was passed, which has given to the Board of Trade a certain degree of control over the formation, and of surveillance over the conduct of railways. But this measure, though a step in the right direction, is comparatively feeble and inefficient, and hardly, in fact, touches those matters in which the public have the greatest interest; and from interference having been so long delayed, and large and powerful private interests been allowed to grow up under the old system, it will now be very difficult to introduce a better.

A TREATISE on RAILROADS. By NICHOLAS WOOD, Esq. 3rd ed., 1 vol., 8vo. London, 1839.

There are good and popular accounts of railways in the last edition of the 'Encyclopædia Britannica,' and in the 'Penny Cyclopædia,' especially the former.

The following is, perhaps, the most easily understood and generally interesting account of that extraordinary engine to which we are indebted for almost all the mechanical superiority of the present age.

The Steam-Engine Explained and Illustrated: with an Account of its Invention and Progressive Improvement (including a Life of Watt), and its Application to Navigation and Railways. By DIONYSIUS LARDNER, D.C.L. 7th edition, illustrated with numerous Engravings. 1 vol. 8vo. London, 1840.

The following are also useful publications:—

THE STEAM-ENGINE; being a popular Description of the MODE of ACTION of that Engine, as applied to Raising Water, Machinery, Navigation, Railways, &c.; with a Sketch of its History, and an Account of the Laws of Heat and Pneumatics. Illustrated with Engravings. By HUGO REID. 1 vol. Fcap. 8vo., cloth. London, 1840.

ON THE NATURE, PROPERTIES, and APPLICATION of STEAM, and on STEAM NAVIGATION. By J. S. RUSSELL, M.A. 1 vol. Post 8vo. London, 1841.

A TREATISE on the STEAM-ENGINE. By J. S. RUSSELL, M.A. 1 vol. Post 8vo. London, 1841.

In 1836 a commission was appointed to inquire into the policy of a general system of railways for Ireland, the lines in which they would be most advantageous, and the ports whence intercourse by steam might be most advantageously carried on with the United States. The second report of this commission is of peculiar importance. Besides a great deal of scientific information with respect to the laying out and construction of railways, it embodies many authentic and most valuable statements with respect to the physical capacities of Ireland, her internal and external trade, the condition of the inhabitants, &c. This interesting report was written by the late Mr. Thomas Drummond, then under-secretary for Ireland, and will be a lasting monument of his industry, and of his extensive scientific and political attainments.

Sketch of the Civil Engineering of North America; comprising Remarks on the Harbours, River and Lake Navigation, Lighthouses, Steam-Navigation, Canals, Roads, Railways, &c., of that Country. By DAVID STEPHENSON, Civil Engineer. 1 vol., 8vo. London, 1838.

A highly instructive and valuable volume.

A DESCRIPTION of the CANALS and RAILROADS of the UNITED STATES. By H. S. TANNER. 1 vol. 8vo. New York, 1840.

Histoire des Grands Chemins de l'Empire Romain; contenant l'Origine, Progrès, et Etendue quasi incroyable de Chemins Militaires, Pavez depuis la Ville de Rome jusques aux extrémités de son Empire. Par M. NICOLAS BERGIER.

The first edition of this important work, in 1 large 4to. vol., appeared at Paris in 1622; but having become rare, it was reprinted at Brussels in 1728, and again in 1736, with the addition of Peutinger's Itinerary Chart, in 2 vols. 4to. These editions are equally accurate, but that of 1728 is the handsomest and best printed.

The Romans have never been equalled in the difficult art of effacing national and local prejudices, and of consolidating different and distant nations into one great homogeneous people. A considerable portion of their success in this respect is to be ascribed to their colonies and their great roads. No country was considered as fully taken possession of and united to the empire, till colonies of Roman citizens had been established in it, and till highways communicating with those leading from Rome had been carried to its remotest extremities. The former served at once to bridle the subjugated people, and to communicate to them the language and the arts of the conquerors; while the latter served as channels by which information could be speedily conveyed from and to the Imperial city, and by which the victorious legions could be marched wherever disturbance or danger was apprehended. Hence the intimate relation that subsisted amongst the various parts of the Roman empire, and which was said to give it more the appearance of a city than of a vast territory stretching from the Euphrates to the Severn, and from Atlas to the Rhine.

"Fecisti patriam diversis gentibus unam:
Profuit injustis te dominante capi.
Dumque offert victis proprii consortia juris,
Urbem fecisti, quod prius orbis erat."—(Rutilii Itin., lib. i.)

"The public highways," says Gibbon, "issuing from the Forum of Rome traversed Italy, pervaded the provinces, and were terminated only by the frontiers of the empire. If we carefully trace the distance from the wall of Antoninus to Rome, and from thence to Jerusalem, it will be found that the great chain of communication from the north-west to the south-east part of the empire was drawn out to the length of 4080 Roman miles. The public roads were accurately divided by mile-stones, and ran in a direct line from one city to another, with very little respect either for the obstacles of nature or of private property. Mountains were perforated, and bold arches thrown over the broadest and most rapid streams. The middle part of the road, raised into a terrace which commanded the adjacent country, consisted of several strata of sand, gravel, and cement, and was paved with large stones, or in some places, near the capital, with granite. Such was the solid construction of the Roman highways, whose firmness has not entirely yielded to the effort of fifteen centuries. * * * The advantage of receiving the earliest intelligence, and of conveying their orders with celerity, induced the emperors to establish throughout their extensive dominions the regular institution of posts. Houses were everywhere erected at the distance only of five or six miles; each of them was constantly provided with forty horses, and by the help of these relays it was easy to travel an hundred miles a day along the Roman roads. The use of the posts was allowed to those who claimed it by an imperial mandate; but though originally intended for the public service, it was sometimes indulged to the business or conveniency of private citizens."—(i. 81, ed. 1807.)

Bergier is quoted as the authority for the greater number of these interesting details; and he has collected with unwearied industry almost everything that can be learned with respect to the construction, repair, uses, and police of the Roman roads. He undertook the task at the suggestion of Peiresc, the Mæcenas of his day, who supplied him with part of the materials for his work.—(Biographie Universelle.) It might, perhaps, have been advantageously condensed, though the minuteness and amplitude of its details make it in some respects more valuable. It was translated into Latin, and published in the 10th volume of Grævius' *Thesaurus Antiquitatum Romanorum;* but Dufresnoy says "*que l'ouvrage de Bergier est défiguré dans cette version.*"—(Méthode d'Etudier l'Histoire xi., 106, ed. 1772.)

ORIGINE des POSTES chez les ANCIENS et chez les MODERNES. Par M. de NEUVILLE. 1 vol., 12mo. Paris, 1708.

TRAITÉ de la CONSTRUCTION des CHEMINS. Par GAUTIER. 1 vol., 8vo. Paris, 1728; reprinted in 1751.

DE L'ADMINISTRATION des CHEMINS. Par M. DUPONT. 8vo. Paris, 1767.

DES CANAUX de NAVIGATION, et spécialement du CANAL de LANGUEDOC. Par M. de la LANDE. 1 vol., fol. Paris, 1778.

HISTOIRE du CANAL du MIDI. Par M. ANDREOSSY. 1 vol., 4to. Paris, 1804.

HISTOIRE du CANAL de LANGUEDOC. Publiée par les Descendants du P. RIQUET de BONREPOS. 1 vol. 8vo. Paris, 1805.

The last two works are of a controversial character, having reference to the claims of rival engineers to the honour of having planned the canal of Languedoc, the greatest and most perfect work of its kind that had then been constructed in any part of the world. It is in truth one of the most splendid monuments of the reign of Louis XIV.

The direction of all that relates to the planning, construction, and repair of roads, bridges, and canals in France has been for a lengthened period placed under the control of a peculiar department of the government, entitled the *Direction Générale des Ponts-et-Chaussées, et des Mines.* The roads are divided into the three classes of *Routes Royales*, or great lines of road, traversing different departments; *Routes Départmentales*, including the principal local lines, or those leading from one place to another in the same departments; and the *Chemins Vicinaux*, corresponding to our cross or parish roads. These have all, but especially those belonging to the first and second classes, been greatly improved within the last twenty years; but France has still *beaucoup à faire pour porter ses routes à un état d'entretien comparable à ce qu'on voit en Angleterre.*—(Chevalier, 'Economie Politique,' p. 290.)

The fullest information respecting the roads, railways, canals, and public works of France will be found in the publication now referred to (see *ante*, p. 26), and in the following works:—

Des Intérêts Matériels en France—Travaux Publics, Routes, Canaux, et Chemins de Fer. Par M. MICH. CHEVALIER. 1 vol. 8vo. Paris, 1838.

Histoire de la Navigation Intérieure de la France. Par M. DUTENS. 2 vol. 4to. Paris, 1829.

A comprehensive and important work.

MÉMOIRES sur les TRAVAUX PUBLICS. Par M. J. CORDIER. 2 vol. 4to. Paris, 1841–42.

Histoire et Description des Voies de Communication aux Etats-Unis, et des Travaux d'Art qui en dépendent. Par M. MICH. CHEVALIER. 2 vol. 4to., avec un Atlas in-fol. Paris, 1840–43.

CHAPTER VI.

POLITICAL ARITHMETIC, STATISTICS, AND AGRICULTURAL ECONOMY.

"Est enim cognitio reipublicæ et privato homini et publico utilissima et maxime necessaria; atque scientiam illam, qua duce cognitionem reipublicæ nobis comparamus, imprimis dignam esse, quam studiosius colamus et prosequamur, non est, quod jure negare vel adeo dubitare possimus."—Mone, *Hist. Statisticæ*, p. 4.

Several Essays in Political Arithmetic. By Sir WILLIAM PETTY, F.R.S., &c. 4th ed. 1 vol. 8vo. London, 1755.

A portion of these Essays appeared originally in 1682; but they were greatly enlarged and improved in subsequent editions. That most elaborate and valuable essay on the 'Extent and Value of Lands, People, Buildings, &c.' was a posthumous publication, having appeared for the first time in 1691, four years after the death of the author.

MAGNÆ BRITANNIÆ NOTITIA; or the Present State of Great Britain, with divers Remarks upon the Ancient State thereof, in Two Parts (England and Scotland). By JOHN CHAMBERLAYNE, Esq. 1 vol. 8vo. London, 1737.

This work, compiled originally in the reign of Charles II., enjoyed for a lengthened period a very extensive sale, having gone through from 30 to 40 editions. It continued, indeed, down almost to the accession of George III., to be in very extensive demand. It owed this great success principally, no doubt, to the variety of useful information which it contained, and which made it in some sort a year book, or companion to the Almanac, and partly to the want of other publications of a similar kind. Its statistical information is meagre in the extreme; but, however singular, it appears to have fallen into neglect from those to whom it belonged not making the necessary improvements upon it, and accommodating it to the altered circumstances and advanced knowledge of the age, without being superseded by any better work: in fact, till the present century, there were none better by which to supersede it.

Natural and Political Observations and Conclusions upon the State and Condition of England in 1696. By GREGORY KING, Esq., Lancaster Herald.

This tract gives the best account of the population and wealth of England at the close of the 17th century that is anywhere to be met with. Some extracts from it were published by Davenant, but the tract itself was not published till 1801, when Chalmers added it, with a notice of King, to the edition of his 'Comparative Estimate' published in the course of that year.

Political Survey (or Anatomy) **of Ireland,** with the Establishment of that Kingdom when the Duke of Ormond was Lord Lieutenant, &c. By Sir WILLIAM PETTY. 1 vol. 8vo. 1st ed., London, 1691 ; 2nd ed., with Additions, London, 1719.

This, perhaps, is the best of Petty's works; and is valuable alike for the authentic information it affords respecting the state of Ireland in the latter part of the 17th century, and for the judicious suggestions of the author with a view to its improvement. We subjoin his account of the number and condition of the inhabitants in 1676.

"The number of the people in Ireland is about 1,100,000, viz., 300,000 English, Scotch, and Welsh Protestants, and 800,000 Papists, whereof one-fourth are children unfit for labour, and about 75,000 of the remainder are, by reason of their quality and estates, above the necessity of corporal labour; so as there remain 750,000 labouring men and women, 500,000 whereof do perform the present work of the nation.

"The said 1,100,000 people do live in about 200,000 families or houses, whereof there are about 16,000 which have more than one chimney in each; and about 24,000 which have but one; all the other houses, being 160,000, are wretched, nasty cabins, without chimney, window, or door shut, even worse than those of the savage Americans, and wholly unfit for the making merchantable butter, cheese, or the manufacture of woollen, linen, or leather."—(p. 114, ed. 1719.)

Like all men of sense who have ever reflected for a moment on the subject, Sir William Petty was strongly in favour of an incorporating union between Great Britain and Ireland, and of the establishment of a perfectly free commercial intercourse between them. Speaking of the act passed in 1664, prohibiting the importation of cattle and beef from Ireland, he says, "If it be good for England to keep Ireland a distinct kingdom, why do not the predominant party in parliament, suppose the western members, make England beyond Trent another kingdom, and take tolls and customs upon the borders? or why was there ever any union between England and Wales? and why may not the entire kingdom of England be further cantonised for the advantage of all parties?"—(p. 34.)

Sir William Petty was one of the most remarkable persons of the seventeenth century. He was born at Rumsey, in Hampshire, in 1623; and was successful alike in the acquisition of knowledge and of wealth. He was educated partly at the grammar-school of his native town, and partly at some of the most celebrated foreign universities. Having studied medicine and taken the degree of M.D., he was appointed physician-general to the army in Ireland, which had suppressed the rebellion of 1641. When thus employed he perceived that the admeasurement and division of the forfeited estates was very much mismanaged; and having represented this to government, and obtained a contract for the execution of the work, he performed the task in a manner not more for his own advantage than for that of the public. The estates in question comprised a very large proportion of the entire kingdom; the maps of them drawn by Petty making what is called the "Down Survey." * And considering the time when, and

* Copies of part of the maps composing the Down Survey were taken by Petty for his own use; but being shipped for England, the vessel in which they were embarked was captured by a privateer and carried to France, when the maps came into the possession of the French court. A number of the originals that remained in Ireland were subsequently much injured by fire, and some of them altogether destroyed; but their place has been supplied by copies taken by General Vallancey and others, from the captured maps, now in the Royal Library at Paris.—(Report of 1824, on the Survey, &c. of Ireland. Append., p. 133, &c.)

the circumstances under which, these maps were executed, their accuracy is wonderful, being such that they continue to be referred to as evidence in the courts of law even at this day. By laying out the sums which he received for the survey in the purchase of soldiers' debentures and of portions of the forfeited estates, Petty acquired large landed and monied property, which he afterwards improved and augmented in various ways. He died in 1687, in the 65th year of his age.

Few men have possessed so great a variety of attainments as Sir William Petty. In addition to his talents as a political and statistical writer, he was distinguished by his proficiency in polite literature, medicine, mathematics, and mechanics, in which he made many inventions, and by his shrewdness and sagacity in practical matters. Evelyn and Pepys, who knew him well, speak of him in the highest terms of commendation. The former says, "The map of Ireland made by Sir William Petty is believed to be the most exact that ever yet was made of any country. He did promise to publish it; and I am told it has cost him neare 1000*l.* to have it engrav'd at Amsterdam. There is not a better Latine poet living when he gives himselfe that diversion; nor is his excellence less in council and prudent matters of state; but he is so exceeding nice in sifting and examining all possible contingencies, that he adventures at nothing which is not demonstration. There were not in the whole world his equal for a superintendent of manufacture and improvement of trade, or to govern a plantation. If I were a prince, I should make him my second counsellor at least. There is nothing difficult to him. * * * He was, with all this, facetious and of easy conversation, friendly and courteous, and had such a faculty of imitating others, that he would take a text and preach, now like a grave orthodox divine, then falling into the Presbyterian way, then to the phanatical, the quaker, the monk, and frier, the Popish priest, with such admirable action, and alteration of voice and tone, as it were not possible to abstain from wonder, and one would sweare to heare severall persons, or forbear to think he was not in good earnest an enthusiast and almost beside himselfe; then he would fall out of it into a serious discourse; but it was very rarely he would be prevail'd on to oblige the company with this faculty, and that only amongst most intimate friends. My Lord Duke of Ormond once obtain'd it of him, and was almost ravish'd with admiration. He never could get favour at court, because he outwitted all the projectors that came neere him. Having never known such another genius, I cannot but mention these particulars amongst a multitude of others which I could produce." —(Memoirs, i. 474-475, 4to. edit.)

Among other things Pepys says of Petty, "He is in discourse, methinks, one of the most rational men that I ever heard speak with a tongue, having all his notions the most distinct and clear."—(Diary, ii. 145, 8vo. ed.)

It is to be regretted that we have nothing like a complete or respectable edition of the works of this extraordinary man. Mr. J. W. Croker informed the Committee of the House of Commons of 1824, on the Survey and Valuation of Ireland, that there was "in the possession of the Dowager Marchioness of Lansdowne a volume carefully written and in excellent preservation, entitled 'Sir William Petty's History of the Survey of Ireland,' in eighteen chapters. There is also, in the same collection, a very curious and detailed account of the population of Ireland, distinguishing the English inhabitants from the Irish, and their respective numbers and property." Treatises of such importance and authenticity should not be buried in obscurity. Nor could the noble successors of Petty, to whom much of his talent as well as his estates have descended, raise any better monument to his memory than the publication of a complete edition of his works.

Essays on Husbandry. By the Rev. WALTER HARTE, A.M. (Author of the Life of Gustavus Adolphus). 2nd ed. 1 vol. 8vo. London, 1770.

This is the work of a scholar and a gentleman; and is attractive from the variety and interest of the subjects treated of, its learning, and good taste.

A POLITICAL SURVEY of BRITAIN; being a Series of Reflections on the Situation, Lands, Inhabitants, Revenues, Colonies, and Commerce of this Island. By JOHN CAMPBELL, LL.D. 2 vols. royal 4to. London, 1774.

This is a work of great labour and research; but it is ill-arranged, overlaid with details, tedious, and of little practical value. The author is one of our most voluminous writers; and his works are for the most part carefully compiled from original sources. He was born at Edinburgh in 1708, and died in London in 1775.

The following Works of Arthur Young, Esq., should have a prominent place in every Economical library, viz.:—

1. THE FARMER'S LETTERS to the PEOPLE of ENGLAND, containing the Sentiments of a Practical Husbandman on various subjects of great importance, &c. 3rd ed. 2 vols. 8vo. London, 1771.

2. A SIX WEEKS' TOUR through the SOUTHERN COUNTIES of ENGLAND and WALES, describing particularly the Present State of Agriculture and Manufactures, &c. By the Author of the 'Farmer's Letters.' 1 vol. 8vo. 2nd ed. London, 1769.

3. A SIX MONTHS' TOUR through the NORTH of ENGLAND, containing an Account of the Present State of Agriculture, Manufactures, and Population in several counties of this Kingdom. 2nd ed. 4 vols. 8vo. London, 1771.

4. THE FARMER'S TOUR through the EAST of ENGLAND; being the Register of a Journey through various Counties in this Kingdom to inquire into the State of Agriculture, &c. By the Author of the 'Farmer's Letters,' &c. 4 vols. 8vo. London, 1771.

5. POLITICAL ARITHMETIC, containing Observations on the Present State of Great Britain, and the Principles of her Policy in the Encouragement of Agriculture, &c. 1 vol. 8vo. London, 1774.

6. POLITICAL ARITHMETIC, Part II., containing Observations on the Means of Raising the Supplies within the Year. 8vo. London, 1779.

7. A TOUR in IRELAND; with General Observations on the Present State of that Kingdom, made in the years 1776, 1777, and 1778, and brought down to the end of 1779. 1 vol. 4to. London, 1780.

8. TRAVELS during the Years 1787, 1788, and 1789; undertaken more particularly with a view of ascertaining the Cultivation, Wealth, Resources, and National Prosperity of the Kingdom of France (but extending also into parts of Italy and Spain). 2nd ed. 2 vols. 4to. Bury St. Edmunds, 1794.

9. ANNALS of AGRICULTURE and other USEFUL ARTS. 45 vols. 8vo. Bury St. Edmunds, 1784, &c.

The works of Arthur Young, of which the above make a part only, did incomparably more than those of any other individual to introduce a taste for agriculture and to diffuse a knowledge of the art in this and other countries. They are written in an animated, forcible, pure English style; and are at once highly entertaining and instructive. In his different Tours, and, indeed, in all his publications, his grand object is not so much to describe the existing state of things as to point out objectionable and approved practices; and to show the mischievous consequences of the former, and the advantages of the latter. Though sometimes rash and prejudiced, his statements and inferences may in general be depended upon. His activity, perseverance, and devotedness to agriculture were unequalled. It has been truly said, that "If great zeal, indefatigable exertions, and an unsparing expense in making experiments, can give any one a claim to the gratitude of agriculturists, Arthur Young deserved it more than most men. We will not affirm that in all cases his conclusions were correct, or his judgment unimpeachable; but even his blunders, if he committed any, have tended to the benefit of agriculture, by exciting discussion and criticism."—(Kirwan, 'Irish Transactions,' as quoted in 'Penny Cyclopædia.')

His Tours, especially those in Ireland and in France, which are both excellent, are his most valuable publications. The latter is admitted by the ablest French writers to contain the best account of the state of France previously to the Revolution; and the numerous defects in the agricultural economy of that kingdom were never so clearly pointed out as by Young. The 'Tour in Ireland' is also the first work that made the British public fully acquainted with the real state of that kingdom, the fertility of its soil, and the badness of its agriculture; and which exhibited the degraded taste of the lower classes of the population, the oppressions of which they were the victims, their poverty and wretchedness. His English Tours contain, also, the best account of the state of the country, and the condition of the agriculturists, between 1760 and 1780.

Young died in 1820, in his 80th year. In the earlier period of his life he combined for some years the apparently irreconcileable pursuits of a reporter for a morning paper in town, and a practical farmer in Essex. We need not, under such circumstances, be surprised at his little success in the latter department. He was secretary to the Board of Agriculture from its formation till its extinction. In this capacity he carried on an immense correspondence.

REMARKS upon the HISTORY of the LANDED and COMMERCIAL POLICY of ENGLAND, from the Invasion of the Romans to the Accession of James I. 2 vols. 8vo. London, 1785.

A valuable, though desultory work; less known than it deserves to be.

THE HUSBANDRY of the ANCIENTS. By the Rev. ADAM DICKSON, A.M., Minister of Whittingham. 2 vols. 8vo. Edinburgh, 1788.

This, though the best work on the subject in the English language, is inferior to that of Butel Dumont, referred to below. It was a posthumous publication, the author having been killed by a fall from his horse in 1776. Mr. Dickson was also the author of a tract published in 1773, on the Causes of the High Price of Provisions. See *ante*, p. 193.

A View of the British Empire, more especially Scotland, with some Proposals for the Improvement of that Country, the Extension of its Fisheries, and the Relief of the People. By John Knox. 3rd ed. 2 vols. 8vo. Edinburgh, 1785.

A Journey through Spain in 1786 and 1787; with particular attention to the Agriculture, Manufactures, Commerce, Population, Taxes, and Revenues of that Country. By the Rev. Joseph Townsend, A.M. 2nd ed. 3 vols. 8vo. London, 1792.

One of the best works of the kind that has ever appeared, throwing a great deal of light on the political economy of Spain, and on the causes of her decline.

The Statistical Account of Scotland, drawn up from the Communications of the Ministers. By Sir John Sinclair, Bart. 21 vols. 8vo. Edinburgh, 1791–99.

The Reports on the Agriculture, &c. of the different Counties of Great Britain and Ireland, drawn up for the Information of the Board of Agriculture and of the Dublin Society, viz.—

ENGLAND.

Bedford . . .	by	Batchelor . . .	1 Vol. 8vo.	London	1808
Berkshire. . .	„	Mavor	ditto	„	1808
Buckinghamshire	„	Priest	ditto	„	1810
Cambridgeshire .	„	Gooch	ditto	„	1811
Cornwall . . .	„	Worgan . . .	ditto	„	1811
Cheshire . . .	„	Holland . . .	ditto	„	1808
Cumberland . .		(see Northumberland).			
Derbyshire . .	„	Farey	2 Vols. 8vo.	„	1815
Devon	„	Vancouver . . .	1 Vol. 8vo.	„	1813
Dorset	„	Stevenson . . .	ditto	„	1812
Durham . . .	„	Bailey	ditto	„	1810
Essex	„	Young	2 Vols. 8vo.	„	1807
Gloucester . .	„	Rudge	1 Vol. 8vo.	„	1807
Hampshire. . .	„	Vancouver . . .	ditto	„	1810
Herefordshire .	„	Duncomb . . .	ditto	„	1805
Hertfordshire .	„	Young	ditto	„	1804
Huntingdonshire	„	Parkinson . . .	ditto	„	1811
Kent	„	Boys.	ditto	„	1796
Leicestershire .	„	Pitt	ditto	„	1809
Rutland . . .	„	Parkinson . . .			
Lancashire . .	„	Dickson & Stevenson	ditto	„	1815
Lincolnshire . .	„	Young . (2nd Ed.)	ditto	„	1813
Middlesex. . .	„	Middleton (2nd Ed.)	ditto	„	1798
Monmouthshire .	„	Hassall	ditto	„	
Norfolk . . .	„	Young	ditto	„	1804
Northampton . .	„	Pitt	ditto	„	1813
Northumberland, Cumberland, and Westmoreland .	„	Bailey, Cully, and Pringle	ditto	Newcastle	1797
Nottingham . .	„	Lowe	ditto	London	1798
Oxfordshire . .	„	Young	ditto	„	1808
Rutland . . .		(see Leicestershire).			
Shropshire . .	„	Plymley . . .	ditto	„	1813
Somerset . . .	„	Billingsley . . .	ditto	Bath	1797
Stafford . . .	„	Pitt . (2nd Ed.)	ditto	London	1813
Suffolk . . .	„	Young	ditto	„	1797

SURREY	by	Stevenson	1 Vol. 8vo.	London	1809
SUSSEX	„	Young	ditto	„	1808
WARWICK	„	Murray	ditto	„	
WORCESTERSHIRE	„	Pitt	ditto	„	1811
WESTMORELAND		(see Northumberland).			
WILTSHIRE	„	Davis	ditto	„	1811
YORKSHIRE (West Riding)	by	Brown	ditto	Edinburgh	1799
Ditto (North Riding)	„	Tuke	ditto	London	1800
Ditto (East Riding)	„	Strickland	ditto	„	1812

NORTH WALES (Anglesey, Caernarvon, Denbigh, Flint, Merionydd, and Montgomery)	by	Davies,	1 Vol. 8vo.	London,	1810
SOUTH WALES (Brecon, Caermarthen, Cardigan, Glamorgan, Pembroke, and Radnor)	by	Davies,	2 Vols. 8vo.	„	1815
JERSEY and GUERNSEY	„	Quayle.	1 Vol. 8vo.		
ISLE of MAN	„	Quayle.	1 Vol. 4to.	„	1794

SCOTLAND.

ABERDEENSHIRE	by	Keith	1 Vol. 8vo.	Aberdeen	1811
ARGYLL	„	Smith	ditto	Edinburgh London	1798 1805
AYRSHIRE	„	Aiton	ditto	Glasgow	1811
BERWICK	„	Kerr	ditto	London	1809
BUTE	„	Aiton	ditto	Glasgow	1816
CAITHNESS	„	Henderson	ditto		1812
CLYDESDALE	„	Naismith	ditto	Glasgow	1798
DUMBARTON	„	White & Macfarlane	ditto	„	1811
DUMFRIES	„	Singer	ditto	Edinburgh	1812
EAST LOTHIAN	„	Somerville	ditto	London	1813
FIFE	„	Thomson	ditto	Edinburgh	1800
FORFAR	„	Headrick	ditto	„	1813
GALLOWAY (Kirkcudbright and Wigton)	„	Smith	ditto	London	1810
HEBRIDES	„	Macdonald	ditto		1811
INVERNESS	„	J. Robertson	ditto	London	1808
KINCARDINESHIRE	„	ditto	ditto	„	1811
MID-LOTHIAN	„	G. Robertson	ditto	Edinburgh	1795
NAIRN and MORAY	„	Leslie	ditto		1811
PEEBLES	„	Findlater	ditto	Edinburgh	1802
PERTH	„	J. Robertson (2nd Ed.)	ditto	Perth	1813
RENFREW	„	Wilson	ditto		
ROSS and CROMARTY	„	Mackenzie	ditto	London	1810
ROXBURGH & SELKIRK	„	Douglas	ditto	Edinburgh	1798
SHETLAND ISLES	„	Shirreff	ditto	„	1814
SUTHERLAND	„	Henderson	ditto	London	1812
WEST LOTHIAN	„	Trotter	ditto		1812

IRELAND.

ANTRIM	by	Dubourdieu	2 Vols. 8vo.	Dublin	1812
ARMAGH	„	Sir C. Coote	1 Vol.	„	1804
CAVAN	„	ditto	1 Vol.	„	1802
CLARE	„	Dutton	ditto	„	1808
CORK	„	Townsend	2 Vols.	Cork	1815

DERRY	by	Sampson . .	1 Vol.	Dublin	1802
DONEGAL	„	McParlan . .	ditto	„	1802
DOWN	„	Dubourdieu. .	ditto	„	1802
DUBLIN	„	Archer . . .	ditto	„	1801
GALWAY	„	Dutton . . .	ditto	„	1824
KILDARE	„	Rawson . . .	ditto	„	1801
KILKENNY	„	Tighe . . .	ditto	„	1801
KING'S COUNTY . .	„	Sir C. Coote .	ditto	„	1801
LEITRIM	„	Dr. McParlan .	ditto	„	1802
LONDONDERRY . . .	„	Sampson . .	ditto	„	1802
MAYO	„	McParlan . .	ditto	„	1802
MEATH	„	Thompson . .	ditto	„	1802
MONAGHAN. . . .	„	Sir C. Coote .	ditto	„	1801
QUEEN'S COUNTY . .	„	Sir C. Coote. .	ditto	„	1802
ROSCOMMON . . .	„	Weld . . .	ditto	„	1832
SLIGO	„	McParlan . .	ditto	„	1801
TYRONE	„	McEvoy . .	ditto	„	1802
WEXFORD	„	Fraser . . .	ditto	„	1802
WICKLOW	„	Fraser . . .	ditto	„	1801

These publications are of very unequal merit, some of them being vastly superior to others. In general, however, they supply much useful information; and we incline to think that it would conduce materially to the improvement of agriculture, and of the country generally, were a series of analogous works undertaken at present. They might be made to furnish accurate information with respect to the state of the population, of agriculture, and of the most important branches of industry carried on in the different counties. And supposing them to be interspersed with judicious criticisms on improper or defective practices, and to embody the latest and best information in regard to the various topics touched upon, they could hardly fail to be of material service. Neither do we suppose there would be any great difficulty in getting such works respectably executed. A little exertion on the part of a few leading gentlemen in each county would go far to insure their accuracy and utility.

A VIEW of the NATURAL, POLITICAL, and COMMERCIAL CIRCUMSTANCES of IRELAND. By THOMAS NEWENHAM, Esq. (Author of the Work on the Population of Ireland). 1 vol. 4to. London, 1809.

A Treatise on Agriculture and Rural Affairs. By ROBERT BROWN, of Markle, co. Haddington. 2 vols. 8vo. Edinburgh, 1811.

Perhaps the best work on agriculture that had appeared when it was published.

An Estimate of the Comparative Strength of Great Britain, and of the Losses of her Trade from every war since the Revolution. By GEORGE CHALMERS, F.R.S. 1st ed. 1 vol. 8vo. London, 1783. Last ed. Edinburgh, 1812. But the best ed. is that of 1802, from its having annexed to it Gregory King's tract, previously noticed.

This work, by the author of 'Caledonia,' was written to dispel the gloomy apprehensions of those who supposed that the country was in a ruined state at the close of the American war; and it successfully accomplished its object. It exhibits the constant progress made by the country in wealth and population, from the Revolution down to 1812; and shows that complaints of the decline of trade, the impoverished condition of the people, and the oppressiveness of taxation, have been constantly occurring, and have been usually put forward with the greatest confidence when there was least foundation for them. But though generally correct, the work is deficient in criticism, and partakes too much of the nature of a panegyric. Chalmers died in 1825, at the age of 82. His library, which comprised a valuable collection of books and tracts with respect to trade, colonial policy, and finance, was sold by auction in 1842, and brought a large sum.

General Report on the Agricultural State and Political Circumstances of Scotland. Drawn up for the Consideration of the Board of Agriculture and Internal Improvement, under the directions of Sir John Sinclair, Bart. 5 vols. 8vo. Edinburgh, 1814.

An unequal, and, in some respects, antiquated, but still a very valuable work.

An Account of Ireland, Statistical and Political. By Edward Wakefield. 2 vols. 4to. London, 1812.

The best and most complete work that has appeared on Ireland since the publication of Young's Tour. So many and such very extensive changes have, however, been effected in Ireland since 1812, that this work is now valuable rather as a record of what Ireland was at the above epoch, than of what she now is. A large portion of the information given by Mr. Wakefield is, however, of an abiding character, and applicable at all times.

A Treatise on the Wealth, Power, and Resources of the British Empire, in every Quarter of the World, including the East Indies, &c. By P. Colquhoun, LL.D. 2nd ed. 1 vol. 4to. London, 1815.

This work enjoyed for a while a considerable degree of popularity, to which it certainly had but slender claims. It is, from beginning to end, a tissue of extravagant hypotheses and exaggeration. Nothing was too difficult for this intrepid calculator. Under his transforming hand everything was reduced to figures; and matters, respecting which it is impossible to obtain any certain information, and of which he knew nothing, are set down as if they had been ascertained with the utmost precision. But, it is almost needless to add, that such statements are good for nothing, unless it be to bring statistical computations into discredit.

A Review and Complete Abstract of the Reports to the Board of Agriculture on the several Counties of England. By William Marshall. 5 vols. 8vo. London, 1817.

An Account of the Systems of Husbandry adopted in the more Improved Districts of Scotland. By Sir John Sinclair, Bart. 3rd ed. 2 vols. 8vo. Edinburgh, 1820.

An Encyclopædia of Agriculture, comprising the Theory and Practice of the Management and Cultivation of Land, &c. By J. C. Loudon, F.L.G.Z., &c. 1 thick and closely-printed 8vo. vol., best edition. London, 1844.

Mr. Loudon was one of the first who introduced the practice of condensing a vast body of matter into a single volume. His industry and perseverance have seldom been equalled, and could hardly be surpassed. His works give the fullest and best information on the subjects of which they treat, and are compiled with the greatest diligence and good faith. The volume now referred to is one of his most useful performances; but his great work, the *Arboretum et Fruticetum Britannicum*, is that by which he will be longest remembered. Considering the very delicate state of his health, it is astonishing he should have been able to produce so many elaborate publications.

THE PRESENT STATE of ENGLAND in regard to AGRICULTURE, TRADE, FINANCE, &c. By JOSEPH LOWE, Esq. 1 vol. 8vo. London, 1822.

AN ANALYSIS of the STATISTICAL ACCOUNT of SCOTLAND, with a General View of the History of that Country, and Discussions on some Important Branches of Political Economy. By Sir JOHN SINCLAIR, Bart. 2 vols. 8vo. Edinburgh, 1825.

This work is very inferior to the 'General Report' on Scotland, referred to above, and is of little value. Its political economy is puerile.

The Present State of the Tenancy of Land in Great Britain, showing the Principal Customs and Practices between Incoming and Outgoing Tenants, and the usual Methods under which Land is now held in the several Counties. By L. KENNEDY and T. B. GRAINGER. 1 vol. 8vo. London, 1828.

The prosperity of agriculture and the well-being of a large proportion of the population depend, in a great degree, on the nature of the conditions under which land is held or occupied by the cultivators. And there is no work that contains so much information respecting its occupancy in England as that of Messrs. Kennedy and Grainger. It was reviewed in the 59th vol. of the 'Edinburgh Review.'

Rural Recollections, or the Progress of Improvement in Agriculture and Rural Affairs (in Scotland). By GEORGE ROBERTSON. 1 vol. 8vo. Irvine, 1829.

The author of this work was actively engaged in agricultural affairs in different parts of Scotland, either as a practical farmer or as a manager of estates, for about half a century previously to the publication of this volume; and his recollections extended to a still more remote period. He had, consequently, the most favourable opportunities for becoming acquainted with the progress of the country during the period referred to; and he did not fail to profit by them. His work is highly interesting. The advance made by Scotland in industry, wealth, and improved accommodations of all sorts since 1765, when these Recollections commence, has, we believe, been quite unprecedented in any old-settled country, and is hardly, indeed, surpassed by anything that has taken place in Kentucky and Illinois. Mr. Robertson does not, however, pretend to give anything like a detailed or systematic account of this wonderful progress, but judiciously confines himself to a statement of such changes in agriculture, and in the condition of the agricultural population, as fell under his own observation.

Reports to the British Government, by JOHN BOWRING, M.P. and LL.D., viz.:—

1. FIRST REPORT on the COMMERCIAL RELATIONS between FRANCE and GREAT BRITAIN. Folio. 1834.

2. Second Report on the Commercial Relations between France and Great Britain. Folio. 1835.

3. Report on the Commerce and Manufactures of Switzerland. Folio. 1836.

4. Report on the Statistics of Tuscany, Lucca, the Pontifical and the Lombardo-Venetian States; with Special Reference to their Commercial Relations. Folio. 1837.

5. Report on the Prussian Commercial Union (including the Commercial Statistics of Germany). Folio. 1840.

6. Report on Egypt and Candia. Folio. 1840.

7. Report on the Commercial Statistics of Syria. Folio. 1840.

Mr. Villiers (now Earl of Clarendon) was associated with Dr. Bowring in drawing up the first of these reports, but the others are exclusively the work of the learned gentleman. They comprise a great body of information not otherwise accessible to the English reader. And though their conclusions may not perhaps be always relied upon, and they sometimes evince too much of the spirit of a partisan, and of a desire to make out what are called points, they are, on the whole, highly creditable to the talents and the industry of the author.

Ordnance Memoir, or Survey of the Parish of Templemore, including the City of Londonderry, in the County of the same name. 1 vol. 4to. Dublin, 1837.

This memoir, which was compiled by gentlemen engaged in the Ordnance survey of Ireland, contains extremely full and circumstantial accounts of the geology; antiquities; agriculture; natural, civil, military, and ecclesiastical history; trade, statistics, &c., of Londonderry, and the immediately adjacent country. It is consequently of very considerable value. No doubt, however, it might have been advantageously compressed within much shorter limits; and the entire county of Londonderry might have been included within the Memoir with little additional trouble and expense. It has been proposed to compile surveys on something like the same plan of other parts of Ireland; and if irrelevant matter were excluded, and they were made to embrace sufficiently extensive districts, and were executed by competent parties, they would be of great national importance.

Elements of Practical Agriculture. By David Low, Esq., Professor of Agriculture in the University of Edinburgh. 2nd ed. 1 vol. 8vo. London, 1838.

A work of high and, we believe, well-deserved reputation.

A Statistical Account of the British Empire, exhibiting its Extent, Physical Capacities, Population, Industry, and Civil and Religious Institutions. By J. R. M'Culloch, Esq., assisted by numerous contributors. 2nd ed. 2 vols. 8vo. London, 1839.

The Progress of the Nation in its various Social and Economical Relations, from the beginning of the 19th century to the present time. By G. R. PORTER, Esq. (of the Board of Trade). 3 vols. crown 8vo. London, 1836—1843.

REPORT to the BRITISH GOVERNMENT on the COMMERCIAL STATISTICS of the KINGDOM of the TWO SICILIES. By JOHN MACGREGOR, Esq. (now one of the Secretaries to the Board of Trade). Folio. London, 1840.

A Dictionary, Geographical, Statistical, and Historical, of the various Countries, Places, and principal Natural Objects in the World. By J. R. M'CULLOCH, Esq. 2 thick and closely printed 8vo. vols. London, 1841.

Ireland before and after the Union with Great Britain. By R. M. MARTIN, Esq. 1 vol. 8vo. London, 1843.

A useful compilation, conclusively showing (which, however, was no very difficult task), in opposition to the statements put forth by the leaders of the Repeal faction, that Ireland has made very great advances since the Union; that many of her grievances have been redressed, and the most important benefits conferred upon her by the legislature of the United Kingdom. If those by whom the cry for the repeal of the Union has been raised were really sincere, it would evince an almost unparalleled degree of folly and absurdity. It is probable, however, that few will be disposed to give them credit for being such simpletons; and that it will be generally supposed, how erroneously soever, that a wish to excite a susceptible and confiding population, and thereby to further their own beggarly purposes, has had quite as much to do in the matter as any more exalted motives.

The opinion of Sir William Petty in favour of an incorporating union with Ireland has been already noticed; but having touched upon this topic, we may perhaps be allowed to avail ourselves of this opportunity to state that Molyneux, the friend of Locke, and the ablest defender of the independence of the Irish parliament, speaks of a union with England as of "an happiness we can hardly hope for!"—(The Case of Ireland, &c., p. 98, ed. Dublin, 1698.) And Lord Charlemont, the general of the volunteers, states that in the course of his conversations with the most illustrious political philosopher of last century, Ireland and its interests were often the topic. "Upon these occasions," says his Lordship, "I always found Montesquieu an advocate for an union between that country and England. 'Were I an Irishman,' said he, 'I should certainly wish for it; and as a general lover of liberty I sincerely desire it, and for this plain reason, that an inferior country, connected with one much her superior in force, can never be certain of the permanent enjoyment of constitutional freedom unless she has, by her representatives, a proportional share in the legislature of the superior kingdom.'"—(Hardy's 'Life of Lord Charlemont,' i. 70.)

The New Statistical Account of Scotland, compiled by the Ministers of the respective Parishes, under the superintendence of a Committee of the Society for the Benefit of the Sons and Daughters of the Clergy.

This work will comprise in all about 26 vols. 8vo., of which 24 are already published. Edinburgh, 1834, &c.

This account is in various respects superior, as indeed a second work of the same kind could hardly fail to be, to the old statistical account of Scotland, executed under the superintendence of Sir John Sinclair. It adopts, like the former, the parochial division; but in the present work the accounts of the parishes belonging to particular counties are all brought together and paged consecutively; whereas in the former they were distributed, without any sort of order, throughout the work. A summary is added to the close of each county of such particulars, in its statistical condition, as admit of being thrown into a tabular form; and the work is to be concluded by a general summary applicable to the entire kingdom. This national undertaking is, speaking generally, well executed, and reflects, as did the former work, much credit on the clergy of Scotland. The contrast between the condition of most parishes at present, and their condition from forty to fifty years ago, when the old account was published, is most striking, and generally, also, most gratifying.

Tables of the Revenue, Population, Commerce, &c., of the United Kingdom and its Dependencies, from 1820 downwards, compiled from Official Returns. By G. R. PORTER, Esq. 12 Parts, folio. London, 1833, &c.

In 1832, a Statistical Department was organised in the Board of Trade for preparing, classifying, and publishing official returns and information respecting the statistics of the United Kingdom and its dependencies, and also respecting foreign states. Mr. Porter was placed at the head of this department; and the numerous volumes of well-digested, commodiously arranged returns he has since given to the world afford the best evidence of his zeal and industry.

Progress of the United States in Population and Wealth in Fifty Years, as exhibited by the Decennial Census. By GEORGE TUCKER, Professor of Philosophy and Political Economy in the University of Virginia. 1 vol. 8vo. New York, 1843.

This work exhibits the censuses of the United States, taken in 1790, 1800, 1810, 1820, 1830, and 1840, and their results, as respects the progress of the population, and its distribution according to age, sex, race, &c. It also contains the statements obtained under the last census of the annual produce of the various branches of industry carried on in the different States, with the amount of capital and the number of hands engaged in each. But it is needless to add, that returns of this description can have no pretensions to anything like accuracy; and we doubt whether, under such circumstances, it would not be better to dispense with them altogether. Theories founded upon, or inferences deduced from such slippery data, must necessarily be worth little or nothing.

Companion to the Almanac: an Annual Volume, in post 8vo. London, 1828–44.

A well-compiled, useful publication. In addition to abstracts of important official documents and Acts of Parliament, and a chronological notice of the more prominent events of the previous year, it is enriched with numerous original papers on topics of interest. No publication has done so much to diffuse a taste for statistical inquiries. The 'North American Almanac,' which is compiled on the same plan, is also a very valuable work.

The Book of the Farm. By HENRY STEPHENS, F.R.S.E., &c. 3 vols. 8vo. Edinburgh, 1844.

This work was intended to be, and we have been assured is, a complete body of practical agriculture, embracing all the latest discoveries and improvements.

The Industrial Resources of Ireland. By ROBERT KANE, M.D. 1 vol. 8vo. Dublin, 1844.

One of the earliest systematical efforts to obtain accurate statistical information appears to have been made in France towards the end of the seventeenth century. It was then resolved, in order that the Duke of Burgundy, the grandson of Louis XIV., and the pupil of Fénélon, might have accurate information with respect to the state of the country, which it was highly probable he might be called to govern, to direct the Intendants to prepare accounts of their respective provinces, describing the state of agriculture, manufactures, and commerce; the number and classification of the inhabitants; their taxes and revenues, means of communication, peculiar laws, privileges, &c. There was of course the greatest inequality in these accounts. That of Languedoc, by M. Lamoignon de Baville, was by far the best; and to use the words of Voltaire, *si l'on avait rempli les vues du roi sur chaque province comme elles le furent dans le dénombrement du Languedoc, ce recueil de mémoires eût été un de plus beaux monumens du siècle.*—(Siècle de Louis XIV., c. 29.) But, notwithstanding the defects of the greater number, they contained a vast deal of authentic information respecting the state of France at the period referred to; and their non-publication is much to be regretted. A valuable abstract or abridgment of them was, however, given by the Comte de Boulainvilliers, under the title of *Etat de la France*, 6 vol. 12mo. Londres (Rouen), 1737. Lamoignon's Memoir was published separately *in extenso*, under the title of *Mémoires pour servir à l'Histoire du Languedoc*, 1 vol. 8vo. Amsterdam (Marseille), 1734; and deserves all that has been said in its commendation. The Memoirs now referred to, the *Dixme Royale* of Maréchal Vauban, the works on population of Messance and Moheau (see *post*), and the geographical works of Piganiol de la Force and the Abbé Expilly being excepted, few works having any very close connexion with statistics appeared in France till a comparatively late period.

Recherches Historiques et Critiques sur l'Administration Publique et Privée des Terres chez les Romains. (Par M. BUTEL-DUMONT: see p. 34). 1 vol. 8vo. Paris, 1779.

RICHESSES et RESSOURCES de la FRANCE, pour servir de suite aux Moyens de simplifier la Recette et la Comptabilité des Deniers Royaux. Par M. BONVALLET DESBROSSES. 1 vol. 4to. Paris, 1789.

APERÇU de la RICHESSE et des REVENUS de la FRANCE. Par MM. LAVOISIER, la GRANGE, et autres. 8vo. Paris, An IV, 1795.

The statements in this tract are alike interesting and valuable. Its authors were among the most distinguished philosophers of the age.

STATISTIQUE GÉNÉRALE et PARTICULIÈRE de la FRANCE et de ses COLONIES. Par une Société de Gens de Lettres et de Savans (MM. PEUCHET, HERBIN, SONINI, &c.) 7 vol. 8vo. et Atlas. Paris, An XII (1803).

STATISTIQUE ELÉMENTAIRE de la FRANCE. Par M. PEUCHET. 1 vol. 8vo. Paris, 1805.

Though no longer of much use in reference to the existing statistics of France, there is not, perhaps, a better model than this of what an elementary statistical work should be.

DE l'INDUSTRIE FRANÇAISE. Par M. le COMTE CHAPTAL. 2 vol. 8vo. Paris, 1819.

RECHERCHES sur les CONSOMMATIONS de la VILLE de PARIS en 1817, comparées à ce qu'elles étaient en 1789. Par M. BENOISTON de CHATEAUNEUF. 8vo. 2 Parties. Paris, 1820–21.

The imposition of *octrois*, or duties, on the principal articles of consumption imported into the great towns, affords facilities for compiling this description of works in France which do not exist in this country. In addition, however, to the official returns, which any one may get together, this tract contains various illustrative discussions on collateral topics, highly creditable to the discernment and research of the author. M. de Châteauneuf has published other valuable statistical tracts, some of which are elsewhere noticed in this work.

RECHERCHES STATISTIQUES sur la VILLE de PARIS. Par M. le Comte CHABROL. 3 vol. 4to. Paris, 1821, &c.

Consisting principally of very elaborate statistical tables.

DE l'ECONOMIE PUBLIQUE et RURALE des CELTES; des PERSES et des PHŒNICIENS; des ARABES et des JUIFS; des EGYPTIENS et des CARTHAGINOIS; et des GRECS. Par M. Z. REYNIER. 5 vol. 8vo. Genève, 1818–25.

VOYAGE de M. le Baron DUPIN dans la GRANDE BRETAGNE, en 1816, 1817, et 1819.

1re Part.	Force Militaire.	2 vol.	4to. avec un Atlas.	Paris,	1821.
2de ,,	Navale.	,,	,,	,,	,,
3me ,,	Commerciale.	,,	,,	,,	1824.

These volumes are principally occupied with descriptions of the great public works constructed in this country in each of the departments to which they refer. The *Force Commerciale* was translated into English under the title of

THE COMMERCIAL POWER of GREAT BRITAIN; exhibiting a Complete View of the Public Works of this Country, &c., with an Atlas of Plans, Elevations, &c. 2 vols. 8vo. London, 1825.

FORCES PRODUCTIVES et COMMERCIALES de la FRANCE. Par M. DUPIN. 2 vol. 4to. Paris, 1827.

Statistique Génerale de l'Empire de la Russie. Par M. J. H. SCHNITZLER. 1 vol. 12mo. Paris, 1829.

The best and most comprehensive work of its kind on Russia. A new edition is now, however, very much wanted.

LA RUSSIE, la POLOGNE, et la FINLANDE; ou Tableau Statistique, Géographique, et Historique de toutes les Parties de la Monarchie Russe prises isolément. Par M. SCHNITZLER. 1 vol. 8vo. Paris, 1835.

This work has been compiled with great care from the best sources; but it wants the interest and completeness of the 'Statistique Génerale.'

APERÇU STATISTIQUE de la FRANCE. Par M. GIRAULT de St. FARGEAU. Ed. 2de. 8vo. Paris, 1836.

A comprehensive and valuable sketch of the statistics of France previously to and since the Revolution.

STATISTIQUE GÉNÉRALE de la BELGIQUE. Par M. HEUSCHLING. 1 vol. 12mo. Bruxelles, 1838.

TRAITÉ de STATISTIQUE, ou Théorie de l'Etude des Lois d'après lesquelles se développent les Faits Sociaux. Par M. DUFAU. 1 vol. 8vo. Paris, 1840.

ESSAI COMPARATIF sur la FORMATION et la DISTRIBUTION du REVENU de la FRANCE en 1815 et 1835. Par M. DUTENS. 8vo. Paris, 1842.

This tract contains some curious details with respect to the increase of the town and country population, and the progressive subdivision of the land occasioned by the law of equal partition. In 1815, according to M. Dutens, the agricultural population of France amounted to 17,100,000, and in 1835 to 19,582,000; the town population having amounted at the former epoch to 11,732,745, and at the latter to 13,744,575. This increase of the town population has been, no doubt, mainly owing to the growth and improvement of manufactures and commerce in the interval. But the increase of the rural population would appear to be wholly a consequence of the increasing subdivision (*morcellement*) of the land; the first effect of the introduction of an improved system of agriculture into a country like France being the diminution of the number of persons living upon the land. M. Dutens estimates that, in 1835, there were in France above 2,000,000 *landed* properties, of which 312,500 did not exceed 1 hectare (about $2\frac{1}{2}$ acres), 507,500 did not exceed 5 hectares, and 150,000 did not exceed 10 hectares: there were only 1000 properties of 400 hectares (1000 acres) and upwards. M. Dutens appears to have formed a much more judicious estimate than most part of his countrymen of the consequences of the continued subdivision of the land that is now going forward. "Si donc," says he, "quelque chose peut nous étonner, c'est la persistance avec laquelle les esprits qui s'occupent principalement des progrès de l'industrie et de l'extension du commerce poursuivent l'idée de la division des terres; ils ne prennent pas garde qu'en substituant ainsi la petite à la grande culture, et en réduisant de cette manière le nombre des grands propriétaires, ils enlèvent à l'industrie des manufactures et aux différentes classes d'artisans la classe des consommateurs qui éprouvent le plus de besoin de leurs produits. Dira-t-on que cette opinion est moins celle des hommes voués aux progrès de l'industrie et du commerce que de ceux qui, par un sentiment de philanthropie, voudraient, en réunissant le travail agricole et le travail industriel, voir s'améliorer le sort des classes ouvrières? Mais ce partage de temps et d'efforts entre des occupations si différentes n'est-il pas un obstacle à tout perfectionnement dans les deux branches d'industrie auxquelles se livrerait presque simultanément un seul homme? Et est-ce bien à l'éventualité d'un adoucissement très-incertain dans la position de quelques individus qu'on pourrait sacrifier les énergiques moyens de production que le gouvernement ne peut attendre que de l'emploi des grands capitaux? La subdivision des terres poussée au-delà de certaines limites nous paraît affectée d'un double et grave inconvénient: premièrement, de nuire constamment aux intérêts de l'agriculture, en mettant à sa disposition des bras qu'elle ne réclame pas et en s'opposant à la formation des capitaux qui lui manquent; secondement, d'être en certaines circonstances en opposition avec les intérêts du gouvernement, en le privant des ressources que, dans des momens difficiles, il ne peut espérer que des grandes propriétés et des grands revenus. Sous ce double rapport, c'est donc, en principe, aux forces de l'agriculture et à l'application de ces forces à l'exploitation des grandes fermes, que les nations et les gouvernemens peuvent être redevables de si éminens services."—(pp. 78, 79.)

De la Création de la Richesse, ou des Intérêts Matériels en France: Statistique comparée et raisonnée. Par M. J. H. Schnitzler. 2 vol. 8vo. Paris, 1842.

Two more volumes, treating *Des Intérêts Moraux*, are required to complete this valuable work, which is not, however, what we should have expected from the author of the 'Statistique Générale de la Russie.'

Latterly the French Government have published several quarto volumes of very valuable official returns respecting the extent, population, productions, internal and external commerce, &c. of France, comprising most part of the statistical information respecting the kingdom capable of being embodied in tables. Of course the returns are not all equally authentic, and entitled to the same attention. In illustration of this remark, we may observe that, amongst others, accounts are given of the extent of land under different crops, the quantity of seed, and the amount of the produce per hectare in different years. But, as already stated, seeing that no such information can be obtained with anything like accuracy, we doubt whether it had not better be withheld.

Filosofia della Statistica. Da Gioja. 2nda ediz., con Aggiunte di Romagnosi. 4 vol. 8vo. Milano, 1829.

Cenzo de la Riqueza Territorial, &c., de España. Por J. Polo y Catalina. Folio. Madrid, 1803.

Informe de la Sociedad Economica de Madrid al Real y Supremo Consejo de Castilla en expediente de Ley Agraria. Por Don Gaspar M. de Jovellanos.

This memoir was presented to the Council of Castile in 1795, and was printed in 4to., at Madrid, in the same year. It was reprinted in 4to., Palma, 1814.

In this famous memoir the author exhibits the influence of the laws of entail and mortmain, the privileges of the *mesta*,* the want of roads, and of a free intercourse among the different provinces, the inequality and oppressiveness of the taxes, the ignorance of the cultivators, &c., in depressing industry, and preventing agriculture from making any progress. But instead of receiving, as he well deserved, the thanks of government for his efforts to open their eyes and those of the public to the circumstances by which the national energies were paralyzed and the kingdom overspread with pauperism, the imbecile bigots who then ruled over Spain threw Jovellanos into prison, where he remained for

* The Spanish name for the migratory flocks of sheep.

some years, or till the invasion of the country by the French. An English version of this memoir is given in the translation of Laborde's work on Spain, of which it is the most valuable portion, vol. iv. pp. 111–315. It is also noticed in an article in the 14th volume of the 'Edinburgh Review.'

MONE, HISTORIA STATISTICÆ ADUMBRATA. 1 vol. 4to. Lovanii, 1828.

Scriptores Rei Rusticæ Veterum Latinorum, illustravit J. G. SCHNEIDER. 4 vol. 8vo. Lipsiæ, 1794.

An excellent translation of Columella, the best by far of the ancient writers on agriculture and rural economy, was published with notes in 1 vol. 4to. London, 1745.

CHAPTER VII.

COAL TRADE.

It is hardly possible to exaggerate the advantages England derives from her vast beds of coal. In this climate fuel ranks among the principal necessaries of life; and it is to our coal mines that we owe abundant and cheap supplies of so indispensable an article. Had they not existed, wood must have been used as fuel; and it is quite impossible that any attention to the growth of timber could have furnished a supply equal to the wants of the present population of Great Britain, even though a large proportion of the cultivated land had been appropriated to the raising of trees. But however great, this is not the only advantage we derive from our coal-mines; they are the principal source and foundation of our manufacturing and commercial prosperity. Since the invention of the steam-engine coal has become of the highest importance as a moving power; and no nation, however favourably situated in other respects, not plentifully supplied with this mineral, need hope to rival those that are, in most branches of manufacturing industry.

To what is the astonishing increase of Glasgow, Manchester, Birmingham, Leeds, Sheffield, &c., and the comparatively stationary or declining state of Canterbury, Winchester, Salisbury, and other towns in the south of England, to be ascribed? It cannot be pretended, with any show of reason, that the inhabitants of the former are naturally more ingenious, enterprising, or industrious, than those of the latter. The abundance and cheapness of coal in the north, and its scarcity, and consequent high price, in the south, is the real cause of this striking discrepancy. The citizens of Manchester, Glasgow, &c. are able, at a comparatively small expense, to put the most powerful and complicated machinery in motion, and to produce results quite beyond the reach of those who have not the same command over coal, or, as it has been happily defined, "hoarded labour." Our coal-mines have been sometimes called the "Black Indies;" and they have certainly conferred a thousand times more real advantage on us than we have derived from the conquest of the Mogul empire, or than we should have reaped from the dominion of Mexico and Peru. They have supplied our manufacturers and artisans with a power of unbounded energy and of easy control, and enabled them to overcome difficulties insurmountable by those to whom Nature has been less liberal of her choicest gifts.

There are no mines of coal in either Greece or Italy; and no evidence has been produced to show that the ancients had learned to avail themselves of this most useful mineral. Even in England it does not seem to have been used previously to the beginning of the thirteenth century; for the first mention of it occurs in a charter of Henry III., granting licence to the burgesses of Newcastle to dig for coal. In 1281 Newcastle is said to have had a considerable trade in this article. About the end of this century, or the beginning of the fourteenth, coals began to be imported into London, being at first used only by smiths, brewers, dyers, soap-boilers, &c. This innovation was, however, loudly complained of.

A notion got abroad that the smoke was highly injurious to the public health; and in 1316 parliament petitioned the king, Edward I., to prohibit the burning of coal, on the ground of its being an intolerable nuisance. His Majesty issued a proclamation conformably to the prayer of the petition; but it being but little attended to, recourse was had to more vigorous measures; a commission of oyer and terminer being issued out, with instructions to inquire as to all who burned sea-coal within the city, or parts adjoining, to punish them for the first offence by "pecuniary mulcts," and upon a second offence to demolish their furnaces; and to provide for the strict observance of the proclamation in all time to come.

But notwithstanding the efforts that were thus made to prohibit the use of coal, and the prejudice that was long entertained against it, it continued progressively to gain ground. This was partly, no doubt, owing to experience having shown that coal-smoke had not the noxious influence ascribed to it, but far more to the superior excellence of coal as an article of fuel, and the growing scarcity and consequent high price of timber. In the reign of Charles I. the use of coal became universal in London, where it has ever since been used to the exclusion of all other articles of fuel. At the Restoration, the quantity imported was supposed to amount to about 255,000 tons. In 1670, the imports had increased to 340,000 tons, and have since gone on increasing with the growing magnitude and population of the city; being, in 1750, about 630,000 tons; in 1800, about 1,200,000 tons; and at present, 1844, nearly 3,000,000 ditto!

The best account, perhaps, of the rise and progress of the coal-trade is that given by Brand in his 'History of Newcastle' (2 vols. 4to. London, 1789), ii. pp. 241-311.

A LETTER addressed to ROWLAND BURDON, Esq., M.P., on the present state of the carrying part of the COAL TRADE, with TABLES of the DUTIES on COAL raised by the CORPORATION of the CITY of LONDON (from 1700 to 1801). By NATHANIEL ATCHISON, F.A.S., &c. 8vo. London, 1802.

The duties on coal, referred to in this tract, partly originated in the corporation of the city of London having early undertaken the task of weighing and measuring coal; and having been allowed a greater sum for this duty than it cost to perform, the surplus formed a portion of the city's nett revenue. But, in addition to the above, a duty on all coal brought into the city was granted subsequently to the great fire in 1666, to enable the corporation to rebuild churches, &c. And a duty of this sort has, under one pretence and another, been continued down to the present day.

Exclusive, however, of the corporation duties, a duty payable to government was laid on *all sea-borne* coal in the reign of William III., which was not finally repealed till 1831. This duty was at once glaringly unjust and oppressive: unjust, inasmuch as it fell only on those parts of the empire to which coals had to be carried by sea; and oppressive, inasmuch as it amounted to full *fifty* per cent. upon the price paid to the coal-owner for the coal. This tax, after being long stationary at 5*s.* a chaldron, was raised to 9*s.* 4*d.* during the late war; but was reduced to 6*s.* in 1824. But the inequality of the tax was not confined to its affecting those parts only of the empire to which coal had to be carried by sea. Even there its pressure was not equal; for, while it amounted to 6*s.* a chaldron, or 4*s.* a ton, in the metropolis and all the south of England, it only amounted to 1*s.* 7¼*d.* a ton on coal carried by sea to Ireland, and to 1*s.* 8*d.* on that carried to Wales; while Scotland was for many years entirely exempted from the duty.

A General View of the Coal Trade of Scotland, chiefly that of the River Forth, and Mid-Lothian, &c. By ROBERT BALD, Civil Engineer. 8vo. Edinburgh, 1808.

The best work on the subject.

A TREATISE on the COAL TRADE; with Strictures on its Abuses, and Hints for their Amendment. By ROBERT EDINGTON. 2nd ed., 1 vol., 8vo. London, 1814.

REPORTS from the SELECT COMMITTEES of the HOUSES of LORDS and COMMONS on the STATE of the COAL TRADE. Folio, 1830.

These reports contain the most ample information on almost every matter connected with the coal-trade: and especially with respect to the various charges on coal in the port of London, and in its passage thence to the consumer.

OBSERVATIONS on the DUTY on SEA-BORNE COAL, and on the Peculiar Duties and Charges on Coal in the Port of London. (By J. R. M'CULLOCH, Esq.) 8vo. London, 1830.

This tract preceded, and we believe promoted, the repeal of the duty on sea-borne coal.

The History and Description of Fossil Fuel—the Collieries and Coal Trade of Great Britain. By the Author of 'Manufactures in Metal' in the Cabinet Cyclopædia (Mr. JOHN HOLLAND). 1 vol., 8vo. London, 1841.

OBSERVATIONS on the PROPOSED DUTIES (those in the TARIFF of 1842) on the EXPORTATION of COALS; with Tables and Statements from Parliamentary Returns and other Authentic Sources. 8vo. London, 1842.

CHAPTER VIII.

HERRING AND OTHER FISHERIES.

It would be useless to attempt giving any notice of any considerable number of the works respecting the British fisheries, more especially of those relating to the herring fishery. A library might, in fact, be filled with the books, tracts, reports, and acts of parliament having reference to the latter; and yet among these myriads there are but few entitled to attention. The false estimates that were long current of the extent and value of the Dutch herring fishery appear to have generated, on this side the Channel, the most exaggerated ideas of the importance of the business. "It has given the Dutch," said Andrew Yarranton, in 1681, "their mighty numbers of seamen, their vast fleets of ships, and a foundation for all their other trades." (England's Improvement, 2nd Part, p. 129.) And it is affirmed in a statement said (though, perhaps, on no good grounds) to have been drawn up by Sir Walter Raleigh, for the information of James I., in 1618, that 3000 Dutch vessels, having on board 50,000 men and boys, were then employed in the herring fishery on the coasts of Great Britain, and that no fewer than 9000 additional vessels and 150,000 "persons more are employed by sea and land, to make provision to dress and transport the fish they take, and return commodities, whereby they are enabled, and do build yearly 1000 ships and vessels, &c." (Raleigh's Works, by Birch, i. 130.) The gross exaggeration of this statement, both as respects the number of vessels and the number of hands employed, is obvious. At the period referred to, the entire population of the United Provinces did not certainly exceed 2,400,000 persons, of which fully a half may be set apart as being, from age, youth, &c., unfit for active pursuits; and to suppose that a sixth part, or 200,000 persons, of the remaining portion of the population, including females, should have been engaged in the herring fishery and the employments immediately connected therewith, is so very absurd, that one is astonished it should have been believed for a moment. Most probably, indeed, it never would have obtained much currency, but for the circumstance of its having been introduced by M. Delacourt into his 'Memoirs of John de Witt' (p. 24, Eng. trans.), which, having been erroneously ascribed to that statesman (see chapter on Miscellaneous Works), acquired an influence and authority to which they were not really entitled.

But, though vastly exaggerated, the Dutch herring fishery far exceeded that of any other country; and for this superiority the Hollanders were indebted to the skill which they had early acquired in the business; to the economy with which all their operations were conducted, which made Andrew Yarranton say that "we fish intolerably dear and the Dutch exceeding cheap" (*ubi supra*, p. 131); and to the easy access afforded by the great rivers that traverse their country to the interior of Europe, where the herrings were principally disposed of. The English had no similar advantages on their side; and the use of fish has never been popular among the bulk of our people. Hence, though pamphlet after pamphlet was written, holding out the example of the Dutch, and calling upon the public to patronize the fishery as the surest means of increasing the national wealth; though company after company was formed for its encouragement; and though immense sums were lavished upon bounties for its encouragement, which at one time rose to the all but incredible amount of 159*l.* 7*s.* 6*d.* per barrel of merchantable fish (Wealth of Nations, p. 231), the fishery made no real progress. It merely dragged out a sickly, miserable existence; and it is only in our own times, and since it was left to depend on its own resources, that it has become of importance.

The bounty system was not merely objectionable from the waste of the national resources which it occasioned, but also from its tempting crowds of landsmen to engage in the business, generally to their own ruin, and always to the injury of the regular fishermen, for whose encouragement the bounties were said to be granted. But notwithstanding its costliness, and its all but obvious defects, it was persevered in till 1830, when it finally ceased: and we are gratified to have to state that the fishery has increased most materially since that epoch, and that the "take" of herrings in 1842 exceeded by more than 200,000 barrels what it had ever amounted to in any year during the bounty system!

Even if the bounty system had been productive of any real advantage, which was certainly not the case, it would have been more than countervailed by the operation of the salt-duties. The influence of the latter was most mischievous. It is true that salt was allowed to be used *duty free* in the fisheries; but so many and such troublesome forms and conditions had to be complied with before it could be procured, while the penalties for non-compliance with the regulations respecting its use were so numerous and heavy, that every individual engaged in the fishery would have preferred using salt charged with a moderate duty. To such an extent did the grievance growing out of the salt-laws affect the fishery, that Mr. M'Donald, the well-informed author of the 'Survey of the Hebrides,' mentions, that he had repeatedly seen whole cargoes of the finest herrings thrown into the sea in a putrid state, through the inability of the fishermen to procure a supply of duty-free salt! (p. 513). The repeal of the salt-laws was, in fact, indispensable to give the fisheries a chance of success; and this measure may be said to be the only real encouragement ever given to the latter by the Legislature.

Those who wish to inquire further into this matter may, in addition to the references in Anderson and Macpherson's Histories of Commerce, refer to the following works, viz.:—

ENGLAND'S PATH to WEALTH and HONOUR. In a Dialogue between an Englishman and a Dutchman. By J. PUCKLE. 8vo. London, 1707, and reprinted in 1750.

THE WEALTH of GREAT BRITAIN in the OCEAN; including an HISTORICAL and CRITICAL STATE of the BRITISH FISHERIES. 8vo. London, 1749.

THE FISHERIES REVIVED; or, BRITAIN'S HIDDEN TREASURE DISCOVERED. 8vo. London, 1750.

An unusual degree of attention was directed towards the fisheries at this period in consequence of the formation of a society for their encouragement, with the Prince of Wales at its head, and a subscribed capital of 500,000*l.* But of this society Adam Smith says there was hardly a vestige in 1784. Its capital had been wholly spent, and the fishery was, if anything, in a worse condition than when the society was established.

Knox's 'View of the British Empire, more especially Scotland,' was published in 1785 (see *post*). The first volume contains a lengthened account of the herring and other fisheries, with various suggestions for their improvement.

Two Reports from the Select Committee of the House of Commons, appointed in 1785 to Inquire into the State of the British Fisheries, on the Pilchard Fisheries. Folio. 1786.

Seven Reports from the same Committee on the State of the British Fisheries; and on the most effectual means for their Improvement, Encouragement, and Extension. Folio. 1786.

A new society was formed about the time that these reports were published, for improving the fisheries. Under its auspices harbours were formed in sundry places, and several useful undertakings of that kind were completed. But in other respects the influence of the society appears to have been very limited, and no dividend has ever been realized on its funds.

A Review of the Domestic Fisheries of Great Britain and Ireland. By Robert Fraser, Esq. 1 vol. 4to. Edinburgh, 1818.

Sir T. C. Morgan has added an 'Historical Sketch of the British and Irish Fisheries' to the 'First Report of the Commissioners of Inquiry into the State of the Irish Fisheries,' folio, Dublin, 1836. Sir John Barrow has contributed a valuable article on the Fisheries to the last edition of the 'Encyclopædia Britannica.' And there is an article on the Herring Fishery in the 'Commercial Dictionary,' &c. But a good work on the history, state, and prospects of the latter continues to be a desideratum.

A View of the Greenland Trade and Whale-Fishery, with the National and Private Advantages thereof. (By Henry Elking.) 8vo. London, 1722.

This valuable tract embodies, within a short compass, a great deal of information respecting the early history of the whale-fishery. The object of the author, who had been extensively engaged in the trade, as stated by himself, was to give—

1.—" An account how the whale fishery is and ought to be performed, from the first outset to the return of the ships.

2.—" By whom this fishing is chiefly carried on, viz., by the Hollanders, Hamburghers, and Bremeners; and how much it appears to their advantage.

3.—" A brief recapitulation of what happened in the infancy of the Greenland trade; how the English were first in it, how they lost it, and what have been the causes that all their attempts to retrieve it have been unsuccessful.

4.—" A full proof that England may retrieve this trade, and is able to carry it on to more advantage than any other nation; and all the known objections to the contrary answered and removed."

Elking's statements on each of these heads are clear, concise, and satisfactory. His tract is, indeed, of the highest authority, and is repeatedly referred to by Mr. Scoresby.

An Account of the Arctic Regions, with a History and Description of the Northern Whale-Fishery. By W. SCORESBY, jun., F.R.S.E. 2 vols. 8vo. Edinburgh, 1820.

This standard work comprises all that most persons can wish to know of the subjects of which it treats. A useful compendium of the most important information with respect to the Arctic regions and the northern whale-fishery may be found in the volume of the Edinburgh Cabinet Library, entitled

NARRATIVE of ADVENTURE and DISCOVERY in the POLAR SEAS and REGIONS, including an Account of the Whale-Fishery. By HUGH MURRAY, Esq., F.R.S.E. 1 vol. 12mo. Edinburgh, 1830.

A VIEW of the PRESENT STATE of the SALMON and CHANNEL FISHERIES. By J. CORNISH, Esq. 1 vol. 8vo. London, 1824.

OBSERVATIONS respecting the SALMON FISHERY of SCOTLAND, especially with reference to the Stake-net mode of Fishing. 8vo. Edinburgh, 1824.

This tract was written by a learned gentleman, now a Judge of the Court of Session, in Scotland.

REPORTS from and MINUTES of EVIDENCE taken before the SELECT COMMITTEE of the HOUSE of COMMONS on the State of the Salmon Fisheries of the United Kingdom, and on the modes of Improving them. Folio. 1824—25.

REPORT from the SELECT COMMITTEE of the HOUSE of COMMONS appointed to Inquire into the Present State of the British Channel Fisheries, and the Laws affecting the Fishery Trade of England, with a view to their Amendment. Folio. 1833.

The Natural History of the Sperm Whale (including an Account of the Rise and Progress of the Sperm-Whale Fishery), with a Sketch of a South-Sea Whaling Voyage. By THOMAS BEALE, Surgeon. 1 vol. 8vo. London, 1839.

We have given in the article Whale-Fishery, in the 'Commercial Dictionary,' an account of the number of ships annually absent from Great Britain on South-Sea whaling expeditions, from 1800 to 1842, both inclusive; the quantities of sperm and of common oil annually imported during the same period; the prices of such oils, &c.

A good deal of information respecting the Newfoundland fisheries, and those carried on along the coast of Labrador, may be found in Mr. Macgregor's work on British North America, 2nd ed. 2 vols. Edinburgh. Mr. Pitkin has described the origin and progress of the American fisheries in his 'Statistical View of the Commerce, &c., of the United States' (pp. 36-46). See *ante*, p. 60.

TRAITÉ GÉNÉRAL des PÊCHES MARITIMES, des RIVIÈRES, etc., des POISSONS. Par M. DUHAMEL DU MONCEAU. 3 vol. gr. in-fol. Paris, 1769-82; avec 74 pp. du tome IV.

MÉMOIRE sur l'ANTIQUITÉ de la PÊCHE de la BALEINE. Par NOEL. 1 vol. 12mo. Paris, 1795.

Histoire des Pêches, des Découvertes, et des Etablissemens des Hollandois dans les Mers du Nord, ouvrage traduit du Hollandois. Par BERNARD de RESTE. 3 vol. 8vo. Paris, an IX (1801).

CONSIDÉRATIONS sur la PÊCHE de la BALEINE. Par M. de la JONKAIRE. 8vo. Paris, 1830.

CHAPTER IX.

MANUFACTURES, ARTS, &c.

Reasons for a Limited Exportation of Wool. 4to. (London), 1677.

From the Conquest down to the æra of the Commonwealth, the exportation of wool was either quite free, or free under payment of a duty. But in 1647 its exportation was prohibited by an ordinance of the parliament; and at the Restoration this prohibition was confirmed, and the exportation of wool made felony by the 12 Car. II. c. 32, and the 13 and 14 Car. II. c. 18. This prohibition, which continued down to a very late period, was enacted to favour the woollen manufacture, of the importance of which the most exaggerated notions have generally been entertained; and the influence of the measure was farther promoted by allowing Spanish wool to be imported free of duty, and by compelling all Irish wool to be sent to England; the market of which was, in this way, completely glutted. We may remark, by the way, that the fact of the landed interest having consented for so long a period to the existence of regulations by which the market value of one of their most considerable products was materially reduced, is rather a curious commentary on the statements so frequently put forth of their readiness to sacrifice every interest to their own; and shows that they must have been deeply impressed with the belief of the paramount importance of the woollen manufacture.

The tract referred to above is one of the very few that were written in opposition to the prohibition of exportation; which it contends should be allowed under a reasonable duty. It is short, comprising only 24 pages, and ably written. We have already laid before the reader a remarkable passage from it, in which the fundamental principles of Quesnay's theory are clearly enunciated.—(See p. 9.)

The Ancient Trades Decayed Repaired Again. By a Country Tradesman. 8vo. London, 1678.

In this year (1678) the act was passed 29 and 30 Car. II. c. 1, prohibiting, for three years, the importation of all French commodities.

The woollen manufacture is said to have made some considerable progress in Ireland in the interval between 1640 and the Revolution; though, considering the convulsed state of that country during that period, and the wars and proscriptions of which she was the theatre, it is difficult to believe that it could have been very perceptible. But such as it was, it excited the fears and jealousy of the English manufacturers, who prevailed, in 1698, on both Houses of parliament to address William III., praying that he would take measures for the discouragement of the woollen manufacture in Ireland! And soon after the Act 10 and 11 Will. III. c. 10 was passed, prohibiting, under excessively heavy penalties, the exportation of wool and woollens from Ireland to any place except England, where the woollens were loaded with duties that were, in effect, prohibitory! The extreme injustice, tyranny, and impolicy of such proceedings are too obvious to require being pointed out. We do not, however, believe that in point of fact they had any considerable practical influence, or that the woollen manufacture of Ireland would have been in a much more advanced state than it really is had the measures referred to never been heard of. The superior facilities enjoyed by England for the prosecution of manufacturing industry are such that it is visionary to suppose she should, under any circumstances, have had anything to fear from the competition of Ireland.

At the same time that the English parliament evinced this spirit of hostility to the woollen manufacture of Ireland, it gave every sort of encouragement to her linen manufacture. It may however be doubted whether this was really of advantage. At all events two very eminent authorities, Messrs. Young and Wakefield, concur in thinking that the linen manufacture, so long at least as it was carried on in the houses of the peasantry, was prejudicial, rather than otherwise, to the country.

A good deal of information with respect to the manufactures then existing in England is given in the 'British Merchant,' originally published in 1713-1714. See *ante*, p. 45.

PROVISION for the POOR; or a View of the Decayed State of the Woollen Manufacture, with Remarks on the Causes and Evil Consequences thereof, and a Scheme of Proper Remedies, &c. By JOHN HAYNES. 2nd ed. 4to. London, 1715.

For a statement of the proceedings with respect to the importation of calicos, see *ante*, p. 99, &c.

THE CASE of the BRITISH and IRISH MANUFACTURE of LINEN, THREADS, and TAPES FAIRLY STATED, and all the Objections against the Encouragement proposed to be given to that Manufacture fully answered. 8vo. London, 1738.

A vast number of tracts were published in the interval between 1720 and 1750 in reference to the state of the woollen trade and the woollen manufacture. They mostly all represent the latter as being in a declining state, mainly occasioned, as they allege, by the clandestine exportation of British wool to France and other parts of the continent. But though the manufacture made but little progress during the period referred to, it certainly did not decline. The statements respecting the smuggling abroad (*running* *) of British wool were, however, well founded; this being a necessary consequence of the low price of wool in England as compared with its price on the continent. The severest punishments were inflicted on those found engaged in its exportation, and every possible effort was made to prevent its being carried on; but if we may believe the statements of contemporary writers, with very little effect. In truth it is quite as difficult to prevent the clandestine exportation of low-priced native articles as it is to prevent the clandestine importation of low-priced foreign articles.

Chronicon Rusticum-Commerciale; or Memoirs of Wool, &c. By JOHN SMITH, LL.B. 1st ed. 2 vols. 8vo. London, 1747. 2nd ed. 2 vols. 4to. London, 1756–7.

This is one of the most carefully compiled and valuable works that has

---

* This offence was called *owling*, from its being principally carried on at night.

been published on the history of any branch of trade. It brings together from every source, however remote, and mostly in the words of the authors, almost all the information that had been previously given to the world respecting the progress of the woollen trade and manufacture, more especially in Great Britain; and incidentally throws a strong and steady light on other departments of economical history. Smith is opposed to the restriction on the exportation of wool; and approves, in respect to it, of the course suggested by the author of the 'Reasons for a Limited Exportation of Wool,' referred to above.

THE STATE of the TRADE and MANUFACTORY of IRON in GREAT BRITAIN CONSIDERED. 8vo. (London), 1750.

This tract is curious from the information which it affords respecting the production of iron at the time, which the author estimates at 18,000 tons. He states the difficulties with which the manufacture had to contend from the scarcity and high price of timber; and yet, not very consistently, complains of the importation of Swedish iron, and still more bitterly of the establishment of iron-works in our North American colonies. It is curious that not a word is said in this tract about the employment of pit-coal in the manufacture of iron; though Lord Dudley had taken out a patent for its application in 1619; and the practice of making iron by its means had been carried on to some extent at the works in Colebrook Dale since about 1740, or for ten years previously to the publication of this tract. It is singular, indeed, to observe how slowly this great invention, to which this country owes more perhaps than to any one else, made its way. The works of the inventor were destroyed by an ignorant rabble; and when Dr. Campbell published his elaborate work on Great Britain, in 1774, upwards of thirty-four years after the process had been again introduced, he merely alludes to it in a note, and in a way that shows he had no conception of its value (ii. 43). In fact it was not till about 1780 that the superiority of this practice began to be apparent. And the most sanguine speculator of those days could not have formed an idea of its prodigious importance, and of the astonishing results of which it was to be productive.

SOME ACCOUNT of the RISE, PROGRESS, and PRESENT STATE of the BREWERY. (By MICHAEL COMBRUNE, Esq., Brewer.) 8vo. London, 1757.

THE CONTRAST; or a Comparison between the Woollen, Linen, Cotton, and Silk Manufactures. 8vo. London, 1782.

The project for allowing a free exportation of wool having been again brought forward about this period, gave occasion to the following tracts:—

THE QUESTION CONSIDERED, whether WOOL should be allowed to be Exported when the Price is Low at Home, on Paying a Duty to the Public? By Sir JOHN DALRYMPLE, Bart. 8vo. London, 1781.

A well-written pamphlet, in which the question is answered in the affirmative.

AN ANSWER to Sir JOHN DALRYMPLE'S PAMPHLET on the EXPORTATION of WOOL. By NATHANIEL FORSTER, D.D. (author of the Work on Prices, see p. 193). 8vo. Colchester, 1782.

REFLECTIONS on the PRESENT LOW PRICE of COARSE WOOLS, its Immediate Causes, and its Probable Remedies. By JOSIAH TUCKER, D.D., Dean of Gloucester. 8vo. London, 1782.

This pamphlet exhibits, though in an extreme degree, that singular medley of sense and nonsense that is found in some of Tucker's other tracts. He shows that wool being at a very low price, it would be good policy to permit exportation on payment of a moderate duty; and he then proposes that the produce of the duty should be expended in bounties on the exportation of woollen goods. Had he stopped here, there would have been little to object to in his tract; but not satisfied with the above suggestions, he goes on to recommend, with a view to increase the home consumption of coarse wool (the price of which was the most depressed), by increasing the numbers of the peasantry, that cottages should be erected at the public expense on heaths, wastes, &c.; that the occupiers of these cottages should serve as permanent militia-men and enjoy sundry privileges; and that the preference should be given in their selection to those having the greatest number of children, and so on!

AN ESSAY on the MANUFACTURES of IRELAND, &c. By THOMAS WALLACE, M.R.I.A. 1 vol. 8vo. Dublin, 1798.

REPORT of the SECRETARY (General Hamilton) of the UNITED STATES on the Subject of MANUFACTURES, presented to the House of Representatives on the 5th December, 1791. 8vo. London, 1793.

This is a well drawn-up *résumé* of the arguments in favour of the mistaken policy of encouraging manufactures applied to the case of America. But without taking up the time of the reader by entering into any detailed exposition of their sophistry and fallacy, we may shortly observe that it would have been well for the United States had they rejected General Hamilton's advice; and left manufactures to grow up in the Union as they would have done, without any artificial encouragement, according as the circumstances of the country enabled them to be carried on with advantage. All that she has realised by her attempts prematurely to stimulate their growth, has been a heavy loss. She has forced, by her ill-judged policy, a large portion of her capital and industry into employments which cannot be carried on without laying heavy duties on the products of similar employments when imported from abroad; that is, without imposing a heavy tax upon her own people! It would not be difficult to show that America expends at present from ten to twelve millions sterling a year in protection to her manufactures, exclusive of the injury this policy inflicts on her agriculture and trade! And it is impossible to show that she has gained a single real advantage by this heavy sacrifice. Indeed all those manufactures for which the country is adapted, and which may be carried on without loss to the public, are injured by the protective system.

AN ACCOUNT of the PROCEEDINGS of the MERCHANTS, MANUFACTURERS, and others concerned in the WOOL and WOOLLEN TRADE of GREAT BRITAIN, &c. 1 vol. 8vo. London, 1800.

These proceedings refer to the strenuous opposition made by the woollen manufacturers and others interested in the trade, to the provisions in the treaty of Union between Great Britain and Ireland, which went to introduce a more liberal system into the trade between the two countries. Happily their opposition was unsuccessful.

Report from the Select Committee of the House of Commons on the State of the Woollen Manufacture of England. Folio, 1806.

This is a very valuable and interesting report. It gives a history of the manufacture and an account of the modes in which it is carried on in the West of England and the West Riding of Yorkshire. The comparative advantages and disadvantages of the domestic and factory systems are also fully and fairly stated.

REPORTS from the SELECT COMMITTEE of the HOUSE of COMMONS of 1817 and 1818, on the Petitions of the Watchmakers of Coventry, and on the Laws relating to Watchmakers.

These Reports supply ample information with respect to the progress and state of the watch trade.

REPORT from the SELECT COMMITTEE of the HOUSE of COMMONS on the LINEN TRADE of IRELAND. Folio. 1825.

This Report includes a previous Report of 1822 on the Laws which regulate the Linen Trade of Ireland; and the two give a very complete view of the history and state of the manufacture.

Speeches in the House of Commons on the 24th of February, 1826, on the Motion for a Committee on the State of the Silk Trade. 8vo. London, 1826.

This tract contains Mr. Huskisson's defence of his measures with respect to the silk trade, and the famous speech made by Mr. Canning in vindication of their policy.

REPORT from the SELECT COMMITTEE of the HOUSE of LORDS on the STATE of the BRITISH WOOL TRADE. Folio. 1828.

REPORT of the SELECT COMMITTEE of the HOUSE of COMMONS on the SILK TRADE, with Minutes of Evidence, Appendix, &c. Thick folio. 1832.

THE CIVIL, POLITICAL, and MECHANICAL HISTORY of the FRAMEWORK KNITTERS in EUROPE and AMERICA. By GRAVENOR HENSON. 1 vol. 8vo. (all published). Nottingham, 1831.

This, though in several respects a shallow and prejudiced, is, on the whole, a curious and interesting work; and it is to be regretted that it was not finished.

REPORT from and EVIDENCE taken before the SELECT COMMITTEE of the HOUSE of COMMONS on the PRESENT STATE of MANUFACTURES, COMMERCE, and SHIPPING in the UNITED KINGDOM. Folio. 1833.

The evidence annexed to this Report is peculiarly valuable.

The Economy of Machinery and Manufactures. By CHARLES BABBAGE, Esq., A.M. 2nd ed. 1 vol. 12mo. London, 1833.

The merits and defects of this book are exhibited in an article upon it in the 56th volume of the 'Edinburgh Review.'

A TREATISE on MANUFACTURES in METAL. (By Mr. JOHN HOLLAND.) 3 vols. fcap. 8vo. London, 1834.

History of the Cotton Manufacture in Great Britain; with a Notice of its early History in the East, and in all the Quarters of the Globe, &c. By EDWARD BAINES, Esq. 1 vol. 8vo. London, 1835.

"Mr. Baines's work discovers much laborious research, and is both interesting and valuable. With the exception of Smith's 'Memoirs of Wool,' published so far back as 1747, it is the only work that gives a clear and copious account of the rise, progress, and present condition of any of the great branches of manufacture carried on in the kingdom. Besides being of much interest in an economical point of view, the history of the British cotton manufacture exhibits a combination of invention, sagacity, and enterprise, unequalled in the history of industry. Owing to the difficulty of acquiring accurate information, it is possible Mr. Baines may be mistaken on some points, and imperfectly informed on others; but, speaking generally, the work appears to be worthy of the subject."—(Edinburgh Review, lxi., 471.)

A HISTORY of the GLOVE TRADE, with the CUSTOMS connected with the Glove. By WILLIAM HULL, Jun. 1 vol., post 8vo. London, 1834.

A Comprehensive Treatise of the Iron Trade throughout the World, from the earliest Periods to the present Time. By HARRY SCRIVENOR. 1 vol. 8vo. London, 1839.

A useful work, though rather deficient in learning and research.

A Dictionary of Arts, Manufactures, and Mines; containing a clear Exposition of their Principles and Practice. By ANDREW URE, M.D., &c. 3rd ed., 1 large vol. 8vo. London, 1843.

A Comprehensive History of the Woollen and Worsted Manufactures, and the Natural and Commercial History of the Sheep. By JAMES BISCHOFF, Esq. 2 vols. 8vo. London, 1842.

This useful work is formed on the plan of Smith's 'Memoirs of Wool,' from which, indeed, it is partly taken; but it is neither so minute, so learned, nor so able.

LETTERS on the FACTORY ACT, as it affects the Cotton Manufacture. By N. W. SENIOR, Esq. 2nd edit., 8vo. London, 1844.

The business of hand-loom weaving being easily learned, those engaged in it have seldom been in the receipt of good wages; and of late years they have been involved in the greatest distress and difficulty by the introduction of power-looms. Committees of the House of Commons have repeatedly inquired into the case of the hand-loom weavers: and in 1837 a commission was appointed to investigate their condition, and to report whether any, and if any what, measures could be suggested for their relief. Mr. Senior and Mr. Loyd were members of this commission; and as might in consequence be expected, the Report of the Commissioners, published in 1841, is entitled to especial attention. The greater number of the suggestions embodied in it have not, however, any very peculiar application to the case of the hand-loom weavers, but are mostly of a general character, referring to the corn laws, the releasing of the work-people from the tyranny of combinations, and so forth. The truth is, that all that can be done for the hand-loom weavers is to discourage as much as possible fresh entrants into their business, and to facilitate the transfer of those engaged in it to other employments. It may drag on a few years more of a sickly, declining existence; but there can be no doubt that in the end hand-looms will be wholly superseded by power-looms.

MÉMOIRE sur les MOYENS qui ont amené le grand DÉVELOPPEMENT que l'INDUSTRIE FRANÇAISE a pris depuis vingt ans. Par M. COSTAZ. 1 vol. 8vo. Paris, 1816.

De l'Industrie en Belgique; Causes de Décadence et de Prospérité; sa Situation actuelle. Par M. BRIAVOINNE. 2 vol. 8vo. Bruxelles, 1839.

This is a superior work. The author has pointed out some of the circumstances which have occasioned revolutions in manufacturing industry, and has described its present state and its progress in Belgium during the last half century. But he has hardly touched upon the important inquiry respecting the probable future influence of the extension of manufacturing employments upon the condition of the labouring classes, and the well-being of society. No doubt this inquiry is as difficult as it is important; but it can no longer be neglected. We have stated some considerations with respect to it in the last edition of the 'Principles of Political Economy,' pp. 181-188, to which we beg to refer the reader.

CHAPTER X.

INSURANCE OF LIVES, SHIPS, HOUSES, &c.

AN ESSAY towards illustrating the SCIENCE of INSURANCE, &c. By the Author of the 'Letter from a By-stander' (CORBYN MORRIS, Esq., F.R.S.). 8vo. London, 1747.

AN ESSAY towards deciding the QUESTION, whether BRITAIN be permitted by right Policy to Insure the Ships of her Enemies? (By CORBYN MORRIS, Esq.) 2nd ed. 8vo. London, 1748.

This is a practice, as to the policy of which, and its legality at common law, much doubt has been entertained. We think, however, notwithstanding the deference due to Lord Mansfield, who held the opposite opinion, that Mr. Morris, in the tract now referred to, and others, have sufficiently shown the extreme impolicy of insuring enemies' property, and it would also appear to be clearly illegal. There is, in fact, no real difference between it and insuring against British capture, which would on the face of it be illegal and void.—(Marshall on Insurance, book i., cap. ii., § 1.)

An Essay on Insurances, explaining the Nature of the various kinds of Marine Insurance practised by the different Commercial States of Europe, and showing their Consistency or Inconsistency with Equity and the Public Good. By NICÓLAS MAGENS, Merchant. 2 vols. 4to. London, 1755.

This work, which was first published at Hamburg in 1753, in 1 vol. 4to., consists principally of calculations of averages; of the acts, regulations, and ordinances of this and other countries in relation to insurance and maritime affairs; and of commercial treaties.

A COMPLETE DIGEST of the THEORY, LAW, and PRACTICE of INSURANCE. By F. WESKETT. 1 vol. folio. London, 1781.

THE PRINCIPLE of the DOCTRINE of LIFE ANNUITIES, with a variety of New Tables. By FRANCIS MASERES, Cursitor Baron of Exchequer. 1 vol. 4to. London, 1783.

A voluminous work, useful at the epoch of its publication. The Baron gives a good deal of information respecting the efforts that had been made to provide annuities for the poor.

The Doctrine of Life Annuities and Insurances. By FRANCIS BAILY, of the Stock Exchange. 1 vol. large 8vo. London, 1810.

Until the appearance of Mr. Milne's treatise on Annuities (see Works on Interest, Annuities, &c.), this was the best work that had been published on the principles of life assurance. And notwithstanding the important labours of Mr. Milne, Mr. Jones, and other late writers, it continues to be held in high estimation.

Mr. Baily added to some of the copies of this work a paper read before the Royal Society on an improved method of calculating life annuities discovered by Mr. Barrett. This method has been still further improved by Mr. Griffith Davies, and affords great facilities for the calculation of deferred and increasing life annuities and assurances. Mr. Baily's work is now become scarce; and copies with the appendix fetch a high price.

The 14th chapter of this work being of a popular nature, and on a subject with respect to which the public are much in want of accurate information, Mr. Baily published it separately as a pamphlet, entitled

An Account of the Several Life-Assurance Companies established in London; containing a View of their respective Merits and Advantages. By Francis Baily, of the Stock Exchange. 8vo. London, 1811.

System of Marine Insurances, with Chapters on Bottomry, on Insurance on Lives, and on Insurances against Fire. By J. A. Park, Esq.; (subsequently Mr. Justice Park.) 8th ed., with additions, by F. Hildyard, M.A. 2 vols. 8vo. London, 1842.

A Treatise on the Law of Insurance. By Samuel Marshall, Esq., Serjeant-at-Law. The 3rd ed., with additions, by C. Marshall, Esq. 2 vols. 8vo. London, 1823.

One of the most learned and best reasoned works that has appeared on marine insurance.

Report from and Evidence taken before a Committee of the House of Commons on Marine Insurance. Folio. 1810.

On the Principles and Doctrine of Assurances, Annuities on Lives, and Contingent Reversions. By William Morgan, F.R.S. Actuary to the Equitable Society. 1 vol. 8vo. London, 1821.

A Comparative View of the various Institutions for the Assurance of Lives. By Charles Babbage, Esq., M.A., F.R.S., &c. 1 vol. 8vo. London, 1826.

This work was very ably reviewed in an article in the 45th volume of the 'Edinburgh Review.'

A View of the Rise and Progress of the Equitable Society, and of the Causes which have contributed to its Success. By William Morgan, F.R.S., Actuary to the Society. 8vo. 2nd ed. London, 1829.

Principles of Life Annuities and Assurances practically illustrated. By an Accountant. 8vo. Edinburgh, 1829.

Life Tables, founded upon the Discovery of a Numerical Law regulating the Existence of every Human Being: illustrated by a New Theory of the Causes producing Health and Longevity. By T. R. Edmonds, B.A. 1 vol. royal 8vo. London, 1832.

An Essay on Probabilities, and on their Application to Life Contingencies and Insurance Offices. By AUGUSTUS de MORGAN, M.A. 1 vol. foolscap 8vo. London, 1838.

GUIDE to MARINE INSURANCES, containing the POLICIES of the PRINCIPAL COMMERCIAL TOWNS in the WORLD; with Remarks on the mutual Relation between Insured and Insurers, and comparative Tables, &c. By J. VAUCHER. 1 vol. 8vo. London, 1834.

ESSAY on AVERAGE and other Subjects connected with the CONTRACT of MARINE INSURANCE. By R. STEVENS, Esq. 5th ed. 1 vol. 8vo. London, 1835.

Tables showing the Total Number of Persons Assured in the Equitable Society, from its commencement in September, 1762, to January, 1829, &c.; to which are added Tables of the Probabilities and Expectations of the Duration of Human Life, deduced from these Documents, &c. Folio (pp. 29). London, 1834.

This paper contains a correct statement of the experience of the Equitable Society, in a convenient form. The tables which Mr. Griffith Davies published in 1825 of the experience of the same society were not deduced from these returns, but from the 'Statements' of Mr. Morgan, and are consequently not quite so valuable as they would otherwise have been.

The example of the Equitable Society, in publishing correct returns of their experience, has been followed by the Amicable Life Office, and the results are given in the

Tables of Mortality, deduced from the Experience of the Amicable Society for a Perpetual Assurance Office, during the period of 33 years, ending the 5th of April, 1841.

The results of later returns from several of the London assurance offices are embodied in the following work of Mr. Jones:—

A SERIES of TABLES of ANNUITIES and ASSURANCES, calculated from a New Rate of Mortality among Assured Lives. By JENKIN JONES, Esq. 1 vol. 8vo. London, 1843.

LE GUIDON DE LA MER, the earliest treatise on the subject of maritime insurance, is comprised in the collection entitled *Us et Coutumes de la Mer*, by Cleirac, already referred to (p. 124). "This work," says Mr. Sergeant Marshall, "is evidently the production of a much earlier period than that of its publication (1647); and yet its contents plainly show that it could not have been written till after the practice of insurance had become pretty general, and most of the principles which govern it were ascertained and well understood. We may, therefore, reasonably conclude that it could not have been written long before the 15th century. Cleirac informs us, 'that it was originally composed for the use of the Merchants of Rouen, and is so complete in itself, that it fully explains all that it is necessary to know on the subject of marine contracts and naval commerce; and that nothing is wanting to it but the author's name.' Many faults which had crept into it through time and the carelessness of copiers, have been corrected by the editor, who has enriched the whole by a very learned and excellent commentary of his own."—(Preliminary Discourse, p. 22.)

Traité des Assurances et des Contrats à la Grosse. Par M. B. M. Emérigon. 2 vol. 4to. Marseille, 1782.

The author of this work, an advocate in the parliament of Aix and a councillor in the admiralty court of Marseilles, died in 1784, at the age of 68. He had by long practice and study acquired a very extensive and profound knowledge of maritime and commercial law. This treatise is of the highest authority. It is said by Lord Tenterden, in the preface to his work on maritime law, to be "peculiarly valuable for its extent of learned research, and the numerous and apt citations of the texts of the civil law and of the marine ordinances, the opinions of former writers, and the adjudications of the courts of justice of his own country, which are to be found in every part of it." It is not limited to the subject specified in the title; but, to use the words of M. Pardessus, "*Il embrasse la presque totalité du droit maritime, et ne saurait être trop recommandé à ceux qui s'occupent de cette importante partie de la législation.*"

Traité des Contrats Aléatoires. Par M. Pothier. 1 vol. 12mo. Paris, 1777.

The name of the author is a sufficient eulogy of this work. An edition with useful notes was published in 8vo., in 1810, at Marseilles.

Coup d'Œil sur les Assurances sur la Vie des Hommes. Par Juvigny. 8vo. 4me éd. Paris, 1825.

A popular, useful tract.

Trattato dell' Assecurazione Maritime, del Cambio Maritime, dell' Avaria, e Leggi e Costumi, &c. Del Signor Ascanio Baldasseroni. 5 vol. 4to. Firenze, 1801, &c.

The author of this very complete and valuable work was a judge in the revenue court of Leghorn. He is also the author of the first two volumes of a dictionary of mercantile jurisprudence (*Dizzionario della Giurisprudenza Mercantile*), Florence, 1810–11. The *Dizzionario delle Legge e Costumi del Cambio* (see p. 190) is by his brother Pompeo Baldasseroni.

Kuricke, Diatribe de Assecurationibus. 1 vol. 4to. Hamburgi, 1667.

"Il est cité par tous ceux qui ont traité ces matières, et mérite d'être entre les mains de tous ceux qui en font leur étude."—(Pardessus.)

Essai sur les Probabilités de la Durée de la Vie Humaine. Par M. Deparcieux. 1 vol., 4to. Paris, 1746.

"Information much wanted is here given in a very clear and popular manner, and the work no doubt contributed greatly to the advancement of the science."—(Milne.)

Halley first called attention to the *vie probable*, or age to which it is probable, or, in Halley's words, to which "it is an even wager" that a person will live. Deparcieux appears to have been the first who adverted to and defined the "*vie moyenne*," by which, he says, "On entend le nombre d'années que vivront encore, les unes portant les autres, les personnes de l'âge correspondant à cette vie moyenne. Ainsi selon l'ordre de mortalité de M. Simpson, les personnes de l'âge de 50 ans ont encore 15 ans et 10 mois à vivre, les unes portant les autres."—(p. 56.) We may remark that our term "expectation of life" corresponds precisely with the "vie moyenne" of Deparcieux, and not, as might at first sight be supposed, with the *vie probable*.

N.B.—Works on Annuities and Interest (which see) mostly treat of Insurance.

CHAPTER XI.

INTEREST AND ANNUITIES, USURY, &c.

The rate of interest, supposing there were no legal restrictions of any kind on the borrowers and lenders, and that the principal lent were perfectly secure, would obviously depend on what might be made at the time by the employment of capital in industrious undertakings, or on the rate of profit. Where profits are high, as in the United States, interest is also high; and where they are comparatively low, as in Holland and England, interest is proportionally low. In fact, the rate of interest is nothing more than the *nett* profit on capital: whatever returns are obtained by the borrower, beyond the interest he has agreed to pay, accrue to him on account of risk, trouble, or skill, or of advantages of situation and connexion.

But besides fluctuations in the rate of interest caused by the varying productiveness of industry, the rate of interest on each particular loan must, of course, vary according to the supposed solvency of the borrowers, or the degree of risk supposed to be incurred by the lender, of either not recovering payment at all, or not recovering it at the stipulated term. No person of sound mind would lend on the personal security of an individual of doubtful character and solvency, and on mortgage over a valuable estate, at the same rate of interest. Wherever there is risk, it must be compensated to the lender by a higher premium or interest.

And yet, obvious as this principle may appear, all governments have interfered with the adjustment of the terms of loans; some to prohibit interest altogether, and others to fix certain rates which it should be legal to charge, and illegal to exceed. The prejudice against taking interest seems to have principally originated in a mistaken view of some enactments of the Mosaical law (see *Michaelis on the Laws of Moses*, vol. ii. pp. 327-353, Eng. ed.), and a statement of Aristotle to the effect that, as money did not produce money, no return could be equitably claimed by the lender! But whatever may have been the origin of this prejudice, it was formerly universal in Christendom, and is still supported by law in all Mohammedan countries. The famous reformer Calvin was one of the first who saw and exposed the absurdity of such notions (see an extract from one of his epistles in the *Principles of Political Economy*, 3rd ed. p. 520); and the abuses caused by the prohibition, and the growing conviction of its impolicy, soon after led to its relaxation.

In England, down to the reign of Henry VIII., the taking of interest was absolutely forbidden to all persons within the realm except Jews and strangers. But the disorders and inconveniences thence arising became at length so obvious that in 1546 an Act (the 37 Henry VIII. c. 7) was passed, legalising the taking of interest to the extent of 10 per cent. In 1552, however, the prejudice against usury, or the taking of interest, seems to have revived in its full force; and it was then prohibited by the 5 Edward VI. c. 20, as a "vice most odious and detestable, and contrary to the word of God!" But the lenders of money having now to be insured against the threatenings of the law, as well as the ordinary chances of non-payment, the rate of interest, instead of being reduced, is said to have risen from 10 to 14 or 15 per cent., and continued at about this rate till 1571, when the 13 Eliz. c. 8 was passed, repealing the Act of Edward VI., and reviving the law of Henry VIII. because, as stated in the preamble to the Act of Elizabeth, the "prohibitory Act of Edward VI. had not done so much good as was hoped for; but that rather the vice of usury hath much more exceedingly abounded, to the utter undoing of many gentlemen, merchants, occupiers, and others, and to the importable hurt of the commonwealth."

The legal or statutory rate of interest continued at 10 per cent. till 1624, when it was reduced to 8 per cent.

On this occasion the following tract was published, in which the advantages to be derived from reducing the rate of interest to 6 per cent. are strongly insisted upon:—

A TRACT against the HIGH RATE of USURIE. Presented to the High Court of Parliament, A.D. 1623. (By Sir THOMAS CULPEPER, Knt.) 4to. London, 1623.

The legal rate of interest was farther reduced by an ordinance, passed the 8th of August, 1651, from 8 to 6 per cent., which was confirmed at the Restoration, by the 12 Car. II. c. 13.

But notwithstanding this reduction various efforts were made, during the remaining portion of the seventeenth century, still further to lower the rate of interest. In this view Sir Josiah Child published, as already stated (p. 42), in 1668, the first edition of his treatise on trade. It was entitled

BRIEF OBSERVATIONS concerning TRADE, and the INTEREST of MONEY. By J. C. 4to. London, 1668.

Sir Thomas Culpeper's treatise is annexed to this tract by way of Appendix.

In this remarkable tract Child has given reasons for the rapid progress made by the Hollanders in commerce and the accumulation of wealth, which do honour to his discernment. For the most part they differ but little from the statements of the Dutch merchants on the same subject nearly a century later. (See p. 47.)

It is not a little singular that Child, who had so ably traced the more prominent causes of the superiority of the Dutch in wealth and commerce, should go on to say that "*the lowness of the rate of interest is the* CAUSA CAUSANS *of all the other causes of the riches of that people.*" This is a signal instance of the mistake of an effect for a cause; for it is almost needless to say that the lowness of interest was in reality a consequence of their great wealth, and of the low rate of profit occasioned by the heaviness of taxation and other circumstances.

The error of Child did not, however, escape immediate detection; but was skilfully and clearly pointed out at the time in the following tract:—

Interest of Money Mistaken, or a Treatise Proving that the Abatement of Interest is the Effect and not the Cause of the Riches of a Nation, &c. 4to. London, 1668.

In the reign of Queen Anne the legal rate of interest was reduced by the statute, 12 Anne, c. 16, to 5 per cent. And it was then enacted, that "all persons who shall receive, by means of any corrupt bargain, loan, exchange, chevizance, or interest of any wares, merchandise, or other thing whatever, or by any deceitful way or means, or by any covin, engine, or deceitful conveyance for the forbearing or giving day of payment, for one whole year for their money or other thing, above the sum of 5*l.* for 100*l.* for a year, shall forfeit for every such offence the *treble* value of the moneys, or other things, so lent, bargained," &c.

It is needless to waste the reader's time by entering into any arguments to show the inexpediency and mischievous effect of such interferences. This has been done over and over again. It is plainly in no respect more desirable to limit the rate of interest than it would be to limit the rate of insurance, or the prices of commodities. And though it were desirable, it cannot be accomplished. The real effect of all legislative enactments having such an object in view, is to increase, not diminish, the rate of interest. When the rate fixed by law is less than the market or customary rate, lenders and borrowers are obliged to resort to circuitous devices to evade the law; and as these devices are always attended with more or less trouble and risk, the rate of interest is proportionally enhanced. During the late war it was not uncommon for a person to be paying 10 or 12 per cent. for a loan, which, had there been no usury laws, he might have got for 6 or 7 per cent. Neither was it by any means uncommon, when the rate fixed by law was more than the market-rate, for borrowers to be obliged to pay more than they really stipulated for. It is singular that an enactment which contradicted the most obvious principles, and had been repeatedly condemned by committees of the Legislature, should have been allowed to preserve a place in the statute-book for so long a period; but at length it was substantially repealed by the Act 2 & 3 Victoria, c. 37, which exempts bills of exchange not having more than twelve months to run, and contracts for loans of money above 10*l.*, from its operation.

Tables of Interest, Discount, Annuities, &c. By JOHN SMART, of Guildhall, London, Gent. 1 vol. 4to. London, 1726.

These tables are carried to eight decimal places, and their accuracy and excellence have been universally admitted. They were republished with a few additions in 1780; and portions of them have since repeatedly appeared in other works, generally, however, without acknowledgment.

Annuities upon Lives, or the Valuation of Annuities upon any Number of Lives, as also of Reversions, &c. By ABRAHAM de MOIVRE, F.R.S. 1st ed. 1 vol. 8vo. London, 1725. 3rd ed. 1 vol. 8vo. London, 1750.

The author of this valuable work was honoured by the friendship of Newton, and the eulogy of Pope—

> "Who made the spider parallels design,
> Sure as De Moivre, without rule or line?"

De Moivre, who was a French refugee, died in 1754, at the age of eighty-seven.

THE DOCTRINE of ANNUITIES and REVERSIONS, deduced from General and Evident Principles, with useful Tables, showing the Values of Single and Joint Lives, &c. By THOMAS SIMPSON. 1 vol. 8vo. London, 1742.

Down to about the middle of last century the notion of Locke, that the rate of interest depends on the abundance of money, being low where money is plentiful and high where it is scarce, had been usually taken for granted.

Hume is generally supposed to have been the first to point out, in his Essay on Interest, the fallacy of this opinion, by showing that the rate of interest really depends on the abundance and scarcity of disposable capital compared with the demands of the borrowers and the rate of profit. This, however, is a mistake, the doctrine in question being fully established in the following tract published two years previously to the essay of Hume:—

AN ESSAY on the GOVERNING CAUSES of the NATURAL RATE of INTEREST, &c. 8vo. London, 1750.

Mr. Joseph Massie, the author of this tract, published a great many other tracts during the next dozen years, some of which are noticed elsewhere in this work. The above seems to be one of the best of his publications.

Observations on Reversionary Payments, Annuities, &c. By RICHARD PRICE, D.D. 1st ed. 1 vol. 8vo. London, 1769. 7th ed., by MORGAN, 2 vols. London, 1812.

One of the most important and long the most popular work on the subject of annuities and life insurance. "The publication of the 4th edition of Dr. Price's 'Observations on Reversionary Payments,' in 1783, formed a new æra in the science; and showed the necessity of abandoning the hypothesis of De Moivre, and of deducing the value of life annuities and assurances from real observations."—(Baily.)

Defence of Usury, showing the Impolicy of the Present Legal Restraints on the Terms of Pecuniary Bargains. By JEREMY BENTHAM, of Lincoln's Inn, Esq. 3rd ed., with a Protest against Law Taxes. 1 vol. 12mo. London, 1816.

Sir Francis Baring, than whom few have been better versed in trade and money matters, said of this work that it was "perfectly unanswerable," a decision the justice of which has been generally acquiesced in.

TABLES for the PURCHASING and RENEWING of LEASES, &c. By FRANCIS BAILY. 1 vol. 8vo. London, 1802.

The Doctrine of Interest and Annuities. By FRANCIS BAILY. 1 vol. 4to. London, 1808.

A Treatise on the Valuation of Annuities and Assurances on Lives and Survivorships; on the Construction of Tables of Mortality; and on the Probabilities and Expectations of Life, &c., with a variety of new Tables. By JOSHUA MILNE, Actuary to the Sun Life Assurance Society. 2 vols. 8vo. London, 1815.

This is a work of great value and importance both in a scientific and practical point of view. Previously to its publication almost all annuities and insurances on lives were calculated according to the results deduced from Dr. Price's table of mortality, founded on the burial registers of the parish of All Saints in Northampton. But however near at the time when it was framed, the rate of mortality, as represented by this table, has been for a lengthened period considerably above the average mortality of England and Wales. And in the view of getting a more correct representation of the latter, Mr. Milne published in the present work a new table of mortality, deduced from returns and observations made with great care by Dr. Heysham, on the deaths at

Carlisle. And this table, which gives a decidedly lower rate of mortality than the Northampton table, has now gone far to supersede the use of the latter, and has in consequence been productive of much advantage to the public. It is believed, indeed, to represent the average mortality of the kingdom with much more accuracy than might have been expected from the narrow basis on which it is framed. In this work Mr. Milne has also given tables of the law of mortality in Sweden and Finland, and in Montpellier in the South of France.

CONSIDERATIONS on the RATE of INTEREST, REDEEMABLE ANNUITIES, and FOREIGN LOANS. By E. B. SUGDEN, Esq. (now Chancellor of Ireland). 8vo. London, 1817.

REPORT by and EVIDENCE taken before the SELECT COMMITTEE of the HOUSE of COMMONS on the USURY LAWS. Folio. 1818.

REPORT of JOHN FINLAISON, Actuary of the National Debt, on the Evidence and Elementary Facts on which the Tables of Life Annuities are founded. Printed by Order of the House of Commons. Folio. 1829.

REPORT and EVIDENCE from the SELECT COMMITTEE of the HOUSE of COMMONS on the Proposal of Mr. Cadogan Williams, recommending the purchase of Life Annuities under the authority of Government. Folio. 1829.

ON the VALUE of ANNUITIES and REVERSIONARY PAYMENTS, with numerous Tables. By DAVID JONES, Esq., Actuary to the Universal Life Assurance Office. 2 vols. 8vo. London, 1843.

An able scientific treatise.

CALCUL des RENTES VIAGÈRES sur une et sur plusieurs TÊTES. Par M. de St. CYRAN. 1 vol. 4to. Paris, 1779.

RECHERCHES sur les RENTES, les EMPRUNTS, et les REMBOURSEMENTS. Par M. DUVILLARD. 1 vol. 4to. Paris, 1787.

NOUVELLE THÉORIE du CALCUL des INTÉRÊTS SIMPLES et COMPOSÉS, des Annuités, des Rentes, et des Placemens Viagers. Par M. GRÉMILLIET. 1 vol. 8vo. Paris, 1823.

CHAPTER XII.

PROGRESS OF POPULATION.

THE CAUSE of the GREATNESSE of CITIES, from the Italian of BOTERO. By Sir T. H. 1 vol., 12mo. London, 1635.

The work from which this is translated is entitled 'Della Ragione di Stato libri X., con tre libri delle Cause della Grandezza delle Città, di Giovanni Botero, Benese.' 1 vol., 8vo. Venezia, 1598.

This is a very remarkable treatise. The causes to which Botero ascribes the increase of cities are mostly identical with those mentioned by Seneca (see Miscellaneous Works), the influence of each being traced and estimated. But the work is principally worthy of notice from its showing that the author was fully master of all that is really true in the theory of Malthus. This is particularly evinced in his reasonings to show that colonies do not depopulate the mother countries, and in his investigation of the circumstances which limit and determine the growth of cities. It was a great oversight to omit giving Botero's work a place in the collection of Italian Economists.

Botero was a native of Benna, in Piedmont, where he first saw the light in 1540. He died at Turin in 1617. Besides those referred to above, he was the author of several other publications.—(See Tiraboschi, 'Letteratura Italiana,' vii., 920; Biog. Universelle, &c.)

THE PRIMITIVE ORIGINATION of MANKIND considered and explained. By Sir MATTHEW HALE. Folio. London, 1677.

ORIGINES GENTIUM ANTIQUISSIMÆ; or Attempts for Discovering the times of the first Planting of Nations. By Dr. CUMBERLAND, Bishop of Peterborough. 1 vol., 8vo. London, 1724.

See especially Tract IV., "Concerning the possibility of a sufficient increase of men from the three sons of Noah, to a number large enough to found all the nations mentioned in the oldest credible histories," &c.

Observations Concerning the Increase of Mankind, Peopling of Countries, &c. By BENJAMIN FRANKLIN. 8vo. Philadelphia, 1751; and since frequently reprinted.

This short essay is an excellent specimen of the penetrating sagacity, and compressed and clear style, for which its eminent author was so remarkable. The circumstances on which the increase and diminution of population depend are succinctly and accurately stated. We subjoin a considerable portion of this remarkable tract:—

"1.—Tables of the proportion of marriages to births, of deaths to births, of marriages to the number of inhabitants, &c., formed on observations made upon the bills of mortality, christenings, &c., of populous cities, will not suit countries; nor will tables formed and observations made on full-settled old countries, as Europe, suit new countries, as America.

"2.—For people increase in proportion to the number of marriages, and that is greater in proportion to the ease and convenience of supporting a family. When families can be easily supported, more persons marry, and earlier in life.

"3.—In cities, where all trades, occupations, and offices are full, many delay marrying till they can see how to bear the charge of a family; which charges are greater in cities, as luxury is more common; many live single during life, and continue servants to families, journeymen to trades, &c. Hence cities do not by natural generation supply themselves with inhabitants; the deaths are more than the births.*

"4.—In countries full settled the case must be nearly the same, all lands being occupied and improved to the height; those who cannot get land must labour for others that have it; when labourers are plenty their wages will be low; by low wages a family is supported with difficulty; this difficulty deters many from marriage, who therefore long continue servants and single. Only, as the cities take supplies of the people from the country, and thereby make room in the country, marriage is a little more encouraged there, and the births exceed the deaths.

"5.—Great part of Europe is fully settled with husbandmen, manufacturers, &c., and therefore cannot now much increase in people. America is chiefly occupied by Indians, who subsist mostly by hunting. But as the hunter, of all men, requires the greatest quantity of land from whence to draw his subsistence (the husbandman subsisting on much less, the gardener on still less, and the manufacturer requiring least of all), the Europeans found America as fully settled as it well could be by hunters; yet these, having large tracts, were easily prevailed on to part with portions of territory to the new-comers, who did not much interfere with the natives in hunting, and furnished them with many things they wanted.

"6.—Land being thus plenty in America, and so cheap that a labouring man, that understands husbandry, can, in a short time, save money enough to purchase a piece of new land sufficient for a plantation, whereon he may subsist a family, such are not afraid to marry; for if they even look far enough forward to consider how their children, when grown up, are to be provided for, they see that more land is to be had at rates equally easy, all circumstances considered.

"7.—Hence marriages in America are more general, and more generally early, than in Europe. And if it is reckoned there that there is but one marriage per annum among 100 persons, perhaps we may here reckon two; and if in Europe they have but four births to a marriage (many of their marriages being late), we may here reckon eight, of which, if one half grow up, and our marriages are made, reckoning one with another, at twenty years of age, our people must at least be doubled every twenty years.

"8.—But, notwithstanding this increase, so vast is the territory of North America, that it will require many ages to settle it fully; and till it is fully settled, labour will never be cheap here, where no man continues long a labourer for others, but gets a plantation of his own: no man continues long a journeyman to a trade, but goes among those new settlers, and sets up for himself, &c. Hence labour is no cheaper now, in Pennsylvania, than it was thirty years ago, though so many thousand labouring people have been imported from Germany and Ireland.

"9.—The danger, therefore, of the colonies interfering with their mother country in trades, that depend on labour, manufactures, &c., is too remote to require the attention of Great Britain.

"13.—As the increase of people depends on the encouragement of marriages, the following things must diminish a nation, viz.:—1. The being conquered; for the conquerors will engross as many offices, and exact as

* This was the case in London formerly; but it has not been the case during any part of the present century.

much tribute or profit on the labour of the conquered, as will maintain them in their new establishment; and this diminishing the subsistence of the natives discourages their marriages, and so gradually diminishes them, while the foreigners increase. 2. Loss of territory. Thus the Britons, being driven into Wales, and crowded together in a barren country, insufficient to support such great numbers, diminished, till the people bore a proportion to the produce; while the Saxons increased on their abandoned lands, till the island became full of English. And were the English now driven into Wales by some foreign nation, there would in a few years be no more Englishmen in Britain than there are now people in Wales. 3. Loss of trade. Manufactures, exported, draw subsistence from foreign countries for numbers who are thereby enabled to marry and raise families. If the nation be deprived of any branch of trade, and no new employment is found for the people occupied in that branch, it will soon be deprived of so many people. 4. Loss of food. Suppose a nation has a fishery, which not only employs great numbers, but makes the food and subsistence of the people cheaper: if another nation becomes master of the seas, and prevents the fishery, the people will diminish in proportion as the loss of employ and dearness of provisions makes it more difficult to subsist a family. 5. Bad government and insecure property. People not only leave such a country, and settling abroad, incorporate with other nations, lose their native language, and become foreigners; but the industry of those that remain being discouraged, the quantity of subsistence in the country is lessened, and the support of a family becomes more difficult. So heavy taxes tend to diminish a people. 6. The introduction of slaves. The negroes brought into the English sugar islands have greatly diminished the whites there: the poor are by this means deprived of employment, while a few families acquire vast estates, which they spend on foreign luxuries; and, educating their children in the habits of those luxuries, the same income is needed for the support of one that might have maintained one hundred. The whites, who have slaves, not labouring, are enfeebled, and therefore not so generally prolific; the slaves being worked too hard, and ill fed, their constitutions are broken, and the deaths among them are more than the births; so that a continual supply is needed from Africa. The northern colonies having few slaves increase in whites. Slaves also pejorate * the families that use them; the white children become proud, disgusted with labour, and, being educated in idleness, are rendered unfit to get a living by industry.

"14.—Hence the prince that acquires new territory, if he finds it vacant, or removes the natives to give his own people room; the legislator, that makes effectual laws for promoting trade, increasing employment, improving land by more or better tillage, providing more food by fisheries, securing property, &c.; and the man that invents new trades, arts, or manufactures, or new improvements in husbandry—may be properly called fathers of their nation, as they are the cause of the generation of multitudes by the encouragement they afford to marriage.

"15.—As to privileges granted to the married (such as the *jus trium liberorum* among the Romans), they may hasten the filling of a country that has been thinned by war or pestilence, or that has otherwise vacant territory, but cannot increase a people beyond the means provided for their subsistence.

"21.—The importation of foreigners into a country that has as many inhabitants as the present employment and provisions for subsistence will bear, will be in the end no increase of people unless the new-comers have more industry and frugality than the natives, and then they will provide more subsistence, and increase the country: but they will gradually eat the natives out. Nor is it necessary to bring in foreigners to fill up any occasional vacancy in a country; for such vacancy

* *Sic* in original.

(if the laws are good, § 14, 16) will soon be filled by natural generation. Who can now find the vacancy made in Sweden, France, or other warlike nations, by the plague of heroism forty years ago; in France, by the expulsion of the Protestants; in England, by the settlement of her colonies; or in Guinea, by a hundred years' exportation of slaves, that has blackened half America? The thinness of the inhabitants in Spain is owing to national pride and idleness, and other causes, rather than to the expulsion of the Moors, or to the making of new settlements.

"22.—There is, in short, no bound to the prolific nature of plants or animals, but what is made by their crowding and interfering with each other's means of subsistence. Was the face of the earth vacant of other plants, it might be gradually sowed and overspread with one kind only, as, for instance, with fennel: and were it empty of other inhabitants, it might, in a few ages, be replenished from one nation only, as, for instance, with Englishmen. Thus there are supposed to be now upwards of one million of English souls in North America (though it is thought scarce 80,000 have been brought over sea), and yet perhaps there is not one fewer in Britain, but rather many more, on account of the employment the colonies afford to manufacturers at home. This million, doubling, suppose but once in twenty-five years, will, in another century, be more than the people of England, and the greatest number of Englishmen will be on this side the water. What an accession of power to the British empire by sea as well as land! What increase of trade and navigation! What numbers of ships and seamen! We have been here but little more than a hundred years, and yet the force of our privateers in the late war, united, was greater both in men and guns than that of the whole British navy in Queen Elizabeth's time! How important an affair then to Britain is the present treaty [1749] for settling the bounds between her colonies and the French? and how careful should she be to secure room enough, since on the room depends so much the increase of her people?

"23.—In fine, a nation well regulated is like a polypus:* take away a limb, its place is soon supplied: cut it in two, and each deficient part shall speedily grow out of the part remaining. Thus if you have room and subsistence enough, as you may by dividing make ten polypuses out of one, you may of one make ten nations equally populous and powerful; or, rather, increase the nation ten-fold in numbers and strength."

Dr. Franklin's conjecture that the million of whites in America in 1750, when the above tract was written, would in a century thereafter, or in 1850, exceed the number of people in England, how extravagant soever it may have appeared at the time, would have turned out to be perfectly well-founded but for the extraordinary and unlooked-for increase that has taken place in the numbers of the latter. And even with this increase it is but little, if anything, wide of the mark; the white population of the United States having amounted in 1840 to 14,189,555, while that of England and Wales amounted in 1841 to 15,911,725; but it is next to certain that the white population of the United States will exceed that of England in 1850; and the fair presumption is, that in 1860 it will very materially exceed the population of Great Britain, which, in 1841, amounted to 18,532,335. The total population of the United States, including slaves and free coloured persons, did not, in 1750, exceed 1,300,000, whereas in 1840 it had increased to 17,069,453.

It is impossible, however, to foretell from the rate at which population has increased in any country, how it will continue to increase, seeing that this depends wholly, or almost wholly, on the facility with which food and

* A water-insect, well known to naturalists.

other accommodations may be supplied. It is, however, sufficiently established that, had it not been for the facilities the Americans have had of spreading themselves over the vast and fertile valley of the Mississippi, their former progress in population would have been already very materially checked. But considering the immense extent of fertile and hitherto all but unoccupied land to the west of the Mississippi, it seems not unreasonable to suppose that the present rate of increase may be maintained for the next fifty or sixty years; and if so, the population, including slaves, would, according to Mr. Tucker (Progress of the United States, &c., 8vo., New York, 1843), amount in the year 1900 to about 74,000,000! And gigantic as this may seem, there is really nothing in the estimate to make one suppose that it may not be fully realised.

Hume's essay 'Of the Populousness of Ancient Nations,' the most perfect specimen ever published of an inquiry into any matter connected with the public economy of the ancients, appeared in his Political Essays, Edinburgh, 1752 (see p. 32). An answer to this Essay was published in the following year in the Appendix to a work entitled 'A Dissertation on the Numbers of Mankind in Ancient and Modern Times, in which the Superior Populousness of Antiquity is Maintained.' 1 vol. 8vo. Edinburgh, 1753.

This Dissertation was written by the Rev. Dr. Wallace of Edinburgh. But though the reverend gentleman succeeded in pointing out a few errors in Hume's statements, which were rectified in subsequent editions of the Essay, he wholly failed to shake its foundations, or to prove in opposition to Hume that Europe was more populous in ancient than in modern times.

Exclusive of the above, Dr. Wallace published the following works:—

CHARACTERISTICS of the PRESENT POLITICAL STATE of GREAT BRITAIN. 1 vol., 8vo. Lond. 1758.

VARIOUS PROSPECTS of MANKIND, NATURE, and PROVIDENCE. 1 vol., 8vo. Lond. 1761.

These works embrace sundry speculations, which evince considerable boldness and ingenuity, on matters connected with the condition and prospects of society, the influence of public debts and taxes, the increase of riches, &c. It has been alleged that Malthus was under considerable obligations to some of Wallace's speculations; and no doubt they may have afforded him hints, though of a less palpable kind than those afforded by the works of Sir James Steuart, Franklin, Townsend, Bruckner, and others. Dr. Wallace died at Edinburgh on the 29th July, 1771.

A Comparative History of the Increase and Decrease of Mankind in England and several Countries abroad, &c. By THOMAS SHORT, M.D. 1 vol., 4to. London, 1767.

Dr. Short was the author of other treatises on allied subjects, some of which are noticed in other parts of this work.

PROPOSALS to the LEGISLATURE for NUMBERING the PEOPLE. (By ARTHUR YOUNG, Esq.) 8vo. London, 1771.

OBSERVATIONS on the STATE of the POPULATION in MANCHESTER and other adjacent Places. By THOMAS PERCIVAL, M.D. 8vo. London, 1778.

This valuable tract is also published in the author's 'Essays Medical, Philosophical, and Experimental,' 1767-1778.

A famous controversy was carried on, during and after the American War, between Dr. Price on the one side, and Mr. Wales and Mr. Howlett on the other, with respect to the population of England. Dr. Price maintained that the population had gradually decreased from the Revolution down to the period referred to; and that the ratio of decrease had increased during the twenty years ending with 1780. The Doctor principally relied, in supporting this opinion, on the returns of houses by the window-light surveyors. He concluded, from a statement of Dr. Davenant—or rather of Gregory King, from whom it was borrowed by Davenant—that there were 1,319,215 houses in England and Wales in 1690: and as it appeared from the returns of the window-light surveyors that there were only 952,734 houses in 1777, Dr. Price inferred, supposing *five* to be the average number of persons to a house, that the population had declined in the course of eighty-seven years, or in the interval between 1690 and 1777, from 6,596,075 to 4,763,670! There were some collateral circumstances on which Dr. Price founded; and he further endeavoured to show, that the diminution of population was not only directly proved, in the way now mentioned, but that though such direct proof had not been obtainable, there were circumstances in the condition of the country from which the same conclusion might have been confidently arrived at: the increased emigration to the colonies, the drains occasioned by foreign wars, the increase of enclosures and of the size of farms, the overgrown magnitude of the metropolis, the progress of luxury, and so forth—being, as he affirmed, at once causes and consequences of a decrease of population. It is plain, however, that Price, had he been aware of the laws which really govern the increase of population, would not have drawn any such inferences. With the exception of the statement respecting the decrease in the number of houses, which, however, was too vague to be depended upon, the circumstances from which he deduced the conclusion that population must have diminished were in truth either quite immaterial, or went to show that it had really increased. But as the circumstances which determine the amount of population were then very imperfectly known, the statements and reasonings of the learned author, enforced as they were by very considerable talent and great earnestness, made a considerable impression, and excited a good deal of attention and discussion. Various replies were made to Dr. Price; but those by Mr. Wales, who had accompanied Captain Cook in the capacity of astronomer in some of his voyages; and Mr. Howlett, vicar of Dunmow, in Essex, were by far the best. The Essay of the latter is indeed a very able one. Mr. Howlett examines both the facts and collateral reasonings on which Price built his theory; and shows that no reliance can be placed on the former, and that the latter are founded on mistaken and erroneous notions. But Mr. Howlett does not stop here: he gives accounts of the births and burials in a great number of parishes in all parts of the country, for two periods of twenty years each—the first beginning with the Revolution, and the latter with 1758 or 1760; and he shows by this comparison that the number of births and deaths, and consequently the population, had been nearly doubled since the Revolution. Mr. Howlett also procured accounts of the actual number of houses in different places of the country; and by comparing the enumerations so obtained with those given in the returns by the window-duty collectors, he formed a general estimate of the deficiencies in the latter, and consequently of the total number of houses; and multiplying this number by $5\frac{2}{3}$, which he supposed he had ascertained, by actual investigation, to be the average number of persons in a house, he estimated the population in 1780 at 8,691,600, being nearly *four* millions more than the estimate made by Dr. Price. The accounts of births and deaths obtained under Parliamentary authority, and the careful examination that the registers have since undergone, have occasioned the population in 1780 to be estimated, in the Parliamentary Reports, at somewhat less than eight millions. But Mr. Howlett's estimate, though apparently a little exaggerated, was infinitely more accurate than any that had previously been made. His Essay displays great sagacity in the application of principles, and great patience and industry in the investigation of facts. It was supposed at the time, by those qualified to form an opinion, completely to overthrow the principles and statements advanced by Dr. Price; and the census of 1800 showed that that supposition had been well founded. We subjoin the titles of the three works referred to above:—

An Essay on the Population of England, from the Revolution to the present time, &c. By RICHARD PRICE, D.D., F.R.S. 8vo. London, 1780.

An Inquiry into the Present State of Population in England and Wales, and the Proportion which the Present Number of Inhabitants bears to the Number at former Periods. By WILLIAM WALES, F.R.S. 8vo. London, 1781.

An Examination of Dr. Price's Essay on the Population of England and Wales, and the Doctrine of an increased Population in this Kingdom established by Facts. By the Rev. JOHN HOWLETT, A.B. 8vo. Maidstone (1781).

An Essay on the Principle of Population, as it Affects the Future Improvement of Society. (By the Rev. T. R. MALTHUS.) 1st ed. 1 vol., 8vo. London, 1798. 6th and best edition, 2 vols., 8vo. London, 1826.

This work made, when published, a powerful impression; and was supposed, for awhile, to have exhausted the important department of the science of which it treats. It had, however, but few claims to attention on the score of originality, the fundamental principle maintained by Mr. Malthus, that population never fails, without any artificial stimulus, to rise to the level of subsistence, having been already set in the clearest point of view by a great number of the most eminent writers. But Mr. Malthus did not stop here. He contended, with Mr. Townsend (see *post*), that population has a necessary tendency to outrun the means of subsistence, and that unless this tendency be effectually countervailed by the prudence and forethought of the mass of the people, of which there has not hitherto been any example, it must necessarily keep the lower classes in a state of want and destitution. Mr. Malthus drew this conclusion from observing that population, deducting immigrants, has gone on doubling itself in newly settled colonies and other favourable situations, for a lengthened period, once every twenty-five or thirty years: and as the principle of increase is everywhere the same, it follows that were food and other necessary accommodations as easily procured in England, France, Holland, and other densely peopled countries, the population would increase with equal rapidity. But every one knows that the means of supporting population cannot be so easily increased in the countries referred to. Indeed, Mr. Malthus lays it down as a general principle, that food and other accommodations increase in old settled countries in an arithmetical progression only, whereas the inhabitants having a uniform tendency to increase in a geometrical progression, their numbers are constantly getting beyond the means of subsistence, and the land is overspread with poverty and misery. And he endeavours to support this theory by an examination of the state of population and subsistence in different countries.

Such, in a few words, is the theory of Malthus; and no one can deny that it embodies a large admixture of truth. Undoubtedly population has, under favourable circumstances, been doubled in twenty-five or thirty years; and undoubtedly the same power which has effected this doubling of the population in Kentucky and Illinois exists in England and Holland. But it is, at the same time, to be borne in mind that man is not the mere slave of appetite or instinct; and it is everywhere found that the principle of increase adjusts itself to the means of supporting additional population. Despite all that has been alleged by Malthus and others to the contrary, population, unless it has been excited by artificial means, is not, as compared with the means of subsistence, more dense in old settled than in new countries. Indeed every one, who has any acquaintance, however slight, with the history of society and the condition of the people of this or any other European country, a thousand, five hundred, or a hundred years ago, knows that it has been vastly improved in the interval; that instead of population outrunning subsistence, the latter has outrun population; and that the mass of the people have been gradually acquiring an increased command over necessaries and conveniences. And where are the grounds for supposing that it should be otherwise in time to come? In his anxiety to establish his theory, Mr. Malthus has overlooked and undervalued the influence of the principles which countervail the tendency to increase, and which uniformly keep it within due bounds. He has stated a part of the truth; but he has not stated the whole truth. "*Esclave d'une idée dominante, l'auteur de l' 'Essai sur la Population' s'y abandonne sans réserve; en combattant des exagérations, il se livre à des exagérations contraires; à des vérités utiles, se mêle des aperçus qui ne sont que spécieux; et pour vouloir en tirer des applications absolues, il en fausse les conséquences.*" (Degerando, 'Bienfaisance Publique,' I., Introd. p. 23.) Food is indispensable to existence; and it might be correctly laid down as a general principle that the necessity of a supply of food on the one hand, and the difficulty of getting it on the other, have a tendency to make every man die of hunger. Happily, however, the countervailing influences are so very powerful, that, though many die of repletion, not one individual in ten thousand dies of want; and such being the case, a theory, or a work on the subject, which should in a great measure overlook these influences, would not, we imagine, be considered good for much. And this, we apprehend, is the case with the 'Essay on the Principle of Population.'

Mr. Malthus's work is chiefly valuable for the attention which it drew to the subject of population, and for its showing that the principle of increase is sufficiently powerful, without any artificial stimulus, to keep population on a level with the supply of food and other accommodations. In other respects it leads to false conclusions. The principle of increase is not the bugbear, the invincible obstacle to all improvement it appeared to be as described by him, and still more by Dr. Chalmers and others of his school. A vast improvement has everywhere taken place. And it is easy to see that the principle of increase, instead of being adverse to, has really occasioned this progress. It is, in fact, the great cause of the advance of mankind; inasmuch as by keeping population on a level with the means of subsistence, it makes the demand for fresh discoveries and inventions as great at one period as another, and insures the continued improvement of the arts and of civilization.

Mr. Malthus was born in 1766. In 1797 he entered into holy orders, and in 1805 he was appointed Professor of Political Economy and History in the East India Company's College at Haileybury, in which situation he continued till his death in 1834. He was one of the founders of the Political Economy Club, and was a constant attendant at its meetings.

AN ESTIMATE of the NUMBER of INHABITANTS in GREAT BRITAIN and IRELAND. By Sir F. M. EDEN, Bart. 8vo. London, 1800.

A Statistical and Historical Inquiry into the Progress and Magnitude of the Population of Ireland. By THOMAS NEWENHAM, Esq. 1 vol., 8vo. London, 1805.

A Treatise on the Records of the Creation, &c., showing the Consistency of the Principle of Population with the Wisdom and Goodness of the Deity. By J. B. SUMNER, A.M. (Bishop of Chester). 2 vols., 8vo. 1st ed., London, 1815. 4th. ed. London, 1825.

An excellent work. The doctrines laid down by Malthus are not, perhaps, sufficiently modified; but the main object in view, that of showing that the theory of population is in perfect harmony with the Divine wisdom and goodness, is fully accomplished.

Two Lectures on Population, to which is added a Correspondence between the Author and Mr. Malthus. By N. W. SENIOR, Esq. 8vo. London, 1829.

THE LAW OF POPULATION: a Treatise in six books, in Disproof of the Superfecundity of Human Beings, and developing the real Principle of their Increase. By M. T. SADDLER, Esq., M.P. 2 vols., 8vo. London, 1830.

This work attracted some attention when it was published; but that arose out of extrinsic and adventitious circumstances, and it has already well nigh sunk into oblivion. It is quite unworthy of the subject. We certainly have no desire to extenuate or conceal either the faults or the errors of the author of the 'Essay on Population;' but whatever they may be, Mr. Saddler was not the person by whom they were to be pointed out, and the true theory of population established. His work consists principally of declamatory abuse, and of lengthened statements, to show that the fecundity of human beings is inversely as their numbers! A law which never had any existence except in his own distempered imagination, and which is contradicted by universal experience.

Researches into the Physical History of Mankind. By J. C. PRICHARD, M.D., &c. 4th ed., 4 vols., 8vo. London, 1841–1844.

A profoundly learned, elaborate, and in all respects excellent work. It will be completed in another volume.

The Principles of Population, and their Connexion with Human Happiness. By ARCHIBALD ALISON, Esq., F.R.S.E., &c. 2 vols., 8vo. Edinburgh, 1840.

This treatise discovers the same excellencies and defects that characterise the author's great historical work. Mr. Alison appears to have taken a pretty correct view of the relation between population and subsistence in the different states of society, and has shown how in its progress the principle of increase is restrained within proper limits. But exclusive of the inquiries necessary to the elucidation of the principles of population, we have lengthened disquisitions on a host of irrelevant topics, such as 'Church Establishments and the Voluntary System,' 'The Advantages and Disadvantages of Popular Instruction,' 'The Corn Laws,' and so forth. The style is also diffuse and declamatory; and the work has too much of a sermonising tone. But despite its defects, it is able and comprehensive; and contains, amid much that is questionable, much, also, that is well established and important.

CENSUSES of the POPULATION of GREAT BRITAIN in 1801, 1811, 1821, 1831, and 1841. Numerous vols. folio.

CENSUSES of the POPULATION of IRELAND in 1821, 1831, and 1841. Folio.

We beg to subjoin, for the convenience of the reader, the results of these enumerations:—

ACCOUNT of the POPULATION of the UNITED KINGDOM at the undermentioned Periods.

	1801.	1811.	1821.	1831.	1841.
England	8,331,434	9,538,827	11,261,437	13,091,005	14,995,138
Wales	541,546	611,788	717,438	806,182	911,603
Scotland	1,599,068	1,805,688	2,093,456	2,365,114	2,620,184
Army abroad and in Ireland, Seamen afloat, &c.	470,598	640,500	319,300	277,017	193,469
Islands in the British Seas	..	..	89,508	103,710	124,040
Ireland	No census	No census	6,801,827	7,767,401	8,175,124
TOTALS . . .	—	—	21,282,966	24,410,429	27,019,558

L'AMI des HOMMES, ou Traité de la Population. (Par M. le Marquis de MIRABEAU.) 5 vol. 12mo. Paris, 1755.

The author of this *ennuyeux fatras*, as it has been correctly termed, was one of the most zealous of the disciples of Quesnay; but this work was published before the latter had laid the foundations of his theory. Mirabeau's writings and his life are said to have exhibited rather a striking contrast; the former being full of all manner of fine sentiment, while the latter was in no ordinary degree sensual and tyrannical. He is commonly called Mirabeau père, to distinguish him from his son, the famous revolutionary leader.

In 1755 M. Herbert published his *Essai sur la Police Générale des Grains*, to which reference has been already made. In that able, and, as Smith justly calls it, "elegant" work, he refers as follows to the laws which govern the increase of population:—

"Nous n'examinerons point de quelle façon la race des hommes se multiplie. Il est évident que leur nombre augmenteroit à l'infini, sans des obstacles physiques, politiques, et moraux. Il nous suffit de savoir, que les hommes sont toujours en abondance, par-tout où ils se trouvent bien : que des pays ont été successivement bien ou mal peuplés, suivant la nature du gouvernement. La Palestine, l'Egypte, d'où sortoient des armées innombrables, sont désertes depuis long-tems. La Hollande et l'Angleterre, autrefois mal habitées, se remplissent tous les jours de nouveaux sujets. Des loix et des usages favorables à la culture, et à la population, font cette différence ; et l'on remarque aisément, que les états ne se peuplent point suivant la progression naturelle de la propagation, mais en raison de leur industrie, de leurs productions, et des différentes institutions.

"La guerre, la famine, les maladies épidémiques, ont souvent ravagé la terre ; ces maux se réparent ; et une nation renaît de générations, par les soins du législateur. Ces fléaux si terribles sont moins redoutables que des vices intérieurs, qui minent un état par dégrés imperceptibles. Un peuple s'anéantit, si l'on ne remédie aux maladies de langueur, qui affoiblissent l'agriculture ; et les sujets se dissipent ou dépérissent, sans qui l'on s'en apperçoive. Tout ce qui tend à détériorer le travail de la terre, tend à dépeupler un état, et à l'appauvrir.

"On ne voit point d'habitans dans des champs incultes ; la nature même y paroît triste et languissante. Tout semble respirer dans des terres bien travaillées. Des côteaux rians, des vergers, des troupeaux, des sillons, annoncent une multitude de cultivateurs ; et l'on croiroit, que la terre en produit à mesure que la culture s'anime.

"Les hommes en effet se multiplient comme les productions du sol, et à proportion des avantages et des ressources qu'ils trouvent dans leurs travaux. Leur premier soin est celui des besoins ; quand ils trouvent à les satisfaire, nulle inquiétude ne s'oppose à leur augmentation. Le colon n'appréhende point de voir croître sa famille, quand il prévoit pouvoir la soutenir : mais des gens découragés, ou dans la misère, prisent trop peu la vie, pour avoir soin de celle des autres. On ne songe point à arroser des plantes, quand on a besoin d'eau pour soi-même. * * * *

"Cette abondance dépend moins de la fertilité du terrain, que des causes qui attachent chaque particulier à son pays, ou qui l'en dégoûtent. Des contrées fécondes se dépeuplent quand l'habitant ne peut jouir sans inquiétude du fruit de ses peines. Des pays ingrats se repeuplent par l'aisance, et par l'encouragement des sujets.

"L'industrie l'emporte toujours sur la qualité du sol, et la nation économe est la ruche qui s'accroît par son travail. Le peuple s'augmente à proportion de la facilité qu'il trouve à vivre ; et les hommes se multiplient naturellement comme les denrées, quand leur vie n'est point traversée par les besoins, ou par la crainte. Protéger l'agriculture, c'est aider la nature dans ses opérations.

"De la supériorité de la culture, naît une supériorité de population ; du plus grand nombre d'habitans, vient une plus grande industrie ; de l'industrie bien dirigée, suit un commerce plus étendu : et ces différens accroissemens forment les sources inaltérables des revenus publics. Tout ce qui n'en découle point, n'est qu'un torrent passager, plus destructif que fécond. La culture, la population, le commerce, étendent la puissance ; et toutes ces branches partent de l'agriculture."—(pp. 319-325.)

THÉORIE du SYSTÈME ANIMAL. 1 vol., post 8vo., à Leide, 1767.

This scarce and curious work was written by Mr. Bruckner, a scholar of Valcknaer, and subsequently pastor of the German church and teacher of the German language at Norwich. It contains an exposition of the theory of population; and an attempt to show that the extreme profusion of animal life, and the consequent destruction to which it leads, is the arrangement best fitted to promote the well-being of man and of the lower animals.

Bruckner is noticed in Robberds' 'Life of Mr. William Taylor, of Norwich;' but we derived the above statements from a note by Dr. Parr, in a copy of the *Théorie Animal* (now in our possession), which he states had been given him by the author.

Recherches sur la Population des Généralités d'Auvergne, de Lyon, de Rouen, &c., depuis 1674 jusqu'en 1764. Par M. MESSANCE. 1 vol., 4to. Paris, 1766.

It was customary in France, during the reign of Louis XV., as it was at the same time in England, to represent the population of the kingdom as declining. This work is intended to show the real worth of these representations, by giving the results of enumerations of the people in various parts of the kingdom, with extracts from a great many parish registers, &c., for periods of from ten to upwards of forty years previously to 1760. These returns show beyond a doubt that, instead of decreasing, the population had increased very considerably during the period to which they extend; and they also supply valuable data with respect to various matters of interest connected with the state of the population.

Recherches et Considérations sur la Population de la France. Par M. MOHEAU. 1 vol., 8vo. Paris, 1778.

This when published was certainly the best work that had appeared on the population of any country. It is, says Peuchet, "*un livre classique et bien écrit*" (Statistique Elémentaire, p. 226). A work on the population of France or Great Britain, modelled after that of Moheau, and embodying the latest information on the subject, would be a very valuable acquisition.

TABLEAU de la POPULATION de toutes les PROVINCES de la FRANCE, &c. Par M. de POMMELLES. 8vo. Paris, 1789.

The most ample accounts of the progress and distribution of population in France since 1815 are given in the Statistical Works published by order of the French government; for which see the chapter entitled Political Arithmetic, Statistics, &c. In the mean time we may state that, according to the best attainable information, the progress of population in France has been—

Years.	Population.	Years.	Population.
1700	19,670,000	1821	30,464,875
1784	24,800,000	1831	32,569,223
1801	27,349,000	1836	33,540,910
1811	29,092,000	1841	34,136,695

RECHERCHES sur la POPULATION, les NAISSANCES, les DÉCÈS, &c., dans le PAYS BAS. Par M. QUETELET. 8vo. Bruxelles, 1827.

RIFLESSIONI sulla POPULAZIONE delle NAZIONE per Rapporto all' ECONOMIA NAZIONALE. Di GIAMMARIA ORTES. 1 vol., 8vo. Venezia, 1790.

It is also printed in the 24th volume of the modern part of the *Economisti Italiani*.

This work has been a good deal referred to by various foreign writers, from its anticipating in some respects the conclusions of Malthus. Ortes contends that population, were it not restricted by the difficulty of providing food and other accommodations, would increase in a geometrical proportion, doubling every thirty years; and he further contends that the difficulty of providing the means of subsistence, by operating on the reason of mankind, and restraining the principle of increase, keeps the latter within the necessary limits, and prevents the extreme poverty and misery that would otherwise result from the tendency to increase. But notwithstanding the soundness of some of his conclusions, its obscurity and prolixity must have prevented the work of Ortes from having any practical influence. Most probably it was unknown to Malthus, at the period when he published his Essay; and besides, there is nothing in it that had not been previously stated by others.

The economical writings of Ortes are very voluminous, filling no fewer than seven volumes of the *Economisti Italiani*. Certainly, however, they might have been advantageously omitted; and, with the exception of the one now referred to, are not worthy of notice.

CHAPTER XIII.

FOUNDLINGS AND FOUNDLING HOSPITALS.

THE establishment of an hospital in London for exposed children, or foundlings, was recommended by Addison in the 'Guardian,' No. 105. It was not, however, till 1739 that this recommendation was acted upon; but in that year a foundling hospital was organized, through the exertions of a benevolent individual of the name of Coram, who left his property for its support. Originally it was intended for the indiscriminate admission of deserted children. The funds belonging to the hospital being, however, quite inadequate to admit of this being done, Parliament was applied to for assistance, which being granted, the numbers of children on the establishment and its expense increased so very rapidly as to attract the attention of Government and of the public. The policy of the institution was called in question; and it was contended that, instead of being advantageous, the indiscriminate admission of children was really productive of a great increase of profligacy and immorality. Parliament having concurred in this opinion, it was decided, in 1760, that the practice should be abandoned; and the mode of admission to the charity was then so much altered, and placed under so many limitations, that it has since been nominally only a foundling hospital. This is the only institution of its kind in Great Britain; and measures are now in progress for the suppression of the foundling hospital in Dublin. In France, however, and most other continental states, these institutions are extremely numerous, and occupy an important place in their domestic economy.

Considérations sur les Enfans-Trouvés dans les Principaux Etats de l'Europe. Par M. BENOISTON DE CHATEAUNEUF. 8vo. Paris, 1824.

An elaborate and valuable tract.

HISTOIRE STATISTIQUE et MORALE des ENFANS-TROUVÉS. Par M. TERME et M. MONFALCON. 1 vol., grand in-8vo. Paris et Lyon, 1837.

RECHERCHES sur les ENFANS-TROUVÉS, les ENFANS NATURELS, et les ORPHELINS. Par M. l'Abbé GAILLARD. 1 vol., 8vo. Poitiers, 1837.

Recherches sur les Enfans-Trouvés et les Enfans Illégitimes, en Russie, dans le reste de l'Europe, en Asie, et en Amérique, précédés d'un Essai sur l'Histoire des Enfans-Trouvés depuis les Temps les plus Anciens jusqu'à nos Jours. Par M. de GOUROFF. 1 vol. (all that has been published), 8vo. Paris, 1839.

This work, in so far as it has been completed, is undoubtedly the best that has appeared on the subject. The essay on the history of foundlings in antiquity and in modern times is most valuable and interesting, and reflects high credit on the learning and ability of the author. A small impression (120 copies) of this essay was published separately at Paris in 1829; and to it various succeeding writers have been more indebted than they have always thought proper to acknowledge.

On the whole we should, speaking generally, be disposed to agree in opinion with those who think that foundling hospitals are disadvantageous, or that the evils to which they give rise exceed those which they obviate. At the same time it must be admitted that this is a subject which is encumbered with not a few difficulties, and that much depends on the condition and habits of the society in which the hospitals are erected. The arguments on both sides have been fairly and ably stated by Degerando (Bienfaisance Publique, ii. pp. 201-226), to whom there appears to be a balance of advantage on the side of the hospitals.

CHAPTER XIV.

NATURALIZATION

AN antipathy to resident foreigners seems to be indigenous to all rude and uncivilised nations. Whatever is done by them appears to be so much taken from the employment, and, consequently, from the subsistence of the citizens; while the advantages resulting from the new arts or improved practices they seldom fail to introduce for the most part manifest themselves only by slow degrees, and rarely make any impression on the multitude. Hence the jealousy and aversion with which foreigners are uniformly regarded in all countries not far advanced in civilization. The early Greeks and Romans looked upon strangers as a species of enemies, with whom, though not actually at war, they maintained no sort of friendly intercourse. "*Hostis*," says Cicero, "*apud majores nostros is dicebatur, quem nunc peregrinum dicimus*,"—(De Off. lib. i. cap. 12) It may, therefore, be considered as a striking proof of the good sense and liberality of those by whom it was framed, that a clause is inserted in the Magna Carta which has the encouragement of commerce for its object; being to the effect, that "all merchants (if not openly prohibited before) shall have safe and sure conduct to depart out of and to come into England, to reside in and go through England, as well by land as by water; to buy and sell without any manner of evil tolls, by the old and rightful customs, except in time of war; and if they be of a land making war against us, and such be found in our nation at the beginning of the war, they shall be attached without harm of body or goods, until it be known unto us, or our chief justice, how our merchants be entreated in the land making war against us; and if our merchants be well entreated there, shall be so likewise here."

But until the era of Edward I, this stipulation seems to have been little attended to. It is doubtful whether, previously to his reign, foreigners could either hire houses of their own, or deal except through the medium of some Englishman. But this intelligent prince saw the advantage that would result to the trade and industry of his subjects from the residence and intercourse of Germans, Flemings, Italians, and other foreigners, who, at that time, were very superior to the English in most branches of manufacture and commerce. He therefore exerted himself to procure a repeal of some of the more oppressive restrictions on aliens, and gave them a charter which conveyed considerable privileges. Down, however, to the reign of Edward III., it continued to be customary in this, as in most other countries, to arrest one stranger for the debt, and even to punish him for the crimes and misdemeanors of others; but the practice was then put an end to by the 27 Edw. III. stat. 2, cap. 17.

In consequence of the encouragement given by Edward III., a good many of the woollen manufacturers of Flanders came over to England; and it is from their immigration that we may date the improvement and importance of the woollen manufacture in this country. But this policy, however wise and judicious, was exceedingly unpopular. The foreigners were openly insulted, and their lives endangered, in London and other large towns; and a few of them in consequence returned to Flanders. Edward, however, was not to be driven from his purpose by an unfounded clamour of this sort. A proclamation was issued, in which every person accused of disturbing or attacking the foreign weavers was ordered to be committed to Newgate, and threatened with the utmost severity of punishment. In a parliament held at York, in 1335, an act was passed for the better protection and security of foreign merchants and others, by which penalties were inflicted on all who gave them any disturbance. This seems to have had the effect, for a while, at least, of preventing any outrages.

During the troubled period that intervened between the demise of Edward III. and the accession of Elizabeth, the hostility to aliens was again revived. Our sovereigns were then too much occupied in maintaining themselves on the throne, or in other matters of more immediate and pressing interest, to think of opposing any effectual resistance to the popular prejudices against aliens, who were, in consequence, subjected to many indignities. But under the vigorous government of Elizabeth the outrages of which they had been the victims were repressed; the advantages, also, of a more indulgent treatment of foreigners began to be better appreciated; and the political and religious circumstances under which the country was then placed conspired to promote the immigration, and to procure for them a better reception than they would otherwise have met with.

The influx of foreigners during the reign of Elizabeth was occasioned chiefly by the persecutions of the Duke of Alva and the Spaniards in the Low Countries. The friends of the reformed religion, which at the time was far from being firmly established, and the Government, were glad to receive such an accession of strength; and from the superiority of the Flemings in commerce and manufactures, the immigrants contributed materially to the improvement of the arts in England. It would seem, however, that the ministers of Elizabeth contented themselves, perhaps that they might not excite the old prejudice of the public, with declining to enforce the laws against aliens, without taking any very active steps in their favour.

Since the Revolution more enlarged and liberal views respecting the conduct to be followed with respect to aliens have continued to gain ground: several of the restraining statutes have fallen into disuse, while others have been so much modified by the interference of the courts, which have generally been inclined to soften their severity, that their more offensive provisions have long been inoperative. In 1709 an Act was passed (7 Anne, c. 5) for the naturalization of all foreign Protestants; but the prejudice against them was still so powerful that it was repealed in 1712. Some unsuccessful attempts have since been made to carry a similar measure. One of these, about the middle of last century, occasioned the publication of the following pamphlets:—

Reflections on the Expediency of a Law for the Naturalization of Foreign Protestants: in Two Parts, the first being Historical Remarks on the late Naturalization Bill, and the second Queries occasioned by the same. By JOSIAH TUCKER, M.A. 8vo. London, 1751 and 1752.

These tracts are both excellent. The arguments in favour of the naturalization of foreigners have never been more clearly and forcibly stated, nor those in opposition to the measure more skilfully answered.

It is curious that, notwithstanding the failure at this period of the attempt to effect the naturalization of foreign Protestants, an Act should have passed in 1753 for naturalizing Jews. But the passing of this Act occasioned so violent a ferment that it was repealed in the course of next year. On this occasion, also, Tucker was in the field.

A Letter to a Friend concerning Naturalizations, &c. By JOSIAH TUCKER, M.A. 8vo. London, 1753.

A Second Letter to a Friend concerning Naturalizations, &c. By JOSIAH TUCKER, M.A. 8vo. London, 1753.

In these tracts Tucker defends the Act for the Naturalization of the Jews with equal ingenuity, vigour, and boldness. But his efforts were far too feeble to have any influence over the current of popular prejudice.

We have already seen (p. 48) that the merchants of Holland considered the liberty given to strangers to settle in that country, and the efficient protection given to them while there, as one of the circumstances that had conduced most to increase the wealth and prosperity of the Republic: and so long as aliens conduct themselves properly, it is not very easy to see what is to object to in their residence, or to allowing them, under such conditions as may be deemed necessary, to hold fixed property, and to enjoy the other privileges of natural-born subjects. It is, however, quite another thing when they come amongst us, not for the sake of an asylum, or for the prosecution of industrious pursuits, but to make this country a theatre for carrying on plots and hatching conspiracies against the governments of countries with which we may be in amity. In that case they forfeit all claim to hospitality; and have no just ground for complaint should they be forthwith compelled to quit our shores.

REPORT from the SELECT COMMITTEE of the HOUSE of COMMONS appointed to Inquire into the State of the Laws affecting Aliens, with Minutes of Evidence. Folio. 1843.

This Report,* and the evidence annexed to it, comprise pretty full information respecting the disabilities under which aliens laboured in this country previously to the late act, the 7 and 8 Victoria, c. 66. This act authorises the Secretary of State for the Home Department, on his receiving such evidence as he may think necessary in regard to any application by an alien for a certificate of naturalization, to grant, if he think fit, such certificate. And the certificate so granted conveys to him (unless some special reservation be made in it) all the rights and capacities of a natural-born British subject, except that of being a member of either House of Parliament, and of being a Privy Councillor. Probably this is as good a law as can be enacted in reference to this matter.

---

* The compilers of this Report have been pleased, for what reason is best known to themselves, to call the *Richesse de la Hollande* a "state document!" They might, with quite as much propriety, apply the same designation to Scott's Novels, or Gibbon's Decline and Fall. The *Richesse de la Hollande* (with which we suspect they are but indifferently acquainted) is a work written by a foreigner, in 2 vols. 4to., and 4 vols. 8vo., in which many of the acts and proceedings of the Dutch Government are severely criticised. (See p. 63.)

CHAPTER XV.

BILLS OF MORTALITY, AND WORKS HAVING REFERENCE TO HEALTH AND MORTALITY.

Natural and Political Observations upon the Bills of Mortality, by Captain JOHN GRAUNT, F.R.S.; chiefly with reference to the Government, Religion, Trade, Growth, Air, Diseases, &c., of the City of London. 1st ed. 4to. London, 1662. 5th ed. 8vo. London, 1676.

This work is not only one of the earliest but also one of the best of its class. It is said by Evelyn, in his Memoirs (i. 475, 4to. ed.), and by Dr. Halley, in his paper referred to below, that Sir William Petty was the real author of the 'Observations.' But notwithstanding the deference due to their authority, it may be doubted whether there be any good ground for this statement. Dr. Sprat, the historian of the Royal Society, and also a contemporary, ascribes, without hesitation or qualification of any kind, the work to Graunt, who, he says, had been elected a member of the Society by desire of Charles II.—(Hist. of Royal Society, 2nd ed. p. 67.) But, independently of this circumstance, it would be contrary to all that is known of Petty to suppose, had he been the author of the work, he would have allowed any one else to enjoy the credit thereof. He was always forward to acknowledge his writings; and there is certainly nothing in this work that should have made him wish to disown it. Admitting, however, that he had for some unimaginable reason published the first edition under a borrowed name, it is not very likely he would have continued a useless deception of this sort after the extraordinary merit of the work had been acknowledged on all hands, and after the death of Graunt. And yet in a private letter to his intimate friend, Sir Robert Southwell, written five years after Graunt's demise, and when he had no motive for disguise or concealment, he refers to the work as Graunt's, without indulging in any insinuation of any kind, direct or indirect, respecting its paternity.—(Pepys' Life, Journals, &c., ii. 317.) The subjects treated of in it are similar to those treated of by Petty, and the last edition, published after Graunt's death, which took place in 1674, being edited by Petty, that circumstance may perhaps have given rise to the notion of his being the author.

The first table of mortality that appeared in modern Europe was constructed by Dr. Halley, and published in the 'Transactions of the Royal Society' for 1693. The paper in which it appears is entitled—

AN ESTIMATE of the DEGREES of the MORTALITY of MANKIND, drawn from curious TABLES of the Births and Funerals at the city of BRESLAW, with an attempt to ascertain the Price of Annuities upon Lives. By E. HALLEY, R.S.S.

The tables referred to by Halley comprised the numbers, ages, and sexes of the persons who died at Breslaw during each of the five years ending with 1691, compared with the number of the births for the same years. The paper contains, exclusive of the table of mortality, many judicious observations on the useful purposes to which such tables may be applied.

A TREATISE of the DISEASES of TRADESMEN, &c. Translated from the Latin of BERNARD RAMAZZINI, M.D. 1 vol. 8vo. London, 1705.

This work was long held in high estimation, and has been referred to by Smith.

New Observations, Natural, Moral, Civil, Political, and Medical, on City, Town, and Country Bills of Mortality, &c. By THOMAS SHORT, M.D. 1 vol. 8vo. London, 1750.

"Dr. Short collected, with incredible labour, extracts from the mortuary and baptismal registers in a great many market towns and country parishes of England, chiefly in the northern counties, and in almost every variety of soil and situation, and reduced them into tables in various ways so as to enable him to draw useful inferences from them. He likewise procured both the number of families and of souls in seven of the market towns and fifty-four of the country parishes, for which he had registers; and thus arrived at satisfactory information on several points which, till then, had been very imperfectly understood. But the sexes were not distinguished in his enumerations; neither were the ages, in any of the enumerations or registers of which he has given accounts, except in the London Bills of Mortality, and what he has taken from Dr. Halley, respecting those for Breslaw.

"But though Dr. Short took so much trouble in collecting materials, and has generally reasoned well upon them, he has shown but little skill, and does not appear to have taken much pains in communicating his information to his readers, so that it costs them considerable labour to find what they want; and when found to understand it."—(Milne, 'Encyc. Br.')

OBSERVATIONS on the PAST GROWTH and PRESENT STATE of the CITY of LONDON. (By CORBYN MORRIS, Esq., F.R.S.) Folio. London, 1751.

A Collection of the yearly Bills of Mortality, from 1657 to 1758, inclusive: to which are subjoined Graunt's Essay; Sir William Petty's Essay on the Growth of the City of London; Morris's Observations; and a tract by Morris, entitled 'Observations, Political and Natural, &c., on the Bills of Mortality,' written for this volume; with a Table of the Probability of Life, by J. P., Esq., F.R.S. (James Postlethwayt, Esq.). 1 vol. 4to. London, 1759.

This valuable publication has been usually ascribed to Dr. Birch; secretary to the Royal Society. But it appears from the statement of Mr. Milne (Mortality, Law of, 'Encyc. Brit.'), that we are principally indebted for it to the exertions of the elder Dr. Heberden.

A COMPARATIVE VIEW of the MORTALITY of the HUMAN SPECIES at all AGES; and of the Diseases and Casualties by which they are Destroyed or Annoyed. By WILLIAM BLACK, M.D. 1 vol. 8vo. London, 1788.

OBSERVATIONS on MARRIAGES, BAPTISMS, and BURIALS, as preserved in Parochial Registers; with sundry Specimens of the Entries of Marriages, &c., in Foreign Countries. By RALPH BIGLAND, Esq., Garter King-at-Arms. 4to. London, 1764.

OBSERVATIONS on the INCREASE and DECREASE of different DISEASES in LONDON. By WILLIAM HEBERDEN, M.D. 4to. London, 1801.

REPORTS on the DISEASES in LONDON, particularly during the years 1796, 1797, 1798, 1799, and 1800. By ROBERT WILLAN, M.D. 1 vol., 12mo. London, 1801.

Mr. Milne's standard work on annuities and assurances was published in 1815 (see Works on Interest and Annuities); and in it, and his article on Mortality, in the new edition of the 'Encyclopædia Britannica,' the reader will find the best information respecting the history and construction of tables of mortality.

OBSERVATIONS on the MORTALITY and PHYSICAL MANAGEMENT of CHILDREN. By Mr. ROBERTON. 1 vol., 8vo. London, 1829.

ELEMENTS of MEDICAL STATISTICS, &c. By F. B. HAWKINS, M.D. 1 vol., 8vo. London, 1829.

THE EFFECTS of ARTS, TRADES, and PROFESSIONS, and of CIVIC STATES and HABITS of LIVING, on HEALTH and LONGEVITY. By C. T. THACKRAH, Esq. (Surgeon, Leeds). 1 vol. 8vo. London, 1832.

A valuable publication: it may be regarded as a modern Ramazzini.

THE MORAL and PHYSICAL CONDITION of the WORKING CLASSES employed in the COTTON MANUFACTURE in MANCHESTER. By J. P. KAY, M.D. 8vo. London, 1832.

Annual Reports of the Registrar-General. Folio. London, 1839, &c.

Previously to 1833, the system followed in London, and most other parts of England, for the registration of births, marriages, and deaths was exceedingly defective; and it was in consequence very difficult to arrive at any satisfactory conclusion with respect to the duration of human life, and the comparative healthiness of particular districts and businesses. But in the above year a new and vastly-improved system of registration was introduced by the Act 6 & 7 Will. IV. c. 86. It is carried on under the superintendence of a Registrar-General, resident in London, to whose office the returns from the local registrars in different parts of the country are sent, to be classified under their proper heads, and brought into general results. The Annual Reports of the Registrar-General are most valuable, and furnish by far the best accounts of the health and mortality of the population. Some of the most elaborate and important papers in these reports have been written by Mr. W. Farr, and reflect the highest credit on his ability, extensive mathematical and medical learning, and industry.

ARTISANS and MACHINERY: the Moral and Physical Condition of the Manufacturing Population considered with Reference to Mechanical Substitutes for Labour. By P. Gaskell, Esq., Surgeon. 1 vol., post 8vo. London, 1836.

Report to Her Majesty's Principal Secretary of State for the Home Department, from the Poor Law Commissioners, on an Inquiry into the Sanitary Condition of the Labouring Population of Great Britain, with Appendices, and Local and Supplemental Reports. 3 vols., in folio, and in 8vo. 1842.

In the first of these reports, written by Edwin Chadwick, Esq., secretary to the Poor Law Commissioners, a great deal of authentic and very valuable information has been brought together with respect to the habitations of the labouring classes and their condition generally. The interesting and elaborate report, by the same gentleman, on interment in towns, discloses some really frightful abuses.

FIRST REPORT of the COMMISSIONERS for INQUIRING into the STATE of LARGE TOWNS and POPULOUS DISTRICTS. Folio. 1844.

The statements and details in this extremely bulky volume add but little to the information in the reports of Mr. Chadwick; and, perhaps, it may be supposed by some that the time and talents of the Commissioners would be employed to greater advantage in sifting the information previously obtained, and in framing available plans and schemes for obviating the evils complained of, than in adding to the unwieldy mass of superfluous evidence already before the public.

ANNALES d'HYGIÈNE PUBLIQUE, et de MÉDECINE LÉGALE. 32 vol. 8vo. Paris, 1829–44.

This quarterly journal, which is still going on, contains many valuable articles on population, public health, &c., by Villermé, Benoiston-de-Chateauneuf, and other able writers.

ANALYSE et TABLEAUX de l'INFLUENCE de la PETITE VÉROLE sur la Mortalité à chaque âge, et de celle qu'un Préservatif tel que la Vaccine peut avoir sur la Population et la Longévité. Par M. DUVILLARD. 1 vol., 4to. Paris, 1806.

CHAPTER XVI.

WAGES, PAUPERISM, POOR-LAWS, SAVINGS BANKS, FRIENDLY SOCIETIES, &c.

SOME PROPOSALS for the EMPLOYING the POOR, especially in and about the City of LONDON; and for the Prevention of Begging. By T. F. (THOMAS FIRMIN). 4to. London, 1678.

The author of this tract, a native of Ipswich in Suffolk, was an intimate friend of Archbishop Tillotson. He was as much distinguished by his Socinianism as by his charity and zeal for the poor; and it was principally owing to his intimacy with Firmin that the archbishop was subjected to the unfounded imputation of favouring the same heterodox opinion. Firmin died in 1697.

In the 2nd edition of Sir Josiah Child's 'Discourse about Trade,' published in 1690, is a chapter (the second) respecting the poor, in which he proposes a scheme for their improvement that has been a good deal referred to.

A DISCOURSE touching PROVISION for the POOR. (Ascribed to Sir MATTHEW HALE.) 8vo. London, 1683.

Sir F. M. Eden supposes that this tract, if it be really the production of Hale, had been written during his retirement in 1659. It is written, like that of Firmin, to recommend the establishment of workhouses where poor people should be employed in manufactures.

PROPOSALS for raising a COLLEGE of INDUSTRY of all USEFUL TRADES and HUSBANDRY, &c. By JOHN BELLERS. 4to. London, 1696.

REPORT of the BOARD of TRADE to the LORDS JUSTICES respecting the Relief and Employment of the Poor. (Drawn up by LOCKE, one of the original Commissioners of the Board.) See Sir F. M. EDEN, i. 244.

Giving Alms no Charity; and EMPLOYING the POOR a GRIEVANCE to the NATION. Being an Essay, &c. (By DANIEL DEFOE.) 4to. (pp. 28.) London, 1704.

This tract has been a good deal referred to. It is written with considerable cleverness; and is principally directed against a Bill then before Parliament, introduced by Sir Humphrey Mackworth, for setting up manufactures in workhouses. Defoe's arguments in opposition to this project are as follows:—

"Suppose now a workhouse for the employment of poor children sets them to spinning of worsted. For every skein of worsted these poor children spin, there must be a skein the less spun by some poor family or person that spun it before; suppose the manufacture of making bays to be erected in Bishopsgate Street, unless the makers of these bays can find out at the same time a trade or consumption for more bays than were made before, for every piece of bays so made in London, there must be a piece the less made at Colchester.

"I humbly appeal to the Honourable House of Commons what this may be called; and, with submission, I think it is nothing at all to employing the poor; since it is only transposing manufacture from Colchester to London, and taking the bread out of the mouths of the poor of Essex, to put it into the mouths of the poor of Middlesex.

"If these worthy gentlemen, who show themselves so forward to relieve and employ the poor, will find out some new trade, some new market, where the goods they make shall be sold, where none of the same goods were sold before: if they will send them to any place where they shall not interfere with the rest of that manufacture, or with some other made in England; then indeed they will do something worthy of themselves, and they may employ the poor to the same glorious advantage as Queen Elizabeth did, to whom this nation, as a trading country, owes its peculiar greatness.

"If these gentlemen could establish a trade to Muscovy for English serges, or obtain an order from the Czar, that all his subjects should wear stockings, who wore none before, every poor child's labour in spinning and knitting those stockings, and all the wool in them, would be clear gain to the nation, and the general stock would be improved by it; because all the growth of our country, and all the labour of a person who was idle before, is so much clear gain to the general stock.

"If they will employ the poor in some manufacture which was not made in England before, or not bought with some manufacture made here before, then they offer at something extraordinary.

"But to set poor people at work on the same thing that other poor people were employed on before, and at the same time not increase the consumption, is giving to one what you take away from another; enriching one poor man to starve another; putting a vagabond into an honest man's employment, and putting his diligence on the tenters to find out some other work to maintain his family."—(pp. 16-17.)

But these arguments are not so conclusive as some have supposed. It is to be borne in mind that the occupiers of prisons and workhouses must be supported whether they are employed or kept in idleness; and such being the case, if it be practicable to employ them so as to furnish produce that will sell for 5,000*l.*, 10,000*l.*, 100,000*l.*, or any other sum over and above the cost of the material, it would surely be the climax of absurdity to refuse to avail ourselves of their services. Whatever they produce while in confinement is so much nett addition to the public wealth; and the taxes required for their support may be reduced accordingly. It is no good reason for refusing to profit by their labour to allege, as Defoe has done, that for every skein of yarn spun in a workhouse a skein the less must be spun elsewhere. The skein spun in the workhouse really costs nothing, for its inmates must be fed and maintained at the public expense whether they spin or not. Neither is the market limited in extent as Defoe supposed; and though it were, there are an infinity of other branches of industry to which the unemployed poor may resort. This, in truth, is the identical sophism that is always in the mouths of those opposed to the introduction of machinery and to every sort of improvement. For every passenger carried per railway, it might be, and indeed was, said, a passenger the less will be carried by the ordinary road; but is that any reason why the former should not be constructed? Were a bountiful Providence to supply us with shoes and hats, should we act wisely or gratefully in rejecting the boon because it would oblige the shoemakers and hatters to employ themselves in some other business? The truth is, that in matters of this sort Defoe was quite as prejudiced and purblind as the bulk of those around him. He had not read, or if he had read he had plainly, at all events, profited nothing by the conclusive reasonings in the Tract on the East India Trade previously referred to. (See p. 100.)

But without insisting further on the question as to the prosecution of employments in workhouses, it is sufficiently obvious that the establishment of the latter may be made materially to forward the relief of the deserving poor, without at the same time encouraging sloth and idleness. The strict discipline and constant labour enforced in all well-conducted workhouses, and the moderate diet of their inmates, make them objects of disgust and aversion to the idle and disorderly; and many persons who would be eager to obtain assistance from the public, could it be procured at their own houses, would reject it if coupled with the condition of residence in a workhouse.

In 1723 the workhouse system was placed on an improved footing, and received a great extension, by the Act 9 Geo. I., cap. 7, which enabled parishes to unite for building workhouses, and conferred on them the important privilege, if they saw cause, of refusing relief except in a workhouse. This formed the principal bulwark, during the next half century, against the progress of fictitious pauperism. Sir F. M. Eden states that on workhouses being erected after the passing of this act, great numbers of persons who had previously received pensions from parishes preferred depending upon their own exertions rather than take up their abode in them; and he further states that the aversion of the poor to these establishments was so great, that some whose humanity seems to have exceeded their good sense, proposed, by way of weakening this feeling, "to call workhouses by some softer and more inoffensive name."—(State of the Poor, i. 285.)

A still more distinguished though not a better authority, Lord Mansfield, expressed himself as follows respecting workhouses, in a case that came before him in 1782:—"If well regulated, workhouses are a most desirable mode of relief; they supply comfort and accommodation for those who cannot work, and employment for those who can. In many instances which have chanced to fall within my knowledge, particularly in the Midland circuit, they have reduced the annual amount of the poor rates a half."

An Account of several Workhouses for Employing and Maintaining the Poor; setting forth the Rules by which they are Governed, &c. 8vo. London, 1725. A 2nd and improved ed. was published in 1732.

An Enquiry into the Causes of the late Increase of Robbers, &c.; with some Proposals for remedying this growing Evil, &c. By Henry Fielding, Esq. 8vo. London, 1751.

A Proposal for making an Effectual Provision for the Poor, for amending their Morals, and for rendering them useful Members of Society. By Henry Fielding, Esq. 8vo. London, 1753.

These tracts having been written by the most eminent of English novelists, have attracted fully as much attention as they were entitled to on account of their intrinsic merits. The first, however, is written with great force, and contains various statements and reasonings that throw a good deal of light on the causes of crime and pauperism, and on the state of the London poor at the time. But like most other writers on the same subject, Fielding has ascribed far too much to legislative and police arrangements, and too little to the care and discretion of individuals. The truth is, that all that is required to provide for the provident and economical management of the poor is to intrust it to the landlords and persons possessed of property in the different parishes or other districts in which the poor reside, giving the latter a power of easy appeal to some properly constituted tribunal. Every other project is sure to end in jobbing and abuse. Those who really defray the charge of providing for the poor have the most powerful of all motives—a regard to their own interest—for taking care that it be not misapplied or perverted to improper purposes; and if they be allowed to take their own way in the matter, they will not be long in discovering methods of getting rid of those who are able to provide for themselves, and of administering the relief required by the really necessitous poor in the cheapest and best manner. Under such a system the danger is not that idleness should be encouraged, or that the poor should be too liberally provided for, but that parsimony should encroach too much on generosity, and that the allowances to paupers would be rendered too scanty; and hence the necessity of giving them a right of appeal from the decisions of the parochial or local tribunals.

Observations on the Defects of the Poor-Laws, and on the Causes and Consequences of the Great Increase and Burden of the Poor. By Thomas Alcock, A.M. 8vo. London, 1752.

One of the best tracts in opposition to a compulsory provision. Mr. Alcock has, however, though without intending it, set a part of its beneficial operation in the clearest point of view; for he bears testimony to the fact, that the obligation of providing for the poor had, by making landed gentlemen and others anxious to guard against the effects of this indefinite liability, tempted them to oppose every obstacle to the building of cottages and the increase of population, and that this conduct had been a means of lessening the numbers of the poor and raising wages! There can be no doubt that this statement is correct; and this influence was more than sufficient to countervail any mischievous consequences of which the poor-laws might otherwise have been productive. (See pp. 19, 20.)

Considerations on several Proposals lately made for the better Management of the Poor. 2nd ed., with an Appendix. 4to. London, 1752.

An able tract, in which the policy, or rather necessity, of the compulsory provision for the support of the poor is set in a striking light; and in which also it is shown that the smaller the districts into which the country is divided as respects the poor, the more likely will it be that their concerns should be carefully and economically administered.

An Account of the Care taken in most Civilised Nations for the Relief of the Poor, more particularly in Times of Scarcity and Distress. By the Rev. Richard Onely. 4to. London, 1758.

The Manifold Causes of the Increase of the Poor distinctly set forth; together with a Set of Proposals for Removing and

Preventing some of the principal Evils, and for Lessening others. (Ascribed to JOSIAH TUCKER, A.M., Dean of Gloucester.) 4to. London, 1760.

The History of the Poor-Laws, with Observations. By RICHARD BURN, LL.D. 1 vol., 8vo. London, 1764.

This publication, by the learned author of the 'Justice of the Peace,' is one of the best that has appeared on the poor-laws. Its object, to use the Doctor's words, is "to set forth what laws for the poor were anciently in this kingdom; what the laws are now; and what proposals have been made by ingenious and public-spirited men from time to time for the amendment of the same." And this much he has accomplished concisely and skilfully. We subjoin Burn's account of the duties of an overseer of the poor. It is no doubt a little caricatured; but it is substantially accurate, and strikingly evinces the influence of the old system in preventing the too great increase of population:—

"In practice, the office of an overseer of the poor seems to be understood to be this: To keep an extraordinary look-out, to prevent persons coming to inhabit without certificates, and to fly to the justices to remove them; and if a man brings a certificate, then to caution all the inhabitants not to let him a farm of 10*l.* a-year, and to take care to keep him out of all parish offices; to warn them, if they will hire *servants*, to hire them half-yearly, or by the month, by the week, or by the day, rather than by any way that shall give them a settlement; or if they do hire them for a year, then to endeavour to pick a quarrel with them before the year's end, and so to get rid of them: To maintain their poor as cheap as possibly they can at all events; not to lay out two pence in prospect of any future good, but only to serve the present necessity: To bargain with some sturdy person to take them by the lump, who yet is not intended to take them, but to hang over them *in terrorem* if they shall complain to the justices for want of maintenance: To send them out into the country a begging (for why cannot they go, as well as others they will mention, who are less able in body? and the feebler they are, the more profitable will be their peregrination): To bind out poor children apprentices, no matter to whom, or to what trade, but to take especial care that the master live in another parish: To move heaven and earth if any dispute happens about a settlement, and in that particular to invert the general rule, and stick at no expense: To pull down cottages: To drive out as many inhabitants, and admit as few, as possibly they can; that is, to depopulate the parish in order to lessen the poor rate: to be generous indeed, sometimes, in giving a portion, with the mother of a bastard child, to the reputed father, on condition that he will marry her; or with a poor widow (for why should she be deprived of the comforts of matrimony?)—always provided that the husband is settled elsewhere: Or if a poor man with a large family appears to be industrious, they will charitably assist him in taking a farm in some neighbouring parish, and give him 10*l.* to pay his first year's rent with: And if any of their poor have a mercantile genius, they will purchase for him a box, with pins, needles, laces, buckles, and such like wares, and send him abroad in the quality of a petty chapman; with the profits whereof, and a moderate knack at stealing, he can decently support himself, and educate his children in the same industrious way."—(p. 211.)

LETTERS on the IMPORTANCE of the RISING GENERATION of the LABOURING PART of our FELLOW-SUBJECTS. By JONAS HANWAY, Esq. 2 vols., 8vo. London, 1767.

The first edition of the 'Farmer's Letters to the People of England' (by Arthur Young, Esq.), in 2 vols. 8vo., appeared in 1767. They embody some valuable observations on the poor-laws. The following statement strikingly corroborates that of Mr. Alcock respecting the influence of the compulsory provision in preventing the increase of cottages and of population :—

"I have said enough to prove of how great importance our labouring poor are to the public welfare: the strength of the state lies in their numbers; but the prodigious restrictions thrown on their settlements tend strongly to prevent an increase. One great inducement to marriage is the finding without difficulty a comfortable habitation—and another nearly as material, when such requisite is found, to be able to exercise in it whatever business a man has been educated to, or brought up in. The first of these points is no such easy matter to be accomplished; for it is too much the interest of a parish, both landlords and tenants, to decrease the cottages in it—and above all, to prevent their increase, that in process of time habitations are extremely difficult to be procured. There is no parish but had much rather its young labourers should continue single; in that state they are not in danger of becoming chargeable; but when married the case alters; all obstructions are therefore thrown in the way of their marrying; and none more immediately than that of rendering it as difficult as possible for the men, when married, to procure a house to live in—and this conduct is found so conducive to *easing the rates*,* that it universally gives rise to an open war against cottages.

"But suppose the young labourer or manufacturer to be inhabitant, by sufferance, of a parish to which he does not belong; the officers of such parish, the moment they hear of his intention to marry, give him notice to quit their parish, and retire to his own, unless he can procure a certificate that neither he nor *his* will ever become chargeable to them. The man applies to his own parish for such certificate.—'No! grant a certificate! Never will we do that. Let marrying alone, and live where you are—but if you come here with your wife—you know what lodging we have for you: our houses are full already.' Such is the language in answer to the request; and in millions of instances it is attended with the desired effect. The intended couple dread the disagreeableness (perhaps impracticability) of living in a little cottage with several other families; one to themselves is not to be had; if any are actually empty, the landlords of the parish take care they shall not be so filled: nay, how often do gentlemen who have possessions in a parish where such cottages come to sale, purchase them, and immediately erase them from the ground, that they may never become the *nests*, as they are called, of *beggars' brats!* by which means their tenants are not so burthened in their rates, and of course their farms let the better; for the *rates* are considered as much by tenants as the *rent* of a new farm.

"In this manner cottages are the perpetual objects of a parish jealousy. The young inhabitants are deterred from marrying, because of the difficulty of procuring an habitation: a hearty stout labourer that earns good wages aims at having a neat comfortable house to live in, and cannot bear the idea of living in common with others; but all his wishes are too often frustrated by the scarcity of cottages. Nor is the hardship of removals less: a man is resident in a parish where, by his connexions or nature of his business, he is much better able to maintain himself than in any other place—this circumstance often is as three to one. He marries; immediately he receives warning to quit this place, where alone he can advantageously support himself, and is driven to another, to live in a ten times more uneasy manner, and where he is unable to make near his former earnings. His lot is hard;

* The italics are in the original.

and his example hangs *in terrorem* to prevent others from being guilty of the folly of marrying."—(i. pp. 300–303.)

A PROPOSAL for establishing LIFE ANNUITIES in PARISHES for the BENEFIT of the INDUSTRIOUS POOR. (By Baron MASERES.) 8vo. London, 1772.

A bill founded on the calculations contained in this tract was introduced into parliament in the course of the ensuing year, and carried through the Commons; but it was thrown out in the Lords, in consequence of the opposition of Lord Camden.

During the period between the termination of the American war and the commencement of the Revolutionary war with France, the poor rates were considerably reduced. In 1782, however, the principle of the system under which these advantageous results had been obtained, was to a considerable extent subverted by the passing of Gilbert's Act (so called from the name of the gentleman by whom it was introduced into parliament), 22 Geo. III. c. 83. This Act repealed the salutary and powerful check imposed by the Act of 1723 on the perversion of the rates to the encouragement of idleness and imposture, in the option given to parishes of refusing relief except in a workhouse; and enacted that able-bodied paupers should not be obliged to resort to these establishments, but that work should be provided for them at or near their own homes! This throwing down of the principal barrier that had hitherto prevented the spread of fictitious pauperism, was the first great inroad on the old system of poor-laws, and had, in the end, the worst possible effects.

A PLAN for rendering the POOR independent on PUBLIC CONTRIBUTIONS, founded on the Basis of the FRIENDLY SOCIETIES commonly called CLUBS. By the Rev. JOHN ACLAND. 8vo. Exeter, 1786.

A Dissertation on the Poor-Laws. By a WELL-WISHER to MANKIND (the Rev. JOSEPH TOWNSEND, Rector of Pusey, Wilts). Small 8vo. London, 1786.

This remarkable tract was republished in 1817, with a preface ascribed to Lord Grenville. It is most ably written, and embodies the same opinions with respect to the mischievous influence of a compulsory provision for the poor, and of a too profuse charity, which are further illustrated in the author's 'Travels in Spain,' one of the best works of its class that has ever been published. But the Tract now referred to is chiefly deserving of attention for its clear and striking exposition of the principle of population.

"In the progress of society," says Mr. Townsend, "it will be found that some must want; and then the only question will be this, Who is most worthy to suffer cold and hunger, the prodigal or the provident, the slothful or the diligent, the virtuous or the vicious? In the South Seas there is an island, which from the first discoverer is called Juan Fernandes. In this sequestered spot John Fernando placed a colony of goats, consisting of one male attended by his female. This happy couple finding pasture in abundance, could readily obey the first commandment, to increase and multiply, till in process of time they had replenished their little island. In advancing to this period they were strangers to misery and want, and seemed to glory in their numbers: but from this unhappy moment they began to suffer hunger; yet continuing for a time to increase their numbers, had they been endued with reason, they must have apprehended the extremity of famine. In this situation the weakest first gave way, and plenty was again restored. Thus they fluctuated between happiness and misery, and either suffered want or rejoiced in abundance, according as their numbers were diminished or increased; never at a stay, yet nearly balancing at all times their quantity of food. This degree of equipoise was from time to time destroyed, either by epidemical diseases or by the arrival of some vessel in distress. On such occasions their numbers were considerably reduced; but to compensate for this alarm, and to comfort them for the loss of their companions, the survivors never failed to meet returning plenty. They were no longer in fear of famine: they ceased to regard each other with an evil eye; all had abundance, all were contented, all were happy. Thus, what might have been considered as misfortunes, proved a source of comfort; and to them at least, partial evil was universal good.

"When the Spaniards found that the English privateers resorted to this island for provisions, they resolved on the total extirpation of the goats, and for this purpose they put on shore a greyhound dog and bitch. These in their turn increased and multiplied, in proportion to the quantity of food they met with; but in consequence, as the Spaniards had foreseen, the breed of goats diminished. Had they been totally destroyed, the dogs likewise must have perished. But as many of the goats retired to the craggy rocks, where the dogs could never follow them, descending only for short intervals to feed with fear and circumspection in the valleys, few of these, besides the careless and the rash, became a prey; and none but the most watchful, strong, and active of the dogs could get a sufficiency of food. Thus a new kind of balance was established. The weakest of both species were among the first to pay the debt of nature: the most active and vigorous preserved their lives.

"It is the quantity of food which regulates the number of the human species. In the woods, and in the *savage state*, there can be few inhabitants; but of these there will be only a proportionable few to suffer want. As long as food is plenty they will continue to increase and multiply; and every man will have ability to support his family, or to relieve his friends, in proportion to his activity and strength. The weak must depend upon the precarious bounty of the strong; and, sooner or later, the lazy will be left to suffer the natural consequence of their indolence. Should they introduce a community of goods, and at the same time leave every man at liberty to marry, they would at first increase their numbers, but not the sum total of their happiness, till by degrees, all being equally reduced to want and misery, the weakly would be the first to perish.

"To procure a more ample, certain, and regular supply of food, should they cut down their woods and take to *breeding cattle*, this plenty would be of long continuance; but in process of time its limits would be found. The most active would acquire property, would have numerous flocks and numerous families; whilst the indolent would either starve or become servants to the rich, and the community would continue to enlarge till it had found its natural bounds and balanced the quantity of food.

"Should they proceed to *agriculture*, these bounds would be much extended, and require ages before the straitness would be felt again. In process of time a complete division of labour would take place, and they would have not only husbandmen, but artists, manufacturers, and merchants, monied men and gentlemen of landed property, soldiers and men of letters, with all their servants, to exchange their various commodities and labours for the produce of the soil. A noble author in the North of Britain is of opinion, that 'a nation can scarce be too populous for husbandry, as agriculture has the singular property of producing food in proportion to the number of consumers.' But is it not clear, that when all that is fertile has been cultivated to the highest pitch of industry, the progress must of necessity be stopped, and that when the human species shall have multiplied in proportion to this increase of food, it can proceed no further? Indeed, as we have remarked already of the savage state, should they establish a community of goods, their numbers for a time would certainly increase; but the quantity of food not being augmented in proportion, and that which had been sufficient only for a given number being now distributed to the increasing multitude, all would have too little, and the weakly would perish sooner than if he who tilled the soil had been left to reap the undivided fruits of his industry and labour. Nations may for a time increase their numbers beyond the due proportion of their food, but they will in the same proportion destroy the ease and comfort of the affluent, and, without any possible advantage, give universality to that misery and want which had been only partial. The course of nature may be easily disturbed, but man will never be able to reverse its laws."

Nothing can be more appropriate than the illustration drawn from Juan Fernandez; and in so far as respects the lower animals, we believe little if anything can be added to the exposition of the law of increase given above. But it seems not to have occurred to Mr. Townsend that men are neither goats nor dogs; and are not alone governed by that animal instinct that governs the latter. Speaking generally, they look forward to the consequences of their actions; and except, perhaps, in the case of the least civilized and most barbarous hordes, population has never been checked by the mere want of food. On the contrary, as has been previously seen, the supply of necessary accommodations has continued in almost all countries to outrun the increase of population, and the condition of society has been proportionally improved. It is singular, indeed, how, with the example of the civilized world before them, Messrs. Townsend, Malthus, Chalmers, and others should have all but wholly lost sight of the circumstances which naturally grow out of the progress of society to countervail the principle of increase, and to make its influence harmonize with, and depend upon, the supplies of food and other accommodations.

The Insufficiency of the Causes to which the Increase of our Poor, and of the Poors' Rates, have been commonly ascribed, &c. By the Rev. John Howlett. 8vo. London, 1788.

The author of this valuable tract is a zealous defender of the compulsory provision for the support of the poor. He endeavours to show that it had not had the effects ascribed to it by its opponents; and that though abuses might have insinuated themselves into its management, they were not of its essence, and might be obviated without affecting its principle. He deals as follows with some statements of Mr. Townsend:—

"A writer of distinguished ingenuity, spirit, and elegance (Mr. Townsend) zealously contends, that our poor laws take away the most powerful motives to diligence and economy, and directly encourage idleness, vice, and profligacy. 'Hope and fear,' says he, 'are the springs of industry. But our laws weaken the one and destroy the other. For what encouragement have the poor to be industrious and frugal, when they know for certain, that should they increase their store, it will be devoured by the drones? Or what cause have they to fear when they are assured that if by their indolence and extravagance, by their drunkenness and vices, they should be reduced to want, they shall be abundantly supplied, not only with food and raiment, but with their other accustomed luxuries, at the expense of others?' These maxims are undoubtedly true; but can anything be more unjust than their application? Is there a kingdom in Europe in which industry, in every form and shape, in the field, in the shop, and at the loom, is more alive and spirited than here? Is there a kingdom in Europe where it is crowned with more distinguished success? Where does trade, commerce, manufactures, agriculture equally flourish? Where do more numerous individuals rise from meanness and poverty to affluence and splendour? Are these proofs that our poor laws have weakened the springs of industry? And as to the removal of fear from the minds of the poor, how is that effected? 'Why the laws,' asserts this writer, 'say that in England no man, even though by his indolence, improvidence, prodigality, and vice, he may have brought himself to poverty, shall ever suffer want.' Can we conceive a stranger perversion of language? Is there a poor man in his senses, and with his eyes open, who does not see that the assertion, in every valuable signification, is utterly groundless? He knows, if really criminal, the laws will punish him; he knows too that the laws, indeed, will not suffer him to be absolutely starved or frozen to death, and that at all events his parish must, at last, maintain him; and, in the moments of thoughtless jollity, he may wantonly declare his confidence of this. But in the hours of serious reflection, which sometimes come to most persons, will he not naturally ask himself, but *how* will it maintain me? Why, as it now maintains many of my neighbours, with hungry bellies in filth and rags, and, if not contented with this, it will deprive me of my liberty, imprison me in a workhouse, and compel me to labour, like an arrant slave, or a senseless beast of burden, as long as I can lift a hand or stir a foot. Did ever any man less stupid than an ass, seriously use such an argument to encourage himself in vice and indolence? or really think it a satisfactory reason for omitting his utmost endeavours to maintain and support himself in tolerable comfort."—(p. 4.)

Some Account of the Shrewsbury House of Industry. By J. Wood, Esq. 8vo. Shrewsbury, 1791.

The History of the Poor; their Rights, Duties, and the Laws respecting them. By Thomas Ruggles, Esq., F.A.S. 2 vols. 8vo. London, 1793.

This work, which is not so good as that of Burn, has been entirely superseded by that of Sir F. M. Eden. (See p. 285.)

An Essay on the best Means of Providing Employment for the People; to which was adjudged the Prize proposed by the Royal Irish Academy for the best Dissertation on that Subject. By Samuel Crumpe, M.D., M.R.I.A. 1 vol., 8vo. 1st ed. London, 1793; 2nd do. London, 1795.

It is but seldom that a prize essay is worth looking into. The present, however, is an exception to the common rule, and is a really valuable publication. The author was an intelligent physician residing in Limerick. The principles which pervade the work are sound; and those parts of it which have special reference to Ireland are distinguished by the absence of prejudice, and by their practical good sense.

The Case of Labourers in Husbandry stated and considered, &c.; with an Appendix, containing a Collection of Accounts, showing the Earnings and Expenses of Labouring

Families in different parts of the Kingdom. By the Rev. DAVID DAVIES (Rector of Barkham, Berks). 4to. London, 1795.

A publication which has been a good deal referred to for its facts and statements.

The price of corn, which had, at a medium of the three preceding years, averaged 48*s.* 2*d.*, rose, in 1795, to 75*s.* 2*d.* As wages continued stationary at their former elevation, the distress of the poor was comparatively great, and many able-bodied labourers, who had rarely before applied for parish assistance, became claimants for relief. But instead of meeting this emergency as it should have been met, by temporary expedients, and by grants of relief proportioned to the exigency of any given case, one uniform system was adopted. The magistrates of Berks, and some other southern counties, issued tables, showing the wages which, as they affirmed, every labouring man should receive, according to the number of his family and the price of bread; and they accompanied these tables with an order, directing the parish officers to make up the deficit to the labourer, in the event of the wages paid him by his employers falling short of the tabular allowance.

Unhappily this system did not cease with the temporary circumstances which gave it birth, but spread all over the South of England, and was acted upon down to the passing of the Poor Law Amendment Act. Perhaps no more objectionable and mischievous practice was ever introduced into any country. It gave a powerful artificial stimulus to population, by making the wages of a married man with a family very much exceed those of an unmarried individual: it made the poor indifferent to character by insuring them of reasonably good wages whether they were employed or not: and it tempted many of the employers of labourers to reduce their wages below the fair level, that their neighbours, the occupiers of villas, might have to pay a portion of them out of the rates. Nothing, in truth, could be more perfectly monstrous than this system: and yet it kept its ground, as stated above, for upwards of 35 years; and produced an extent of artificial pauperism and moral degradation that could hardly have been conceived possible.

The State of the Poor; or, an HISTORY of the LABOURING CLASSES in ENGLAND, from the CONQUEST to the PRESENT PERIOD; in which are particularly considered, their Domestic Economy, with respect to Diet, Dress, Fuel, and Habitation; and the various Plans which from time to time have been proposed and adopted for the Relief of the POOR, &c., &c. By Sir F. M. EDEN, Bart. 3 vols., 4to. London, 1797.

This important work contains a vast body of authentic information respecting the condition of the labouring classes of the population, from the Conquest down to the close of last century. The first volume comprises a general history of the poor, the fruit of much laborious and pains-taking research; the second volume, and part of the third, consist principally of parochial Reports on the state of the poor from all parts of the country, some of which extend to remote epochs. The Appendix includes an extensive and elaborate table of prices, a collection of statutes relating to the poor, a notice of the poor of Scotland, and the most complete catalogue that has ever been published of the various works in the English language that had then appeared relative to the poor. Altogether this is the grand storehouse of information respecting the labouring classes of England, and should have a prominent place in every library. Exclusive of this standard work, Sir F. M. Eden published tracts on insurance, population, &c., some of which are specified in other parts of this work. He died in 1809, at the house of the Globe Insurance Company, of which he had been long the chairman.

Mr. Malthus' Essay on the Principle of Population, which, as already seen, was first published in 1798, may in some respects be considered as a treatise on the poor-laws; and the authors of the works that have since appeared on population have almost all referred largely, in the course of their reasonings and illustrations, to the state of the poor; while the writers on the latter have since made similar references to the law of increase.

A SHORT INQUIRY into the POLICY, HUMANITY, &c. of the POOR-LAWS. By One of His Majesty's Justices of Peace for the Three Inland Counties (JOHN WEYLAND, Esq.). 1 vol., 8vo. London.

A TREATISE on INDIGENCE, exhibiting a General View of the National Resources for Productive Labour, with Propositions for Ameliorating the Condition of the Poor. By PATRICK COLQUHOUN, LL.D. (Author of the Work on the Statistics of the British Empire, see p. 218). 1 vol., 8vo. London, 1808.

Collections relative to Systematic Relief of the Poor, at different Periods and in different Countries, with Observations on Charity, &c. (By JOHN DUNCAN, Esq.) 8vo. Bath, 1815.

REPORT from and EVIDENCE taken before the SELECT COMMITTEE of the HOUSE of COMMONS on the STATE of MENDICITY in the METROPOLIS. Folio, 1815.

Observations on the Circumstances which influence the Condition of the Labouring Classes of Society. By JOHN BARTON. 8vo. London, 1817.

This, like Mr. Barton's other tracts, is clever, ingenious, and generally sound; but his statements and reasonings are not in all cases to be depended upon. We have endeavoured to show, in a note added to the 'Principles of Political Economy,' the fallacy of the case Mr. Barton has stated in this tract (pp. 15, 16) in proof of his position that the introduction of machinery most commonly occasions a decline in the demand for labour.

REPORT from and EVIDENCE taken before the SELECT COMMITTEE of the HOUSE of COMMONS on the POOR-LAWS. Folio, 1817.

This Report sets the increase of pauperism in a very striking light; and it then goes on to say that "unless some efficacious check be interposed, there is every reason to think that the amount of the assessment will continue, as it has done, to increase, till at a period more or less remote, according to the progress the evil has already made in different places, it shall have absorbed the profits of the property on which the rate may have been assessed, producing thereby the neglect and ruin of the land, and the waste or removal of other property, to the utter subversion of that happy order of society so long upheld in these kingdoms." After such a statement one might have supposed that the Committee would have proposed some measures fitted to arrest the further progress of so great and imminent an evil; but they did nothing of the sort, and contented themselves with suggesting a few impotent palliatives: and yet it was obvious that all that was necessary to stop the torrent of pauperism was to revert to the system that had existed previously to 1782, and this would have been effected by abolishing the allowance system, and giving parishes power, when they saw fit, to refuse relief except in workhouses.

REMARKS on the REPORT of the SELECT COMMITTEE of the HOUSE of COMMONS on the POOR-LAWS. By a MONMOUTHSHIRE MAGISTRATE (J. H. MOGGRIDGE, Esq.) 8vo. Bristol, 1818.

An Inquiry into the Causes of the Progressive Depreciation of Agricultural Labour in Modern Times, with Suggestions for its Remedy. By JOHN BARTON. 8vo. London, 1820.

In this tract Mr. Barton ascribes to the depreciation in the value of money that deterioration in the condition of the agricultural labourers which he assumes to exist; but it may be doubted whether in fact their condition has, speaking generally, been deteriorated; and whether the value of money, meaning thereby gold and silver, has fallen during the last half century. The rise that took place in the price of corn in this country is sufficiently accounted for by the change which has taken place since 1765, from our being an exporting to our being an importing country; and to the restraints which the war threw, and which the corn-laws have since thrown, in the way of importation. And as respects other articles, it would be easy to show that many more have fallen than have risen in price; and that the fall and the rise are both to be accounted for by circumstances connected with their production, or with their demand and supply, independently altogether of changes in the value of money.

But whatever weight may be attached to Mr. Barton's statements, with respect to the value of money and the condition of the labourers, his arguments in favour of a compulsory provision for the able-bodied poor are equally ingenious and profound. In a manufacturing country like this, where industry is exposed to the greatest vicissitudes, large bodies of labourers must frequently be deprived, without any fault of their own, of the means of subsistence; and it is of the last importance, not merely to the tranquillity of the country, but to the permanent interests of the labouring classes, that provision should then be made for their support.

" It is to be remembered," says Mr. Barton, " that even those who most strongly assert the impolicy and injurious tendency of our poor-laws, admit that causes wholly unconnected with these laws do at times depress the condition of the labourer. Poor families are often thrown into a state of severe necessity by long-continued illness or unavoidable misfortunes, from which it would be impossible for them to return to the enjoyment of decent competence, if not supported by extraneous means. It is well known, too, that a general rise in the price of commodities is seldom immediately followed by a rise in the wages of country labour. In the mean time great suffering must be endured by the whole class of peasantry, if no legislative provision existed for their relief; and when such a rise of prices goes on gradually increasing for a long series of years, as generally happens, the suffering resulting from it must be proportionally prolonged. The question at issue is simply this: whether that suffering be calculated to cherish habits of sober and self-denying prudence, or to generate a spirit of careless desperation?

" During these periods of extraordinary privation, the labourer, if not effectually relieved, would imperceptibly lose that taste for order, decency, and cleanliness, which has been gradually formed and accumulated, in better times, by the insensible operation of habit and example; and no strength of argument, no force of authority, could again instil into the minds of a new generation, growing up under more prosperous circumstances, the sentiments and tastes thus blighted and destroyed by the cold breath of penury. Every return of temporary distress would therefore vitiate the feelings and lower the sensibilities of the labouring classes. The little progress of improvement made in happier times would be lost and forgotten. If we ward off a few of the bitterest blasts of calamity, the sacred flame may be kept alive till the tempest be past; but if once extinguished, how hard is the task of rekindling it in minds long inured to degradation and wretchedness!"—(p. 32.)

OBSERVATIONS on the ADMINISTRATION of the POOR-LAWS in AGRICULTURAL DISTRICTS. By the Rev. C. D. BRERETON, A.M., Rector of Little Massingham, Norfolk. 8vo. Norwich (1823).

AN INQUIRY into the WORKHOUSE SYSTEM and the LAW of MAINTENANCE in AGRICULTURAL DISTRICTS. By the Rev. C. D. BRERETON, A.M. 8vo. Norwich (1825).

A PRACTICAL INQUIRY into the NUMBER, MEANS of EMPLOYMENT, and WAGES of AGRICULTURAL LABOURERS. By the Rev. C. D. BRERETON, A.M. 8vo. Norwich, (1826).

THE SUBORDINATE MAGISTRACY and PARISH SYSTEM, considered in their connexion with the Causes and Remedies of Modern Pauperism, &c. By the Rev. C. D. BRERETON, A.M. 8vo. Norwich (1827).

These tracts are earnestly and vigorously written. The author is opposed to the whole scheme of compulsory charity; and has given a striking picture of the mischiefs arising out of the allowance system, the interference of the justices, and the mismanagement of workhouses. We believe, however, that his statements are, if not palpably exaggerated, at all events too highly coloured; and his acquaintance with the Scotch system might have taught him that profusion is not, as he appears to suppose, of the essence of a compulsory system; and that it may, without any difficulty, be managed so as to be free of all abuse, at least on the side of liberality.

AN INQUIRY into the POOR-LAWS, chiefly with a View to examine them as a Scheme of National Benevolence, and to elucidate their Political Economy. By J. E. BICHENO, Esq., Barrister-at-Law. 2nd ed., 8vo. London, 1824.

Against a compulsory provision.

THE PRINCIPLE of the ENGLISH POOR-LAWS ILLUSTRATED and DEFENDED, &c. By FREDERICK PAGE, Esq., &c. 1st ed., 8vo. Bath, 1822. 3rd ed., with the addition of a Tract on the State of the "Indigent Poor of Ireland." 8vo. London, 1830.

REPORTS from and EVIDENCE taken before the SELECT COMMITTEES of the HOUSE of COMMONS, in 1824 and 1825, on the Condition of the MANUFACTURING POPULATION, and the EXPORTATION of MACHINERY. Folio. 1824-25.

THE CHRISTIAN and CIVIC ECONOMY of LARGE TOWNS. By THOMAS CHALMERS, D.D. 3 vols. 8vo. Glasgow, 1821–26.

Dr. Chalmers is a zealous, or rather a fanatical opponent of poor-laws. His projects for providing for the support of the poor, without resorting to a compulsory provision, which he regards as one of the greatest possible evils, are developed in this work. But, while we admit the goodness of his intentions, nothing, as it appears to us, can be more futile and visionary than his schemes; more inconsistent with principle, experience, and common sense.

REPORT from and EVIDENCE taken before the SELECT COMMITTEE of the HOUSE of COMMONS, on the COMBINATION-LAWS. Folio. 1825.

AN ESSAY on the CIRCUMSTANCES which determine the RATE of WAGES, and the CONDITION of the LABOURING CLASSES. (By J. R. M'CULLOCH, Esq.) 12mo. Edinburgh, 1826.

OBSERVATIONS on the NATURE, EXTENT, and EFFECTS of PAUPERISM, and on the Means of reducing it. By THOMAS WALKER, Esq., Barrister-at-Law, (Author of the 'Original.') 8vo. London, 1826.

ON COMBINATIONS of TRADES. 8vo. London, 1830.

Three Lectures on the Rate of Wages, with a PREFACE on the CAUSES and REMEDIES of the PRESENT DISTURBANCES. By N. W. SENIOR, Esq. 8vo. London, 1830.

SUGGESTIONS for a CHANGE in the ADMINISTRATION of the POOR-LAWS. By FREDERICK CALVERT, Esq. 8vo. London, 1831.

ON WAGES and COMBINATIONS. By Colonel TORRENS. 8vo. London, 1834.

CHARACTER, OBJECT, and EFFECTS of TRADES UNIONS. 8vo. London, 1834.

ESSAY on the RATE of WAGES: with an Examination of the Causes of the Difference in the Condition of the Labouring Population throughout the World. By H. C. CAREY. 1 vol. 8vo. Philadelphia. 1835.

Mr. Carey is the author of works in other departments of this science; see *ante*, p. 19 and p. 186.

We have now arrived at an important æra in the history of the poor-laws of England. No effectual measures having been taken for the abolition of the allowance-system, or for reviving the check on imposture taken away by the repeal of the act 9 Geo. I. c. 7, the rates continued to increase, and the necessity of taking some effectual steps for arresting the progress of pauperism became obvious. Under these circumstances it might have been supposed that experience would have been appealed to; and that as the rates had not increased so rapidly as the population till after the American war, or rather till after 1795, when the allowance-system was introduced, it would have been deemed sufficient to revert to the system which had for about *two centuries* prevented any material abuse of the rates. And supposing this were not enough, the example and experience of Scotland were at hand to supply what might be wanted. It is admitted on all hands that there has been no abuse of the provision for the poor in that part of the kingdom, and that, on the contrary, the complaint is not that the poor get too much, but that they get decidedly too little; that the funds for their support are too sparingly drawn upon, and too parsimoniously administered. And how have these results been brought about? Not certainly by any peculiar sagacity or hard-heartedness on the part of the Scotch, but by the peculiar constitution of the kirk-session, or parochial body, to which the care of the poor is intrusted, and the preponderating influence which the landlords, on whom the rates really fall, have in their distribution, and in the treatment of the poor.

The English vestries and parochial bodies were altogether incompetent properly to transact any business connected with the affairs of the poor; because the vote of a mere occupier of lands or houses, perhaps not a shade removed himself from pauperism, was allowed to countervail the vote of the proprietor of an entire parish.* But supposing that this flagrant abuse had been completely rectified; that the amount of the assessment and the disposal of the provision for the poor had been left to be decided upon by those by whom it was really paid; that the act authorising the refusal of relief to able-bodied paupers, except in a workhouse, had been revived, and that the allowance-system had been abolished, everything would have been done that was necessary to eradicate abuse. The widest experience and the plainest principles concur in demonstrating, that the measures now referred to would have been effectual for the amendment of the poor-laws, and would, with the addition of a right of appeal to the poor, have made them as they were intended to be, and had long been, adequate to the relief of the necessitous and deserving poor without acting as an incentive to idleness and imposture.

But *Diis aliter visum!* Anything so simple as this, so consistent with experience and the plainest principles, did not suit the taste of the day, or the prevalent rage for innovation. In 1832 a Commission was appointed to inquire into the administration and operation of the Laws for the Relief of the Poor; and the Commissioners-in-chief employed a number of Sub-Commissioners, who proceeded to different parts of the country to collect information. The Reports of these Commissioners, and the evidence taken before them, fill several folio volumes; and contain a curious mixture of authentic, questionable, and erroneous statements. The Commissioners, with very few exceptions, appear to have set out with a determination to find nothing but abuses in the old poor-law, and to make the most of them; and this was no more than might have been expected, seeing that this was the most likely way to effect its abolition, and to secure employment for themselves under the system proposed to be adopted in its stead. Hence the exaggeration, one-sidedness, and quackery so glaringly evident in most of their Reports. But such as they were, they became the foundation of, or rather the pretext for, a measure of the most sweeping description, by which, with few exceptions, every vestige of the old system for the administration of the affairs of the poor was wholly abolished. It is, however, much easier to subvert what is established than to construct anything better in its stead; and certainly the Poor-Law Amendment Act, as the statute 4 & 5 Will. IV. c. 76 has been absurdly termed, is a striking instance of this; no statute ever being passed that appears to be more contradictory of the best established principles, or more likely to be productive of mischievous results. We beg to subjoin, in vindication of what has now been stated, the following extract from the last edition of the 'Principles of Political Economy:'—

* This gross abuse was partially, and to a very limited extent, obviated by the 58 Geo. III. c. 69.

"Down to the passing of the Poor-Law Amendment Act it had been generally supposed, that individuals would take better care of their estates and interests than any one else, and that these could nowhere be so safe as in their own keeping. But the act now alluded to proceeds on the extraordinary assumption, that a regard to self-interest is not a principle on which any stress can safely be laid; and that the interests of individuals will be best protected by salaried officers appointed by government, and responsible to it only! To carry this principle, if we may so call it, into effect, in the administration of the poor-laws, a Central Board of three Commissioners has been established in London, which has power to control and direct parishes and unions (of different parishes) in relieving the wants of the poor. For this purpose the Commissioners are authorised to decide as to the kind and amount of pauper relief; to issue rules and regulations with respect to the treatment of the poor, which all inferior officers are bound to obey; to determine as to the erection and government of workhouses, and the education of parish children; to form unions of parishes for the better administration of the law, &c. Boards of Guardians, consisting for the most part of people of property and respectability, are chosen in the different unions for superintending the workhouses and administering relief. But these functionaries, to whom, from their local knowledge, and their obvious interest in the proper administration of the rates, much power might have been safely conceded, are, in fact, rendered all but cyphers; they cannot, however well satisfied of their expediency, adopt any rules or modes of relief not sanctioned by the Central Board in London; and are substantially mere tools or instruments in the hands of the latter and its officers. Justices of the peace have been properly prohibited from interfering, in any way, with the rules laid down by the Central Board, or with the proceedings of the various parties acting under its orders.

"It would be to no purpose to enter into any lengthened inquiries with respect to the working of this novel system. Dr. Smith has said, that it is the highest impertinence in kings and ministers to pretend to instruct private people how they may best employ their capital and industry. But this pretension, like every other put forward by the advocates of mercantile system, appears to be modesty itself, compared with the pretensions put forward by the authors and abettors of the new poor-law. They take for granted that the country gentlemen and people of property in England are simpletons, incapable of managing their own affairs; that they are wholly unfit to take care of their estates and most obvious interests; and unable to do that which every kirk-session in Scotland is admitted to do admirably well! We doubt, indeed, whether in the whole history of the legislation of the least enlightened and most despotically-governed nations, any instance can be pointed out in which the rage for interference (influenced no doubt by the scent of the patronage it was to bring along with it) has been carried to such an extreme, not to say offensive, extent.

"We should never have done, were we to point out a tithe of the pernicious consequences which, it can hardly be doubted, must unavoidably result from this law, supposing it is maintained entire. It may be truly said to have already given birth to a new political power of the most dangerous description. Previously to the passing of this act, the management of the poor, belonging to the different parishes, was the private affair of the parties resident in them, and interested no one else; so that if the poor of a particular parish felt themselves aggrieved, they had nothing for it but to appeal to the parochial authorities or to the courts for redress. But the present state of things is totally different. The poor, no doubt, are distributed over different unions; but these being all subject to the same rules and regulations, the interests of the poor in them, and in the kingdom generally, have been substantially identified. Instead of the authorities, in any single parish, having to deal with some twenty or fifty paupers, the Central Board, or rather the Government, by whose orders it must be directed, has to deal with all the paupers in the kingdom; and has made itself responsible for all the real and fancied abuses that may exist in their treatment! It is not easy to exaggerate the inconveniences of this state of things. The smaller, speaking generally, the divisions into which a country is parcelled out, and the more directly the burden of providing for the poor is brought home to the door of those on whom it must fall, the greater will be the security against the mismanagement of the rates, and the less room will there be for imposture, cabal, and menace on the part of the poor. But in a country like England, with an immense manufacturing population exposed to tremendous vicissitudes, how is the Central Board, or its agents, to deal with masses of paupers? In such cases ministers, however determined, must compromise, and accommodate their policy to the exigencies of the moment. We shall then hear little or nothing of the 'stern path of duty;' but will, on the contrary, be told that—*tempori cedere, id est necessitati parere, semper sapientis est habitum:* the central Commissioners will be instructed to give way; and those offensive regulations in regard to the granting of relief only in workhouses, the separation of married parties, and so forth, that have occasioned so much well-founded disgust, will be quietly thrown overboard.* And when once begun, there will seldom be wanting occasions for fresh relaxations. In such matters, present convenience is sure to be permitted to outweigh prospective and contingent disadvantages. And we may be pretty well assured that this, like every similar project attempted to be carried into effect by government agents instead of the parties naturally interested in its success, will terminate by being made a convenient screen for all sorts of jobbing and malpractices.

"It has been said, that without the supervision of a Central Board it would be impossible to introduce any sort of uniformity into the treatment of the poor; and that, but for it, negligence and abuse in the expenditure of the rates would be sure to spring up. But why should there be any uniformity in such matters? Indeed, any one who reflects for a moment on the subject, must see that the treatment of the poor should vary in different parishes and parts of the country, and that it would be the climax of folly to treat the poor of a manufacturing and an agricultural district in the same way. And does not the example of Scotland demonstrate the inutility of a Central Board for the prevention of waste and abuse? Why should it not be left to people of property on the spot, who pay the rates, and are consequently most interested in their advantageous outlay, and best acquainted with the wants of the poor, to decide respecting the means to be taken in providing for their support?

"We do not mean, by anything now stated, to insinuate a doubt as to the

---

* This has already taken place to an extent that could hardly have been conceived possible in so short a period. During the discussions on the Poor-Law Act of 1844, the 7 and 8 Victoria, c. 101, it was made a boast of by the supporters of the new system, that relief was administered to an immense extent out of workhouses, and it was affirmed that it was never intended that it should be otherwise, or that the workhouse should be made a test of destitution, and so forth. The bastardy and other offensive clauses in the Poor-Law Amendment Act have also been abolished. But however explained or mitigated, this act, being an unwarrantable and uncalled for interference with the property, rights, and duties of individuals, and a means of keeping the labouring classes in a constant state of hostility with government, is not one of which any shred or remnant should be allowed to preserve its place on the statute-book; and we trust that at no distant period it may be wholly expunged.

abstract merit of some of the general rules and regulations framed by the Central Board; though we confess, at the same time, that it seems rather difficult to discover the wisdom or possible utility of the greater number. But the treatment of the poor is obviously a matter in which the most carefully drawn-up general rules can, speaking generally, be of little or no service; it is one in which we have to deal with conflicting interests and opinions, conflicting and perpetually varying circumstances, and in which expediency must be allowed quite as much weight as right or principle. And, such being the case, can any one doubt that the attempt to apply the same rules to so many different and opposite interests must be fraught with gross injustice and extreme danger?

"It is sometimes said, by way of apology for the new system, that under its influence the rates have been materially reduced, and that therefore it must, at least, be in so far advantageous. While, however, we admit the fact, we deny the inference. All changes in the public economy of a great nation, and especially those which deeply affect the interests of the poorer classes, should be brought about gradually and slowly. Had the care of providing for the poor been committed, as it should have been, to the people of property in the different parishes, without any interference on the part of the justices, under the regulations established previously to 1782, it is highly probable that the reduction of rates, though more effectual in the end, would have been less rapid at first than under the new system. At the outset of all projects of this description, the officers have an extraordinary anxiety to discover their zeal; and seldom, indeed, hesitate about availing themselves of any means, however questionable, to evince their desire to be useful to their employers, and to prove the value of their services. But this ultra zeal very soon cools down to something like apathy, or, it may be, connivance at abuse; whereas, the watchful care which individuals take of their own interests is a principle which no fancied security can ever relax or time wear out; so that, while reforms, effected by the agency of those to whom they are profitable, are usually introduced with caution, they are invariably carried out to the fullest extent, and enforced with untiring vigilance.

"Such are some of the contradictions that appear to be involved in the new poor-law, and of the mischievous consequences that will most likely flow from it. It would be inconsistent with the plan and objects of this work to subject it to a more lengthened examination. We do not presume to cast its horoscope, to conjecture how long it is destined to be the law of the land, or to measure the degree of rigour with which its provisions may be enforced. But we are well convinced, that if it be suffered to run its full course, without some very material modifications, it will be found to be, in the end, as expensive and dangerous in its practical results, as it is unconstitutional in its principles and audacious in its pretensions."

The regulation of the hours of labour by legislative enactment has for some years past attracted a large share of the public attention, and has been the subject of much discussion both in and out of parliament. It may, however, appear, on the first blush of the matter, that there can be no real room or ground for such discussions; and that it should be left to the buyers and sellers of labour to settle the terms of the contract as they may think best for themselves. And if the question regarded those only who are or who may be fairly presumed to be in a position to take care of themselves, it is not easy to see on what pretence the interference of government in such matters could be justified. If a person of full age and in the possession of his faculties agree to serve another in any lawful employment, it would appear to be as inexpedient and uncalled-for to interfere to regulate the number of hours he should engage in this employment during the day or the week, as it would be to regulate the rate of wages or the price of necessaries. Such contracts are universally founded on the principle of mutual interest and compromised advantage; and they cannot be fairly adjusted otherwise than by the higgling of the market, or by the free competition of the parties.

But unluckily the question cannot be thus disposed of. Children of both sexes, and perhaps women, cannot be regarded as free agents able to perceive and to pursue their own interests; they are, as it were, in a state of pupilage; and being so, have a just claim to the public protection.

It may, perhaps, be supposed that parents are the natural and proper guardians of children; and that therefore no interference with respect to them can be really necessary, except, perhaps, in the case of orphans. This, however, is not a matter in which we are left to conjecture, or to deduce inferences from general principles; the experience of this and every other country having shown that, wherever legal restraints have not interfered, the real or alleged necessities of the parents have disposed them to task the energies of their children to a most oppressive extent. And such being the case, no one can doubt that it is the bounden duty of governments to provide for the well-being of so very large and important a portion of their subjects, by taking care that their health and strength be not sacrificed to paternal cupidity; and that a few years of precocious exertion be not purchased at the heavy cost of premature decay and decrepitude.

But though it be easy, in a case of this sort, to lay down a general principle, it is extremely difficult to apply it practically, or to say how far it should be carried: to decide, for example, when children should be allowed to engage in factory labour, and for how many hours a day they should be permitted to carry it on. Such questions admit of no very definite answer; and it is in most cases difficult to assign any good reason for one limit rather than another. On the whole, however, we should be inclined to think that the existing regulations respecting factory labour in this country are about as reasonable and judicious as they can well be made. And the vast interests that might be seriously endangered by any rash or ill-considered attempt at introducing new changes should make us oppose every alteration, however trivial, of which the expediency is not clearly and satisfactorily established. The following notice of the regulations now referred to may not, perhaps, be deemed misplaced:—

No statutory restrictions respecting the employment of children in the mills and factories of the United Kingdom existed until the year 1802, when an act of parliament was passed (42 Geo. III.) for the preservation of the health and morals of apprentices and others employed in cotton and other factories, and directing the local magistrates to report whether the factories were conducted according to law, and to adopt such sanitary regulations as they might think fit. This act was followed, in 1816, by an act generally called Sir Robert Peel's Act, imposing various regulations on the employment of children in cotton-mills.

Both of these acts were repealed in 1831, by the 1 and 2 Will. IV. c. 39, commonly called Sir John Hobhouse's Act, which provided, that in cotton factories, to which it alone related, no child could legally be employed till it had attained the age of 9 years; and that no person under 18 years of age should be permitted to remain in the factories more than 12 hours in one day; and that on Saturdays they should only be employed in the factories for 9 hours.

Sir John Hobhouse's Act was repealed in 1833, by the act 3 and 4 Will. IV. c. 103, which, and the 7 Victoria, c. 15 (6 June, 1844), to take effect from 1 October, 1844, enact the following provisions relative to persons employed in all processes incident to the manufacture of cotton, wool, hair, silk, flax, hemp, jute, or tow, separately or mixed together, or mixed with any other material, or any fabric made thereof, with the exception of factories used solely for the manufacture of lace, hats, or paper, or solely for bleaching, dyeing, printing, or calendering.

1. That no person under 18 years of age shall be allowed to work in the night, *i. e.*, from ½-past 8 in the evening to ½-past 5 in the morning, nor on Saturday for any purpose after ½-past 4 in the afternoon, the hours to be regulated by a public clock, marked on a notice put up in each factory.
2. That no child under 8 years of age shall be employed, and that no child between 8 and 13 years old shall be employed more than 6 hours and 30 minutes in any one day, unless the dinner-time of the young persons from 13 to 18 years old in the factory shall begin at one o'clock, in which case the children beginning to work in the morning may work for 7 hours, but any child above 11 years of age employed solely in the winding and throwing of silk may work for 10 hours a day. And any occupier of a factory restricting the labour of young persons between 13 and 18 years old to 10 hours a day, may on certain conditions employ any child 10 hours on three alternate days of every week, provided that such child shall not be employed in any manner in the same or any other factory on two successive days.
3. That no child under 13 years of age shall work in the night for any purpose.
4. That every child under 13 years of age must have a surgical certificate of age, and must attend some school, on five days of every week for certain specified periods, and obtain a weekly certificate of attendance from the schoolmaster, which may be annulled by the Inspector on account of the unfitness of the schoolmaster.
5. That no young person of the age of 13 and under the age of 18 shall be allowed to work for more than 12 hours in any one day, nor more than 69 hours in any one week.
6. That every young person under 16 years of age must have a surgical certificate of age.
7. That no female above the age of 18 years shall be employed in any factory save for the same time and in the same manner as young persons in factories, certificates of age not however being necessary for females above 18 years of age.
8. That in factories, in which any part of the machinery is moved by water, and time lost by stoppages from want of water or too much water, children or young persons may under certain conditions be employed one hour additional, except on Saturday; and that when from the same causes any part of the manufacturing machinery driven by the water-wheel has been during any part of a day stopped, the young persons who would have been employed at such machinery may under certain conditions recover such lost time during the night following the said day, unless the said day be Saturday.
9. That the Inspector of the District, one of the four Inspectors appointed under the Acts, shall have power to appoint a sufficient number of certifying surgeons to examine the children and young persons, and to give certificates of age to children and young persons under 16 years of age according to certain forms and directions, but which certificate may be annulled by the Inspectors or Sub-Inspectors appointed under the Acts, provided they believe the real age of the persons mentioned in the certificates to be less than that mentioned in them, or provided the certifying surgeon of the district deems such persons to be of deficient health or strength at the time when the certificates are annulled.
10. That not less than one and a half hours shall be allowed every day for meals to every young person, to be taken between ½-past 7 A.M. and ½-past 7 P.M., and one hour at least before 3 P.M., and that no child or young person shall be employed more than 5 hours before one P.M. without an interval for meal-time of at least 30 minutes, and that all the young persons shall have the meal-times at the same period of the day.

11. That all children and young persons shall have not fewer than eight half-holidays in the year, four of such half-holidays between 15th March and 1st October, and that no child or young person shall be allowed to work in any factory on Christmas-day or Good Friday in England or Ireland, and in Scotland on any day the whole of which is set apart by the Church of Scotland for the observance of the Sacramental Fast in the parish in which the factory is situated.

It is singular, notwithstanding the magnitude of the interests involved in the discussion, and the keenness with which the proposal for limiting factory labour to ten hours a day has been debated, that it should have produced very few tracts of any merit either on the one side or the other. The few writers who have treated of the subject, and most speakers in parliament, appear to have confined themselves to some particular point of the case, and have either overlooked or passed cursorily over the others. A philosophical and comprehensive discussion of the subject in its various bearings has not, in so far as we know, been hitherto attempted.

The following is perhaps the best tract in opposition to the ten-hours project, while the speeches of Lord Ashley and his supporters contain the most powerful reasonings in its favour.

A LETTER to LORD ASHLEY, on the PRINCIPLES which REGULATE WAGES, and on the MANNER and DEGREE in which WAGES would be REDUCED by the passing of a TEN HOURS' BILL. By R. TORRENS, Esq., F.R.S. 8vo. London, 1844.

Two Discourses concerning the Affairs of Scotland. (By ANDREW FLETCHER of Saltoun, Esq.) 8vo. Edinburgh, 1698; republished in Fletcher's Works. 1 vol. 8vo. London, 1737.

In the second of these discourses, which is principally occupied with details relating to the poor, we find the following statement:—

"There are at this day in Scotland (besides a great many poor families very meanly provided for by the church boxes, with others who by living on bad food fall into various diseases) 200,000 people begging from door to door. These are not only no way advantageous, but a very grievous burden to so poor a country. And though the number of them be, perhaps, double to what it was formerly, by reason of this present great distress, yet in all times there have been about 100,000 of those vagabonds who have lived without any regard or subjection either to the laws of the land, or even those of God and nature: fathers incestuously accompanying with their own daughters, the son with the mother, and the brother with the sister. No magistrate could ever discover or be informed which way one in a hundred of those wretches died, or that ever they were baptized. Many murders have been discovered among them; and they are not only a most unspeakable oppression to poor tenants (who if they give not bread, or some kind of provision, to perhaps forty such villains in one day, are sure to be insulted by them), but they rob many poor people who live in houses distant from any neighbourhood. In years of plenty many thousands of them meet together in the mountains, where they feast and riot for many days; and at country weddings, markets, burials, and other the like public occasions, they are to be seen, both men and women, perpetually drunk, cursing, blaspheming, and fighting together."—(Works, p. 144.)

We suspect there must be some considerable exaggeration in this striking paragraph; for as Scotland did not at the period referred to contain more than 1,000,000 of inhabitants, it is very difficult to suppose, notwithstanding the peculiar distress by which she was then visited,* that 200,000 persons, or a fifth part of the entire population, could be given up to the mendicancy and disorders described above. But the intelligence and good faith of Fletcher are unquestionable; and there cannot be a doubt that the disorders to which he refers were of long standing, and upon the most gigantic scale, and that he did not believe he had in any degree overstated them. Indeed, so impressed was he by the idleness and crime then so prevalent, and by the enormities he had witnessed, that, to introduce good order and industry, he did not scruple to recommend the establishment of a system of predial slavery, to which the vagabonds in question, and their children, should be subjected! The nature of the proposed remedy shows what the disease must have been.

The establishment of schools, and of a more vigorous and impartial system of government, happily succeeded in repressing these disorders. But the people of Scotland continued, till after the peace of Paris, in 1763, without manufactures or trade, and were frequently involved in extreme misery and destitution.

The writer of these discourses, a Scottish gentleman of good estate, born in 1653, was early placed under the tuition of Dr. Burnet, afterwards Bishop of Salisbury. He was elected on his return from his travels, in 1681, representative for Mid-Lothian in the Scotch parliament. Here he distinguished himself by his uncompromising opposition to the arbitrary measures of the government; and having been in consequence compelled to withdraw to the Continent, he took part in the ill-fated attempt of the Duke of Monmouth, and subsequently accompanied our great deliverer, William III., on his expedition to this country in 1688. But he was too independent and too much of a republican to yield a steady support to any government. He died in London in 1716.

"He was a learned, gallant, honest, and every other way well accomplished gentleman; and if ever a man propose to serve and merit well of his country, let him place his courage, zeal, and constancy as a pattern before him; and think himself sufficiently applauded and rewarded if he obtain the character of being like Andrew Fletcher of Saltoun."—(Lockhart's Memoirs, p. 68.)

Inquiries Concerning the Poor. By John M'Farlan, D.D., one of the Ministers of Edinburgh. 1 vol. 8vo. Edinburgh, 1782.

This comprehensive and able treatise, though treating of the poor generally, is principally founded on facts and observations relating to the poor of Scotland. The author is opposed to a compulsory provision.

The appendix to a speech of Mr. Whitbread on the poor-laws, delivered in the House of Commons on the 19th of February, 1807, and published separately in 8vo. in the same year, contains valuable notes by Mr. Horner and Sir Henry Moncrieff, on the poor-laws of Scotland. We subjoin an extract from the note by the former:—

"The act of the Scotch parliament of 1579, c. 74, forms, with a few

* The period from 1693 to 1700, emphatically termed "the seven ill years," was long remembered in Scotland. A scarcity continued throughout; and the severity of its pressure was such as to depopulate several extensive parishes in different parts of the country.

amendments subsequently made, the existing code of Scotch poor-laws. It is almost a literal transcript of an English statute passed seven years before, the 14th Elizabeth, c. 5, which, though not printed in the modern editions of the statutes at large, may be found in the older collections, as in the second volume of Rastell. Sir F. M. Eden, in consequence of having overlooked this original statute of Elizabeth, has fallen into a very remarkable mistake, when he intimates his opinion that the English system of assessment was borrowed from the Scotch act of 1579. On the contrary, the latter is so closely copied from the English statute, that the execution of the act in country parishes is committed "*to them that sall be constitute justices be the King is Commissioners*," justices of the peace not being introduced into Scotland till 1587. It is also worthy of being remarked, that the only general regulation which the Scotch legislature in 1579 did not copy from the 14th of Elizabeth is that which directs the surplus of the poor's fund to be employed in providing work for able-bodied vagrants."

HISTORICAL DISSERTATIONS on the LAW and PRACTICE of GREAT BRITAIN, and particularly of SCOTLAND, with regard to the POOR, &c. By the Rev. ROBERT BURNS, one of the Ministers of Paisley. 2nd ed., 1 vol. 8vo. Edinburgh, 1819.

Hardly worth notice, the useful matter being of limited amount, and buried under a load of irrelevant rubbish.

Report for the Directors of the Town's Hospital of Glasgow, on the Management of the City Poor, the Suppression of Mendicity, and the Principles of the Plan for the New Hospital. 1 vol. 8vo. Glasgow, 1818.

An able, well-written, and interesting report. It was drawn up by James Ewing, Esq., of Levenside, Merchant, Glasgow.

A Treatise on the Law of Scotland relative to the Poor. By ALEXANDER DUNLOP, Esq., Advocate. 2nd ed., 1 vol. 8vo. Edinburgh, 1828.

Decidedly the best work on the subject.

REMARKS on the POOR-LAWS, and on the Method of Providing for the POOR of SCOTLAND. By DAVID MONYPENNY, Esq. (formerly a Lord of Session). 2nd ed., improved, 1 vol. 8vo. Edinburgh, 1836.

This is a work of considerable authority; but its value is impaired by the author's extreme partiality for the existing Scotch system, in which he can see nothing defective.

REPORT by a COMMITTEE of the GENERAL ASSEMBLY (of the Church of Scotland), on the MANAGEMENT of the POOR in SCOTLAND. Folio and 8vo. 1839.

This report, which was laid by Her Majesty's command before both Houses of Parliament, gives a luminous exposition of the existing system for providing for the poor of Scotland, and of the mode in which it is administered, with ample statistical details respecting the number and classes of paupers in the different parishes, the funds for their support, &c. Those, however, who should form their estimate of the Scotch system from this report, would be apt to entertain a very exaggerated opinion of its merits; for it says nothing that could lead any one to suspect that the allowances made to the really necessitous poor are so wretchedly inadequate as they frequently are, or that misery, destitution, and disease are so very prevalent as they are found to be in most of the great towns of Scotland.

Observations on the Management of the Poor in Scotland, and its Effects on the Health of the Great Towns. By W. P. ALISON, M.D., &c. 8vo. Edinburgh, 1840.

This tract, written by an accomplished physician, brother to the historian of the Revolutionary war, has had a very powerful influence. It unveiled a state of things of which most people in the upper and middle classes of society had no idea; and showed that the really necessitous poor were reduced, through the ultra parsimony of the kirk sessions, and the inadequate means provided for their support, in most of the great Scotch towns, to a state of destitution and suffering disgraceful to a civilized and Christian country. This shameful neglect of the rights and duties of humanity has, however, brought a frightful retribution along with it; and fever, or rather we should say pestilence, originating in the abodes of wretchedness, periodically spreads its destructive ravages through all classes of the inhabitants of Edinburgh, Glasgow, Dundee, Paisley, &c. In Glasgow the rate of mortality rose in 1832 to the enormous amount of 1 in 21·7, and in 1837 to 1 in 24·63 of the population; and in the old town of Edinburgh, the population of which is not exposed to the privations occasioned by sudden changes in the channels of trade, the mortality is still greater! Surely such a state of things calls loudly for the interference of the legislature. People of property in Scotland, and even the majority of the clergy, have long felt, or affected to feel, a horror of assessments for the support of the poor. But a selfish unfounded prejudice of this sort should not be allowed to fill the land with destitution and typhus. Whatever enthusiasts may say, the voluntary system is not a resource on which reliance can be placed in matters of this sort. It is well enough by way of supplement to the bounty of the state; but the interests of humanity imperatively require that, while waste and idleness are prevented, effectual provision be made for the prompt and adequate relief of the really necessitous. And this might be done, without making any change on the principle of the existing Scotch system, which we should be the first to deprecate, by organising means, through an appeal to the sheriffs or otherwise, for compelling the kirk sessions and landlords to make something like a sufficient allowance to the destitute poor.

PROPOSED ALTERATION of the SCOTTISH POOR-LAWS, and of the Administration thereof, as stated by Dr. Alison in his 'Observations on the Management of the Poor in Scotland,' considered and commented on by DAVID MONYPENNY, Esq. 8vo. Edinburgh, 1840.

It is needless to say more of this tract than that it is principally made up of extracts from the reports of the Commissioners of Inquiry into the administration of the poor-laws in England, from "Lord Chancellor Brougham's speech in the House of Lords on the 21st of July, 1834" (!), and from Dr. Chalmers' works. Dr. Alison, however, thought it worthy the following answer:—

REPLY to the PAMPHLET entitled 'Proposed Alteration of the Scottish Poor-Law Considered and Commented on.' By W. P. ALISON, M.D. &c. 8vo. Edinburgh, 1840.

The powerful impression made by Dr. Alison's tracts, and the appalling nature of the facts which they brought for the first time fully before the public, having awakened the attention of government, a commission was appointed early in 1843 to inquire into the state of the Scotch poor-laws, and the management of the poor in Scotland. This commission has since made a Report, and has collected several folio volumes of evidence. The Report is not, perhaps, such a document as might have been expected, and discovers greater anxiety to preserve the existing system with as little change as possible, than to grapple with admitted and glaring evils. The latter have, we apprehend, principally resulted from the want of any readily accessible tribunal to which the poor who felt themselves aggrieved by the decisions of the kirk sessions and heritors (landlords) might appeal. And it was generally supposed that the commissioners would have recommended authorising that appeal to the sheriffs which at present can only be made to the court of session; and that they would also have recommended the establishment of officers for the supervision, under the parochial tribunals, of the poor in all great towns. The commission has not, however, done this, but has contented itself with recommending that a salaried officer, or clerk, should be appointed in every parish, who should be bound, when called upon, to make reports respecting the mode of providing for the poor, to a Board of Supervision to be established in Edinburgh, which, however, is merely to have power to advise, not to interfere in the management of parochial affairs.

But though quite ineffectual for anything like a reform of the existing evils, the adoption of these recommendations may do something towards their discouragement; and we incline to think that an effort will, at no very distant period, be made for their total suppression. It would be a libel on the people of Scotland to suppose that the present state of things should be allowed to continue. Should the proposed board be established, it will most likely become, in the end, a court of appeal; and that duty may, we believe, be quite as well or better done by the sheriffs.

An Address to the Public on the Expediency of a regular Plan for the Maintenance and Government of the Poor, &c. To which is added, an Argument in support of the Right of the Poor of Ireland to a National Provision. By Richard Woodward, LL.D., Dean of Clogher (afterwards Bishop of Cloyne). 8vo. Dublin, 1775.

The first part of this tract contains a satisfactory vindication of the compulsory provision for the poor of England, from the attacks made upon it by Lord Kames in his 'Sketches of the History of Man,' 2 vols. 4to., Edinburgh, 1774. The second part is remarkable for its being one of the earliest as well as ablest pleadings for the introduction of a compulsory provision for the poor into Ireland, which, as everybody knows, had no footing in that country till very recently.

A Letter to Thomas Spring Rice, Esq., M.P. (now Lord Monteagle), on the Establishment of a Legal Provision for the Irish Poor, and on the Nature and Destination of Church Property. By the Right Rev. James Doyle, D.D. 8vo. Dublin, 1831.

Poor-Laws in Ireland considered in their probable Effects upon the Capital, the Prosperity, and the Progressive Improve-

MENT of that COUNTRY. By Sir JOHN WALSH, Bart. 8vo. London, 1830.

Incomparably the best pamphlet in opposition to the project for introducing poor-laws into Ireland.

A LETTER to LORD HOWICK on a LEGAL PROVISION for the IRISH POOR, a COMMUTATION of TITHES, and a PROVISION for the CATHOLIC CLERGY. By N. W. SENIOR, Esq. 8vo. London, 1831.

But despite the opposition to the measure, and the many difficulties in its way, the conviction gained ground in England that it would be highly advantageous to introduce a compulsory provision for the poor into Ireland. To pave the way for such a measure, a Commission was appointed in 1832 to inquire into the condition of the poorer classes in that country, and the means by which it might be meliorated. This Commission collected much valuable evidence, which, among other things, fully established the existence of a vast mass of pauperism in Ireland; and that there were few, and those very inadequate, means either for checking its increase or for relieving the wants of the really necessitous paupers. The Commissioners did not, however, propose any scheme for building workhouses, or for providing for the wants of the able-bodied poor; but recommended that employment should be provided for them by carrying on and enforcing the drainage of bogs, the culture of waste land, and so forth, under the superintendence of a "Board of Improvement"! And they farther recommended that Poor-Law Commissioners should be appointed, and rates levied, for the support of lunatics, of maimed and impotent poor persons, the construction of penitentiaries to which vagrants might be sent, &c. The reader need hardly be told that these recommendations met with but little attention. All ordinarily intelligent and unprejudiced parties saw that the project for undertaking the improvement of bogs and waste lands by a public board would be productive of nothing but a waste of public money, jobbing, and every sort of abuse. The other measures proposed by the Commissioners, though of a very different character, were not reckoned of sufficient importance to justify the organising of machinery to carry them into effect.

The unfavourable Report of the Commissioners did not, however, hinder the bringing of bills into Parliament in 1836 for the introduction of a system of poor-laws into Ireland on the model of the new English system, with workhouses as tests of destitution, and so forth. Mr. Nicholls, one of the English Poor-Law Commissioners, was despatched to Ireland in 1836 to report upon the subject; and he, as was to be expected, saw no difficulties in the way of the proposed system, or none that might not be easily overcome; and, fortified by this authority, the act 2 Victoria, c. 56, was passed, providing for the compulsory relief of the Irish poor, the erection of workhouses, &c., under the superintendence of the English Commissioners.

This system has wrought exceedingly ill, though not worse perhaps than might have been anticipated. The idea of making workhouses tests of destitution in Ireland is as absurd as can well be imagined; and owing to the endless division and subdivision of the soil, the occupiers are in great part so very poor as to be themselves little better than paupers. The attempt to levy rates from such persons necessarily, we may say, led to serious riots, and has had to be relinquished. How the system may work in future it is impossible to foretell, seeing that almost everything depends on the discretion with which it may be administered; though, after the salutary pruning it has undergone in England, its more offensive features will no doubt be equally softened down in Ireland. We incline, however, to think that relief should at first have been provided only for the aged, infirm, and impotent poor. Those who, in such matters, attempt a great deal at once, generally do little or nothing in the end.

THE POOR-LAW BILL for IRELAND Examined, its Provisions, and the Report of Mr. Nicholls contrasted with the Facts proved by the Poor Inquiry Commission, in a Letter to Lord Viscount Morpeth, M.P., &c. By ISAAC BUTT, LL.B., M.R.I.A., &c. 8vo. London, 1837.

A clever, well-written pamphlet, which deserved more attention than it appears to have met with.

THREE REPORTS by GEORGE NICHOLLS, Esq., to HER MAJESTY'S PRINCIPAL SECRETARY of STATE for the HOME DEPARTMENT. Folio and 8vo. 1838.

These Reports, whatever estimate may be otherwise formed of them, are clearly and ably written. The third Report, on the poor of Holland and Belgium, is peculiarly valuable.

FIVE LECTURES on the Principles of a LEGISLATIVE PROVISION for the POOR in IRELAND. By HERMAN MERIVALE, A.M. 8vo. London, 1838.

AN ESSAY on the NATURE and ADVANTAGES of PARISH BANKS for the SAVINGS of the INDUSTRIOUS. By the Rev. HENRY DUNCAN (formerly Minister of Ruthwell, Dumfriesshire). 2nd and enlarged ed., 8vo. Edinburgh, 1816.

OBSERVATIONS on BANKS for SAVINGS, &c. By J. H. FORBES, Esq., Advocate (now a Lord of Session). 8vo. Edinburgh, 1817.

SHORT ACCOUNT of the EDINBURGH BANK for SAVINGS. (Ascribed to Mr. FORBES.) 4th ed., 8vo. Edinburgh, 1816.

ANNALS of BANKS for SAVINGS, containing an Account of their Rise and Progress, with Reports and Essays on their National Importance, Constitution, &c. 8vo. London, 1818.

Report on Friendly or Benefit Societies, exhibiting the Law of Sickness as deduced from Returns by Friendly Societies in different parts of Scotland; to which are subjoined Tables, &c. By a COMMITTEE of the HIGHLAND SOCIETY of SCOTLAND. 1 vol. 8vo. Edinburgh, 1824.

Drawn up with much care and ability by Mr. Oliphant, W.S.

THE CONSTITUTION of FRIENDLY SOCIETIES, upon LEGAL and SCIENTIFIC PRINCIPLES, exemplified by the Rules and Tables of Calculations adopted under the advice and approbation of WILLIAM MORGAN, Esq., F.R.S., and WILLIAM FREND, Esq.,

A.M., for the Government of the Friendly Institution at Southwell, &c. 8vo. Newark, 1822.

Two Reports from, with the EVIDENCE taken before the SELECT COMMITTEE of the HOUSE of COMMONS, on the LAWS respecting FRIENDLY SOCIETIES. Folio. 1825 and 1827.

These Reports and the Evidence are extremely valuable. They contain statements by some of the ablest mathematicians and most experienced actuaries of the present century.

OBSERVATIONS upon the REPORT of the SELECT COMMITTEE of the HOUSE of COMMONS, on the LAWS respecting FRIENDLY SOCIETIES; exemplifying and vindicating the Principles of Life Assurance adopted in calculating the Southwell Tables, &c. By the Rev. JOHN THOMAS BECHER, M.A. 8vo. Newark, 1826.

A TREATISE on FRIENDLY SOCIETIES, &c. By CHARLES ANSELL, Esq., F.R.S. 1 vol. 8vo. London, 1835.

An able scientific treatise, but too mathematical to be of much use to ordinary readers.

The constitution of all savings banks and friendly societies, which claim to participate in the valuable privileges granted by law to such institutions, must be submitted to, and certified as approved by, the officer (John Tidd Pratt, Esq.) appointed by Government for that purpose.

The History of Savings Banks in England, Wales, Ireland, and Scotland, with the Period of the Establishment of each Institution, the Place where it is held, and the Number of Depositors classed according to the latest Official Returns, &c. By JOHN TIDD PRATT, Esq., &c. 1 vol. royal 8vo. London, 1842.

An interesting and perfectly authentic publication.

The early French works on the subject of pauperism and the poor are but few in number and of little value (Bienfaisance Publique, i. Introd., p. 54); but subsequently to the middle of last century, public attention began to be strongly fixed on the subject. In 1777 the Academy of Châlons-sur-Marne proposed a prize for the best memoir on the best means of suppressing mendicity, for which there were above a hundred competitors; and from these memoirs the following work was drawn up:—

Les Moyens de Détruire la Mendicité en France, en rendant les Mendians utiles à l'Etat sans les rendre Malheureux. Tirés des Mémoires qui ont concouru pour le Prix accordé en l'Année 1777, par l'Académie de Châlons-sur-Marne. 2 parties en 1 vol. 8vo. Châlons-sur Marne, 1780.

An excellent judge, the Baron Degerando, says of this work, "Il forme un résumé méthodique qui présente assurément le travail le plus complet qui ait encore vu le jour sur cet important sujet. On y distingue les divers genres de mendicité et les diverses classes des mendians; on y trace l'histoire des moyens politiques, moraux, repressifs employés jusqu'à ce jour pour détruire ce fléau; on y traite de toutes les branches de secours publics; on en discute le mérite; on indique les moyens de les perfectionner; on recherche surtout les moyens de prévenir la mendicité par le travail, par la réforme des mœurs, par des mesures d'économie politique. C'est un vaste traité qui embrasse à-la-fois la théorie et les applications, qui, aujourd'hui encore, n'est point assez connu, et qui pourrait être consulté avec fruit."—(Bienfaisance Publique, Introd., p. 55.)

RAPPORTS du COMITÉ de MENDICITÉ de l'ASSEMBLÉE CONSTITUANTE. Paris, 1790–91.

RECUEIL des MÉMOIRES sur les ETABLISSEMENS d'HUMANITÉ. Traduit de l'Anglois et de l'Allemand, par M. DUQUESNOY. 39 No. en 15 vol. 8vo. Paris, 1799–1804.

Histoire de l'Administration des Secours Publics, ou ANALYSE HISTORIQUE de la LÉGISLATION des SECOURS PUBLICS. Par M. le Baron DUPIN. 1 vol. 8vo. Paris, 1821.

"La législation Française sur les pauvres et sur les établissemens de bienfaisance, a trouvé dans le Baron Dupin un historien érudit, judicieux, chez lequel l'amour du bien s'associait à un fort bon esprit. Son ouvrage est devenu déjà fort rare."—(Degerando, i. Introd., p. 61.)

ESSAI HISTORIQUE et MORAL sur la PAUVRETÉ des NATIONS, la POPULATION, la MENDICITÉ, les HÔPITAUX, et les ENFANS-TROUVÉS. Par M. FODERÉ. 1 vol. 8vo. Paris, 1825.

LE VISITEUR du PAUVRE. Par M. DEGERANDO. Ouvrage couronné en 1820 par l'Académie de Lyons, et, en 1821, par l'Académie Française. 4me. éd., 1 vol. 12mo. Paris, 1829.

DE la CHARITÉ dans ses RAPPORTS avec l'ETAT MORAL et le BIEN-ÊTRE des CLASSES INFÉRIEURES de la SOCIÉTÉ. Par M. DUCHATEL. 1 vol. 8vo. Paris, 1829.

A GENERAL, MEDICAL, and STATISTICAL HISTORY of the present Condition of PUBLIC CHARITY in FRANCE, comprising a detailed Account of all the ESTABLISHMENTS destined for the SICK, the AGED, and INFIRM, CHILDREN, LUNATICS, &c. By DAVID JOHNSTON, M.D. 1 vol. 8vo. Edinburgh, 1829.

RECUEIL des RÈGLEMENS et INSTRUCTIONS sur l'ADMINISTRATION des SECOURS à DOMICILE. 1 vol. 4to. Paris, 1829.

DES BANQUES PUBLIQUES de PRETS sur GAGES, et de leurs INCONVÉNIENS. Par M. BEUGNOT. 8vo. Paris, 1829.

ECONOMIE POLITIQUE CHRÉTIENNE; ou RECHERCHES sur la NATURE et les CAUSES du PAUPERISME en FRANCE et en EUROPE. Par M. le Vicomte VILLENEUVE-BARGEMONT. 3 vol. 8vo. Paris, 1834.

If a strong feeling for the poor, and an anxious desire to improve their condition, were all that were required to make a good work on pauperism, the *Economie Politique Chrétienne* would be all that could be wished for; but other qualifications are quite as indispensable, and of these M. de Bargemont is all but wholly destitute.

De la Charité Légale, de ses Causes, et spécialement des Maisons de Travail, et de la Proscription de la Mendicité. Par M. Naville, Pasteur à Genève. 2 vol. 8vo. Genève, 1836.

M. Naville and M. Duchâtel have adopted the opinion espoused by Chalmers and others in this country, but which has been shown over and over again to be wholly erroneous, that a compulsory provision for the poor is, in all cases, productive of the poverty it seeks to relieve, and is, consequently, injurious to the real interests of the poor and of society.

De la Prostitution dans la Ville de Paris, considérée sous le Rapport de l'Hygiène Publique, de la Morale, et de l'Administration. Par M. Parent-Duchatelet. Ed. 2de., 2 vol. 8vo. Paris, 1837.

Des Moyens de Soulager et de Prévenir l'Indigence. Par Ducpetiaux. 8vo. Bruxelles, 1837.

Tableau de l'Etat Physique et Moral des Ouvriers employés dans les Manufactures de Coton, de Laine, et de Soie. Ouvrage entrepris par l'Ordre et sous les Auspices de l'Académie des Sciences Morales et Politiques. Par M. le Docteur Villermé. 2 vol. 8vo. Paris, 1840.

The authentic statements of M. Villermé give, we regret to say, the most unfavourable representation of the condition of the labouring classes in Lille, Rouen, Lyons, and other manufacturing towns in France. It appears to be in almost all respects decidedly inferior to the condition of the same classes in this country.

De la Misère des Classes Laborieuses en Angleterre et en France; de la Nature de la Misère, de son Existence, de ses Effets, de ses Causes, et de l'Insuffisance des Remèdes qu'on lui a opposés jusqu'ici, &c. Par M. Eugène Buret. 2 vol. Paris, 1840.

Many very questionable doctrines are advanced in this work, which, however, is ably and forcibly written. The subjects discussed are mostly of great importance; and some of them have attracted too little attention on this side the Channel.

Des Classes Dangereuses de la Population des Grandes Villes, et des Moyens de les rendre Meilleures. Par M. Fregier. 2 vol., 8vo. Paris, 1839.

De la Bienfaisance Publique. Par M. le Baron Degerando. 4 vol., 8vo. Paris, 1839.

A very learned, comprehensive, and most valuable work. It contains a more ample and careful investigation of the causes and remedies of pauperism than is elsewhere to be met with; and is decidedly the best of the many publications on the subject.

DU PAUPERISME, ce qu'il était dans l'Antiquité, ce qu'il est de nos Jours. Par M. de CHAMBORANT. 1 vol., 8vo. Paris, 1842.

HISTOIRE des MONTS-DE-PIÉTÉ. Par M. CERETTI. 1 vol., 12mo. Padoue (Paris), 1752.

"Ceretti a exposé la vrai nature de ces établissemens, peu ou mal connus de la plupart des économistes; il a montré que les prêts faits par eux n'ont réellement pas le caractère qu'on leur reproche."—(Bienfaisance Publique, iii. 48.)

PLAN d'un CAISSE de PRÉVOYANCE et de SECOURS. Par M. MOURGUES. 8vo. Paris, 1809.

LES CAISSES d'EPARGNES de la SUISSE. Par M. ALPH. de CANDOLLE. 1 vol., 8vo. Genève, 1838.

ETUDES HISTORIQUES et CRITIQUES sur les MONTS-DE-PIÉTÉ en BELGIQUE. Par M. DECKER. 1 vol., 8vo. Bruxelles, 1844.

RIFORMA degl' ISTITUTI PII della CITTA di MODENA. Del Signor LODOVICO RICCI. 1 vol., 8vo. Modena, 1787.

Reprinted in the *Economisti Italiani*, vol. xli., *Parte Moderna*.

Remarkable for being one of the first works published in Italy, in which the utility of such institutions was called in question. Ricci's researches and statements show, indeed, that their effectual reform was highly necessary; but they go no farther than this. Abuse is not necessarily inherent in such institutions; and they may be made, and have been made, powerful means for the prevention of poverty, as well as for the relief of the necessitous poor.

DEGL' INSTITUTI di PUBLICA CARITA, &c., in ROMA. Del Monsignor MORICHINI. 1 vol., 8vo. Roma, 1835.

SAGGIO sul BUON GOVERNO della MENDICITÂ, &c. Del CONTE PETITTI di RORETO. 2 vol., 8vo. Torino, 1837.

These two works have been spoken of in terms of commendation by Degerando.

THE POOR-LAWS, and their BEARING on SOCIETY; being a Series of Political and Historical Essays in English. By E. G. GEIJER, Professor at Upsal (Sweden). 8vo. Stockholm, 1840.

CHAPTER XVII.

RIGHT OF PROPERTY, LAW OF SUCCESSION, COPYRIGHTS, &c.

It would be useless in a work of this kind to enter into any disquisitions with respect to the origin and advantages of the right of private property. It is enough to state that it is coeval with the origin of society; that it is perfected with the advance of the latter; and that without a right of private property in land and in the various products of art and industry, there could be neither wealth nor civilization in the world.

It is singular, considering their vast importance, how little attention has been paid in this country to questions connected with the succession to property, or its transmission from one generation to another, and that we have not so much as one respectable work on the subject.

In cases of intestacy, where a deceased party, possessed of property, leaves a number of descendants, or where he leaves no direct descendants, the law, in order to prevent endless disputes and litigation, must interfere to regulate the succession to the property; and it will necessarily follow that the rule to be observed on such occasions will be determined in different countries by local circumstances, depending partly on the peculiar state and institutions of each country, and partly on the views entertained by its legislators of what is just and proper, and most conducive to the public advantage.

In most countries a preference has been given, in regulating the succession to property vacant by intestacy, and in defining the power to leave property by will, to male heirs; and in some countries, and especially in modern times, a marked predilection has been shown in favour of the eldest son, or, as it is usually termed, in favour of the right of primogeniture. Among the Jews, the eldest son was entitled to a double share of the paternal inheritance; but among the Greeks, Romans, and our Saxon ancestors, all inheritances, whether consisting of land or moveables, were equally divided, in some cases among all the male children, and in others among all the children, whether male or female. The growth of the feudal system appears, however, to have put an end to this rule of inheritance in most European nations. When titles of nobility were created, it was necessary to limit their descent to the eldest son; and it was also necessary that the estate required to maintain the dignity of the possessor of the title should descend according to the same rule of primogeniture. And even when estates were not held by noble proprietors, various inconveniences were found to result from their partition, in the division of military services; the number of infant tenants incapable of performing any kind of duty; and, more than all the rest (though its importance was the last to be perceived), the injurious influence of the system of equal partition in occasioning the too great subdivision of the land, in emancipating the younger sons from the control of their parents, in tempting them to remain at home and to indulge in the pleasures and idleness of a country life, and lastly, in overspreading the country with a proud and a beggarly gentry. In consequence, the old rule of succession to landed property was changed in most countries; and in England, except in Kent and a few other places, when a person dies intestate his estate descends entire to his eldest son. And there are good grounds for thinking, notwithstanding the statements of Adam Smith and others to the contrary, that this rule, though not without its disadvantages, is, on the whole, the best that can be devised. Females being incapable of performing any personal feudal service, it is the common rule, when a person seized of an estate dies intestate, leaving only daughters, that they should succeed as co-heiresses. Such is the law of England; and, when thus limited, little harm can ensue from the subdivision that is thus occasioned. It has, speaking generally, been the usual practice in cases of intestacy to divide the money or other moveable property in equal portions among the children or kinsmen of the deceased, without respect of sex or seniority. This however, though a general, is by no means to be regarded as a constant rule. Thus, in the case of the Jews, daughters were excluded from all participation in the inheritance, and apparently were left to depend on the bounty of their father's heirs.—(Michaelis, 'Law of Moses,' i. 420.) In Athens also, daughters inherited nothing when there were sons alive; and when there was no son, and a daughter succeeded to the inheritance, she was bound to marry her nearest relation, so that the property might not be taken out of the family.—(Michaelis, *ubi supra.*) In Rome, however, all sorts of property were divided equally among sons and daughters. And as the inconveniences found to result in modern times from the splitting of landed property do not follow in anything like the same degree, or at all, from the subdivision of moveable property, it is the practice in this and most modern countries to admit females of the same propinquity to share in the succession to such property, when left intestate, equally with males, excluding all preference on account of primogeniture.

The length to which testators have been allowed to go in selecting those who are to succeed them, and the conditions under which they are to be allowed to devise their property, have varied widely in different countries and different conditions of society. In some countries the power of bequeathing is much more extensive than in others. In England, for example, a man may leave his property to whomsoever he pleases, and may regulate its destination till the first unborn heir be 21 years of age, when his authority over it ceases. In Scotland, on the other hand, a man may entail his estate on an endless series of unborn heirs, and prescribe the conditions under which they are respectively to hold it. In France, again, the practice is quite different from what obtains either in England or Scotland: the power of the possessor of property to dispose of it by will or deed *mortis causa*, is there very much restricted; the law making nearly the whole of it divisible equally amongst his successors without respect of sex or seniority.

We have inquired at considerable length, in a note added to our edition of Adam Smith, into the influence of the various methods of disposing of property by will, and to it we beg to refer the reader.

De Successionibus apud Anglos: the Law of Hereditary Descents; showing the Rise, Progress, and successive Alterations thereof. By Sir MATTHEW HALE. 1 vol. 12mo. London, 1700.

This instructive little work forms the 11th chapter of Sir Matthew Hale's 'History of the Common Law of England,' published in 1713. It contains the following striking and, we believe, perfectly well-founded statements respecting the influence of the custom of equally dividing inheritances among the children.

"It seems that until the Conquest the descent of lands was, at least to all the sons, alike, and, for aught appears, also to all the daughters, and that there was no difference in the hereditary transmission of lands and goods, at least in reference to the children. This appears by those laws of King Edward confirmed by the Conqueror, and recited in Lambard, fol. 167, and also by Mr. Selden upon Eadmerus, Lege 36, tit. *De Intestatorum bonis* 184. *Siquis intestatus obierit, Liberi ejus Haereditatem equaliter dividant.*

"But this equal division of inheritances among the children was found to be very inconvenient: for, first, it weakened the strength of the kingdom, for by frequent parcelling and subdividing of inheritances, in process of time inheritances were so crumbled that there were few persons of able estates left to undergo public charges or offices: secondly, it did by degrees bring the inhabitants to a low kind of country living, and families were broken, and the younger sons, which, had they not had these little parcels of land to apply themselves to, would have betaken themselves either to trades, or military, or civil, or ecclesiastical employments, neglected those opportunities, and applied themselves to their small dividends of land, whereby they neglected opportunities of greater advantage to enrich themselves and the kingdom. And therefore," &c.

We may take this opportunity to mention that Sir John Davis, in his famous tract entitled 'Discourse of the True Causes why Ireland was never Subdued,' makes a precisely similar statement. Speaking of the Irish custom of gavelkind, he says, "It did breed another mischief; for thereby everybody being born to land, as well bastard as legitimate, they all held themselves to be gentlemen; and though their portions were ever so small, and themselves ever so poor (for gavelkind must needs in the end make a poor gentility), yet they scorned to descend to husbandry or merchandise, or to learn any mechanical art or science; and this is the true cause why there were never any corporate towns erected in the Irish counties. Besides, these poor gentlemen were so much affected unto their small portions of land, as they rather chose to live at home by theft, extortion, and coshering, than to seek to better their fortunes abroad."—(Davis, Tracts, p. 130, ed. 1787.)

An Essay towards a General History of Feudal Property in Great Britain. By JOHN DALRYMPLE, Esq. 1 vol. 8vo. London, 1757; and in 12mo. London, 1759.

Considerations on the Polity of Entails in a Nation. By JOHN DALRYMPLE, Esq. 8vo. Edinburgh, 1765.

The author of these works, afterwards a Baron of Exchequer in Scotland, and father to the present Earl of Stair, died in 1810 at the age of 84. He states, in the dedication of the 'Treatise on Feudal Property' to Lord Kames, that parts of it had been revised by Montesquieu, and it was not unworthy even of his supervision. "*Cet ouvrage, écrit avec goût et plein de philosophie politique, contient plus que ce titre ne l'annonce, même l'histoire de la constitution du parlement d'Angleterre. Il serait désirable qu'on le traduisit en Français, et qu'on nous donnât un ouvrage semblable pour notre pays.*"—(Dupin.) The Considerations on Entails is one of the best defences that has been put forth of their policy. It appears to have been principally intended as an answer to the following tract, in which entails are vigorously and ably attacked.

A Free Disquisition concerning the Law of Entails in Scotland, occasioned by some late Proposals for Amending that Law. 8vo. Edinburgh, 1765.

ESSAYS on several SUBJECTS concerning BRITISH ANTIQUITIES. (By HENRY HOME, Lord Kames.) 3rd ed., with additions, 1 vol. 12mo. Edinburgh, 1763.

Among other essays in this volume is one upon 'Succession, or the Transmission of Estates from the Dead to the Living.'

AN ESSAY on the RIGHT of PROPERTY in LAND, with respect to its Foundation in the Law of Nature; its present Establishment by the Municipal Laws of Europe; and the Regulations by which it might be rendered more Beneficial to the Lower Ranks of Mankind. 1 vol. 8vo. London. No date, but probably about 1786.

This essay was written by Mr. Ogilvie, Professor of Latin in the University of Aberdeen. Sir James Mackintosh, who had been a pupil of the author, indulgently says: "The essay is full of benevolence and ingenuity, but it is not the work of a man experienced in the difficult art of realizing projects for the good of mankind. Its bold agrarianism attracted some attention during the ferment of speculation occasioned by the French Revolution."—(Memoirs of Mackintosh, i. 17.) But in truth, the author's schemes, however well intended, are not impracticable only, but mischievous; and his principles and reasonings are alike false, shallow, and sophistical. Probably, however, it was hardly necessary to say so much of a work that never had any influence, and which has long been forgotten.

THE COMMON LAW of KENT, or CUSTOM of GAVELKIND. By THOMAS ROBINSON, Esq. 3rd ed., with Notes by J. Wilson, Esq. 8vo. London, 1821.

Considerations on the Inexpediency of the Law of Entail in Scotland. By PATRICK IRVINE, Esq., W.S. 8vo. Edinburgh, 1826.

An ably written historical and philosophical tract in opposition to the practice of entail.

THE RIGHT of PRIMOGENITURE EXAMINED, in a Letter to a Friend. By a YOUNGER BROTHER (Samuel Bailey, Esq., of Sheffield). 8vo. London, 1837.

De la Propriété dans ses Rapports avec le Droit Politique. 1 vol. 18mo. Paris, 1792.

This little work reflects infinite credit on the memory of its author, the Marquis Garnier, the translator and annotator of Smith. At a period when the most pernicious sophisms were in the highest favour, and an invasion of the right of property in land was strongly recommended, and partially carried into effect, by the more violent section of the revolutionists, Garnier did not hesitate, though at great danger to himself, to undertake its defence, and to show that the maintenance of this right was essential to the very existence of society; and that political power could nowhere be so safely placed as in the hands of persons possessed of landed property. The essay is not less remarkable for the clear and forcible manner in which it is written, than for the soundness of its principles and the boldness with which they were advanced. The author gives (p. 31) a striking picture of the evils to be feared, and which, indeed, were then on the eve of being fatally realised, from the ascendancy in revolutionary periods of those apostles of sedition without fortune, principle, or character, which swarm in Paris, in London, and in all great cities.

Du Droit d'Ainesse. Par M. Dupin ainé. 8vo. Paris, 1826.

Traité de la Propriété. Par M. Ch. Comte. 2 vol. 8vo. Paris, 1834.

Etudes d'Economie Politique sur la Propriète Territoriale. Par Dupuynode. 1 vol. 8vo. Paris, 1840.

This is an able essay. Like the greater number of his countrymen, M. Dupuynode is a defender of the present French law of succession.

The question with respect to the establishment of a right of private property, or as it is called, a copyright, in books and literary productions, is one of considerable importance and difficulty. There can, indeed, be no manner of doubt that an author should have unlimited control over his works for a certain period; but it is difficult to say what that period should be, and it is contended by many that copyright in books should be perpetual.

For a considerable time after the invention of printing, no questions seem to have occurred with respect to copyrights. This was occasioned by the early adôption of the licensing system. Governments soon perceived the vast importance of the powerful engine that had been brought into the field; and they endeavoured to avail themselves of its energies by interdicting the publication of all works not previously licensed by authority. During the continuation of this system, piracy was effectually prevented. The licensing act (13 and 14 Chas. II., c. 2), and the previous acts and proclamations to the same effect, prohibited the printing of any book without consent of the owner, as well as without a licence. In 1694 the licensing act finally expired, and the press then became really free. Instead, however, of the summary methods for obtaining redress for any invasion of their property enjoyed by them under the licensing acts, authors were now left to defend their rights at *common law;* and as no author or bookseller could procure any redress for a piracy at common law, except in so far as he could *prove damage*, property in books was virtually annihilated; it being in most cases impossible to prove the sale of one printed copy out of a hundred. Under these circumstances, applications were made to parliament for an act to protect literary property, by granting some speedy and effectual method of preventing the sale of spurious copies; and the statute 8 Anne, c. 19, was passed, which secured to authors and their assignees the exclusive right of printing their books for 14 years certain, from the day of publication, with a contingent 14 years, provided the author were alive at the expiration of the first term. Persons printing books protected by this act, without the consent of the authors or their assignees, were to forfeit the pirated copies, and 1*d.* for every sheet of the same. Books not entered at Stationers' Hall were excluded from the benefit of this act.

The act of Anne did not, however, put to rest the questions respecting copyright. The authors contended that it did not affect their natural ownership; and that they or their assignees were entitled to proceed at *common law* against those who pirated their works after the period mentioned in the statute had expired. The publishers of spurious editions resisted these pretensions, and contended that there was either no right of property at common law in the productions of the mind; or that, supposing such a right to have existed, it was superseded by the statute of Anne. There was some difference of opinion in the courts upon these points; but Lord Mansfield, Mr. Justice Blackstone, and the most eminent judges, were favourable to the claims of the authors. However, it was finally decided, upon an appeal to the House of Lords in 1774, that an action could not be maintained for pirating a copyright after the term specified in the statute.—(Godson on the Law of Patents and Copyrights, p. 205.)

Every one must be satisfied that 14 years' exclusive possession is too short a period to indemnify the author of a work the composition of which has required any considerable amount of labour and research; though 28 years is, perhaps, all things considered, not a very improper period. But the grand defect of the statute of Anne consisted in its making the right to the exclusive possession for 28 years contingent on the fact of a person having lived a day more or less than 14 years after the publication of his work. This was making the enjoyment of an important right dependent on a mere accidental circumstance over which man has no control. Could anything be more unjust than to hinder an author from bequeathing that property to his widow and children, that would have belonged to himself had he been alive? Nothing, as it appears to us, can be more obvious than the expediency of extending all copyrights to the same period, whether the authors be dead or alive.

But though the extreme hardship, not to say injustice, of the act of Queen Anne had been repeatedly pointed out, its provisions were continued down to 1814, when the copyright act, 54 Geo. III. c. 156, was passed. This act extended the duration of all copyrights, whether the authors were dead or alive, to 28 years certain; with the further provision, that if the author should be alive at the end of that period, he should enjoy the copyright during the residue of his life.

This act conferred a most important advantage on authors and publishers; but it did not satisfy their pretensions, and repeated attempts were subsequently made to have copyrights declared perpetual, or, at all events, to have their term considerably extended. In consequence, after a great deal of discussion, the existing copyright act, 5 and 6 Vict. cap. 45, was passed in 1842. This statute extends the duration of all copyrights, whether the authors be dead or alive, to *forty-two* years certain; providing, further, that if the author be alive at the expiration of this period of 42 years from the publication of his work, he shall enjoy the copyright to his death, and that his heirs or assignees shall enjoy it for 7 years after that event.

We beg to subjoin, from the 'Commercial Dictionary' (Art. Books), the following remarks on the proposal for making copyrights perpetual:— "It is argued by many that copyrights should be made perpetual; that, were this done, men of talent and learning would devote themselves much more readily than at present to the composition of works requiring great labour; inasmuch as the copyright of such works, were it perpetual, would be an adequate provision for a family. But we doubt much whether these anticipations would be realised. Most books or manuscripts are purchased by the booksellers, or published upon the presumption that there will immediately be a considerable demand for them; and we apprehend that when copyrights are secured for 42 years certain, very little more would be given for them were they made perpetual. When an annuity, or the rent or profit arising out of any fixed and tangible property, with respect to which there can be no risk, is sold, if the number of years for which it is to continue be considerable, the price which it is worth, and which it fetches, does not differ materially from what it would bring were it perpetual. But the copyright of an unpublished work is of all descriptions of property in which to speculate the most hazardous, and the chances of reaping contingent advantages from it, at the distance of 42 years, would be worth very little indeed.

"Those who write books, and those who publish them, calculate on their obtaining a ready and extensive sale, and on their being indemnified in a few years. Very few authors, and still fewer booksellers, are disposed to look forward to so distant a period even as 28 years for remuneration. They are, with very few exceptions, sanguine enough to suppose that a much shorter term will enable them to reap a full harvest of fame and profit from the publication: and we doubt much whether there be one case in a hundred, in which an author would obtain a larger sum for a perpetual copyright, than for one that is to continue for the period stipulated in the late act.

"But while the making of copyrights perpetual would not, as it appears to us, be of any material advantage to the authors, there are good grounds for thinking that it would be disadvantageous to the public. Suppose an individual computes a table of logarithms to five or seven places; if his computations be correct, no improvement can be made upon them, to the extent at least to which they go. But is he or his assignees to be entitled, in all time to come, to prevent other individuals from publishing similar tables, on the ground of an invasion of private property? Such a pretension could not be admitted without leading to the most mischievous consequences; and yet there is no real ground (though the courts have attempted to make one) on which the claim in question and others of the same description could be resisted, were copyrights made perpetual, and placed in all respects on the same footing as other property. We therefore are clearly of opinion that good policy suggests the limitation of the exclusive right of printing and publishing literary works to some such reasonable period as may secure to authors the greater part of the profit to be derived from their works; and that this period being expired, they should become public property.

"Perhaps the period of 28 years has been advantageously extended to 42; but we are satisfied that more injury than benefit would result to literature by extending it beyond this term. In France, copyrights continue for 20 years after the death of the author. In most of the German states they are perpetual; this, however, until very recently, hardly indemnified the authors for the ease with which spurious copies might be obtained from other states. But by a late resolution of the Diet, a copyright secured in one state is good in all."

The law with respect to patents for inventions is encumbered with nearly the same difficulties as that respecting copyright in books. The expediency of granting them has been disputed; though, as it would seem, without any sufficient reason. Were they refused, the inducement to make discoveries would, in many cases, be very much weakened; at the same time that it would plainly be for the interest of every one who made a discovery, to endeavour, if possible, to conceal it. And notwithstanding the difficulties in the way of concealment, they are not insuperable; and it is believed that several important inventions have been lost, from the secret dying with their authors. On the other hand, it is not easy to decide upon the term for which the patent, or exclusive privilege, should be granted. Some have proposed that it should be made perpetual; but this would be a very great obstacle to the progress of improvement, and would lead to the most pernicious results. Perhaps the term of 14 years, to which the duration of a patent is limited in England, is as proper a one as could be suggested. It may be too short for some inventions, and too long for others; but, on the whole, it seems to be a pretty fair average

The following is one of the ablest papers on the subject of literary property that we have met with.

Information (addressed to the Lords of Session, Scotland) **for Messrs. Donaldson, Wood, &c. against John Hinton,** Bookseller, London. 4to., 82 pages. Edinburgh, 1773.

This information was written by Mr. Ilay Campbell, afterwards President of the Court of Session.

The various arguments for and against the perpetuity of literary property, whether founded on statute or common law, are embodied in the following report:—

The Question concerning Literary Property, determined by the Court of King's Bench on the 20th of April, 1769, in the Case between, &c., with the Opinions of the Judges (Justices Willes, Aston, Yates, and Lord Mansfield), and the Reasons given by each in support of his opinion. 4to. London, 1773.

TREATISE on the LAWS of LITERARY PROPERTY, comprising the Statutes and Cases relating to Books, Manuscripts, Lectures, &c. By R. MAUGHAM, Esq. 1 vol. 8vo. 1826.

A Practical Treatise on the Law of Patents for Inventions and of Copyright, with an Introductory Book on Monopolies. By RICHARD GODSON, Esq., M.P., Barrister-at-Law. 2nd ed. 1 vol. 8vo. London, 1840.

A clear, comprehensive, and useful work. A supplement containing the modifications introduced by the late statute has been recently published.

OBSERVATIONS on the LAW of COPYRIGHT, in reference to the Bill introduced into the House of Commons by Mr. Sergeant TALFOURD. 8vo. London, 1838.

A PLEA for a PERPETUAL COPYRIGHT, in a Letter to Lord Monteagle. By W. D. CHRISTIE, Esq. 8vo. London, 1840.

The act of Anne, at the same time that it gave to authors a statutory copyright of fourteen years, with a contingent right for an equal term, made the enjoyment of this right depend on the circumstance of their having delivered *nine* copies of their works, free of expense, at Stationers' Hall, for the use of so many public libraries; and when the Act of 1801 was passed, this tax was increased to *eleven* copies. Upon expensive books, or books having a limited sale, this was a most oppressive burden, and in some cases prevented their being printed. But we are glad to have to state that within these few years the assessment has been reduced to *five* copies; and were it reduced to *three* copies—one for England, one for Scotland, and one for Ireland—there would be little to object to in it.

Traité des Droits d'Auteurs dans la Littérature, les Sciences, et les Beaux-Arts. Par A. C. RENOUARD. 2 tomes, 8vo. Paris, 1838.

CHAPTER XVIII.

SLAVERY.

A SLAVE, in the ordinary sense of the term, is an individual at the absolute disposal of another, who has a right to employ and treat him as he pleases. But the state of slavery is susceptible of innumerable modifications; and it has been usual, in most countries where it has been long established, to limit in various ways the power of the master over the slave.

It is singular that though slavery has existed from the remotest antiquity, and has prevailed at one period or other to a less or greater extent in most countries, and though the policy of colonial slavery has been for many years past the subject of the most animated discussion, there is not, so far as we know, a single good or even respectable work on the subject. In this country slavery has been treated, since it became a subject of speculative inquiry, as if it were everywhere the same, and as if it were in every case a crime and an outrage on humanity. This, however, is to confound the most obvious distinctions, to substitute abuse for reasoning, assertion for inquiry, and prejudice for principle. Those who inquire more dispassionately into the matter will perhaps see reason for abating a little of this dogmatism; and may even come to be of opinion that though slavery has many evils, it may also have some advantages; and that while there are countries and states of society in which the former would very decidedly predominate, there may be those also in which the preponderance may be on the side of the latter. See on this subject Michaelis' learned and admirable Commentary on the Laws of Moses, ii. 155, &c., Eng. Trans.; and Grotius, de Jure Belli, lib. ii. c. 27.

AN HISTORICAL ACCOUNT of GUINEA: its Situation, Produce, and the General Disposition of its Inhabitants; with an Inquiry into the Rise and Progress of the Slave Trade, its Nature and lamentable Effects. By ANTHONY BENEZET. 8vo. London, 1772.

AN ESSAY on the TREATMENT and CONVERSION of AFRICAN SLAVES in the BRITISH SUGAR COLONIES. By the Rev. JAMES RAMSAY, M.A. 8vo. London, 1784.

Report of the Lords of the Committee of Council for Trade; with the Evidence and Information collected under an Order in Council of the 11th of February, 1788, concerning the Present State of the Trade to Africa, particularly the Trade in Slaves, and concerning the Effects and Consequences of this Trade, as well on Africa and the West Indies, as on the General Commerce of this Kingdom. 1 large vol. folio, 1789.

This bulky volume, the statements in which must however be received with caution, contains an immense variety of details respecting the trade in slaves from Africa to the West Indies, the treatment of the slaves in the colonies, &c.

A LETTER on the ABOLITION of the SLAVE TRADE, addressed to the FREEHOLDERS and other INHABITANTS of YORKSHIRE. By WILLIAM WILBERFORCE, Esq., M.P. 1 vol. 8vo. London, 1807.

THE HISTORY of the RISE, PROGRESS, and ACCOMPLISHMENT of the ABOLITION of the SLAVE TRADE. By THOMAS CLARKSON (one of the most distinguished of the Abolitionists). 2 vols. 8vo. London, 1808; a new edition, with Additions, 1 vol. 8vo. London, 1839.

The Slavery of the British West India Colonies, as it exists both in Law and Practice, &c. By JAMES STEPHEN, Esq. (Under-Secretary for the Colonies). 2 vols. 8vo. London, 1824–30.

An Inquiry into the State of Slavery among the Romans. By WILLIAM BLAIR, Esq. 1 vol. 12mo. Edinburgh, 1833.

A learned and valuable little work. The author is a son of Mr. Blair, the late distinguished President of the Court of Session, and grandson of the author of the 'Grave.'

Some Account of the Trade in Slaves from Africa, as connected with Europe and America; from the Introduction of the Trade into Modern Europe down to the Present Time; especially with reference to the Efforts made by the British Government for its Extinction. By JAMES BANDINEL, Esq. 1 vol. royal 8vo. London, 1842.

A concise and well-written account of the various matters referred to in the title-page of the work.

CODE NOIR; ou Recueil des Règlemens concernant les Colonies et le Commerce des Nègres. 1 vol. 24mo. Paris, 1752; 1 vol. 4to. et 1 vol. 18mo. ibid. 1767.

TRAITE et COMMERCE des NÈGRES. 1 vol. 12mo. Paris, 1764.

LA CAUSE des ESCLAVES NÈGRES. Par M. FROSSARD. 2 vol. 8vo. Lyon, 1789.

Portions of the 3rd and 4th volumes of the *Cours d'Economie Politique* of M. Storch, Paris, 1823, contain the best account that we have anywhere seen of the rise, progress, and decline of slavery in Europe, and of its influence on civilization and morals.

RECHERCHES STATISTIQUES sur l'ESCLAVAGE COLONIAL, et sur

les Moyens de le Supprimer. Par M. MOREAU de JONNÈS. 1 vol. 8vo. Paris, 1842.

POPMÆ (TIT.), de OPERIS SERVORUM, LIBER. Ed. opt. 1 vol. 12mo. Amstelœdami, 1672.

PIGNORII (LAUR.), de SERVIS et eorum apud VETERES MINISTERIIS, COMMENTARIUS. 4to. Patavii, 1656; 1 vol. 12mo. Amstelœdami, 1674.

CHAPTER XIX.

REVENUE AND FINANCE.

" Neque quies gentium, sine armis; neque arma, sine stipendiis; neque stipendia sine tributis haberi queunt."—*Taciti Hist.* iv. 74.

A Treatise of Taxes and Contributions; showing the Nature and Measures of Crown Lands, Assessments, Customs, Poll-Money, Lotteries, Benevolence, &c., &c. (By Sir William Petty.) 4to. London, 1679.

One of the most remarkable of the early tracts in any branch of political economy. Petty touches in this treatise on various subjects of great interest and importance, and his remarks are uniformly distinguished by their depth and appropriateness. He has in different parts of this tract indicated, with considerable distinctness, the fundamental principle, by establishing which Mr. Ricardo gave a new aspect to the whole science, that the value of commodities is, speaking generally, determined by the quantities of labour required to produce them and bring them to market. Our readers, we doubt not, will be well pleased to see the first germs of this theory:—

" A collateral question may be, how much English money this corn or rent is worth? I answer, so much as the money which another single man can save within the same time, over and above his expense, if he employed himself wholly to produce and make it: viz., let another man go travel into a country where is silver, there dig it, refine it, bring it to the same place where the other man planted his corn, coyn it, &c., the same person, all the while of his working for silver, gathering also food for his necessary livelihood, and procuring himself covering, &c., I say the silver of the one must be esteemed of equal value with the corn of the other—the one being perhaps twenty ounces, and the other twenty bushels. From whence it follows that the price of a bushel of this corn ought to be an ounce of silver.

" And forasmuch as possibly there may be more art and hazard in working about silver than about the corn, yet all comes to the same pass; for let a hundred men work ten years upon corn, and the same number of men the same time upon silver, I say that the neat proceed of the silver is the price of the whole neat proceed of the corn, and like parts of the one the price of like parts of the other. Although not so many of those who wrought in silver learned the art of refining and coyning, or outlived the dangers and diseases of working in the mines. And this also is the way of pitching the true proportion between the values of gold and silver, which many times is set by popular error, sometimes more, sometimes less diffused in the world; which error (by the way) is the cause of our having been pestered with too much gold heretofore, and wanting it now."—(p. 24.)

" If a man can bring to London an ounce of silver out of the earth in Peru, in the same time that he can produce a bushel of corn, then one is the natural price of the other. Now, if by reason of new and more easy mines, a man can get two ounces of silver as easily as he formerly did one, then corn will be as cheap at ten shillings the bushel as it was before at five shillings, *cæteris paribus*."—(p. 31.)

"Natural dearness and cheapness depend upon the few or more hands requisite to necessaries of nature: as corn is cheaper where one man produces corn for ten than where he can do the like but for six; and withal, according as the climate disposes men to a necessity of spending more or less. Corn will be twice as dear where are two hundred husbandmen to do the same work which an hundred could perform."—(p. 67.)

The History and Antiquities of the Exchequer of the Kings of England, from the Norman Conquest to the End of the Reign of Edward II., &c. By THOMAS MADOX, Esq. 1 vol., folio. London, 1711. Reprinted in 1769 in 2 vols., 4to., with an Index.

In this learned and standard work, among an immense variety of other subjects, the different sources of the royal revenue are specified, and their history minutely traced.

A COLLECTION of TREATISES relating to the NATIONAL DEBTS and FUNDS; to which is added a Collection of Treatises relating to the South Sea Stock and Scheme, &c. By ARCHIBALD HUTCHESON, Esq., M.P. 1 vol., folio. London, 1721.

In the second and other essays in this work Mr. Hutcheson gives an outline of the scheme he had previously proposed in the House of Commons for paying off the public debt, and the means by which he proposed to carry it into effect. This scheme has continued to attract some notice even in our own times, from its having been referred to by Hume, as follows:—

"There was indeed a scheme for the payment of our debts which was proposed by an excellent citizen, Mr. Hutcheson, above thirty years ago, and which was much approved of by some men of sense, but never was likely to take effect. He asserted that there was a fallacy in imagining that the public owed this debt; for that really every individual owed a proportional share of it, and paid in his taxes a proportional share of the interest, beside the expenses of levying these taxes. Had we not better then, says he, make a proportional distribution of the debt amongst us, and each of us contribute a sum suitable to his property, and by that means discharge at once all our funds and public mortgages? He seems not to have considered that the laborious poor pay a considerable part of the taxes by their annual consumptions, though they could not advance, at once, a proportional part of the sum required. Not to mention that property in money, and stock in trade, might easily be concealed or disguised, and that visible property in lands and houses would really at last answer for the whole—an inequality and oppression which never would be submitted to. But though this project is never likely to take place, 't is not altogether improbable that when the nation become heartily sick of their debts, and are cruelly oppressed by them, some daring projector may arise with visionary schemes for their discharge; and as public credit will begin by that time to be a little frail, the least touch will destroy it, as happened in France, and in this manner it will die of the doctor."—(Essay on Public Credit.)

The explosion of the South Sea scheme, in 1720, produced an extraordinary sensation, and led to the publication of myriads of forgotten tracts. In order to give the reader some idea of this famous scheme, we may shortly mention that a joint-stock company, called the South Sea Company, was formed in 1711. It consisted of the holders of navy and army bills, and other unfunded debts, to the amount of about 9,000,000*l.*, who were induced to agree to fund their debts on reasonable terms by being incorporated into a Company, with the monopoly of the trade to the South Sea (whence the name) or Spanish America. In 1712 the Company borrowed 200,000*l.* on bonds for carrying on their trade; and in 1713 they obtained the assiento contract, by which they acquired the privilege, on certain conditions, of importing negroes into the Spanish colonies, of the value of which, as well as the trade to South America generally, very exaggerated notions were entertained. Soon after this a project was set on foot between the Government and the Company for converting the long or irredeemable annuities, for which the public paid a high rate of interest, into perpetual (but redeemable) annuities, bearing a lower rate of interest; and had the scheme been managed with ordinary prudence, it would have been in all respects advantageous; but it was soon extended and perverted, partly by the South Sea Directors wishing to convert it into a source of influence and emolument to themselves, and partly and principally by the corruption and folly of the Government and public. The negotiations between the Government and the Company terminated by the latter making proposals, which were in the end accepted, for the assumption not merely of the long annuities, but of the whole public debt not already held by them, into their stock, on terms very favourable to the public; and as the transaction resolved itself into the Company taking the public debts at a fixed price, and giving the holders an equivalent in their stock at the prices for which it might be subscribed, the Company's profit was made to depend on the price which their stock bore in the market. The Directors were consequently tempted to resort to all manner of artifices for raising its value; but though they had not pandered to their prejudices, such was the infatuation of the public—their disposition to take *omne ignotum pro magnifico*, and their belief in the extraordinary profits to be made by the assiento contract and the trade to the South Seas—that the Company's stock could not have failed to rise to a very high premium; and in no long time, by dint of roguery on the one hand, and of unmeasured gullibility on the other, the price of 100*l.* stock attained to about 1000*l.* or to 900 per cent. premium! As might be expected, the fall was as rapid as the rise, and involved a vast number of persons of both sexes and of all ranks in ruin. The vengeance of Parliament fell with its full weight on the Directors, who certainly deserved to suffer; but Government was far from blameless in the affair, which had its real origin in public corruption, ignorance, and folly. A good history and exposition of the South Sea Scheme has yet to be written; and when it is properly executed it will make an instructive, if not a very creditable, chapter in our financial history.

Sir Robert Walpole's sinking fund was established in 1716; but an opinion having gained ground that, notwithstanding its institution, the public debts had increased rather than otherwise, the following tract appeared in defence of the sinking fund :—

An Essay on the Public Debts of this Kingdom, wherein the Importance of Discharging them is considered; the Provisions for that purpose by the Sinking Fund, and the Progress therein hitherto made, are stated and explained, &c. 8vo. London, 1726.

The author of this "very curious and important pamphlet" (Price), who is believed to have been Sir Nathanael Gould, M.P., an eminent merchant, and Director of the Bank of England, contends that the debt had been considerably reduced in the interval between 1716 and 1726; and he farther endeavours to demonstrate the efficacy of a sinking fund, operating at compound interest.

A State of the National Debt, as it stood on the 24th of December, 1716, with the Payments made towards its Discharge out of the Sinking Fund, &c., compared with the Debt at Michaelmas, 1725. 4to. London, 1727.

This tract, written in answer to that of Sir Nathanael Gould, has been usually ascribed to Mr. Pulteney (afterwards Earl of Bath), then leader of the Opposition in the House of Commons. It was replied to in

A Defence of 'An Essay on the Public Debts of this Kingdom,' &c. in answer to 'A State of the National Debt,' &c. By the Author of the Essay. 8vo. London, 1727.

The following extract from the 'History and Proceedings of the House of Commons,' vol. v., refers to this controversy:—"Feb. 23, 1727-28, the Committee of Supply resolved to raise 1,700,000*l.* on the coal-duty. Hereupon Mr. Pulteney observed that the shifting of funds was but perpetuating taxes, and putting off the evil day; and that, notwithstanding the great merit that some had built on the sinking fund, it appeared that the national debt had been increased since the setting up of that pompous project. On which Sir Nathanael Gould, an eminent merchant, said he apprehended that gentleman had his notions out of a treatise entitled 'A State of the National Debt,' supposed to be written by that very gentleman; but that if he (Sir Nathanael Gould) understood anything it was numbers, and he durst pawn his credit to prove that author's calculations and inferences to be false. To this Mr. Pulteney replied that he took them to be right, and he would likewise pawn his credit to make good his assertion. Upon this, Sir Robert Walpole took up the cudgels, and said he would maintain what Sir Nathanael Gould had advanced. Several warm expressions having passed on both sides, Mr. Hungerford interposed in a jocular speech that put the House in good humour, and so the dispute ended."

In 1733 an open inroad was made upon the sinking fund established in 1716, by taking from it 500,000*l.* for the current service of the year. The motion was strongly opposed, but Sir Robert Walpole having declared that if it were defeated, he should be obliged to move that the land-tax be raised from 1*s.* to 2*s.* per pound, it was carried by 245 votes to 135. Various tracts were published on this occasion; some of which, though strongly tainted with party asperity, are worth the attention of those who take an interest in such subjects. Among others may be specified

An Enquiry into the Conduct of our Domestic Affairs from 1721 to Christmas 1733, in which the Case of our National Debts, the Sinking Fund, &c., are particularly considered. (Ascribed to Mr. Pulteney.) 8vo. London, 1734.

Some Considerations concerning the Public Funds, the Public Revenues, and the Annual Supplies, occasioned by a late Pamphlet, entitled 'An Enquiry,' &c. (Said, by Mr.

Coxe,* to be written by Sir Robert Walpole from p. 8 to p. 81.) 8vo. London, 1735.

The Case of the Sinking Fund and the Right of the Public Creditors to it considered, &c.; being a Defence of 'An Enquiry,' &c., and a full Reply to a late Pamphlet entitled 'Some Considerations,' &c. (Ascribed to Mr. Pulteney.) 8vo. London, 1735.

An Essay on the Sinking Fund, wherein the Nature thereof is fully explained, and the Right of the Public to that Fund asserted and maintained. 8vo. London, 1736.

At a later period (see his 'Appeal,' p. 332) Dr. Price lamented this perversion of the sinking fund in the most piteous terms. "Thus," said he, "after an existence of a few years, expired the sinking fund, that sacred blessing, once the nation's only hope, prematurely and cruelly destroyed by its own parent. Could it have escaped the hands of violence, it would have made us the envy and terror of the world, by leaving us at this time not only tax-free, but in possession of a treasure greater, perhaps, than ever was enjoyed by any kingdom." And all this was said in good faith and believed of a fund that had never paid off, and never could pay off by any efficacy of its own, a single sixpence of debt!

The year 1733 is, however, chiefly memorable in the financial and parliamentary history of the country, from its being the epoch of the famous excise scheme. At that period, and down even to the present century, the customs duties on imported articles, which amount to a very large proportion of the public revenue, had either to be paid at the moment when the goods were imported, or a *bond*, with sufficient security, for their future payment had to be given to the revenue officers. The hardship and inconvenience of such a practice are obvious. Sureties were often difficult to be obtained; and, in order to raise funds to pay the duties, the merchant was frequently reduced to the ruinous necessity of selling his goods immediately on their arrival, when perhaps the market was already glutted. Neither was this the only inconvenience entailed on the country by this system; for, the duties being payable at once, and not by degrees as the goods were sold for consumption, the price of the latter was raised by the amount of the profit accruing on the capital advanced to pay the duties. Competition, too, was diminished in consequence of the greater command of funds required to carry on trade under such disadvantages; and a few rich individuals were thus, in a great measure, enabled to monopolize the business of importing commodities charged with heavy duties. The system had, besides, an obvious tendency to discourage the carrying trade, and to endanger the security of the revenue. For the necessity of paying import duties even on those articles which were destined for re-exportation obstructed the importation of most foreign goods, excepting those colonial products of which we had a monopoly, that were not likely to be speedily required for home consumption; at the same time that the difficulties attending the granting of a really equivalent drawback to the exporters of such as had paid the duty opened a door for the commission of every species of fraud.

Sir Robert Walpole had a clear perception of the injurious consequences of this system; and it was the object of the Scheme, proposed by him in

* Life of Walpole, vol. ii. p. 182, 8vo. ed.

1733, to assimilate the customs regulations to those of the excise, by obliging the importers of articles chargeable with duties to deposit them in public warehouses, relieving them, at the same time, from the necessity of paying the duties chargeable on such articles till they withdrew them for home consumption. The celebrity of this scheme, and the misconceptions that have been so generally entertained respecting it, incline us to think that we shall gratify our readers by laying before them the following passages from the speech made by Walpole, when he submitted his plan to the consideration of the House of Commons.

"The duties now payable upon tobacco,* on importation," he said, "amount to sixpence and one-third part of a penny per pound weight; all which must be paid down in ready money upon importation, with the allowance of ten per cent. upon prompt payment; or otherwise there must be bonds given, with sufficient sureties, for the payment thereof; which is often a great loss to the public, and is always a great inconvenience to the merchant importer. Whereas, by what I am to propose, the whole duties to be paid for the future will amount to no more than fourpence and three farthings per pound weight; and this duty not to be paid till the tobacco comes to be sold for home consumption. So that, if the merchant exports his tobacco, he will be quite free from all payment of duty, or giving bond therefor, or finding out proper sureties for joining in such bond: he will have nothing to do but unload his tobacco on board a ship for exportation, without being at the trouble to attend for having his bonds cancelled, or for taking out debentures for the drawbacks; all which, I conceive, must be a great ease to the fair trader; and to every such trader the preventing of frauds must be a great advantage, because it will put all the tobacco-traders in Britain upon the same footing; which is but just and equal, and what ought certainly to be accomplished, if it be possible.

"Now, in order to make this case effectual to the fair trader, and to contribute to his advantage by preventing as much as possible any frauds in time to come, I propose, as I have said, to join the laws of excise to those of the customs, and to leave the one penny, or rather three farthings per pound, called the farther subsidy, to be still charged at the custom-house upon the importation of any tobacco; which three farthings shall be payable to his Majesty's civil list, as heretofore. And I propose that all tobacco, for the future, after being weighed at the custom-house, and charged with the said three farthings per pound, shall be lodged in the warehouse or warehouses to be appointed by the commissioners of the excise for that purpose, of which warehouse the merchant importer shall have one lock and key, and the warehouse-keeper to be appointed by the said commissioners shall have another, in order that the tobacco may lie safe in that warehouse till the merchant finds a market for it, either for exportation or home consumption. And if his market be for exportation, he may apply to his warehouse-keeper, and take out as much for that purpose as he has occasion for, which, when weighed at the custom-house, shall be discharged of the three farthings per pound with which it was charged upon importation; so that the merchant may then export it without any further trouble. But if it be taken out for home consumption, he shall then pay the three farthings charged upon it at the custom-house upon importation; and then, upon calling his warehouse-keeper, he may deliver it to the buyer, on paying an inland duty of fourpence per pound weight to the proper officer appointed to receive the same."

Walpole concluded his speech by saying, "I look upon this as a most

* Tobacco and wine were the articles to which the new system was to be first applied.

innocent scheme; it can be hurtful to none but smugglers and unfair traders. I am certain it will be of great benefit to the revenue, and will tend to make LONDON A FREE PORT, AND, BY CONSEQUENCE, THE MARKET OF THE WORLD. If I had thought otherwise of it I should never have ventured to propose it in this place."*

Nothing can be clearer than this statement; and had the project been *permissive* only and not compulsory, it would have been wholly unexceptionable. But, as it was, no doubt can now remain in the mind of any one that its adoption would have been of the greatest advantage to the commerce and revenue of the country. But such and so powerful was the delusion generated in the public mind with respect to it, that its proposal nearly caused a rebellion. Most merchants had availed themselves of the facilities which the existing system afforded of defrauding the revenue; and they dexterously endeavoured to thwart the success of a scheme which would have given a serious check to such practices, by making the public believe that it would be fatal to the commercial prosperity of the country. The efforts of the merchants were powerfully assisted by the spirit of party, which then ran very high. The opponents of the ministry in the House of Commons, anxious for an opportunity to prejudice them in the public estimation, contended that the scheme was only the first step towards the introduction of such a universal system of excise as would absorb the wealth and destroy the liberties of the subject! In consequence of these artful misrepresentations, the most violent clamours were everywhere excited against the scheme. On one occasion the minister narrowly escaped falling a sacrifice to the fury of the mob, which beset all the avenues to the House of Commons; and after many violent and lengthened debates the project was abandoned.

The disadvantages of the old plan, and the benefits to be derived from the establishment of the warehousing system, were very clearly stated by Dean Tucker in his 'Essay on the Comparative Advantages and Disadvantages of Great Britain and France with respect to Trade' (see p. 50). But so lasting was the impression made by the opposition to Sir Robert Walpole's scheme, and such is the force of prejudice, that it was not until 1803 that this signal improvement—the greatest, perhaps, that has been made in the financial and commercial system of the country—was adopted.

SOME GENERAL CONSIDERATIONS concerning the ALTERATION and IMPROVEMENT of the PUBLIC REVENUES. 8vo. London, 1733.

Published by government in the view of facilitating the introduction of the excise scheme.

There are, perhaps, no better subjects for taxation than spirituous and fermented liquors. They are essentially luxuries; and while, in consequence of their being very generally used, moderate duties on them are exceedingly productive, the increase of price which they occasion tends to lessen their consumption by the poor, to whom, when taken in excess, they are exceedingly pernicious. Few governments, however, have been satisfied with imposing moderate duties on spirits; and partly in the view of increasing the revenue, and partly to place them beyond the reach

* Tindal's 'Continuation of Rapin,' viii. p. 154, ed. 1769; Coxe's 'Sir R. Walpole,' vol. i. p. 372, 4to. ed. Had the resolutions with respect to tobacco been carried, those regarding wine, which were to have been exactly similar, would have been proposed.

of the lower classes, have almost invariably loaded them with such oppressively high duties as have entirely defeated both objects. The imposition of such duties does not take away the appetite for spirits; and as no vigilance of the officers or severity of the laws has been found sufficient to secure a monopoly of the market to the legal distillers, the real effect of too high duties has been to throw the supply of a large proportion of the demand into the hands of the illicit distiller, and to superadd the atrocities of the smuggler to the idleness and dissipation of the drunkard.

During the latter part of the reign of George I., and the earlier part of that of George II., gin-drinking was exceedingly prevalent; and the cheapness of ardent spirits, and the multiplication of public houses, were denounced from the pulpit, and in the presentments of grand juries, as pregnant with the most destructive consequences to the health and morals of the community. Under such circumstances it could not be supposed the press would be idle, and there appeared the following tracts:—

Distilled Spirituous Liquors the Bane of the Nation, &c., to which is added an Appendix containing the Presentments of the Grand Juries of London, Middlesex, &c. 8vo. London, 1736.

"This tract was composed by a very learned divine, with the assistance of several physicians."—(Fielding, 'On the Increase of Robbers, &c.' p. 19.)

Various answers were made to this tract; but it is not necessary to do more than refer to that which follows.

An Impartial Enquiry into the Present State of the British Distillery; plainly demonstrating the evil consequences of imposing any additional Duties on British Spirits, &c.; wherein the Manifest Absurdities and Gross Impositions contained in the pamphlet entituled 'Spirituous Liquors, &c.,' are fully detected and exposed. 8vo. London, 1736.

The author of this tract has fulfilled the promises in his title-page; and has conclusively shown the exaggeration and fallacy of the statements put forth by the reverend author of 'Spirituous Liquors the Bane, &c.,' and his coadjutors; and the impolicy of imposing any additional duty on spirits.

But despite the efforts of the distillers to the contrary, the clamour against gin-drinking was so very powerful that ministers were compelled to take measures for its suppression by prohibiting the use of spirituous liquors except as a medicine. In this view an act was passed, 9 Geo. II. c. 23, the history and effects of which deserve to be studied by all who think it possible suddenly to change the public taste by dint of legislative interference. Its preamble is to this effect:—"Whereas the drinking of spirituous liquors, or strong water, is become very common, especially among people of lower and inferior rank, the constant and excessive use of which tends greatly to the destruction of their health, rendering them unfit for useful labour and business, debauching their morals, and inciting them to perpetrate all vices; and the ill consequences of the excessive use of such liquors are not confined to the present generation, but extend to future ages, and tend to the destruction and ruin of this kingdom." The enactments were such as might be expected to follow a preamble of this sort. They were not intended to repress the vice of gin-drinking, but to root it out altogether. To accomplish this, a duty of *twenty shillings* a gallon was laid on spirits, exclusive of a licence duty of 50*l.* a-year on retailers, the sale of any less quantity than *two* gallons being at the same time prohibited! Extraordinary encouragements were also held out to informers, and a fine of 100*l.* was ordered to be rigorously exacted from those who, were it even through inadvertency, should vend the smallest quantity of spirits which had not paid the full duty. Here was an act which might, one should think, have satisfied the bitterest enemy of gin. But instead of the anticipated effects, it produced those directly opposite. Respectable dealers withdrew from a trade proscribed by the legislature; so that the spirit business fell almost entirely into the hands of the lowest and most profligate characters, who, as they had nothing to lose, were not deterred by penalties from breaking through all the provisions of the law. The populace having in this, as in all similar cases, espoused the cause of the smugglers and unlicensed dealers, the officers of the revenue were openly assaulted in the streets of London and other great towns; informers were hunted down like wild beasts; and drunkenness, disorders, and crimes increased with frightful rapidity. "Within two years of the passing of the act," says Tindal, "it had become *odious and contemptible*, and policy as well as humanity forced the commissioners of excise to mitigate its penalties."—(Continuation of Rapin, viii. 358, ed. 1759.) The same historian mentions (viii. 390), that during the two years in question, no fewer than 12,000 persons were convicted of offences connected with the sale of spirits. But no exertion on the part of the revenue officers and magistrates could stem the torrent of smuggling. According to a statement made by the Earl of Cholmondeley, in the House of Lords (Timberland's Debates in the House of Lords, viii. 388), it appears, that at the very moment when the sale of spirits was declared to be illegal, and every possible exertion made to suppress it, upwards of SEVEN MILLIONS of gallons were annually consumed in London, and other parts immediately adjacent! Under such circumstances, government could do nothing but give up the unequal struggle. In 1742 the high prohibitory duties were accordingly repealed, and such moderate duties imposed as were calculated to increase the revenue, by increasing the consumption of legally distilled spirits. The bill for this purpose was vehemently opposed in the House of Lords by most of the bishops, and many other peers, who exhausted all their rhetoric in depicting the mischievous consequences that would result from a toleration of the practice of gin-drinking. To these declamations it was unanswerably replied, that whatever the evils of the practice might be, it was impossible to repress them by prohibitory enactments; and that the attempts to do so had been productive of far more mischief than had ever resulted, or could be expected to result, from the greatest abuse of spirits. The consequences of the change were highly beneficial. An instant stop was put to smuggling; and if the vice of drunkenness was not materially diminished, it has never been stated that it was increased.

But it is unnecessary to go back to the reign of George II. for proofs of the impotency of high duties to take away the taste for such an article, or to lessen its consumption. The experience of later times is equally decisive of this question.

Perhaps no country has suffered more from the excessive height to which duties on spirits have been carried than Ireland. If heavy taxes, enforced by severe fiscal regulations, could have made a people sober and industrious, the Irish would have been the most so of any on the face of the earth. In order to make the possessors of property join heartily in suppressing illicit distillation, the novel expedient was here resorted to, of imposing a heavy fine on every parish, town land, manor land, or lordship, in which an unlicensed still was found; while the unfortunate wretches found working it were subjected to *transportation for seven years*. But instead of putting down illicit distillation, these unheard-of severities rendered it universal, and filled the country with bloodshed, and even rebellion. It is stated by the Rev. Mr. Chichester, in the following pamphlet on the Irish Distillery Laws, that "the Irish system seemed to have been formed in order to perpetuate smuggling and anarchy. It has culled the evils of both savage and civilised life, and rejected all the advantages which they contain. The calamities of civilised warfare are, in general, inferior to those produced by the Irish distillery laws; and I doubt whether any nation of modern Europe, which is not in a state of actual revolution, can furnish instances of legal cruelty commensurate to those which I have represented."—(pp. 92-107.)

Oppressions and Cruelties of Irish Revenue Officers; being the Substance of a Letter to a British Member of Parliament. By the Rev. EDWARD CHICHESTER, A.M. 8vo. London, 1818.

The statements in this excellent tract are borne out to the fullest extent by the official details in the *Reports of the Revenue Commissioners*. In 1811, say the commissioners (Fifth Report, p. 19), when the duty on spirits was 2*s*. 6*d*. a gallon, duty was paid in Ireland on 6,500,361 gallons; whereas, in 1822, when the duty was 5*s*. 6*d*., only 2,950,647 gallons were brought to the charge. The commissioners estimate, that the annual consumption of spirits in Ireland was at this very period not less than TEN MILLIONS of gallons; and, as scarcely *three* millions paid duty, it followed that *seven* millions were illegally supplied; and "taking *one* million of gallons as the quantity fraudulently furnished for consumption by the licensed distillers, the produce of the unlicensed stills may be estimated at *six millions of gallons*." —(Ib. p. 8.) Now, it is material to keep in mind that this vast amount of smuggling and of illicit distillation was carried on in the teeth of the above barbarous statutes, and in despite of the utmost exertions of the police and military to prevent it; the only result being the exasperation of the populace, and the perpetration of revolting atrocities both by them and the military. "In Ireland," say the commissioners, "it will appear, from the evidence annexed to this Report, that parts of the country have been absolutely disorganised, and placed in opposition not only to the civil authority, but to the military force of the government. The profits to be obtained from the evasion of the law have been such as to encourage numerous individuals to persevere in these desperate pursuits, notwithstanding the risk of property and life with which they have been attended."

To put an end to these evils the commissioners recommended that the duty on spirits should be reduced from 5*s*. 6*d*. to 2*s*. the wine gallon; and government having judiciously carried this recommendation into effect, smuggling and illicit distillation immediately ceased; the quantity of spirits brought to the charge was trebled; and the revenue very considerably augmented!

Similar results followed the reduction of the duties which then also took place on spirits in Scotland and England. But we beg to refer the reader for further information respecting these reductions, and the history of the spirit trade generally, to our work on the 'Principles and Practice of Taxation,' or to the article 'Spirits' in the 'Commercial Dictionary.'

A LETTER from a BY-STANDER (CORBYN MORRIS, Esq., F.R.S.)

to a MEMBER of PARLIAMENT, wherein is examined what necessity there is for the Maintenance of a large Regular Land Force in this Island; and what Proportion the Revenues of the Crown have borne to those of the People, from the Restoration to his present Majesty's Accession. 8vo. London, 1741.

A FULL ANSWER to the LETTER from a BY-STANDER, wherein his False Calculations, Misrepresentations of Facts in the Time of Charles II. are refuted, &c. By R. H., Esq. (said to be THOMAS CARTE, the Jacobite Historian). 8vo. London, 1742.

A LETTER to the Rev. THOMAS CARTE, Author of the 'Full Answer to the Letter from a By-stander.' By a Gentleman of Cambridge. 8vo. London, 1743.

A FULL and CLEAR VINDICATION of the 'Full Answer to the Letter from a By-stander,' &c. 8vo. London, 1743.

These tracts embody much curious discussion and information with respect to taxation and the expenditure of the public revenue for a lengthened period.

A SURVEY of the NATIONAL DEBTS, the SINKING FUND, the CIVIL LIST, &c. Inscribed to Sir JOHN PHILIPPS, Bart. 8vo. London, 1745.

In 1744 Sir Matthew Decker (or Mr. Richardson) published his famous 'Essay on the Causes of the Decline of Foreign Trade, and of the Value of the Lands of Britain' (see *ante*, p. 46), in which he gives the outline of a project or scheme for obviating these evils.

This scheme, which attracted a good deal of attention at the time, was to the effect that the existing excise and customs duties should be repealed, and replaced by duties on licences to consume certain specified goods, which were to be payable by all parties using the same. But though ingenious, there are insuperable objections to the proposal. It was animadverted upon by Adam Smith as follows:—

"The object of Decker's scheme was to promote all the different branches of foreign trade, particularly the carrying trade, by taking away all duties upon importation and exportation, and thereby enabling the merchant to employ his whole capital and credit in the purchase of goods and the freight of ships, no part of either being diverted towards the advancing of taxes. The project, however, of taxing in this manner goods of immediate or speedy consumption, seems liable to the four following very important objections:—First, the tax would be more unequal or not so well proportioned to the expense and consumption of the different contributors, as the way in which it is commonly imposed. The taxes upon ale, wine, and spirituous liquors, which are advanced by the dealers, are finally paid by the different consumers, exactly in proportion to their respective consumption. But if the tax were to be paid by purchasing a licence to drink those liquors, the sober would, in proportion to his consumption, be taxed much more heavily than the drunken consumer. A family which exercised great hospitality would be taxed much more lightly than one who entertained fewer guests. Secondly, this mode of taxation, by paying for an annual, half-yearly, or quarterly licence to consume certain goods, would diminish very much one of the principal conveniences of taxes upon goods of speedy consumption, the piecemeal payment. In the price of threepence-halfpenny which is at present paid for a pot of porter, the different taxes upon malt, hops, and beer, together with the extraordinary profit which the brewer charges for having advanced them, may perhaps amount to about three-halfpence. If a workman can conveniently spare those three-halfpence, he buys a pot of porter; if he cannot, he contents himself with a pint, and, as a penny saved is a penny got, he thus saves a farthing by his temperance: he pays the tax piecemeal, as he can afford to pay it, and when he can afford to pay it, and every act of payment is perfectly voluntary, and what he can avoid if he chooses to do so. Thirdly, such taxes would operate less as sumptuary laws. When the licence was once purchased, whether the purchaser drunk much or drunk little, his tax would be the same. Fourthly, if a workman were to pay all at once by yearly, half-yearly, or quarterly payments, a tax equal to what he at present pays, with little or no inconveniency, upon all the different pots and pints of porter which he drinks in any such period of time, the sum might frequently distress him very much. This mode of taxation, therefore, it seems evident, could never, without the most grievous oppression, produce a revenue nearly equal to what is derived from the present mode without any oppression."—(p. 396.)

It may be right to observe that Decker has been generally taken for the author of a very remarkable tract, published nearly at the same time with the essay now referred to, entitled

Serious Considerations on the several High Duties which the Nation in General, as well as Trade in particular, labours under, &c., with a Proposal for raising the Public Supplies by One Single Tax. By a Well-Wisher to the Good People of Great Britain. 8vo. London, 1743.

But to whomsoever we may be indebted for this tract,* it certainly was not written by the author of the 'Essay on the Decline of Foreign Trade,' which has also been most commonly ascribed to Decker. They agree in recommending the repeal of the existing taxes and the substitution in their stead of a single tax (*impôt unique*); but there the agreement between them ends. The author of 'Serious Considerations' proposes that the revenue should be raised by a tax on houses proportioned to their rent; and though there are insuperable objections to any scheme of the kind, yet, supposing the expediency of consolidating the infinite variety of existing duties into a single duty were admitted, it would be no easy matter to suggest a better substitute. It is infinitely preferable to that proposed by the author of the 'Essay on the Decline, &c.' No doubt it is quite impracticable, and it would be unjust and inexpedient, if it were practicable, to raise the entire revenue by a tax on houses. Certainly, however, this, when kept within due bounds and

* Mr. Fauquier states distinctly, in his 'Essay on Ways and Means' (see p. 331), that this tract was written by Decker; and he farther states that a gentleman named Richardson was the author of the 'Essay on the Causes of the Decline of Foreign Trade.'—(Ways and Means, 3rd ed. p. 56.) Fauquier, being a contemporary, and apparently well informed on the subject, is most probably right: it appears, however, to have been taken for granted by most subsequent writers, and among others by Adam Smith, that Decker was the author of the Essay; and following in their wake, we have ascribed it to him (*ante*, p. 46). At all events it is clear that the same person could not be the author of it and of the 'Serious Considerations.'

properly assessed, is a most unexceptionable tax. Its recent repeal was an impolitic and ill-judged concession to unfounded clamour. Instead of being repealed or diminished, it should have been considerably increased.

THE PROPOSAL, commonly called Sir MATTHEW DECKER'S SCHEME, for ONE GENERAL TAX upon HOUSES, laid open, &c. (By Mr. JOSEPH MASSIE.) 8vo. London, 1757.

The impracticability and the really objectionable parts of the project for commuting the existing taxes for a house-tax are hardly touched upon in this tract. Its author, though capable of better things, appears in this instance to have mistaken abusive for vigorous writing; and criticises the project for doing that which is its principal merit, that is, for putting down smuggling and freeing commerce from every sort of restraint.

Considerations on the Proposal for Reducing the Interest on the National Debt. (By Sir JOHN BARNARD, M.P.) 8vo. London, 1750.

This well-timed tract was written to recommend the project of Mr. Pelham, then under consideration, for reducing the interest on the public debt from 4 to 3 per cent.; to the success of which it materially contributed by its forcible reasonings, and by the confidence placed by the public in the integrity and intelligence of the author. Sir John Barnard had himself brought forward a similar project in 1737, when it might have been carried into effect with equal facility. It was, however, opposed by the minister, Sir Robert Walpole; and though the resolutions on which the bill for the reduction of the interest was to be founded were carried on a division in a pretty full house, the bill itself was rejected by a large majority.

AN ESSAY on the NATIONAL DEBT and NATIONAL CAPITAL; or, the Account truly stated, Debtor and Creditor, &c. By ANDREW HOOKE, Esq. 8vo. London, 1750.

The author of this tract endeavours to trace and exhibit the increase of the national capital from 1600 downwards; but it is needless to say that there must always be more of conjecture than of certainty in such estimates. Mr. H. supposed that in 1750 the public debt was to the national capital in about the ratio of 1 to 12.

THE HISTORY of our NATIONAL DEBTS and TAXES, from the Year 1688 to the Present Time. 1 vol., 8vo., in four Parts. London, 1751–52.

This work was republished under the title of the 'History of our Customs, Aids, Subsidies, National Debts, and Taxes, from William the Conqueror to the present year, MDCCLXI.' 1 vol. 8vo., in four parts. London, 1761. But the additions are of little value, and, being more than balanced by retrenchments, the former edition is the best of the two.

ESSAYS on the PUBLIC DEBT, on PAPER MONEY, and on FRUGALITY. 8vo. Edinburgh, 1753.

These essays were written by Patrick, fifth Lord Elibank. Dr. Wallace noticed and controverted some of his Lordship's conclusions in his 'Characteristics of the Present State of Great Britain' (see *ante*, p. 257).

A SCHEME for PREVENTING a FURTHER INCREASE of the NA-

TIONAL DEBT, and for REDUCING the same, inscribed to the Earl of Chesterfield. By BOURCHIER CLEEVE, Esq. 4to. London, 1756.

AN ESSAY on WAYS and MEANS for RAISING MONEY for the SUPPORT of the PRESENT WAR, without increasing the Public Debts. By FRANCIS FAUQUIER. 8vo., 3rd ed. London, 1757.

These tracts have nothing original, the leading idea in them being borrowed from the 'Serious Considerations,' already referred to. Their object is to show the advantage which, in the estimation of the authors, would result from imposing a pretty heavy tax on houses, and repealing an equivalent amount of taxes on commodities.

OBSERVATIONS on Mr. FAUQUIER'S 'ESSAY on WAYS and MEANS for RAISING,' &c. By J. M. (JOSEPH MASSIE). 8vo. London, 1756.

CALCULATIONS of TAXES for a FAMILY of each RANK, DEGREE, or CLASS, for ONE YEAR. (By JOSEPH MASSIE.) 8vo. London, 1756.

LETTER to BOURCHIER CLEEVE, Esq., concerning his CALCULATIONS of TAXES, from the AUTHOR of 'CALCULATIONS,' &c. (Mr. JOSEPH MASSIE). 8vo. London, 1757.

Mr. Cleeve gave, in his 'Letter to Lord Chesterfield,' referred to above, sundry calculations, or estimates, to show the portions of the incomes of different classes abstracted by taxation. These, however, as is commonly the case with such calculations, were exceedingly exaggerated; but it does not often happen that their exaggeration is so completely established as it has been by Mr. Massie in this instance. He demonstrates that the taxes could not amount to anything like half the sum stated by Cleeve.

HISTORY of the PUBLIC REVENUE from the REVOLUTION to the PRESENT TIME. By JAMES POSTLETHWAITE, Esq. 1 vol., oblong folio. London, 1758.

THE BRITISH CUSTOMS, containing an Historical and Practical Account of each Branch of that Revenue. By HENRY SAXBY. 1 vol. 8vo. London, 1757.

SMUGGLING LAID OPEN in all its EXTENSIVE and DESTRUCTIVE BRANCHES, with Proposals for the Effectual Remedy of that most Iniquitous Practice. (Ascribed to Sir S. T. JANSSEN, Bart., M.P.) 1 vol. 8vo. London, 1763.

OBSERVATIONS on that PART of a late ACT of PARLIAMENT which lays an additional Duty on Cider and Perry. By THOMAS ALCOCK, A.M. 8vo. Plymouth (1764).

The author of this tract is most probably the same Mr. Alcock who wrote the tract on the Poor Laws previously noticed (see p. 278). This, like that now referred to, is an able pamphlet. The duty of 4*s*. per hhd. on cider, to which it strongly objects, was imposed in 1763, but being extremely unpopular, it was repealed in 1766.

CONSIDERATIONS on TAXES as they are supposed to affect the PRICE of LABOUR in our MANUFACTURES: also, some Reflections on the General Behaviour and Disposition of the Manufacturing Populace of this Kingdom; showing, by Arguments drawn from Experience, that nothing but Necessity will enforce Labour; and that no State ever did, or ever can make any considerable Figure in Trade, where the Necessaries of Life are at a low Price. 8vo. London, 1765.

The title of this tract sufficiently explains its object; and there can be no doubt that the theory of the author is, under certain circumstances, perfectly well-founded. An increase of taxation or of the price of provisions has the same influence over a state that an increase of their families or of their necessary expenses has over individuals; and by acting as an additional stimulus to industry, economy, and invention, may do more than maintain them in their previous condition; and, instead of deteriorating, frequently increases the wealth and improves the condition of the bulk of society. But it must not be supposed that because an increase of taxation has this effect in certain cases, and under certain conditions, it will have the same effect in all cases and under all conditions. To render an increase of taxation productive of greater exertion, economy, and invention, it should be slow and gradual; and it should never be carried to such a height as to incapacitate individuals from meeting the sacrifices it imposes by such additional exertions and economy as it may be in their power to make without requiring any very sudden or violent change in their habits. The increase of taxation should never be so great as to make it impracticable to overcome its influence, or to induce the belief that it is impracticable. Difficulties that are seen to be surmountable sharpen the inventive powers and are readily and vigorously grappled with; but an apparently insurmountable difficulty, or such an excessive increase of taxation as it was deemed impossible to defray, would not stimulate but destroy exertion. Whenever taxation becomes so heavy that the wealth it takes from individuals can no longer be replaced by fresh efforts, these efforts uniformly cease to be made; industry is paralysed, and the country, which is unfortunate enough to be subject to such a scourge, rapidly declines.

PUBLIC ACCOUNTS of SERVICES and GRANTS from 1721 to 1771. By Sir CHARLES WHITWORTH, Bart. Folio. 1771.

An Appeal to the Public on the Subject of the National Debt. By RICHARD PRICE, D.D., F.R.S. A new edition, with an Appendix. 8vo. London, 1774.

This pamphlet contains a pretty full development of what its author believed to be the peculiar and distinctive properties of a sinking fund, and is important from its being the foundation of Mr. Pitt's famous project. Among the answers to Price's work were the two immediately following, viz.:—

THE CHALLENGE, or PATRIOTISM PUT to the TEST, in a Letter to the Rev. Dr. PRICE, occasioned by his late Publications on the National Debt. By JOS. WIMPEY. 8vo. London, 1772.

REMARKS upon Dr. PRICE'S APPEAL to the PUBLIC on the SUBJECT of the NATIONAL DEBT, addressed to the Author. 8vo. London, 1772.

This is a clever and, in some respects, conclusive tract.

Facts Addressed to the Landholders, &c., and generally to all the Subjects of Great Britain and Ireland. 8vo. London, 1780.

This pamphlet rose out of the debates in parliament on certain contracts which it was alleged the Ministry had entered into on exceedingly disadvantageous terms for the public. The financial parts of it were written by Dr. Price, and the others by Horne Tooke. Lord Shelburne was privy to the writing of this pamphlet; but when it was ready for publication he objected to some passages in it, and recommended that it should be suppressed. Tooke, however, thought differently, and published it forthwith, which produced an irreparable breach between his Lordship and him. The pamphlet, as might be anticipated from its parentage, is sufficiently pungent. It went through seven or eight editions in a very few weeks.—(Morgan's 'Life of Dr. Price,' p. 83.)

Considerations on the Present State of Public Affairs, and the Means of Raising the Necessary Supplies. By William Pulteney, Esq. 8vo. 3rd ed. London, 1779.

On the Debt of the Nation, Compared with its Revenue; and the Impossibility of Carrying on the War without Public Œconomy. 8vo. London, 1781.

Tracts, by John Earl of Stair, on the Public Debts of the Kingdom. 8vo. London, 1782–83.

His Lordship seems to have been an alarmist of the first magnitude. But a very brief experience sufficed to show the error of those who apprehended we should be ruined, or, indeed, sensibly injured, by the unsuccessful termination of the American war. The emancipation of the colonies was, in fact, the event most advantageous for us.

The State of the Public Debts and Finances at Signing the Preliminary Articles of Peace, in January, 1783, &c. By Richard Price, D.D. and F.R.S. 8vo. London, 1783.

Postscript to a Pamphlet by Dr. Price, on the State of the Public Debts and Finances at the Signing, &c. 8vo. London, 1784.

An Essay on the Nature and Principles of Public Credit. (By Mr. S. Gale, of Charleston, South Carolina.) 1 vol. 8vo. London, 1784.

After the termination of the American war, and the consolidation of his ministry, the devising of means for the reduction of the public debt became the object of Mr. Pitt's special attention. To accomplish this he adopted one of three projects furnished to him by Dr. Price for establishing a sinking fund. This fund was managed by commissioners appointed for the purpose, and consisted of 1,000,000*l.* a-year set apart by parliament for that peculiar service, with what were called its accumulations at compound interest. These were formed as follows: at the outset of the scheme the commissioners would purchase with the million assigned to them (which be it observed was wholly derived from taxation) a million's worth of stock, on which they would receive a dividend say of 4 per cent.: consequently at the end of the first year the commissioners would have their annual million plus the dividend accruing on the stock previously bought by them, or 1,040,000*l.*

to lay out in the purchase of fresh stock; at the end of the second year they would have 1,081,600*l.*, at the end of the third year 1,124,864*l.*, and so on. Now, this is what Sir Nathanael Gould, Dr. Price, and Mr. Pitt call paying off the public debt by a sinking fund increasing at compound interest; but it is obvious that whatever diminution is effected in the amount of the public debt in the way now stated, is brought about by devoting a portion of *the produce of taxation* to its extinction. It is true that by applying any given sum to purchase stock, and then constantly applying the dividends upon the stock so purchased to the extinction of debt, its reduction is effected in the same way as if the original sum had really been increasing, by an inherent energy of its own, at compound interest; but it is essential to know, that though the results be the same, the means are totally different. The debt is reduced because the taxes required to pay the dividends or interest on the stock purchased by the Sinking Fund Commissioners, instead of being remitted to the contributors, continue to be taken from them, and applied to the purchase of fresh stock. It is the merest delusion to suppose that the debt either has been or ever can be reduced by the agency of any independent fund increasing at compound interest. To make capital increase in this way, it must be employed in some sort of productive industry; and the profits, instead of being consumed as income, must be regularly added to the principal, to form a new capital. It is unnecessary to say that no such sinking fund ever existed. Those that have been set on foot in this and other countries have all been supported either by loans or by the produce of taxes, and have never paid off, and never by any possibility could pay off, a single shilling of debt by their own agency.

In 1792 some further additions were made to Mr. Pitt's sinking fund; and it was then also enacted, that besides providing for the interest of any loan that might henceforth be contracted, additional taxes should be imposed to form a sinking fund of *one* per cent. on the capital stock created by such loan. As there was a considerable excess of revenue in the period between 1786 and 1793, the debt was reduced by about 10½ millions, and this reduction was ascribed to the effect of the sinking fund increasing at compound interest, though it is plain it entirely resulted from the application of surplus revenue to the purchase of stock. Subsequently to the commencement of the revolutionary war, the income of the country uniformly fell greatly short of the expenditure, and the debt rapidly increased. But though there was no *annual million* in the Treasury to transfer to the Commissioners, the juggle of the sinking fund was kept up. Dr. Price had been sanguine, or rather we may say absurd, enough to allege that "any suspension of the sinking fund during war would be the madness of giving it a mortal stab *at the very time it was making the quickest progress towards the accomplishment of its end*."—(Appeal, &c., p. 17.) And even this was believed! In consequence the loans for the service of the year were uniformly increased, by the whole amount of the sums placed at the disposal of the Sinking Fund Commissioners; so that, for every shilling's worth of stock transferred to them by this futile proceeding, an equal or greater amount of new debt had to be contracted, exclusive of the loss incurred on account of management!

Such was the sinking fund, the object of the laudation of all parties. It was universally considered as the great bulwark of the country, as a means by which "a vast treasure was to be accumulated out of nothing!" And so lasting and powerful was the infatuation, that after fourteen years' experience of its absolute nullity, when a new financial project was introduced in 1807, it contained a system of checks to prevent the evils likely to result from allowing the sinking fund to accumulate without any limit, and deluging the country with a flood of wealth, by "a too prompt discharge of the public debt!" The history of the world does not furnish another instance of so extraordinary a delusion. Had the sinking fund involved any unintelligible dogmas, had it addressed itself to popular feelings and passions, or had the notion of its efficacy originated with the mob, the prevalence of the delusion would have been less unaccountable. But it was from the first a matter of mere calculation; it was projected by some of the best informed persons in the country, who continued for upwards of twenty years to believe that they were rapidly diminishing the public debt by the agency of a fund, which was all the while kept on foot by borrowed money! Dr. Hamilton, of Aberdeen, has the merit of having dissipated this delusion—the grossest, certainly, by which any civilised people was ever blinded and deceived. He showed that the sinking fund, instead of reducing the debt, had increased it: and he proved to demonstration, that the excess of revenue above expenditure is the only real sinking fund by which any part of the public debt can be discharged. "The increase of revenue," he observes, "or the diminution of expense, are the only means by which this sinking fund can be enlarged, and its operations rendered more effectual; and all schemes for discharging the national debt, by sinking funds operating at *compound* interest, or in any other manner, unless in so far as they are founded upon this principle, are completely illusory." The act of 10 Geo. IV. consecrated this sound principle; and terminated the sinking fund.

Dr. Price was a distinguished Non-Conformist minister; and it would be unjust not to mention that, notwithstanding the entire fallacy of his views with respect to the sinking fund, he was an excellent mathematician. His work on Annuities (see p. 251) was of essential service, by effecting a great improvement in the method of transacting insurances on lives, and in the constitution of friendly societies. His moral, political, and metaphysical works will be differently estimated, according to the opinions and biases of those by whom they may be read; but there can be no difference respecting the candour, benevolence, and piety of the writer. He died in 1791, in the 68th year of his age.

Manufactures Improper Subjects of Taxation, addressed to the Merchants and Manufacturers of Great Britain, &c. 8vo. London, 1785.

Considerations on the Annual Million Bill, and on the Real and Imaginary Properties of a Sinking Fund. 8vo. London, 1787.

Observations on the Land Revenue of the Crown. (By the Hon. John St. John.) 1 vol. 4to. London, 1787. 2nd ed. 1 vol. 8vo. London, 1792.

An Inquiry into the Principles of Taxation. 1 vol. 4to. London, 1790.

A Sketch of the Revenue and Finances of Ireland. By R. V. Clarendon, Esq. 1 vol. 4to. London, 1791.

A Practical Arrangement of the Laws Relative to the Excise, with Cases, &c. By Anthony Highmore, Jun., Solicitor. 2 vols. 8vo. London, 1796.

Preliminary observations on taxation are prefixed to this work, principally taken from Smith and other writers of authority; and it is interspersed with statements drawn from the same sources.

A REVIEW of Dr. PRICE'S WRITINGS on the SUBJECT of the FINANCES of this KINGDOM; to which are added the three Plans communicated by him to Mr. Pitt, in 1786, for Redeeming the National Debt. By WILLIAM MORGAN, Esq., F.R.S. (Actuary to the Equitable Insurance Company, and nephew to Dr. PRICE). 8vo. London, 1792.

The History of the Public Revenue of the British Empire, containing an Account of the Public Income and Expenditure from the Remotest Periods recorded in History to Michaelmas, 1802; with an Account of the Revenue of Scotland and Ireland, &c. By Sir JOHN SINCLAIR, Bart., M.P. 3rd and best ed. 3 vols. 8vo. London, 1804.

This is one of the best of the many works published by its really patriotic and laborious author. It is, however, very unequally executed; and contains various extracts from speeches made by Sir John in the House of Commons, and other documents of a temporary interest, that should have been omitted.

Sir John Sinclair died in 1835, at the age of 82. He is probably best known by the old statistical account of Scotland in 21 vols., which he projected, and in the completion of which he displayed extraordinary perseverance and incurred great labour and not a little expense. His fecundity was so extreme that he is said to have produced, including the Statistical Account, no fewer than 106 vols. and 367 pamphlets! —('Shetland,' &c., by Miss Sinclair, p. 80.)

Observations on the Produce of the Income Tax, and on its Proportion to the whole Revenue of Great Britain. By the Rev. HENRY BEEKE, D.D. (Dean of Bristol). A new and greatly improved edition. 8vo. London, 1800.

An excellent tract, affording the best example of the successful application of statistical reasonings to finance that had then appeared.

THE INCOME-TAX SCRUTINISED, and some Amendments proposed to render it more agreeable to the British Constitution. By JOHN GRAY, LL.D. 8vo. London, 1802.

A BRIEF EXAMINATION into the INCREASE of the REVENUE, COMMERCE, and NAVIGATION of GREAT BRITAIN during the Administration of the Right Hon. William Pitt, &c. By the Right Hon. GEORGE ROSE. 8vo. London, 1806.

An Enquiry concerning the Influence of Tithes upon Agriculture, whether in the hands of the Clergy or the Laity, with some Thoughts respecting their Commutation, &c. By the Rev. JOHN HOWLETT, Vicar of Great Dunmow, Essex. 8vo. London, 1801.

One of the ablest, though not in all respects the soundest, of Mr. Howlett's tracts.

SUBSTANCE of the SPEECH of the Right Hon. LORD HENRY PETTY (now Marquis of Lansdowne), in the House of Commons, on proposing his New Plan of Finance. 8vo. London, 1807.

This plan was only acted upon for one year. Its extreme inexpediency has been shown by Dr. Hamilton, in the following work, pp. 208-219:—

An Inquiry concerning the Rise and Progress, the Redemption and Present State, and the Management of the National Debt of Great Britain and Ireland. By ROBERT HAMILTON, LL.D., &c. 3rd and best ed. 1 vol. 8vo. Edinburgh, 1818.

The author of this important work, which, as already seen, first opened the eyes of the public to the delusive nature of the sinking fund, was a native of Edinburgh, where he was born in 1743. Having been intended for commercial pursuits, he spent some time, after leaving college, in a banking-house, where he obtained that practical acquaintance with business and with money matters, of which he afterwards availed himself in several of his publications. His taste for study and a literary life having, however, predominated, he became rector of the academy of Perth in 1769, and thereafter, in 1779, professor of mathematics in the university of Aberdeen. His work on the National Debt was not published till 1813, when he was above seventy years of age. He died in 1829, at the advanced age of eighty-six.

Exclusive of this work, by which he will be long remembered, Dr. Hamilton published, in 1777, his 'Introduction to Merchandise, &c.,' previously referred to (see p. 139); he also published a 'System of Arithmetic and Book-keeping,' and some smaller tracts. In 1830, after his death, his family published a treatise of his, entitled 'The Progress of Society,' which embraces a wide range of interesting topics; but it is feebly written, and might without injury to his fame or to the public interests have been allowed to continue in manuscript.

Case of the Salt Duties, with Proofs and Illustrations. By Sir THOMAS BERNARD, Bart. 1 vol. 12mo. London, 1817.

This striking exposition of the mischievous influence of the salt duties contributed considerably to bring about their repeal, which took place in 1823.

ELEMENTS of a PLAN for the LIQUIDATION of the PUBLIC DEBT of the UNITED KINGDOM, &c. By RICHARD HEATHFIELD, Gent. 8vo. London, 1820.

FURTHER OBSERVATIONS on the PRACTICABILITY and EXPEDIENCY of LIQUIDATING the PUBLIC DEBT of the UNITED KINGDOM. By RICHARD HEATHFIELD, Gent. 8vo. London, 1820.

In these tracts Mr. Heathfield has revived (though without making any allusion to it) the project of Mr. Hutcheson, previously noticed (p. 319), for paying off the national debt by an assessment on capital. The most, perhaps, that can be said in favour of this project is that it was approved of by Mr. Ricardo.

In 1820 Mr. Ricardo contributed an essay on the Funding System to the Supplement to the 'Encyclopædia Britannica,' which has been reprinted in the last edition of the 'Encyclopædia.' Though incomplete, and omitting, indeed, all mention of some most important topics, this essay is marked by that perfect acquaintance with the subject, depth, and originality, that distinguish everything put forth by its author. Mr. Ricardo approved highly of the policy of endeavouring to provide by increased taxes for a much larger proportion of the funds necessary to carry on wars than has been usual in this country; and he also approved of Mr. Hutcheson's project, already referred to, for assessing the property of the country to pay off some considerable portion of the national debt.

COMPENDIUM of the FINANCES of GREAT BRITAIN and other COUNTRIES. By BERNARD COHEN, Esq. 1 vol. royal 8vo. London, 1822.

OBSERVATIONS on the EFFECTS PRODUCED by the EXPENDITURE of GOVERNMENT during the RESTRICTION of CASH PAYMENTS. By WILLIAM BLAKE, Esq., F.R.S. 8vo. London, 1823.

By the author of the celebrated tract on Exchange: see p. 174.

AN ACCOUNT of the PUBLIC FUNDS TRANSFERABLE at the BANK of ENGLAND, &c. By WILLIAM FAIRMAN. The 7th ed., revised and enlarged by WILLIAM COHEN. 1 vol. 8vo. London, 1824.

ESSAY on the SUPPOSED ADVANTAGES of a SINKING FUND. By LORD GRENVILLE. 8vo. London, 1828.

A LETTER to LORD GRENVILLE on the SINKING FUND. By T. P. COURTENAY, Esq., M.P. London, 1828.

SPEECH of C. POULETT THOMSON, Esq. (afterwards Lord Sydenham), in the House of Commons, on the 26th of March, 1830, on moving the Appointment of a Select Committee to Inquire into the State of the Taxation of the United Kingdom. 8vo. London, 1830.

On Financial Reform. By Sir HENRY PARNELL, Bart., M.P. (afterwards Lord Congleton). 1st ed. 1 vol. post 8vo. London, 1830. 4th and enlarged ed. 1 vol. 12mo. London, 1832.

A comprehensive and valuable work, comprising a large amount of well-digested and authentic information respecting the revenue, expenditure, and debt of the nation. It is concisely and clearly written, and the principles on which it is bottomed are, for the most part, unexceptionable.

REMARKS on the REVENUE of CUSTOMS; with a few Observations on a late work of Sir H. Parnell on Financial Reform, in a Letter to the Right Hon. Henry Goulburn, &c. (By R. B. DEAN, Esq., Chairman of the Board of Customs.) 8vo. London, 1830.

A LETTER to the Right Hon. LORD ALTHORPE, &c., on the SUBJECT of the DUTY on PRINTED COTTONS. By a CALICO PRINTER. 8vo. London, 1830.

A duty of 3*d*. per square yard on all printed cottons manufactured in this country, imposed in 1774, was increased to 3½*d*. per square yard in 1806. The injurious operation of this duty, which had been long seriously felt and loudly complained of, is forcibly pointed out in this pamphlet. It was repealed in 1831.

For an account of the duties on coal, which were repealed in 1831, see ante, p. 229.

In 1832 a commission was appointed, of which Sir Henry Parnell was chairman, for inquiring into the management and collection of the excise revenue of the United Kingdom. This commission collected a great mass of documentary and other evidence, and presented no fewer than twenty reports, some of which are very able. Taking them altogether, they contain, along with the evidence, the most ample information respecting this important department of the public revenue.

An Attempt to show the Justice and Expediency of Substituting an Income or Property Tax for the Present Taxes, or part of them, &c. (By — SAYER, Esq.) 1 vol. royal 8vo. London, 1833.

This is a valuable work. Its author having been long engaged in the supervision of the collection of the income or property tax repealed in 1815, it embodies much practical as well as theoretical information. We dissent from the views taken by Mr. Sayer of taxes on income; but we are not on that account the less ready to admit the ability and judgment he has displayed in recommending their adoption.

Taxes on Knowledge: a Financial and Historical View of the Taxes which Impede the Education of the People. By JOHN CRAWFURD, Esq., F.R.S., &c. 8vo. London, 1836.

By "taxes on knowledge" are meant in this and some other tracts on the same subject, the stamp-duty on newspapers, and the duty on paper. These, however, were both reduced in 1836—the former from about 3½*d.* to 1*d.* per sheet, and the latter about 50 per cent.

OBSERVATIONS ILLUSTRATIVE of the PRACTICAL OPERATION and REAL EFFECT of the DUTIES on PAPER, showing the Expediency of their Reduction or Repeal. (By J. R. M'CULLOCH, Esq.) 8vo. London, 1836.

As stated above, the paper duties were reduced in the course of the same year.

Post-Office Reform, its Importance and Practicability. By ROWLAND HILL. 8vo. London, 1837.

This pamphlet is important from its having paved the way for the introduction of the new system of penny postage. At the period when this tract was published the rates of postage on letters conveyed any considerable distance were oppressively high, being no less than 11*d.* on a single letter between London and York, and 13*d.* on a single letter between London and Glasgow, and so on. To avoid such oppressive charges vast numbers of letters were sent by other channels than the post; and, notwithstanding the rapid increase of population, and the diffusion of education, the post-office revenue continued for twenty years nearly stationary. Under such circumstances a reduction of the rates of postage was plainly indispensable; and had they been reduced so as to make the postage of a single letter between London and Dublin, and London and Edinburgh, 3½*d.* or 4*d.*, and so in proportion, everything would have been done that was necessary to facilitate correspondence, at the same time that the revenue would have lost little or nothing. But government, which should have taken the lead in the matter, did neither one thing nor other; and the natural consequences of this indecision soon became manifest. The clamour for a uniform penny rate of postage, recommended in this pamphlet, progressively gained ground, till at length it became too strong to be successfully resisted; and the Act 2 and 3 Victoria, c. 56, was passed, by which the postage of all pre-paid letters, not exceeding a quarter of an ounce in weight, was reduced to 1*d*., whether they were carried across the street or to the Orkneys, and whether 2 or 200,000 were conveyed in a parcel!

A very large increase has taken place, under this system, in the number of letters and parcels conveyed by post; though it may be doubted whether there has been any material increase of correspondence. But, notwithstanding this increase of posted letters, the measure has led to the sacrifice of above 1,000,000*l*. a-year of nett revenue; and, coupled with the repeal of the house-tax, has compelled recourse to be had to the existing income-tax.

REPORT from the SELECT COMMITTEE of the HOUSE of COMMONS on IMPORT DUTIES, with Minutes of Evidence, Appendix, &c. Folio. 1840.

The evidence annexed to this report has become, as it were, a sort of arsenal to which those who wish to declaim on the oppressiveness of English taxation and the ruinous operation of restrictions, resort to supply themselves with facts and arguments; and certainly it does contain some astounding statements. We are assured, for example, that taking the public revenue paid into the Treasury at 50,000,000*l*. a-year, the indirect taxes arising out of restrictions on trade are "probably much more than double the amount of the other!" and we are farther assured that the taxation raised on the article corn itself amounts to 90,000,000*l*. a-year! But, while we admit the influence of certain restrictions in raising prices, and in entailing a burden on those who have to buy restricted articles from their producers, the extreme exaggeration of the above statements is palpable and obvious. If such sums be paid in taxes, surely it can be no difficult matter to say by whom they are paid and by whom they are received; and it is to be regretted that the committee did not put a question or two to elucidate this point. Supposing the ordinary rate of wages to be 30*l*. a-year, the 90,000,000*l*. which is said to be forced out of the pockets of certain parties by the corn monopoly, will amount to the entire wages of no fewer than 3,000,000 labourers: it is, therefore, pretty clear that the labourers do not pay it, and it is equally clear that the landlords do not receive it—seeing that it amounts to about double the entire landed rental of the United Kingdom! The truth is, that such statements contradict and confute themselves. They were no doubt made *per incuriam*, without reflecting upon their absurdity, and the impossibility of their being true; and our respect for their authors would have prevented our noticing them, had they not been printed in a report published by order of the House of Commons, and daily referred to.

The Budget: a Series of Letters on Financial, Commercial, and Colonial Policy. By a Member of the Political Economy Club (COLONEL TORRENS). 8vo. London, 1841–43.

Remarks on the State of the Sugar Trade, &c. (By JAMES COOK, Esq.) 8vo. London, 1839.

The Effect of an Alteration of the Sugar Duties on the Condition of the People of England and the Negro race considered. By MACGREGOR LAIRD, Esq. 8vo. London, 1844.

THE MINISTRY and the SUGAR DUTIES. 8vo. London, 1844.

The question respecting the duties on sugar agitated in these tracts is of great importance, and also of considerable difficulty, sugar having in this country become a necessary of life, and yielding a large amount of revenue, while, owing to the peculiar situation in which our sugar-growing colonies have been placed by the emancipation of the slaves, it is not easy to say what measures should be adopted in regard to the sugar-trade. Down to within these few years our own colonies furnished a quantity of sugar which, besides supplying our own wants, left a surplus for exportation to other countries; and while this was the case, the cost of sugar in this country, exclusive of the duty, could not exceed its cost in other countries; and the prohibitive duty of 66*s.* 2*d.* (63*s.*+5 per cent.) on foreign sugar was consequently inoperative. But the great falling off in the supply of British colonial sugars subsequently to the commencement of the proceedings for the emancipation of the slaves, has entirely put an end to its export to foreign countries, and has so far increased its price that British sugar in bond has brought nearly double the price of foreign sugar in bond. Under such circumstances the prohibitory duty on foreign sugars has had a powerful influence, and government has been called upon either to reduce it to the same level as the duty of 25*s.* 2*d.* (24*s.*+5 per cent.) a cwt. on British sugar, or at all events materially to diminish the preference in favour of the latter.

But, independently of the duty, this question is embarrassed with another difficulty. We have abolished slavery in our colonies, and placed them under considerable difficulties as respects the supply of labour; and it is further contended that, by admitting slave-grown sugar, we should be acting contradictorily, and be, in fact, encouraging that slavery in Cuba and Brazil which we have, at great cost to ourselves, put down in Jamaica and Demerara.

We are not, however, inclined to attach much weight to this last consideration, or to the encouragement we should give to slavery in foreign countries by admitting slave-grown sugars to our markets. The raw material of the most important of our manufactures is almost wholly produced by slaves; and really when such is the case, when Manchester, Glasgow, Paisley, Bolton, Preston, Bury, and a host of other great towns, depend for existence on supplies of slave-grown cotton, it looks more like affectation or hypocrisy than anything else to be so very squeamish about importing a few thousand tons of slave-grown sugar. And after all we do the very thing we affect to deprecate. The encouragement to slavery in Cuba and Brazil consists in the purchase of their sugar, and has nothing to do with the mode in which that sugar is disposed of. We send manufactured goods to the Havannah and Rio and exchange them for sugar; and having done that, we carry the sugar to Hamburgh and Petersburgh and exchange it for wool and flax; so that we in effect transmute the slave-grown sugar into other things, and consume it under its new form! But suppose we had been a little more Quixotic, and that after getting the sugar we had thrown it into the sea, the result, as respects Cuba and Brazil, would have been the same: they have got value for their sugar. We English have, by buying it, given all the encouragement in our power to the slavery that exists in these countries. What we shall do with the sugar is our own affair; and whether we use it, sell it to others, or destroy it, is, as far as slavery is concerned, quite immaterial.

But obvious as these considerations may appear, they have not hitherto had much practical influence. And while, in the sugar act of last session, the duty on foreign sugar raised by free labour has been reduced from 63*s.* to 34*s.* a cwt., slave-grown sugar has been wholly excluded. We doubt, however, whether, supposing this exclusion to be desirable, it be practicable. Certificates of origin will, we apprehend, turn out to be rather a slender security for the exclusion of slave-grown sugar. But supposing them to be effectual, the only result will be that, a larger quantity of Java and Manilla sugar being consumed in England, less of it can be sent to the Continent, where, by means of our policy, a corresponding market will be opened for slave-grown sugar.

An Inquiry into the Taxation and Commercial Policy of Great Britain. By David Buchanan. 1 vol. 8vo. Edinburgh, 1844.

Report from the Select Committee of the House of Commons on the Tobacco Trade, with Minutes of Evidence, Appendix, &c. Thick folio. 1844.

This bulky volume contains a great deal of curious evidence with respect to the smuggling and adulteration of tobacco occasioned by the high duty.

A Treatise on the Principles and Practical Influence of Taxation and the Funding System. By J. R. M'Culloch, Esq. 1 vol. 8vo. London, 1845.

Exclusive of the revenue raised for public purposes, or rather for purposes under the control of the general government, a very large revenue is raised in the United Kingdom for local purposes, or for purposes under the control and supervision of local boards or other authorities. The principal taxes of this description are the poors'-rate, the county-rate, the highway-rate, and the church-rate; the gross amount of these in England only being at this moment from 8,500,000*l.* to 9,000,000*l.* a-year! But to these have to be added the sums levied on account of tithe, tolls on highways, port and lighthouse dues, the rates and fines levied by municipal corporations, with a great variety of smaller rates. And if to the local burdens of England be added those of Scotland and Ireland, the aggregate sum will appear to be immense, and will not certainly be under 16 or 17 millions sterling!

There is an absolute deficiency of information with respect to the amount of several branches of local revenue; and the greatest discrepancy exists with respect to the mode in which it is assessed. But all the existing information with respect to the history and present state of local taxation in England and Wales has been collected with the most laudable care and industry, and ably digested, in the

Report of the Poor Law Commissioners on the Subject of Local Taxation. Folio and 8vo. 1843.

The appendixes to the Report, which contain summaries of the statute law relating to the different local taxes, have not been published in octavo.

Projet d'une Dixme Royale, qui, supprimant la Taille, les Aydes, et les Douanes d'une Province à l'autre, &c., produiroit au Roy un Revenu certain et suffisant, &c. Par M. le Maré-

CHAL de VAUBAN. 1 vol. 4to. Rouen, 1707; and frequently republished in 12mo.

This work is creditable alike to the heart and the head of its illustrious author. Though high in the favour of Louis XIV., he did not suffer his respect for his prince to efface his sense of the duty which he owed to his country. Boisguilbert had, in his work entitled 'Détail de la France,' published twelve years previously to the 'Dixme Royale,' exhibited a striking picture of the state to which the occupiers of the soil in most parts of the country were reduced by the inequality and oppressiveness of the system of taxation; and Vauban has fully corroborated his statements, and has added many additional details which set in the strongest light the miserable condition of the cultivators, from the increasing demands upon them occasioned by the enormous expense of the contests in which France had been so long engaged, and still more from the gross abuses in the assessment of the taille and other taxes. "Pour peu," says Vauban, "qu'on ait de connoissance de ce que se passe à la campagne, on comprend aisément que les tailles sont une des causes de ce mal, non qu'elles soient toujours et en tout temps trop grosses; mais parce qu'elles sont assises sans proportion, non seulement en gros de paroisse à paroisse, mais encore de particulier à particulier; en un mot, elles sont devenuës arbitraires, n'y ayant point de proportion du bien du particulier à la taille dont on le charge. Elles sont de plus exigées avec une extrême rigueur et de si grands frais, qu'il est certain qu'ils vont au moins à un quart du montant de la taille. Il est même assez ordinaire de pousser les exécutions jusqu'à dépendre les portes des maisons, après avoir vendu ce qui étoit dedans; et on en a vu démolir, pour en tirer les poutres, les solves, et les planches qui ont été venduës cinq ou six fois moins qu'elles ne valoient, en déduction de la taille.

"L'autorité des personnes puissantes et accréditées, fait souvent modérer l'imposition d'une ou de plusieurs paroisses, à des taxes bien au dessous de leur juste portée, dont la décharge doit conséquemment tomber sur d'autres voisines qui en sont surchargées; et c'est un mal invétéré auquel il n'est pas facile de remédier. Ces personnes puissantes sont payées de leur protection dans la suite, par la plus-valuë de leurs fermes, ou de celles de leurs parens ou amis, causée par l'exemption de leurs fermiers et de ceux qu'ils protègent, qui ne sont imposez à la taille que pour la forme seulement; car il est très-ordinaire devoir qu'une ferme de trois à quatre mil livres de revenu, ne sera quotisée qu'à quarante ou cinquante livres de taille, tandis qu'une autre de quatre à cinq cens livres en payera cent, et souvent plus; ce qui fait que les terres n'ont pas ordinairement la moitié de la culture dont elles ont besoin.

"Il en est de même de laboureur à laboureur, ou de païsan, le plus fort accable toujours le plus foible: et les choses sont réduites à un tel état, que celuy qui pourroit se servir du talent qu'il a de sçavoir faire quelqu'art ou quelque trafic, qui le mettroit luy et sa famille en état de pouvoir vivre un peu plus à son aise, aime mieux demeurer sans rien faire; et que celuy qui pourroit avoir une ou deux vaches, et quelques moutons ou brebis, plus ou moins, avec quoy il pourroit améliorer sa ferme ou sa terre, est obligé de s'en priver, pour n'être pas accablé de taille l'année suivante comme il ne manqueroit pas de l'être, s'il gagnoit quelque chose, et qu'on vît sa recolte un peu plus abondante qu'à l'ordinaire. C'est par cette raison qu'il vit non seulement très pauvrement luy et sa famille, et qu'il va presque tout nud, c'est-à-dire, qu'il ne fait que trèspeu de consommation; mais encore, qu'il laisse déperir le peu de terre qu'il a, en ne la travaillant qu'à demy, de peur que si elle rendoit ce qu'elle pourroit rendre étant bien fumée et cultivée, on n'en prît occasion de l'imposer doublement à la taille. Il est donc manifeste que la première cause de la diminution des biens de la campagne est le défaut de culture, et que ce défaut provient de la manière d'imposer les tailles, et de les lever."—(pp. 28-31, ed. 1708.)

To get rid of these and other monstrous abuses, and to subject the whole kingdom to the same equal tax, Vauban proposed that the taille and most other existing taxes should be suppressed, and that their place should be supplied by a royal tithe, consisting of one-twentieth part or 5 per cent. of the produce of the land, and of certain rates charged on those engaged in manufactures, trade, &c. It is unnecessary to enter into any details respecting this plan. When brought forward its enemies contended that it was impracticable, and in this, perhaps, they were right. The abuses in the system of taxation in France were, in truth, too deeply seated, and too much interwoven with the rights and privileges, not merely of individuals, but of great classes, to be got rid of otherwise than by a revolution. Vauban died in the same year that his tract appeared; and, but for this, it is probable it would have exposed him to a persecution from which his high character and eminent services would with difficulty have afforded him protection.

Histoire du Système des Finances sous la Minorité de Louis XV., pendant les Années 1719 et 1720. (Par M. Duverney.) 6 vol. post 8vo. La Haye (Paris), 1739.

"Cette histoire renferme les détails les plus curieux sur l'agiotage, et le personnel des agioteurs."—(Thiers, 'Encyc. Progressive.')

Réflexions Politiques sur les Finances et le Commerce. (Par M. Dutot.) 2 vol. post 8vo. La Haye (Paris), 1738. Republished, with a new title-page, La Haye, 1754.

"Ces Réflexions de Dutot sont incontestablement ce qu'il y a de plus profond sur le système de Law, et sur la cause de sa chute."—(Thiers.) But though this work displays great acuteness and ability, we doubt whether it gives as fair and able an exposition of the system as is given in the following work of Duverney. Dutot, like Thiers, was an apologist of the system.

Examen du Livre intitulé 'Réflexions Politiques sur les Finances et le Commerce.' (Par M. Duverney.) 2 vol. post 8vo. La Haye (Paris), 1740.

The Mississippi scheme, projected by the famous John Law, of Lauriston, had many points in common with the South Sea scheme, with which it was also coeval. It began by the establishment of a bank at Paris, the notes of which were payable on demand. But we doubt whether Law ever seriously contemplated abiding by this regulation, which was totally at variance with his views in relation to money. He held that things are valuable only according to the purposes they serve in society, and that it is indifferent whether notes or coins are employed to represent the value of land and other things. But it is needless to say that this statement, which was at the bottom of Law's schemes, involves two fundamental errors; things not being valuable according to the purposes they serve, but according to the cost of their production; and notes circulating only because it is believed they will be paid in coin when presented, or because they are made compulsory. In his work entitled 'Money and Trade Considered,' which appeared at Edinburgh in 1705, Law lays it down that "credit (or confidence) depends on the quantity of money in the country, and increases or decreases with it" (p. 70). A theory of this sort would, it is obvious, if acted upon, necessarily lead to over-issue, depreciation, and bankruptcy. But, as France had not been accustomed to credit, Law said it would be enough at the commencement of his project to double the amount of the currency, by adding to the specie in circulation an equal value in notes. But gold and silver in France being of the same value as in other countries, it might have been foreseen that the issue of the paper notes would force all the specie abroad; and that in the event of any additional notes being issued, there would be no means of exchanging them for coins, and the currency would be depreciated from excess. Inasmuch, however, as the paper which Law proposed to issue could not be thrown upon the market at once, but only by degrees as the public became habituated to its use, no depreciation took place in the first instance, the notes were paid when presented, and all parties were pleased by the facility with which loans and discounts were obtained. This apparent and temporary success of the bank led Law and the government to entertain the most extravagant notions of the purposes to which it might be made subservient, and made them engraft upon it the most gigantic trading and financial projects; and though these had no solid foundation, so great was the credulity and cupidity of the public, that the company's stock rose to an immense premium; and many, who had sagacity to sell out before the bubble burst, and to vest the produce in land, made vast fortunes. As might have been anticipated, the recoil was tremendous. It is, however, abundantly certain that, though the trading and financial projects referred to had never been heard of, the bank must have come to a stop. The principles on which it was avowedly conducted could not have failed to involve it in ruin.

The Scotch parliament had sagacity enough to reject Law's schemes; and but for the ruinous state to which the finances of France were then reduced, and the consequent anxiety of the regent and his ministers to grasp at any project, however extravagant, that promised to afford any relief, it is most probable that neither the bank nor the Mississippi scheme would ever have had any existence.

The public resentment against Law rose to such a height on the explosion of his schemes, that he was compelled, from regard to his personal safety, clandestinely to leave France. Whether it were from confidence in his projects, or from their having exploded sooner than he had expected, Law did not remit any part of the funds he might have realised to foreign countries, so that on leaving France he had but very slender means of support. He passed the latter part of his strangely chequered life in Venice, where he was visited by Montesquieu. He died in 1729, in the fifty-eighth year of his age. The following epitaph appeared soon after, in the Paris papers:—

> "Ci-gît cet Ecossois célèbre,
> Ce calculateur sans égal,
> Qui par les règles de l'algèbre
> A mis la France à l'Hôpital."

Duverney, the author of two of the works referred to above, besides being an able writer, was a skilful and successful practical financier. Having associated Voltaire with him in some of his speculations, he made a considerable fortune for his celebrated friend; and by relieving the latter from the necessities that so frequently accompany genius, enabled him to assert his independence, and to follow the pursuits most congenial to his taste.

M. Thiers has written an elaborate article on the Mississippi scheme in the *Encyclopédie Progressive* (1826); but, like Dutot, whom he has principally followed, he is too favourable to Law. We are inclined to think that the account of the scheme given by Storch, in his *Cours d'Economie Politique* (vol. iv. pp. 130-151, éd. de Paris), is, on the whole, the best that has hitherto appeared. The mere English reader will find, in the

'Memoirs of the Life of John Law, of Lauriston,' by J. P. Wood, Esq. (post 8vo., Edinburgh, 1824), a full, but not a very distinct or philosophical, view of the system.

RECHERCHES et CONSIDÉRATIONS sur les FINANCES de FRANCE, depuis 1595 jusqu'en 1721. (Par M. F. V. de FORBONNAIS.) 2 vol. 4to. Basle, 1758; et 6 vol. petit in-8vo., Liège, 1758.

The best work on the history of French finances. The author died in 1800, at the age of 78.

MÉMOIRES pour servir à l'HISTOIRE GÉNÉRALE des FINANCES. Par M. DEON de BEAUMONT. 2 vol. 12mo. Amsterdam, 1760.

LETTRES d'un CITOYEN à un MAGISTRAT sur les VINGTIÈMES et les autres IMPÔTS. 1 vol. 12mo. Amsterdam (Paris), 1768.

These letters were written by M. Le Trosne, one of the most decided of Quesnay's supporters.

THÉORIE de l'IMPÔT. (Par M. le MARQUIS de MIRABEAU.) 1 vol. 4to., et en 12mo. (Paris), 1760.

Conformable, in all respects, to the doctrines of Quesnay.

MÉMOIRE sur les EFFETS de l'IMPÔT INDIRECT, qui a remporté le Prix proposé par la Société Royale d'Agriculture de Limoges. (Par M. SAINT PERAVY.) 1 vol. 12mo. Paris, 1768.

Saint Peravy being a zealous disciple of Quesnay, this work is entirely founded on his principles, and is written to show the advantages which the author supposes would result from repealing the existing taxes, and imposing in their stead a single tax laid directly on the rent of the land. It is needless, perhaps, to say more of this project than that a tax on rent is, by obstructing improvements in agriculture, about the most inexpedient that can be imagined; that it would be grossly unjust to assess, were it practicable, the public burdens on a single class; and that, were it otherwise desirable, the scheme is impossible, inasmuch as there is hardly a country in Europe the rent of which, supposing it were wholly appropriated to the purpose, would suffice to defray the public expenditure.

ESSAI ANALYTIQUE sur la RICHESSE et sur l'IMPÔT. (Par M. GRASLIN.) 1 vol. 8vo. Londres (Paris), 1767.

This work, like that of Saint Peravy, was written for the prize offered by the Society of Limoges. The author is a decided opponent of the Economists; but though he happened to be right in his condemnation of their peculiar doctrines, he has not been able to produce any satisfactory reasons for such being the case. His book is not a bad specimen of the art of writing plausibly about a subject of which the writer knows little or nothing.

Mémoires concernant les Impositions et Droits en Europe. 1re éd. 4 vol. 4to. Paris, 1768; 2de éd., avec des Supplémens, 5 vol. 4to. Paris, 1787.

"This work was compiled (by M. Moreau de Beaumont) by order of the court for the use of a commission employed for some years past in considering the proper mode for reforming the finances of France. The account of the French taxes, which takes up 3 vols. 4to., may be regarded as perfectly authentic. That of those of other European nations was compiled from such information as the French ministers at the different courts could procure. It is much shorter (1 vol. 4to.), and probably not quite so exact as that of the French taxes."—(Wealth of Nations, p. 367.)

TRAITÉ de la CIRCULATION et du CRÉDIT. (Par M. PINTO, a Portuguese Jew established in Holland.) 1 vol. 8vo. Amsterdam, 1771.

This book contains much that is sound and ingenious, but it is now remembered only for the extravagance of its paradoxes; the leading proposition maintained by the author being that the national debt has been the principal source of the wealth and power of this country! But though a national debt brings with it some advantages, and is not the unmixed evil many have supposed, reasonings to prove that it is the chief source of national wealth are much too absurd to deserve notice; and are fit only, as Hume has stated, to rank with the panegyrics on folly and fever, on Busiris and Nero. But such as it is, this book excited when published a good deal of attention. It was translated into English by the Rev. S. Baggs, M.A., and published in 4to. with notes, London, 1774.

Besides the above, M. Pinto was the author of several other publications. He even entered the lists with Voltaire, against whom he undertook the defence of the Portuguese and Spanish Jews; and his treatise on this subject, published in 1762, is believed to have suggested to the Abbé Guéné the idea of his admirable and most successful work, the *Lettres de quelques Juifs à M. de Voltaire.* Pinto died in 1787.—(See 'Biog. Universelle,' art. Pinto, &c.)

De l'Administration des Finances de la France. Par M. NECKER. 3 vol. 8vo. Paris, 1784.

This work gives the only authentic account of the finances of France previously to the Revolution. Owing to the popularity of its author, and the peculiar circumstances of the country at the time when it was published, the Revolution having all but commenced, the demand for the work was so very great that 80,000 copies were sold in the course of a few days!

DES FINANCES de la RÉPUBLIQUE FRANÇAISE en l'AN IX. Par M. RAMEL. 8vo. Paris, An IX.

ESSAI sur l'ETAT ACTUEL de l'ADMINISTRATION des FINANCES et de la RICHESSE NATIONALE de la GRANDE BRETAGNE. Par M. GENTZ. 1 vol. 8vo. Hambourg, 1800.

An able and interesting work. It exhibits, however, more of the talent of a partisan than of a philosopher; the author being determined to see everything in the British system of finance *en couleur de rose.*

QUELLE INFLUENCE ont les DIVERSES ESPÈCES d'IMPÔTS sur la MORALITÉ. Par M. MONTHION. 1 vol. Paris, 1808.

DES IMPÔTS INDIRECTS et des DROITS de CONSOMMATION; ou, Essais sur l'Origine et le Système des Impositions Françaises, comparé avec celui d'Angleterre. Par M. d'AGOULT. 8vo. Paris, 1817.

NOTICE HISTORIQUE sur les FINANCES de la FRANCE, de l'An

1800 au 1er Avril, 1814. Par M. le Duc de Gaete. 8vo. Paris, 1818.

"Ce livre est certainement le plus intéressant à consulter sur les finances de l'Empire."—(Blanqui.)

Des Impôts et des Charges des Peuples en France. Par M. Boislandry. 1 vol. 8vo. Paris, 1824.

Etudes de Crédit Public et des Dettes Publiques. Par M. Dufresne St. Leon. 1 vol. 8vo. Paris, 1824.

"L'un des meilleurs ouvrages élémentaires que nous possédions sur la science pratique des finances. Il est écrit avec un talent du style et une netteté des vues bien rares dans ces sortes des matières. L'auteur avait été employé pendant long-temps dans les bureaux du trésor, et son livre est le fruit de sa haute expérience."—(Blanqui.)

Recherches sur l'Origine de l'Impôt en France. Par M. P. de Thou. 1 vol. 8vo. Paris, 1838.

Essai sur la Science des Finances. Par M. Gandillot. 1 vol. 8vo. Paris, 1840.

Système Financier de la France. Par M. le Marquis d'Audiffret. 2 vol. 8vo. Paris, 1840.

Histoire Financière de la France depuis l'Origine de la Monarchie jusqu'à l'Année 1828. Par M. Bresson. 2de éd., 2 vol. 8vo. Paris, 1843.

A rapid and superficial, but useful sketch.

Du Crédit Public et de son Histoire depuis les Temps anciens jusqu'à nos jours. Par M. Augier. 1 vol. 8vo. Paris, 1842.

Des Finances et du Crédit Public de l'Autriche, de sa Dette, de ses Ressources Financières, et de son Système d'Imposition, avec quelques rapprochemens entre ce pays, la Prusse, et la France. Par M. de Tegoborski, Conseiller Privé de sa Majesté l'Empereur de la Russie. 2 vol. 8vo. Paris, 1843.

A valuable work, comprising a large body of important information respecting the taxes, public debts, and financial systems of Austria and Prussia.

La Magia del Credito Svelata, Istituzione Fondamentale di Pubblica Utilita. Di Giuseppe de Welz. 2 vol. 4to. Napoli, 1824.

"M. de Welz est le premier économiste Italien qui ait arboré avec hardiesse le drapeau du crédit. Quoique ses idées à cet égard soient exagérées, au point de lui faire dire que le crédit multiplie réellement les capitaux, il n'en a pas moins rendu un véritable service à la science en appelant l'attention de ses concitoyens sur les avantages d'un système de circulation mieux entendu."—(Blanqui.) We doubt, however, whether the work have any merits sufficient to countervail the erroneous view which it gives of the nature and influence of credit. It is also excessively prolix, and might have been advantageously condensed into a very moderate-sized octavo volume.

DELLA STORIA delle FINANZE del REGNO di NAPOLI. Del Signor BIANCHINI. Ediz. 2da, 3 vol. 8vo. Napoli, 1839.

A work containing much information respecting a subject of which but little is known in this country.

Petri Burmanni, de Vectigalibus Populi Romani, Dissertatio. 1 vol. 4to. Leidæ, 1734.

TRAITÉ des FINANCES et de la FAUSSE MONNOIE des ROMAINS, &c. (Par M. CHASSIPOL.) 1 vol. 12mo. Paris, 1740.

This book, though so late in being printed, was written at the request of Colbert. It was translated into English, and published in 8vo., London, 1741, under the title of 'A Treatise on the Revenue and False Money of the Romans,' &c.

DE l'IMPÔT du VINGTIÈME sur les SUCCESSIONS, et de l'IMPÔT sur les MARCHANDISES chez les ROMAINS. Par M. BOUCHAUD. 1 vol. 8vo. Paris, 1766.

A prolix and ill-arranged, but at the same time learned and trustworthy work.

The best account of the taxes and finances of the Romans is to be found in the learned and excellent work of Dureau de la Malle, entitled *Economie Politique des Romains:* see *post*.

CHAPTER XX.

MISCELLANEOUS.

A Compendious or Briefe Examination of Certayne Ordinary Complaints of Divers of our Countrymen in these our Days; which, although they are in some part unjust and frivolous, yet they are all by way of Dialogues thoroughly debated and discussed. By W. S., Gentleman. 4to. London, 1587.

This tract has been ascribed to Shakespeare; but it has been fully shown that it was not written by him, but by William Stafford.—(Wood's 'Fasti,' 2nd ed. i. 208; see also Farmer, 'On the Learning of Shakespeare.') It contains some curious statements respecting the rise of prices that was then taking place (in consequence of the influx of gold and silver from America), and the increase of pasturage. The subject of enclosures is also discussed with considerable ability.

Bread for the Poor, and Advancement of the English Nation Promised by Enclosure of the Wastes and Common Grounds of England. By Adam Moore, Gent. 4to. London, 1653.

One of the earliest tracts in favour of the division and enclosure of commons and wastes. It is written with considerable talent. The beneficial influence of the measures which the author recommends is set in rather a striking light, and means suggested for carrying them into effect.

England's Improvement by Sea and Land: To Out-do the Dutch without Fighting, to Pay Debts without Moneys, &c. By Andrew Yarranton, Gent. 4to. London, 1677.

England's Improvement by Sea and Land, &c. By Andrew Yarranton, Gent. Part II. 4to. London, 1681.

These publications present a curious medley of practicable and useful, and of impracticable and useless, or pernicious, suggestions. Having been a good deal abroad, and made himself acquainted with the policy of the Dutch, Yarranton strongly recommends the institution of a registry of lands and houses, which no doubt would be of the greatest advantage. He also recommends the establishment of public granaries, or corn-banks; the improvement of rivers and internal navigation; the improvement of the fisheries and of the iron and linen trades; and having shown, as he believes, the great detriment occasioned by the importation of calicoes and other Indian manufactures, he recommends their exclusion, and so forth.

An Apology for the Builder; or, a Discourse showing the

Cause and Effects of the Increase of Building. 4to. London, 1685.

A well-written, well-reasoned tract, showing the futility of the complaints that were then common of the bad consequences resulting from the continued increase of London and other great towns.

The State of the Nation, in respect to her Commerce, Debts, and Money. (By ERASMUS PHILIPS, Esq.) 2nd edition, with Additions. 8vo. London, 1726.

This is a very superior tract. Mr. Philips shows, in opposition to the statements current at the time, both in and out of parliament, that the wealth of England was then (1726) greater, and her commerce and manufactures more extensive, than at any former period. At the same time he shows how they might be augmented and improved; and he has the courage and good sense to express himself strongly in favour of a more liberal policy in regard to the trade with France, and regrets the rejection (in consequence of the stupid prejudices entertained by the public) of the commercial treaty negociated with that power in 1713. (See *ante*, p. 142.) The following brief paragraph is not surpassed by anything in Smith or Ricardo:—"A trading nation," says Mr. Philips, "should be an open warehouse, where the merchant may either buy what he pleases, or sell what he can. Whatever is brought to you, if you want it not, you will not purchase it: if you do want it, the largeness of the impost will not keep it from you."—(p. 14.) Mr. Philips estimated the land rental of England in 1726 at about 20,000,000*l.*

HUSBANDRY and TRADE IMPROVED; being a Collection of many valuable Materials relating to Corn, Cattle, Coal, Hops, Wool, &c. By JOHN HOUGHTON, F.R.S., &c. 2nd ed. 4 vols. 8vo. London, 1728.

These papers, which originally appeared at different periods between 1680 and 1695, contain a great variety of curious particulars and discussions.

THE POLITICAL and COMMERCIAL WORKS of CHARLES DAVENANT, LL.D. Collected and revised by Sir CHARLES WHITWORTH, M.P. 5 vols. 8vo. London, 1771.

The commercial and financial writings of Dr. Davenant, Inspector-General of Imports and Exports in the reign of Queen Anne, were published in the interval between 1695 and 1712. Though a partisan of the mercantile system, Davenant was free from some of the prejudices of its more indiscriminate and zealous supporters. He considers a "watchful attention to the balance of trade, and its right government," as of the greatest importance; but he does not consider wealth as consisting wholly of gold and silver, or that prohibitions and restrictions should be rashly imposed, even on the intercourse with those countries with which the balance is supposed to be unfavourable. There seem, however, to be but slender grounds for the eulogies bestowed on his writings, or for thinking that they at all accelerated the progress of sound commercial knowledge. They contain little that is valuable that may not be found in the work of Sir Josiah Child. Some detached paragraphs are exceedingly good; but the treatises of which they form parts are remarkably inconclusive, and are for the most part pervaded by the narrowest and most illiberal views. There is no evidence to show that Davenant had ever reflected on the influence of commerce in facilitating the production of wealth, by its enabling the division of labour to be carried to the farthest extent;

that is, by its enabling the people of different countries to apply themselves, in preference, to those employments for the prosecution of which they have some natural or acquired advantage.

THE FABLE of the BEES; or, Private Vices Public Benefits. By BERNARD DE MANDEVILLE, M.D.

The little poem entitled the 'Grumbling Hive, or Knaves turned Honest,' which is the foundation of this work, was published in 1714. Mandeville afterwards republished this poem, with lengthened notes, or dissertations, in 1723, under the title of 'The Fable of the Bees.' He subsequently added to it an Essay on Charity and Charity-Schools, and a Search into the Nature of Society. It was published complete with the latter. 2 vols. 8vo. London, 1732.

Though licentious and in many respects objectionable, there are a great number of valuable remarks and of just and profound observations in this work, especially with reference to the improvement of arts and the increase of wealth. Mandeville, indeed, by way of establishing his leading doctrine, that "private vices are public benefits," has represented sundry passions and desires as vicious which do not deserve any such character. Thus, the desire to rise in the world, to enjoy an increased command over necessaries and luxuries, and to attain to distinction, is said by him to be a vice: but it would be more correct to call it a cardinal virtue. So long as it is pursued by fair and proper means, and without injury or prejudice to the rights and interests of others, it is worthy of every commendation; and is, in fact, the prolific source of wealth, science, and civilization. Luxury and ostentation is also one of the vices on which Mandeville lays the greatest stress, as contributing to national opulence. But luxury is a most ambiguous term, and it is very difficult to say when it is or is not censurable. The use of coaches and claret by a man of good fortune may be as proper and judicious as the use of street cabs and small-beer by another. If there be anything blameable in the matter, it is not in the consumption of certain articles more than others, but in the consumption of articles which the consumers are unable to afford; and even in this case the wish to enjoy such articles may be so powerful a motive to increased industry and economy in other things, that the consumption may, taking all considerations into account, be not unobjectionable merely, but advantageous.

But however incorrect his classification of virtues and vices, and however lax his morality, his book contains a great many paragraphs that strikingly illustrate the progress of society, and may, therefore, be advantageously referred to by the political economist. The famous passage in the first chapter of the 'Wealth of Nations' on the extraordinary combination of art, industry, and ingenuity required to furnish the woollen coat and other accommodations of the poorest labourer in England, may perhaps have been suggested by the following paragraph of Mandeville:—

"What a bustle is there to be made in several parts of the world, before a fine scarlet or crimson cloth can be produced; what multiplicity of trades and artificers must be employed! Not only such as are obvious, as wool-combers, spinners, the weaver, the cloth-worker, the scourer, the dyer, the setter, the drawer, and the packer; but others that are more remote, and might seem foreign to it,—as the mill-wright, the pewterer, and the chymist, which yet are all necessary, as well as a great number of other handicrafts, to have the tools, utensils, and other implements belonging to the trades already named. But all these things are done at home, and may be performed without extraordinary fatigue or danger; the most frightful prospect is left behind, when we reflect on the toil and hazard that are to be undergone abroad, the vast seas we are to go over, the different climates we are to endure, and the several nations we must be obliged to for their assistance. Spain alone, it is true, might furnish us with wool to make the finest cloth; but what skill and pains, what experience and ingenuity are required to dye it of those beautiful colours! How widely are the drugs and other ingredients dispersed thro' the universe that are to meet in one kettle! Allum, indeed, we have of our own; argol we might have from the Rhine, and vitriol from Hungary; all this is in Europe; but then for saltpetre, in quantity, we are forced to go as far as the East Indies. Cochenille, unknown to the ancients, is not much nearer to us, tho' in a quite different part of the earth: we buy it, 'tis true, from the Spaniards; but, not being their product, they are forced to fetch it for us from the remotest corner of the new world in the West Indies. While so many sailors are broiling in the sun, and sweltered with heat in the East and West of us, another set of them are freezing in the North to fetch potashes from Russia."—(i. 411.)

A Collection of Tracts concerning the Present State of Ireland, with respect to its Riches, Revenue, Trade, and Manufactures. 8vo. London, 1729.

An Apology for the Business of Pawnbroking. By a Pawnbroker. 8vo. London, 1744.

A remarkably acute and able, though not, perhaps, an unanswerable pamphlet.

The True Interest and Political Maxims of the Republic of Holland. By John de Witt. Translated from the Original Dutch, with Memoirs of Cornelius and John de Witt, by John Campbell, Esq. (Dr. Campbell). 1 vol. 8vo. London, 1746.

We have been assured by an eminent Dutch professor that the commonly received opinion of this work having been written by John de Witt is incorrect; and that its real author was M. Delacourt, an intimate friend of De Witt, and the author of other political works. It was originally published in 1667, in Dutch, in 4to.—(Communication from M. Ackersdyck of Utrecht.)

A Miscellany containing several Tracts on various Subjects. By the Bishop of Cloyne (Dr. Berkeley). 8vo. London, 1752.

This miscellany contains the 'Querist,' which, however, was originally published in 1735. The queries, some of which are of the most searching description, are brief and precise, and strikingly illustrate the advantages of industry and economy. They involve, however, sundry grave errors. Of these the most prominent, perhaps, is the notion that wealth may be increased by the aid of sumptuary laws, and the proscribing of luxurious accommodations. An edition of the 'Querist,' with notes, was published in 8vo., London, 1829.

The Present State of the Nation: particularly with respect to its Trade, Finances, &c. (By the Right Hon. George Grenville.) 8vo. London, 1769.

Observations on a late 'State of the Nation.' (By the Right Hon. Edmund Burke.) 8vo. London, 1769, and in Mr. Burke's Works.

An Appendix to 'The Present State of the Nation,' containing a REPLY to the 'OBSERVATIONS' on that Pamphlet. (By Mr. GRENVILLE.) 8vo. London, 1769.

These tracts, but more especially the second, are eminently worthy of perusal. Mr. Grenville takes in his first tract a very gloomy and unfavourable view of the situation of public affairs at the peace of Paris in 1763, and during the next half-dozen years, representing the country as suffering from an oppressive load of taxes, her commerce declining, her control over the American colonies shaken by the injudicious repeal of the Stamp Act, and the government rendered feeble and inefficient through the prevalence of faction and party. But it is not going too far to say that there is scarcely one of Mr. Grenville's positions, except the last, which Mr. Burke has not completely overthrown. His tract is indeed one of the very best specimens of a review that has ever been published, displaying all his deep thinking, with much of his eloquence and sarcasm. Mr. Burke argues strongly against the attempt to tax the American colonies, and vindicates the conduct of the administration which repealed the Stamp Act of which Mr. Grenville was the author.

But if we could neither tax the colonies nor control their trade, it is plain our ascendancy over them was nominal merely, and could be productive of nothing save a heavy expense to this country. It was visionary indeed to imagine that a great nation, rapidly advancing in wealth and population, on the other side of the Atlantic, should continue to submit to receive governors from England, and to be legislated for by the parliament of Great Britain. The attempt to tax America merely hastened a crisis that could not by any possibility have been long averted. There was, in fact, no practicable middle course between the coercive system of Grenville and the unconditional emancipation of Tucker. The half-conciliatory and half-threatening policy of Lords Rockingham and Chatham was vague enough to bind them to nothing, and left them at liberty to assail any measure that might be proposed by the friends or the opponents of colonial independence; but it was good for nothing else. And it may well excite surprise that a person of Mr. Burke's penetration should not have appreciated the real nature of the differences with the colonies, and have seen the folly of attempting to obviate them otherwise than by enforcing their submission, or by acknowledging their independence.

FOUR LETTERS to the EARL of CARLISLE, from WILLIAM EDEN, Esq. (afterwards Lord Auckland). The third edition, to which is added a Fifth Letter. 1 vol. 8vo. London, 1780.

A respectable though feeble publication. It contains some judicious remarks respecting the influence of different descriptions of taxes.

LETTERS on CREDIT. The second edition, with a Postscript, and a Short Account of the Bank at Amsterdam. By JOHN HOPE, Esq. 8vo. London, 1784.

This publication is of very little value; but as the subject of which it treats, though of great importance, is much misunderstood, we shall take this opportunity to submit a few observations with respect to it.

By credit is meant the trust or confidence placed by individuals in others when they lend money or other property, or when they sell goods without stipulating for their immediate payment. And, consistently with this definition, it follows that all the advantages, and the extensive and complicated operations originating in or depending upon credit, resolve themselves into a change in the holders of property, or in the property of the lenders, or of those who give credit, coming into the hands of their debtors, or of those who borrow or receive credit. Nothing, indeed, is more common than to hear it stated that commodities are produced, and the most expensive undertakings completed, by means of credit or confidence; but this is an obvious mistake. Wealth cannot be produced, nor can any sort of industrious enterprise be entered upon, or carried on, without the aid of labour and capital; and all that credit does, or can do, is, by facilitating the transfer of capital from one set of individuals to another, to bring it into the hands of those who, it is probable, from their wishing to borrow, may be able to employ it to greater advantage.

The following extract from the evidence of Mr. Ricardo, before the Committee appointed by the House of Lords in 1819, to inquire into the expediency of the resumption of cash payments by the Bank of England, sets the nature of credit, and the distinction between it and capital, in a very clear point of view:—

"Do you not know," Mr. Ricardo was asked, "that when there is a great demand for manufactures, the very credit which that circumstance creates enables the manufacturer to make a more extended use of his capital in the production of manufactures?" To this Mr. Ricardo answered, "I have no notion of credit being at all effectual in the production of commodities; commodities can only be produced by labour, machinery, and raw materials; and if these are to be employed in one place, they must necessarily be withdrawn from another. Credit is the means, which is alternately transferred from one to another, to make use of capital actually existing; it does not create capital; it determines only by whom that capital shall be employed: the removal of capital from one employment to another may often be very advantageous, and it may also be very injurious."

Mr. Ricardo was then asked, "May not a man get credit from a bank on the security of his capital which is profitably employed, whether vested in stock or land; and may he not, by means of that credit, purchase or create an additional quantity of machinery and raw materials, and pay an additional number of labourers, without dislodging capital from any existing employment in the country?" To this Mr. Ricardo answered, "Impossible! an individual can purchase machinery, &c., with credit; he can never create them. If he purchase, it is always of some one else; and, consequently, he displaces some other from the employment of capital."—(Report, p. 192.)

A History of Inventions and Discoveries. Translated from the German of BECKMANN. By WILLIAM JOHNSTON. 4 vols. 8vo. London, 1797–1814.

This work is the result of the most extensive, varied, and profound research and learning. It exhibits the origin and traces the progress of a great number of useful arts, practices, and institutions. "Beckmann en cherche le premier germe jusque dans les temps les plus reculés de l'antiquité; il en suit le développement à travers les ténèbres du moyen âge, et en montre le perfectionnement chez les nations civilisées de l'Europe moderne, avec une patience et une érudition qui ne peuvent être égalées que par la sagacité et la variété des connaissances déployées dans ses recherches."—(Biog. Universelle.)

EIGHT LETTERS on the PEACE, and on the COMMERCE and MANUFACTURES of GREAT BRITAIN. By Sir F. M. EDEN, Bart. (author of the work on the Poor). 8vo. London, 1802.

On the Policy and Expediency of Granting Insurance Charters. 8vo. London, 1806.

This able tract, which should have been noticed in a previous chapter (10th), was also written by Sir F. M. Eden. The arguments to show the expediency of granting charters to insurance companies are quite conclusive, and their validity is now universally admitted. There is, from page 69 to page 83, an estimate of the amount of insurable property in the kingdom, the fruit of very extensive and laborious research.

Aristotle's Ethics and Politics, comprising his Practical Philosophy. Translated from the Greek, &c. By JOHN GILLIES, LL.D., &c. 3rd ed. 2 vols. 8vo. London, 1813.

Aristotle's treatise on politics is the most valuable work on that branch of philosophy that has descended to us from antiquity. The version of it given in this work is sufficiently close to make the reader acquainted with all that is really valuable in the original. The translation into French by Thurot (see *post*) is said to be well executed.

THE PAST, PRESENT, and probably the FUTURE STATE of the WINE TRADE, &c. By JAMES WARRE. 2nd ed. 8vo. London, 1824.

AN HISTORICAL INQUIRY into the PRODUCTION and CONSUMPTION of the PRECIOUS METALS. By WILLIAM JACOB, Esq., F.R.S. 2 vols. 8vo. London, 1831.

Though, perhaps, the best on the subject, this work is very defective. It was reviewed, and some of its deficiencies pointed out, in the 55th volume of the 'Edinburgh Review.'

The Public Economy of Athens; to which is added, a Dissertation on the Silver Mines of Laurion. From the German of BOECKH, by G. C. LEWIS, Esq. 1st ed. 2 vols. 8vo. London, 1828; 2nd ed. 1 vol. 8vo. London, 1842.

A work of great research and value. Had the author's knowledge of modern science borne any proportion to his knowledge of antiquity, the book would have been all that could have been desired.

THE AGE of GREAT CITIES; or, Modern Society viewed in Relation to Intelligence, Morals, and Religion. By ROBERT VAUGHAN, D.D. 1 vol. 8vo. London, 1843.

The clear and comprehensive account given by Seneca (which Dr. Vaughan has not referred to), of the motives which drew so great a concourse of people to Imperial Rome, applies, without the alteration of a syllable, to London:—"*Aspice agedum hanc frequentiam, cui vix urbis immensæ tecta sufficiunt. Ex municipiis et coloniis suis, ex toto denique orbe terrarum confluxerunt. Alios adducit ambitio, alios necessitas officii publici, alios imposita legatio, alios luxuria, opulentum et opportunum vitiis locum quærens; alios liberalium studiorum cupiditas, alios spectacula; quosdam traxit amicitia, quosdam industria, latam ostendendæ virtuti nacta materiam: quidam vænalem formam attulerunt, quidam vænalem eloquentiam. Nullum non hominum genus concurrit in urbem, et virtutibus et vitiis magna præmia ponentem.*"—(Consolat. ad Helviam, cap. 6.)

De l'Esprit des Loix. Par M. de MONTESQUIEU.

The first edition of this immortal work appeared at Geneva, in 2 vols. 4to. (without a date), in 1748. There have since been innumerable editions, of which the best are said to be those in the 'Œuvres de Montesquieu,' 6 vol. 8vo., Paris, 1816; and 8 vol. 8vo., Paris, 1819.

The great and distinguishing merits of the 'Spirit of Laws' are least obvious perhaps in those parts that refer to economical subjects. Montesquieu does justice to the humanising influence of commerce; but he appears to have been so far influenced by the theories of the ancient philosophers as to regard the indefinite accumulation of wealth, and the increase of refinement and luxury, as unfavourable to morality, and to simplicity and elevation of character. The history of society affords, however, a conclusive refutation of such opinions, by showing that wherever countries are enriched by industry and commerce, their manners and morals have been equally softened and improved, at the same time that the manly and martial virtues of the people, and their love of independence, appear to gather new strength and vigour with every increase of their riches. The examples of the Tyrians and Athenians in antiquity, and of the Dutch and English in modern times, seem to be conclusive as respects the truth of what has now been stated.

In accordance with his usual respect for authority in matters of fact, Montesquieu defers more, in treating of commerce, to what is than to what ought to be. It must also be admitted that he has no fixed or well-defined opinions with respect to the real sources of national wealth and the influence of trade. On this subject, indeed, his observations are in an extraordinary degree without sequence or connexion, and wholly fail of establishing any practical conclusion. He is so far subjugated by the spirit of the time as to entitle one of his chapters (liv. xx. c. 23) '*A quelles Nations il est Désavantageux de faire le Commerce.*'

Montesquieu expresses himself as follows, with respect to the circumstances which determine the progress of population:—"Partout où il se trouve une place où deux personnes peuvent vivre commodément, il se fait un mariage. La nature y porte assez lorsqu'elle n'est point arrêtée par la difficulté de subsistance. Les peuples naissants se multiplient et croissent beaucoup. Ce seroit chez eux une grande incommodité de vivre dans le célibat; ce n'en est point une d'avoir beaucoup d'enfants. Le contraire arrive lorsque la nation est formée. * * * Mais les gens qui ne sont pauvres que parcequ'ils vivent dans un gouvernement dur, qui regardent leur champ moins comme le fondement de leur subsistance que comme un prétexte à la vexation; ces gens-là, dis-je, font peu d'enfants—ils non pas même leur nourriture; comment pourroient-ils songer à la partager? Ils ne peuvent se soigner dans leurs maladies; comment pourroient-ils élever des créatures qui sont dans une maladie continuelle, qui est l'enfance?"—(Liv. xxiii. caps. 10, 11.)

It is singular, considering the soundness of these observations, that Montesquieu should have supposed that the amount of population could be sensibly influenced by the premiums and advantages that have sometimes been given to those who rear the greatest number of children, or that he should have concluded that population had declined in modern times. Had he seen Hume's essay on this subject, he would no doubt have been of a different opinion.

The chapter on taxation, though desultory in the extreme, and of no value in a scientific point of view, contains many profound as well as ingenious remarks; and contributed powerfully to open the eyes of the people and government of France and other continental states to the nature and disastrous influence of various taxes.

But whatever, either in these or other matters, may be its defects, the 'Esprit des Loix' is one of the noblest monuments of genius; and has had a more powerful and beneficial influence over public opinion than any work of last century, the 'Wealth of Nations' only excepted. Its illustrious author died in 1755, in the 66th year of his age. The following notice of this event, from the pen of the Earl of Chesterfield, with whom he had long been in habits of intimacy, appeared soon after in the 'London Evening Post:'—

"On the 10th of this month (February, 1755) died at Paris, Charles de Secondat, Baron de Montesquieu, and président-à-mortier of the parliament of Bordeaux. His virtues did honour to human nature—his writings to justice. A friend to mankind, he asserted their undoubted and inalienable rights with freedom, even in his own country, whose prejudices in matters of religion and government he had long lamented, and endeavoured (not without some success) to remove. He well knew and justly admired the happy constitution of this country, where fixed and known laws equally restrain monarchy from tyranny, and liberty from licentiousness. His works will illustrate his name, and survive him as long as right reason, moral obligations, and the true spirit of laws, shall be understood, respected, and maintained."

The 'Spirit of Laws' has been made the subject of numerous commentaries, of which the best by far is the

COMMENTAIRE sur l'ESPRIT des LOIX de MONTESQUIEU, suivi, &c. 1 vol. 8vo. Paris, 1811.

This work, by M. Destutt Tracy, is written with great clearness, vigour, and talent. It is not so much a commentary on the 'Spirit of Laws' as a complete and independent work on the same subjects. Perhaps, in some parts, justice is not done to Montesquieu. His merits cannot be fairly estimated without taking his position into view, and the state of political science and information in France, and Europe generally, at the time when he gave his speculations to the world. Those who do this will see how greatly he was in advance of the age, and will cease to wonder at the extraordinary influence of his work.

Puffendorff, Vattel, Burlamaqui, and most writers on the law of nature and nations, enter at considerable length into disquisitions with respect to the right of property, the regulation of commerce, the coinage of money, and other topics more or less connected with this science. But it appears to be unnecessary to refer particularly to their speculations on these subjects; for the most part, indeed, they are not distinguished by any peculiar novelty or vigour.

The Baron de Bielfeld has, in his 'Institutions Politiques,' 3 vol. 4to. La Haye, 1760-62 (frequently reprinted), sundry chapters on trade, manufactures, finance, &c. His speculations are mostly, however, of a commonplace character, and are rather what might be expected from an intelligent and liberal public officer than from a philosopher. The twelfth chapter of his first volume, 'Continuation des Finances,' is one of the best. Bielfeld is decidedly hostile to all partial, unequal, and arbitrary methods of taxation; and his maxims with regard to taxes will bear a comparison even with those of Smith, with which indeed they appear to have something more than an accidental resemblance. "Les contributions," says he, "doivent avoir trois propriétés—1. Une égalité proportionnelle, c'est-à-dire, que tous les citoyens, et s'il est même possible les etrangers qui se trouvent dans l'état, concourrent, chacun selon ses facultés et ses richesses, à la payer. 2. Que le payement cause au citoyen le moins de distraction qu'il est possible, et qu'on lui évite toutes sortes des vexations à ce sujet. 3. Que chaque contribuable puisse acquitter sa quote part de la manière qui lui est la plus commode, dans le tems qu'il est le mieux en état de payer. Tout est réductible à ces trois principes."—(i. 215.)

The fourteenth chapter of his second volume, 'Des Calculs Politiques,' is also deserving of notice. It comprises a history and a statement of the principles and uses of political arithmetic. Bielfeld was well acquainted with the works of Graunt, Petty, Davenant, &c., as well as with those of the French and German writers in this department. He gives, in the course of this essay, a statement, arranged in parallel columns, of the circumstances which tend to increase, and of those which tend to diminish population; and except in the erroneous view he takes of the influence of emigration, and perhaps also of foundling hospitals, this statement leaves little to be added or desired.

Bielfeld died in 1770, in the fifty-fourth year of his age. An account of his life, and a lengthened analysis of the 'Institutions Politiques,' are given by Robinet in his 'Dictionnaire d'un Homme d'Etat,' viii. 243-293.

La Noblesse Commerçante. 8vo. Paris, 1756.

This brochure was written by the Abbé Coyer, author of the 'Life of John Sobieski, King of Poland.' It has been severely but ably animadverted upon by Grimm (see his 'Correspondance,' i. 486).

De la Félicité Publique; ou, Considérations sur le Sort des Hommes dans les Différentes Epoques de l'Histoire. Par le Marquis de Chastellux. 1re éd. 1 vol. 8vo. Amsterdam, 1772. Nouvelle édition, avec un Notice de la Vie de l'Auteur, 2 vol. 8vo. Paris, 1822.

This ingenious work was highly praised by Voltaire. It is a conclusive answer to the paradoxes and spurious philosophy of the Abbé Mably and other real or pretended admirers of antiquity, rusticity, and poverty. "L'auteur s'y est proposé de prouver par l'histoire, que le sort du genre humain s'est amélioré à mesure que les lumières se sont étendues, et que le bonheur général s'accroîtra à mesure qu'elles s'augmenteront. Des recherches profondes, des connaissances variées, des vues ingénieuses se réunissent à l'appui de cette importante vérité." —(Biog. Universelle.)

Œuvres de M. Turgot, Ministre d'Etat, précédées et accompagnées de Mémoires et de Notes sur sa Vie, son Administration, et ses Ouvrages. (Par M. Dupont de Nemours.) 9 vol. 8vo. Paris, 1811.

It is truly stated by M. Say, that the publication of this edition of the works of Turgot was the most important service rendered by Dupont to the science. Turgot's economical writings are extremely valuable, not merely for the depth and general soundness of his views, but for the skill with which he applies them to the resolution of many complex and difficult practical questions. Most of them, indeed, grew out of his proceedings as Intendant of Limoges, and Comptroller-General of Finance. He was appointed to this important situation on the 24th of August, 1774, amid the plaudits of the philosophical party and the ardent hopes of all who were really anxious for a reform of the many abuses under which the country laboured. These, however, were too deeply seated, and were identified with too many and too powerful interests, to be subverted otherwise than by a Revolution. And despite his extensive knowledge, his unquestionable integrity, and his devotion to the public interests, Turgot wanted the tact and address necessary to conciliate those around him, which was indispensable alike to his continuance in power and to the success of his schemes. He trusted too much to the goodness of his measures and the rectitude of his intentions. Had he attempted less, and introduced his projects with greater *ménagement*, the chances are he would have accomplished more. He did not hold office for quite two years, having been dismissed in May, 1776. He was carried off by an attack of gout in 1781, in the

54th year of his age. A new edition of his works has recently been published at Paris in 2 vols. large 8vo., making a part of the collection of the principal economists.

Turgot's principal work, the *Réflexions sur la Formation et la Distribution des Richesses*, was translated into English, and published in 8vo., London, 1793.

La Morale et la Politique d'Aristote. Traduites du Grec par M. Thurot. 2 vol. 8vo. Paris, 1824.

De l'Esprit d'Association dans tous les Intérêts de la Communauté. Par M. le Comte de la Laborde. 3me éd. 1 vol. 8vo. Paris, 1834.

Considérations sur les Causes de la Grandeur et de la Décadence de la Monarchie Espagnole. Par M. Sempéré. 2 vol. petit in-8vo. Paris, 1826.

Economie Politique des Romains. Par M. Dureau de la Malle. 2 vol. 8vo. Paris, 1841.

A work of very great merit, distinguished alike by its learning, critical sagacity, and the variety and interest of its researches.

We beg to subjoin, from the 'Geographical Dictionary,' the following observations on the population of ancient Rome, principally founded on this work :—

"It is extremely difficult to arrive at any just conclusions with respect either to the population of Rome, or of any other of the great cities of antiquity. Generally it has been exceedingly exaggerated. The great actions of the Romans, the vast extent of their empire, and the magnificence and splendour of their capital, the original seat of their power, seem naturally enough to lead to the conclusion that its population must have been immense. The strong national spirit of the Roman writers led even the most cautious among them to magnify the power and importance of the eternal city, which were exaggerated beyond all bounds by orators and poets, anxious to gain the favour of the public by flattering their prejudices, and exalting their power and greatness. The statements, too, of the classical writers respecting the population of Rome and other great towns are not only in themselves very vague, but, being extremely liable to mistakes in copying, have no doubt in many instances been magnified by copyists and others, always prone to exaggerate what is really great, and of which they have no distinct knowledge. And in addition to this, all inquiries into the population of Rome, Athens, and other ancient cities, are rendered peculiarly difficult from the circumstance of the returns of the censuses, and the statements in the classical authorities founded on them, usually or always referring to such free citizens only as were capable of bearing arms, without including children or slaves, though the latter formed in most instances a large, if not the largest portion of the population. Our limits will not, however, permit of our entering into any detailed examination of the various statements that have been put forth with respect to the population of Rome. The exaggerations of Vossius, Lipsius, Châteaubriant, and others, who gave to imperial Rome fourteen, five, and three millions of inhabitants, are too absurd to deserve notice. Hume, who, in his masterly *Essay on the Populousness of Ancient Nations*, has discussed the question of the population of Rome with his usual learning and good sense, arrives at the conclusion that Rome, when in the zenith of her greatness, might have been as populous as London in 1760; in other words, that she might then have had from

700,000 to 800,000 inhabitants. Gibbon estimated the population at 1,200,000 (v. 286, 8vo. ed.); but it would appear that the more moderate estimate of Hume is the more accurate, though the probability be that even it is beyond the mark. It appears from the very learned and elaborate researches of M. Dureau de la Malle (Economie Politique des Romains, liv. ii. cap. 10), that the area of Rome included within the walls of Aurelian, which have been traced and laid down with the utmost precision, amounts to very near 1396½ hectares, being about three-fifths the area of Paris: and the fair presumption is, from the numerous forums, and other open spaces in Rome, the number of public buildings, and the great magnitude of many of the private residences, that its population, as compared with that of Paris, would be in a still less proportion. To the population within the walls has, however, to be added that of the suburbs, the amount of which is the subject of elaborate inquiry by the same learned critic. On the whole, he concludes, apparently on good grounds, that the population of imperial Rome, including its suburbs, in its most flourishing period, may be fairly estimated, allowing for troops and strangers, at between 560,000 and 570,000 (i. 403). And although we would not be understood as agreeing with M. Dureau de la Malle in all his statements, we have no doubt of their general accuracy, and of his estimate coming very near the mark. And, in fact, how small soever it may appear when contrasted with the statements that have been long current as to its vast magnitude, a population of 600,000 is really immense for a city like Rome, without either manufactures or trade, and the inhabitants of which chiefly depended for subsistence on the gratuitous distribution of the corn supplied by the conquered provinces."

M. Dureau de la Malle is also the author of a learned and valuable work, entitled

RECHERCHES sur la TOPOGRAPHIE de CARTHAGE. 1 vol. 8vo. Paris, 1838.

In this work he shows that the population of Carthage, which had been said by Strabo to amount to 700,000 persons, could not exceed 200,000 or at most 250,000, including slaves.—(p. 38, &c.)

Discurso sobre el Fomento de la Industria Popular. 8vo. Madrid, 1774.

Discurso sobre la Educacion Popular de los Artesanos, y su Fomento. 1 vol. 8vo. Madrid, 1775.

Appendice a la Educacion Popular. 4 vol. 8vo. Madrid, 1775—1777.

Count Campomanes, the author and editor of these works, was one of the most intelligent and distinguished Spanish statesmen of last century. He published the two discourses, now referred to, by direction of the Council of Castile, of which he was the fiscal advocate, or attorney-general, previously to his being made minister of state. They are intended to show the dignity and importance of arts and manufactures; the patronage to which they are entitled; the drawbacks under which they laboured in Spain from corporation privileges and vicious taxes and regulations; and the many advantages that would result from the systematic and judicious training of those engaged in them. The appendix to the 'Educacion Popular' consists principally of a collection of memoirs by different authors, on various matters connected with the domestic economy of Spain, illustrative partly of the former state of industry in the kingdom, and partly of the causes of its backwardness, and of the means by which it might be improved. These are accompanied with learned notes and introductions by Campomanes.

"Almost every point of importance," says Robertson, "with respect to interior police, taxation, agriculture, manufactures, and trade domestic as well as foreign, is examined in the course of these works; and there are not many authors, even in the nations most eminent for commercial knowledge, who have carried on their inquiries with a more thorough knowledge of their various subjects, and a more perfect freedom from vulgar and national prejudices, or who have united more happily the calm researches of philosophy with the ardent zeal of a public-spirited citizen."—(America, iii. 421, 8vo. ed.)

But, while we agree in the greater part of this eulogium, it is at the same time right to state that while Campomanes denounces many gross and scandalous abuses, he supports the vicious policy of encouraging home manufactures by prohibiting those of foreign countries; and, consequently, has lent the weight of his authority to the principle of those oppressive tariffs which have filled Spain with smugglers, and have ruined her industry and trade.

"El comercio Español," says he, "está obligado, conformandose á un espiritu patriotico, y constante en los principios, á valerse con preferencia de las manufacturas nacionales; y á promoverlas eficazmente. Con mayor razon, debe observar las leyes, promulgadas á beneficio de las artes y oficios, que se hallan establecidos en el reyno, ó que se vayan perfeccionando, ó plantificando de nuevo.

"Si quebranta la execucion de estas leyes el comerciante, con introducciones contrarias á este systema patriotico, debe suffrir la confiscacion, y demás penas, que contienen nuestras leyes.

"Toda nacion tiene obligacion de cuidar su propria prosperidad, y contener debidamente á los que la impiden. Hartos objetos de comercio se presentan, sin adoptar los que sean esencialmente ruinosos á los officios." (Discurso sobre la Educacion Popular, p. 389.) This is a different philosophy, certainly, from that of Smith and Quesnay.

Exclusive of the above, and of the learned and excellent treatise on Carthage, previously referred to (see p. 154), Campomanes was the author of several other works, all of which had the promotion of the public good for their object. After his retreat, or rather dismissal, from the ministry, he lived in dignified retirement, till his demise in the early part of this century. Mr. Townsend speaks in high terms of his intelligence, liberality, and want of pretension.

HISTORIA del LUXO, y de las LEYES SUNTUARIAS de ESPAÑA. Por Don JUAN SEMPERÉ y GUARINOS. 2 vol. post 8vo. Madrid, 1788.

INDEX.

I.—INDEX OF AUTHORS.

A.

B.

C.

D.

H.

I.

J.

K.

L.

M.

N.

Q.

R.

S.

U.

V.

W.

Y.

Z.

II.—INDEX OF BOOKS.

A.

B.

C.

D.

E.

G.

H.

I.

J.

L.

M.

O.

P.

Q.

R.

S.

T.

U.

V.

W.

Z.

London: Printed by William Clowes and Sons, Stamford Street.